THE·SOTHEBY'S·GUIDE
···to···

CLASSIC
WINES
AND THEIR
LABELS

This book is dedicated to my wife, Aziza, and
to all the people in the international wine trade
who have given me such help and guidance
over the last 25 years.

THE·SOTHEBY'S·GUIDE
TO
CLASSIC
WINES
AND THEIR
LABELS

DAVID MOLYNEUX-BERRY MW

DORLING KINDERSLEY
LONDON

A DORLING KINDERSLEY BOOK

CONTRIBUTORS
Tom Stevenson
Andrew Jefford
Brian Cooper

PROJECT EDITOR
Josephine Buchanan

EDITORS
Corinne Hall
Roger Smoothy

ART EDITORS
Gail Jones
Caroline Murray

DESIGNER
Carol Briggs

WINE CONSULTANT
Wink Lorch

MANAGING EDITOR
Victoria Davenport

MANAGING ART EDITOR
Nick Harris

FIRST PUBLISHED IN GREAT BRITAIN IN 1990 BY
DORLING KINDERSLEY LIMITED, 9 HENRIETTA STREET, LONDON WC2E 8PS

British Library Cataloguing in Publication data
Molyneux-Berry, David
Sotheby's guide to classic wines and their labels.
1. Wines. Selection
I. Sotheby's. Firm
641.22

ISBN 0-86318-483-9

REPRODUCED IN SINGAPORE BY COLOURSCAN
PRINTED IN GREAT BRITAIN BY BUTLER AND TANNER

CONTENTS

~ INTRODUCTION ~

To THE VAST MAJORITY of wine drinkers, the label is the key to the wine that they wish to purchase. It plays an important part in creating an identity for the wine itself. Today there are tens of thousands of wines available throughout the world. Each one requires its own identity, yet must be seen as part of a similar group if it is to be successful, for few wines are so significant that they can stand alone. Even the First Growths of Bordeaux, with their distinctive individual identites, are part of a group that has helped make them famous. It is this group identity that I find so fascinating, for it is a reflection not only of the wines but also of the winemakers and the tradition and culture of the wine-producing region.

The importance of the wine label

Wine labels in their present form, that is paper labels, are relatively new. They began to be seen regularly in the middle of the nineteenth century. In the UK, for example, it only became legally compulsory for wines to be labelled in the mid-1960s. Many wine regions have labels that have hardly altered over the last hundred years or so, but even in the most traditional areas there are signs of experimentation that could lead to changes. In the newer wine-producing areas, where there is no tradition to follow, it is interesting to see what styles have emerged. Some designs are highly

Taittinger Champagne collection From a traditional wine region comes this new style of packaging. Each release has a different design: the second release, 1981 vintage (left) was designed by Arman; the 1983 by Vieira da Silva.

imaginative, whereas others appear to be imitations of older styles. Either way the label is a statement: it informs the buyer that the wine has been made by someone who is attempting to do something different or perhaps merely trying to mimic a wine from a more traditional source.

Choosing classic wine

This is a book about classic wine, although it is hard to define exactly what "classic" is. Many wines detailed in the book are from new wineries and others are "new" wines from established wineries. In fact, the industry is developing so rapidly that it is difficult to find truly classic wines. However, if classic implies quality, durability and tradition, then these wines are surely classic.

No book of this nature can be totally comprehensive and there are bound to be some unintentional omissions. The wines profiled in this book are a personal selection of some of the finest of their type, and I apologize for any that, either through ignorance, lack of space or the impossibility of obtaining a label, have not been included.

Since there are such rapid changes happening in the wine industry, certain observations in this book may have become redundant even before the ink had dried. With a far greater degree of mobility among winemakers, together with the employment of a growing number of vinicultural techniques, the style of some wines has changed dramatically, often without warning. Most of the change has been for the better, and in every wine-producing region more fine wine is being made today than ever before.

Information on the label

In various countries around the world there are mandatory requirements on what should appear on the label; indeed, unless a particular term is on an approved list it may not appear at all. This is particularly true of countries within the European Community and the United States. But these regulations are not universally accepted, which can lead to certain confusions. For instance, the term "Port" is protected within the EC as being the produce of the delimited area of the Douro valley in Portugal, but countries like the USA, South Africa and the USSR use the term for their own produce. However, should these countries wish to sell such wines within the EC they would be obliged to find a new name. Many other famous names are similarly copied, and the growers and merchants in such places as Champagne, Chablis, Burgundy and Sauternes have had to fight hard and long to protect their names and reputations.

The restrictions on what must or may appear on the label - or indeed what must *not* appear - can be overcome by using a back label. This practice has been taken to the extreme in Italy where the back label is effectively the main label, containing all the mandatory information, and the front label is quite often a simple but eye-catching advertisement of the brand name.

Some of the mandatory information is of great help to the consumer. For instance, wines within the EC are controlled under an appellation system, which denotes their origin and, through this, their quality and style. As yet, these controls do not apply in the same way in most other important wine-producing countries, although definite and positive steps are being taken in the right direction to create similar systems.

Grape varieties

We have tried to give the *cépage* or grape varieties that go into making a particular wine, but this information should be treated with a degree of caution. Most fine wine is made in regions of temperate climate, where the weather is often unpredictable and changeable. Although the *cépage* reflects the way a particular vineyard is planted, it does not necessarily correspond to the percentage of each grape variety that goes into the final blend. One should also make allowances for this when assessing wines, particularly New World wines, which are made from grapes purchased from other growers. This can result in one wine having a substantially different *cépage*, and therefore style, from vintage to vintage. To overcome this problem, many of the New World's producers give a lot of additional information, including grape variety percentages, on back labels.

Recommended vintages

The most up-to-date labels have been chosen to illustrate the wines throughout the book. Some labels hardly change in decades, while others differ each year. The vintages depicted are not necessarily recommended, for with all fine wine there can be substantial variations from one year to the next. It is hard to give vintage recommendations across the board: most vintage charts are generalizations that do not take into account particular micro-climates or the skills of individual producers. They may condemn excellent wines produced in relatively poor years or promote substandard ones in generally fine vintages.

As modern viticultural and vinification techniques improve, more wine is made of a high standard. There are fewer disappointing vintages and the ever-greater variety of excellent wine should provide the consumer with a wide choice. Even so merchants are always keen to exploit new sources of supply, particularly if they provide value for money. One can predict an increasing awareness of South American wines, and it may not be long before we receive a new challenge of different names, grapes and styles from the USSR and other countries that have, until now, been rather remote. With an ever-increasing variety of classic wines, this is truly a golden age for wine.

David Molyneux-Berry MW

KEY TO SYMBOLS AND ABBREVIATIONS

SYMBOLS	
2	Second wine
❧	Grape varieties

FRENCH ABBREVIATIONS	
CB	Cru Bourgeois
CBE	Cru Bourgeois Exceptionnel
CBS	Cru Bourgeois Supérieur
CGB	Cru Grand Bourgeois
CGBE	Cru Grand Bourgeois Exceptionnel
GC	Grand Cru
GCC	Grand Cru Classé
GM	Grande Marque

GRAPES	
ALB	Albillo
AUX	Auxerrois
BLC	Bourboulenc
BO	Bastardo
CAB	Cabernet (Franc and/or Sauvignon)
CAN	Canaiolo
CB	Chenin Blanc
CES	Cesanese
CF	Cabernet Franc
CH	Chardonnay
CL	Clairette
CN	Cinsault
CO	Counoise
CS	Cabernet Sauvignon
G	Grolleau
GR	Grenache/Garnacha
GRB	Grenache Blanc
JUR	Jurançon
M	Merlot
MAM	Mammolo
MB	Malbec
MBPG	Muscat Blanc à Petit Grains
MCD	Muscardin
MCL	Muscadelle
MO	Muscat Ottonel
MRPG	Muscat Rosé à Petit Grains
MUSC	Muscat
MV	Mourvèdre
PAR	Parellada
PB	Pinot Blanc
PM	Pinot Meunier
PMG	Petit Manseng
PN	Pinot Noir
PV	Petit Verdot
RAM	Ramisco
ROUS	Roussanne
SGV	Sangiovese
SB	Sauvignon Blanc
SEM	Sémillon
SYR	Syrah
TA	Tinta Amerella
TAN	Tannat
TB	Tinta Barroca
TC	Tinto Cão
TEMP	Tempranillo
TF	Touriga Francesca
TN	Touriga Nacional
TR	Tinta Roriz
VAR	Various
VIO	Viognier
VRA	Viura

~ F R A N C E ~

I N THE WORLD OF WINE France has no equal. Not only is it one of the largest producers of wine but also one of the greatest consumers. While much of the wine is of a relatively basic quality, France can claim to produce the finest wines in the world across a broad spectrum of styles. Every wine-producing country has tried to emulate France's success, by introducing either the vines or winemaking techniques that have made France the envy of the world.

The scale of production

France produces some 61 million hectolitres of wine each year, equivalent to nearly 680 million cases. While this falls short of Italy's massive output of over 850 million cases, it does account for one-fifth of the world's production.

Yet, much more significant is the high level of quality, which no other European country can match. For the first time since the introduction of the *Appellation Contrôlée* system in 1935, France can boast more vineyard area planted to vines classified as *Appellation d'Origine Contrôlée* (AC or AOC) or *Vin Délimité de Qualité Supérieure* (VDQS) than that classified simply as *Vin de Table*. However, although the former, superior categories are greater in vineyard area - 442,700 hectares (1,094,000 acres) as opposed to 425,000 hectares (1,050,175 acres) of *Vin de Table* - the volume of production is still swayed in favour of the latter. Of the total 61 million hectolitres, 28.6 million are *Vin de Table* and 23.7 million are AOC and VDQS, the balance being sent for distillation as being surplus to requirements or of such sub-standard quality as to be unsaleable.

If a comparison is made with the vineyard area of Spain, one can clearly see that France's viticulture is highly efficient, producing in excess of 50 per cent more wine from roughly half the vineyard area. In effect, this means France is over four times as efficient at growing wine grapes as Spain.

The supremacy of French wine

One only has to take Bordeaux as an example to see the sheer volume of superb wine that is produced year after year. These wines have an endless attraction for consumers; as new markets develop around the world, it is often French wine that the consumer turns to first, as if to establish the yardsticks by which others must be judged.

One of France's greatest assets is its climate, which varies from relatively warm to relatively cool, but is always temperate. The vineyards in western France, such as those of Bordeaux, are influenced by the Atlantic, while those further east, such as Burgundy, have a continental climate. In the south the Mediterranean Sea is the major influence, and both Alsace and the Jura on the eastern borders are basically continental - although they are also affected by their altitude. This, combined with the variety of soil types and structures and a multiplicity of good sites, is responsible for France's wide range of wines. And even if not all the heavily planted regions produce fine wine, modern technical developments and the increasing willingness of winegrowers to experiment with new varieties should result in even greater supplies of quality wines in future.

Other principal factors that make French wine so interesting are the grape varieties and the traditions that have been established over a number of centuries. The first French vineyards were planted in the Midi as long ago as the seventh and sixth centuries BC , but it was the Romans, around the time of Christ, who were responsible for planting all but one of the great vineyards that we know so well today: Burgundy, Rhône, Bordeaux, Loire and Champagne. Only the Alsace region was to have much later origins.

The appellation system

Despite this long history, it was not until 1935 that the first official government regulations were introduced in order to help control the industry. Largely based on the pioneering work carried out by Baron Le Roy in Châteauneuf-du-Pape earlier in the twentieth century, the *Institut National des Appellations d'Origine* (INAO), founded in Paris, began to draw up a set of rules, which today govern all wine production in France.

The principles of the *Appellation d'Origine Contrôlée* system relate basically to the grower rather than consumer and cover such essential aspects as grape variety, growing methods, yields, alcoholic strength, colour and, of course, delimitation of suitable vineyard sites. In recent years the added requirement that all *Appellation Contrôlée* wines should be approved by tasting panels made up of specialists should have added the guarantee of quality for the consumer. However, in reality, practical constraints have meant that these panels have not always been of the greatest help. For instance, it is virtually impossible to find sufficiently unbiased yet experienced tasters to work their way through literally thousands upon thousands of wines each year, particularly when they are probably at their busiest time. The other countries that have tried to enforce requirements similar to those of France have all suffered the same problem. The guarantee of quality today still remains, as it has always done in the past, on the reputations of the grower and wine merchant involved. Of course, not all of France's vineyards are classified under the *Appellation Contrôlée* system. Of lesser status, but still defined and controlled, are those wines entitled to VDQS.

Some of these have managed to gain promotion to AC status in recent years. Below this level there is *Vin de Pays*, which controls origin and basic quality, and finally *Vin de Table*, which is not entitled to any regional designation at all. *Vin de Pays* status offers growers the flexibility to experiment with different grape varieties and methods not permitted for AC wines.

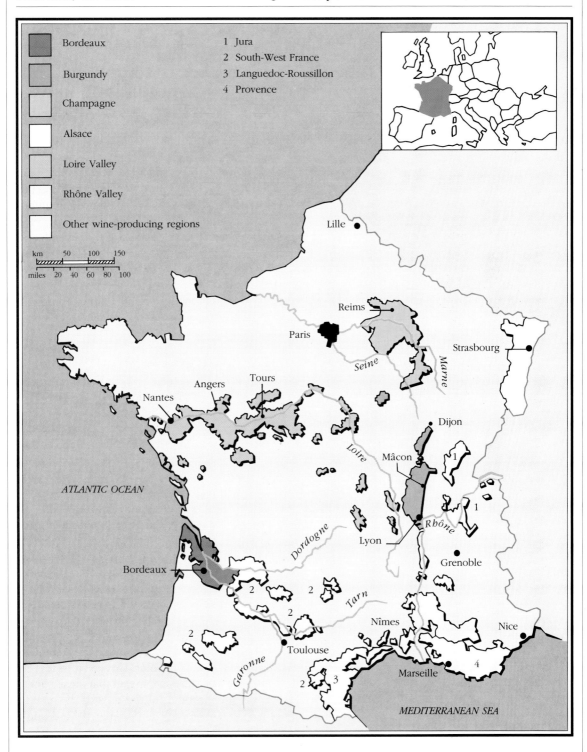

The largest classic wine producer
One-quarter of European wine production comes from France.

Its major wine-producing regions enjoy a multiplicity of good sites, which combine a broadly temperate climate with a variety of soil types and structures to produce wines that are emulated all over the world.

There is tremendous variation in the traditions of winegrowing in France and in the way they are controlled. A good example of the differences can be seen in Bordeaux and Burgundy. In the latter region, each commune is subdivided into vineyards that may be classified as *Grands Crus, Premiers Crus* or *Crus* of lesser status. Not all of a given vineyard, however, may share the same classification, particularly if some of the soil or part of the aspect does not come up to the required standard. It is therefore possible to have a vineyard classified partly as a *Premier Cru* and partly not. In this instance, the delineation will be made right down to the last vine.

This is a very different principle to the manner in which Bordeaux vineyards are classified. Here, the wine carries the status of the producer or château, who can select grapes grown anywhere within one commune to sell under their label. For this purpose, it would be possible for a great château like Latour to grow grapes anywhere within the Commune of Pauillac and bottle the wine under their famous label. The fact that they never do so is based more on their long-standing traditions and the determination to maintain standards than any other factor.

The grape varieties

One of the major distinctions between the various regions of France is the different varieties of grapes that are grown, and whether the wines are made from a single variety or a combination of

---

FRENCH TERMS

AC	Appellation Contrôlée
AOC	Appellation d'Origine Contrôlée
Barrique	Small 225-litre oak cask
Blanc de Blancs	White wine solely from white grapes (often sparkling)
Blanc de Noirs	White wine solely from black grapes (often sparkling)
Brut	Dry (for sparkling wines)
Cave	Cellar
Cave Coopérative	Cooperative cellar
Cépage	Grape variety
Château	Property with vines, usually making/bottling its own wine
Climat	Individual named vineyard within an AC (Burgundy)
Clos	Walled vineyard
Commune	Village
Côte	Slope of a hill
Crémant	Sparkling (until recently in Champagne denoted a wine with less pressure/sparkle than usual)
Cru	"Growth" - a specific vineyard
Cru Bourgeois	Classification used for Médoc properties
Cru Classé	Classed growth (Bordeaux)
Cuve	Wine vat or tank
Cuve Close	Bulk method for sparkling wine making, also called *Charmat*
Cuvée	Blend
Demi-Sec	Semi-dry or semi-sweet
Département	Official French regional division
Domaine	Property with vines that usually makes/bottles its own wine
Doux	Sweet
Élevage	Maturation and pre-bottling treatment
Foudre	Large wooden vat
Fût	Small oak cask
Grand Vin	Château's main wine (Bordeaux)
Grand Cru	"Great growth". Classed Growth (Bordeaux); official AC vineyard classification (Burgundy; Alsace). Highest vineyard classification (Champagne)
Grand Cru Classé	Classified "great growth" (Graves; St Emilion)
Grande Marque	Champagne house belonging to the Syndicat des Grandes Marques de Champagne
INAO	Institut National des Appellations d'Origine
Lieu-dit	See Climat
Macération carbonique	Fermentation of uncrushed black grapes in a carbon dioxide atmosphere
Marque	Brand
Méthode Champenoise	Champagne method of making sparkling wines
Mis en bouteille	Bottled
Moelleux	Fairly sweet
Monopole	Exclusive brand name; or a vineyard with a single owner (Burgundy)
Négociant	Merchant
Pétillant/Pétillance	A light sparkle
Pigeage	Process of pushing down "cap" of skins in a fermenting vat
Premier Cru	First Growth (Bordeaux); official AC vineyard designation (Burgundy); second highest vineyard classification (Champagne)
Récolte	Harvest or vintage
Réserve	Usually a superior wine
Sec	Dry
Sous-marque	Secondary brand
Sur lie	Wine bottled directly from the lees
Tête de Cuvée	Wine from first pressing
Trie	Selected picking of nobly rotted grapes (dessert wines)
Vendange	Harvest or vintage
VDQS	Vin Délimité de Qualité Supérieure
Vigneron	Vine grower
Vin de Paille	Wine from grapes dried on straw mats (Jura)
Vin de Pays	Country wine; table wine from a specific origin
Vin de Table	Table wine
Vin Jaune	Wine matured under *flor* (Jura)

varieties. Perhaps the extreme is Châteauneuf-du-Pape where a dozen permitted varieties can still be employed, although many estates now use as little as two or three. In contrast, Burgundy's wines are made from a single grape variety, mainly Pinot Noir for reds and Chardonnay for whites. The Loire, Beaujolais and Alsace follow this pattern, but Bordeaux and most southern areas usually rely on a blend of several different grapes.

A home for classic grape varieties

Although France is not home to all the more important varieties of *vitis vinifera*, it can boast of having developed to perfection some of the very best, as well as one or two obscure ones. If one were to mention only a few, the list would have to include Cabernet Sauvignon, Cabernet Franc, Merlot, Pinot Noir, Syrah, Grenache and Gamay among the reds, and Chardonnay, Sauvignon Blanc, Sémillon and Chenin Blanc among the whites, although this leaves out both Riesling and Gewürztraminer, which are of Germanic origin but also highly successful in Alsace. In all *Appellation Contrôlée* regulations the grape variety or varieties are carefully controlled, which, of course, tends to minimize the possibilities of experimentation. However, most quality wine growers in France are generally satisfied with their lot and have little need to change the style of their wines.

The pressure for change

The changes that have been made in recent years have usually been initiated from outside France. Research and development in Germany, Australia and California have resulted in the production of much better wines (in the New World in particular), threatening to catch up on France's quality level. Initially France appeared to take little notice of these developments and during the 1970s it was in danger of losing its reputation as the producer of the world's finest wines. This apparent inactivity was short-lived: however traditional the French may be, they have not rejected the best of the technological advances from other countries, or indeed their own. There have been substantial improvements since the late 1970s, especially in that most difficult of all regions, Burgundy, where overall standards had fallen dangerously low.

Not all the innovations were greeted with instant approval. Rumours were rife when both Château Haut-Brion and Château Latour introduced new fermentation *cuves*, replacing the old wooden ones with stainless steel: it was commonly thought that the quality of their wines would surely fall. To the contrary, however, the new wines that were produced were even better, and this important lead was to be followed, if rather slowly, by many others.

Invariably, improvements in quality cost money. Bearing in mind the small scale on which much wine is produced in France, where individual holdings can be smaller than one hectare (2½ acres), there are obvious limitations to the rate of progress. One way in which major improvements have been achieved without enormous individual expenditure has been in the development of co-operatives, which now make an important contribution both in terms of quality and volume. There are several significant cooperatives in the Gironde, of which by far the most important is the one in St Emilion. Other well-known ones are to be found in Alsace, Champagne, Chablis, the Chalonnaise and Beaujolais, as well as an increasing number in the more southerly wine districts.

Modern developments

Today, France sits proud once again as the country of the finest wines, despite the constant pressure from the ever-improving and ever-increasing number of wines, not only from the New World, but also from important nearby competitors, such as Italy and Spain. France's winemakers are now often at the forefront of development; even the First Growths of the Médoc and Graves have announced publicly that they have been conducting joint research on viticulture since 1981. No longer is the sight of machine-harvesting uncommon. A helicopter at Château Pétrus has been seen drying the grapes before harvesting with the down-thrust of air from its rotor blades!

A tradition of fine wines *The style of French wine and its packaging have changed little over the years: these bottles of 1868 Château Margaux (left) and 1890 Château Yquem are just two of the many names that survive the centuries.*

BORDEAUX

THE GIRONDE, THE largest *département* in France, is the largest quality vineyard in the world. Its unique geographical situation, with its special soil structures and ideal climate, combine to make the world's finest dry reds, some of the finest sweet whites (including almost certainly *the* finest) and some quite exceptional dry whites. It would be wrong, however, to believe that everything that Bordeaux produces is either fine or great. For the reputation of this important and long-standing region is based today on a few more than 100 estates, perhaps 200 wines at the most, and far fewer in the past.

The sheer size of the region, however, needs to be understood in order to grasp fully its importance. In the mid-1980s there were some 22,000 growers producing in excess of 44 million cases (over 500 million bottles) of wine per year, from about 100,000 hectares (247,000 acres) of vineyard. Much of this wine is sufficiently good to qualify for *Appellation Contrôlée* status, which puts it amongst the best wines of France. Although the greater wines of Bordeaux account for as little as 1 per cent of the total, this still amounts to nearly half a million cases. In fact Bordeaux is the only region in the world where its greatest wines are available in significant quantities. Most of the first growths, for instance, produce in excess of 20,000 cases each per year.

The significance of water

Water is responsible for much of the essential soil structure of the region, from the substantial gravel deposits to be found mainly in the west (Médoc and Graves), to sand, limestone and clay, which predominate in the east (St Emilion and Pomerol). There are exceptions to this rule, but even the exceptions have their origin in water.

A further, important significance of water was, of course, trade. From 1152 to 1453 Aquitaine, as the region was then called, owed its allegiance to the English crown, which inevitably made it look to the sea and overseas markets. The English occupation was significant and led to the creation of the city of Libourne, the other major port apart from Bordeaux itself, for shipping the region's fine wines. After the departure of the English, Bordeaux went through a period of stagnation, only to be revived by wealth created from the West Indies in the eighteenth century, when the great Médoc estates began to be built up. These had become so powerful that to a large extent they survived the French Revolution (1789), even though

they may have had to change ownership to do so. During the eighteenth and nineteenth centuries many *négociants* (wine merchants) made fortunes upon which they thrived until the present day. These included many foreign nationals such as the English, Irish, Dutch and Germans.

The 1855 classification

Over the centuries these *négociants* kept records of the price paid for, and the quality of, the various wines. This led to the most famous classification of all, when the Bordeaux Chamber of Commerce asked them to produce a classification of the red and white wines of the Gironde for the 1855 *Exposition Universelle* in Paris. All the wines of the Gironde were to be assessed, yet only wines from the Médoc were included in the red wine classification, with the sole exception of Château Haut-Brion in the Graves, and only sweet wines from Sauternes and Barsac were included in the white wine classification. There were no dry whites suitable for inclusion (Sauternes, a sweet wine as we know it today, was only "discovered" in 1836); none of the reds from St Emilion or Pomerol were up to scratch. The 1853 inauguration of the Paris-Bordeaux railway had a profound effect on the distribution and development of these wines. Pomerol was still a rural backwater, with the only relatively important property being Château Certan (now Vieux Château Certan/Château Certan de May); Pétrus was as yet very much a farmhouse until the early part of the twentieth century.

Bordeaux's golden age

Another influence in the 1850s was Napoleon III's creation of the Second Empire (1851), which led to several important Parisian bankers investing in Bordeaux. These included the Rothschilds (Lafite and Mouton) and the Pereires (Palmer). Shortly after the 1855 classification came the greatest period of Bordeaux wine production. Known as the Golden Age, or *La Belle Epoque*, the vintages 1858 to 1878 provided an almost unbroken run of superb wines in plentiful quantity. But disaster struck with the accidental introduction of *phylloxera*, the vine-attacking louse that was to change the shape not only of the Bordeaux vineyard but virtually every wine-producing region of the world.

Bordeaux in the twentieth century

Bordeaux had a hard time of it for over half a century. Two world wars and economic depression interrupted the progress in winemaking. It was not until after the Second World War, and particularly the late 1950s and early 1960s, that investment in the industry looked worthwhile. The growing importance of the American market created a rapid rise in prices in the early 1970s, which was then brought to an abrupt halt and sudden collapse with the oil crisis of 1974.

However, the following year, 1975, was to herald the second golden age of Bordeaux, although no one realized it at the time. With substantial new investment, greatly enhanced winemaking techniques and a more than exceptional run of fortunate climatic conditions, there has not been a seriously poor vintage since 1975. Even the lesser years of 1977, 1980, 1984 and 1987 have increasingly provided excellent drinking wine for early consumption, whilst the greatest years have produced an abundance of top quality wine. Bordeaux has never produced so much exceptionally fine wine as it does today.

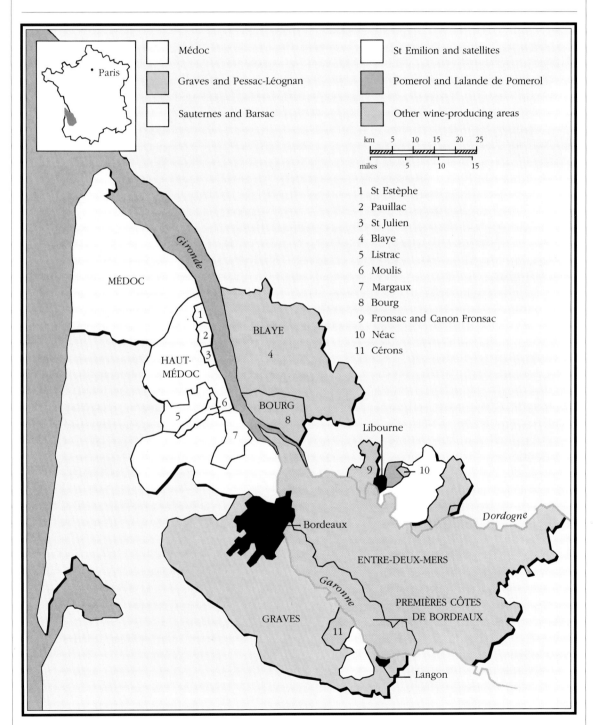

Médoc

Graves and Pessac-Léognan

Sauternes and Barsac

St Emilion and satellites

Pomerol and Lalande de Pomerol

Other wine-producing areas

km 5 10 15 20 25
miles 5 10 15

1 St Estèphe
2 Pauillac
3 St Julien
4 Blaye
5 Listrac
6 Moulis
7 Margaux
8 Bourg
9 Fronsac and Canon Fronsac
10 Néac
11 Cérons

MÉDOC

Gironde

HAUT-MÉDOC

BLAYE

BOURG

Libourne

Bordeaux

Dordogne

ENTRE-DEUX-MERS

Garonne

PREMIÈRES CÔTES DE BORDEAUX

GRAVES

Langon

Paris

Temperate climes *The Atlantic Ocean and the Gulf Stream, as well as the Gironde, Garonne and Dordogne, influence the Bordeaux climate, preventing extremes of temperature, thereby producing sufficiently ripe yet not overripe fruit. In the last three decades there has only been a handful of really cold winters.*

THE 1855 CLASSIFICATION OF THE GIRONDE

RED WINES

Current name	Commune	Original name
PREMIERS CRûS (First Growths)		
Château Lafite-Rothschild	Pauillac	Château Lafite
Château Margaux	Margaux	Château Margaux
Château Latour	Pauillac	Château Latour
Château Haut-Brion	Pessac (Graves)	Haut-Brion
SECONDS CRûS (Second Growths)		
Château Mouton-Rothschild*	Pauillac	Mouton
Château Rausan-Ségla	Margaux	Rauzan-Ségla
Château Rauzan-Gassies	Margaux	Rauzan-Gassies
Château Léoville-Las-Cases	St Julien	Léoville
Château Léoville-Poyferré	St Julien	Léoville
Château Léoville-Barton	St Julien	Léoville
Château Durfort-Vivens	Margaux	Vivens Durfort
Château Gruaud-Larose	St Julien	Gruau-Laroze
Château Lascombes	Margaux	Lascombe
Château Brane-Cantenac	Cantenac	Brane
Château Pichon-Longueville-Baron	Pauillac	Pichon Longueville
Château Pichon-Longueville Comtesse-de-Lalande	Pauillac	Pichon Longueville
Château Ducru-Beaucaillou	St Julien	Ducru Beau Caillou
Château Cos d'Estournel	St Estèphe	Cos Destournel
Château Montrose	St Estèphe	Montrose
TROISIÈMES CRûS (Third Growths)		
Château Kirwan	Cantenac	Kirwan
Château d'Issan	Cantenac	Château d'Issan
Château Lagrange	St Julien	Lagrange
Château Langoa-Barton	St Julien	Langoa
Château Giscours	Labarde	Giscours
Château Malescot-St Exupéry	Margaux	St Exupéray
Château Boyd-Cantenac	Cantenac	Boyd
Château Cantenac-Brown	Cantenac	Boyd
Château Palmer	Cantenac	Palmer
Château La Lagune	Ludon	Lalagune
Château Desmirail	Margaux	Desmirail
No longer exists	Margaux	Dubignon
Château Calon-Ségur	St Estèphe	Calon
Château Ferrière	Margaux	Ferrière
Château Marquis d'Alseme-Becker	Margaux	Becker
QUATRIÈMES CRûS (Fourth Growths)		
Château St Pierre	St Julien	St Pierre
Château Talbot	St Julien	Talbot
Château Branaire-Ducru	St Julien	Du-Luc
Château Duhart-Milon-Rothschild	Pauillac	Duhart
Château Pouget	Cantenac	Poujet/Poujet-Lassale
Château La-Tour-Carnet	St Laurent	Carnet
Château Lafon-Rochet	St Estèphe	Rochet
Château Beychevelle	St Julien	Château de Beychevelle
Château Prieuré-Lichine	Cantenac	Le Prieuré
Château Marquis-de-Terme	Margaux	Marquis de Thermes
CINQUIÈMES CRûS (Fifth Growths)		
Château Pontet-Canet	Pauillac	Canet
Château Batailley	Pauillac	Batailley
Château Haut-Batailley	Pauillac	Batailley
Château Grand-Puy-Lacoste	Pauillac	Grand Puy

* Elevated to Premier Cru in the 1973 Classification of Wines of the Médoc

RED WINES CONTD.

Current name	Commune	Original name
Château Grand-Puy-Ducasse	Pauillac	Artigues Arnaud
Château Lynch-Bages	Pauillac	Lynch
Château Lynch-Moussas	Pauillac	Lynch Moussas
Château Dauzac	Labarde	Dauzac
Château Mouton-Baronne-Philippe	Pauillac	Darmailhac
Château du Tertre	Arsac	Le Tertre
Château Haut-Bages-Libéral	Pauillac	Haut Bages
Château Pédesclaux	Pauillac	Pedesclaux
Château Belgrave	St Laurent	Coutenceau
Château de Camensac	St Laurent	Camensac
Château Cos-Labory	St Estèphe	Cos Labory
Château Clerc-Milon	Pauillac	Clerc Milon
Château Croizet-Bages	Pauillac	Croizet-Bages
Château Cantemerle	Macau	Cantemerle

WHITE WINES

Current name	Commune	Original name
PREMIER CRû SUPERIEUR (Superior First Growth)		
Château d'Yquem	Sauternes	Yquem
PREMIERS CRûS (First Growths)		
Château La Tour Blanche	Bommes	Latour Blanche
Château Lafaurie-Peyraguey	Bommes	Peyraguey
Clos Haut-Peyraguey	Bommes	Peyraguey
Château Rayne-Vigneau	Bommes	Vigneau
Château de Suduiraut	Preignac	Suduiraut
Château Coutet	Barsac	Coutet
Château Climens	Barsac	Climens
Château Guiraud	Sauternes	Bayle
Château Rieussec	Fargues	Rieussec (Sauternes)
Château Rabaud-Promis	Bommes	Rabeaud/Pexoto
Château Sigalas-Rabaud	Bommes	Rabeaud
DEUXIÈMES CRûS (Second Growths)		
Château Myrat	Barsac	Mirat
Château Doisy-Daëne	Barsac	Doisy
Château Doisy-Dubroca	Barsac	Doisy
Château Doisy-Védrines	Barsac	Doisy
Now part of Rabaud-Promis	Bommes	Pexoto
Château d'Arche	Sauternes	d'Arche
Château Filhot	Sauternes	Filhot
Château Broustet	Barsac	Broustet Nérac
Château Nairac	Barsac	Broustet Nérac
Château Caillou	Barsac	Caillou
Château Suau	Barsac	Suau
Château de Malle	Preignac	Malle
Château Romer	Preignac	Romer
Château Romer-du-Hayot	Fargues	Romer
Château Lamothe	Sauternes	Lamothe
Château Lamothe-Guignard	Sauternes	Lamothe

The 1855 classification can never be altered because no provision was made for any changes. However, because of the determination of late Baron Philippe de Rothschild, who considered that Château Mouton Rothschild had been unfairly ranked as the first of the second growths, a new classification was ordered and Mouton was elevated to First Growth status in 1973. This classification was only of the wines of the Médoc and only assessed the First Growths. Château Haut Brion, a First Growth in its own right in 1855, was included because of its preeminence, even though it is in the Graves. Thus it has three classifications: *Premier Cru Classé* (1855), *Premier Cru Classé* (1973) and *Grand Cru Classé* in the 1953 classification of red wines of the Graves.

BORDEAUX VINTAGES

YEAR	CHARACTER
1989	Earliest harvest since 1893. Some red varieties picked end of August; most white picked before. Potentially great vintage, but low acidity could pose maturation problems. Too early to judge.
1988	Variable. Very high yields in Médoc, Graves; the best excellent, stringent selection essential. Some very fine wines in Pomerol and St Emilion where yields were low. Good dry white Graves. Great Sauternes vintage with excellent botrytis.
1987	Played down by the media, but some attractive wines made. The best have good fruit and elegance; for early consumption. Dry whites have good acidity balance and fresh fruit style.
1986	Superb for Cabernet grapes; less so for Merlot, especially in Médoc and Graves. Some great, long-lived Médocs and above-average Pomerols. St Emilions variable. Dry whites very good; Sauternes exceptional, with high degrees of botrytis.
1985	Merlot vintage year. Most red wines have exceptional balance and charm. Successful in the southern Médoc (Margaux) and Graves; exceptional in Pomerol and St Emilion. Attractive dry whites, but a little low in acidity. Sauternes are sweet but lack botrytis unless harvested very late.
1984	Cold, wet, difficult year. Merlot vine suffered the worst *coulure* in living memory, so some Médocs are 100 per cent Cabernet. Some wines very attractive but a little hollow and short on the palate. Early maturing vintage. St Emilion and Pomerol generally disappointing. Dry white good and understated; Sauternes better than expected.
1983	In many ways a classic vintage. Generally well-structured, fruity wines for bottle ageing. Médoc and Graves very stylish; exceptional wine from Margaux and the northern Graves. St Emilion and Pomerol variable, but a few outstanding wines. Very good dry whites; superb Sauternes vintage.
1982	A very distinctive vintage. Many wines intensely ripe; few overripe. Best Médoc and Graves since 1961. Great wines from St Emilion and Pomerol - very ripe and rich, like 1947. Dry whites need drinking young. Sauternes did not fare so well: average wines with a couple of marvellous exceptions, Château d'Yquem for one.
1981	Special vintage, but wet harvest. Médoc/Graves and St Emilion/Pomerol produced stylish wines with fine flavour and elegance. A real "claret" vintage. Dry whites need drinking young. Sauternes are fine, with good botrytis.
1980	Salvaged by modern techniques. Best in the Médoc and Graves, but most should be drunk up. St Emilion and Pomerol quite good at best, variable at worst. Dry whites now showing age. Some attractive Sauternes with good botrytis.

YEAR	CHARACTER
1979	A big vintage of well-coloured, fruity wines which lack the weight of the 1978s but have charm and depth. Médoc and Graves rich in flavour, slightly coarse, although they should develop further. St Emilion and Pomerol produced richer, deeper wines. A very good dry white vintage which is drinking well now. A fine Sauternes vintage, perhaps inferior to 1980s and 1981s.
1978	"Miracle" vintage. Atrocious weather until mid-August, then perfect through harvest. Médoc and Graves have good colour and great breed; well-structured, developing well. St Emilion and Pomerol have less depth, although the top Pomerols are excellent. Very fine dry white year, the best still developing. Sauternes disappointing, with perfect ripeness but absence of botrytis.
1977	The only poor year between 1975 and 1989, but modern technology helped produce quite reasonable wines. Most red wines need drinking now. Dry whites surprisingly good but not special. Sauternes was a non-event.
1976	Hot, dry year, diluted at the last minute. Variable vintage, many wines showing "burnt" character. Médoc and Graves produced interesting wines, most now requiring drinking. Some St Emilion and Pomerol show more signs of dilution. Most dry whites now "over the top"; best Graves can be fine. Sauternes very rich and concentrated.
1975	Very tannic vintage. Finest wines superb; many minor ones lacked fruit for long-term development. Some outstanding Médoc and Graves, but requiring patience. Pomerol and St Emilion follow suit: the best exceptional, the worst very unattractive. Some very good St Emilion *Grands Crus Classés*. Some fine dry white Graves. Potentially very fine Sauternes vintage, but some too big and heavy. At their best, however, they are brilliant (like Château d'Yquem).
1974 1973 1972	Almost without exception these vintages are fully mature and need drinking. Some wines will be well past their best. The 1974s lack flesh, the 1973s were soft, almost sweet clarets, now fading; the 1972s were hollow and short. As with all vintages, there were a few marvellous exceptions.
1971	Uneven flowering created a variety of styles. The Médocs and Graves are mostly mature, flavoury and stylish: drink up. St Emilions opulent, also need drinking. Some Pomerols very special. Some great dry white Graves and classic Sauternes.
1970	A ripe, extremely well-balanced vintage, resulting in fine fruity wines which continue to pick up weight and will continue to age well. Best in the Médoc and Graves; the Pomerols also very fine. One or two of the St Emilions lack structure, but the best are very good. Dry white Graves still very good; Sauternes are big, rich long lasting wines.

THE MÉDOC

THE MÉDOC COVERS THE whole area from the Pointe de Grave in the north, at the mouth of the Gironde estuary, to just north of the city of Bordeaux in the south, where it borders the Graves. The name of Médoc is quite confusing because it covers a number of different areas. The Médoc is split into two basic parts, the Haut Médoc, closest to Bordeaux, and the Bas Médoc which is invariably just called Médoc. The Haut Médoc includes the six communes of St Estèphe, Pauillac, St Julien, Margaux, Moulis and Listrac, which contain the vast majority of the famous *crus classés* of the 1855 classification. It is particularly from these communes that the world's greatest red wines are produced, although there is also a handful of fine whites.

Reasons for the Médoc's greatness

The supreme quality of these great wines is the sum of a number of different factors. First, the excellent soil, which invariably means extensive and very deep gravel banks that provide exceptional drainage, yet warmth, for the vine as the sun heats up and reflects from the stones. Second, the multiplicity of different blends of the predominant grape varieties which make up the essential character of the wine. No great château sells its wine as Cabernet Sauvignon or Cabernet/Merlot blend, but that is what they are. The stress here is on the individual and unique make-up of the wine rather than any one of its constituent parts.

The third and extremely important factor is the use of oak casks (called *barriques* locally although they have long been referred to as hogsheads in the UK) for the maturation of the wine. The oak cask has two fundamental effects. It concentrates the wine and, depending on how new it is, imparts wood tannin, an excellent preservative. In so doing it provides additional flavours, such as vanilla and a smoky, charcoal texture, which increase the complexity of the wine.

The *Grand Vin* and second wines

For centuries, wine had to be consumed within a short period of its manufacture otherwise it "went bad", usually turning to vinegar. It was the development of wine that would keep that made Bordeaux famous, and it was the wooden cask that made the wines keep. Such wine was called *Grand Vin*, and it was this wine that was capable of travel to foreign shores, thus opening up entirely new markets. Some of the Médoc's finest wines are still proud to display this fact today, such as "Grand Vin de Château Latour". The implication here is that only the best is sold under the *Grand Vin* label. So where does the rest go?

In recent years there has been a dramatic increase in the number of second wines marketed by the big châteaux. It is into these that the less-than-perfect wine is put, and indeed even perfect casks that are not required to make up the blend which will become the essence of the *Grand Vin*. It is in the second wines that the produce of young vines is usually included. For many of the leading châteaux, vines are considered young until they are 12 years old, even though they can produce a good quantity of grapes in their third year. Some châteaux can even boast a third and indeed a fourth wine, although they may not be regularly marketed. However, it is this critical selection which makes the *Grand Vin* so good, a luxury that smaller properties find difficult to copy and one of the reasons why the small estates in St Emilion and Pomerol seldom sell under more than one label.

Médoc classifications

The Médoc is home to a much larger number of châteaux than were classified in 1855. Over 400 of these were classified as Bourgeois growths in 1932, but this is now very much out of date. A new grading was made in 1966, and this was updated in 1978 and is due to be revised again in the early 1990s. This latest classification divides the various properties into three distinct categories, although present EC regulations do not allow more than the words "*Cru Bourgeois*" to appear on the label.

These categories do not necessarily guarantee any particular style, but they point to potential quality wines. The criteria used are as follows:

Crus Bourgeois must be of acceptable (good) quality and be made at the estate, which must be at least 7 hectares (17 acres) in size.

Crus Grands Bourgeois must be matured in *barriques* in addition to the *Crus Bourgeois* rules.

Crus Grands Bourgeois Exceptionnels have to be château-bottled and be located within the Haut-Médoc area from where the *crus classés* originate, as well as conforming to the above rules.

In reality, some *Crus Bourgeois* easily exceed the necessary criteria and should more readily be thought of as *crus classés* quality. Certain properties may still use their old 1932 classification, such as *Cru Bourgeois Supérieur* or *Cru (Bourgeois) Exceptionnel*, on the label, particularly if they are not represented in the latest classification. However, despite the confusion, one thing is certain: the *Crus Bourgeois* continue to improve their quality and can provide exceptionally good value.

1978 CLASSIFICATION OF CRUS BOURGEOIS OF THE MÉDOC

CRU GRAND BOURGEOIS EXCEPTIONNEL

NAME OF CHÂTEAU	COMMUNE
Agassac	Ludon
Andron-Blanquet	St Estèphe
Beausite	St Estèphe
Capbern	St Estèphe
Caronne-Ste-Gemme	St Laurent
Chasse-Spleen	Moulis
Cissac	Cissac
Citran	Avensan
Le Crock	St Estèphe
Dutruch-Grand-Poujeau	Moulis
Fourcas-Dupré	Listrac
Fourcas-Hosten	Listrac
du Glana	St Julien
Haut-Marbuzet	St Estèphe
Marbuzet	St Estèphe
Meyney	St Estèphe
Phélan-Ségur	St Estèphe
Poujeaux	Moulis

CRU GRAND BOURGEOIS

NAME OF CHÂTEAU	COMMUNE
Beaumont	Cussac
Bel-Orme	St Seurin-de-Cadourne
Brillette	Moulis
La Cardonne	Blaignan
Colombier-Monpelou	Pauillac
Coufran	St Seurin-de-Cadournne
Coutelin-Merville	St Estèphe
Duplessis-Hauchecorne	Moulis
Fontesteau	St Sauveur
La-Fleur-Milon	Pauillac
Greysac	Bégadan
Hanteillan	Cissac
Lafon	Listrac
Lamarque	Lamarque
Lamothe	Cissac
Larose-Trintaudon	St Laurent
Laujac	Bégadan
Liversan	St Sauveur
Loudenne	St Yzans
MacCarthy	St Estèphe
Malleret	Le-Pian
Martinens	Margaux
le Meynieu	Vertheuil
Morin	St Estèphe
Moulin-à-Vent	Moulis
les Ormes-Sorbet	Conquèques
les Ormes-de-Pez	St Estèphe
Patache d'Aux	Bégadan
Paveil-de-Luze	Soussans
Peyrabon	St Sauveur
Pontoise-Cabarrus	St Seurin-de-Cadourne
Potensac	Potensac
Reysson	Vertheuil
Ségur	Parempuyre
Sigognac	St Yzans
Sociondo-Mallet	St Seurin-de-Cadourne
du Taillan	Le Taillan
la Tour-de-By	Bégadan
la Tour-du-Haut-Moulin	Cussac
Tronquoy-Lalande	St Estèphe
Verdignan	St Seurin-de-Cadourne

CRU BOURGEOIS

NAME OF CHÂTEAU	COMMUNE
Aney	Cussac
Balac	St Laurent-de-Médoc
Bellerive	Valeyrac
Bellerose	Pauillac
La Bécade	Listrac
Bonneau-Livran	St Seurin-de-Cadourne
le Bosq	St Christoly
le Breuil	Cissac
la Bridane	St Julien
de By	Bégadan
Castéra	St Germain-d'Esteuil
Chambert-Marbuzet	St Estèphe
Cap-Léon-Veyrin	Listrac
Carcanieux	Queyrac
la Clare	Bégadan
la Closerie	Moulis
Duplessis-Fabre	Moulis
Fonréaud	Listrac
Fonpiqueyre	St Sauveur
Fort Vauban	Cussac
la France	Blaignan
Gallais Bellevue	Potensac
Grand-Duroc-Milon	Pauillac
Grand-Moulin	St Seurin-de-Cadourne
Haut-Bages-Monpelou	Pauillac
Haut-Canteloup	Couquèques
Haut-Garin	Bégadan
Haut-Padarnac	Pauillac
Hourbanon	Prignac
Hourtin-Ducasse	St Sauveur
de Labat	St Laurent
Lamothe-de-Bergeron	Cussac
Landon	Bégadan
Crû Lassalle	Potensac
Lartigue-de-Brochon	St Seurin-de-Cadourne
le Landat	Cissac
Lestage	Listrac
Mac-Carthy-Moula	St Estèphe
Monthil	Bégadan
Moulin Rouge	Cussac
Panigon	Civrac
Pibran	Pauillac
Plantey-de-la-Croix	St Seurin-de-Cadourne
Pontet	Blaignan
Ramage-la-Bâtisse	St Sauveur
la Roque-de-By	Bégadan
de la Rose Maréchal	St Seurin-de-Cadourne
St-Bonnet	St Christoly
Saransot	Listrac
Soudars	Avensan
Tayac	Soussans
la Tour-Blanche	St Christoly
la Tour-du-Mirail	Cissac
la Tour-Haut-Caussan	Blaignan
la Tour-St-Bonnet	St Christoly
la Tour-St-Joseph	Cissac
des Tourelles	Blaignan
Vieux Robin	Bégadan

ST ESTÈPHE

S T ESTÈPHE IS THE largest and most northerly of the Médoc's great wine communes. Bordered by Pauillac to the south - at the point where Château Lafite is situated - and St Seurin to the north, it has only five classed growths: two seconds, one third, one fourth and one fifth. These are supplemented by a host of *bourgeois* growths. St Estèphe is the only major commune where the land planted to *bourgeois* growths exceeds that of the classed growths.

The commune takes its name from the biggest of the six hamlets that exist within its boundaries, but perhaps the most important in vinous terms is the hamlet of Marbuzet, which lends its name to three very successful properties: Château de Marbuzet, the home of Bruno Prats of Cos d'Estournel fame, and effectively its second wine; and Châteaux Haut Marbuzet and Chambert Marbuzet, both owned by Henri Duboscq.

The area is hillier than the other communes of the Médoc and has a richer soil with a higher proportion of clay. Many of the better properties, however, are situated on gravel slopes that run down towards the river.

Characteristics of the wines

Traditionally, the wines of St Estèphe have been noted for their firmness, requiring a great deal of ageing to soften the high level of tannins. In recent years, however, the wines have been more supple and fruity. This has been achieved by changes in the vinification technique and by planting a much higher proportion of the softer, fleshier Merlot grape. The style of wines now ranges from the rich, fleshy, highly concentrated and complex - like Château Cos d'Estournel - to the rather firm, austere and, at worst, mean wines of some of the lesser growths. The wines are at their best when made in hot, dry years, rather than in cool, wet years, since the relatively poor drainage and lack of ripeness of the Merlot grape can result in hollow and pinched wines.

Oriental fantasy Château Cos d'Estournel, near the Pauillac border, was inspired by the Eastern voyages of Louis Gaspard d'Estournel in the nineteenth century.

CHÂTEAU ANDRON BLANQUET

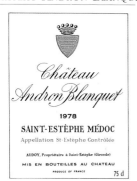

CGBE - This was previously a rather severe style of wine - as has often been the case with lesser St Estèphe wines - but, since the property's purchase in 1971 by the owners of Château Cos Labory, there have been changes. There is now greater fruit in the wine and a noticeable softening of its taste.

    ❦ *M 35%, CS 30%, CF 30%, PV 5%*
    2 *Château St Roch*

CHÂTEAU BEAU-SITE

CGBE - This is a consistent, early-maturing wine, without any harsh tannins. It is usually fairly soft, rounded and supple.

    ❦ *CS & CF 60%, M 40%*
    2 *Château Haut Madrac*

CHÂTEAU BEAU-SITE HAUT-VIGNOBLE

CB (1932) - Although this château is located very close to Château Beau-Site, the wine is dissimilar in that it needs several years' ageing to reduce the hard tannins. Generally, it is a rather firm and unyielding wine in the old style.

    ❦ *CS 60%, M 30%, PV 10%*

CHÂTEAU LE BOSCQ

CBS (1932) - Rather better known some years ago when it had a significant reputation, this wine has been somewhat austere. Recent vintages show much more fruit and richness.
CS 60%, M 40%

CHÂTEAU CALON-SÉGUR

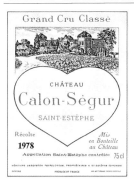

3CC - Although it is rare for Calon-Ségur to reach the very highest peaks of quality, consistency is perhaps one of its greatest assets. It is a well-structured wine that needs time to develop; it also keeps well. Recent vintages have been particularly good.
CS 50%, CF 25%, M 25%
2 Marquis de Ségur

CHÂTEAU CAPBERN GASQUETON

CGBE - An uncompromising wine with classic St Estèphe hallmarks: firm, solid, and with a degree of richness. This wine needs several years to become drinkable, but offers a reliable quality that is worth the wait.
CS 60%, M 25%, CF 15%
2 Grand Village Capbern

CHÂTEAU CHAMBERT-MARBUZET

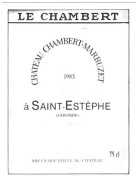

CB - Seldom seen outside France because it is mainly sold to private customers, this has made quite an entrance into the UK market with an outstanding 1982 vintage. The wine is rich, ripe and well structured.
CS 70%, M 30%
2 Château MacCarthy Moula

CHÂTEAU COS D'ESTOURNEL

2CC - For many years regarded as the senior property of St Estèphe. Recently, the wine has been quite superb, with a greater degree of richness and fruit than ever before. The 1982 vintage must be one of the finest wines that has ever been produced in this commune.
CS 50%, M 40%, CF 10%
2 Château de Marbuzet

CHÂTEAU COS LABORY

5CC - Compared to Château Cos d'Estournel, its immediate neighbour, this has been a rather light, one-dimensional and characterless wine. The main problem appeared to be over-production, but recent vintages are a significant improvement.
CS 35%, M 35%, CF 25%, PV 5%

CHÂTEAU COUTELIN-MERVILLE

CGB - In the early 1970s a family division put this estate at risk and the shortage of capital did little to help the quality of the wine. More recently, however, the wine appears to be back on form.
CS & CF 65%, M 30%, PV & MB 5%

CHÂTEAU LE CROCK

CGBE - Another successful property that continues to produce a consistent wine of good quality.
CS 65%, M 35%

CHÂTEAU HAUT-MARBUZET

CGBE - This is another leading bourgeois growth with excellent colour, substantial fruit and a significant level of tannin, largely induced by new oak casks. This is definitely a wine for those who appreciate the added complexity and concentration that oak maturation imparts.
CS 40%, M 50%, CF 10%
2 Château Tour de Marbuzet

CHÂTEAU HOUISSANT

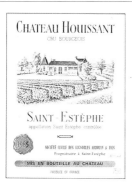

CBS (1932) - Located to the north of Château Cos d'Estournel and west of Château Montrose, this château - although unclassified - is a consistent producer of good quality wine in the classic St Estèphe style.
CS 70%, M 30%

CHÂTEAU LAFFITTE-CARCASSET

CB (1932) - North-west of Château Montrose, this property produces a pleasant, early-maturing wine.
CS 65%, M 35%
2 *Vicomtesse*

CHÂTEAU LAFON-ROCHET

4CC - Recent vintages have shown a significant improvement in the quality of this wine, which is produced adjacent to Château Lafite in Pauillac. Now deep-coloured and rich in fruit and tannin, it will require several years to develop its finer qualities.
CS 70%, M 20%, CF 8%, MB 2%

CHÂTEAU LAVILLOTTE

Until a certain Gault-Milau tasting, this excellent propertly was virtually unknown. This is a very carefully-made wine with outstanding bouquet and a fine, complex palate, enhanced by wood ageing. It certainly merits close attention.
CS 75%, M 25%

CHÂTEAU MAC-CARTHY

CGB - One of the smallest properties in the area producing little more than 1,000 cases per year of good, rather than exceptional, wine.
CS 65%, M 35%

CHÂTEAU MEYNEY

CGBE - A consistently good and highly popular wine from the giant and excellent Cordier "stable". It ages particularly well because of the relatively high acidity that is to be found in most vintages. Excellent value.
CS 70%, M 26%, CF 4%
2 *Prieur de Meyney*

CHÂTEAU MONTROSE

2CC - Always known as one of the biggest and most powerful wines of Bordeaux, much in the style of Château Latour, this has in recent years become much lighter and more approachable at an earlier age. The wine used to show enormous potential and then often seemed to disappoint. However, old vintages can still be excellent.
CS 65%, M 30%, CF 5%
2 *La Dame de Montrose*

CHÂTEAU MORIN

CGB - A high quality wine helped by the age of its vines. It tends to be relatively soft and elegant rather than severe and firm.
CS 65%, M 35%

CHÂTEAU LES ORMES DE PEZ

CGB - Consistent quality and excellent value have made this wine extremely popular. It is pleasantly rounded and fruity, showing none of the meanness that some St Estèphe wines display.
CS 55%, M 30%, CF 10%, PV 5%

CHÂTEAU DE PEZ

CBS (1932) - Although unclassified, this wine is unquestionably one of the leading growths of the commune and can compare with many a classed growth. Deep in colour and with plenty of tannin, but at the same time well-structured and fruity, this wine ages extremely well and needs time to develop.
CS 70%, CF 15%, M 15%

CHÂTEAU PHÉLAN SÉGUR

CGBE - A well-known and popular wine with an easy-going style. The high proportion of Merlot in the wine gives it softness and openness, but in recent years it has tended to be a little light.
CS 50%, M 40%, CF 10%

CHÂTEAU TRONQUOY-LALANDE

CGBE - Usually a consistent wine with plenty of colour and extract, although a little earthy and lacking finesse. Its firmness requires ageing.
CS & CF 50%, M 50%

A SELECTION OF SECOND WINES

CHÂTEAU DE MARBUZET

2nd wine of Château Cos d'Estournel. CGBE - Although a separate property, the wine of Château de Marbuzet is now substantially augmented with the lesser casks of Cos d'Estournel. It is consistently well made and definitely worth trying.

PRIEUR DE MEYNEY

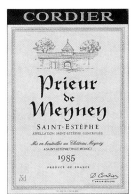

2nd wine of Château Meyney - This wine is rather more advanced and earlier maturing than the *Grand Vin* Château Meyney, which can take many years to develop properly.

LA DAME DE MONTROSE

2nd wine of Château Montrose

NUMERO 2 DU CHÂTEAU LAFON-ROCHET

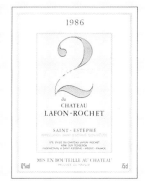

2nd wine of Château Lafon-Rochet

CHÂTEAU MACCARTHY-MOULA

2nd wine of Château Chambert Marbuzet

CHÂTEAU TOUR DE MARBUZET

2nd wine of Château Haut Marbuzet

CHÂTEAU MARQUIS DE SÉGUR

2nd wine of Château Calon-Ségur

PAUILLAC

O F ALL THE MÉDOC communes, Pauillac is by far the most important, both in size of vineyard and volume of top-quality wine production. It boasts no less than three of the five first growths, two important second growths, one fourth and an incredibly twelve - or two-thirds - of the fifth growths. In total, it accounts for approximately one-third of the 1855 classification and probably more in terms of actual volume.

The soil in Pauillac is predominantly gravel; at Châteaux Pontet-Canet and Mouton Rothschild it forms banks up to 30 metres (100 feet) deep. It is this soil, with its excellent drainage and heat retention, which makes the commune of Pauillac the world's finest piece of land for the cultivation of the Cabernet Sauvignon grape, which in turn is responsible for some of the most majestic and long-lived wines produced anywhere.

The first growths
It is difficult to generalize about the Pauillac wines, except to say that they are highly individual and seem to follow no set pattern. To the north, bordering St Estèphe, lies Château Lafite and its sibling Duhart-Milon. The former is renowned for its exquisite perfume, finesse and elegance. At the other end of the commune lies Château Latour, a giant among wines: powerful, slow to develop, long-lived and extraordinarily consistent. If these two wines are in many ways opposites, then Mouton Rothschild - lying close to Lafite - could hardly be more different in style, with its exotic bouquet of blackcurrants and cedarwood and its opulent, richly, fruity structure.

The style of the wines
Broadly speaking, the wines follow either the style of Lafite or Mouton Rothschild, although one marvellous exception is Château Pichon Longueville, Comtesse de Lalande. Part of this vineyard actually lies in St Julien, which can lead to its wine having a "split personality". In some years it tastes like a Pauillac and in others a St Julien, but whatever its style, this is one of Bordeaux's most consistently brilliant wines, reaching - and occasionally surpassing - first growth quality.

The eighteen *crus classés* take up much of the Pauillac vineyard, so there is little space for *crus bourgeois*. However, some of the finest bargains are to be found among the second wines of the leading châteaux, many of which have a long history either as independent *bourgeois* growths, or as true second wines. Mouton Cadet, the world-famous brand created by the late Baron Philippe de Rothschild was first produced for the declassified crop of Mouton Rothschild 1931, although it was soon to include other wines and is now a straightforward although excellent Bordeaux blend. Les Forts de Latour certainly existed in the early 1920s and probably earlier.

CHÂTEAU BATAILLEY

5CC - A very dependable wine that is rarely a failure, although it seldom hits the high spots. It tends to be a little one-dimensional in a rather solid, rustic way, but it has the ability to age well. Generally good value.
CS 70%, M 20%, CF 9%, PV 1%

CHÂTEAU CLERC MILON

5CC - Known for many years as Château Clerc Milon Mondon, this only recently abandoned the name Mondon, even though it was purchased in 1970 by Baron Philippe de Rothschild. The wine is usually fairly soft, quick-maturing and on the light side, although the most recent vintages have shown a little more complexity and length.
CS 65%, CF 20%, M 15%

CHATEAU COLOMBIER-MONPELOU

CGB - I have always had a soft spot for this wine, having enjoyed both the 1962 and 1966 vintages enormously. It is a typical Pauillac wine in style, with deep colour and a slightly chunky fruit, which nevertheless exhibits the classic Cabernet structure.
CS 70%, M 20%, CF 5%, PV 5%
2 Grand Canyon

CHÂTEAU CROIZET-BAGES

5CC - For many years this was a fairly robust, fruity wine with a tendency to mature quickly, but more recently there have been a few disappointingly light and simple wines. Fortunately, the owner has intimated that things will change for the better.
CS 70%, CF 10%, M 20%
2 *Enclos de Moncabon*

CHÂTEAU DUHART-MILON ROTHSCHILD

4CC - It has taken the Rothschilds of Lafite fame a long time to bring this property back to top quality wine production, but since 1978 a series of excellent wines have been made. Located next to Château Lafite, this château produces wine very similar in style but obviously not to the same elevated standard. Recent vintages will need several years to develop.
CS 70%, M 25%, CF 5%
2 *Moulin de Duhart*

CHÂTEAU LA FLEUR MILON

CGB - Although fairly well-known, this château is not among the leading producers in Pauillac. The wine is usually very pleasant, but seldom has the distinctive hallmarks of wines from this commune.
CS 70%, M 30%

CHÂTEAU FONBADET

CBS (1932) - One of the better wines of Pauillac - well-coloured, big and fruity, with the blackcurrant bouquet often associated with this commune.
CS 60%, M 19%, CF 15%, MB & PV 6%
2 *Château Tour du Roc Milon*

CHÂTEAU GRAND-PUY DUCASSE

5CC - An example of the fruity, softer style of Pauillac; it is seldom hard and tannic. Even though it is easy to drink when young, it has considerable ageing ability. Modestly priced.
CS 65%, M 35%
2 *Château Artigues Arnaud*

CHÂTEAU GRAND-PUY-LACOSTE

5CC - Since 1978, when the Château came into the control of Xavier Borie, the wines have been excellent: concentrated, powerful and well-structured. The high level of tannin demands 10 or more years' cellaring.
CS 70%, M 25%, CF 5%
2 *Château Lacoste-Borie*

CHÂTEAU HAUT-BAGES LIBÉRAL

5CC - Another wine with a very high percentage of Cabernet. The result is a wine not dissimilar to Château Lynch Bages, with excellent deep colour and a big, powerful blackcurrant bouquet. It is relatively inexpensive and provides outstanding value.
CS 92%, M 5%, PV 3%

CHÂTEAU HAUT-BAGES MONPELOU

CB - Another property in the Borie-Manoux "stable" that, like Château Batailley, produces consistent rather than special wine. Very dependable and relatively inexpensive.
CS 75%, M 25%

CHÂTEAU HAUT-BATAILLEY

5CC - Under the expert management of Jean-Eugène Borie and his son, Xavier, this property has been making much better wine in recent years. The wine tends to be more St Julien in style, being lighter and quicker-maturing than most Pauillac wines. Definitely in ascendancy in quality, the price has remained relatively modest and offers good value.
CS 65%, M 25%, CF 10%
2 *La Tour d'Aspic*

CHÂTEAU LAFITE-ROTHSCHILD

1CC - In the famous 1855 classification, and indeed for many years before, Lafite was and has always been the first of the first growths. Little has changed, and with the exception of a few uncharacteristic falters, Lafite must surely remain one of the world's greatest red wines.

It is noted for its longevity, which may be a little surprising as it is not the biggest or most robust wine by any means. But the secret of its success is its near perfect balance and remarkable bouquet, which is neither too powerful nor obvious. It is this refined elegance, often hauntingly beautiful, that gives Lafite its legendary reputation. In the best vintages, this wine needs many years before it reaches its peak - about 20 years, although it can be enjoyed sooner. In off-vintages its performance is somewhat erratic and it has been known to produce some decidedly substandard wines. Since 1975, however, its performance has been electrifying. It will never be inexpensive, but currently it certainly deserves its price.

CS 70%, M 20%, CF 5%, PV 5%
2 *Carruades de Lafite Rothschild (original name and used again from 1987), Moulin des Carruades (for several vintages up to 1986)*

CHÂTEAU LATOUR

1CC - In many ways Latour is the antithesis of Lafite. The châteaux are located at opposite ends of the commune and on opposite sides of the road. Latour is consistently one of the most highly-coloured wines in Bordeaux and has the structure of a giant in comparison to Lafite's lighter hue and more delicate, supple style. Latour is one of the most consistent producers of quality wine, particularly in off-vintages, whereas Lafite does tend to be erratic. Yet there are

similarities. Both have enormous ageing potential, with wines in fine drinking condition even a century old; both have undoubted quality; and, of course, both are Pauillacs and first growths. As a general rule, a good vintage of Latour needs at least 20 years' ageing and probably 25 to 30 to reach its peak. Exceptional vintages may even need 40. Recent vintages, however, appear to be slightly lighter and more accessible, although this may prove to be a short-lived phase.

CS 80%, M 10%, CF 10%
2 *Les Forts de Latour,* **3** *Pauillac*

CHÂTEAU LYNCH BAGES

5CC - Of all the fifth growths, this the most misplaced, for unquestionably it deserves and actually commands far greater recognition - its free market price places it firmly among the second growths. Château Lynch Bages is often referred to as "the poor man's Mouton" (Rothschild) and although it certainly exhibits much of the same exuberant character and style, the description is a little unfair.

I have attended tastings when the Lynch Bages of the same vintage was actually superior. The wine is usually very deeply coloured and has a pronounced blackcurrant and cedarwood bouquet. It is well-structured, big-boned and mouth-filling.

CS 75%, M 15%, CF 10%
2 *Château Haut-Bages Averous*

CHÂTEAU LYNCH-MOUSSAS

5CC - This is a small property that produces a relatively light, pleasant, early-maturing wine. It is certainly not among the leaders of the commune, but its price is modest and provides good value.

CS 75%, M 25%

CHÂTEAU MOUTON BARONNE PHILIPPE

Originally known as Château Mouton d'Armailhacq, this was purchased by Baron Philippe de Rothschild in 1933, although its name was not changed to to Château Mouton Baron Philippe until the mid-1950s. In the mid-1970s - in honour of his late second wife - the "Baron" was changed to "Baronne". The wine is a typical Pauillac but without the concentration, depth or extrovert character of the *Premier Cru*. It also matures relatively quickly, with most vintages drinking well within 10 years.

CS 70%, M 17%, CF 13%

CHÂTEAU MOUTON ROTHSCHILD

1CC - This famous estate and its wine owe a lasting debt to the late Baron Philippe de Rothschild. It was his guidance that led, in 1973, to the promotion to first growth status, the only château to be elevated from its 1855 classification. The wine is almost pure Cabernet, producing a classic, often opulent and even exotic bouquet of *cassis*, cedarwood and spices. On the palate it is rich, powerful, concentrated and tannic in its youth, developing into a mouth-filling, ripe, fruity wine of considerably complexity and length. It is superlative in great vintages, requiring 20 years or so ageing, but has had its failures in lesser years.

CS 76%, CF 16%, M 8%

CHÂTEAU MOUTON ROTHSCHILD LABELS

In 1923, at the age of 21, Baron Philippe took over the management of Mouton and immediately commissioned Jean Carlu, a talented graphic artist, to design a new label - the now famous sheep's head and five arrows - for the 1924 vintage. The label was used for several vintages, including some produced before the Baron's arrival at Mouton. The design changed for the vintages of 1928 and 1929, then changed again for the 1933 vintage, remaining the same until 1944. Since 1945 the Baron has commissioned a leading artist each year to design part of the label, so creating a brilliant marketing idea that has more recently been widely copied. These labels are highly sought after by collectors, to the point where certain vintages can command astonishing prices, regardless of the wine's quality.

The original 1924 label designed by Jean Carlu

Salvador Dali - 1958

Henry Moore - 1964

Marc Chagall - 1970

Pablo Picasso - 1973

CHÂTEAU PÉDESCLAUX

5CC - One of the least well-known *crus classés* probably because of its small production. The wine is lightweight and straightforward, although it does exhibit good fruit. Generally inexpensively priced.
CS 65%, M 20%, CF 5%, PV 5%, MB 5%
2 *Château Bellerose*

CHÂTEAU PIBRAN

CB - Situated in the northern half of Pauillac, close to Château Pontet-Canet, this is a small property producing a well-made wine of good value.
CS 60%, M 24%, CF 10%, PV 6%

CHÂTEAU PICHON-LONGUEVILLE-BARON

2CC - An important estate, more correctly called Château Longueville, au Baron de Pichon Longueville. The wine can be quite big and powerful, but it has not been producing as well as it should. The wines of the 1980s show substantial improvement and the recent sale of the estate should result in further elevation.
CS 75%, M 24%, MB & PV 1%
2 *Les Tourelles de Pichon*

CHÂTEAU PICHON LONGUEVILLE COMTESSE DE LALANDE

2CC - Affectionately known as Pichon Lalande, this is currently one of Bordeaux's and the world's high fliers. Since Madame May de Lencquesaing took control of the property in 1978, it has produced a succession of brilliant wines. But Pichon Lalande's ability to achieve excellence is not new, as the Desai tasting in Los Angeles in 1987 proved, with vintages dating back to 1875. The estate is located in part in St Julien, and the wine does tend to have a "split personality", being more like a St Julien wine in some vintages and a Pauillac wine in others. Whatever its style, the wine is noted for outstanding balance, charm and finesse. It can be drunk relatively young, but ages beautifully over many decades.
CS 50%, M 35%, CF 7%, PV 8%
2 Réserve de la Comtesse

CHÂTEAU PONTET-CANET

5CC - There should be no difficulty in obtaining this wine as it has the largest production of the classed growth Médocs. In recent years, substantial sums have been spent on this property that have resulted in greatly improved wines, especially the most recent vintages. A wine to watch.
CS 68%, M 20%, CF 12%
2 Les Haut de Pontet

A SELECTION OF SECOND WINES

CARRUADES DE LAFITE ROTHSCHILD

2nd wine of Château Lafite-Rothschild - For many years this was called Carruades de Château Lafite, but the Rothschilds decided to change it when they found that unscrupulous merchants were passing it off as genuine Lafite. Made from the younger vines, it is very similar to the senior wine, although not as good and maturing more quickly. This is the original second label, and used again since 1987.

LES FORTS DE LATOUR

2nd wine of Château Latour - Since its inception with the 1966 vintage, this has been an outstanding wine. It is not a true second wine because it always contains some wine produced from part of the estate that never goes into the *Grand Vin*. However, it is almost identical to Latour but slightly lower quality level and maturing more quickly.

LACOSTE-BORIE

2nd wine of Château Grand-Puy-Lacoste

CHÂTEAU HAUT-BAGES AVEROUS

2nd wine of Château Lynch Bages - This was originally a small estate on its own that produced some excellent little wines. These are now blended with the lesser casks of Château Lynch Bages and are similar in style, with excellent colour and a noticeable blackcurrant bouquet. Certainly worth looking for.

RÉSERVE DE LA COMTESSE

2nd wine of Château Pichon Longueville Comtesse de Lalande - This is a recent innovation and certainly one of the best second wines in Bordeaux. Its style can vary surprisingly, depending on the selection made for the *Grand Vin*. The delicious 1984 vintage, for instance, is 100 per cent Cabernet wine, because all the available Merlot went into the *Grand Vin*.

MOULIN DE DUHART

2nd wine of Château Duhart-Milon Rothschild

St Julien

S T JULIEN IS THE smallest of the four most important communes in the Médoc, although nearly all the available vineyard area is taken up by the 11 classed growths, and most of what little remains is planted to some excellent *bourgeois* growths. The overall quality of its wines is unmatched by any other areas for consistency and breeding. Very little poor wine is made in this commune, the home of quintessential claret.

Yet St Julien has no first growths. All 11 classed growths are closely grouped together, rather like the vineyards themselves, with five second growths, two thirds and four fourth growths. This tight grouping tends to hide the great individuality of the wines, for none of them is really like another. They have the finesse and elegance of the wines of Margaux, and the power and body of those from Pauillac. The most Pauillac-like of all is Château Léoville Las Cases, which adjoins Château Latour on the north St Julien border.

The soil is similar to that of Pauillac and Margaux, in that it contains a high proportion of gravel, but there is a little more clay and sand here. So excellent is the drainage that in poor climatic and particularly wet years the commune can still make wines that are consistently above average.

Those châteaux closest to the river Gironde exhibit the greatest finesse and bouquet, whilst those further inland are bigger in colour and body. All the wines tend to be a little tough in youth, but when the tannins mellow the resultant wines are elegant, soft and flavoursome. Of the *bourgeois* and unclassified growths, Château Gloria stands proud, often matching the *crus classés* for quality.

CHÂTEAU BEYCHEVELLE

4CC - One of the most beautiful estates in France, producing a very popular, internationally-known wine. Generally uncomplicated yet with a lot of character and St Julien finesse, this wine regularly commands a second growth price. Recent vintages suggest an even greater quality level.
CS 60%, M 28%, CF 8%, PV 4%
2 *Amiral de Beychevelle*

CHÂTEAU BRANAIRE-DUCRU

4CC - Another fourth growth and, in my opinion, a wine superior to its classification. Very traditional, with excellent extract and a highly individual spicy, herby bouquet and flavour. Underrated and excellent value.
CS 60%, M 25%, CF 10%, PV 5%

CHÂTEAU LA BRIDANE

CB - A moderate-sized property, located to the north of the commune next to Château Leoville Las Cases. This is generally a dependable wine, which shows the typical St Julien style but seldom hits the high notes.
CS & CF 55%, M 45%

CHÂTEAU DUCRU-BEAUCAILLOU

2CC - This is consistently one of the finest wines in Bordeaux. Noted for its sheer balance and elegance rather than power and rich fruit, it is a slow developer, needing all of ten years and often longer to develop its finer points. At its best the wine is the epitome of claret.
CS 65%, M 25%, CF 5%, PV 5%
2 *Château La Croix*

CHÂTEAU DU GLANA

CGBE - This is a substantial estate, ideally located close to Château Ducru-Beaucaillou. The quality of the wine has been a bit patchy in the past, but recent vintages have been more consistent, although still not of the highest quality.
CS & CF 70%, M 25%, PV 5%

CHÂTEAU GLORIA

CB (1932) - Henri Martin, mayor of St Julien and former wine maker at Château Latour, has developed Château Gloria into a wine that regularly competes with many of the *crus classés*. It is full-bodied, rounded and fruity, which shows well in its youth but will keep for many years.
CS 65%, M 25%, CF 5%, PV 5%

CHÂTEAU GRUAUD LAROSE

2CC- The flagship of the substantial Cordier estate and a great wine, too. It used to be called "commercial" because of its rich, chunky fruit and popular style, but in my opinion it is consistently one of Bordeaux's finest wines, with lots of fruit, balance and excellent ageing potential.

❧ CS 64%, M 24%, CF 9%, PV 3%
2 *Sarget de Gruaud- Larose*

CHÂTEAU HAUT-BEYCHEVELLE GLORIA

Not to be confused with either Châteaux Gloria or Beychevelle, this is a separate wine made by Henri Martin. In view of Château Gloria's reputation, this wine has no difficulty in finding buyers and commands an above-average price.

❧ CS 65%, M 25%, CF 10%

CHÂTEAU HORTEVIE

One of the best unclassified growths of St Julien. Made from the older vines at Château Terrey-Gros-Cailloux, it is a rich, fruity wine, capable of 10 years' ageing. Production is small, so it may be difficult to find.

❧ CS & CF 70%, M 25%, PV 5%

CHÂTEAU LAGRANGE

3CC - Located further inland than the other leading St Julien classed growths, this has been under-performing for some time. That is, until Suntory, the giant Japanese drinks concern purchased it in 1984. They have spent several years and a great amount of money totally reorganizing and rebuilding the estate. There is little doubt that this will be a wine to keep a close eye on in the future.

❧ CS 58%, M 40%, PV 2%
2 *Les Fiefs de Lagrange*

CHÂTEAU LALANDE-BORIE

CBS (1932) - This estate was replanted by Jean-Eugène Borie shortly after he purchased it in the early 1970s. Now that the vines are reaching maturity the resultant wine is beginning to show its true class. This is a typical, well-made St Julien.

❧ CS 65%, M 25%, CF 10%

CHÂTEAU LANGOA BARTON

3CC - The home of Anthony Barton, who is also proprietor of Château Léoville Barton. The two wines are very similar in style and quality and only on rare occasions does this wine actually surpass that of Château Léoville Barton. Nearly always very competitively priced.

❧ CS 70%, M 15%, CF 8%, PV 7%
2 *St Julien*

CHÂTEAU LÉOVILLE BARTON

2CC - One of the most traditional and uncompromising wines of the Médoc. It is slow to develop and can appear rather firm and lacking in fruit when young, but it develops into a classic St Julien wine in time. The high percentage of Cabernet tends to produce great wines in good years, but can be a little weak in difficult vintages.

❧ CS 70%, M 15%, CF 8%, PV 7%
2 *St Julien*

CHÂTEAU LÉOVILLE LAS CASES

2CC - The most northerly of the three Léovilles, bordering Château Latour, it produces a deep-coloured, powerful, well-structured tannic wine that is consistently one of Bordeaux's finest. It needs at least 10 years' ageing and some vintages much more.

❧ CS 67%, M 17%, CF 13%, PV 3%
2 *Clos du Marquis*

CHÂTEAU LÉOVILLE POYFERRÉ

2CC - Until very recently Poyferré was producing the least fine wine of the three Léovilles. But since the 1982 vintage it seems that it is back to first-class production and a wine to watch.

❧ CS 65%, M 30%, CF 5%
2 *Château Moulin Riche*

Château Moulin de la Rose

CB (1932) - This small property is situated in the hamlet of Beychevelle, close to Château Gloria.
CS 55%, M 30%, CF & PV 15%

Château Saint-Pierre

4CC - Prior to Henri Martin's purchase in 1982, this estate was known as Saint Pierre Sevaistre. Although little known, the wine is a classic St Julien. It can be a little firm and unyielding on the palate, but it has one of the finest bouquets of all St Julien wines. Under its new management the wine is more generous and fruity.
CS 70%, M 25%, CF 5%
2 Château St Louis Le Bosq

Château Talbot

4CC - Similar in many ways to Gruaud Larose, the other *cru classé* in St Julien owned by Cordier, this wine tends to be more spicy but with slightly less grip and definition than the second growth. Occasionally, it makes a superior wine, as is the case with the magnificent 1971 vintage.
CS 70%, M 20%, CF 5%, PF 5%
2 Connetable Talbot

Château Talbot Caillou Blanc

White wine of Château Talbot - One of the few white wines made commercially in the Médoc. This is a particularly successful wine made exclusively from Sauvignon. It is very attractively priced, compared with its other competitors.

A Selection of Second Wines

Amiral de Beychevelle

2nd wine of Château Beychevelle - In view of Beychevelle's history it seems appropriate that a wine should be named after the Duc d'Epernon, Premier Admiral of France. Amiral de Beychevelle is a typical St Julien wine in style - soft, fruity and fairly quick-maturing.

Clos du Marquis

2nd wine of Château Léoville Las Cases - One of the best of Bordeaux's second wines, largely because of the rigorous selection made by the proprietor Michel Delon. Similar to the *grand vin* and great value.

Château Terrey-Gros-Cailloux

Not well-known, but a good wine. See also Château Hortevie.
CS & CF 65%, M 30%, PV 5%

Connetable Talbot

2nd wine of Château Talbot

Les Fiefs de Lagrange

2nd wine of Château Lagrange

Sarget de Gruaud-Larose

2nd wine of Château Gruaud Larose

MARGAUX

THERE ARE NO FEWER than five communes entitled to the appellation Margaux. Besides Margaux itself, there are Cantenac, Labarde and Arsac which lie to the south, and Soussans to the north. The wines are very similar, although Margaux makes the most exquisitely perfumed wine, while Cantenac, Labarde and Arsac make the more full-bodied wine, but with less finesse.

Distinctive features of Margaux

Taking all five communes together, there are more *crus classés* (21) than even Pauillac can boast, and the total vineyard area is nearly as large as St Estèphe. However, Margaux is in no way similar to either commune. First, it has the thinnest soil of the great Médoc appellations, although - like Pauillac - it does have deep gravel beds that in outstanding years help create some of the world's greatest wines. In poor vintages, however, the wines can be rather lean and charmless. Second, many of the vineyards are very intermingled, with some châteaux owning plots in literally dozens of different locations: even though a château may be located in Margaux, its vineyards can be spread over several of the other sub-communes. So unless the vineyard happens to be a single plot - or at least closely grouped - the soil becomes less important than the wine-making style of the château. Much vineyard-swapping has taken place in an attempt to consolidate these fractured holdings, but it will be years before the commune loses its patchwork-quilt appearance.

Margaux is the only commune to have properties classified in all five growths. Château Margaux itself, now unquestionably one of the greatest of the world's wines, is a first growth; there are five seconds, no less than ten thirds, three fourth growths and two fifth growths (although these are actually in Arsac and Labarde). Of all these *crus classés*, very few have been consistent producers of quality wine in the last 30 years, but since the late 1970s and early 1980s there appears to have been an incredible change in pace, leading to a substantial improvement virtually across the board.

Château Margaux The great first growth of Margaux is the only château to have a commune named after it.

CHÂTEAU D'ANGLUDET

Cantenac, CBSE (1932) - This wine was omitted from the 1855 classification because of neglect to the property. Nevertheless, by 1932 it had recovered sufficiently to be classed "Exceptionnel" and today it is producing excellent wines again. The wine is a relatively light- to middle-weight Margaux wine, but displays great elegance and charm. The 1983 vintage is quite exceptional.
CS 50%, M 35%, CF 8%, PV 7%
2 *Château Baury*

CHÂTEAU BEL AIR-MARQUIS D'ALIGRE

Soussans, CBSE (1932) - Located in Soussans on excellent soil, this château is certainly capable of making top quality wine, as it did in the nineteenth century and early in the twentieth century. In fact, it was one of only six "Exceptionnel" wines in the 1932 classification. Today, however, the wine is made in a rather rustic fashion, resulting in a deep-coloured, chunky, fat, but rather coarse wine, which has fruit without the classic Margaux finesse.
M 35%, CS 30%, CF 20%, PV 15%
2 *Marquis de Pomereu*

CHÂTEAU BOYD-CANTENAC

Cantenac, 3CC - This wine is in the same ownership as Château Pouget, and the two wines were made together for many years until 1982, when a new winery was built for Château Pouget. Although vintages prior to 1982 have been good, the younger vintages will obviously have more individuality. The wine tends towards the big, powerful, full-bodied style with deep colour and quite a lot of tannin. A wine to watch for future developments.
CS 67%, M 20%, CF 7%, PV 6%

CHÂTEAU BRANE-CANTENAC

Cantenac, 2CC - Definitely one of the lighter Margaux wines, noted for its excellent bouquet and elegant, stylish flavour, rather than for its weight and power. The wine is drinkable very young, though it does have a great capacity for ageing - the 1928 vintage is still beautiful today.
❧ *CS 70%, CF 15%, M 13%, PV 2%*
2 *Château Notton and Domaine de Fontarney*

CHÂTEAU CANTENAC BROWN

Cantenac, 3CC - This wine tends to be very traditional, being rather firm and tannic in its youth and requiring many years to soften. What it lacks in finesse and elegance, it makes up for in body and concentration.
❧ *CS 75%, M 17%, CF 8%*
2 *Château Canuet*

CHÂTEAU DAUZAC

Labarde, 5CC - Since its purchase in 1978 great improvements have been made by the new owner. The wine is rather light, probably because of the young vines, but shows an elegance that bodes well for future vintages.
❧ *CS 65%, M 30%, PV 5%*
2 *Château Labarde*

CHÂTEAU DESMIRAIL

Margaux, 3CC - In 1957 Desmirail's vineyards were absorbed into those of Château Palmer and for many years no wine was made under its name. Then in 1981 Lucien Lurton resuscitated the *cru* and the first vintages have been stylish, elegant wines with lots of finesse.
❧ *CS 69%, M 23%, CF 7%, PV 1%*
2 *Château Daubry*

CHÂTEAU DURFORT-VIVENS

Margaux, 2CC - Rather disappointing because of its irregular performace, although I have enjoyed the 1966, 1970 and 1978 vintages. Only recently has Lucien Lurton managed to get the château back on track.
❧ *CS 80%, CF 12%, M 8%*
2 *Domaine de Curebouise*

CHÂTEAU FERRIÈRE

Margaux, 3CC - By far the smallest production of the existing classed-growth Médoc wines, making about 1,000 cases per annum. The estate is managed by Château Lascombes, where the wine is made. The wine is bigger and more powerful than that of Lascombes, but lacks such finesse.
❧ *CS 46%, M 33%, PV 12%, CF 8%, MB 1%*

CHÂTEAU GISCOURS

Labarde, 3CC - Out of all the Margaux appellations, Château Giscours is consistently one of the best wines. It is highly distinctive, very dark-coloured and full-bodied, with tremendous tannin reserves. This wine usually requires at least 10 to 15 years to develop.
❧ *CS 70%, M 25%, CF 3%, PV 2%*

CHÂTEAU D'ISSAN

Cantenac, 3CC - This is a property that is very much in ascendancy. The wine is deep coloured - because of the exceptionally high Cabernet Sauvignon content - but it is soft and forward in style. In many ways this wine is not typical of the Margaux style, although it has obvious quality.
❧ *CS 75%, M 25%*

CHÂTEAU KIRWAN

Cantenac, 3CC - Recent vintages of this wine have been a great improvement over those produced for many years, which have been very one-dimensional. Although it was originally classified as the first of the third growths, Château Kirwan has definitely not retained its exalted position. However, it is now beginning to show its potential once again. The wine is approachable relatively early and is best drunk young.
❧ *CS 40%, M 30%, CF 20%, PV 10%*

CHÂTEAU LABÉGORCE

Margaux, CBS (1932) - One of three properties to include the Labégorce name (once all part of the same estate). The wine is light, soft and fruity, although a little inconsistent.
🍷 *CS 55%, M 40%, CF 5%*

CHÂTEAU LABÉGORCE ZÉDÉ

Soussans, CBS (1932) - Since its purchase in 1979 by a member of the Thienpont family this wine has greatly improved. It is made traditionally and has a good deal of depth that needs at least eight years to develop.
🍷 *CS 50%, M 35%, CF 10%, PV 5%*
2 *Château Amiral*

CHÂTEAU LASCOMBES

Margaux, 2CC - The reputation of this large estate, once owned by Alexis Lichine, fell during the 1970s under new ownership. But it can produce elegant and refined wines; the 1982 vintage was particularly promising.
🍷 *CS 63%, M 33%, PV 3%, MB 1%*
2 *Château Ségonnes*

CHÂTEAU MALESCOT ST EXUPÉRY

Margaux, 3CC - I have always thought Malescot to be a rather light yet elegant Margaux wine, but it requires a few years to develop these characteristics. Initially, it can be a little hard and apparently short of fruit, but it ages well and probably should be judged only when it reaches some maturity. A good performer in the best vintages.
🍷 *CS 50%, M 35%, CF 10%, PV 5%*
2 *Château de Loyac,*
3 *Domaine de Bulardin*

CHÂTEAU MARGAUX

Margaux, 1CC - Château Margaux has always been classified among the leading growths of Bordeaux, and is the only château to have a commune named after it. Its performance during the 1960s and 1970s, however, was rather disappointing, until its change of ownership in 1977. Beginning with the 1978 vintage, there has been a series of wines that in quality terms I doubt could have been produced during any other period in history. Quite simply, Château Margaux is producing one of the finest, most elegant red wines in the world. Even in its youth, and well before the wine is truthfully drinkable, it shows a concentration and balance that is remarkable. None of these great new vintages are ready yet, but the 1980 - reckoned to be an off-vintage - will give you some idea of what to expect.
🍷 *CS 75%, M 20%, PV & CF 5%*
2 *Pavillon Rouge du Château Margaux*

PAVILLON BLANC DU CHÂTEAU MARGAUX

White wine of Château Margaux Bordeaux - For many years this was made as a non-vintage wine, but it now carries a vintage. Clean, dry and with good character and length, it can take considerable bottle age. It tends to be expensive but is worth trying.
🍷 *SB 100%*

CHÂTEAU MARQUIS D'ALESME BECKER

Margaux, 3CC - A great deal of time and money has been spent on this property in recent years, with a corresponding improvement in quality. The wine is rather chunky but shows good colour and some depth, requiring about 10 years to develop.
🍷 *CS 40%, M30%, CF 20%, PV 10%*

CHÂTEAU MARQUIS DE TERME

Margaux, 4CC - This wine is little known outside Europe because most is sold direct to the French consumer. The wine tends to require a considerable amount of ageing to reduce the relatively high level of tannin, although the 1982 and 1983 vintages both display a much softer style.
🍷 *CS 45%, M 35%, CF 15%, PV 5%*
2 *Domaine de Condats*

CHÂTEAU MARTINENS

Cantenac, CGB - This property has been virtually reconstructed since 1960 and now produces a relatively straightforward wine that has a certain degree of Margaux elegance. Best drunk when reasonably young.
M 40%, CS 30%, PV 20%, CF 10%

CHÂTEAU MONBRISON

Arsac, CBS (1932) - This château is currently considered to be under reconstruction; the 1983 vintage was certainly very drinkable, showing a fair degree of elegance and balance, and the 1985 is excellent.
M 35%, CS 30%, CF 30%, PV 5%
2 *Clos Cordat*

CHÂTEAU PALMER

Cantenac, 3CC - With its very high percentage of Merlot and traditional winemaking practices, this wine is big, deep, richly fruity and supple, although it has excellent longevity. Its reputation as one of the best of all the Margaux is based on a whole series of vintages, although perhaps its most famous is the brilliant 1961.
CS 55%, M 39%, CF 6%
2 *La Réserve du Général*

CHÂTEAU PAVEIL DE LUZE

Soussans, CGB - An easygoing, straightforward style of wine that can be drunk young. Consistently well made, but lacking excitement.
CS 70%, M 30%
2 *Château de la Coste*

CHÂTEAU POUGET

Cantenac, 4CC - Until 1982 this wine was made with Château Boyd-Cantenac. It is now made separately, and shows the difference of not only the soil, but also the slightly different grape varieties that make up the blend. There are two labels - one for the French market and one, as here, for export markets.
CS 66%, M 30%, CF 4%

CHÂTEAU PRIEURÉ-LICHINE

Cantenac, 4CC - The late Alexis Lichine devoted much of his time to create a typical Cantenac with good colour and body, yet still retaining a good degree of finesse and subtlety.
CS 52%, M 33%, PV 8%, CF 7%
2 *Château de Clairefont*

CHÂTEAU RAUSAN-SÉGLA

Margaux, 2CC - A classic Margaux with elegance, depth and a fine bouquet, this wine improved greatly in the 1980s, although the entire 1987 crop was sold under the second label.
CS 66%, M 28%, CF 4%, PV 2%
2 *Château de Lamouroux*

CHÂTEAU RAUZAN-GASSIES

Margaux, 2CC - A deep-coloured, chunky style of Margaux. The last 25 years have been poor, but there have been recent improvements.
CS 40%, M 39%, CF 20%, PV 1%
2 *Enclos de Moncabon*

CHÂTEAU SIRAN

Labarde, CBS (1932) - This wine has a deep colour, a beautiful bouquet and lovely elegance and finesse. It is very consistent and can be drunk relatively young. It now has a different "picture" label for each vintage.
CS 50%, M 25%, PV 15%, CF 10%
2 *Château Bellegarde*

CHÂTEAU TAYAC

Soussans, CB - A good example of a *bourgeois cru* that makes consistent, fruity wine that is easy to drink. The wine is ready for drinking after four to six years.
CS & CF 70%, M 25%, PV 5%

CHÂTEAU DU TERTRE

Arsac, 5CC - Another property that is very much in ascendancy. Château du Tertre is the only *cru classé* in Arsac, but recent vintages show just how good the soil is. The wine tends towards the Cantenac style, with a deep colour, good concentration and an excellent bouquet. It needs about 10 years to develop.
CS 80%, CF 10%, M 10%

CHÂTEAU LA TOUR DE MONS

Soussans, CBS (1932) - For many years this wine was a contender for elevation to classed growth status, but was not quite good enough. The wine is particularly slow to evolve for a non-classified growth, often requiring 10 years to develop its classic Margaux finesse. It is deep-coloured, fairly tannic, but with good concentration. Worth looking out for.
CS 45%, M 40%, CF 10%, PV 5%

A SELECTION OF SECOND WINES

CHÂTEAU NOTTON

2nd wine of Château Brane-Cantenac. Cantenac - Originally classified as a *Cru Bourgeois* in 1932, this is now the second wine of Château Brane-Cantenac.

PAVILLON ROUGE DU CHÂTEAU MARGAUX

2nd wine of Château Margaux. Margaux - A really outstanding second wine, and perhaps one of the few to match the quality of Les Forts de Latour. Like the *Grand Vin*, it is also matured in new oak casks and although it is lighter in colour it is still of excellent quality, showing much of the finesse of the premier wine.

CHÂTEAU CANUET

2nd wine of Château Cantenac Brown

CHÂTEAU DE CLAIREFONT

2nd wine of Château Prieuré-Lichine

CHÂTEAU DE LAMOUROUX

2nd wine of Château Rausan-Ségla

LA RÉSERVE DU GÉNÉRAL

2nd wine of Château Palmer

CHÂTEAU SÉGONNES

2nd wine of Château Lascombes

LISTRAC & MOULIS

L ISTRAC AND MOULIS LIE slightly further away from the river Gironde than the four big communes of Médoc. Because of their relative obscurity, the wines of both communes offer excellent value. The wines of Moulis tend to be deep-coloured, with body and vigour. Often hard in their youth, they develop into well-structured, ripe, interesting wines after a decade of bottle ageing.

Ground rules *Gravelly soil provides excellent drainage, and has helped Listrac and Moulis gain their appellations.*

In Moulis, Château Chasse-Spleen has been making wine of classed growth standard for many years. Several other properties elsewhere in Moulis are nearly the equal of Chasse-Spleen, including Châteaux Brillette, Maucaillou and Poujeaux.

The best area in Moulis is around the village of Grand Poujeaux, on a high plateau containing a good amount of gravel. No less than four châteaux link their names with Grand Poujeaux - other than Château Poujeaux itself - and all make significantly good wine. They are Châteaux Branas, Dutruch, Gressier and Lestage-Darquier.

The wines of Listrac

Listrac lies to the west of Moulis further inland and on higher ground and, if anything, the wines often exaggerate the characteristics of those of Moulis. They are more severe when young, but develop well if given sufficient time. In Listrac the gravel to be found in the soil overlaps chalk, which is probably responsible for the firmness of some of Listrac's wines.

Neither Listrac nor Moulis can boast any *crus classés,* although there are a couple of properties in Listrac that are strong contenders. Its leading estate at the moment is Château Fourcas Hosten, which has been producing exceptional wines recently, with a great deal of attractive, rich fruit.

LISTRAC

CHÂTEAU CLARKE

CBS (1932) - Enormous sums of money have been spent by Baron Edmund de Rothschild in completely renovating and restructuring this property. The vines are very young, but already the vintages of the 1980s are beginning to show great promise.
CS 49%, M 37%, CF 10%, PV 4%
2 *Granges de Clarke*

CHÂTEAU FONRÉAUD

CB - A large property, producing a pleasant, rather light wine made for early consumption. Generally a good value, everyday Médoc wine.
CS 66%, M 31%, PV 3%

CHÂTEAU FOURCAS DUPRÉ

CGBE - Another rather traditional, austere style of wine that requires several years to mellow. Recent vintages have shown a greater degree of suppleness.
CS 50%, M 38%, CF 10%, PV 2%
2 *Bellevue Laffont*

CHÂTEAU FOURCAS HOSTEN

CGBE - The best wine in Listrac today, showing excellent deep colour and a considerable amount of fruit, depth and length. This was not always so, as the wines of the pre-1980 period tended to be very severe and tannic.
CS 55%, M 40%, CF 5%

CHÂTEAU LESTAGE

CB - A very high percentage of Merlot makes this a soft, fruity, supple wine for relatively early consumption. Another good value property.
M 55%, CS & CF 41%, PV 4%

MOULIS

CHÂTEAU BRILLETTE

CGB - An above-average Moulis wine, largely sold through Euromarché and Viniprix in France, although a small amount is exported. Relatively early maturing, it displays good fruit with pleasant oak overtones.
CS 55%, M 40%, PV 5%

CHÂTEAU CHASSE-SPLEEN

CGBE - An outstanding *bourgeois* growth that has been producing *cru classé* quality for many years. Deep-coloured, firm, structured wine, with excellent depth of fruit, especially popular on the continent of Europe, but well-known elsewhere. Very consistent.
M 45%, CS 50%, PV 3%, CF 2%
2 *Ermitage de Chasse-Spleen*

CHÂTEAU DUTRUCH GRAND POUJEAUX

CGBE - A well-made, firm and slightly one-dimensional style of wine that requires a certain amount of ageing to soften its rough edges. Best in the finer vintages, it is a wine for Médoc lovers who prefer the drier style.
CS & CF 60%, M 35%, PV 5%

CHÂTEAU GRESSIER GRAND POUJEAUX

CBS (1932) - Another "Poujeaux" wine, softer than Dutruch and lighter than Château Poujeaux itself. It is rarely seen outside France.
CS 50%, M 40%, CF 10%

CHÂTEAU MAUCAILLOU

CB (1932) - This is an excellent, supple, early-maturing wine that is very drinkable within four years, but is still nice after ten. Good colour, fine bouquet and savoury palate.
CS 45%, M 35%, CF 15%, PV 5%

CHÂTEAU MOULIN À VENT

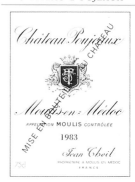

CGB - An improving property that could be worth following. The deep-coloured wine has been very Cabernet in style, owing to the low production of the very old Merlot vines.
CS 65%, M 30%, PV 5%
2 *Moulin de St Vincent*

CHÂTEAU POUJEAUX

CGBE - Perhaps the longest-lived and most traditional style of wine in Moulis; a deep-coloured, well-structured, fairly tannic, high-quality wine that requires ageing to show its finer qualities.
CS 35%, M 35%, CF 15%, PV 15%
2 *Salle de Poujeaux*

HAUT-MÉDOC

BORDERING THE REGION of the Graves to the south near Taillan and Blanquefort, which have effectively become the northern suburbs of the city of Bordeaux, Haut-Médoc stretches north to the southern borders of the communes of St German d'Esteuil and St Yzans de Médoc.

There are no fewer than 15 communes entitled to this appellation, but the most significant are St Seurin de Cadourne, St Laurent, Cussac, St Sauveur, Cissac and Vertheuil. The region surrounds and indeed includes the six communes of St Estèphe, Pauillac, St Julien, Margaux, Moulis and Listrac, which, of course, have their own appellations, although they have the right to be declassified to Haut Médoc. Some parts of these communes, particularly parts of Margaux, are only entitled to the Haut-Médoc appellation.

As well as the many single properties, there are well-organized cooperatives which account for 17 per cent of production and make an important contribution to the quality of the wines in the area.

The effect of the soil

Most of the vineyard land, and certainly the best of it, lies within 10 kilometres (6 miles) of the Gironde. It is basically a long, thin strip of land protected to the west from the Atlantic Ocean by miles of pine forest. This is the area where the *crus bourgeois* reign supreme, with over 60 per cent of the vineyard land planted to them. The soil often contains substantial deposits of gravel, like the more famous communes mentioned above, but not in such quantity. Nevertheless, the soil is good enough to support a number of *crus classés*, accounting for nearly 6 per cent of the area, with three located in the commune of St Laurent and one each in the communes of Ludon and Macau.

Recent developments

The whole region is undergoing a major new lease of life. During the earlier part of this century the area under vines fell dramatically. This sad state of affairs has been completely reversed, with the number of vines being increased by over two-thirds in the last 15 years or so. Many of the wines are now matured in oak barrels, with an increasing amount of new oak. This fortunate development means that the appellation can provide high-quality wine at a relatively modest price.

Qualities of the wines

The wines vary substantially in quality. At best they are at least as good as many of the *crus classés* and at worst they are little more than everyday drinking wines. Most show a pronounced Cabernet Sauvignon style and require bottle ageing to develop their full fruit flavours and the finesse that is associated with this grape. Even the lesser wines show a pleasing fruit and their relative austerity makes them ideal for drinking with food. The best display considerable complexity and will reach their zenith between 10 and 20 years.

In the south the wines are lighter, softer and more obviously fruity, and are very suitable for early drinking. Further north they show greater colour, depth and concentration and require time.

CHÂTEAU D'AGASSAC

Ludon, CGBE - Following an excellent 1966, most of the wines of the 1970s were rather light and lacking in character, but the wines of the 1980s show a stunning return to form. They are deeply coloured, rich and plummy, with sufficient tannin for medium- to long-term cellaring.
 CS 60%, M 40%
2 *Château Pomiès-Agassac*

CHÂTEAU D'ARSAC

Arsac, CBS (1932) - A deep-coloured wine with substantial body and tannin, becoming soft and perfumed with age. It should be a Margaux, but the estate was not planted when *Appellation Contrôlée* was introduced.
 CS 70%, M 25%, CF 5%
2 *Château Ségur d'Arsac, Château Le Monteil d'Arsac*

CHÂTEAU BEAUMONT

Cussac, CGB - Known as Château Beaumont de Bolivar until the death of the owner in 1978. Until this time the wines were big-boned and made to last. Today, they have a much more forward, easy-drinking style and represent excellent value for money.
 CS 56%, M 36%, CF 7%, PV 1%
2 *Château Moulin d'Arvigny*

CHÂTEAU BELGRAVE

St Laurent, 5CC - Located close to Château Lagrange in St Julien, this château had been underperforming during the 1960s and 1970s, but new ownership in 1980 and substantial investment since have helped to raise the quality markedly. Its performance is erratic, but worth watching, especially as its price is very competitive.
CS 60%, M 35%, PV 5%

CHÂTEAU BEL ORME TRONQUOY DE LALANDE

St Seurin de Cadourne, CGB - A truly uncompromising wine made in the old style and requiring considerable cellaring to develop. Older vintages can be exceptional, but do not expect to drink younger ones until they are 15 to 20 years old.
M 45%, CS 30%, CF 20%, MB 3%, PV 2%

CHÂTEAU LE BOURDIEU

Vertheuil, CB - A well-made wine that is perhaps more in the style of a St Estèphe (the commune that it borders). The proprietress also owns Châteaux Victoria and Picourneau.
CS 50%, M 30%, CF 17%, PV 3%

CHÂTEAU DE CAMENSAC

St Laurent, 5CC - In virtual dereliction until its purchase in 1965 by its present owners, this property now produces a good quantity of medium-weight wine, with a noticeable St Julien style. The wines are good value, if seldom exciting, and can be safely kept for a decade or more.
CS 60%, M 20%, CF 20%

CHÂTEAU CANTEMERLE

Macau, 5CC - Perhaps unfairly listed last in the 1855 classification, this château produced some outstanding wines from the 1920s to the early 1960s, but then fell into decline. Now managed by Cordier, it has returned to top form - the 1983 vintage is superb. The wine is fairly deep-coloured, with outstanding depth of rich, ripe fruit and subtle, oaky hints.
CS 40%, M 40%, CF 15%, PV 5%
2 *Baron Villeneuve de Cantemerle*

CHÂTEAU CARONNE STE GEMME

St Laurent, CGBE - This property benefits from a good gravelly soil. The wines are big in colour and tannin, but have sufficient body and fruit to develop well. More recent vintages, particularly of the 1980s, appear to be more fruity, but even these need time to develop.
CS 65%, M 33%, PV 2%
2 *Château Labat*

CHÂTEAU CISSAC

Cissac, CGBE - An excellent property that produces a deep-coloured, tannic, powerful wine that is particularly popular in the UK. The wine requires considerable ageing and seldom reaches its peak before 10 years; it can easily last for 20 or more.
CS 75%, M 20%, PV 5%
2 *Château Abiet*

CHÂTEAU CITRAN

Avensan, CGBE - A large estate and the most important in Avensan. It has a high proportion of Merlot vines for the Médoc. The wine can be soft and fruity, but there has been a tendency to produce large crops, which can result in one-dimensional wines.
M 60%, CS 35%, PV 5%

CHÂTEAU COUFRAN

St Seurin de Cadourne, CGB - With an even higher proportion of Merlot than Château Citran, this is a fairly big, rich, fleshy wine that has been very successful during the 1980s. Although it is easy to drink quite young, it does improve with up to 10 years bottle age.
M 85%, CS 10%, PV 5%
2 *Domaine de la Rose Maréchale*

CHÂTEAU LA DAME BLANCHE

An unique Médoc property, producing only white wine which, because of the *Appellation Contrôlée* regulations, can only carry the Bordeaux appellation. The unusual blend of grapes results in an attractive, flowery wine, suitable for early consumption.
SB 67%, COL 33%

CHÂTEAU DILLON

Blanquefort, CB (1932) - Owned by the Ministry of Agriculture, this is a light, attractive wine, best drunk young. Perhaps because it is made by the school of agriculture, it has been uneven in quality over the years.
CS 48%, M 48%, CF 2%, PV 1%, CAR 1%

CHÂTEAU FONTESTEAU

St Sauveur, CGB - Made very traditionally, this is neverthess a light, forward wine that does not benefit from long ageing. Recent new ownership may see some change in style.
CS 35%, CF 30%, M 30%, PV 5%

CHÂTEAU HANTEILLAN

Cissac, CGB - Completely replanted in 1972, this property is already showing some of its real potential. As the vines mature, the wine should get deeper and more complex.
CS 45%, M 42%, CF 8%, MB & PV 5%
2 Tour de Vatican, Château Larrivaux Hanteillan

LE HAUT-MÉDOC DU PRIEURÉ

Cantenac (Margaux) - Owned by and made at Château Prieuré Lichine, this carefully made oak-aged wine is not easy to find - it has an annual production of less than 500 cases.
CS 60%, M 35%, CF 5%

CHÂTEAU LACHESNAYE

Cussac - Located next to Château Lanessan, this property was purchased by the Bouteiller family in 1961. Today both are run by Hubert Bouteiller. With a higher proportion of Merlot, this wine is softer than Lanessan and easier to drink younger.
CS 50%, M 50%

CHÂTEAU LA LAGUNE

Ludon, 3CC - A consistent wine in both off-vintages as well as great ones; it is deep in colour, remarkably supple and always seems to have an outstanding amount of ripe fruit. Since its virtual total reconstruction in the 1960s, this château - now owned by the Ayala Champagne firm - has been producing an outstanding wine of second-growth quality. It is one of the best values amongst the classed growths, as it is usually offered at an attractive price. When young, it can have an oaky character, as 100 per cent new casks are invariably used.
CS 55%, CF 20%, M 20%, PV 5%

CHÂTEAU DE LAMARQUE

Lamarque - This substantial property, once an important fort with parts dating back to the eleventh century, is certainly worth a visit. The vineyards were totally refurbished in the 1960s, but the wine can still be a little inconsistent, especially in lesser vintages, when it tends to be rather light. So it pays to choose the better years for fuller fruit and elegance.
CS 50%, CF 20%, M 25%, PV 5%
2 Réserve du Marquis d'Evry

CHÂTEAU LANESSAN

Cussac, CBS (1932) - Celebrating 200 years in the hands of the same family, this fine property makes well above-average wines, which tend to be firm in their youth. Since it is located on a gravel outcrop that is an extension of the soil of St Julien, there is a resemblance to wines of that commune.
CS 75%, M 20%, CF 5%

CHÂTEAU LAROSE-TRINTAUDON

St Laurent, CGB - A huge vineyard, the largest in the Médoc, which produces lightweight, but interesting, fruity wines for early consumption. Despite its vast production, its price is inexpensive and the wine consistent.
CS 60%, CF 20%, M 20%
2 *Larose Mascard, Larose Perganson, Larose Sieujean*

CHÂTEAU LESTAGE SIMON

St Seurin de Cadourne, CB - Located next to Château Coufran, this wine is also Merlot based. Although fairly solid in structure, it matures quickly and is meant for early drinking.
M 68%, CS 22%, CF 10%

CHÂTEAU LIVERSAN

St Sauveur, CGB - Under new ownership since 1983 this is a property to watch, as all the facilities have been improved. Previously rather severe in style, the wine is now very attractive, with much more fruit and body.
CS 49%, M 38%, CF 10%, PV 3%
2 *Château Fonpiqueyre*

CHÂTEAU DE MALLERET

Le Pian, CGB - This vineyard, bordering part of Château La Lagune in Ludon, produces a well-structured, fairly firm wine with good tannin and a subtle hint of oak. Its large production makes it fairly easy to find.
CS 75%, M 10%, CF 5%, MB 5%, PV 5%
2 *Château Lemoine Nexon, Château Barthez*

CHÂTEAU LE MEYNIEU

Vertheuil, CGB - Made by Jacques Pedro, the local mayor, this is a well-structured Cabernet Sauvignon style wine with excellent depth, good fruit and plenty of tannin. Several years are required for the elegant, soft, fruit flavours to develop.
CS 70%, M 30%

CHÂTEAU PEYRABON

St Sauveur, CGB - An increasing quantity of Merlot in the blend (it was once a 90 per cent Cabernet wine) has resulted in a softer, rounded, easy style of wine with good colour and reasonable depth. This attractive wine can be drunk young.
CS 50%, M 27%, CF 23%
2 *Château Pierbone*

CHÂTEAU RAMAGE LA BATISSE

St Sauveur, CB - A very attractive wine with excellent scented bouquet and a richly fruity soft taste that has immediate appeal. Although it can be drunk young, it ages well.
CS 60%, M 40%
2 *Château Tourteran*

CHÂTEAU SÉNÉJAC

Le Pian, CBS (1932) - A truly international set-up with an American owner of French descent and a New Zealand winemaker married to an English *négociant* husband. The wine is very traditional - deep-coloured, aromatic and tannic - and requires many years to develop its full potential.
CS 47%, CF 25%, M 23%, PV 3%, MB 2%
2 *Domaine de L'Artigue*

CHÂTEAU SOCIANDO-MALLET

St Seurin de Cadourne, CGB - Unquestionably one of the best wines of the Haut Médoc appellation, this is a true *vin de garde*. Made in a very traditional style with a high percentage of new oak, it is a deep-coloured, well-structured, tannic, yet deeply fruity wine that needs plenty of ageing to show off its best qualities. *Cru classé* quality.
CS 60%, M 25%, CF 10%, PV 5%
2 *Château Lartigue de Brochon*

CHÂTEAU SOUDARS

St Seurin de Cadourne, CB - One of the three properties in this commune belonging to the Miailhe family, this is a particularly rounded, soft, fruity wine that drinks very well young but continues to develop for up to eight years or so. Excellent value.
CS 60%, M 40%

CHÂTEAU DU TAILLAN

Le Taillan, CGB - Owned by Henri Cruse, this is effectively the other half of Château La Dame Blanche. The wine is relatively soft, light and supple, suitable for early drinking.
CS 55%, M 40%, CF 5%

CHÂTEAU LA TOUR CARNET

St Laurent, 4CC - After an enormous effort to bring this property back to quality production after a long period of serious decline, it was particularly tragic that the owner's husband should die in an accident. However, the wine in the 1980s has shown a significant improvement and now has more depth and richness which one hopes will be maintained and developed further.
CS 66%, M 33%, PV 1%
2 *Le Sire de Camin*

CHÂTEAU TOUR DU HAUT-MOULIN

Cussac, CGB - A rich, powerful wine with excellent deep colour: this is one of the better wines of the commune and indeed of the Haut-Médoc. With a good proportion of new oak used each year, its tannic structure requires 10 years or so to soften. Good value.
CS 50%, M 45%, PV 5%

CHÂTEAU TOUR DU MIRAIL

Cissac, CB - Owned by the daughters of the proprietor of Château Cissac, this is a consistently well-made wine of good quality that is mainly sold in the UK. Even with its noticeable Cabernet style, it can be drunk after about five years or so.
CS 70%, M 25%, PV 5%

CHÂTEAU VERDIGNAN

St Seurin de Cadourne, CGB - Of the three Miailhe wines, this is the biggest and firmest, but it does have good fruit and can be drunk with pleasure after five to six years. The wines of the 1980s are definitely superior to those of the 1960s and 1970s, which tended to lack fruit.
CS 55%, M 40%, CF 5%
2 *Château Plantey de la Croix*

CHÂTEAU DE VILLEGEORGE

Avensan, CBSE (1932) - One of only six wines classified as *Exceptionnel* in 1932, this is a most atypical Médoc because of its very high Merlot content. The wine has a deep colour with a pronounced flavour. In the past it has often lacked a little fruit, but under the guiding hand of Lucien Lurton it appears to be improving.
M 60%, CS 30%, CF 10%

CHÂTEAU LES VIMIÈRES

Lamarque - A real rarity and probably unique for the Médoc, this is made only from Merlot grapes. Its tiny production means it will be difficult to find, but it should be worth the effort.
M 100%

MÉDOC

MARGINALLY BIGGER IN area under vines than the appellation Haut-Médoc, at just under 3,000 hectares (7,400 acres), the appellation Médoc continues north from Haut-Médoc's border to the tip of the Médoc region at La Pointe de Grave. There are few vines, however, planted north of St Vivien and the most important communes within the appellation are located in the more southerly area, with Bégadan being by far the most significant. Of the remaining 15 communes, St Yzans de Médoc, Prignac, Ordonnac, St Christoly, Blaignan and St Germain d'Esteuil are all important.

There is much less gravel here than in the Haut-Médoc and Graves, and a correspondingly higher level of rich earth, including clay and some sand. These conditions tend to favour the Merlot grape more than the Cabernet Sauvignon, so it is not surprising to see much more Merlot in the blends. This results in wines that are relatively light in body but with good flavour and an attractive bouquet. They never have the finesse of the wines of Haut-Médoc, although the best of them are certainly very good and a few can command a high price. This is an area of excellent value.

CHÂTEAU LE BOSCQ

St Christoly, CB - Produced by the owners of Château Patache d'Aux, this is a big, fleshy, fruity wine, made for relatively early consumption.
CS over 50%

CHÂTEAU LA CARDONNE

Blaignan, CGB - Immense change has taken place here after Domaines Barons de Rothschild of Lafite fame took over the property in 1973. The wine, however, remains relatively light and one-dimensional in style, although it is very pleasing.
CS 72%, M 23%, CF & PV 5%

CHÂTEAU CASTÉRA

St Germain d'Esteuil, CB - Owned by Alexis Lichine and Co., the Bordeaux *négociants*, this important property produces attractively fruity, rounded, soft wines that can be drunk young.
CS 60%, M 40%

CUVÉE DE LA COMMANDERIE DU BONTEMPS

Not produced every year, this used to be a blend of wines donated in cask by members of the Bontemps and included the leading *crus classés* of the Médoc. Following the introduction of compulsory château-bottling for the *crus classés* in 1972, this has beome a carefully selected wine marketed by Ulysse Cazabonne. Always a wine of high quality, it represents good value. A Sauternes has recently been added to the range.

CHÂTEAU GREYSAC

Bégadan, CGB - Brought to great popularity in the USA by the late Baron François de Gunzburg, this is a well-made, medium-bodied, elegant, fruity wine, capable of ageing at least 10 years, but usually ready for drinking rather sooner.
CS 50%, M 38%, CF 10%, PV 2%
2 *Château Les Bertins*

CHÂTEAU LAUJAC

Bégadan, CGB - This significant property is owned by the Cruse family. Made along traditional lines, the wine is deeply coloured and firm in its youth, but develops an attractive soft fruit after 10 years or so.
CS 60%, M 25%, CF 10%, PV 5%

CHÂTEAU LOUDENNE

St Yzans, CGB - This outstanding property produces a soft, supple, fruity claret, which is easy to drink when young but has excellent keeping properties. A true Médoc, it lacks the grip and depth of a great wine but rarely fails to please. The white Château Loudenne, classified only as AC Bordeaux and made with equal amounts of Sémillon and Sauvignon, is delightfully fresh, clean and fruity.

CS 55%, M 38%, CF 7%

CHÂTEAU LES ORMES SORBET

Couquèques, CGB - Seldom seen outside France, this is a classic Médoc with good colour and firm structure, with enough fruit and balance to be worth ageing for five to eight years.

CS 65%, M 35%

CHÂTEAU PATACHE D'AUX

Bégadan, CGB - A wine with a high Cabernet content and good colour, but made for early consumption: a soft, supple style with little tannin. Drink within eight years or so.

CS 70%, M 20%, CF 10%

CHÂTEAU POTENSAC

Ordansac, CGB - This excellent, highly sought-after wine is very much a Cabernet one in style. With 75 per cent Cabernet in the blend, and the expert hand of Michel Delon of Château Léoville Las Cases, it has deep colour, fruit and a positive oak character. One of the more expensive Médocs, but well worth the extra.

CS 55%, M 25%, CF 20%

2 *Château Lassalle, Château Gallais Bellevue, Château Goudy La Cardonne*

CHÂTEAU SAINT BONNET

St Christoly, CB - This château is located close to the Gironde, although the vineyards lie further inland. The property produces well-structured, full-bodied wines with plenty of flavour. Good value.

M 50%, CS 28%, CF 22%

CHÂTEAU SIGOGNAC

St Yzans, CGB - A medium-bodied, well-made wine that lacks the class of its neighbour, Château Loudenne, but nevertheless offers good drinking at a modest price. A wine for early drinking, rather than laying down.

CS 33%, CF 33%, M 33%

CHÂTEAU LA TOUR BLANCHE

St Christoly, CB - A medium-bodied wine, very Médoc in style, which has enough good fruit for it to be enjoyed after four to five years. Good value for money.

CHÂTEAU LA TOUR DE BY

Bégadan, CGB - A popular and consistent wine with good structure and ageing potential. Always well-coloured, it can be a little firm to begin with, but develops an excellent palate after six to ten years.

CS 70%, M 25%, CF 5%

2 *Château Caillou de By, Château La Roque de By, Moulin de la Roque*

CHÂTEAU LA TOUR ST BONNET

St Christoly, CB - Deep-coloured, full-bodied and tannic in its youth, this wine requires several years to soften. Usually best in the finest vintages, when it shows a greater depth of fruit and complexity.

M 50%, CS 28%, CF 22%

2 *Château La Fuie St Bonnet*

GRAVES

I N RECENT YEARS THE GRAVES has undergone a renaissance that is quite remarkable, considering the slow but serious decline of this once famous and important commune. For three centuries (1152-1453) all wine shipped from Bordeaux was from the Graves. At this time Aquitaine, as it was then known, belonged to the English crown. However, in the twentieth century - until very recently - Graves was seldom identified or listed separately. The expansion of Bordeaux and its suburbs, combined with the economic depression until well after the Second World War, resulted in a catastrophic reduction in the vineyard area.

During the 1950s and most of the 1960s Graves was associated with poor quality, heavily sulphured, clumsy and often oxidized semi-sweet white wines. The few quality wines were invariably red; indeed, much of the commune's reputation could be attributed to Château Haut-Brion, one of the oldest and most illustrious wine châteaux of Bordeaux, and classified as a first growth in the 1855 classification of the wines of the Gironde.

The renaissance of the Graves

Much has changed and today the commune is again expanding, its reputation rapidly on the rise. Although this resurgence is the product of a large number of people, three individuals stand out: André Lurton, for his determination to prevent concrete from destroying further prime vineyards and indeed the replanting of long-since derelict sites; Peter Vinding-Diers, for his outstanding contribution to wine-making techniques, especially his research into yeast cultures; and Pierre Coste for his leadership in the southern Graves.

The new appellation of Pessac-Léognan

The Graves surrounds the city of Bordeaux, bordering the Médoc to the north, and today extends southwards a further 48 kilometres (30 miles) to beyond St Pierre de Mons and indeed effectively surrounding the vineyards of Sauternes and Barsac. Because of the disparate nature of the commune, there is an element of conflict between the north, where all the *crus classés* are, and the south, where the majority of growers are situated.

The conflict may have been overcome with the introduction, on 9 September 1987, of the new appellation of Pessac-Léognan. This covers 10 communes in the north of the Graves region: Cadaujac, Canéjan, Gradignan, Léognan, Martillac, Pessac, St Médard d'Eyrans, Talence and Villenave d'Ornon. All the *crus classés,* which were originally classified in 1959, and many other significant properties are included in this new appellation. It will be interesting to see if these properties benefit from this change and if they decide to disassociate themselves from the Graves, calling their wines Pessac-Léognan instead.

Characteristics of the wines

Until very recently only three white wines were of particularly high quality - Châteaux Haut-Brion Blanc, Laville-Haut-Brion, and Domaine de Chevalier Blanc - but now there are a host of rising stars. Some are made from 100 per cent Sauvignon, whilst others are the more traditional blend of Sémillon with Sauvignon. At their best, they are as individual and good as top-quality white Burgundy and, like them, they are relatively expensive. Almost without fail, the best wines are aged in oak barrels, most of which are new.

The reds are at their finest in the Pessac-Léognan appellation, although some very drinkable, inexpensive, early maturing, fruity wines are made in the southern area. They show various qualities, among which are often noted earthy, milky, soft, tobacco and mineral scents. They develop quite quickly, but last well. Some of the older vintages were made in a very severe style and took many years to mellow, but the increasing use of Merlot has reduced this characteristic.

1959 GRAVES CLASSIFICATION

CHÂTEAU	COMMUNE
Red wines	
Bouscaut	Cadaujac
Carbonnieux	Léognan
Domaine de Chevalier	Léognan
de Fieuzal	Léognan
Haut-Bailly	Léognan
Haut-Brion	Pessac
Latour-Haut-Brion	Talence
Malartic-Lagravière	Léognan
La Mission-Haut-Brion	Talence
d'Olivier	Léognan
Pape-Clément	Pessac
Smith-Haut-Lafitte	Martillac
La Tour-Martillac	Martillac
White wines	
Bouscaut	Cadaujac
Carbonnieux	Léognan
Domaine de Chevalier	Léognan
Couhins	Villenave d'Ornon
Laville-Haut-Brion	Talence
Malartic-Lagravière	Léognan
d'Olivier	Léognan
La Tour-Martillac	Martillac

PESSAC-LÉOGNAN REDS

CHÂTEAU BARET

Villenave d'Ornon - Made with old vines and a high percentage of Cabernet Sauvignon, this is a well-coloured but relatively straightforward Graves that had a better reputation during the 1960s and 1970s than now.
CS 72%, M 25%, CF 3%

CHÂTEAU BOUSCAUT

Cadaujac, CC - In serious decline in the 1960s, this château was resuscitated by an American group who sold it to Lucien Lurton in 1980. The wine is well made and its modest price makes it worth trying.
M 55%, CS 35%, CF 5%, MB 5%
2 *Château Valoux*

CHÂTEAU BROWN

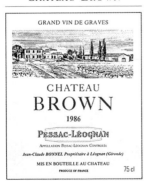

Léognan - Only red wine is made on this estate. Well-structured, yet relatively easy to drink, even when young. Capable of long-term ageing.
CS 60%, M 40%

CHÂTEAU CARBONNIEUX

Léognan, CC - Until very recently this wine has been relatively light, simple and for early drinking. Recent use of oak ageing, some in new wood, has added an extra dimension.
CS 55%, M 30%, CF 10%, MB 3%, PV 2%
2 *Château La Tour Léognan*

CHÂTEAU LES CARMES HAUT BRION

Pessac - A much underrated property. The wine has unusually deep colour and needs at least five to eight years' ageing to soften its firm structure. Consistent even in poor vintages.
M 60%, CS 20%, CF 20%

DOMAINE DE CHEVALIER

Léognan, CC - One of the finest wines of Graves. It has a spicy, mineral and tobacco bouquet, with a well-structured flavour and long, powerful finish. Wines of the 1960s and 1970s reached their peak within 10 to 15 years; recent vintages appear to be deeper and may need longer.
CS 65%, M 30%, CF 5%

CHÂTEAU COUHINS

Villenave d'Ornon - An estate that is better known for its white wine, it nevertheless makes more red than white. The vines are young, but the wine has a good colour and plenty of tannin for long-term cellaring.
CS 54%, M 31%, CF 11%, PV 4%

CHÂTEAU DE CRUZEAU

St Médard d'Eyrans - Once an important estate that was seriously run-down before André Lurton's purchase in 1974. The wine has a spicy, scented bouquet; supple yet full-bodied, fruity palate. It is easy to drink while young, but will age well.
CS 60%, M 40%

CHÂTEAU DE FIEUZAL

Léognan, CC - Highly underrated, this is a well-structured wine with plenty of tannin, but with the Graves softness that makes it relatively easy to drink young. Good value.
CS 60%, M 30%, CF 5%, PV 4%, MB 1%
2 *L'Abeille de Fieuzal*

FRANCE

CHÂTEAU DE FRANCE

Léognan - Another Graves property that has been much expanded and improved in recent years. Although not amongst the finest of the region, its deep colour and firm palate make it a worthy glass of wine.
CS 60%, M 40%

CHÂTEAU LA GARDE

Martillac - This large property produces a consistent, medium-bodied, soft, fruity wine that is best drunk between five and ten years old. Usually very good value.
CS 62%, M 27%, CF 9%, PV 2%

CHÂTEAU GAZIN

Léognan - An ancient property that was abandoned in 1960 and only replanted from 1972. It makes only red wine. The vines have now reached maturity and are beginning to make some interesting wines with deep colour and positive Cabernet characteristics. A wine to watch.
CS 80%, M 10%, CF 10%

CHÂTEAU HAUT-BAILLY

Léognan, CC - A high percentage of very old vines help to produce a well-coloured, supple wine with lots of fruit and sufficient tannin for medium- to long-term ageing. Certainly one of the best Graves and usually very good value. Red wine only.
CS 60%, M 30%, CF 10%
2 *La Parde de Haut Bailly*

CHÂTEAU HAUT-BERGEY

Léognan - A consistent source of good, rather than great wine. Fine colour and bouquet. Inexpensive and good value.
CS 70%, M 30%

CHÂTEAU HAUT BRION

Pessac, 1CC (1855), GCC - One of Bordeaux's truly great wines and the only red wine in the famous 1855 classification that did not come from the Médoc. Its current production could hardly be bettered, with very impressive and elegant wines being made since the mid-1970s. For a wine that is medium- rather than full-bodied it has an extraordinary amount of flavour and length. It ages well: examples over 60 years old are still in excellent drinking condition.
CS 55%, M 25%, CF 20%
2 *Bahans Haut Brion*

CHÂTEAU HAUT-GARDÈRE

Léognan - Well-positioned opposite Château de Fieuzal, this estate produces a relatively full-bodied wine with a degree of elegance and a delicate bouquet.
CS 58%, M 35%, CF 7%

CHÂTEAU LARRIVET-HAUT-BRION

Léognan - A typical, fine Léognan Graves, of *cru classé* quality, with excellent colour and spicy bouquet. Suitable for relatively early drinking, but will keep for many years.
CS 55%, M 40%, MB & PV 5%

CHÂTEAU LA LOUVIÈRE

Léognan - Better known for its suberb white wine, this estate deserves to be classified for both red and white wines. Under the able direction of André Lurton, who has increased the amount of Merlot in the blend, this wine has changed from a firm, lean Graves during the mid-1960s to a full, fruity and altogether more complex wine. Significantly underpriced.
CS 70%, M 20%, CF 10%
2 *Château Coucheroy*

Château Malartic-Lagravière

Léognan, CC - For many years rather lightweight wine, but with a certain grip and some bitterness in the finish. Recent vintages are an improvement, showing more body and depth.
✣ *CS 50%, CF 25%, M 25%*

Château La Mission Haut Brion

Talence et Pessac, CC - This exceptional estate is now under the same ownership as its neighbour, Château Haut Brion. La Mission has always been the bigger and more tannic of the two, making up in vigour what it loses in finesse. Very consistent, particularly in off-vintages.
✣ *CS 60%, M 30%, CF 10%*
2 was Château La Tour Haut Brion

Château Olivier

Léognan, CC - Very young vines have been the cause of lightweight wines for some years, but vintages of the 1980s have shown more body and personality, as well as more fruit.
✣ *CS 65%, M 35%*

Château Le Pape

Léognan - Under the same direction as Château Carbonnieux, this is an unusual Graves because of its very high percentage of Merlot. Well-coloured, soft and supple.
✣ *M 95%, CS 5%*

Château Pape Clément

Pessac, CC - A classic Graves with the typical spicy tobacco bouquet and fine, supple, mineral flavour on the palate. It made some excellent wines in the 1950s and 1960s, but was rather inconsistent during the 1970s and early 1980s. The wine can be enjoyed when young; recently it has shown a tendency to fade quickly.
✣ *CS 60%, M 40%*

Château Picque Caillou

Mérignac - Sadly the only remaining château producing wine in Mérignac, where once dozens used to abound. Fortunately the wine is very well made, with deep-colour and a full-flavoured, rich, supple, fruity style. Can be drunk young, but ages well.
✣ *CS 35%, CF 35%, M 30%*
2 Château Chênevert

Château de Rochemorin

Martillac - A famous property with a long history, but from 1919 until 1973 (when it was purchased by André Lurton) it was given over to forestry. Although the vines are still young, the wine already shows a spicy Graves bouquet and elegant, fruity palate.
✣ *CS 50%, M 50%*

Château Smith Haut Lafitte

Martillac, CC - Until recently a source of simple, fruity wines that developed quickly. Vintages since the mid 1980s show extra depth and concentration. The property was sold in 1989 to the Brent Walker group.
✣ *CS 70%, M 20%, CF 10%*
2 Château Les Hauts de Smith

Château La Tour Haut Brion

Talence, CC - For many years this was effectively the second wine of Château La Mission Haut Brion, but today the new proprietors ensure that it is made separately. The wine is very similar to La Mission Haut Brion with very deep colour, masses of tannin and plenty of flavour, but perhaps lacks the former's richness.
✣ *CS 70%, CF 15%, M 15%*

CHÂTEAU LA TOUR MARTILLAC

Martillac, CC - Once one of the least interesting classified growths because it was lightweight but still had a fair amount of tannin. Recent vintages have shown greater body and fruit.
CS 60%, M 25%, CF 6%, MB 5%, PV 4%
2 *Château Lespault*

SOUTHERN REDS

CHÂTEAU LA BLANCHERIE-PEYRET

La Brède - One of the finest wines of southern Graves, with fine bouquet and full palate. Easy to drink young, but capable of ageing. The vines are still young, so greater results can be expected. The white wine is sold as Château La Blancherie.
CS 75%, M 25%

CHÂTEAU DE CHANTEGRIVE

Podensac - A well-made, attractive, supple and fruity wine that is a good example of the modern Graves style.
CS 60%, M 40%
2 *Château Mayne Lévêque*

CHÂTEAU CHERET-PITRES

Portets - Old vines help to make an old-style Graves that needs time to develop and soften its firm structure. Usually good value.
CS 50%, M 50%

CHÂTEAU FERRANDE

Castres - An excellent, easy-to-drink, deep-coloured, fruity, supple wine that can be drunk young but holds well. Very good value.
CS 33%, CF 33%, M 33%

DOMAINE LA GRAVE

Portets - A deep-coloured, supple, almost fat style of Graves, with noticeable oak overtones and good length. Consistently well-made.
CS 50%, M 50%

CHÂTEAU MILLET

Portets - Its large production makes this wine fairly easy to obtain. It is a well-made, stylish, supple, early-maturing wine of consistent standard.
M 60%, CF 40%
2 *Château du Clos Renon*

CHÂTEAU RAHOUL

Portets - One of the finest wines of this area, with a lovely spicy, fleshy style and noticeable new oak, both on the nose and palate. It is particularly good to drink when young, but improves with ageing up to about 10 years old.
M 70%, CS 30%

CHÂTEAU RESPIDE-MÉDEVILLE

Toulenne - This medium-bodied wine has good colour, a savoury palate with new oak overtones and has a pleasant, supple style that makes it useful for early drinking.
CS 50%, M 50%

CHÂTEAU DE ROQUETAILLADE LA GRANGE

Mazères - Recently one of the best wines of the region, with excellent deep colour, lovely soft fruit and real individuality. A wine to watch.
M 40%, CS 25%, CF 25%, MB 5%, PV 5%
2 *Château de Roquetaillade Le Bernet*

CHÂTEAU TOUR BICHEAU

Portets - A full-bodied, solid wine with deep colour. It ages well - it is best at about eight to ten years old.
CS 40%, M 60%

PESSAC-LÉOGNAN WHITES

CHÂTEAU BARET

Villenave d'Ornon - A typical old style, white Graves with a high percentage of Sémillon that gives a fairly full but cleanly-made wine, capable of some ageing.
SEM 70%, SB 30%

CHÂTEAU BOUSCAUT

Cadaujac, CC - An increased percentage of Sauvignon in the blend in recent years has led to a more stylish and refined wine. Still typically Graves in style, it requires five to ten years to be at its best.
SEM 60%, SB 40%
2 *Château Valoux*

CHÂTEAU CARBONNIEUX

Léognan, CC - A medium-weight, fresh, modern-syle Graves that needs three to five years to be at its best, but will keep longer. Usually reasonably priced.
SB 65%, SEM 34%, MCL 1%
2 *Château La Tour Léognan*

DOMAINE DE CHEVALIER

Léognan, CC - Unquestionably one of the finest white Graves, consistently good even in off-vintages, it is very oaky when young, but develops great complexity and an intense bouquet. Expensive, but worth the search.
SB 70%, SEM 30%

CHÂTEAU COUHINS

Villenave d'Ornon, CC - This rare wine is produced by the Institut National de la Réchèrche Agronomique and differs from Château Couhins-Lurton, which is part of the same vineyard, because it is not matured in wood at all. Fresh and aromatic, it is best drunk young.
SB 100%
2 *Château Cantebau*

CHÂTEAU COUHINS-LURTON

Villenave d'Ornon, CC - An excellent, clean, fresh and complex wine with citrus overtones produced by fermentation and maturation in new oak casks. Delicious young, but capable of ageing for many years.
SB 100%

CHÂTEAU DE CRUZEAU

St Médard d'Eyrans/Martillac - Another excellent, dry white wine from the André Lurton stable, this develops a rich citrus bouquet and flavour with ageing. Excellent value.
SB 85%, SEM 15%

CHÂTEAU DE FIEUZAL

Léognan - One of the finest white Graves, even though it is unclassified. Recent vintages have been quite exceptional - and expensive, too. Pronounced oak and ripe, almost exotic, fruit flavours.
❦ *SB 60%, SEM 40%*
2 *L'Abeille de Fieuzal*

CHÂTEAU HAUT BRION

Pessac - Unclassified at the express wish of the owners because of the very small production, this is never-thelesss an exceptional white wine. Firmer, more oaky, but less exotic than its close neighbour Laville Haut Brion, it develops extremely well and can still be drunk after over 20 years. Very expensive and difficult to obtain.
❦ *SB 50%, SEM 50%*

CHÂTEAU HAUT-GARDÈRE

Léognan - Fermented in new wood, this wine displays excellent balance and ages well. Good value.
❦ *SB 60%, SEM 40%*

CHÂTEAU LAVILLE HAUT BRION

Talence, CC - The finest dry white Bordeaux, but one that has recently seen a change. Traditionally big, buttery and lemony, with an exotic richness that can lead one to confuse it with a top-quality white Burgundy. Following the purchase of Laville by the owners of Château Haut Brion in 1983, the wine has been made with greater elegance and finesse. It is capable of substantial ageing - 20 years or more.
❦ *SEM 60%, SB 40%*

CHÂTEAU LA LOUVIÈRE

Léognan - A very fine wine that really should have been classified. Fermented in new oak, it shows great finesse, length and fruit and ages extremely well. Excellent value.
❦ *SB 85%, SEM 15%*

CHÂTEAU MALARTIC-LAGRAVIÈRE

Léognan, CC - An outstanding, crisp white Graves, with an excellent Sauvignon bouquet that is now fattened with the use of 100 per cent new oak. Underrated and worth searching for.
❦ *SB 100%*

CHÂTEAU OLIVIER

Léognan, CC - Certainly one of the easiest classified white Graves to obtain, because of its substantial production. It is relatively dull when young, probably because of the high percentage of Sémillon. Recent vintages appear fresher. It ages reasonably well.
❦ *SEM 70%, SB 25%, MCL 5%*

CHÂTEAU PAPE CLÉMENT

Pessac - An exceptional, but sadly exceedingly rare, white wine, which heralds the re-emergence of this property at the forefront of Graves producers. New plantings should increase its availability shortly.
❦ *SEM 33%, SB 33%, MCL 33%*

CHÂTEAU PONTAC MONPLAISIR

Villeneuve d'Ornon - For many years one of the best of the lesser-known Graves properties. Recent vintages have been equally good, perhaps even better. Outstanding value.
❦ *SB 70%, SEM 30%*

CHÂTEAU DE ROCHEMORIN

Martillac - Another of André Lurton's resuscitated Graves estates, which is already achieving excellent results. The wine is similar in style to Château de Cruzeau.
❦ *SB 80%, SEM 20%*

CHÂTEAU SMITH HAUT LAFITTE

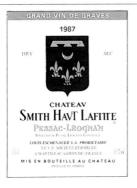

Martillac - In the 1980s this wine has been outstanding. Highly perfumed, flowery, a pure expression of Sauvignon. Since 1986 it has been matured for eight months or so in new oak. Excellent value.
❦ *SB 100%*

CHÂTEAU LA TOUR MARTILLAC

Martillac; CC - Some 7 per cent of very old mixed vines help to make this one of the better and more interesting white Graves. Since 1983 vinified and matured in oak casks. Worth looking for.
❦ *SEM 55%, SB 35%, VAR 7%, MCL 3%*

SOUTHERN WHITES

CHÂTEAU D'ARCHAMBEAU

Illats - A delicious wine that can be drunk young, but ages well. It is always elegant and refined, with good depth of flavour.
❦ *SEM 70%, MCL 20%, SB 10%*

CHÂTEAU LA BLANCHERIE

La Brède - From the most important property in the commune, this is an excellent, full-bodied, fruity wine. The red wine is sold under the La Blancherie-Peyrat label.
❦ *SEM 60%, SB 30%, MCL 10%*

CHÂTEAU CABANNIEUX

Portets - Not to be confused with Château Carbonnieux in Léognan, this is a typical, high-quality white Graves that ages well. It can occasionally reach *cru classé* quality.
❦ *SEM 75%, SB 25%*

DOMAINE LA GRAVE

Portets - Under the expert guidance of Peter Vinding-Diers, this wine has set the pace for many in the region. Aged in new oak, it has a positive, full flavour and length.
❦ *SEM 100%*

CHÂTEAU MAGENCE

St Pierre de Mons - One of the front-runners of "modern" white Graves, this was initially 100 per cent Sauvignon. Now a blend, it still produces an excellent value, fresh, interesting wine.
❦ *SB 64%, SEM 36%*

CHÂTEAU RAHOUL

Portets - Until recently under the control of Peter Vinding-Diers, during which time a number of exciting wines were made. It will be interesting to see if the standard can be maintained after his departure.
❦ *SEM 100%*

SAUTERNES & BARSAC

THIS WORLD-FAMOUS region lies to the south-east of the city of Bordeaux, surrounded by the Graves and bordered to the north by Cérons. Five communes are entitled to use the appellation Sauternes. They are Sauternes itself, Bommes, Fargues, Preignac and Barsac. The latter is strangely allowed its own appellation as well as Sauternes.

In 1855 the red and white wines of the Gironde were classified for the great Paris exhibition (see page 16). Only the wines of Sauternes and Barsac were considered good enough to be included amongst the white wines. Over the years there have been a few changes: many châteaux have failed to maintain their initial standards, and others not originally classified have deserved to be included. But, like the classification of red wines, it will never be altered, although one day it may be superseded. The best wines usually come from the hillier commune of Sauternes. Indeed, this is where the magnificent estate of Château Yquem lies, but perhaps more depends upon the individual efforts of the producers than the actual location of the vineyards.

The effect of *botrytis cinerea*

Barsac, sited on low-lying land, is separated from the other communes by the Ciron, a small tributary of the river Garonne. The Ciron is said to be the cause of the high humidity that permits the development of the all-important mould called *botrytis cinerea,* which attacks ripe grapes (in particular the Sémillon variety), puncturing their skins and concentrating their contents. The result is a rather unattractive, mouldy-looking, raisined grape, which has not only an extremely high sugar content but also concentrated acidity and extract.

Sadly, nature is not very consistent. Only a few vintages each decade can be considered special, and even in good years the grapes are not attacked at an even rate. This necessitates a series of harvests or *tries,* as individual berries, which are perfectly "ripe", are selected. Such a process is exceedingly laborious and highly uncommercial, with the result that many producers cannot afford to continue the practice.

The great châteaux of Sauternes

Fortunately, Yquem, amongst others, refused to bow to these pressures, and fashion, as fickle as ever, swung back in their favour. Today there is a major renaissance in the demand for these great wines, and standards have consequently risen. But the region hangs on a knife edge. It will always take dedicated proprietors who are determined to

fight the unequal odds and take the long-term view for this exquisite wine to survive, let alone thrive. The great first growths of the Médoc today can reckon on a yield of between 30 to 50 hl/ha and command a suitably high price. In Sauternes the maximum permitted yield is 25 hl/ha, and Château Yquem had averaged less than 10 over many years. The 1980s have brought not only an increased interest in these sumptious wines, but a series of much better vintages, some of which are truly great. It appears that Sauternes has been granted a temporary reprieve.

Red and dry white production

During the depression in the region's fortunes in the 1960s and 1970s, some properties turned partly to red and dry white wine production in order to make a living. One of the *crus classés* pulled up its vines, and others began to harvest whole bunches of unbotrytized grapes. The inevitable consequence was a lowering in standards and a further decline in sales. Unfortunately, the *Appellation Contrôlée* laws were less than helpful, permitting the dry whites to use only the "Bordeaux" appellation and the reds to use "Bordeaux Supérieur". This was in spite of the adjoining area of Cérons being permitted the higher and most useful "Graves" appellation for both. Today, few châteaux make red wines, although the dry whites seem to be on the increase, as they are very helpful in taking up those grapes that do not reach the botrytized stage. Invariably these wines have a higher percentage of Sauvignon grapes. Château Yquem was the first to use a single letter, "Y", to sell this wine. Many others have since followed.

Great Sauternes have an ability to age well because of their relatively high sugar, alcohol and acidity levels. Wines of the late nineteenth and early twentieth centuries are still very pleasurable, despite the fact that they take on a totally different style and flavour. After a period of time, they tend to dry out, developing an interesting barley sugar and caramel bouquet and palate.

A case of quality *The case end of the world's most famous dessert wine: Château d'Yquem.*

CHÂTEAU D'ARCHE

Sauternes, 2CC - After a long period of indifferent performance, this old property now has Pierre Perromet making its wines. Since 1981 the wine has been matured in oak casks, with up to 50 per cent new, and the result is a more interesting wine, although it remains lighter than many Sauternes.

❦ *SEM 90%, SB 10%*

2 *Château d'Arche Lafaurie*

CRU D'ARCHE-PUGNEAU

Preignac - Old vines here produce a rich wine of high quality, certainly the *cru classé* status which the estate claims. It has a particularly high percentage of Sauvignon in the blend.

❦ *SB 72%, SEM 18%, MCL 10%*

CHÂTEAU D'ARMAJAN DES ORMES

Preignac - Another property owned by the Perromet family, which produces well-made wines. Better known for its long history and famous visitors over the centuries, this estate deserves more attention, given the quality of its wines in recent years.

❦ *SEM 60%, SB 30%, MCL 10%*

2 *Château des Ormes*

CHÂTEAU BASTOR-LAMONTAGNE

Preignac - One of the bigger properties in the area and a serious contender for *cru classé* status, this estate produces excellent, well-concentrated wines of great class. Excellent value and worth trying.

❦ *SEM 70%, SB 20%, MCL 10%*

CHÂTEAU BROUSTET

Barsac, 2CC - Under the able direction of Eric Fournier, this wine has shown great improvement in recent years and now benefits from much more new oak. It is a stylish, fairly rich wine with a good degree of complexity and length.

❦ *SEM 63%, SB 25%, MCL 12%*

2 *Château de Ségur*

CHÂTEAU CAILLOU

Barsac, 2CC - Little-known outside France, mainly because it is sold to private customers either at the cellar door or by mailing list, this is nevertheless a well-made, elegant, fruity wine that in recent years has shown greater depth and concentration.

❦ *SEM 90%, SB 10%*

2 *Château Petit Mayne*

CHÂTEAU CLIMENS

Barsac, 1CC - One of the many *crus classés* owned by Lucien Lurton, this is an exceptional property that consistently produces one of the finest wines, not only of Barsac but of the whole region. Past vintages, such as 1921, 1937 and 1967, rival Château d'Yquem for quailty, if not style. It has an exceptional balance of acidity and refined, elegant fruit, with an excellent degree of botrytis that makes this such an outstanding, long-lived wine. Best after 10 years.

❦ *SEM 98%, SB 2%*

CHÂTEAU COUTET

Barsac, 1CC - This is often mentioned in the same breath as Climens, but it has not been quite as good recently. It is a slightly lighter wine, although there have been some very elegant and refined examples.

CHÂTEAU COUTET CUVÉE MADAME

Barsac, 1CC - Occasionally a *crème de tête* is made at Coutet. Always made in small quantities - usually less than 200 cases - and not available through normal commercial channels, it is unquestionably their finest wine. Vintages made to date are 1943, 1949, 1959, 1971, 1975 and 1981.

CHÂTEAU DOISY-DAËNE

Barsac, 2CC - This is one of the leading second growths that in recent years has produced wines of first-growth quality. They have outstanding balance, with a refined elegance and excellent creamy fruit. The dry white wine of this estate is made from Sémillon with the addition of Sauvignon and some Riesling.
☙ *SEM 100%*
2 *Château Cantegril*

CHÂTEAU DOISY DUBROCA

Barsac, 2CC - This small property, owned by the Lurton family, produces less than 500 cases a year of very consistent, light, elegant wine that keeps well but can be drunk when young. Made at Château Climens.
☙ *SEM 90%, SB 10%*

CHÂTEAU DOISY-VÉDRINES

Barsac, 2CC - The third of the Doisys that made up the original estate and the largest, although it does not produce the most quantity of sweet wine. This is a bigger, richer wine, often more akin to a true Sauternes rather than a Barsac. Vintages since 1983 have been very impressive.
☙ *SEM 80%, SB 20%*

CHÂTEAU DE FARGUES

Fargues - This small estate is the hereditary home of the Comtes de Lur-Saluces, owners of Château Yquem. Although not a *cru classé*, it produces wine as fine as most *Premiers Crus* and commands a similar or higher price. Like d'Yquem, the wine is made and matured in 100 per cent new oak and can be brilliant, combining great richness with elegance and finesse.
☙ *SEM 80%, SB 20%*

CHÂTEAU FILHOT

Sauternes, 2CC - This substantial and potentially important estate - the biggest in the area - is sadly not producing the quality of which it is capable. This must be owing in part to the selection of grapes and the lack of oak in the maturation process. However, the wine can be very pleasant, even if it is on the light side.
☙ *SEM 60%, SB 35%, MCL 5%*

CHÂTEAU GILETTE

Preignac - An extraordinary wine, made by an extraordinary process. After fermentation the wine is stored in concrete vats for up to 20 years before bottling and release for sale. Recent releases have been the 1953, 1955 and 1959 vintages, which, although mature, show a remarkable freshness and great botrytis concentration. First growth quality.
☙ *SEM 83%, SB 15%, MCL 2%*

CHÂTEAU GUIRAUD

Sauternes, 1CC - A once great estate that had fallen on hard times until its dramatic renovation following its purchase by the Narby family in 1981. Located on excellent soil, this is a rapidly rising star, although the high percentage of Sauvignon prevents the wine being richer. Watch closely. The dry wine is Vin Blanc Sec 'G'.
☙ *SEM 54%, SB 45%, MCL 1%*
2 *Le Dauphin de Lalogue*

CHÂTEAU GUITERONDE DU HAYOT

Barsac - An attractive and well-made wine from the du Hayot family, who also own part of Château Romer. Its fairly large production is reflected in a very reasonable price.
☙ *SEM 65%, SB 25%, MCL 10%*
2 *Château Brassens Guiteronde*

CHÂTEAU CLOS HAUT-PEYRAGUEY

Bommes, 1CC - Once part of the Peyraguey estate, from which the more famous Lafaurie-Peyraguey also comes, this has been a rather light and inconsistent wine. The most recent vintages, however, have far more concentration, which suggests a much better selection of grapes and improved wine-making techniques. A wine to watch.
☙ *SEM 83%, SB 15%, MCL 2%*
2 *Château Haut Bommes*

CHÂTEAU LES JUSTICES

Preignac - An excellent rich, ripe, fruity wine that deserves greater recognition. Owned by the Médeville family of Château Gilette, who bottle this wine in the more conventional way after four years. Great value.
SEM 84%, SB 12%, MCL 4%

CHÂTEAU LAFAURIE-PEYRAGUEY

Bommes, 1CC - These are consistently made, if rather unexciting wines, until the exceptional 1983 vintage, which seems to be the turning point for this important property (which is part of the giant Cordier estate). The wine is elegant, yet ripe, and displays a lot of botrytis character.
SEM 80%, SB 15%, MCL 5%
2 *Château Vimeney*

CHÂTEAU LAFON

Sauternes - Neighbouring Château Yquem, and for many years sold as Château Lafon contigu Yquem, this small property sells its wine direct or through the well-known *négociant* Dourthe. This is a good-value, consistently made wine.
SEM 89%, SB 8%, MCL 3%

CHÂTEAU LAMOTHE

Sauternes, 2CC - Purchased by the Despujots family in 1961, this half of the original estate makes a light, commercial wine that lacks the true intensity of botrytis of a leading Sauternes. Its price reflects this.
SEM 70%, SB 15%, MCL 15%

CHÂTEAU LAMOTHE GUIGNARD

Sauternes, 2CC - This is the other half of the estate, the part without the château, which was known as Lamothe Bergey until its purchase by the Guignard family in 1981. This is a serious wine with good concentration of botrytis and fruit, matched by a degree of elegance.
SEM 90%, SB 5%, MCL 5%

CHÂTEAU LIOT

Barsac - This excellent property has been a consistent producer of elegant, light, yet fine wine for many decades. Recent vintages show even better finesse, following the reduction of Muscadelle in the blend.
SEM 80%, SB 15%, MCL 5%

CHÂTEAU DE MALLE

Preignac, 2CC - A beautiful château with part of the estate in Graves. The wine tends to lack botrytis, but makes up for it in sweetness from ripe grapes and an attractive elegance. Good value. They make a dry wine called "M" de Malle.
SEM 75%, SB 22%, MCL 3%
2 *Château de Ste Hélène*

CHÂTEAU DU MAYNE

Barsac - With the richness of a Sauternes rather than a Barsac, this full-bodied wine benefits from old vines and a special micro-climate. The property is owned by the Sanders of Château Haut-Bailly in Graves.
SEM 80%, SB 20%

CHÂTEAU NAIRAC

Barsac, 2CC - Completely refurbished since 1972, this estate is producing classic Barsac wine of great elegance and longevity. The use of new wood for fermentation and maturation requires extra ageing time to bring the best out in the wines. Floodwater caused serious damage in 1982, but this seems to have been overcome.
SEM 90%, SB 6%, MCL 4%

CHÂTEAU RABAUD-PROMIS

Bommes, 1CC - The larger part of the Rabaud estate, which now incorporates the second-growth Château Pexoto, had been producing variable and unexciting wine for many years. But a dramatic improvement since 1983 has produced wine that is now almost opulent.

🍷 *SEM 80%, SB 18%, MCL 2%*
2 *Château Jasaga*

CHÂTEAU RAYMOND-LAFON

Sauternes - Adjoining Château Yquem and owned by Pierre Meslier, the *régisseur* there, this estate produces wines of *cru classés* quality - concentrated and richly fruity.

🍷 *SEM 80%, SB 20%*

CHÂTEAU DE RAYNE VIGNEAU

Bommes, 1CC - Another wine that has improved out of all recognition. Until 1985 this was a commercial Sauternes showing little botrytis and lacking concentration. The most recent vintages display a creamy ripeness and exotic fruit flavours. A wine to watch. The dry wine is Rayne Sec.

🍷 *SEM 75%, SB 25%*
2 *Château L'Abeilley*

CHÂTEAU RIEUSSEC

Farques, 1CC - One of the finest properties in the whole region. In recent years, before its acquisition by Domaines Rothschild of Lafite fame in 1984, it was producing highly botrytized wines of enormous concentration. Under new management, the wine appears to have regained some elegance without losing its inherent ripeness.

🍷 *SEM 80%, SB 18%, MCL 2%*
2 *Clos Labère*

CHÂTEAU DE ROLLAND

Barsac - An excellent property under the same ownership as part of Château Lamothe. This is a well-made wine with good botrytis and an elegant, fruity finish. The château is now a hotel, the only one in the area.

🍷 *SEM 60%, SB 20%, MCL 20%*
2 *Château Arnaudes*

CHÂTEAU ROMER DU HAYOT

Farques, 2CC - A most attractive and well-balanced wine that is made at Château Guiteronde du Hayot. This estate is split into halves and has two owners, but since 1977 the wines of both parts have been made together. Good value.

🍷 *SEM 65%, SB 25%, MCL 10%*
2 *Château Andoyse*

CHÂTEAU ROUMIEU

Barsac - Located between Climens and Doisy-Védrines, this château claims second growth status. It makes a rich wine for Barsac that is well above average in quality.

🍷 *SEM 95%, SB 5%*

CHÂTEAU SAINT-AMAND

Preignac - A consistently good wine with some weight and yet quite elegant. Usually excellent value. Also sold under the Château de la Chartreuse label as an exclusivity of Maison Sichel.

🍷 *SEM 85%, SB 15%*

CHÂTEAU SIGALAS RABAUD

Bommes, 1CC - The smallest but best part of the Rabaud estate, which has been making serious Sauternes for many years. This is a rich, flavoury wine with elegance and breeding. In spite of its high quality, it has not been expensive.

🍷 *SEM 93%, SB 7%*
2 *Château Jean Blanc,*
Château Perroy

CHÂTEAU SUAU

Barsac, 2CC - The least well-known of the classified growths, this is grown on heavier soils, producing a rather less elegant wine that can nevertheless be quite rich. The wine is actually made at the owners' property, Château Navarro, in the commune of Illats in the Graves, along with his Sauternes, Domaine du Coy.
SEM 85%, SB 15%

CHÂTEAU SUDUIRAUT

Preignac, 1CC - This magnificent and important estate has been responsible for some truly great wines in the same mould as Château d'Yquem, whose property it adjoins. It went through a dull period in the 1970s, although the 1976 is a great exception, but now appears to be back on track in the 1980s. Potentially great, if inconsistent wines, which are opulent and highly coloured.
SEM 80%, SB 20%

CHÂTEAU LA TOUR BLANCHE

Bommes, 1CC - Classified second only to the great Château d'Yquem in the 1855 classification of sweet white wines of the Gironde, it is a sad fact that the wine now rates as only average. Perhaps this is because the property is now an agricultural school owned by the state. Very recent vintages appear to show more character, but time will tell.
SEM 78%, SB 19%, MCL 3%
2 Cru St Marc

CHÂTEAU D'YQUEM

Sauternes, 1CC - To describe this wine in a few lines is virtually impossible, but the fact that in the 1855 classification of the wines of the Gironde it was given the unique rank of *Premier Grand Cru Classé* says it all. The finest Sauternes then and the finest now, this is a majestic wine of unparalleled concentration, depth, complexity, length and balance. It is made to the highest standards that many would like to copy, but few can afford. Few vintages should be drunk before they are at least 15 years old; many reach their peak after 25 years; and the greatest may live for decades more without deterioration, slowly evolving an interesting caramel flavour. Expensive, but worth the treat. The dry wine is "Y".
SEM 80%, SB 20%

A SELECTION OF DRY WHITE WINES

Labels of some of the leading dry white wines of the region are illustrated here. "Y" (pronounced Ygrec) the 50 per cent Sauvignon, 50 per cent Sémillon production of Château Yquem, is often the finest. It has a botrytis nose, which leads one to think it will be sweet, followed by a dry, yet full taste, which appears as a something of a surprise.

CHÂTEAU CAILLOU

Dry white of Château Caillou

G CHÂTEAU GUIRAUD

Dry white of Château Guiraud

R RIEUSSEC

Dry white of Château Rieussec

LE SEC DE RAYNE VIGNEAU

Dry white of Château de Rayne Vigneau

"Y" LUR-SALUCES

Dry white of Château d'Yquem

ST EMILION

THE TOWN OF ST EMILION, one of the most beautiful of all wine centres, is east of Bordeaux, overlooking the Dordogne valley to the west. It dates from Roman times, and some of the surrounding vineyards were in production during the third and fourth centuries; in fact, Château Ausone is named after Ausonius, the fourth-century poet. The region was laid waste by the Visigoths in the fifth century and again in the eighth century by the Moors, after whom Château Villemaurine takes its name.

The region came to pre-eminence again when it became English territory, following the marriage in 1152 of Henry II of England to Eleanor of Aquitaine. Charters granted by the English kings John and Edward I gave privileges to the people of St Emilion, and by 1289 their vineyards had been clearly delineated. But the region once again lapsed into relative obscurity following the Hundred Years War, only to surface with any real force after the Second World War, so the omission of St Emilion wines from the famous 1855 classification of the wines of the Gironde (see page 16) was not unexpected. It took until 1954 for a St Emilion classification to be produced (enacted in 1955 and rectified in 1958).

The styles of St Emilion wines

In St Emilion the Merlot grape is king, making wines fuller, softer and quicker to mature than those of the Médoc. There are five main areas in soil terms, although only two are commonly spoken of - the *côtes* and the *graves* (not to be confused with the region of the same name). Most of the famous vineyards are located, at least in part, on the *côtes*, where there is a substantial deposit of limestone in which there are many *caves*, or cellars. The wines of the *côtes*, and of the plateau on which the town of St Emilion stands, are generally not very deep in colour, but are fuller, softer and more alcoholic than Médocs. Although the wines mature relatively quickly, they succeed in ageing extremely well, and fine vintages are still outstanding up to 40 years old or so. Of the *Premiers Grands Crus Classés*, Châteaux Ausone, Beauséjour, Belair, Canon, La Gaffelière, Magdelaine, Pavie, Trottevieille and Clos Fourtet are all located here.

The *graves* is a very small area bordering Pomerol to the west. It takes its name from the substantial amount of fine gravel (mixed with sand) in the soil and is more consistent with the soil of Pomerol than the other areas of St Emilion. Two very important châteaux are located here, Cheval Blanc and Figeac.

The hierarchy of St Emilion wines

The 1954 classification divided the region's wines into four major groups, each with its own appellation: *Premiers Grands Crus Classés*, subdivided into categories A and B, *Grands Crus Classés, Grands Crus* and straight St Emilions. It only lists the two former groups. *Grands Crus* are only granted on an annual basis after assessment, and the remainder are called "St Emilion", provided they satisfy the *Appellation Contrôlée* regulations. The St Emilion system allows a review every 10 years, and in 1969 there were eight additions to the existing *Grands Crus Classés*, but no changes to *Premiers Grands Crus Classés*.

In 1985 another amendment was proposed that surprisingly included six demotions. After lengthy deliberations this amendment was enacted in 1986, setting the precedent for demotions in official classifications, a possibility that had long been resisted by the French wine establishment. Château Berliquet was the single and long-overdue promotion, so there are now 11 *Premiers Grands Crus Classés* and 63 *Grands Crus Classés* (see table opposite).

The 1985 classification changes

The 1985 classification made two other important departures. The first of these was that the existing four appellations, *Premiers Grands Crus Classés, Grands Crus Classés, Grands Crus* and St Emilion should be reduced to only two, that is *Grands Crus* and St Emilion. This change was the result of a wise decision, as the criteria for granting the first three appellations were identical, although wines officially classified could state so on the label.

The second change came with the placing of a limit of 90 on the total number of *Premiers Grands Crus Classés* and *Grands Crus Classés*. Indeed, this

The top of the **graves** *Château Cheval Blanc has been owned by the Fourcaud-Laussac family for over 150 years.*

development has a great deal more significance than may at first meet the eye. In the 1985 St Emilion classification there is a total of 74 classified properties, and it is to be expected that in the next revision those that were demoted, as well as many others, will wish to be included. As there are about 200 such properties in this category, of which about 150 or so gain *Grand Cru* status on an annual basis, the 90 limit can only be a welcome move, as there is substantial variation in quality amongst the *crus classés*. The greater competition for the limited number of places that now results should play an important part in encouraging an improvement in standards.

The structure of St Emilion

It is noticeable that - with the exception of just two properties - all the classified wines are actually produced from the commune of St Emilion itself. There are, however, seven other communes entitled to the appellation of St Emilion, which are St Christophe des Bardes, St Etienne de Lisse, St Hippolyte, St Laurent des Combes, St Pey-d'Armens, St Sulpice de Faleyrens and Vignonet. In addition, there are the St Emilion satellites - Lussac, Puisseguin, Montagne (which incorporates Parsac) and St Georges (see page 71).

With members throughout the region of St Emilion, the superb *Union de Producteurs de St Emilion* should not be overlooked. Not only is it the finest *coopérative* in all France, but it also accounts for roughly one-third of all St Emilion production. The *coopérative* undertakes the bottling of Château Berliquet, *Grand Cru Classé*, which, in order to conform to the necessary classification requirements, has to be carried out inside the château.

St Emilion wines make ideal choices for restaurant supplies because they have a strong tendency to drink well when young as well as continuing to improve in bottle over a number of years. Traditionally the most important markets for St Emilion producers are within France itself and Belgium. Both Switzerland and the United Kingdom are significant importers, even though the latter's preoccupation is with wines from the Médoc region.

Vintage tableau *In the St Emilion region, bullock-drawn carts were used to collect the harvested grapes.*

1985 Classification of the Wines of St Emilion

PREMIERS GRANDS CRUS CLASSÉS		
	Cap de Mourlin	Laniote
	le Châtelet	Larcis-Ducasse
	Chauvin	Lamarzelle
A Ausone	Clos des Jacobins	Larmande
Cheval-Blanc	Clos la Madelaine	Laroze
	Clos de l'Oratoire	Matras
B Beauséjour	Clos Saint-Martin	Mauvezin
(Duffau-Lagarrosse)	la Clotte	Moulin du Cadet
Belair	la Clusière	Pavie-Decesse
Canon	Corbin-Michotte	Pavie-Macquin
Clos Fourtet	Corbin	Pavillon Cadet
Figeac	Couvent des Jacobins	Petit Faurie de Soutard
La Gaffelière	Croque-Michotte	le Prieuré
Magdelaine	Curé Bon la Madelaine	Ripeau
Pavie	Dassault	Sansonnet
Trottevieille	la Dominique	Saint Georges Côte Pavie
	Faurie de Souchard	la Serre
GRANDS CRUS CLASSÉS	Fonplégade	Soutard
	Fonroque	Tertre Daugay
l'Angélus	Franc-Mayne	la Tour du Pin-Figeac (Giraud-
l'Arrosée	Grand Barrail Lamarzelle-Figeac	Belivier)
Balestard-la-Tonnelle	Grand Corbin Despagne	la Tour du Pin-Figeac (Moueix)
Beauséjour (Bécot)	Grand Corbin	la Tour-Figeac
Bellevue	Grand Mayne	Trimoulet
Bergat	Grand Pontet	Troplong-Mondot
Berliquet	Guadet Saint-Julien	Villemaurine
Cadet-Piola	Haut Corbin	Yon-Figeac
Canon-la-Gaffelière	Haut Sarpe	

CHÂTEAU L'ANGÉLUS

GCC - The attempt by Angélus to be upgraded to *Premier Grand Cru Classé* status seems to have failed temporarily, but vintages since 1980 have been matured in 100 per cent new oak, so this is now a wine to watch.

CF 50%, M 45%, CS 5%

CHÂTEAU L'ARROSÉE

GCC - A rising star in St Emilion that was previously bottled by the local *coopérative*. This is a top-quality wine with great depth; richly fruity and with great ageing capacity.

M 50%, CS 35%, CF 15%

CHÂTEAU AUSONE

1GCC (A) - The smallest production of all the first growths and since 1975 one of the most sought-after and expensive wines in the world. Although difficult to taste when young, the wine develops a beautiful fragrance and flavour and keeps exceptionally well.

CF 50%, M 50%

CHÂTEAU BALESTARD LA TONNELLE

GCC - This is a big, meaty, full-bodied wine that has few complications, yet enough vigour to develop well over a relatively long time. The unusual label quotes a fifteenth-century poem that mentions Balestard's pre-eminence. Good value.

M 65%, CF 20%, CS 10%, MB 5%

CHÂTEAU BEAUSÉJOUR (DUFFAU LAGARROSSE)

1GCC (B) - The least well-known of the *Premiers Grands Crus Classés*, and deservedly so. Even though a substantial quantity is sold directly to private clients, this does not detract from the fact that this is a relatively light but very tannic wine that lacks the elegance or true class of a leading St Emilion. Recent vintages, perhaps spurred on by the latest classification revision, show more depth.

M 50%, CS 25%, CF 25%
2 La Croix de Mazerat

CHÂTEAU BEAU-SÉJOUR BÉCOT

GCC - An historic situation arose when this château was demoted to *Grand Cru Classé*. It was certainly not the worst of the *Premiers Crus*, but the owner's integration of two *Grands Crus Classés*, also owned by him, into the estate seems to have been the cause. Recent vintages have been rich, rounded and easy to drink.

M 70%, CF 15%, CS 15%

CHÂTEAU BELAIR

1GCC (B) - Owned by the co-owner of Château Ausone, the wine can be as fine as that of Ausone and a little more fruity, but quicker maturing. Not inexpensive, but worth its price.

M 60%, CF 40%

CHÂTEAU BERLIQUET

GCC - The only addition to the *Grands Crus Classés* in 1985. The wine is still made by the local *coopérative*; it is highly perfumed and has depth, strength and finesse.

M 70%, CS & CF 30%

CHÂTEAU CADET-PIOLA

GCC - A tannic wine, because of the use of new oak; it is well-structured and requires ageing to develop its excellent bouquet and fruit flavours.
🍷 *M 51%, CS 28%, CF 18%, MB 3%*

CHÂTEAU CANON

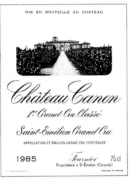

1GCC (B) - An outstanding vineyard, situated more on the plateau rather than the *côtes*, which produces magnificent wine, being rich, powerful and full of fruit. This is consistently one of the finest wines of St Emilion and, in recent years, of the whole of Bordeaux.
🍷 *M 55%, CF 40%, CS 3%, MB 2%*

CHÂTEAU CANON-LA-GAFFELIÈRE

GCC - Until recently, a producer of pleasant, relatively light and early maturing wines that were best drunk young. Some of the latest vintages have more body and fruit.
🍷 *M 55%, CF 40%, CS 5%*

CHÂTEAU CAP DE MOURLIN

GCC - Until 1983 there was confusion in that the estate was split between mother and son (both J. Capdemourlin); their wines were made separately but sold under the same label. The estate is now united and the wine has good structure, plenty of fruit and an attractive bouquet.
🍷 *M 60%, CF 25%, CS 12%, MB 3%*

CHÂTEAU LE CHÂTELET

GCC - One of the lesser-known *Grands Crus Classés*, which now appears to be making fine, fruity wine that merits more attention.
🍷 *M 34%, CF 33%, CS 33%*

CHÂTEAU CHAUVIN

GCC - A chunky mouth-filling style of wine, with lots of fruit and a rounded, corpulent body. Lots of flavour, rather than finesse. Very drinkable.
🍷 *M 60%, CF & CS 40%*

CHÂTEAU CHEVAL BLANC

1GCC (A) - Located in the *graves* on the border with Pomerol. Unquestionably the greatest of all St Emilions, unique in style and one of the finest and most consistent red wines in the world. One of its finest qualities is that it can usually be drunk when young, but continues to develop class and finesse for up to 30 years. Its greatest vintages, such as 1947, now nearing its peak, and 1921, which is still very good, suggest that the 1982 might have a similarly long life.
🍷 *CF 60%, M 34%, MB 5%, CS 1%*

CHÂTEAU LA CLOTTE

GCC - Although not owned by them, J.-P. Moueix manage this small estate and make the wine, which is sold only in the USA, the UK, and at the owner's restaurant in St Emilion, the Logis de la Cadène. This is an elegantly soft, refined St Emilion, with an excellent bouquet.
🍷 *M 85%, CF 15%*

CHÂTEAU LA CLUSIÈRE

GCC - Made at Château Pavie, who own this property, the wine is full-bodied, but less tannic and earlier maturing than Valette's other wines. Annual production of only 100 cases.
🍷 *M 70%, CF 20%, CS 10%*

CHÂTEAU CORBIN

GCC - A deep-coloured, rich, supple, full-bodied wine, very typical of the wines made in this part of St Emilion, on the Pomerol border. Most of the production is sold in Belgium.
M 66%, CF & CS 34%

CHÂTEAU CORBIN MICHOTTE

GCC - Another of the five properties originating from the Grand Corbin estate. Typical of the wines made in this area, it is a rich, full, fruity, deep-coloured wine, with an excellent mouth-filling quality. Very good.
M 65%, CF 30%, CS 5%

CHÂTEAU CORMEIL-FIGEAC

GC - As its name suggests, this property is located near Château Figeac, but on sandy soil rather than gravel. The wine is fruity and soft, with a very attractive, yet early drinking, style. Very good value.
M 70%, CF 30%

CHÂTEAU CÔTE DE BALEAU

GC - Sadly demoted in the 1985 classification, for reasons that are still not quite clear, this is where Clos St Martin and Les Grands Murailles are also made. The wine is well structured and has ageing potential and a reasonable degree of finesse.
M 70%, CF 15%, CS 15%

CHÂTEAU LE COUVENT

GC - A miniscule quantity of fine wine is produced from this very small vineyard located within the town of St Emilion itself. It is no longer a *Grand Cru Classé* because its new owners - Marne & Champagne - did not apply for reclassification in 1985. A charming wine with good colour, supple, rich fruit and sufficient backbone for medium-term ageing.
M 55%, CF 25%, CS 20%

COUVENT DES JACOBINS

GCC - A well-made wine with excellent structure, more tannin than many others, but with a silky, ripe fruit. This is a particularly old property that once belonged to a religious order, hence its name.
M 65%, CF 25%, CS 9%, MB 1%

CHÂTEAU CROQUE MICHOTTE

GCC - One of the better-known and consistently fine wines of St Emilion. Located on the border with Pomerol at the extreme north-west of the region, this large estate produces a surprisingly big, tannic wine, considering the very high percentage of Merlot used. However, the wine also has considerable depth of fruit and excellent balance.
M 90%, CF & CS 10%

CHÂTEAU CURÉ BON LA MADELEINE

GCC - Ideally situated between Châteaux Ausone, Belair and Canon, this small estate produces a wine not dissimilar to its neighbours', although without the same degree of finesse. It is a dark-coloured, big, firmly-structured wine that is capable of a decade or more of ageing.
M 95%, MB 5%

CHÂTEAU DASSAULT

GCC - Originally known as Château Couperie, its name was changed under new ownership in 1955. This is a good, elegantly balanced, full-flavoured wine, made for relatively early consumption. Well-made and very consistent, it provides ideal drinking at a reasonable price.
M 65%, CF 20%, CS 15%
2 *Château Merissac*

CHÂTEAU LA DOMINIQUE

GCC - Neighbouring Cheval Blanc in the *graves*. A rising star, producing big, powerful wines of great quality. Presently moderately priced.
M 60%, CS 15%, CF 15%, MB 10%

CHÂTEAU FAURIE DE SOUCHARD

GCC - Confusingly, this château used to be called Petit Faurie de Souchard and was always being mixed up with its neighbour, Petit Faurie de Soutard. The wines are elegant, light and a little bit hollow, but they do last well. The last few vintages suggest rather more body. Made by the owners of Cadet-Piola, but as yet not as good.
M 65%, CF 26%, CS 9%

CHÂTEAU DE FERRAND

GC - Owned by Baron Bich of Bic ballpoint pens fame. A significant property, located in St Hippolyte, which makes powerful tannic wines that require suitable ageing to develop their rich fruit content.
M 67%, CS 33%

CHÂTEAU FIGEAC

1GCC (B) - Neighbouring Cheval Blanc and similarly on the *graves*. Its best wines are outstanding and are easier to drink when young than most *Premiers Crus*. It does not have the weight of Cheval Blanc, but has an exquisite elegance that sets it apart. Often very special.
CS 35%, CF 35%, M 30%

CHÂTEAU LA FLEUR

GC - An excellent, lesser-known growth owned by Lily Lacoste, who also owns the outstanding Château Latour à Pomerol and is part-owner of Château Pétrus. This relatively simple wine has excellent balance and charming, moderately rich fruit.
M 75%, CF 25%

CHÂTEAU FOMBRAUGE

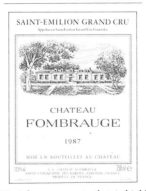

GC - A large property that is highly respected for making attractive, fruity wines that drink early, but age well. The wine is popular in the UK, but now that the château is owned by 10,000 Danes, it is likely to gain recognition elsewhere!
M 60%, CF 25%, CS 15%

CHÂTEAU FONPLÉGADE

GCC - Owned by Armand Moueix, who is also the proprietor of part of Château La Tour du Pin Figeac. Noted for producing a rather firm, tannic, unyielding wine until very recently, when the style has changed to a much more fruity, opulent, soft flavour. A wine to watch.
M 60%, CF 35%, CS 5%

CHÂTEAU FONROQUE

GCC - These wines take much longer to develop than most of those in the region, but patience is nearly always rewarded with well-balanced, mellow wine with elegance and finesse. Made by the J.-P. Moueix team.
M 70%, CF 30%

CLOS FOURTET

1GCC (B) - Some of the finest cellars in Bordeaux, but erratic and uninspiring wines were produced here until 1978, when the great improvements made in the early 1970s began to take effect. A slow developer. Recent vintages show greater depth of fruit and enormous promise.
M 60%, CS 20%, CF 20%

Château Franc Grace-Dieu

GC - Rapidly building a good reputation for itself since it has been under the management of Eric Fournier of Château Canon. An excellent fruity wine with good structure and some finesse.
🍇*M 52%, CF 41%, CS 7%*

Château Franc-Mayne

GGC - A modest property, located on the *côtes*, with a similarly modest reputation. Like most *côtes* wines, it has good, deep colour with a solid, rather firm palate but lacks the excitement of the better wines.
🍇*M 75%, CF & CS 25%*

Château La Gaffelière

1GCC (B) - Ideally located on the *côtes*, La Gaffelière has only just begun to produce top quality wines again, after a period of inconsistency. The 1980s vintages are promising and show much more depth and concentration. This is a wine that requires ripeness to display its natural charm.
🍇*M 65%, CF 20%, CS 15%*

Château La Grâce Dieu Les Menuts

GC - A popular, lightweight, although very attractive wine, which matures quickly but keeps well. It usually offers very good value.
🍇*M 75%, CF & CS 25%*

Château Grand Barrail Lamarzelle Figeac

GCC - Run in association with Château Marzelle, this is a substantial property. The wine is fruity and soft, with good body, but matures quickly, probably because the vines are grown on sandy soil, even though it is close to Figeac where gravel predominates.
🍇*M 75%, CF & CS 25%*

Château Grand-Corbin-Despagne

GCC - A fairly substantial property that makes deep-coloured, powerful, fruity wines. Its bigger-than-average production results in modest prices.
🍇*M 90%, CF 10%*

Château Grandes Murailles

GCC - The wines are usually richly fruity and soft and easy to drink, but they have attracted controversy and the property - together with Côte de Baleau where the wines are made - was demoted in the 1985 revision.
🍇*M 60%, CS 20%, CF 20%*

Château Grand Mayne

GCC - A substantial property that has had a rather chequered performance, but seems to be making much better and more consistent wine in the 1980s - stylish and fruity, with good structure and bouquet.
🍇*M 50%, CF 40%, CS 10%*

Château Grand-Pontet

GCC - Much more exciting wines, since a change of ownership in 1980. They are now full-bodied and richly fruity, almost opulent. A wine that deserves to be better known.
🍇*M 60%, CF 20%, CS 20%*

CHÂTEAU GUADET-ST JULIEN

GCC - A small property with a slightly confusing name for a St Emilion. The wine is attractively made, with a gentle, soft fruit and a good degree of elegance. It can be drunk young, but it is well worth laying it down for a few years to develop its silky fruit.
M 75%, CF & CS 25%

CHÂTEAU HAUT-PLANTEY

GC - A well-balanced wine from St Laurent des Combes. Good fruit and structure for medium-term ageing. Good value and consistent quality.
M 70%, CF 28%, CS 2%

CHÂTEAU HAUT-SARPE

GCC - A wine that has shown excellent quality in recent years. This is a well-structured, deep-coloured, concentrated, fruity wine that deserves more attention. Owned by the Janoueix family, who have several good properties in both St Emilion and Pomerol.

CHÂTEAU CLOS DES JACOBINS

GCC - A much underrated, fine wine produced by the huge Cordier estate. Even better than usual recently - rich, opulent and deeply fruity. The wine is competitively priced.
M 85%, CF 10%, CS 5%

CHÂTEAU LANIOTE

GCC - A lovely wine with long, elegant, refined fruit flavours. Sadly, its small production means that it is often difficult to find.
M 80%, CF 15%, CS 5%

CHÂTEAU LARCIS DUCASSE

GCC - Located more in St Laurent-des-Combes than St Emilion. One of the few properties not to use oak casks. The wines are rather lacking in depth, but recent vintages appear to have more fruit and complexity.
M 65%, CS & CF 35%

CHÂTEAU LARMANDE

GCC - This is an excellent wine that has attracted much attention in the last 10 years. Situated close to Soutard and Cadet Piola, it makes a beautifully perfumed, deeply rich, spicy wine, with excellent balance and length. A wine to watch.
M 65%, CF 30%, CS 5%

CHÂTEAU LAROQUE

GC - A substantial property, more on the scale of a Médoc estate than one in St Emilion. Located in the commune of St Christophe des Bardes, its wine is exclusively distributed by Alexis Lichine. Well-made, fruity wine, with medium-term keeping potential.
M 65%, CF & CS 35%

CHÂTEAU LAROZE

GCC - This is a lovely, soft, ripe, fruity wine, lacking in complexity but providing excellent early drinking. Its relatively large production allows its price to be very competitive. It offers excellent value.
M 50%, CF 40%, CS 10%

CLOS LA MADELEINE

GCC - A charming wine with seductive bouquet and elegant, refined palate. Its tiny production, mostly reserved for Belgium, makes it a difficult wine to find.
M 50%, CF 50%

CHÂTEAU MAGDELAINE

1GCC (B) - One of the finest of the *côtes* wines and probably the most consistent. It has an exquisite bouquet, perfumed and fine, and the palate shows considerable breeding and length. The wine is charming rather than mouth-filling.
M 80%, CF 20%

CHÂTEAU MAUVEZIN

GCC - A small production sadly makes this wine hard to find, but it is worth the effort as it has an attractive, supple, fruity style, with pleasant oak overtones.
CF 50%, M 40%, CS 10%

CHÂTEAU MONBOUSQUET

GC - A consistently successful wine that is available in large quantities from this substantial estate. It is a delicious, fruity, rich wine made for early consumption, although its excellent balance permits a decade of ageing.
M 50%, CF 35%, CS 15%

CHÂTEAU MOULIN DU CADET

GCC - An excellent but small property run by the Libournais company of J.-P. Moueix. The wine is typically elegant, refined and with an attractive bouquet. Lighter in style but with more finesse than its neighbour, Fonroque, which is also out of the Moueix stable.
M 90%, CF 10%

CLOS DE L'ORATOIRE

GCC - There is no château or house on this estate, and the wine is made at Château Peyreau. The wines are consistent; they are very Merlot in style, with a good depth of flavour, and are easy to drink.
M 75%, CF 25%

CHÂTEAU PATRIS

GC - A well-made wine from the owner of another good property, Château Mazeyres in Pomerol. This is an attractive, supple wine, which has a moderate intensity and a pleasant bouquet.
M 70%, CS 20%, CF 10%

CHÂTEAU PAVIE

1GCC - Double the production of most *Premiers Crus*, and 10 times that of Ausone, keeps Château Pavie reasonably priced. The wines have a soft openness and fruity charm that makes them very popular. Recent vintages have shown much greater depth and concentration. They offer excellent value.
M 55%, CF 25%, CS 20%

CHÂTEAU PAVIE DECESSE

GCC - Usually rather lighter in style than its neighbour, Pavie, which is also owned by the Valette family. Some vintages are at least as good, particularly the 1978. This is a well-made, very good-value wine.
M 65%, CF 20%, CS 15%

CHÂTEAU PAVIE MACQUIN

GCC - This vineyard, located close to Château Pavie, produces an attractive wine that is rather lighter than Pavie Decesse or Pavie itself. It is of consistently high quality and good value.
M 80%, CF 10%, CS 10%

CHÂTEAU PETIT-FAURIE-DE-SOUTARD

GCC - Once part of the larger Soutard estate and often confused with (Petit) Faurie de Souchard, this château is now owned by Jacques Capdemourlin. It produces an elegant, fruity wine, with great elegance and breed, which ages well.
M 60%, CF 30%, CS 10%

CHÂTEAU LE PRIEURÉ

GCC - A small property owned by the proprietors of Vray Croix de Gay in Pomerol and Château Siaurac in Lalande de Pomerol. The wine is attractive, light and elegant, with very good length. Small production and difficult to find.
M 70%, CF 30%

CHÂTEAU RIPEAU

GCC - Well-known during the 1950s and early 1960s, this property was modernized after its new owners took possession in the mid 1970s. Situated close to Cheval Blanc, its wine tends to be well-structured, with an attractive bouquet and a fairly deep, fruity taste. Younger vintages should be worth looking for.
M 40%, CF 40%, CS 20%

CHÂTEAU LA ROSE-POURRET

GC - An excellent *cru* that produces richly concentrated, deep-coloured, ripe, fruity wines. It deserves to be much better known. The wine is a local favourite in Switzerland.

CHÂTEAU ST GEORGES (CÔTE PAVIE)

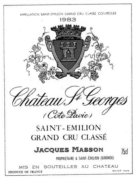

GCC - Situated opposite Château Ausone and neighbouring Château la Gaffelière and Pavie, this estate has been the site of winegrowing for many centuries. A delightful, plump, easy-to-drink wine with obvious Merlot character.
M 50%, CS 25%, CF 25%

CHÂTEAU CLOS ST MARTIN

GCC - A small property owned together with Grands Murailles and Côte Baleau by the *Société Civile des Grands Murailles*. The wine of all three properties was made at Côte Baleau, but in 1985 all but Clos St Martin were declassified for reasons not entirely clear. This wine is rather inconsistent, but can be fairly rich, fruity and with good length.
M 66%, CF 17%, CS 17%

CHÂTEAU SANSONNET

GCC - A relatively light, yet firm, style of wine that requires ageing to develop its fruit flavour. Not in the top league of St Emilion wines, but quite rewarding nevertheless.
M 60%, CF 20%, CS 20%

CHÂTEAU LA SERRE

GCC - A good example of a plateau wine that shows good fruit with a marked oak character that develops into a solid, reliable flavour. Recent vintages have more style and depth.
M 80%, CF 20%

CHÂTEAU SOUTARD

GCC - An impressive property producing big, deep-coloured backward wines that deserve lengthy ageing. Although popular in Belgium and the UK, it is usually modestly priced, considering its quality, so it is a notable find.
M 65%, CF 30%, CS 5%

CHÂTEAU TERTRE DAUGAY

GCC - Recently acquired by the owner of Château La Gaffelière, this property is well-placed to make top-quality wines. Since the 1980s the best have been gloriously perfumed and fruity, with good tannin structure and the potential to age well.
M 60%, CF 30%, CS 10%

CHÂTEAU TERTRE ROTEBEOUF

This excellent estate is located in St Laurent des Combes and has rapidly made a name for itself, with its carefully produced wines, which show excellent structure, good fruit and a fine degree of elegance.
M 80%, CF 20%

CHÂTEAU LA TOUR FIGEAC

GCC - Once part of Château Figeac, this estate produces excellent, rich, ripe, easy-to-drink, fruity wines that have considerable breed. Good value.
M 60%, CF 40%

CHÂTEAU LA TOUR DU PIN FIGEAC (MOUEIX)

GCC - There are two properties of this name, both *Grands Crus Classés*. This label represents the better of the two. It is particularly good, like many of the wines in this area. Good full flavour and structure.
M 60%, CF 30%, CS & MB 10%

CHÂTEAU LA TOUR DU PIN FIGEAC (GIRAUD-BÉLIVIER)

GCC - The less exciting half of this estate, which is now owned and managed by the Giraud family, who also own Château Le Caillou in Pomerol. Located on good soil, the results should be finer than they are, for this is a modest, but not unattractive wine, with few pretensions.
M 75%, CF 25%

CHÂTEAU TRIMOULET

GCC - A large property that uses a substantial amount of new oak for its wines; perhaps rather too much, as the wines are well-structured but can be a little aggressive. The best are pleasantly fruity and have a nice oak vanillin flavour.
M 60%, CF 20%, CS 15%, MB 5%

CHÂTEAU TROPLONG MONDOT

GCC - A large estate whose wines have been very popular in Belgium and the UK. Recent vintages have tended to be rather light but pleasant.
M 65%, CF & MB 20%, CS 15%

CHÂTEAU TROTTE VIEILLE

1GCC (B) - Located well away from the other *Premiers Grands Crus Classés* on the eastern side, this château produced superb wines until the devastating frost of 1956. Since then the wines have been inconsistent and, occasionally, very disappointing. Since the 1980s, however, with the exception of the 1981, most vintages have shown a substantial improvement. Clearly now back on top form.
M 60%, CF 25%, CS 15%

CHÂTEAU VIEUX SARPE

GC - This is one of the many properties that is owned by the Janoueix family of Haut-Sarpe. The wine is consistently well made and always displays good fruit and firm structure.

CHÂTEAU VILLEMAURINE

GCC - These are the most extensive cellars in the area, and are worth visiting. The rather lean wines require ageing to develop their potential. More recent vintages show a greater level of fruit, but still have substantial tannin. This is a wine to watch.
M 70%, CS 30%

CHÂTEAU YON-FIGEAC

GCC - A big estate, once part of the Figeac domaine, which now matures its wine in new oak. This is a stylish wine with scented bouquet, silky soft palate of rich fruit and good finish. The estate is now producing much better wines than 10 years ago.
M 34%, CF 33%, CS 33%

ST EMILION SATELLITES

Four areas can hyphenate their name with that of St Emilion. Referred to as the St Emilion satellites, they are Lussac, Puisseguin, Montagne (which incorporates Parsac) and St Georges. Whereas most of the properties in St Emilion are very small, many producing a mere 2,000 cases or so per annum, those in the St Emilion satellites are big - for instance, Château des Tours in Montagne-St Emilion produces over 45,000 cases per annum. Generally, these wines tend to lack the sheer breed and elegance of the great St Emilion wines, but they provide excellent value for money.

CHÂTEAU CALON
St Georges

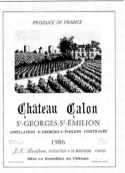

CHÂTEAU DURAND-LAPLAGNE
Puisseguin

CHÂTEAU DES LAURETS
Puisseguin

CHÂTEAU LYONNAT
Lussac

CHÂTEAU ROUDIER
Montagne

CHÂTEAU ST GEORGES
St Georges

CHÂTEAU DES TOURS
Montagne

POMEROL

THIS ATTRACTIVE RURAL commune is Bordeaux's smallest top-quality wine-producing region. Even though vines stretch as far as the eye can see, broken only by the odd clump of trees or little clusters of buildings here and there, the total vineyard area covers as little as one-seventh of that of St Emilion. In size it is most comparable with St Julien in the Médoc, and it produces about 400,000 cases of wine per year. As there are nearly 200 growers, the average size of each property is obviously very small, with a number of them producing as little as 200 to 300 cases. Only one estate (Château de Sales) produces over 20,000 cases, the equivalent quantity of a Médoc first growth. There are no great châteaux, although there are a few more prominent buildings, but the majority are attractive, but modest, farmhouses.

Styles of wine

Like the wines of St Emilion, those of Pomerol tend to be slightly more alcoholic, by almost one degree, than those of the Médoc. Usually the harvest is a week or so earlier because of its inland location and the preponderance of earlier-ripening grape varieties. The wines have a good deep colour and are vividly fruity. They are intense, rich, full and rounded with good tannin, but the overall impression is one of plumpness rather than aristocratic finesse. This enables them to be drunk young, and many are attractive between four to eight years old, although the best require a longer time to develop fully. Surprisingly, for such early maturing wines, they are quite long-lived, and vintages of the 1940s and 1950s can still be outstanding. It is rare to find older vintages even of Château Pétrus, but when discovered they can still be drinkable from the 1920s and 1930s.

The effect of the soil

The soil is the important factor that determines the style of the wine. To the west of the commune it is predominantly sandy, and on the eastern side - where nearly all the best properties are located - it is sand and gravel with *crasse de fer*, or iron subsoil. This is the same soil that helps make the great wines of Châteaux Cheval Blanc and Figeac over the border in St Emilion. In the centre of this *graves* lies the summit of Pomerol, a modest rise of 16 metres (50 feet) above the surrounding area on which Château Pétrus lies. Here the soil is unique, for the gravel and sand give way to a remarkable form of clay created by the decomposition of the molasse bedrock which lies beneath it. It is this clay that determines that Pétrus is

planted with Merlot rather than Cabernet vines. In fact Pétrus is often a 100 per cent Merlot wine because the very small percentage of Cabernet Franc is not added unless totally ripe.

Vine varieties

The two most important vine varieties are Merlot and Cabernet Franc, the latter known locally as Bouchet. Generally, very little Cabernet Sauvignon is planted (although there are a couple of significant exceptions) because this variety dislikes cold soil and the clay in the ground tends to encourage water to lie just beneath the surface. The Cabernet Franc is less affected by this problem and the Merlot actually seems to like clay.

Recent fame

Pomerol's fame and fortune is very recent. The commune only became a separate wine region in 1923. No wines, not even Pétrus, were listed in the 1855 classification of the Gironde (see page 16). At that time they were considered inferior, not only to the wines of the Médoc, but also to those of St Emilion and even Fronsac.

Nearly all the wine produced in this area was sold locally in France or to Belgium, which has been the most important market for many years. It was only in the early 1950s that some of the leading wines were actively promoted by the important firm of Jean-Pierre Moueix, with the result that two famous Bristol wine merchants, Avery's and Harvey's, imported Pétrus for the first time into the UK. It was not until the 1960s, however, that prices began to increase. Today, Pétrus has become the world's most expensive red wine, if not at opening price then certainly when traded at auction. In fact it is auction that has created the substantial rise in price of these once little-known wines, first with the meteoric rise of Pétrus, followed by the other leading properties.

The contribution of Jean-Pierre Moueix

One cannot mention Pomerol without the name of Jean-Pierre Moueix for it is he, and the firm that carries his name, that has been largely responsible for the pre-eminent position that this region finds itself in today. With outstanding promotional flair and a matching determination to improve, where necessary, the quality of the wines, Jean-Pierre Moueix has transformed the international image of these exceptional wines. The region today no longer has to rely on Pétrus as the sole standard-bearer, but can count on a dozen or more outstanding wines to further the cause of Pomerol.

CHÂTEAU BEAUREGARD

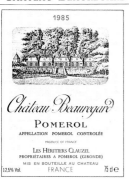

A large property by Pomerol standards, making over 5,000 cases of fairly full-flavoured, rich, but relatively firm wine that requires about 8 to 10 years' ageing. Moderately priced, good value.

M 48%, CF 44%, CS 6%, MB 2%
2 *Domaine des Douves*

CHÂTEAU BONALGUE

Located on the south-west border of Pomerol, away from the great wine properties, this typically sized estate produces a very good example of a fruity, relatively early-maturing wine.

M 75%, CF 19%, CS 5%, MB 1%

CHÂTEAU LE BON PASTEUR

An excellent property located on the St Emilion border, opposite Château Croque Michotte. The wine is rich, deeply fruity and complex, with a lovely long supple finish. Particularly popular in the USA.

M 90%, CF 10%

CHÂTEAU BOURGNEUF VAYRON

A large property, producing about 6,000 cases of well-made, relatively light, supple, fruity wine that can be drunk young. It is a good wine, but not amongst the leaders.

M 80%, CF 20%

CHÂTEAU LA CABANNE

This is a medium-weight wine, with excellent fruit and good structure. Best known in Belgium; some old bottles are still excellent. Quite a large production for the area.

M 90%, CF 10%
2 *Château de Compostelle*

CHÂTEAU LE CAILLOU

Owned by the proprietors of Château La Tour du Pin Figeac, the *Grand Cru Classé* in St Emilion, this is a fairly deep, old-fashioned style wine, with good body and keeping qualities.

M 80%, CF 20%
2 *Domaine de Lacombe,*
Château Priourat

CHÂTEAU CERTAN DE MAY DE CERTAN

Better-known as Château Certan de May, and once part of the Vieux Château Certan estate, this property makes superb wines - big, rich, concentrated, fairly solid and with excellent fruit flavours. Recent years have seen a string of very successful wines, which regrettably have become expensive because of high demand and the small production.

M 65%, CF 25%, CS & MB 10%

CHÂTEAU CERTAN-GIRAUD

Another property that was part of Vieux Château Certan, but was not making wine of such stature until recently. Traditionally, the wine has been rather light and early maturing, but now it appears much fuller, riper and with real depth. This is a wine to watch closely.

M 70%, CF 30%
2 *Château Certan Marzelle,*
Château Clos du Roy

CHÂTEAU CLINET

A rather firm and austere wine for Pomerol, perhaps because of the large proportion of Cabernet Sauvignon in the blend. Nevertheless, in good vintages it has sufficient fruit and body to be very good.

M 75%, CS 15%, CF 10%

CLOS DU CLOCHER

A popular wine with a good "fat" style, and well-coloured and generous fruit. Can be drunk quite early, but also keeps well. Vintages of the 1920s can still be enjoyable.
M 66%, CF 34%
2 *Clos du Rocher,*
Château Monregard-La Croix

CHÂTEAU LA CONSEILLANTE

One of the great Pomerols, but it has shown a slightly disturbing inconsistency. The wine obviously has depth and concentration, and displays an elegance and fine structure. The 1985 vintage is quite special.
M 50%, CF 40%, MB 10%

CHÂTEAU LA CROIX

One of the many properties owned by the Janoueix family, this is a rising star that has been producing better and better wines. They are styled in an open, fruity way, yet have considerable ability to age. Worth looking for, as they are modestly priced and the production is quite large.
M 60%, CF 25%, CS 15%

CHÂTEAU LA CROIX DU CASSE

Situated on the southern border of Pomerol and owned by the Georges Audy family, like Château Clinet, this property has been particularly successful in recent years. It produces a spicy, fat wine with excellent flavour and long finish. Well worth its relatively modest price.
M 60%, CF 40%

CHÂTEAU LA CROIX DE GAY

A neighbour of Château Le Gay, but much lighter in style. This is an open-knit, fruity wine, made for early drinking. Very attractive.
M 80%, CF 10%, CS 10%
2 *Château Le Commandeur,*
Vieux Château Groupey

CHÂTEAU DU DOMAINE DE L'EGLISE

A respectable Pomerol of good colour. Relatively lightweight, but with a degree of elegance and class. Consistent rather than outstanding.
M 75%, CS 20%, CF 5%

CLOS L'EGLISE

Perhaps the best of all the estates with the name "L'Eglise". A rising star in recent years, this winery produces well-structured, full, richly fruity wines that age well. Although production is currently small, this is one wine to watch.
M 50%, CS 28%, CF 22%

CHÂTEAU L'EGLISE-CLINET

Another small property located near the church, which has been producing very good wines recently. A high percentage of old vines, which survived the devastating frosts of 1956, help to make a big wine with supple, rich fruit flavours. Difficult to find, but worth looking for.
M 60%, CF 30%, CS 10%

CHÂTEAU L'ENCLOS

A consistent producer of very drinkable Pomerol in the second tier. These wines are succulent and soft, suitable for early drinking, but with a good ability to age. Very good value.
M 80%, CF 19%, MB 1%

CHÂTEAU L'EVANGILE

One of the great Pomerols, which like so many went through a patchy period during the 1960s and 1970s. Now back on form, this is a big, dark-coloured wine with a lot of chewy fruit and firm structure. Potentially one of Bordeaux's great red wines.
M 66%, CF 34%

CHÂTEAU FEYTIT-CLINET

Managed by the J.-P. Moueix team, this estate produces a deeply coloured, very plummy wine of consistent good quality. Not in the front rank of Pomerols, it is nevertheless well worth buying. Slightly greater than average production.
M 75%, CF 25%

CHÂTEAU LA FLEUR DE GAY

This is the prestige *cuvée* of Château La Croix de Gay, produced from a 1-hectare (2.5-acre) plot of 100 per cent Merlot grapes and matured in 100 per cent new oak casks. Definitely richer, bigger and made to last, it has a much better quality than its parent. Well worth looking for, although its very small production makes it rare.
M 100%

CHÂTEAU LA FLEUR-PÉTRUS

Located next to Château Pétrus, but on gravel rather than clay soil, this important estate produces one of the most elegant, perfumed wines of all Pomerol. It has great complexity of flavour and a good degree of vigour. Its distinctive label is well worth looking for.
M 75%, CF 25%

CHÂTEAU LE GAY

Owned by the proprietors of Château Lafleur and neighbouring it, this property is capable of producing an excellent, deeply coloured, powerful, fruity wine. It lacks the sheer power and concentration of Lafleur and has been rather inconsistent, yet remains one of the best value Pomerols today.
M 50%, CF 50%

CHÂTEAU GAZIN

One of the larger estates, which was bigger still until it sold a parcel of land to Château Pétrus, which it neighbours. The wine is fairly big and opulent in style, but lacks the finesse and character of a top growth.
M 80%, CF 15%, CS 5%

CHÂTEAU GOMBAUDE-GUILLOT

This is one of the better-known lesser growths of the area. The wine is made from an unusual blend of each of the three main grape varieties, with a high percentage of Malbec. Mainly sold in France, the wine is well-structured, with good fruit, and ages well.
M 60%, CF 32%, MB 8%

CHÂTEAU LA GRAVE À POMEROL
TRIGANT DE BOISSET

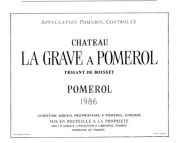

Owned by Christian Moueix of J.-P. Moueix, this is a rising star in the second league of Pomerols. The wine has good structure, being fairly rich and tannic.
M 95%, CF 5%

CHÂTEAU LAFLEUR

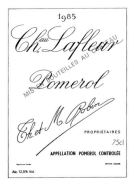

The only wine in the area that has the weight and potential of Château Pétrus. Now made by the J.-P. Moueix team, it is producing some of the finest wines of all time, although it will take a lot to surpass the 1947 vintage. The wine is deeply coloured, rich, very powerful and requires considerable ageing. The 1978 may be better than Pétrus.
M 50%, CF 50%

CHÂTEAU LAFLEUR-GAZIN

Located slightly north of and between Châteaux Lafleur and Gazin - hence the name. Another of the many wines under the expert control of the J.-P. Moueix team. It is a fairly big, powerful wine, yet supple with an underlying firm structure.
M 65%, CF 35%

CHÂTEAU LAGRANGE

Owned by the firm of J.-P. Moueix, this is a consistently good second-tier Pomerol. The wine is middle-weight, elegant and fruity, and is attractively priced. Not to be confused with the third-growth château of the same name in St Julien.
M 80%, CF 20%

CHÂTEAU LATOUR À POMEROL

Managed by the J.-P. Moueix team and owned by the co-proprietor of Château Pétrus, this has always been a fine wine, although it has been a little inconsistent at times. Recent vintages have been superb, with great complexity of flavour, concentration and length. Certainly one of the best wines of the region.
M 80%, CF 15%, MB 5%

CHÂTEAU MAZEYRES

Owned by the Querre family, this is a well-made, middle-weight, elegant, fruity wine with a positive Merlot character. Very good value.
M 70%, CF 30%

CHÂTEAU MOULINET

One of the biggest Pomerol estates, located to the north-west of the region on the border with Lalande de Pomerol. Owned by Armand Moueix, it produces an attractively perfumed middle-weight wine that drinks well young. Good value.
M 66%, CF & MB 34%

CHÂTEAU NENIN

Besides Château de Sales, this is the largest in Pomerol and was widely known for its consistent quality and availability. However, recent vintages have been rather one-dimensional, and, although pleasantly fruity, do not have the weight of a truly great wine.
M 50%, CF 30%, CS 20%

CHÂTEAU PETIT VILLAGE

Until very recently, this was owned by Bruno Prats, who had to sacrifice it in order to keep control of Château Cos d'Estournel, the outstanding second growth in St Estèphe. Under his able direction, this property - like that of Cos d'Estournel - reached new heights. Recent vintages have had deep colour, a beautiful aroma and excellent, deep, rich flavour.
M 75%, CS & CF 25%

CHÂTEAU PÉTRUS

Unquestionaly the greatest of all Pomerols, and one of the greatest red wines of the world. Perhaps only Château Latour can match it for consistency through good and poor vintages. The unique clay soil here favours the almost pure Merlot wine, which is of great intensity, depth and concentration. Light vintages reach their best within 12 to 15 years, but most great ones need 20 to 30 years to develop their true potential. Although very expensive, it is worth the effort to obtain, if only to see what such care in the vineyard and cellar can achieve - for the secret of Pétrus starts with the vines.
M 95%, CF 5%

LE PIN

A new estate now owned by the Thienpont family of Vieux Château Certan fame. A tiny production of around 350 cases of brilliant (though expensive) wine made to the highest specifications - highly concentrated, rich, ripe, and superbly crafted.
M 90%, CF 10%
2 *Domaine de la Vieille Ecole*

CHÂTEAU PLINCE

Owned by the Moreau family, who are proprietors of Clos L'Eglise. This wine has been a bit patchy, but recent vintages suggest a return to form. It is a relatively light, open-knit wine, which can be drunk young, but has sufficient structure to age well.
M 68%, CF 24%, CS 8%

CHÂTEAU LA POINTE

One of the biggest estates in Pomerol. After a brilliant 1970 vintage, La Pointe produced a series of light-weight wines of little consequence; vintages since 1975 show a serious improvement. At its best, a very stylish, middle-weight fruity wine.
M 75%, CS 20%, MB 5%

CLOS RENÉ

Part of the crop is sold as Moulinet Lasserre for family reasons, but it is the same wine. A dense, plummy wine with a powerful bouquet and lots of rich fruit flavours. Lacking the elegance of the finest wines, this is one of the best of the second tier.
M 60%, CF 30%, MB 10%
2 *Château Moulinet Lasserre*

CHÂTEAU ROUGET

One of the bigger estates, with modestly-priced wine. The style of wine is old-fashioned, with substantial tannins and excellent depth of flavour that needs long-term ageing to develop its full potential.
M 40%, CF 30%, CS 30%

CHÂTEAU DE SALES

Easily the largest property in Pomerol, making 10 times as much wine as many of the other estates, although about 40 per cent is sold under the second labels. The wine has been improving since the 1970s and now provides tremendous value. Rich and plummy, with good bouquet, it develops quite quickly.
M 70%, CF 15%, CS 15%
2 *Château Chantalouette, Château de Délias*

CHÂTEAU DU TAILHAS

Tucked in the south-west corner of Pomerol, opposite Château Figeac in St Emilion, this property produces a consistently fine, middle-weight wine of deep colour and attractive fruit. Good value.
M 70%, CF 15 %, CS 15%

CHÂTEAU TAILLEFER

Owned by Armand Moueix, this property has been producing attractive ripe, fruity wines for some time. It is a big estate, roughly the size of Château Nenin. The wine is made for early consumption, although it will develop for a decade or so.
M 66%, CF & CS 34%
2 *Clos Beauregard, Clos Toulifaut*

CHÂTEAU TROTANOY

A truly great wine, made much in the Pétrus style. Like Pétrus, the wine is made by the J.-P. Moueix team, and is owned by the family. Trotanoy has a deep colour, a rich, spicy bouquet and a powerful, almost opulent, deep flavour, which requires considerable ageing. Its great vintages command prices similar to Médoc first growths.
M 80%, CF, CS & MB 20%

VIEUX CHÂTEAU BOURGNEUF

Situated almost exactly in the centre of Pomerol, this is a fine little property producing fairly substantial, full-bodied, rounded wines that develop well with keeping.

M 60%, CF 30%, CS 10%

VIEUX CHÂTEAU CERTAN

Ideally situated on the high plateau, this property is one of the finest - it used to be considered the finest of all Pomerol. Its high percentage of Cabernet Sauvignon produces wines of exquisite breed and great longevity. Less deep in colour than many of the other great Pomerols, it has great finesse, elegance and class. Not over-priced for its quality.

M 50%, CF 25%, CS 20%, MB 5%
2 La Gravette de Certan

CLOS VIEUX TAILLEFER

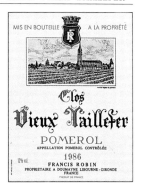

A very small property, producing between 400 and 600 cases of wine per year. Also owners of Château Sansonnet in St Emilion, the Robin family make a well-structured, medium-bodied fruity wine.

M 100%
2 Château Le Castelet

CHÂTEAU LA VIOLETTE

As its name implies, and the label suggests, the wine is said to have the aroma of violets. This is not always noticeable, but the wine does have rich fruit and a full body, particularly in good years. A little inconsistent, but appears to be improving. Small production but modest price.

M 95%, CF 5%
2 Château La Nouvelle Eglise

CHÂTEAU VRAY CROIX DE GAY

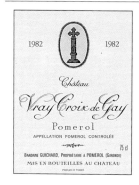

Owned by the proprietor of Châteaux Siaurac in Lalande de Pomerol and Le Prieuré in St Emilion, this is a small property that is noted for making deep, tannic wines with lots of fruit and power. However, like its name - which appears to have a number of spellings - the wine can be a little inconsistent.

M 80%, CF 15%, CS 5%

LALANDE-DE-POMEROL

Pomerol has two satellites, which lie to the north and are called Lalande and Néac. Both have their own appellation although Néac has the added advantage of being allowed to sell its wine under the appellation Lalande-de-Pomerol as well. This area has surprisingly good soil, mostly of sand and more recent gravel. The wines produced here are very similar to the lesser Pomerols, and, because they have a tendency to develop quickly and are produced in large quantities, they often provide outstanding value for money.

CHÂTEAU DE BEL AIR
Lalande-de-Pomerol

CHÂTEAU LES HAUTS-CONSEILLANTS
Néac

Sold as Château Les Hauts Tuileries for export

CHÂTEAU MONCETS
Néac

CHÂTEAU SIAURAC
Néac

LESSER-KNOWN BORDEAUX

BESIDES THE GREAT appellations of Bordeaux, there are some that deserve more attention than they receive. Even in the less exciting areas there are inevitably one or two properties that produce wine that is consistently above average.

Fronsac

One of the finest and least-known areas is that of Fronsac. Traditionally, Fronsac, which today also includes the slightly superior appellation of Canon Fronsac, was included among the wines of St Emilion, as indeed were all the wines on this side of the Dordogne.

It is only very recently that this significant area, which lies close to the bustling town of Libourne, has been rediscovered. The wines produced here are a cross between those of Pomerol and St Emilion, yet they have a greater firmness than either, and generally require much more ageing than most wine guides suggest.

For many years the comment "will soon become popular" has been heard about the wines in Fronsac, but their relative obscurity and the general dilapidation of the estates has meant a much longer period of rediscovery than expected. However, the recent move of the notable firm of Jean-Pierre Moueix into the area strongly suggests that matters will move more quickly in future.

Rising star of Fronsac *Château de la Rivière is not just an imposing building; its wines enjoy increasing success.*

Other developing areas

Another potentially exciting area is the Côtes de Francs which together with the Côtes de Castillon is located on the other (east) side of St Emilion. The Côtes de Francs was a major winegrowing area that sold its produce as St Emilion until just before the development of the *Appellation Contrôlée* laws. The region declined and fell into disrepute, virtually ceasing production altogether. Today, some of the leading producers of St Emilion and Pomerol have boldly moved back to this area in order to develop some of the finer sites. Early results suggest wines as rich and interesting as the better Pomerols.

Supplies of attractive, everyday wine

The Côtes de Castillon is a source of extremely good yet relatively simple wine, which is sold at a very competitive price. It is no longer a secret that Bordeaux's most popular branded wine draws much of its supply from here.

It is impossible to discuss Bordeaux wines without mentioning both the Côtes de Bourg and Premières Côtes de Blaye on one hand, and the Entre-deux-Mers on the other. Blaye, and Bourg in particular, provide a substantial quantity of excellent, attractively fruity everyday red wine. Although suitable for early consumption, the wine can also be matured for several years. The Entre-deux-Mers, which once had the unenviable reputation of producing some of the worst wine of the Gironde, has since discovered how to make both attractive red wine and deliciously fruity dry white wine in large quantities. The area represents exceptional value, and, although the quality of the wine will never be particularly special, there should always be a demand for it.

Appellation complications

One of the typical complications of the *Appellation d'Origine Contrôlée* system is often apparent here, for many wines can be sold under more than one appellation. For instance, red wine could be sold under its regional appellation, such as "Premières Côtes de Blaye" or "Blayais", as well as "Bordeaux Supérieur" or plain "Bordeaux".

Red wines of the Entre-deux-Mers may not even be sold as such but simply as "Bordeaux Supérieur" or "Bordeaux". Similar rules apply to white wines. As always, the guarantee of quality tends to rest with the château rather than the appellation.

Grape varieties

In the entire area the predominant grape is Merlot, particularly in Blaye and Fronsac where it may constitute 40 to 80 per cent of grapes grown (and can reach as high as 100 per cent). Malbec used to be widely planted - especially in the Bourg, where the traditional blend comprised one-third of Malbec, Merlot and Cabernet Sauvignon. Recently there has been a tendency to increase Merlot at the expense of Malbec, which is harder to grow.

CANON FRONSAC

CHÂTEAU CANON

This is a tiny vineyard now owned by Christian Moueix, which produces a deep-coloured, concentrated yet fairly tannic wine that requires ageing. It is one of the very best of the region and one that is bound to gain further recognition in the near future.

CHÂTEAU CANON DE BREM

For many years the leading property of the region, this is now owned by the J.-P. Moueix family. Like the wines of Canon, these wines are deep in colour, richly fruity, but also firm and tannic and require ageing.
M 50%, CF 50%
2 Château Pichelèbre

CHÂTEAU COUSTOLLE

A very good, ripe, concentrated fruity wine with excellent length and finish. Recent vintages show real class.
M 60%, CF 30%, CS & MB 10%

CHÂTEAU DU GABY

A well-structured wine that requires substantial ageing to be at its best. It is deep in colour and extract, with a deep fruit and positive tannic structure. Worth the wait.

CHÂTEAU JUNAYME

Perhaps not of the highest quality level as the top Canon Fronsacs, but this is still a very popular wine with an elegance and breed that merit some attention.
M 80%, CF & CS 20%

CHÂTEAU MAZERIS

This is an attractive wine with a full, fat bouquet, but lacking any obvious oak ageing. It is usually well-balanced between ripe fruit and refreshing acidity. Worth ageing.

CHÂTEAU MAZERIS-BELLEVUE

With a high percentage of Cabernet Sauvignon in the blend, this wine can easily be mistaken for a Médoc when young. It develops an attractive deep fruit, with a lovely flavour when mature. One of the best Canon Fronsacs at the moment.
M 50%, CS 40%, MB 10%

CHÂTEAU TOUMALIN

Owned by the proprietors of Châteaux La Pointe in Pomerol and La Serre in St Emilion, this is also well-run and produces an attractive, fruity wine that can be enjoyed while young. Average production and an attractive price.
M 70%, CF 30%

CHÂTEAU VRAI CANON BOUCHÉ

One of the many wines on this side of the Dordogne that claims to be the "true" (*vrai*) château. This leading property makes well-structured, fruity wines that deserve a modest amount of ageing.

CHÂTEAU VRAY CANON BOYER

This is a good example of the style of wine of the region, which lacks the depth of the best yet offers a full, fruity mouthful for early drinking. Its name is obviously in conflict with the many properties named Canon.

FRONSAC

CHÂTEAU DALEM

One of the leading properties, producing soft, ripe wines with an exquisite perfume. Drinkable when young, but excellent even after 20 years.

CHÂTEAU DE LA DAUPHINE

Perhaps the best-known wine of the region and now owned by J.-P. Moueix, this is a lovely, attractive, fairly forward style of wine, suitable for early drinking. Like all Fronsac wines, it keeps well. It is actually part of Canon de Brem, but outside the appellation of Canon Fronsac.
M 66%, CF 34%

CHÂTEAU MAYNE VIEIL

A substantial estate that makes very attractive wines of classic Fronsac style. Well-structured and fruity, the wine is usually drinkable within a relatively short period of time.
M 80%, CF 20%

CHÂTEAU MOULIN HAUT-LAROQUE

A fairly full, rich wine with a spicy flavour and good structure that deserves a little ageing. A good overall impression; this is one of the better wines of the area.
M 65%, CF 20%, CS 10%, MB 5%

CHÂTEAU LA RIVIÈRE

These are the most important cellars in the Gironde and the biggest and best property in the region. The wines are particularly big, rich and tannic and require considerable ageing to reach their best. The proprietor, Jacques Borie, is especially proud of his wine and is prepared to challenge some of Bordeaux's greatest wines to prove his point.
M 60%, CS 30%, CF 5%, MB 5%

CHÂTEAU ROUET

Owned by Patrick Danglade, who is President of the Syndicat de Fronsac, this is a carefully run estate and one of the leaders of the area.

CHÂTEAU LA VALADE

An excellent property, located on the Fronsac plateau and côte, that makes lovely wines with outstanding bouquet and well-balanced, almost chunky, fruity taste. Very fine and deserving of attention. Perhaps unique to the region, this is a 100 per cent Merlot wine.
M 100%

CHÂTEAU VILLARS

A very soft, fruity style of wine that is at its best within the first three to four years of its life. The property is located in Saillans, both on the plateau and *côte*. Its production is in the region of 12,000 cases.
M 60%, CF 30%, CS 10%

CÔTES DE FRANCS

CHÂTEAU PUYGUERAUD

A superb, "new" property, resurrected by the Thienpont family of Vieux Château Certan fame. This is a particularly good, deep, fruity wine, with excellent structure that can be mistaken for a top-quality Pomerol in blind tastings. A wine to watch.

CÔTES DE CASTILLON

CHÂTEAU DE BELCIER

A well-coloured, rounded, fruity wine that offers excellent value for youthful drinking. Although it lacks complexity, it has a depth of fruit that makes it worth its modest price. Unusually, it claims both Côtes de Francs and Côtes de Castillon appellations.

CHÂTEAU MOULIN ROUGE

A significant property producing in excess of 15,000 cases per year. The wine is pleasantly fruity, of medium body, and made for early drinking.

CHÂTEAU PITRAY

This is not the biggest, but certainly one of the best properties of the whole region. Consistently very good, well-structured wines of excellent value are produced, which although best drunk young are still very good after 10 years or so.

CHÂTEAU ROCHER BELLEVUE

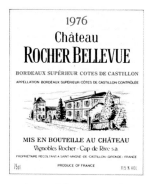

A regular medal winner at domestic French wine shows, this is an excellent wine that could easily be mistaken for a minor St Emilion. Great value.

CHÂTEAU LA TERRASSE

A well-made, deeply fruity, chunky style of wine that deserves to be amongst the leaders here. Recent vintages have been especially good.

CÔTES DE BOURG

CHÂTEAU DE BARBE

A well-known, substantial estate that makes an attractively fruity, soft, early-drinking wine. Consistently good value.
M 70%, C 25%, MB 5%

CHÂTEAU DU BOUSQUET

This property has an even bigger production than de Barbe with around 35,000 cases per annum. The wine is deeper in colour and richer, more plummy and fruity than de Barbe. Ideal for early drinking, but does develop well for up to 10 years or so.
M 45%, CS 45%, MB 10%

CHÂTEAU EYQUEM

A relatively small quantity (5,000 cases) of attractively light wine is made here each year. The name is confusingly similar to the illustrious Château d'Yquem in Sauternes.
M 34%, C 33%, MB 33%

CHÂTEAU DE LA GRAVE

A large and important property located on the high point of the Bourg. The wine is one of the deepest of the Bourg and shows noticeable oaky character in its youth. Worth a few years' ageing to soften.
M 60%, CS 30%, MB 10%

CHÂTEAU LA GROLET

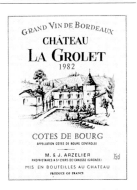

A supple, fruity wine, made for early consumption, this has a Merlot-dominated style that gives it an open frankness rather than great depth.
M 50%, C 35%, MB 15%

CHÂTEAU GUERRY

This is one of the leading wines of the area. It is all cask-aged and has a high percentage of the Malbec grape. The wine is rich yet supple, powerful yet fine. An excellent example of Bourg at its best.
M 34%, CS 33%, MB 33%

CHÂTEAU GUIONNE

A modest-sized property that makes attractively fruity wines with a degree of elegance. Well-known in the UK.
C 50%, M 45%, MB 5%

CHÂTEAU ROUSSET

Another well-placed property that still retains a fair proportion of Malbec. This is a good, fairly rich, fruity wine that is ideal for drinking when two to four years old.
M 45%, CS 33%, MB 16%, CF 6%

PREMIÈRES CÔTES DE BLAYE

CHÂTEAU HAUT SOCIONDO

This is a fairly large-boned wine, that has a spicy deep fruit of mouth-filling proportions. Well-coloured and with good structure, it does keep but is at its best when young.

CHÂTEAU LE MENAUDAT

A fruity, attractively supple yet well-structured wine that is best in the first four years of its life. Excellent value.

ENTRE-DEUX-MERS

CHÂTEAU BONNET

André Lurton, the highly successful proprietor of many of Bordeaux's leading growths, especially in the Graves and Médoc, chooses to live at this splendid property. The substantial production of red and white wine is of high quality and typical of the best the area can produce.

CHÂTEAU THIEULEY

Best-known for its excellent crisp, dry white wine made from Sauvignon, this is an exemplary estate run by the former professor of viticulture and oenology, Monsieur Courselle. The red wine is also fresh and fruity. Note this example is sold under the Bordeaux appellation, an alternative to Entre-Deux-Mers.

BURGUNDY

EACH WINE-GROWING region of the world is like a jigsaw puzzle that the wine drinker pieces together, in whole or in part, as resources permit. Burgundy is no exception. What distinguishes Burgundy from other regions, making the puzzle more than usually difficult, is scale: the pieces are tiny and manifold, the picture mockingly complicated. These difficulties - combined with the high price of the puzzle in the first place - have caused many to throw the board over, scattering the fragments, before storming from the room, slamming the door, and swearing never to return. Others, of more ample resource, continue with the jigsaw, from time to time uttering cries of delight; these attract newcomers to the puzzle, and the cycle of frustration, palliated by momentary success, continues.

Questions of scale

In 1983 (an average year in respect of size of crop) the Côte d'Or produced nearly 336,000 hectolitres (3.7 million cases) of *Appellation Contrôlée* wine. In the same year, the Bordeaux Rouge appellation alone was responsible for three times this total.

Not only is there very little Burgundy, but what is produced comes from a huge number of different sources. There are nearly 10,000 growers in greater Burgundy (an area that includes Chablis, the Côte d'Or, the Côte Chalonnaise, the Mâconnais and Beaujolais), and the average holding is only a single hectare ($2^1/2$ acres). The French laws of succession (by which each child has an inalienable right to inherit a share of their parents' propety) is often blamed for having fragmented estates, yet the law has not led to similar problems in France's other fine winegrowing areas. A more likely explanation is the question of scale itself: because there is little suitable land, the pressures

Artist's impression *This engraving of the Clos de Vougeot, in the Côte de Nuits, dates from 1719.*

on that land are great. Everybody wants a piece. But not everybody knows the best means of making use of it.

Enter the *négociant*

The answer to this problem should be the *négociant*: someone who will put certain parts of the jigsaw together on your behalf. The *négociant* makes a profession of advising, and buying from, small growers, blending small quantities of wine into larger quantities, and trading on his name as a quality standard in a notoriously mobile and unpredictable market. The theory is a good one; in practice, and for a variety of reasons, merchants' wines have often been as unsatisfactory as growers' wines. Although merchants' wines may not have been as bad as the worst, they were rarely as good as the best. They often blurred village or vineyard character - for decades merchants in Beaune or Nuits-St Georges understood greater Burgundy to include large tracts of Algeria, parts of the Midi, and most of the Rhône valley, blending in a proportion of wines from these areas to beef up their wines. This led to popular misconceptions about the taste of red Burgundy which persist today, as well as earning *négociants* a questionable reputation for honesty.

The taste of Burgundy

The taste of Burgundy is the taste of Pinot Noir and Chardonnay, grown on well-exposed, predominantly limestone slopes in a climate in which grapes are only just able to ripen.

The Chardonnay, a Burgundian grape variety now grown and revered throughout the world, loves the limestone soils of its homeland, and finds the stresses and strains of its continental climate a great incentive to quality. Traditional white-wine vinification here includes alcoholic fermentation in cask; malolactic fermentation at a pace decreed by the seasons; and often a period of ageing on lees before bottling: a "hands-off" approach that requires few interventions from the grower. Careful vineyard husbandry and a well-maintained cellar were the only essential complements to tradition, with the result that fine white Burgundies have never been as hard to find as their red counterparts.

Ironically, perhaps the main threat to these fine, traditional wines comes from the increasing competence and rising aspirations of the small grower - and from Chardonnay's globetrotting. There is now an appreciable "international" style for white Chardonnay: it dictates a fleshy white wine of generous fruit - perhaps tropical in style (pineapple and mango) or lemony - harnessed and informed by a spell in new oak that lends the wine a toasty vanilla richness. The easy charms of these largely warm-climate Chardonnays are completely alien to the traditional style of white Burgundy, which varies from a flinty austerity in Chablis to a nutty but still nervous richness in Meursault, with highish acidity and plenty of secondary aromas and flavours. Yet there are white Burgundies today which fit the former rather than the latter profile; the customer gets a wine that is easy to enjoy, and so does not complain or feel cheated, but a part of French culture has been lost. The situation is not critical yet, as most white

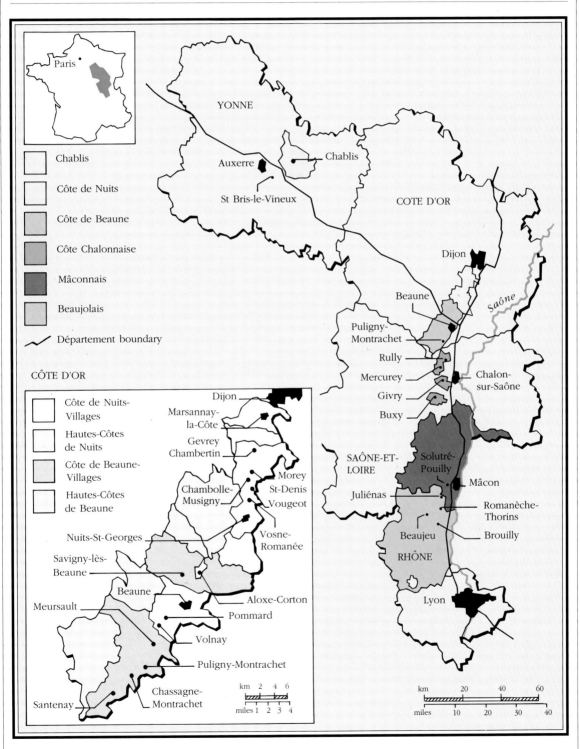

Chablis

Côte de Nuits

Côte de Beaune

Côte Chalonnaise

Mâconnais

Beaujolais

Département boundary

CÔTE D'OR

Côte de Nuits-Villages

Hautes-Côtes de Nuits

Côte de Beaune-Villages

Hautes-Côtes de Beaune

The range of Burgundy *Burgundy's vineyards offer a remarkable spectrum of wines. The region is driven from the south by the red- and white-wine generators of Beaujolais and the Mâconnais. Quality and finesse grow as the Côte d'Or is approached: this is the nerve centre of Burgundy. Chablis marks an elegant conclusion.*

Burgundy Vintages

YEAR	WHITE WINES	RED WINES
1989	Rich, ripe wines, though acidity levels lower than usual	An early harvest of very ripe fruit, giving big, powerful wines
1988	Well-balanced, concentrated wines of good quality	Consistent wines of great presence, structure and depth
1987	Soft, easy and attractive wines for early drinking	Rounded and harmonious wines; some Côtes de Nuits lack concentration
1986	An excellent vintage with wines of concentration and style. Some great	The best are firmly tannic, with high acid levels, for keeping; others are light and thin
1985	Magnificently rich, layered wines that will develop well	A superb vintage, producing wines which combine elegance and power. They will age splendidly
1984	Clean, fresh and lively wines	A small vintage of small-scale wines (though many have appealing fruit)
1983	Big, rather blowsy wines unlikely to develop much with further age, though they will hold their qualities until 1993	Difficult conditions (heat and rot) have produced inconsistent and often badly balanced wines. The best have the structure and the tannins for long ageing
1982	A large harvest of easy, supple wines for drinking soon	Attractive wines from the start, with plenty of fruit aroma and flavour, though some lack backbone. Not for keeping
1981	A small harvest of good quality fruit, giving sinewy wines of great intensity	Aromatic, middle-weight wines showing well after eight years
1980	An average year for white wines, and most are past their best	Underestimated wines with the structure and flesh to please into the early 1990s

Previous vintages of merit: 1979, 1978, 1976, 1972, 1971, 1969, 1966, 1964, 1962, 1961

Burgundy is still made within the tradition rather than without, but the trend is there, emphasized by the warm summers of the 1980s which produced super-ripe fruit, and it may increase in importance in the future.

A tradition to re-find

Red Burgundy is an altogether different matter. Rather than a tradition in danger of being lost, here there is a tradition still struggling to be found again: that of authentic Pinot Noir from a fillet of hillside in northern France, unbolstered by wines from other regions and unfalsified by excessive chaptalization. The struggle is consequent on the fact that the Pinot Noir of pure tradition is considerably less attractive to the ordinary consumer than its Chardonnay counterpart; for this grape in this climate gives wines that often seem ungrateful and ungracious at first, full of harsh tannin and green acidity. They generally improve with time and, once in a while, may seem rich and perfumed from the outset, but all too often they are difficult and unlikeable in youth. High yields have not helped, for they have added a lack of concentration to the charge sheet of those who have paid for fine wines and found these wanting.

Welcome aspirations

The increasing competence and rising aspirations of the small grower look set to improve matters considerably. Red-wine vinification in Burgundy involves more decision making than does white-wine vinification. A number of optional measures can alter the nature of the wines for the better, such as the exclusion or inclusion of stalks in the fermentation vat, and, if included, in what proportion. Adding stalks is a traditional Burgundian stratagem for enlarging the tannic structure of the wine, but it is a good idea only when the fruit is big enough to support such a structure, and when the stalks themselves are ripe and their tannins not too greenly astringent. Other decisions need to be taken regarding the length of time fermentation takes place in the presence of the grape skins (or even, in some cases, a period of skin maceration before fermentation begins); the extent of chaptalization; the degree and frequency of *pigeage*; the use of press wine; inducement of malolactic fermentation; and the proportion of new oak casks in which the wines age. By varying all these factors to suit the nature of the vintage, by keeping yields low, and by scrupulously discarding any rot-affected fruit, palatable wines can be produced even after the most ungenerous years. (In any case, ungenerous years became uncommon during the 1980s.)

The growers and the *négociants* are by no means all ready or able to be painstaking to this

CLASSIFICATIONS AND APPELLATIONS

There are four levels of Burgundy classification. A minimum requirement for decoding them is the ability to recognize the names of Burgundy's wine-producing villages as distinct from those of its vineyards. Village names often take a hyphenated, two-part form (e.g. Gevrey-Chambertin), whereas vineyards are generally a single name (Chambertin) or a descriptive name (Clos du Roi, Les Bonnes Feuves).

1: GRAND CRU

Each *grand cru* vineyard enjoys its own appellation, independently of the village in which it is found. The label will only mention the name of the vineyard (e.g. Chambertin. Appellation Chambertin Contrôlée). It is a village's most important vineyard (often *grand cru*) that often forms the second hyphenated part.

2: PREMIER CRU

Each *premier cru* vineyard is classified together with the village in which it is found, and the label will mention the names of both vineyard and village, and in the clearest cases the fact that the vineyard is a *premier cru* (e.g. Beaune-Clos du Roi Appellation Beaune Premier Cru Contrôlée).

The fatal flaw in the legislation is that there is no obligation incumbent on the grower to state whether his wine meets *premier cru* requirements or not, or whether the vineyard is *premier cru* or not. As many vineyards are only classified *premier cru* in part, and other, non-*premier cru* vineyards may also be mentioned on labels, the purchaser may understandably be in doubt as to the true status of the wine. (Another label, for example, may read Beaune-Clos du Roi Appellation Contrôlée or Beaune-Clos du Roi Appellation Beaune Contrôlée, and who is to say whether the wine comes from the *premier cru* or the non-*premier cru* part of Clos du Roi?)

Technically, wine from unclassified vineyards (Beaune-Les Bonnes Feuves, for example) must indicate the fact, albeit coyly, by labelling the vineyard name in letters not more than half the size of the lettering of the village name, and using only the village appellation (for example, BEAUNE-Les Bonnes Feuves. Appellation Beaune Contrôlée): such wines are emphatically not *premier cru*. If wine is made from a number of different *premier cru* vineyards, then it will simply be labelled (for example) Beaune Premier Cru, with no vineyard name.

3: "VILLAGE" WINES

These are wines made from the fruit of vineyards enjoying classification for the Appellation Communale or "village" appellation (Appellation Gevrey-Chambertin Contrôlée, for example). Recognized vineyards or *lieux-dits* may be specified if wished, in letters not more than half the size of those used for the village name.

4: REGIONAL WINES

Wines from the least promising vineyards are only eligible for Burgundy's regional appellations, Bourgogne Rouge, Rosé, Clairet, Blanc and Mousseux, Crémant de Bourgogne, Bourgogne Ordinaire or Grand Ordinaire, Bourgogne Passetoutgrains and Bourgogne Aligoté. Wines from the Hautes Côtes de Nuits and Hautes Côtes de Beaune, and from Irancy, Coulanges-la-Vineuse and Epineuil in the Yonne, are also "regional" Burgundy, and their names are linked to Bourgogne in the appellation formula. Côte de Nuits Villages and Côte de Beaune Villages are appellations allowed for certain villages not entitled to a communal appellation in their own right.

degree, but some are, and their number increases yearly. Those who are prepared to make the effort to produce fine wines every year are rewarded by buoyant sales. The question may soon no longer be simply "Good Burgundy or bad Burgundy?", but "What sort of Burgundy?" And there may be up to 10,000 answers to that question.

The price of Burgundy

The question of scale dominates every aspect of Burgundy production. A small vineyard area means a small number of bottles for sale each year; a global repuation means intense competition to acquire those bottles, and this means high prices. The wines of the Domaine de la Romanée-Conti, for example, are always more expensive than any first-growth claret of comparable age, and are far more difficult to obtain.

For the consumer, the usual reflex has been to seek out Burgundies made by an ambitious but little-known grower, or sourced from a village with a less well-known name. Perhaps they did exist once, perhaps they still exist, but they get harder to find each year. The spotlight of demand shines more and more intensely on Burgundy. Immediately a grower achieves any sort of distinction, there will be a gaggle of clamouring wine-buyer suitors at the cellar door.

There is no help for it: fine Burgundy is expensive now and will only become more so in the future. Every other wine-producing region of the world offers better value for money. But two strategies are possible in combatting the difficulties. The first plan of attack is to select the very best examples of Pinot Noir and Chardonnay from greater Burgundy, in order to see what magic the climate and soils can work here: choose carefully from the Mâconnais, the Côte Chalonnaise and the Hautes Côtes. The second strategy is to select fine (but not fashionable) Côte d'Or Burgundy from fine (but not fashionable) growers. The price will be high; the project will be a long-term one; but eventually the pieces of the jigsaw puzzle will begin to fit into place.

CHABLIS & DISTRICT

CHABLIS IS A DISTANT outpost of greater Burgundy, midway between Paris and Beaune. Its nearest fellow vines are those of the Aube region of Champagne, some 30 kilometres (19 miles) away; Dijon lies 100 kilometres (62 miles) to the south-east.

Growth and diversity

The soils of this frontier zone are clays of calcareous origin (they have an "active lime" level as high as 14 per cent), divided into two types: Kimmeridgian and Portlandian. Traditionally, Chablis vineyards have been sited only on Kimmeridgian clay, but in recent years the area has been extended to Portlandian clay, amid controversy. The move was inevitable, given the decision of the Institut National des Appellations d'Origine (INAO) to authorize 1,600 hectares (3,954 acres) of new plantings between 1967 and 1985; in 1966, only 733 hectares (1,811 acres) were given over to viticulture. In total, Chablis' vineyards have expanded fourfold since 1945.

Has the quality of Chablis been quartered in the process? Even the most vociferous opponent of the move to Portlandian clay (William Fèvre of the Domaine de la Maladière is unchallenged in this role) would stop short of such criticism. He would, rather, claim that the distinctive profile of Chablis has been lost; that the wine has been *banalisé* (robbed of its originality); that its crystal-clear flavours have been muddied; and that the finely honed edge of Chablis has been blunted.

Those who remember the Chablis of 50 years ago are inclined to agree, and those who have tasted widely in Chablis recently acknowledge that there is now more diversity of style in the little region than ever before. Whether this is alone due to the move to Portlandian clay is questionable; other significant factors include changes in weather patterns and in viticultural techniques (increased chaptalization; fermentation and sometimes *élevage* in stainless steel; use of the malolactic fermentation to reduce acidity and of cold stabilization to precipitate tartrates). Chablis can no longer be assumed to be keen-edged and slender; it may now be softer and richer, taller and broader, plumper and fuller. The little region has grown.

The future for Chablis

The end of Chablis is not yet nigh. Some producers (like René Dauvissat and Jean-Marie Raveneau) produce wines of the sort that their forebears were making 100 years ago; while others make wines that may not fit the traditional image of Chablis, but that would certainly have been enjoyed by the *bons vivants* of a century ago, just as they are by today's *bon vivants*. Chablis is broadening in other ways: the vineyards of the Yonne, which surround the Chablis zone, are undergoing a modest renaissance, with Pinot Noir reds being made in Irancy, Coulanges-la-Vineuse and Epineuil, and with the Sauvignon Blanc grape lending interest and identity to the wines of Saint-Bris-le-Vineux and its neighbours.

CHABLIS

LA CHABLISIENNE

Cooperatives are usually insignificant in Burgundy, but La Chablisienne is the exception: nearly a third of Chablis production comes from its members' 472 hectares (1,165 acres). Its wines - from the clean, fresh and floral Chablis to the the fat, fruity *Grand Cru* Grenouilles - make a worthy standard for the region.

R. ET V. DAUVISSAT
PREMIER CRU "LA FOREST"

The hallmark of a *premier cru* should be elegance and flavoury brightness, and Dauvissat's Forest (more usually "Forêts", a *climat* sited within Montmains) follows the pattern with characteristic accuracy. The wines are cool-fermented in vat and then receive eight months in oak casks (the family were originally coopers as well as winemakers).

R. ET V. DAUVISSAT
GRAND CRU "LES PREUSES"

The Dauvissat estate produces only *grands* and *premiers crus*. Of the seven *grands crus*, Les Preuses is the fullest and roundest. A delicate hand is needed to draw out the vineyard's richness without sacrificing the steely edge that all great Chablis should have. René Dauvissat has such a hand, and his Preuses is always a perfectly judged wine.

J.P. LOUIS DROIN
PREMIER CRU MONTMAINS

The wines of this domaine are sold by Labouré-Roi, whose president, Armand Cottin, is a member of the Committee for the Promotion of Chablis. Finesse and nuance are all here: when young, the Montmains is almost colourless, with a fine aroma of flint and honey, and a crisp, bracingly fresh flavour; with age, the wines ripen and fill out, but never sink into obviousness.

JOSEPH DROUHIN
GRAND CRU VAUDÉSIR

This Beaune-based *négociant* house actually owns more vineyards in Chablis than on the Côte d'Or: 36 hectares (89 acres) out of a total of 61 hectares (148 acres). This includes a parcel of the *Grand Cru* Vaudésir, from which Robert Drouhin makes a fine, oak-aged, straw-yellow Chablis with lemony scent, ripe hazelnut flavours and a keen balance of acidity.

JEAN DURUP
DOMAINE DE L'ÉGLANTIÈRE

Jean Durup has been at the vanguard of the movement to expand the Chablis AC away from exclusively Kimmeridgian clay and on to favourable sites of Portlandian clay. In recent years, much of the land around Maligny, where the Domaine de l'Églantière is based, has been upgraded from Petit Chablis to Chablis. The Chablis of this estate is fresh and full of clear fruit.

JEAN DURUP DOMAINE DE L'ÉGLANTIÈRE, PREMIER CRU MONTÉE DE TONNERRE

Domaine de l'Églantière is one of four different domaines owned by lawyer Jean Durup. Together, his 73 hectares (180 acres) of vineyard make him one of the largest individual producers in Chablis. Vinification and *élevage* in fibreglass-lined cement or stainless steel produces wines with floral aromas and chalky fruit, exemplified by his striking Montée de Tonnerre.

DOMAINE ALAIN GEOFFROY
PREMIER CRU VAU-LIGNEAU

Vau-Ligneau is a new *premier cru* site near the village of Beines, where the Domaine Alain Geoffroy is based. From the 3 hectares (7½ acres) he owns, Monsieur Geoffroy, who is the mayor of Beines, produces a stylish Chablis, full of grassy aromas and with a good backbone of vinosity. Once a no-oak estate, Alain Geoffroy is now experimenting with cask-ageing for the fruit from his old vines.

LABOURÉ-ROI

Armand and Louis Cottin, the two brothers who own the Nuits-St-Georges-based *négociant* business of Labouré-Roi, take great interest in Chablis, and have recently bought a winery site there. The wines are made with care, and Labouré-Roi does not stint on oak. Its harmonious Chablis is relatively full, with vanilla and hawthorn notes on the nose.

LAMBLIN & FILS
PREMIER CRU BEAUROY

The Lamblin family is a *négociant* based in Maligny, owning 10.4 hectares (25 acres) of vineyards. Beauroy, sited to the north-west of Chablis, about halfway up the hillside overlooking Poinchy, is not one of the best *premiers crus*, but the wine produced by Lamblin from this site is clean and fresh on the nose. It has a good intensity of citrus fruit and finishing length to match - five to seven years see it at its peak.

LAMBLIN & FILS
GRAND CRU "VALMUR"

From a hectare (2½ acres) in Valmur, the Lamblin family produces a full and fleshy wine, lemon-yellow in colour, roundly flavoured and of medium depth. The Lamblins also have a holding in the largest of the *grands crus*, Les Clos.

DOMAINE LAROCHE
PREMIER CRU LES VAILLONS

"Using new oak in vinification is like using salt in cooking", says Michel Laroche. "Too little and the dish is insipid; too much and you hide or alter the flavour of the dish." For the Domaine Laroche *grands crus*, 50 to 75 per cent new oak is used; for the *premiers crus* ("usually wines of lighter structure") 30 per cent new oak is used. The result is a Vaillons of pale straw colour, a grassy or nutty bouquet, and light, nuanced fruit.

DOMAINE LAROCHE GRAND CRU LES BLANCHOTS

This important domaine is now run by the fifth generation of the Laroche family, Michel. The winemaking is a combination of the modern and traditional: pneumatic pressing and must centrifuge is followed by temperature-controlled oak fermentation. This Blanchots, harvested from old vines, has a delicate golden colour with scents of peach and pear, and a long, subtle, faintly smoky flavour.

DOMAINE LONG-DEPAQUIT PREMIER CRU LES VAUCOPINS

Les Vaucopins (or Vaucoupins) is tucked away on a hillside to the south-west of Fleys. Although not the best sited of the *premiers crus*, Long Depaquit usually succeeds in making a sound, vigorous Chablis, tingling with mineral flavours. Its wines show that modern methods need not jeopardize traditional quality.

DOMAINE LONG-DEPAQUIT GRAND CRU MOUTONNE

Moutonne is a 2.35-hectare (6-acre) *climat* lying within the *grands crus* of Preuses and Vaudésir. Once the property of the Abbey of Pontigny, the site belongs exclusively to the Domaine A. Long Depaquit, run by the large Beaune *négociant,* Albert Bichot. Moutonne is one of the finest of the *grands crus*: always imposing, but consistently graceful, especially after a decade in the cellar.

DOMAINE DE LA MALADIÈRE PREMIER CRU LES LYS

Les Lys lies just under the hilltop woodland of Bois des Lys. Its north-east-facing aspect provides a nervous wine, shot with green-gold glints and with a rather flinty aroma. Owner William Fèvre's version is true to this character, but the oak he uses softens and balances the rather harsh, chalky textures found in others' versions.

DOMAINE DE LA MALADIÈRE GRAND CRU BOUGROS

Traditional quality, the hallmark of Domaine de la Maladière, is obtained by traditional methods: fermentation and ageing in oak casks, a quarter of which are replaced every year. This holding in Bougros produces a fragrant Chablis which hints at honey, acacia, vanilla and almond. The domaine is the largest owner of *grand cru* vineyards, with 16 hectares (40 acres) in all.

LOUIS MICHEL & FILS PREMIER CRU FOURCHAUME

This small domaine has a large reputation. Fourchaume, ideally sited on the right bank of the Serein just north of the *grands crus*, is one of the best *premiers crus*, and Michel's silky-smooth version does the site justice. None of Michel's wines sees a cask, but even the keenest oak addict would struggle to find fault with these excercises in clean, fresh fruit.

LOUIS MICHEL & FILS GRAND CRU GRENOUILLES

The domaine's commitment to quality begins in the vineyards (where yields are always kept low); continues in the winery (where the must is scrupulously cleaned, the wines slowly fermented, and malolactic fermentation allowed to proceed at its own pace); and proves itself in the bottle. The Michel Grenouilles is benchmark *grand cru* Chablis: aromatic, lean yet powerful, and with breed and finesse.

J. MOREAU & FILS GRAND CRU VAUDÉSIR

Moreau is the big name in Chablis: this domaine is the largest vineyard owner in the region - with over 70 hectares (173 acres) - and the sibling *négociant* business reaches from Mâcon to Muscadet. The Moreaux pioneered the use of concrete and stainless steel in Chablis, and their big, fruity Vaudésir has the concentration and acidity to last years.

ALBERT PIC & FILS PREMIER CRU MONTÉE DE TONNERRE

"Albert Pic et Fils" is a *sous-marque* used by the *négociant* firm of A. Regnard et Fils. The company owns no vineyards, but buys its fruit wisely, and vinifies and ages it with care - and a little oak - to produce a Montée de Tonnerre with edge and length, full of iodine pungency.

DOMAINE PINSON
PREMIER CRU MONTMAIN

Montmain (or Montmains) is one of the larger *premier cru* sites, situated on a south-east-facing hillside between Chablis and Courgis. This is where Louis Pinson has a portion of the vineyards that make up his small, 4-hectare (10-acre) estate, and from which he produces a carefully crafted Chablis of poise and depth.

JEAN-MARIE RAVENEAU
PREMIER CRU BUTTEAUX

Jean-Marie Raveneau has helped his father François to maintain the high standards of this 7-hectare (17-acre) family domaine for some years. From a plot in Butteaux (a sub-vineyard within Montmains, lying south-west of Chablis itself) comes this beautifully keen-edged, lemony white wine.

A. REGNARD & FILS
GRAND CRU LES CLOS

This *négociant* business, owned by Patrick de Ladoucette of Château du Nozet in Pouilly-Fumé and ably directly by Michel Rémon, also sells wine under the name "Albert Pic et Fils", as well as under Monsieur Rémon's own name. At just under 26 hectares (64 acres), Les Clos is the largest of the *grand cru* vineyards, and the wines produced on the site are close-textured, rich and full. Regnard's Les Clos is an attractive, harmonious and well-balanced wine.

DOMAINE SERVIN
GRAND CRU LES PREUSES

Stoniness and steeliness are touch-stones of fine Chablis, and no *grand cru* better exemplifies these qualities than a good Les Preuses. The Servin family owns just under a hectare (2¹/₂ acres) of land here, where Jean Servin makes a vivid and racy wine, full of mouth-watering flintiness.

DOMAINE SIMONNET

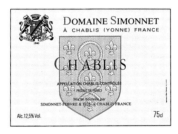

The *négociant* business of Simonnet-Fèbvre, founded in 1840, built much of its prosperity on sparkling Chablis. Today the company is run by Jean-Claude Simonnet: it has small vineyard holdings in Chablis, but most of its products are made from must bought from around 40 growers. The Chablis is a youthful and stylish wine presented in a handsome bottle.

PHILIPPE TESTUT
GRAND CRU GRENOUILLE

Twenty years ago, the Testut family was an important vineyard-owner in the Chablis area, but following family problems, much of the estate has now been sold. Philippe Testut has begun reconstituting what he can of past glories, and his harmonious and seductively aromatic Grenouille is a persuasive argument in favour of the initiative.

DOMAINE ROBERT VOCORET
& SES FILS
GRAND CRU VALMUR

Robert Vorcoret, ex-mayor of Chablis, has now handed over the domaine to his sons. They own just over a third of a hectare (³/₄ acre) in Valmur, a pleasingly aromatic and fleshy *grand cru*. The Vocoret wines, fermented in oak and aged in stainless steel, need time to show their best.

SAUVIGNON
DE ST-BRIS

ROBERT DEFRANCE

Robert Defrance and his son Philippe produce a ripely aromatic Sauvignon Blanc, full of clean gooseberry fruit. Of the 11 hectares (27 acres) of the family domaine, 2.5 hectares (6 acres) are given over to Sauvignon Blanc; the rest are planted with a typical mix of Sacy, Pinot Noir, Chardonnay and, most importantly, Aligoté.

ANDRÉ SORIN ET FILS
DOMAINE DES REMPARTS

The Sauvignon de St-Bris VDQS zone is adjacent to that of Chablis and encloses that of Bourgogne-Irancy. André Sorin produces an aromatic, softly flavoured white wine, in which the pungency of the Sauvignon Blanc is tempered by the local chalky soils.

CÔTE DE NUITS

THE CÔTE D'OR IS divided into two parts. The division is a logical one, as the Côte comes to a natural pause in the middle, where marble quarries replace vineyards, and the soils and aspects of the southern half of the Côte are subtly different from those of the north.

The northern half is around 22 kilometres (13 miles) in length, and varies between 500 metres and 1.5 kilometres (545 and 1,640 yards) in width. It is called the Côte de Nuits, a resonant and suggestive name of mundane origin: the largest town on this stretch of the Côte is Nuits-St Georges, just as the largest town on the Côte de Beaune is Beaune. But Nuits suggests darkness, and darkness suggests red wines; this is as it should be, for bottles of red (and rosé) wine outnumber bottles of white on the Côte de Nuits by a thousand to one. The fame of red Burgundy has been won by splendid wines from Gevrey-Chambertin, Clos de Vougeot and Vosne-Romanée; and, if winemakers the world over are now struggling with the troublesome, temperamental Pinot Noir, it is largely because of the splendour of those wines.

Complex geology

Why is red wine so dominant on the Côte de Nuits? The answer lies in the soils and aspects of this part of the long slope (*la côte*). The geology of the region is extremely complex, complex enough to sow dissent among professionals. In general, it can be said that the topsoils are formed by an interplay between limestone and marl (marl being a mixture of clay and silt, some of it calcareous in origin). Limestone makes for a light, acid soil, giving light, acidic wines; marl is a heavier, richer soil, and the wines it yields mimic this profile. On the Côte de Nuits, marl has the upper hand - it is even red in colour in many vineyards. Furthermore the best sites generally face east, rather than south-east as on the Côte de Beaune; the Nuits vines get a full view of the sun coming up on cloudless summer mornings, and this exposure helps to provide the extra ripening warmth that red grapes need. It is also worth noting that the Côte itself is slightly steeper and narrower in its northern part: the *premiers crus* of Nuits-St Georges, for example, form an extremely thin band only 250 metres wide in places, while at Beaune itself the *premiers* stretch over a gently sloping sea of vines more than a kilometre wide.

The Côte de Nuits begins at Dijon, and the vineyards gradually increase in number and importance from the Dijon suburb of Chenôve, through the villages of Marsannay (one of the best sources today of inexpensive red Burgundy), Couchey, Fixin and Brochon, before the first rumble of kettledrums signals the silky power of Gevrey-Chambertin. With 446 hectares (1,100 acres) under vines, this is one of the most important of all the Côte d'Or's villages; unfortunately, quality (especially among the "village" wines) is variable. Morey-St Denis, the next village, is barely a quarter of the size of Gevrey, but the enthusiasm and proficiency of the growers (chief among them Jacques Seysses of Domaine Dujac) makes it a fertile hunting ground for Burgundy enthusiasts, though it no longer yields the bargains that it once did. Musigny, whose name has been borrowed by the village of Chambolle, is one of Burgundy's steepest *grands crus,* and the soil mix here and throughout the commune is comparatively high in calcareous materials, giving beautifully perfumed, seductive red wines, and even a little white.

Multiple ownership

The Clos de Vougeot's 50 hectares (123 acres) make it Burgundy's biggest *grand cru,* and its 70 owners make it Burgundy's least reliable appellation; red Burgundy should always be chosen with care, but never more so than here. The rest of Vougeot occupies only 16.5 hectares (40 acres).

Neighbouring Flagey-Echézeaux is, in wine terms, a ghost village: the place exists, but wines from its village vineyards are sold as Vosne-Romanée; it has no *premiers crus*; and its *grands crus* are, in practical terms, a continuation of the Vougeot vineyards. Like the Clos de Vougeot, Echézeaux and Grands Echézeaux are geologically heterogeneous and in multiple ownership, with the best winemakers and the best sites combining to produce intense wines that have great presence and finesse.

Perfect conditions

Everything - soils, aspects, winemaking ambitions - is right in Vosne-Romanée; there just are not enough of the village's perfumed wines to go around. The *grands crus* are within reach of the very wealthiest only; the *premiers* may at least be contemplated, and their quality almost justifies their price. After the metaphorical summit of Vosne, the Côte de Nuits comes to an end with the long, tapering vineyards of Nuits-St Georges. There are no *grands crus* here, but some of the Côte's best *premiers,* earthily majestic, provide ample compensation. There are few more satisfying abstracts of red Burgundy than a fine Nuits.

MARSANNAY

DOMAINE BRUNO CLAIR ROSÉ

Launched by Joseph Clair in 1919, Marsannay Rosé is Burgundy's best-quality rosé; that produced by Bruno Clair is a deep strawberry colour, growing coppery after a few years, with scents of currants and berries.

JEAN FOURNIER CLOS DU ROY

The Clos du Roy actually lies in the neighbouring village of Chenôve, but it is entitled to the Marsannay appellation. Jean Fournier's example is full of lean fruit, with a long flavour that finishes with attractively bitter notes.

FIXIN

BOUCHARD AÎNÉ & FILS PREMIER CRU CLOS DU CHAPITRE

Clos du Chapitre, with its steep gradient and rich limestone soils, produces solid, meaty wines that ask for eight to ten years' cellaring. This version has a fruity aroma mingling raspberries and blackcurrants and a rich, mouth-filling flavour.

DOMAINE PIERRE GELIN PREMIER CRU CLOS NAPOLÉON

Clos Napoléon lies within Aux Cheusots, and owes its name to one of Napoleon's guardsmen who created a park in the Emperor's memory next to this vineyard. The largely flat vineyard yields a lighter Burgundy than does Fixin's steeper slopes, but Monsieur Gelin produces a wine that is still structured and firm.

PHILIPPE JOLIET PREMIER CRU "CLOS DE LA PERRIÈRE"

Powerful, full-bodied wines are produced from the pebbly brown limestone soils lying above Clos du Chapitre, wines full of the earthy, mineral flavours so characteristic of this northern end of the Côte de Nuits.

GEVREY-CHAMBERTIN

BOUCHARD AÎNÉ ET FILS GRAND CRU CHAMBERTIN-CLOS DE BÈZE

Bouchard Aîné vinifies the wine of the Domaine Dr Henri Marion, owner of nearly two of the 15 hectares (37 acres) of Chambertin-Clos de Bèze. Together with Chambertin itself, this is the finest vineyard in Gevrey, and Bouchard Aîné makes a traditional example: often rather harsh in youth, but becoming rich and full with time.

ALAIN BURGUET VIEILLES VIGNES

Alain Burguet's vines all lie in the "village" zone of Gevrey, but the results he obtains there are as good as a number of other growers' *premiers crus*. These attractive wines age well; they are deeply coloured, generously aromatic and roundly flavoured, with roasted, spicy notes.

DOMAINE BRUNO CLAIR PREMIER CRU CLOS DU FONTENY

1986 was the first vintage of this wine made by Bruno Clair, following the division of the Marsannay-based Clair-Daü estate. Clos du Fonteny is situated at the same approximate height as the *grands crus*, but faces north rather than east. The wines are lighter than most people expect from Gevrey, but full and flavoury.

JOSEPH DROUHIN GRAND CRU GRIOTTE-CHAMBERTIN

Griotte-Chambertin is a thin-soiled *Grand Cru* lying beneath Clos de Bèze, and it produces one of the more elegant wines of this splendid hillside. Its fruit is said to resemble the bright red, bitter cherries known as *griottes* which, legend has it, once grew here. With Robert Drouhin's expertise, the vines yield a wonderfully fruity, silkily textured Burgundy.

DOMAINE DROUHIN-LAROZE
GRAND CRU
CHAPELLE-CHAMBERTIN

Chapelle-Chambertin is adjacent to Griotte-Chambertin, and shares its thin soils. The wines of Chapelle-Chambertin are the lightest of all the Chambertin *grand cru* family, and the wine produced from Drouhin-Laroze's half-hectare (1¼ acres) are smooth and supple, marked by floral or redcurrant aromas, and develop with comparative speed in bottle.

DOMAINE DROUHIN-LAROZE
GRAND CRU
LATRICIÈRES-CHAMBERTIN

Latricières occupies a site just south of Chambertin itself, yet the fractionally different microclimate and more silicious soils produce a wine that is lighter and more elegant than Chambertin. Domaine Drouhin-Laroze cultivates three-quarters of a hectare (2 acres) here, making wines in which elegance and poise are to the fore, though not at the expense of length.

DOMAINE DUJAC
PREMIER CRU AUX COMBOTTES

Aux Combottes is sited next to the *Grand Cru* Latricières, and a tiny fragment of Combottes has the right to use the Latricières name. Jacques Seysses of Domaine Dujac in the neighbouring village of Morey-St Denis makes a fine Combottes from the hectare (2½ acres) he holds here, with a rich and spicy aroma and a deep, beautifully balanced flavour, full of clear, fresh fruit.

J. FAIVELEY
GRAND CRU
CHAMBERTIN CLOS DE BÈZE

With over 100 hectares (240 acres), Domaine Faiveley is one of the most important landowners in Burgundy. François Faiveley is a great believer in cool fermentation, ageing in new oak and minimum pre-bottling treatments, and the result - in this case - is a concentrated, powerfully aromatic, richly fruited Clos de Bèze.

PHILIPPE LECLERC
PREMIER CRU LES CAZETIERS

Les Cazetiers is one of a bank of nine or so fine *premiers crus* that face south-west, overlooking the exit of the Combe de Lavaux into Gevrey. Philippe Leclerc produces a sensational Cazetiers, entirely aged in new oak, unfined and unfiltered, with huge fruit and length.

PHILIPPE LECLERC
PREMIER CRU
COMBE AUX MOINES

Combe aux Moines is adjacent to Les Cazetiers, but is a little higher up the hillside. Philippe Leclerc achieves a remarkable consistency in his wines, modifying the time they spend in wood to suit the vintages. His Combe aux Moines has a little more finesse and a little less depth than his Cazetiers, acquiring scents of liquorice, coffee and dried fruit with age.

LEROY
GRAND CRU CHAMBERTIN

Chambertin occupies 13 hectares (32 acres), and Chambertin-Clos de Bèze, 15 hectares (37 acres), so in theory wine from 28 hectares (70 acres) may go to market under the Chambertin name, since Clos de Bèze is also allowed to use the Chambertin appellation. Most important *négociants* want to offer a Chambertin, and Leroy is no exception. This is a hugely powerful but tightly structured Chambertin, built like a fortress and priced like a racehorse.

HENRI MAGNIEN
PREMIER CRU
LAVAUX ST-JACQUES

Lavaux St Jacques lies just west of Clos St Jacques in the centre of the fine, curved bench of *premiers crus* that dominates the Brochon end of Gevrey-Chambertin. Henri Magnien produces an intense, mid-weight Gevrey, full of haunting Pinot aromas and liquorice-tinted, red-fruit flavours.

DOMAINE MAUME
GRAND CRU
MAZIS-CHAMBERTIN

Mazis-Chambertin lies north of Chambertin, on gravelly soils close to the limestone bedrock. This combination produces a lighter Burgundy than its southerly neighbour - except when the label reads "Maume". In this case, low-yielding vines produce wines of tannic concentration, opening up after a decade or so to reveal spicy fruit.

PHILIPPE ROSSIGNOL

Plain "village" Gevrey-Chambertin is one of the Côte d'Or's most marketable names, and nowhere else is the appellation boundary drawn so generously. Poor bottles abound, but Philippe Rossignol produces Gevrey-Chambertin worthy of the name: handsome to look at, intriguing to sniff and exhilarating to drink.

JOSEPH ROTY PREMIER CRU "LES FONTENYS"

Les Fontenys shares the soil and elevation of the adjacent Chambertin *grand cru* vineyards, but it has mainly north-facing rather than east-facing aspects. The skills of a winemaker like Joseph Roty make up for nature's slight, and Roty's Fontenys is a dark, rich and sonorous Gevrey, needing time to show at its best.

CHRISTOPHE ROUMIER GRAND CRU RUCHOTTES-CHAMBERTIN

Christophe Roumier has taken over the winemaking from his father at what used to be the Domaine Georges Roumier, a 14-hectare (35-acre) estate based at Chambolle-Musigny. A small parcel is owned in the high-sited Ruchottes *Grand Cru*; the Roumiers give an elegant Chambolle sheen to the natural strength and depth of this Chambertin.

DOMAINE ARMAND ROUSSEAU PREMIER CRU CLOS ST JACQUES

This domaine has a total of 14 hectares (35 acres) in many of the best sites of the Côte de Nuits, including 1 hectare (2¹/₂ acres) in Chambertin. The Clos St Jacques lies in the middle of the broad sweep of super-*premiers* west of Gevrey. Its old vines produce a wine of concentration and controlled power.

DOMAINE ARMAND ROUSSEAU GRAND CRU RUCHOTTES CHAMBERTIN

The *monopole* Clos des Ruchottes takes up a large part of the 3-hectare (7-acre) Ruchottes *Grand Cru*, tucked away above Mazis-Chambertin, and has been acquired relatively recently by this domaine. Charles Rousseau produces a firmly structured, extract-rich Ruchottes that requires long ageing before its cherry fruit turns to perfume.

DOMAINE TORTOCHOT GRAND CRU CHARMES-CHAMBERTIN

Charmes-Chambertin, at nearly 32 hectares (80 acres), is the biggest of all the *grands crus*, and it is worth following the best producers in this appellation to avoid disappointment. Gabriel Tortochot uses destalked fruit that is lengthily fermented and aged in mainly seasoned oak.

LOUIS TRAPET PÈRE & FILS GRAND CRU CHAMBERTIN

With almost 4 hectares (10 acres) in Chambertin, Jean Trapet produces a Vieilles Vignes version as well as "straight" Chambertin. His wines of the 1980s are better than those of the 1970s, with a powerfully aromatic and tannic 1983 and a ripe, rich 1985, aged in 50 per cent new oak.

LOUIS TRAPET PÈRE & FILS GRAND CRU LATRICIÈRES-CHAMBERTIN

Latricières-Chambertin is usually lighter and more accessible than Chambertin, but Jean Trapet's 1985 Latricières reversed this: it is a spicy, earthy wine, full of smoky length and prune fruit, and broader than his 1985 Chambertin. Other years are lighter, but always charming and poised.

DOMAINE DES VAROILLES PREMIER CRU CHAMPONETS

Jean-Pierre Naigeon is co-owner and winemaker for the Domaine des Varoilles; he succeeds in striking a balance between perfume and texture for the short term and tannin and extract for the long. The 1980 Champonets that so impressed the Tastevin jury has a rich, musky, animal odour and a full, velvety taste.

DOMAINE DES VAROILLES
CLOS PRIEUR

This is, in appellation terms, a "village" wine, but as it is made from a recognized *lieu-dit* - called Clos Prieur - the vineyard may be mentioned on the label. Like its mate in the Varoilles stable, Clos du Meix des Ouches, the Clos Prieur makes a satisfying bottle of mid-weight Gevrey, best at five to seven years old.

DOMAINE PHILIPPE
CHARLOPIN-PARIZOT

This 10-hectare (24-acre) domaine has a rigorous regime: fermentation is in wood, with 80 per cent of the stalks retained, and a long maceration period of up to 22 days; the wines then move into heavily toasted oak casks (a quarter new each year), where they acquire coffee and vanilla notes. This is "village" Morey with chewy depth, and it needs bottle age.

DOMAINE DUJAC
GRAND CRU CLOS LA ROCHE

Jacques Seysses's home base is in Morey-St Denis, and the wines he makes from nearly 2 hectares (5 acres) in the 15-hectare (37-acre) Clos la Roche are among his finest. Typically for Morey, they are packed with fruit, and have subtle perfume and a beautifully opulent texture.

DOMAINE DUJAC
GRAND CRU CLOS SAINT-DENIS

This tiny 6.5-hectare (16-acre) fillet of land half way up the hillside is the *Grand Cru* after which Morey styles itself. Jacques Seysses has nearly a quarter of its vines, which he manures organically. He harvests the fruit as late as possible, ferments it slowly (stalks included), ages the wines in oak, fines them with white of egg and bottles them without filtration. The result is intense, fragrant and vivid.

DOMAINE DES LAMBRAYS
GRAND CRU
CLOS DES LAMBRAYS

This *monopole* was sold in 1979 to the Saier brothers (from Mercurey) and Roland de Chambure. In 1981 Clos des Lambrays, previously a *premier cru*, became a *grand cru*. Much replanting has been done and the estate still needs time to prove itself, but a deep and resonant 1985 bodes well for the future.

GEORGES LIGNIER ET FILS
PREMIER CRU CLOS DES ORMES

Georges Lignier has 4.5 hectares (11 acres) of the Clos des Ormes site, situated on the same lines of gradient as the lower part of Mazoyères-Chambertin to its north. Lignier's wines always have great panache: this elegant wine has peppery, spicy aromas and light, almost nutty fruit flavours, sometimes with bitter notes.

ALAIN MICHELOT

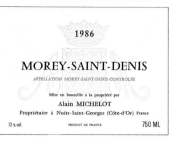

This Morey-St Denis, produced by Nuits-St Georges grower Alain Michelot, has everything a good "village" wine should have: clear fruit, a touch of oak in the bouquet, and balance and length on the palate.

MOMMESSIN
GRAND CRU CLOS DE TART

The 7.5-hectare (19 acre) Clos de Tart owned by Mommessin is sited next to the portion of Bonnes Mares found within Morey-St Denis, at the southern end of the village. Low yields, ultra-traditional vinification and 16 to 18 months in new oak result in fruity, rich wines that are approachable when young but that also age well.

DOMAINE PONSOT GRAND CRU
CLOS DE LA ROCHE
CUVÉE VIEILLES VIGNES

Half of the Domaine Ponsot's 8-hectare (20-acre) estate lies in Clos de la Roche, and the size of this holding allows Jean-Marie Ponsot and his son Laurent produce a version from old vines as well as a standard version. Both are big wines, and the Cuvée Vieilles Vignes, after generous years such as 1985 or 1986, grows monstrous: lock it in the cellar for a decade and a half. The Ponsot Clos de la Roche can be a little hard in lesser years, and also needs time.

DOMAINE ARMAND ROUSSEAU GRAND CRU CLOS DE LA ROCHE

Charles Rousseau places his 1.5-hectare (4 acre) holding in Clos de la Roche only just behind his Clos-St Jacques in quality, ahead of his three lesser Chambertin *grands crus*. Rousseau makes a Clos de la Roche of characteristic elegance and finesse, full of stylish fruit when young but better still after five to ten years, when it acquires the characteristic Burgundian complexities of manure and undergrowth.

DOMAINE B. SERVEAU ET FILS PREMIER CRU LES SORBETS

This is a small domaine with holdings in Morey and neighbouring Chambolle. Bernard Serveau makes a Sorbets of simple excellence: well-structured, firm and long, full of the scent and flavour of loganberries.

CHAMBOLLE-MUSIGNY

BERNARD AMIOT PREMIER CRU LES CHATELOTS

Les Chatelots is centrally positioned directly below the village of Chambolle. Bernard Amiot produces a Burgundy of enormous charm from his plot there, full of floral and fruit aromas. The wine is plumply flavoured, but it has enough soft tannins to coax the fruit into profile.

M. BARTHOD-NOËLLAT

Some of the richer "village" Chambolle-Musigny is produced by Gaston Barthod-Noëllat, president of the local winegrowers' association. His domaine is not a large one - just under 4 hectares (10 acres) - but methods in the vineyard and in the cellar are painstakingly traditional, resulting in wines of stylish, spicy fruit.

DOMAINE DUJAC PREMIER CRU LES GRUENCHERS

The village of Chambolle-Musigny sits wedged into the exit of one of the small *combes* that interrupt the Côte, and beneath the village lies its gaggle of *premiers crus*. Les Gruenchers is found more or less in the middle of these, and from the fruit harvested there Domaine Dujac produces textbook Chambolle: hauntingly fragrant, beautifully weighted in the mouth, long and flavoury.

DOMAINE DUJAC GRAND CRU BONNES MARES

Bonnes Mares is a large *grand cru* of 15.5 hectares (38 acres), 13.7 (34 acres) of which lie in Chambolle-Musigny and 1.8 (4¹/2 acres) in Morey-St Denis, stretching as far as the walls of Clos de Tart. It is a very fine site indeed, and Jacques Seysses produces perhaps his finest wine from a tiny holding there: it is powerfully perfumed, sweetly concentrated, sappy and long.

JEAN GRIVOT LA COMBE D'ORVAUX

This Chambolle-Musigny, from the unclassified vineyard of La Combe d'Orvaux, is made by Etienne Grivot, a talented young winemaker who also makes the wines for the Domaine Jacqueline Jayer. Grivot's style is not dissimilar to Georges Lignier's: both aim for very pure, clean Pinot Noir fruit, moving between the poles of power and elegance as the *terroir* dictates. Here it is elegance: floral aromas and light fruit flavours to charm and seduce.

ALAIN HUDELOT-NOËLLAT

Alain Hudelot-Noëllat's Chambolle-Musigny is a model of fidelity to the light, stony soils of the village, richer in limestone materials than those of its neighbours to north and south. Supple, silky textures, finely drawn fruit and lingering length are all expressions of that fidelity.

GEORGES MUGNERET PREMIER CRU LES FEUSSELOTTES

Georges Mugneret is a qualified doctor, but has given up tending patients in order to devote his full attention to vines. His methods are painstaking and traditional, and result in wines that, like this one, have a deep, limpid intensity, the fruit flavours given an extra sheen by judicious use of new oak.

JACQUES-FRÉDÉRIC MUGNIER PREMIER CRU LES FUÉES

The grace, elegance and delicacy of line so evident in this label is a perfect abstract of the wine contained in the bottle it identifies. Les Fuées is adjacent to Bonnes Mares, and is one of the best *premier cru* sites in this comparatively small village. From his part of the vineyard, Jacques-Frédéric Mugnier produces a wine with plenty of fresh raspberry aroma and rich flavours of tobacco and liquorice.

JACQUES-FRÉDÉRIC MUGNIER GRAND CRU MUSIGNY

Musigny, tucked up against the Clos de Vougeot, can produce wines of faultless construction, and the flavours and aromas Mugnier's wine surrenders are always charming and often entrancing. Few *grands crus* draw rhapsodies from their drinkers as Musigny does.

DOMAINE G. ROUMIER

The Domaine Georges Roumier has over 7 hectares (17 acres) of vine-yards producing "village" Chambolle, and it is almost invariably the supple, cleanly fruity wine that the name promises. Christophe Roumier also produces finely aromatic *Premier Cru* Les Amoureuses; while the Pegasus of the stable is a deep *Grand Cru* Bonnes Mares from old vines, almost inscrutable in youth but ageing over 15 years into opulence.

DOMAINE B. SERVEAU ET FILS PREMIER CRU LES AMOUREUSES

None of Musigny's *Premiers Crus* is better known than Les Amoureuses, a 5-hectare (12-acre) vineyard lying beneath Musigny in the southern part of the village, and the prices its wines command sometimes match those paid for Bonnes Mares. Bernard Serveau produces a fine example: elegant, balanced and long, and full of deep cherry fruit.

DOMAINE COMTE GEORGES DE VOGÜÉ GRAND CRU BONNES MARES

Few Burgundy labels are as distin-guished as that of the 12-hectare (30-acre) de Vogüé estate, and, with 7 hectares (17 acre) in Musigny and nearly 3 hectares (7 acres) in Bonnes Mares, its wines should match the label's grandeur. Unfortunately, the wines have often been inconsistent, but since 1985 greater reliability has been evident. The de Vogüé Bonnes Mares is full and rich, structured after good years, and attractively textured.

DOMAINE COMTE GEORGES DE VOGÜÉ GRAND CRU MUSIGNY BLANC

This domaine is the only one to make a white Musigny, from a half-hectare (1¼ acre) of Chardonnay vines. The result is a supple white Burgundy, fresh and full, with a nutty taste and rich finish. Rarity dictates a high price.

ROBERT ARNOUX GRAND CRU CLOS-VOUGEOT

Robert Arnoux owns a finger of land in the best - the highest - part of the 50-hectare (123-acre) Clos de Vou-geot. From this, he produces a small quantity of deeply coloured, tannic and meaty wine which, with age, grows rich, succulent and aromatic.

DOMAINE BERTAGNA PREMIER CRU CLOS DE LA PERRIÈRE

The Clos de la Perrière lies beneath the *Grand Cru* of Musigny, to the north of the Clos de Vougeot itself, and its wine (there is only one, for this 2-hectare (5-acre) vineyard is a *monopole*) represents a mid-point between the charm and elegance of the former and the latent power of the latter. New oak adds perfume and structure to the rich, choice fruit.

JOSEPH DROUHIN GRAND CRU CLOS DE VOUGEOT

Robert Drouhin's own holdings in the Clos de Vougeot are in the least favourable part of the site, in the south-western corner. Yet Drouhin produces a wine with rich fruit and depth, superior to the offerings of many better-sited domaines.

DOMAINE DROUHIN-LAROZE
GRAND CRU CLOS DE VOUGEOT

Drouhin-Laroze has 1.5 of the best-sited hectares (4 acres) in the Clos. The "house style" of its wines is light and elegant, and the Clos de Vougeot is no exception, often showing aromas of cherry and liquorice and a palate of velvety fullness. Its Vougeot is soon ready to drink.

JEAN GRIVOT
GRAND CRU CLOS-DE-VOUGEOT

Grivot is another owner with vines sited at the bottom of Clos de Vougeot - nearly 2 hectares (5 acres) of them, in fact. Yet the Grivot family believes that its Vougeot vines produce better wine than their plot in Echézeaux does. The Clos de Vougeot 1985 is built in the elegant style favoured by Etienne Grivot, with a full depth of rounded berry fruit and light, ripe tannins.

JEAN GROS
GRAND CRU CLOS DE VOUGEOT
GRAND MAUPERTUIS

The half-hectare (1¼-acres) of the Clos that belongs to the Domaine Jean Gros is sited high, and in generous years it produces one of the best of all Vougeots. The wine is dark and rich, stretching the potential of the fruit towards the limits of suggestive subtlety. Grand Maupertuis is one of the *climats* into which the Clos de Vougeot is divided by tradition.

ALAIN HUDELOT-NOËLLAT
GRAND CRU CLOS DE VOUGEOT

Alain Hudelot's father Noël was long thought to produce one of the best Clos de Vougeots, from around half a hectare (1¼ acres) of vineyard in the upper part of the Clos. Alain continues in this tradition, producing an elegant, peppery Vougeot with long, vegetal flavours and a spicy finish.

JAFFELIN
GRAND CRU CLOS DE VOUGEOT

The Beaune *négociant* Jaffelin, since 1969 the property of the Drouhin family, owns two-thirds of a hectare (1½ acres) in the centre of the Clos de Vougeot. Recent years have seen a switch towards a vigorously fruity style in the company's Vougeot, as in its other wines, with spice and tannin closing in at the finish. The shape is round, the flavours clear and bright.

MONGEARD-MUGNERET
GRAND CRU CLOS DE VOUGEOT

Two-thirds of a hectare (1¾ acres) in the best part of the Clos; long vatting times; long wood ageing, with a high proportion of new oak: all this adds up to a muscular, powerful Vougeot with intense fruit early in life and the tannin and structure for longevity. Like Grivot's Clos-de-Vougeot, this Clos de Vougeot can edge ahead of the Echézeaux (though not the Grands Echézeaux) on occasion.

GEORGES MUGNERET
GRAND CRU CLOS-VOUGEOT

This is another domaine with a small holding in the best, high part of the Clos - so near to the Château, in fact, that the floodlights sit between Dr Mugneret's rows of vines. At present, this is one of the very finest Vougeots of all: impeccable wines of style and impact, full of swirling flavours and textures. One third of a hectare (⅗ acre), though, does not go far.

DOMAINE DANIEL RION & FILS
GRAND CRU CLOS-VOUGEOT

Domaine Rion has just over half a hectare (1¼ acres) of Clos de Vougeot which it cultivates on a *fermage* (tenant farming) basis. The Rion Clos de Vougeot can be very good - as in 1980 or 1985 - but it can also be disappointing, as in 1981 or 1986. When it is good, it is in a rich and round style, with plenty of plum fruit and a kiss of new oak.

DOMAINE DES VAROILLES
GRAND CRU CLOS-VOUGEOT

The Domaine des Varoilles has 2.6 hectares (6½ acres) of the Clos which it vinifies with another grower holding a complementary plot in a different area of the vineyard, much as the monks of old did. The result is a sweetly scented, rich and round Vougeot, needing time to open out and show at its best.

FLAGEY-ÉCHEZEAUX AND VOSNE-ROMANÉE

ROBERT ARNOUX GRAND CRU ECHÉZEAUX

The two Echézeaux vineyards occupy 40 hectares (99 acres); Echézeaux itself is much the larger and higher of the two. The wines are light in comparison with most red *grands crus*, but Arnoux's Echézeaux is fuller than some: elegant and concentrated, often with lovely raspberry scent.

ROBERT ARNOUX GRAND CRU ROMANÉE-ST-VIVANT

Romanée-St-Vivant is the lowest-lying of the Vosne *grand crus*, with the deepest soils, and it produces powerful, aromatic wines. Robert Arnoux's 1985 was perhaps his best of the 1980s: it has a bouquet in which oak mingles with raspberries, redcurrants and violets, and a big, velvety taste.

DOMAINE RENÉ ENGEL PREMIER CRU LES BRÛLÉES

The Domaine René Engel owns 2.5 hectares (6 acres) of the small *Premier Cru* Les Brûlées. This domaine is finding its feet again after a period of disappointing results. The Engel Les Brûlées has, since 1985, been a richly flavoured and well-constituted wine, with meaty, savoury aromas.

JEAN GRIVOT PREMIER CRU LES SUCHOTS

Les Suchots, a large vineyard separating Echézeaux from Richebourg and Romanée-St Vivant, is probably the senior *premier cru* in Vosne. The Grivot family's holding there is small (one-fifth of a hectare/ 1/2 acre), but this wine is considerably better than the Grivot "village" Vosne, with floral and fruit aromas and good structure and length.

JEAN GRIVOT GRAND CRU RICHEBOURG

Richebourg occupies 8 hectares (20 acres) above Romanée-St Vivant, with la Romanée and Romanée-Conti lying adjacent to it to the south. The opulence hinted at in the name should surface in the wine, and Etienne Grivot is a producer who can be trusted to bring this out without losing fruit definition.

JEAN GROS CLOS DES RÉAS

The 2 hectares (5 acres) of Clos de Réas, sited in the lowest part of the village beneath Les Chaumes, belongs exclusively to the Gros family. Madame Gros produces a rich and perfumed wine with a wealth of woodland flavours from its vines. The vineyard, by Vosne-Romanée standards, is not well known, and the wine can therefore be good value.

JEAN GROS GRAND CRU RICHEBOURG

A regal label for a regal wine. From just over half a hectare (1 1/4 acres), with traditional vinification methods and new oak every year, Madame Gros produces a Richebourg of complexity, depth and sumptuousness. The wine is completely successful in "big" years; in lighter years, the new oak can sometimes be a little intrusive and distracting.

HENRI JAYER CROS-PARANTOUX

Henri Jayer, widely considered to be one of the finest winemakers in Burgundy, has now retired; the winemaking at his domaine is today in the hands of his nephew Emmanuel Rouget, though an avuncular eye continues to supervise matters in the cellars. The wines of the unclassified Cros-Parentoux, should you be lucky enough to find them, are deep, tightly structured, and full of raspberry fruit.

J. JAYER GRAND CRU ECHÉZEAUX

The wines of the domaine of Jacqueline Jayer are now made by Etienne Grivot of Domaine Jean Grivot, and they share his hallmarks of pure fruit, suppleness and keen balance. New oak is used to add spicy, toasty notes, and to give the raspberry fruit a rich, tannic structure.

DOMAINE FRANÇOIS LAMARCHE
LA GRANDE RUE

La Grande Rue is the 1.5-hectare (4-acre) *Premier Cru* between *Grand Cru* La Tâche and the three Romanée *Grands Crus*, and such a position generates high expectations. These have not always been satisfied by the generally light, sometimes rough-and-ready wines of Domaine Lamarche, but if you want to try La Grande Rue, these are the wines you must buy, for the vineyard is a *monopole*.

DOMAINE MÉO-CAMUZET
PREMIER CRU LES CHAUMES

Jean Méo owns 2 hectares (5 acres) of Les Chaumes, the *Premier Cru* lying between Malconsorts and the Clos des Réas. From 1985 the widely-admired Henri Jayer has been engaged as a consultant; filters have been thrown out and new casks brought in, and the wines now have a directness and integrity that sets them apart from their peers.

MOILLARD-GRIVOT

In addition to plots of the Vosne *Premiers* Malconsorts and Beaux Monts, the *négociant* Moillard also owns vines within the "village" part of Vosne. The fact that it is labelled Moillard-Grivot indicates that it is highly regarded by its makers; stylistically it is one of the bigger of the "village" Vosnes, full of high-spirited power and extract.

MONGEARD-MUGNERET
GRAND CRU
GRANDS-ECHÉZEAUX

Jean Mongeard's 15-hectare (37-acre) estate offers a mouthwatering range of wines, but none is finer than that made from a 1-hectare (2½-acre) plot in Grands Echézeaux. This is often one of the outstanding Burgundies of its year, with a dazzlingly rich bouquet and flavours that hint of fruit, coffee and chocolate.

DOMAINE DANIEL RION & FILS
PREMIER CRU BEAUX-MONTS

The "handsome peaks" lie up on the high ground above Echézeaux; an aromatically complex but comparatively light Vosne is produced by the Rions from the 1-hectare (2½-acre) holding the family has there. The flavours are delicate and persistent, often with an animal edge to them.

DOMAINE DE LA
ROMANÉE-CONTI
GRAND CRU ROMANÉE-CONTI

Romanée-Conti is just under 2 hectares (5 acres) in size, and is in the sole ownership of the DRC, as this domaine is often called. The fruit is harvested late, macerated lengthily, and always aged in new oak. Richness, opulence and concentration are key words in the lengthy appreciations that this wine's fabulous expense commands.

DOMAINE DE LA
ROMANÉE-CONTI
GRAND CRU LA TÂCHE

La Tâche, just across La Grande Rue from the three Romanées, is 6 hectares (15 acres) in size, and is the other glittering *monopole* of the DRC. The domaine came in for some criticism for over-chaptalization in the 1970s, but the more generous vintages of the 1980s seem to have sidelined this problem and superlatives are now the order of the day. La Tâche's aromatic finesse is legendary, with spices, resin, roses and truffles repeatedly suggesting themselves to the entranced; while the wine's velvety fruit, ample dimensions and fine length of flavour seldom disappoint the expectations aroused by scents of such sublimity.

ROBERT SIRUGUE
GRAND CRU
GRANDS-ECHÉZEAUX

Robert Sirugue's small parcel of vines in Grands Echézeaux is his only *grand cru* holding, and he treats the wines it produces with great respect. The harvest is sorted and unripe or rotten fruit removed; fermentation is in wood, with twice-daily *pigeage*; and the wines are aged in wood, some of it new, for 20 to 24 months. Fining is with egg white and the wines are given only a light filtration. This is an artisan's Grands Echézeaux, full of berry and flower aromas and sweet, round, textured fruit.

CHÂTEAU DE VOSNE-ROMANÉE BOUCHARD PÈRE & FILS GRAND CRU LA ROMANÉE

Exclusively owned by the Comte Liger-Belair, this vineyard is France's smallest *Appellation Contrôlée* - it is under a hectare (2½ acres) in size. Bouchard Père & Fils make and age the wines, which are a deep garnet colour, powerfully aromatic, with fire and fruit on the palate.

NUITS-SAINT GEORGES

ROBERT CHEVILLON PREMIER CRU LES CAILLES

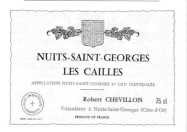

Two hectares of the 13-hectare (32-acre) Chevillon domaine lie in the *Premier Cru* of Les Cailles, a mid-slope vineyard on the southern side of Nuits. Les Cailles normally produces one of the lighter, more elegant wines of Nuits, but Robert Chevillon's parcel is in old vines, and his wine is lushly fruity, with the structure to ripen over a decade.

ROBERT DUBOIS & FILS PREMIER CRU "CLOS DES ARGILLIÈRES"

Clos des Argillières sits on the upper slopes of the stretch of *premiers crus* behind Prémeaux, and from a small holding of under half a hectare (1¼ acres), Robert Dubois produces a red Burgundy of gamey, irony flavour.

J. FAIVELEY PREMIER CRU CLOS DE LA MARÉCHALE

Faiveley's 9.5-hectare (24-acre) leased *monopole,* Clos de la Maréchale, is tucked up beneath the Bois de la Montagne south of Prémeaux. The vineyard produces a fat, ripe, some-times rather rustic but always vigorous and forthcoming wine.

DOMAINE HENRI GOUGES PREMIER CRU CLOS DES PORRETS-ST-GEORGES

The Gouges domaine has for long been one of the standard-bearers of quality and authenticity in Nuits, and its wines of the 1980s have been as good as the fine 1960s offerings. The 3.5-hectare (9-acre) *monopole* Clos des Porrets lies between Nuits and Prémeaux and produces an aromatic, graceful wine, with suggestions of fine leather and tobacco.

DOMAINE MACHARD DE GRAMONT PREMIER CRU "LES DAMODES"

Following the split with Bertrand de Gramont, the Domaine Machard de Gramont is now somewhat smaller than of old, but quality is as good as ever. Les Damodes, a high-sited plot near the Vosne boundary, produces a beautifully rich, powerful and balanced wine, full of earthy, gamey scents and flavours and lightened with a touch of cinnamon.

JEAN GRIVOT PREMIER CRU LES BOUDOTS

Les Boudots is the first *Premier Cru* in Nuits, just across the boundary with Vosne. The wine reflects its geo-graphical position: the silky textures, fine cherry fruit and subtle tannic structure recall the neighbouring Vosne *Premier Cru* of Malconsorts more than the generally sturdy ranks of Nuits *premiers.*

HOSPICES DE NUITS, CUVÉE RICHARD DE BLIGNY, PREMIER CRU, "LES VIGNERONDES"

The Hospices de Nuits is a similar, though smaller, charitable estate to the Hospices de Beaune. As with the Hospices de Beaune wines, *élevage* is as important as site. Here, the *élevage* is by Charles Viénot, a *négociant* owned by Jean-Claude Boisset, prod-ucing a full, sweet-edged wine from a small parcel of vines in the well-sited Les Vignerondes, north of Nuits.

J. JAYER

Jaqueline Jayer's is one of the best "village" Nuits, thanks to fruit from old vines. By replacing 2 per cent of the vines every year, the domaine ensures that they stay old. The wine has real richness and texture, with clear fruit definition. Its power comes from sunshine rather than sugar.

ALAIN MICHELOT
PREMIER CRU
LES PORETS ST-GEORGES

1986

NUITS-SAINT-GEORGES
LES PORETS ST-GEORGES

APPELLATION NUITS-SAINT-GEORGES 1er CRU CONTRÔLÉE

Mise en bouteille à la propriété par
Alain MICHELOT
Propriétaire à Nuits-Saint-Georges (Côte-d'Or) France

13,3% vol.   PRODUIT DE FRANCE   750 ML

Alain Michelot has half a hectare (1¼ acres) in Les Porets from which he produces a *vin de garde* of earthy fruit, battened down with fresh oak: it is an uncompromising Nuits that will reward the patient.

DOMAINE DANIEL RION & FILS
PREMIER CRU HAUTS PRULIERS

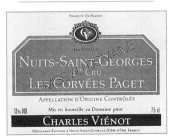

NUITS-ST-GEORGES 1er CRU
HAUTS PRULIERS
APPELLATION CONTRÔLÉE

13% vol.   75 cl
Mis en bouteille au Domaine
DOMAINE DANIEL RION & Fils
PROPRIÉTAIRE-RÉCOLTANT · PRÉMEAUX 21 NUITS-ST-GEORGES (CÔTE-D'OR)
PRODUCE OF FRANCE

The Rion family have something under half a hectare (1¼ acres) of the small Hauts Pruliers *Premier Cru*, sited above les Pruliers just south of Nuits. Careful vinification and 30 per cent new oak results in firmly fleshed wines with plenty of fruit and toasty spice. The Rion wines tend to reflect the nature of the vintage quite closely, though, and difficult vintages are not always adequately handled.

CHARLES VIÉNOT
PREMIER CRU
LES CORVÉES PAGET

NUITS-SAINT-GEORGES
1er CRU
LES CORVÉES PAGET
APPELLATION D'ORIGINE CONTRÔLÉE

13% VOL   Mis en bouteille au Domaine pour   75 cl
CHARLES VIÉNOT
Négociant-Éleveur à Nuits-Saint-Georges (Côte d'Or) France

Les Corvées Paget lies just behind the village of Prémeaux, and its ownership is divided between the *négociant* Charles Viénot and the Hospices de Nuits (Cuvée St Laurent). Viénot's 1.5-hectare (4-acre) holding produces a soundly fruity, well-constituted wine, though one that perhaps lacks the vein of carnal excitement of a good Nuits *premier cru*.

CÔTE DE NUITS-VILLAGES & HAUTES-CÔTES DE NUITS

The wines of the Côte de Nuits-Villages differ from those of the Côte de Beaune-Villages in that they are produced not from vineyards the length of the Côte de Nuits, but from those of five communes at each end of the Côte: from Fixin and Brochon in the north, and from Comblanchien, Corgoloin and Prémeaux-Prissey in the south. This factor limits their quality potential, but scrupulous producers, such as Philippe Rossignol or Robert Dubois, still manage to produce wines of interest and character. The vineyards of the Hautes-Côtes de Nuits got off to a later start than those of the Hautes-Côtes de Beaune, and the vines are still young; as they age, quality will improve, and the next two decades should see exciting wines from this source.

LES CAVES DES HAUTES-CÔTES
HAUTES-CÔTES DE NUITS

ÉLEVAGE EN   FÛTS DE CHÊNE

BOURGOGNE
HAUTES-CÔTES DE NUITS
"LES DAMES HUGUETTES"
Appellation Bourgogne Hautes-Côtes de Nuits Contrôlée
75 cl • Alcohol 12.5% by volume
LES CAVES DES HAUTES-CÔTES
ROUTE DE POMMARD A BEAUNE (CÔTE-D'OR)

ROBERT DUBOIS & FILS
CÔTE DE NUITS-VILLAGES

PRODUCE   OF FRANCE

Côte de Nuits - Villages
APPELLATION CONTRÔLÉE

Mis en bouteille à la propriété par
13% Vol.   DUBOIS Robert & Fils   75 cl
VIGNERONS A PRÉMEAUX, NUITS-St-GEORGES (CÔTE-D'OR)

DUFOULEUR FRÈRES
LE VAUCRAIN
CÔTE DE NUITS-VILLAGES

Product   of France

Côte de Nuits-Villages Le Vaucrain
Appellation Côte de Nuits-Villages Contrôlée
DUFOULEUR FRÈRES
mis en bouteille par
DUFOULEUR FRÈRES, NÉGOCIANTS-ÉLEVEURS   A NUITS-SAINT-GEORGES, FRANCE
75 cl

GEISWEILER & FILS
HAUTES-CÔTES DE NUITS

GEISWEILER
PRODUCT OF FRANCE

MAISON FONDÉE EN 1804

BOURGOGNE
HAUTES COTES DE NUITS
APPELLATION BOURGOGNE HAUTES COTES DE NUITS CONTRÔLÉE

GEISWEILER & FILS 1804   750 ml

DOMAINE DE LA POULETTE
CÔTE DE NUITS-VILLAGES

PARIS   1981

Côte de Nuits-Villages
Appellation d'Origine Côte de Nuits-Villages Contrôlée

RÉCOLTÉ ÉLEVÉ ET MIS EN BOUTEILLE PAR LE
DOMAINE DE LA POULETTE   75 cl
Propriétaire-Récoltant à Corgoloin 21700 Nuits-St-Georges (France)

REINE PÉDAUQUE
CLOS DES LANGRES
CÔTE DE NUITS-VILLAGES

№ 01868

Clos des Langres
CÔTE DE NUITS-VILLAGES
APPELLATION CÔTE DE NUITS-VILLAGES CONTRÔLÉE
MIS EN BOUTEILLE AU DOMAINE A CORGOLOIN PAR
12.5% vol.   REINE PÉDAUQUE   75 cl
NÉGOCIANT-ÉLEVEUR A ALOXE-CORTON, CÔTE-D'OR, FRANCE

PHILIPPE ROSSIGNOL
CÔTE DE NUITS-VILLAGES

Côte de Nuits-Villages
APPELLATION CONTRÔLÉE
Ce vin a été récolté, élevé et mis en bouteille à la propriété
PHILIPPE ROSSIGNOL
PROPRIÉTAIRE-VITICULTEUR A GEVREY-CHAMBERTIN (CÔTE-D'OR)
750 ml   PRODUCE OF FRANCE   13% vol.

DOMAINE THEVENOT-LE
BRUN ET FILS, "LES RENARDES"
HAUTES-CÔTES DE NUITS

Médaille d'Or
au Concours des
Grands Vins de France
MÂCON 1989

Bourgogne
Hautes Côtes de Nuits
"LES RENARDES"
APPELLATION BOURGOGNE HAUTES CÔTES DE NUITS CONTRÔLÉE
Mis en bouteille par
Domaine THEVENOT-LE BRUN et Fils
Propriétaires à Marey-lès-Fussey, par Nuits-St-Georges, Côte-d'Or, France
12,5% Vol.   PRODUCE OF FRANCE

CÔTE DE BEAUNE

IF YOU LOOK AT A MAP of Burgundy, and you let your eye follow the red trace of the N74 motorway south out of Dijon and down to Beaune, you will see a subtle change in orientation from south to south-west after Nuits-Saint Georges. There is a further hiatus at Beaune, where the N74 forks, and by the time Santenay is reached, the Côte is moving very determinedly in a south-westerly direction - and the N74 is no more. That subtle change at Nuits means that the Côte de Beaune vineyards' primary exposure is not easterly·but south-easterly. There are other differences, too. The soils are paler and often limier, though marl is by no means absent; and the geological structure is still more complicated than north of Nuits. The Côte is dislocated and faulted in this southern stretch, particularly towards Santenay, and the slopes are less steep. At Meursault the vines form a large, green millpool, and at Saint Romain, Auxey-Duresses and Saint Aubin they chase off up side valleys away from the main slope. One result of these differences is white Burgundy of power and majesty. There is little of it, though: bottles of red Burgundy still outnumber white by three to one. But that one bottle represents Chardonnay's noblest incarnation.

Soils and aspects

The dust of the marble quarries is beginning to settle by the time the twin villages of Ladoix and Serrigny are reached; just south of them lies the beautiful, wood-crowned hill of Corton. Corton and its village, Aloxe, is a microcosm of the Côte de Beaune, in that both red and white wines of superb quality are produced, almost side by side, in the large *grand cru* zone that sweeps round the hillside from Ladoix to Pernand. The orientation of the vineyards changes by nearly 180° in the process, and it is questions of aspect that decide whether Chardonnay or Pinot Noir is planted, with Chardonnay traditionally predominating towards Pernand and Pinot at the Ladoix end. But soils are crucial, too, with the whiter, thinner soils at the top of the slope yielding the Côte d' Or's first white *grand cru*, Corton-Charlemagne, and the redder, iron-charged soils below yielding the Côte d'Or's last red *grand cru*, Corton.

Dominant reds

Red wines predominate in Savigny-lès-Beaune, a village set back in one of the *combes* that interrupt the Côte: the charmingly named Vallée de la Fontaine-Froide, down which the Rhoin flows. Two banks of *premiers crus* face each other across the Rhoin, and these almost opposite aspects, together with differing soil structures, make for lighter, more aromatic wines on the Pernand side, and richer, deeper, more slowly maturing wines from the Beaune side. Beaune's own *premiers*, by contrast, form a consistent swathe behind the town; the differences between them are more a consequence of winemaking than of aspect, though soil types move through a number of subtle changes with confusing rapidity. Red wine continues to dominate here.

Red wine continues to dominate in the next three villages, too: Pommard, Volnay and Monthélie. The kaleidoscope of soil/slope combinations produces, at Pommard, the Côte de Beaune's biggest and beefiest reds; the lesser "village" wines can be brainless hulks, but some of the top *premiers* combine the intelligence and physical prowess of a Greek hero. A gradual lightening takes place through Volnay to Monthélie, with Volnay's *premiers* being very fine, perfumed and consistent. Monthélie produces no truly fine wine, but much sound wine, and this is also true of Auxey-Duresses, Blagny (red wines only) and Saint-Romain. Auxey-Duresses, tucked away in a little valley to one side of the Montagne de Montmellian, continues the emphasis on red wines (one in three bottles only is white); while Saint-Romain, even further west off the Côte, produces equal quantities of both types. What is happening back on the Côte at this point?

White Burgundy

The answer is Meursault; and also that the level of lime in the soil is creeping up. Marl and brown limestone, rather than the more suitable white limestone, are still found here, and in the old days red Meursault was a deal more common than it is today; but most of the commune's soils provide a perfect medium for the production of deliciously nutty, buttery white Burgundy. Between Puligny and Chassagne lies a 30-hectare (74-acre) block of vineyards of perfect exposure, with a fine mix of well-drained limestone soils; as at Vosne on the Côte de Nuits, everything comes good here. These are the *grand cru* Montrachets: Chardonnay's Everest. It is instructive to compare the rich, firm structure of Corton-Charlemagne with the floral intensity of the Montrachets.

The southern half of Chassagne sees the return of the Pinot Noir, and the trend is confirmed at Santenay and into the three Maranges villages. The Côte d'Or ends, much as it began at Marsannay, with a flourish of frank and fruity red wines.

LADOIX

PRINCE FLORENT DE MERODE PREMIER CRU HAUTES MOUROTTES

Around 1,000 bottles of white Hautes Mourottes are made each year by this estate from a third of a hectare (⁴/₅ acre) of Chardonnay vines. Vinification is traditional, and the oak casks are renewed every other year.

ANDRÉ ET JEAN RENÉ NUDANT LES GRECHONS

This Ladoix, harvested from the unclassified *lieu-dit* of Les Grechons, is full and firm, with the texture and depth to balance its alcohol. Les Grechons is a high-sited, east-facing vineyard with white marl soils, and white wines are produced as well as reds.

ALOXE-CORTON

PIERRE ANDRÉ CHÂTEAU CORTON-ANDRÉ GRAND CRU CORTON

Château Corton-André is made from the fruit of a third of a hectare (⁴/₅ acre) of vines in Corton. The wine is a clear ruby-red colour and has blackcurrant and liquorice aromas with light, lively fruit on the palate.

ADRIEN BELLAND GRAND CRU CORTON-PERRIÈRES

Adrien Belland owns just over two-thirds of a hectare (1²/₃ acres) of Corton-Perrières, a site lying directly above the village of Aloxe-Corton at a mid-point on the slope. The destalked fruit undergoes a lengthy vatting period, during which it is fermented with twice-daily *pigeage*, and is aged in oak to produce a rich, lush wine that is comfortable and round: a Corton for the mid-term.

BONNEAU DU MARTRAY GRAND CRU CORTON-CHARLEMAGNE

The 11-hectare (27-acre) Bonneau du Martray domaine is one of the most tantalizing prospects in Burgundy. There are just two vineyards: 8.5 hectares (21 acres) in mid-slope Corton-Charlemagne and 2.5 hectares (6 acres) in mid-slope Corton. The white Corton-Charlemagne is magnificent: rich with hazelnut and lime flavours.

BOUCHARD PÈRE & FILS GRAND CRU LE CORTON

The vineyard holdings of Bouchard Père et Fils, which total over 80 hectares (200 acres), are the largest in Burgundy, with nearly 4 hectares (9 acres) in Corton. At its best, its Corton can be a commanding wine, many-faceted yet harmonious, with the potential to age for several decades.

DOMAINE CHANDON DE BRIAILLES GRAND CRU CORTON CLOS DU ROI

Comte Aymard-Claude de Nicolay, a cousin of the Champagne Chandons of Moët fame, owns a hectare (2¹/₂ acres) of Corton in the central part of the vineyard known as Clos du Roi. Traditional vinification methods are followed. The wines can be sound and deep, acquiring finesse with the years. However they can also develop rapidly and disappointingly, becoming hollow and tired inside a decade.

MAURICE CHAPUIS GRAND CRU CORTON-PERRIÈRES

Maurice Chapuis took over the domaine in 1985 from his father Louis, since when the high standards have not faltered. The family owns 5 hectares (12¹/₂ acres) in Corton, part of it in Perrières. The wines have delicious stony fruit and acquires tarry, leathery notes with time.

DOMAINE P.DUBREUIL-FONTAINE PÈRE & FILS GRAND CRU CORTON-BRESSANDES

This important domaine of 18 hectares (44 acres) is based in Pernand-Vergelesses; the Dubreil family has two-thirds of a hectare (1²/₃ acres) in Corton-Bressandes, and produces lightly coloured but highly flavoured Corton, full of supple, leafy notes.

ANTONIN GUYON GRAND CRU CORTON-BRESSANDES

Guyon's winemaking methods include destalking of the crop and vinification in wood at around 30°C (54°F). Maturation also takes place in oak (one-third of it new each year) over 18 months. The Guyon Bressandes has good colour and rich raspberry aromas. Its youthful, tannic structure generally leads to elegance.

LOUIS JADOT GRAND CRU CORTON-POUGETS

Louis Jadot, under its capable manager, André Gagey, has become one of Burgundy's finest *négociants*, and its own 25-hectare (60-acre) domaine has been enlarged by many of the vineyards of the Clair-Daü domaine in the mid-1980s. The Corton-Pougets from Jadot is rich and silky, full of cherry and strawberry fruit, attractive in youth but ages well.

LOUIS LATOUR GRAND CRU CORTON-CHARLEMAGNE

The Maison Louis Latour has a holding of 9 hectares (22 acres) in Corton-Charlemagne. The wines are fermented and aged in oak, with a bottling date at around the 12-month mark. They are a straw-gold in colour and complex in aroma, with grilled almonds, cinnamon, honey and vanilla all emerging in time.

LOUIS LATOUR CHÂTEAU CORTON GRANCEY GRAND CRU CORTON

More *grand cru* Burgundy is sold under this label each year than any other - some 60,000 bottles, on average. The wine is a blend from the 17 hectares (42 acres) of Latour vineyards scattered about Corton. Vinification is traditional, and all the wine is aged in oak. This is large, almost corpulent wine, but not without concentration and length.

MOILLARD-GRIVOT GRAND CRU CORTON CLOS DES VERGENNES

To complement its three-quarter-hectare (1³/4-acre) holding in Corton-Clos du Roi, Moillard has recently acquired a parcel of Vergennes, adjacent to Bressandes and stretching into *premier cru* soils - though the Moillard holding is in the *grand cru* part. Vergennes does not have the power of the Clos du Roi, but its spicy, oaky fruit emerges strongly after 10 years.

ANDRÉ ET JEAN RENÉ NUDANT PREMIER CRU LES COUTIÈRES

The *premier cru* of Les Coutières actually lies within the boundaries of Ladoix-Serrigny, but the appellation regulations permit this and other Ladoix *climats* to use the Aloxe-Corton name. The Nudants cultivate a hectare (2¹/2 acres) of Les Coutières, and produce a firm, balanced wine of medium depth and lively fruit.

DOMAINE RAPET PÈRE ET FILS GRAND CRU CORTON-CHARLEMAGNE

The 12-hectare (30-acre) Rapet family estate includes 1.5 hectares (3³/4 acres) in Corton-Charlemagne, from which Roland Rapet produces a statuesque white wine that is rich, full and dry. Its complex secondary aromas are full of spicy, leafy notes.

DOMAINE DANIEL SENARD GRAND CRU CORTON CLOS DES MEIX

In addition to his holding of just over 2 hectares (5 acres) in the Clos des Meix, Daniel Senard also has half a hectare (1¹/4 acres) of Bressandes and Clos du Roi. The Clos des Meix wine is probably the most consistent of the trio, with well-defined fruit engaged in a harmonious duet with oak (a tenth or more renewed each year).

TOLLOT-BEAUT & FILS GRAND CRU CORTON-BRESSANDES

Corton-Bressandes lies towards the bottom of the *grand cru* part of the hill of Corton, nearer to Ladoix than Aloxe, and the Tollot-Beaut domaine owns nearly a hectare (2¹/2 acres) of its prized, iron-rich soils. Low yields and scrupulously traditional vinification, with no fining and minimal filtration, result in a wine of dark good looks, powerful fruit, rich oak, and sonorous, concentrated flavours. It needs at least 10 years of cellaring.

C. TOLLOT & R. VOARICK

This 22-hectare (54-acre) domaine combines two well-known local names; half of its annual production goes to the tasting-cellar/restaurant, Le Bareuzai, which is also owned by Tollot-Voarick. This is one of the lighter Aloxes, but the fruit is well defined and lively, giving an impression of finesse and stylish charm.

DOMAINE MICHEL VOARICK
GRAND CRU CORTON-RENARDES

Michel Voarick is a traditionalist who believes in stem-retention and dislikes new oak. From half a hectare (1¹/₄ acres) of Corton-Renardes he produces wines of massive fruit presence, cloaked in tannin, ready for a march through time. In lesser years, the wines can be a bit charmless.

PERNAND-VERGELESSES

DOMAINE P. DUBREUIL-FONTAINE CLOS BERTHET

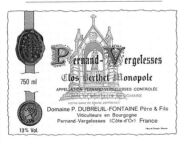

The 1.5-hectare (3³/₄-acre) *Premier Cru* Clos Berthet is Pernand-Vergelesses's only *monopole*. One hectare (2¹/₂ acres) is planted with Chardonnay and half a hectare (1¹/₄ acres) with Pinot Noir to give a concentrated and nutty white wine and a seductively perfumed red. Neither wine needs ageing for long.

DOMAINE JACQUES GERMAIN

From the 15-hectare (37-acre) Domaine Jacques Germain, this "village" Pernand-Vergelesses white wine is aged in 20 per cent new oak, and is full of deft, clear fruit, edged with notes of honey and spice.

DOMAINE RAPET PÈRE & FILS
PREMIER CRU
ILE DES VERGELESSES

Ile des Vergelesses and Basses Vergelesses are two large *premiers crus* contiguous with the Vergelesses vineyards of Savigny-lès-Beaune, and both enjoy south-eastern aspects. Iron and clay in the soils of the Ile favour red wines, and the Rapets produce full and harmonious wines for the mid-term from their holdings there.

SAVIGNY-LÈS-BEAUNE

SIMON BIZE & FILS
PREMIER CRU
"AUX VERGELESSES"

The Vergelesses vineyards are divided between Pernand and Savigny; Aux Vergelesses - the highest of them - is within the Savigny boundary. The Bize family produces a fine Vergelesses from its 3 hectares (7¹/₂ acres) of vineyards. A clear raspberry-red in colour, this wine has aromas of leaf, undergrowth and cherry kernels and a beautifully clear fruit flavour.

DOMAINE CHANDON DE BRIAILLES

The Chandon de Briailles estate is based in the village of Savigny-lès-Beaune, north-west of Beaune. The vineyards lie to each side of the Rhoin, with *premiers crus* up on the slopes and "village" wines - like this one - coming from the vineyards in the plains. In general, Savigny's wines are simple, straightforward and full of easy charm.

PIERRE GUILLEMOT
PREMIER CRU SERPENTIÈRES

Serpentières is one of the largest and sunniest of Savigny's *premiers crus*, lying at mid-slope on the Pernand side of the village. Pierre Guillemot, president of the Savigny winegrower's association, has just over a hectare (2¹/₂ acres) here - his only *premier cru* holding. Old vines and traditional vinification result in a deliciously typical Savigny - lightly, but firmly, structured, full of mouth-filling strawberry fruit.

ANTONIN GUYON

The important Guyon domaine only has "village" vineyards in Savigny, but it turns these to good account in this attractively perfumed wine (hints of sandalwood as well as aromas of *petits fruits rouges*). All Guyon wines respond well to cellaring: give the Savigny six to eight years.

TOLLOT-BEAUT & FILS PREMIER CRU CHAMP CHEVREY

Champ Chevrey, a *premier cru* in the exclusive ownership of Tollot-Beaut, produces one of the deeper and more succulent Savigny wines: the usual sweet fruit aromas are succeeded by lush, almost meaty flavours. Tollot-Beaut also produces an excellent Savigny *Premier Cru* Lavières.

CHOREY-LÈS-BEAUNE

DOMAINE JACQUES GERMAIN CHÂTEAU DE CHOREY-LES-BEAUNE

Chorey-lès-Beaune lies, like the little village of Serrigny, on the "bad" side of the N74 motorway (the flat, deep-soiled eastern side), and that is where most of its vineyards are sited. There are no *premiers crus*. From just over 4 hectares (10 acres) Germain produces this prettily perfumed, graceful red wine, full of supple fruit: the result of careful vinification and *élevage* in wood (25 per cent new each year).

TOLLOT-BEAUT & FILS

Tollot-Beaut's *cave* is situated in Chorey-lès-Beaune. The position may not be propitious, but from nearly 8 hectares (20 acres), this family domaine produces excellent and modestly priced red Burgundy, with rich, fruity aromas and flavours, a firm structure, length and balance.

BEAUNE

ROBERT AMPEAU ET FILS CLOS DU ROI

Clos du Roi is a *premier cru*, but only in part; this label is unclear as to whether the Ampeau's half hectare (1¼ acres) lies in the lower, unclassified part of this vineyard or the higher, *premier cru* part. The wine is full of firm, peppery fruit and earthy, animal flavours. Game for a decade.

ARNOUX PÈRE ET FILS PREMIER CRU

Burgundy labels do not come simpler than this, nor is it difficult to appreciate the lively fruit perfume and supple flavours of the Arnoux family's Beaune *Premier Cru*. The wine is produced from 2 hectares (5 acres) of vineyard parcels in a number of *premier cru* sites: this contributes to its consistency from year to year.

BOUCHARD PÈRE & FILS PREMIER CRU GRÈVES VIGNE DE L'ENFANT JÉSUS

Grèves is one of the largest of Beaune's many *premiers crus* and Maison Bouchard owns a celebrated 4-hectare (10-acre) *clos* within Grèves called Vigne de l'Enfant Jésus. This is one of Bouchard Père's finest wines, earthily luscious in youth, growing silky and rich with the years.

BOUCHARD PÈRE ET FILS PREMIER CRU MARCONNETS

Marconnets lies above Clos du Roi, abutting the Savigny boundary, and the domaine arm of the *négociant* Bouchard Père et Fils (labelled Domaines du Château de Beaune) holds 2 hectares (5 acres) there. Wine from this end of the strip of Beaune *premiers crus* tends to be hard and unyielding at first; after four or five years, though, Bouchard's Marconnets softens into meaty richness.

CHANSON PÈRE & FILS PREMIER CRU CLOS DES FÈVES

Chanson is another Beaune *négociant*; 95 per cent of the 4-hectare (10-acre) Clos des Fèves is Chanson-owned, and it is there that this company produces one of the softer, more elegant Beaune reds, warmly aromatic and discreetly spicy.

DOMAINE BERNARD DELAGRANGE PREMIER CRU BOUCHEROTTES

Meursault-based Bernard Delagrange produces, in addition to a prize-winning "village" Beaune, a fine *premier cru* red from the vineyard of Boucherottes, sited on the Pommard boundary. The limestone soil of Boucherottes contains an admixture of clay, and the vines produce wines with solid fruit, firm tannins and, after a year or two, liquorice flavours.

JOSEPH DROUHIN
PREMIER CRU
CLOS DES MOUCHES

Clos des Mouches is a large *premier cru* on the Pommard boundary; Robert Drouhin owns some 13 hectares (32 acres) there. Both red and white wines are produced: the former is cherry-ripe, the latter nutty and round. In a region of notoriously long odds, these two wines are a couple of the safest bets.

DOMAINE JACQUES GERMAIN
PREMIER CRU VIGNES-FRANCHES

Vignes-Franches lies at the Pommard end of the strip of Beaune *premiers crus*, beneath Clos des Mouches. This domaine has a hectare (2½ acres) of the vineyard's brown, heavy soils. The harvested grapes remain on their stalks, are macerated for several weeks, and the wine is matured in 50 per cent new oak. It is usually garnet in colour, requiring six to ten years to reveal its perfumed intricacies.

DOMAINE MACHARD DE
GRAMONT PREMIER CRU
"LES CHOUACHEUX"

Les Chouacheux, underneath Vignes Franches, does not appear to be a particularly favourable site, yet this wine is usually one of the delights of the Machard de Gramont portfolio and is studded with soft, red-fruit flavours. The 1985 vintage is particularly sumptuous and rich.

LOUIS JADOT CLOS-DES-URSULES
PREMIER CRU
LES VIGNES FRANCHES

The 2.5-hectare (6-acre) Clos des Ursules lies within Les Vignes Franches. André Gagey's meticulous vinification produces a satiny, graceful Burgundy, full of redcurrant fruit, but with enough well-toned muscle to out-distance many of its bulkier peers.

DOMAINE MICHEL LAFARGE
PREMIER CRU GRÈVES

From just under half a hectare (1¼ acres) in the large *premier cru* hillside named Grèves comes this attractive, cherry-scented Burgundy. De-stalking, removal of any rot-affected bunches, fairly rapid fermentations, and over a year in oak give creamy wines of deceptive accessibility. They age most successfully over five to eight years.

DOMAINE CHANTAL LESCURE
CÔTE DE BEAUNE
LA GRANDE CHATELAINE

This appellation covers the vineyards of the town of Beaune, as well as a small number of unclassified named vineyards (or *lieux-dits*) outside the town. La Grande Chatelaine is one of these, and the *négociant* Labouré-Roi, owner of Domaine Chantal Lescure, produces both a red and a white wine there. They are good representatives of the cheerful Beaune style.

DOMAINE DU
CHÂTEAU DE MEURSAULT
PREMIER CRU CENT-VIGNES

Cent-Vignes is a large *premier cru* lying beneath Fèves. The Domaine du Château de Meursault belongs to the *négociant* Patriarche, whose own Burgundies have an indifferent reputation. Yet these wines are generally good: all are aged in new oak, and the Cent-Vignes is a Beaune red of elegance, measured richness and tapered length.

ALBERT MOROT
PREMIER CRU BRESSANDES

Although the Albert Morot labels proclaim the business to be a *négociant's*, 75 per cent of turnover is actually generated by the wines of the 7-hectare (17-acre) Morot domaine. This includes 1.5 hectares (3¾ acres) in Bressandes, a parcel that often produces the top Morot wine of the year: deeply coloured, full of lively blackcurrant and aniseed aromas, and generously structured, with tannin, flesh and fruit in close harmony.

DOMAINE MUSSY
PREMIER CRU EPENOTTES

Epenottes is an almost flat vineyard at the far south of the *premier cru* area. Wines from here can be softer than those from the northern half of the commune, yet the Epenottes of the Pommard-based Domaine Mussy is a deep, tightly structured wine that needs five years to unravel its charms.

DOMAINE JACQUES PRIEUR
PREMIER CRU
CLOS DE LA FÉGUINE

The *premier cru* from which this wine is made is, in fact, the steeply sloped Coucherias. The 2-hectare (5-acre), Prieur-owned Clos de la Féguine is sited within this vineyard, and produces a square-shouldered Beaune, but one which softens to a smooth and mellow middle age.

DOMAINE PRIEUR-BRUNET
PREMIER CRU CLOS DU ROY

The Clos du Roy, which lies on the boundary with Savigny, produces quite sturdy, solid wines. The Santenay-based Domaine Prieur-Brunet's version, made from a half-hectare (1¼-acre) plot there, has a bright colour, and rich spice and fruit aromas, together with a sound depth of fruit on the palate.

DOMAINE THOMAS-MOILLARD
PREMIER CRU GRÈVES

Moillard, Moillard-Grivot, Thomas-Moillard: the variations occur because the vineyards originally came from Marguerite Grivot, and the Thomas family now controls Moillard. From just over 2 hectares (5 acres) of the *premier cru* Grèves, Moillard produces a monster of a wine: dark red; savagely aromatic, with bitter herbal notes; and hugely fruity - the red fruit mixed with orange and chocolate and charged with alcohol.

TOLLOT-BEAUT & FILS
CLOS DU ROI

This wine is produced from Tollot-Beaut's 1-hectare (2½-acre) holding in Clos du Roi (part of which enjoys *premier cru* status, part of which does not). It is built in the big, extract-laden style favoured by this family domaine, which uses wood fermentation with assiduous *pigeage* and keeps temperatures high. The aromas are packed as generously into the bottle as are the roasted fruit flavours; the result is heady and rich.

POMMARD

COMTE ARMAND
PREMIER CRU
CLOS DES ÉPENEAUX

Just over 5 hectares (12½ acres) of the *premier cru* Les Épenots is taken up by Comte Armand's Clos des Épeneaux. The wines produced here are archetypal Pommard: dark in colour; an aroma of oak, pepper and plums; and a rich and structured flavour, with a long, meaty finish.

HOSPICES DE BEAUNE

This label may be found on a range of 34 red and white wines from villages primarily sited within the Côte de Beaune. The vines that yield these wines grow in sites that have been given to the Hospices de Beaune, a hospital for the sick, poor and aged. The Hospices was founded in 1443 by Nicolas Rolin, whose name is commemorated in one of the Beaune *cuvées*. The wines are made by the Hospices itself, sold with much pomp at auction two months later, and then matured and bottled by the purchaser. This is a delicate mission, as the label points out, and purchasers (whose names are shown) do not always fulfil the mission as successfully as might be hoped. As with all Burgundies, selection is therefore the key to enjoyment.

BEAUNE
CUVÉE NICOLAS-ROLIN

MEURSAULT-CHARMES
CUVÉE DE BAHÈZRE-DE-LANLAY

MONTHELIE
CUVÉE LEBELIN

VOLNAY-SANTENOTS
CUVÉE JEHAN-DE-MASSOL

DOMAINE HENRI BOILLOT
PREMIER CRU LES JAROLLIÈRES

Les Jarollières is a large *premier cru* lying at the southern end of Pommard, adjacent to the boundary line with Volnay. Henri Boillot's example, from a parcel of just over 1 hectare (3 acres) in size, reflects this position: its scent and opening flavours suggest Volnay, and its finish Pommard.

DOMAINE DE MADAME BERNARD DE COURCEL
PREMIER CRU GRAND CLOS DES "EPENOTS"

Domaine de Courcel's 5-hectare (12½-acre) *clos* lies within Épenots, one of Pommard's top two *premiers crus*. Maximum skin-contact is sought from the grapes via lengthy maceration with their stalks, and the wines spend two years in new oak. This is a big Pommard, full of rich tannins and toasty fruit, that asks for a decade of darkness to show its best.

MICHEL GAUNOUX
PREMIER CRU RUGIENS

Rugiens is the second of Pommard's two finest *premiers crus*. Like Épenots, it is in two halves, and not all of the lesser half (Rugiens-Hauts) is classified as *premier cru*. Gaunoux's methods are traditional, producing a Rugiens of medium depth and good balance, full of sloe fruit.

BERNARD & LOUIS GLANTENAY

The Volnay-based Glantenay domaine includes just over a hectare (2½ acres) of Pommard "village" vineyards. Bernard Glantenay produces a soundly constructed, richly flavoured Pommard from his family vines there.

DOMAINE MACHARD DE GRAMONT
PREMIER CRU "LE CLOS BLANC"

Le Clos Blanc lies between the village itself and Les Épenots. This outstanding site, in Machard de Gramont's hands, produces one of Pommard's finest wines. Old vines (50-70 years old) and traditional vinification result in a splendidly aromatic and rich fruity wine, with concentration, depth and elegance. There are few better representatives of the village at present than this wine.

LABOURÉ-ROI

The Nuits-based *négociant* Labouré-Roi produces a well-knit, plummy "village" Pommard as well as a *premier cru* Pommard from the les Bertins site near the boundary with Volnay. This *premier cru* wine is also sold under the Chantal Lescure label, while the "village" wine is sold only under the Labouré-Roi name.

DOMAINE LEJEUNE
PREMIER CRU LES ARGILLIÈRES

The 8-hectare (20-acre) Domaine Lejeune holds 1.5 hectares (3¾ acres) of the *Premier Cru* Les Argillières, sited in mid-slope on the Beaune side of Pommard. This is one of the finer Pommards, the lush strawberry fruit tempered by peppery extract, light tannins, and a touch of oak.

LEROY

Maison Leroy is based in Auxey-Duresses, and its head, Lalou Bize-Leroy, is co-proprietor of the Domaine de la Romanée-Conti. The Leroy Pommard is a heady, full-bodied wine, very much in the house style. The company also markets a wine from the *lieu-dit* of les Vignots, which generally shows greater concentration and definition.

DOMAINE MAZILLY PÈRE ET FILS
PREMIER CRU LES POUTURES

The Mazilly family comes down from Meloisey in the Hautes-Côtes to cultivate vines in a small parcel of Poutures, a *premier cru* lying on flattish land between the village and les Bertins. Like Machard de Gramont's Clos Blanc, the Mazilly's Poutures is in old vines, and produces a full-bodied Pommard with plenty of depth and extract, requiring the best part of a decade to soften and unfold.

CHÂTEAU DE MEURSAULT
HOSPICES DE DIJON
PREMIER CRU FREMIERS

Dijon also has a Hospices of its own, and the Cuvée Prieur Louis Berrier is made (by the Partriarche-owned Château de Meursault) from fruit harvested in the *premier cru* of Fremiers, the larger part of which lies in Pommard, and the smaller part in Volnay. The wine has a fine colour, rich cherry and herb aromas, and is well-structured and substantial.

DOMAINE JEAN MONNIER & FILS
PREMIER CRU ÉPENOTS
CLOS DE CITEAUX

The 3-hectare (7¹/₂-acre) Clos des Cîteaux, lying within Épenots was owned for four centuries by the Abbey of Cîteaux. The Monnier family acquired it in 1950, and its wines are now subject to careful and painstaking vinification in order to produce stylish and vibrant Pommard, full of harmonious fruit and gamey warmth.

HUBERT DE MONTILLE
PREMIER CRU PÉZEROLLES

Hubert de Montille is one of the finest winemakers in this part of the Côte de Beaune. Even in difficult vintages he succeeds in producing a wine of finesse, perfectly balanced and full of structured fruit, from his hectare (2¹/₂ acres) of Pézerolles, a *premier cru* lying on the Beaune side of Pommard. Montille is celebrated for his advocacy of minimum chaptalization.

DOMAINE MUSSY
POMMARD PREMIER CRU

From a number of different *premier cru* sites in Pommard, the Domaine Mussy produces this big, beefy, hessian-textured Burgundy. The wine needs at least five years to settle down and soften.

DOMAINE PARENT
PREMIER CRU
LES CHAPONNIÈRES

This old (founded 1650) and distinguished domaine has three-quarters of a hectare (2¹/₂ acres) in the small *premier cru* of Chaponnières, lying just below Rugiens-Bas. Traditional methods produce wines of direct fruit flavour, lightly but firmly structured, and finished with a stamp of oak.

CHÂTEAU DE POMMARD
JEAN LOUIS LAPLANCHE

This 20-hectare (50-acre) walled estate is the largest *clos* under single ownership in Burgundy. The property, which lies on flat land in the "village" area of Pommard, belongs to psychoanalyst and Sorbonne professor Jean Louis Laplanche. Vinification is traditional, with all the wines being aged in new oak for two years. Heavy bottles and a baroque label promise an imposing wine; the promise is kept by this Pommard of velvety depth and lush fruit.

POTHIER-RIEUSSET

Virgile Pothier's 8-hectare (20-acre) domaine includes fine wines from the *premiers crus* of Épenots, Rugiens and Clos de Verger, as well as this sturdy "village" Pommard, one of the deeper and more tannic examples. Behind the tannin is a panorama of rich fruit, which needs four or five years' cellaring to reveal itself.

VOLNAY

ROBERT AMPEAU ET FILS
PREMIER CRU
VOLNAY-SANTENOTS

The curious appellation of Volnay-Santenots indicates a red *premier cru* from Meursault. Ampeau's Santenots is a splendidly deep wine, full of animal aromas and chunky cherry fruit. Let it brood for a few years.

DOMAINE MARQUIS
D'ANGERVILLE
PREMIER CRU CLOS DES DUCS

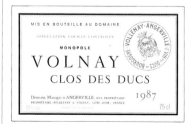

The 2-hectare (5-acre) Clos des Ducs is one of Volnay's best *premiers crus*. Exclusively owned by the Marquis d'Angerville, it is the richest and deepest of the domaine's wines. This historic Volnay estate is an advocate for authentic Burgundy, using selected low-producing vine strains, minimum chaptalization and estate bottling. This wine combines power with ripe, clean and appealing fruit.

DOMAINE MARQUIS D'ANGERVILLE
PREMIER CRU CAILLERETS

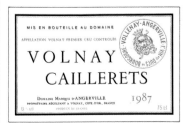

From a half hectare (1¼ acres) of vines in the large, fine *premier cru* of Caillerets comes a Volnay of rich cherry flavour, rounded with vanilla from 25 per cent new oak casks.

HENRI BOILLOT

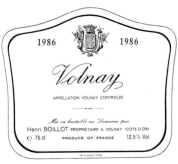

This 22-hectare (54-acre) domaine owns substantial vineyard holdings in the "village" area of Volnay. Careful vinification produces a Volnay of seductive typicality, full of cherry-stone scents, light fruit flavours and silky textures.

BOUCHARD PÈRE & FILS
PREMIER CRU CAILLERETS
ANCIENNE CUVÉE CARNOT

"Ancienne Cuvée Carnot" on this label signifies that the wine is made from a 4-hectare (10-acre) plot of vines that belonged, before his assassination by an Italian anarchist in 1894, to the French President Sadi Carnot. This is very much a wine in the Bouchard style - deep, swish and rich, scented with oak and having, when young, a pinch of tannin.

BITOUZET-PRIEUR
PREMIER CRU TAILLEPIEDS

Vincent Bitouzet, who cultivates 7 hectares (17 acres), is a believer in warm fermentation - as high as 35°C (95°F) - rather than lengthy *macération* as a means of obtaining fruit and extract. For him, it works: the Taillepieds carries a suitcase full of flavours with it, held in admirable balance and harmony, and ready to acquire the characteristic finesse of Volnay over dark years in the cellar.

DOMAINE Y. CLERGET
PREMIER CRU CLOS DU VERSEUIL

This Volnay-based domaine shares the Clerget surname with some half-dozen others in the Côte; the roots of this branch of the family go back to the thirteenth century. Tradition is accorded great respect here, and a well-shaped, fruity red Burgundy is produced from two-thirds of a hectare (1½ acres) between Taille-Pieds and Bousse d'Or.

DOMAINE BERNARD
DELAGRANGE PREMIER CRU
CLOS-DES-CHAMPANS

Bernard Delagrange owns a third of a hectare (⅘ acre) in the *premier cru* of Champans, from which he produces a light and lively Volnay with scents of raspberry and redcurrant. His wines age well, though they are perfectly accessible early on.

DOMAINES BERNARD & LOUIS
GLANTENAY

Following the death of Louis Glantenay in 1980, his son Bernard took over the running of the 8-hectare (20-acre) domaine. The Glantenay "village" Volnay combines great presence with a lot of charm, acquiring musky, gamey aromas after a few years in bottle.

DOMAINE MICHEL LAFARGE
PREMIER CRU CLOS DES CHÊNES

Michel Lafarge has a hectare (2½ acres) in the highest of Volnay's *premiers crus*, the Clos des Chênes, and the wines he produces there are urbane, charming and elegant. The fruit is always carefully sorted and selected, and the vinification is scrupulously overseen.

DOMAINE DES COMTES LAFON
PREMIER CRU
SANTENOTS-DU-MILEU

This is a stylish Pinot Noir from the Lafon family, master white-wine makers of Meursault. As well as 2.5 hectares (6 acres) of Santenots, the domaine has half a hectare (1¼ acres) of the Clos des Chênes and 1 hectare (2½ acres) of Champans. All of their red wines drink well once bottled, but they have the fruit and concentration to last, growing more perfumed with each passing year.

HUBERT DE MONTILLE
PREMIER CRU TAILLEPIEDS

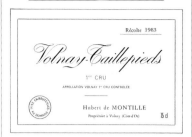

Taillepieds lies below the northern part of Clos des Chênes, and above Champans, on white limestone soils giving a fine, light Volnay. Hubert de Montille has nearly a hectare (2½ acres) here, and he produces a true Volnay, fragrant with the aromas of rose and flowering currant, and bright with warm, berry fruit.

DOMAINE DE LA POUSSE D'OR
PREMIER CRU
CLOS DE LA BOUSSE D'OR

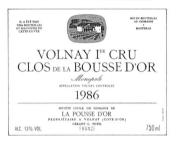

The 2-hectare (5-acre) *monopole* Clos de la Bousse d'Or, owned by the famous Pousse d'Or Domaine, is a wine of delicious richness, its intense, lingering fruit balanced by supple, spicy oak. Scrupulous sorting of the crop in poor years has given this estate a reputation for reliability.

DOMAINE DE LA POUSSE D'OR
PREMIER CRU LES CAILLERETS
"CLOS DES 60 OUVRÉES"

All of the Pousse d'Or's 13 hectares (32 acres) of vineyards are of *premier cru* status, and the Clos des 60 Ouvrées is one of its three Volnay *monopoles*. This *clos* occupies nearly 2.5 hectares (6 acres) of Les Caillerets, and Gérard Potel produces perhaps his biggest wine from its vines: dark in colour, full of cherry and plum aromas and deep, ripely tannic fruit.

DOMAINE JACQUES PRIEUR
PREMIER CRU
CLOS DES SANTENOTS

The Domaine Jacques Prieur's Clos des Santenots occupies 1.2 hectares (3 acres) within Santenots. The Prieur Santenots is firmly structured, with attractive fruit and a solid, bread-like texture in its early years. It often has the tannins for a decade of ageing.

MONTHÉLIE

J. BOIGELOT
PREMIER CRU
"LES CHAMPS FUILLOTS"

Jacques Boigelot produces a raspberry-scented wine from his holding in the *Premier Cru* of Les Champs Fulliots. This vineyard marks a continuation of Volnay's Caillerets, and its brown limestone soils produce bigger wines than the white-soiled vineyards on the Auxey side of Monthélie.

DENIS BOUSSEY
PREMIER CRU
"LES CHAMPS FULLIOTS"

A number of owners have plots in Les Champs Fuillots, and for many of them this is the grandest of their wines. Denis Boussey produces a well-structured and lightly scented wine from the hectare (2½ acres) he cultivates there. It is suitable for ageing for five or more years.

DOMAINE ANDRÉ ET BERNARD
LABRY

The small village of Monthélie, on a hillside between Volnay and Auxey-Duresses, produces a comparatively large amount of "village" wine. In style it is light but fragrant, and that produced by André and Bernard Labry at Melin is typical: a whiff of plums and cherries, mid-weight in the mouth, and a pleasing depth of liquorice and plum flavour.

CHÂTEAU DE MONTHELIE
R. DE SUREMAIN

Robert de Suremain's wines, which are among the most ambitious of the village, age well. Old vines with low yields, long and careful vinification and new oak produce a Monthélie of sombre colour, with rich oaky aromas and a depth of fruit flavour unusual in this part of the Côte de Beaune.

DOMAINE RENÉ THÉVENIN-
MONTHELIE & FILS

René Thévenin's wife's maiden name was Monthélie, and around a quarter of the vineyards of this 10-hectare (25-acre) domaine, based up the road from Auxey in St Romain, lie in the village that shares her name. The Thévenin Monthélie is closer to Volnay than to Auxey-Duresses in character: it is light and scented, but with fairly rich fruit that needs four or five years to soften and round out.

AUXEY-DURESSES

ROBERT AMPEAU ET FILS
ECUSSEAUX

The vineyards that lie to either side of the D973 as it crosses the communal boundaries of Auxey-Duresses are those of Ecusseaux, parts of which are classified as *premier cru*. Robert Ampeau cultivates a hectare (2½ acres) here, and produces a soft red wine, full of earthy fruit.

JEAN-PIERRE DICONNE
PREMIER CRU

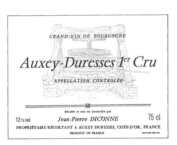

Jean-Pierre Diconne produces this red wine from plots in several *premier cru* sites - hence the absence of a specifying vineyard name. What the wine does specify is its wood-panelled upbringing: oak is evident in both aroma and flavour, to balance out the lively raspberry fruit.

DOMAINE ANDRÉ ET BERNARD
LABRY

Auxey-Duresses, in common with 13 other villages on the Côte de Beaune, can append "Côte de Beaune" to its "village" appellation (red wines only). André and Bernard Labry have taken up the option for their red Auxey-Duresses, a gracefully fruity wine of medium depth, with cherry-kernel aromas and light tannins.

DOMAINE DU DUC DE MAGENTA

The 12-hectare (30-acre) domaine of the Duc de Magenta is based in Chassagne-Montrachet, and produces both a red and a white Auxey-Duresses. The white, a more successful wine than the red, has pleasing aromas of sweet apples and honeysuckle and a soft but harmonious flavour. The red is generally light, with full fruit and glycerine after a warm summer; it can be sharp when the weather has been less kind.

MICHEL PRUNIER
PREMIER CRU CLOS DU VAL

Michel Prunier produces a fine red wine from his holding in the Auxey-Duresses *Premier Cru* of Clos du Val (or Le Val). The grapes are not destalked, giving the wines pronounced tannic structure, but the fruit is clean and concentrated, with a pleasing redcurrant flavour. The austere finish mellows with time.

ROY FRÈRES
PREMIER CRU LE VAL

Of Auxey-Duresses's handful of *premiers crus*, Le Val (also known as Clos du Val) is one of the best, with a south-facing aspect and pebbly, calcareous soils. With the 5 hectares (12 acres) it owns there, the Roy family is the leading producer. Its wine is a sturdy red with attractive blackcurrant scents and rich, chunky fruit that will improve over five to eight years.

ST ROMAIN

RENÉ THÉVENIN-MONTHELIE
SOUS LE CHÂTEAU

Formerly part of the Hautes-Côtes, St Romain is even further west from the main Côte than is Auxey-Duresses. Both red and white wines are produced here, with René Thévenin's white being particularly noteworthy: a wine full of leafy honey and lime flavours.

MEURSAULT

ROBERT AMPEAU ET FILS
LA PIÈCE SOUS LE BOIS

Robert Ampeau's Meursault comes from the vineyard of La Pièce sous le Bois in Blagny. Since the Blagny name can only be used for reds, this brightly fruity, firmly oaked wine is entitled to the Meursault appellation.

BITOUZET-PRIEUR
CLOS DU CROMIN

Bitouzet's Meursault whites are as good as his Volnay reds, thanks to a good proportion of old vines, careful vinification, and eight months in new oak. The Clos du Cromin is full of rich, ripe fruit, suggesting pineapple or guava, but held in check by a cut of acidity and brush of oak.

J.-F. COCHE-DURY PREMIER CRU PERRIÈRES

This modestly-sized, 7-hectare (17-acre) domaine is immaculately run by Jean-François Coche-Dury. His white Burgundies, the majority of them from Meursault, are among the most carefully vinified of the region, with at least 18 months' oak ageing (in up to 50 per cent new oak), two rackings, and unfiltered bottling. The Perrières is a rich, lingering Meursault, complex, balanced and graceful: the kind of Chardonnay that sends Californians back to their drawing boards.

HENRI GERMAIN

Henri Germain is one of the leading producers of "village" Meursault, and his is a textbook example of the genre: a bright green-gold in colour, with toasty, almond perfume; then a flavour of elegant, balanced fruit, light on the tongue, finishing with a swirl of vanilla richness.

PATRICK JAVILLIER CLOS DU CROMIN

Patrick Javillier has taken over the 5-hectare (12-acre) family domaine from broker Raymond Javillier and, like Vincent Bitouzet, he cultivates vines in the unclassified Clos du Cromin. The Javillier version is a wine of smaller proportions than the Bitouzet, but it shares the ripe, full fruit and frank, firm flavour.

FRANÇOIS JOBARD PREMIER CRU PORUZOT

Les Poruzots is one of Meursault's finer *premiers crus*, and François Jobard's Poruzots is one of the finest of the vineyard. The wine's hazelnut richness emerges after several years from an almost austere depth of fruit and an almost bony finishing vinosity.

DOMAINE DES COMTES LAFON CLOS DE LA BARRE

Comtes Lafon is now run by Dominique and Bruno Lafon, who ensure impeccable standards are kept throughout the domaine. The wine from their unclassified *monopole* Clos de la Barre is Meursault at its best: richly nutty with a spicy edge, full of fruit, yet tight and nervy within. This mineral intensity ensures a long life.

DOMAINE DES COMTES LAFON PREMIER CRU PERRIÈRES

The Lafons own three-quarters of a hectare (1⁴/5 acre) in the *premier cru* of Perrières, generally considered to be the finest vineyard in the village. Their wine needs age; after four or five years, it develops a beautiful aroma of lime blossom, vanilla and hazels and a sustained, stony-rich flavour. The Domaine Lafon is renowned for giving its white wines long cask-ageing on their lees.

LOUIS LATOUR PREMIER CRU GOUTTE D'OR

Maison Louis Latour owns no vineyards in Meursault, but purchases from a number of the village's better sites, among them the *premier cru* vineyard of Goutte (or Gouttes) d'Or. This is the nearest of the *premiers* to Meursault itself, and produces full, ripe wines of deep colour (the "golden drop" in the vineyard's name); sweetly nutty and pastry-rich, they are freshened by sound citrus fruit.

DOMAINE RENÉ MANUEL PREMIER CRU CLOS DES BOUCHES CHÈRES

This 6-hectare (15-acre) estate is now owned by Labouré-Roi; 1.5 hectares (3³/4 acres) of the *premier cru* Bouches Chères (elsewhere Bouchères) are held, and a toasty, buttery Meursault is produced from its vines. The label, which is nearly as sumptuous as the wine, is an enlargement of a design from 1830.

PIERRE MATROT PREMIER CRU PERRIÈRES

The 18-hectare (45-acre) Matrot domaine includes a half hectare (1¹/4 acres) in Perrières. Thierry Matrot aims for a Meursault in which fruit is pre-eminent; the wines are oak-aged, but with little new oak, and bottling dates are relatively early. The result is a trim Perrières in which elegance is the keynote.

DOMAINE DU CHÂTEAU DE MEURSAULT

Technically this is "village" Meursault, but of a superior sort, since it contains wines from both Perrières and Charmes as well as from more humbly-sited vineyards. The Comte de Moucheron has sold the domaine to André Boisseaux of Beaune's largest *négociant*, Patriarche Père et Fils. Fermentation and *élevage* both take place in new oak. The wine is a light straw-yellow in colour, has a choice, nutty aroma and a stylish, full-bodied and harmonious flavour.

MICHELOT-BUISSON "LE LIMOZIN"

Le Limozin is one of many unclassified *lieux-dits* in the 29-hectare (72-acre) Michelot domaine that are vinified separately by Bernard Michelot. It yields a big Meursault with fleshy fruit, balanced by generous acidity and alcohol. Three or four years in bottle see it soften and acquire poise.

MICHELOT-BUISSON PREMIER CRU GENEVRIÈRES

The two Genevrières vineyards (Dessus and Dessous) lie north of Perrières and Charmes, and produce some of the most finely drawn of all Meursault. Bernard Michelot owns 1.5 hectares (3³/4 acres) of Genevrières; he is a great devotee of new oak for fermentation as well as for maturation, and he produces a rich, supple, flavoury Genevrières with aromas of honeysuckle and vanilla.

DOMAINE JEAN MONNIER & FILS PREMIER CRU CHARMES

The irresistibly named Meursault-Charmes comes from two large *premier cru* vineyards (as with Genevrières, divided into Dessus and Dessous) lying below Perrières. Jean Monnier has two-thirds of a hectare (1²/3 acres) here, and produces a wine of unusual subtlety, full of leafy, blossomy scents and hazelnut flavours. This is one of his grand wines, but his lesser wines are vinified with equal care.

PIERRE MOREY

Pierre Morey is one of Meursault's better-known growers; in addition to working his own holdings, he also cultivates some of the Domaine Lafon's vineyards on a sharecropping basis (a practice that is still comparatively widespread in Burgundy). His Meursault is full and rich, attractive and approachable right from the start.

DOMAINE PRIEUR-BRUNET PREMIER CRU CHARMES

The 13-hectare (32-acre), Santenay-based domaine of G. Prieur has 1 hectare (2¹/2 acres) in Charmes. The wine produced from these vines has positive, forthcoming aromas and flavours, with a tangy floral scent mingling with hazelnut, and a firm, structured flavour suggesting that this is a Charmes that will age well.

DOMAINE JACQUES PRIEUR CLOS DE MAZERAY

The 14-hectare (35-acre) Domaine Jacques Prieur is sole owner of the 3.2-hectare (8-acre) Clos de Mazeray. The southern half of this walled vineyard is planted with Chardonnay to give a full and fruity white Meursault. The northern half is Pinot Noir, giving a juicy red Meursault, first made there by the monks of Cîteaux some several centuries ago.

DOMAINE GUY ROULOT PREMIER CRU PERRIÈRES

The Domaine Guy Roulot holds over 5 hectares (12 acres) in Meursault, two of its best sites being in the unclassified Tessons and the *Premier Cru* Perrières. The wine Franck Greux produces from vines in the latter are charged with toasty, lime-flower scents and concentrated fruit.

BLAGNY

ROBERT AMPEAU, PREMIER CRU LA PIÈCE SOUS LE BOIS

Blagny lies on the hill between Meursault and Puligny. The Blagny appellation is reserved for reds; its *premier cru* "piece" of vineyard below the wood (*la pièce sous le bois*) produces exuberant, earthy and gamey wines. Ampeau's is typical.

HENRI CLERC & FILS
PREMIER CRU
SOUS LE DOS D'ANE

Sous le Dos d'Ane is a small, spur-sited vineyard with a range of aspects. Puligny-based Henri Clerc produces a rather lighter red than Ampeau's, but it exhibits the same peppery scents and animal flavours, finishing with a hint of marc.

PULIGNY-MONTRACHET

ROBERT AMPEAU ET FILS
PREMIER CRU COMBETTES

Combettes is a *premier cru* site at the northern end of Puligny. The vineyard is rocky with thin soils, at almost the same height and aspect as Montrachet further south. The Meursault-based Ampeau domaine produces a fine white wine from two-thirds of a hectare (1²/₃ acres) of Combettes: full of intense, nutty fruit and built to last.

LOUIS CARILLON ET FILS
PREMIER CRU LES REFERTS

From a holding of under a quarter of a hectare (³/₅ acre) in Referts, beneath Combettes, the Carillon family produces a supple, flavoury white wine for the mid-term. Like the other white wines of the 12-hectare (30-acre) domaine, a year is spent in oak (10-15 per cent new each year), and - with luck - a few years in bottle.

DOMAINE JEAN CHARTRON
PREMIER CRU
CLOS DU CAILLERET

The domaine, until 1984 under contract to Joseph Drouhin, owns 3.5 hectares (8¹/₂ acres) of the Clos du Cailleret, which is promisingly sited next to Montrachet. It is certainly one of the better *premiers crus* of the village, but the wines produced here have still perhaps to acquire the polish and excitement of which the site is almost certainly capable.

GÉRARD CHAVY ET FILS
PREMIER CRU LES CLAVOILLONS

Les Clavoillons is sited in the middle of Puligny's stretch of *premier crus*, beneath the steeply sloping Les Folatières. The Chavy family produces a Clavoillons that is well up to the generally high standards of this village's *premiers*: richly flavoured, full of deep, layered fruit, and often with more finesse than, for example, Combettes has.

DOMAINE HENRI CLERC & FILS

Monsieur Clerc labels his "village" Puligny, as all producers here have the right to, with the suffix "Côte de Beaune". The vines grow in the lower, almost flat land that lies between the village itself and the *premiers* and *grands crus*. The Clerc version is a good example of the sappy, nervous yet still richly flavoured Chardonnay that the village should offer its customers.

JOSEPH DROUHIN

Robert Drouhin's "village" Puligny is as sound as reputation would suggest: it has lively floral aromas and rich, buttered apple fruit, the finish hinting at the lusciously honeyed flavours that characterize the same *négociant's Premier Cru* Folatières.

LOUIS JADOT
PREMIER CRU LES FOLATIÈRES

In addition to its well-known Chevalier-Montrachet "Demoiselles", Louis Jadot also cultivates part of Les Folatières, the most steeply sloped of Puligny's *premier crus*. The consistent quality of Jadot's wines is due in part to a flexibility about whether or not to permit malolactic fermentation to take place: in years of very ripe fruit, such as 1982, 1983 and 1985, malolactic fermentation is inhibited so as to conserve acidity levels. Jadot's Folatières is full of breed and finesse, and matures well in bottle.

PATRICK JAVILLIER
LES LEVRONS

The Meursault-based Javillier domaine owns part of the unclassified vineyard of Les Levrons in Puligny-Montrachet, and from it produces a light golden wine with attractive floral aromas and fine, firm fruit. It is ready at three years, but will last.

HUBERT LAMY
LES TREMBLOTS

Seven children, of whom three wanted to be winegrowers, made the division of Jean Lamy's 22-hectare (54-acre) estate difficult. The parcels in Puligny went to Hubert, and from the unclassified vineyard Les Tremblots he produces a deft white wine, rich with blossomy, honeysuckle aromas yet almost austere on the palate in the early years. It matures over half a decade to a pleasing, nutty fullness.

LOUIS LATOUR TRUFFIÈRES

From vines in yet another of Puligny's many unclassified vineyards comes this richly flavoured white wine, full of exotic fruit notes (mango and pineapple). The keen acidity of the Latour Truffières is balanced and softened by the oak in which this *négociant* and domaine-owner's white wines are fermented and aged.

DOMAINE LEFLAIVE
PREMIER CRU LES PUCELLES

One of the finest of the many fine wines produced by Vincent Leflaive comes from the domaine's 3-hectare (7½ acres) holding in the *Premier Cru* Pucelles vineyard, sited next to Bâtard-Montrachet and Bienvenues-Bâtard-Montrachet. It has an attractive, often acacia-scented, aroma, and there is always beautiful fruit definition on the palate, allied with great power and length.

DOMAINE ETIENNE SAUZET
PREMIER CRU CHAMP-CANET

Champ Canet is a partly classified vineyard situated higher than most of the other Puligny *premiers*; the Sauzet domaine lies in the *premier cru* part. This is a relatively light wine, with charming buttery scents and elegant, lively flavours.

MONTRACHET GRANDS CRUS

BLAIN-GAGNARD
CRIOTS-BÂTARD-MONTRACHET

Criots-Bâtard-Montrachet is the only Montrachet *grand cru* vineyard to be sited exclusively within the Chassagne village boundaries. Blain-Gagnard produces a finely structured and intensely flavoured wine from a small parcel of vines there, its nervy fruit softened and filled out with new oak.

LOUIS CARILLON ET FILS
BIENVENUES-BÂTARD-MONTRACHET

This family of Puligny winegrowers owns a morsel of the 3.7-hectare (9 acre) Bienvenues-Bâtard-Montrachet. The Carillon Bienvenues is matured in oak for a year, then rested in stainless steel for a few months before bottling. The wine has a flowers-and-honey bouquet, a supple and concentrated palate and well-judged acidity.

DELAGRANGE-BACHELET
LE MONTRACHET

Montrachet is sited in the central portion of the hillside between Puligny and Chassagne where soil, aspect and micro-climate combine to such magical effect. This distinguished Chassagne domaine is in the process of subdivision, most of its vineyards being shared by the domaines of Blain-Gagnard and Fontaine Gagnard. The Delagrange-Bachelet Montrachet has been less finely aromatic than wines from rival parcels, but its flavours were always deep and classical, and its potential is unlikely to be squandered by the new generation.

FONTAINE-GAGNARD
CRIOTS BÂTARD-MONTRACHET

Fontaine-Gagnard now owns a small holding in the smallest of the Montrachet *grand crus*, Criots; from it is produced a beautifully blossomy, oaky-rich white wine.

GAGNARD-DELAGRANGE
BÂTARD-MONTRACHET

Jacques Gagnard-Delagrange is also winemaker for the Domaine Fontaine-Gagnard, and the two estates are run in tandem. The Gagnard-Delagrange parcel in Bâtard-Montrachet is only a fifth of a hectare (½ acre), but produces fragrant, richly textured wines in which sweet floral notes meet dark, smoky oak. The wines last well.

JEAN-NOËL GAGNARD
BÂTARD-MONTRACHET

Another Gagnard, Jean-Noël, treasures a third of a hectare (⁴/5 acre) of Bâtard-Montrachet as the jewel in his 7-hectare (17-acre) domaine. His wine is one of the richest Bâtards, seductively perfumed and packed full of honeyed, nutty fruit. Oak adds a further layer of opulence and wealth.

LOUIS JADOT
CHEVALIER-MONTRACHET
"LES DEMOISELLES"

The wine of Chevalier-Montrachet, from vineyards situated on the highest part of the hillside, is generally considered to be second only in quality to that of Montrachet. Les Demoiselles used to be part of the Le Cailleret *Premier Cru*, but has now been upgraded to Chevalier-Montrachet. The two *négociants* Jadot and Latour share half a hectare (1¼ acres) here, and the Jadot wine is unfailingly fine, concentrated, long and fragrant.

MARQUIS DE LAGUICHE JOSEPH
DROUHIN MONTRACHET

The Marquis de Laguiche's 2 hectares (5 acres) of Montrachet form the largest single holding in that vineyard. The wine is entrusted to the Beaune *négociant* Joseph Drouhin for vinification, *élevage* and sales. An overwhelming intensity of fruit, resolved by time and balance into creamy voluptuousness, testifies that Drouhin does not betray this trust.

DOMAINE LEFLAIVE
CHEVALIER-MONTRACHET

This 20-hectare (50-acre) domaine is run with extraordinary zeal by Vincent Leflaive, whose finest wine is certainly that produced from his 2 hectares (5 acres) in Chevalier-Montrachet. Cool fermentation, a cautious use of new oak, spotless cellar cleanliness and bottling just under the 18-month mark produce a Chevalier-Montrachet of complex, aromatic brilliance.

MICHEL NIELLON
CHEVALIER-MONTRACHET

With total holdings of just under 4 hectares (10 acres), Michel Niellon is not one of Chassagne-Montrachet's most important growers, but his Chevalier-Montrachet and Bâtard-Montrachet are always as fine as their vineyards' reputations. The Niellon style is for big wines, opulently and richly aromatic, fat with honeyed fruit on the palate.

DOMAINE DE LA ROMANÉE-
CONTI MONTRACHET

The DRC has just over half a hectare (⁴/5 acre) of Montrachet to its name, and its policy of ripe fruit at any cost (no Montrachet is more expensive) results in stylish, dense wines that require over a decade of cellaring before they begin to show at their statuesque best. As with all fine white Burgundy, do not over-chill.

DOMAINE ETIENNE SAUZET
BIENVENUES BÂTARD-
MONTRACHET

Long lees ageing, replacement of a quarter of the casks each year and minimum filtration ensure that wines of this 12-hectare (30-acre) domaine are of a high standard. The Bienvenues is a delicate member of the Montrachet family, and Sauzet's is freshly flavoured, yet persistent.

DOMAINE THÉNARD
REMOISSENET PÈRE & FILS
LE MONTRACHET

The Domaine Thénard is the second largest landowner in Montrachet, with holdings of over 1 hectare (2¹/2 acres). The wine is vinified at the Thénard cellars in Givry, and bottled and sold by the Beaune *négociant* Remoissenet. Given time, it achieves the greatness that is its birthright.

CHASSAGNE-
MONTRACHET

BLAIN-GAGNARD
PREMIER CRU LA BOUDRIOTTE

The domaine of Blain-Gagnard was created from a large proportion of the vineyards of Edmond Delagrange's Domaine Delagrange-Bachelet. La Boudriotte lies at mid-slope on the Santenay side of Chassagne-Montrachet, and yields a cherry-scented, crisply flavoured red wine.

MARC COLIN PREMIER CRU "LES CHAMP-GAINS"

Champ-Gains as a *premier cru* is typical of Chassagne: both Pinot Noir and Chardonnay vines are found here, and both perform well on appropriate soils, white marl and red gravelly earth occurring in close conjunction. Marc Colin's white Champ-Gains is one of the fleshier, more richly flavoured white Chassagnes.

MICHEL COLIN-DELÉGER PREMIER CRU "LES VERGERS"

Les Vergers lies at mid-slope on the Puligny side of Chassagne, on red clay-gravel soils with a fine south-eastern aspect. The primary vocation of the vineyard is for red wines; but Chardonnay also performs well, as this richly fruity, closely textured white from Colin-Deléger proves.

FONTAINE-GAGNARD PREMIER CRU "LES CAILLERETS"

Chassagne, like Puligny, has a *Premier Cru* Les Caillerets, though the two sites are have little in common. Both red and white vines are found in the Chassagne Caillerets, and the wines made by Jacques Gagnard-Delagrange for Fontaine-Gagnard are full of attractive fruit, softened and given a smoky edge with oak.

JEAN-NOËL GAGNARD PREMIER CRU MORGEOT

The Morgeot *premier cru* is one of the best for red wine in the village. (At one time, a bottle of red Morgeot was worth two of white Montrachet.) Jean-Noël Gagnard produces both red and white wine from his hectare (2 1/2 acres) of vines there; the stylish, summer-fruit red perhaps has the edge on the light but comely white.

GAGNARD-DELAGRANGE PREMIER CRU "LA BOUDRIOTTE"

La Boudriotte is contiguous with Caillerets and Champs-Gains, and lies above Morgeot in the west of Chassagne. Jacques Gagnard-Delagrange's white Boudriotte is made with customary care, the summer fruit lent depth by supple, smoky oak; often his red Boudriotte is a more interesting wine, full of haunting cherry fruit

DOMAINE DU DUC DE MAGENTA PREMIER CRU MORGEOT CLOS DE LA CHAPELLE

Owned by Philippe MacMahon, Duc de Magenta, two-thirds of the vines at the 4.5-hectare (11-acre) Clos de la Chapelle are red and one-third is white. In the past the quality of the wines has mirrored the quality of the vintage rather too faithfully. The Beaune *négociant* Louis Jadot has recently taken over vinification and maturation of the Magenta wines, and the vineyard may be expected to give of its best soon.

CHÂTEAU DE LA MALTROYE A. COURNUT & FILS PREMIER CRU

This 13-hectare (32-acre) domaine, owned by André Cournot, includes a 2.5-hectare (6-acre) *monopole*, the Clos du Château de la Maltroye. Both red and white wines are produced; the red, when successful, is a cherry-scented wine of medium depth, with plenty of expressive fruit; the white is lemony and graceful.

LES DOMAINES ALBERT MOREY ET FILS VIEILLES VIGNES

Bernard Morey runs this fine, 12-hectare (30-acre) domaine, producing red and white wines of great style and panache. Ripeness is looked for in the vineyards; vinification is tailored towards maximum fruit extraction; and *élevage* brings new oak into the equation. The results are deliciously accessible, though they will also age well - especially when produced, as here, from old vines.

JEAN-MARC MOREY PREMIER CRU CHAMPS-GAINS

Champs-Gains lies just south of Chassagne, and from his holding in the vineyard Bernard Morey's brother Jean-Marc produces a red wine of bright ruby colour, rich raspberry aromas and firm, structured flavour, ageing well for up to a decade.

MICHEL NIELLON
PREMIER CRU LES VERGERS

GRAND VIN DE BOURGOGNE

CHASSAGNE-MONTRACHET
"LES VERGERS 1ᵉʳ CRU"
Appellation Chassagne-Montrachet Contrôlée
WHITE BURGUNDY TABLE WINE

Mis en bouteille à la Propriété par
MICHEL NIELLON
VITICULTEUR A CHASSAGNE-MONTRACHET (COTE-D'OR)
Alc. 13,5% by Volume ℮ᵉ 750 ml Produce of France

Niellon's whites are particularly successful and exuberant, produced by cask fermentation and careful *élevage*. Les Vergers is one of the better *premier cru* sites of Chassagne, occupying a mid-slope position with a south-eastern aspect. Both red and white wines are made. Michel Niellon makes one of his lushest, most opulent whites here.

SAINT-AUBIN

RAOUL CLERGET
PREMIER CRU LE CHARMOIS

*Ce vin d'excellente
Cuvée a été sélectionné
[...]*

SAINT-AUBIN 1ᵉʳ CRU
LE CHARMOIS
APPELLATION SAINT-AUBIN 1ᵉʳ CRU LE CHARMOIS CONTROLÉE

Mis en bouteille par
RAOUL CLERGET, NEGOCIANT-ELEVEUR A SAINT-AUBIN, COTE-D'OR
PRODUCE OF FRANCE ℮ 75 cl

For such a small village, Saint Aubin has a complicated pattern of 19 *premiers crus*. Le Charmois is one of the more important, and Maurice Clerget produces both a red and a white wine there. Both see oak, the reds for an extended period. The whites are full and floral.

HUBERT LAMY
PREMIER CRU LES FRIONNES

GRANDS VINS PRODUCT OF FRANCE
DE BOURGOGNE DOMAINE LAMY

Saint-Aubin 1ᵉʳ Cru
LES FRIONNES
APPELLATION SAINT-AUBIN CONTROLÉE

13% vol. *Mis en bouteille par* 750 ml
Hubert Lamy
PROPRIÉTAIRE-RÉCOLTANT A SAINT-AUBIN COTE-D'OR

The Lamy winegrowing roots go back to 1640, and the quality of the family domaines is high. Hubert Lamy's Les Frionnes is a beautiful golden-yellow in colour, with an aroma at times floral, at times fruity (suggesting pear or quince). On the palate it is well-balanced, with a nutty finish.

DOMAINE LAMY-PILLOT
"LES ARGILLIERS"

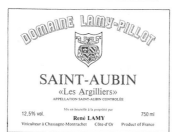

DOMAINE LAMY-PILLOT

SAINT-AUBIN
«Les Argilliers»
APPELLATION SAINT-AUBIN CONTROLÉE

12,5% vol. *Mis en bouteille à la propriété par* 750 ml
René LAMY
Viticulteur à Chassagne-Montrachet Côte-d'Or Product of France

René Lamy, based in Chassagne-Montrachet, is Hubert's brother, and he has built up an 8-hectare (20-acre) domaine, with a further 10 hectares (25 acres) cultivated on a tenancy basis. Les Argilliers is one of Saint-Aubin's unclassified vineyards, and traditional methods are used to produce wines of texture and substance, which improve with age.

HENRI PRUDHON & FILS
PREMIER CRU LES FRIONNES

PRODUIT DE FRANCE

SAINT-AUBIN 1ᵉʳ CRU
LES FRIONNES
APPELLATION D'ORIGINE CONTROLÉE

Mis en Bouteilles au Domaine par
HENRI PRUDHON & FILS
VITICULTEURS A SAINT-AUBIN PAR MEURSAULT COTE-D'OR FRANCE
13% vol. 750 ml

The graceful style of winemaking that marks bottles issuing from the Prudhon *cave* is evident in the red and white wines produced from Les Frionnes, one of Saint-Aubin's best-sited *premiers*. The red has fine summer fruit aromas and a supple, lively texture; the white suggests apricot or peach, is pleasingly oaked and finishes long and bright.

ROUX PÈRE & FILS
PREMIER CRU LA CHATENIÈRE

SAINT-AUBIN
1ᵉʳ Cru - La Chatenière
Appellation Saint-Aubin Contrôlée

Elevé et mis en bouteilles par
12,5% vol. **ROUX PÈRE & FILS** 375 ml
Saint-Aubin par Meursault (Côte-d'Or)
France

A base of marl covered by a mix of limestone debris, brown clay and chalk allows both Pinot Noir and Chardonnay to thrive in this area. The Roux family favours Chardonnay for its 2-hectare (5-acre) parcel of La Chatenière, and from it they make a pungent, characterful white with a nutty, almond-and-hazelnut character.

SANTENAY

ADRIEN BELLAND
PREMIER CRU
CLOS DES GRAVIÈRES

PRODUCE OF FRANCE
GRAND VIN DE BOURGOGNE

Santenay Clos des Gravières
PREMIER CRU
APPELLATION SANTENAY CONTROLÉE

Mis en bouteilles au Domaine
ADRIEN BELLAND 750 ml
PROPRIÉTAIRE A SANTENAY (COTE-D'OR) FRANCE
13% Alc. by vol.

Adrien Belland's Clos de Gravières is a refreshingly leafy white wine, produced from a flattish site near the boundary with Chassagne-Montrachet. As the name suggests, gravelly soils predominate here. (Adrien Belland also produces a red Les Gravières.)

ROGER BELLAND
PREMIER CRU COMMES

Grand Vin *de Bourgogne*

SANTENAY-COMMES
Appellation Santenay Premier Cru Contrôlée

MIS EN BOUTEILLE AU DOMAINE PAR
Roger BELLAND
13% vol. Viticulteur à Santenay (Côte-d'Or) France 750ml

There are at least three Belland domaines in Santenay; that of Roger Belland produces some of the sturdiest red wines of the village. La Comme is probably the finest *premier cru*, from a sloping, well-exposed site above Gravières. Its red wine, which is rich, robust and earthy, requires at least five years to show at its best.

DOMAINE LEQUIN-ROUSSOT
PREMIER CRU LE PASSE-TEMPS

Grands Vins *Vignerons*
de *de père en fils*
Bourgogne *depuis 1334*

SANTENAY
1ᵉʳ CRU LE PASSE-TEMPS
APPELLATION SANTENAY 1ᵉʳ CRU CONTROLÉE

DOMAINE LEQUIN-ROUSSOT
René et Louis LEQUIN Frères
13,5% vol. VITICULTEURS A SANTENAY COTE-D'OR FRANCE 750 ml
MISE EN BOUTEILLE AU DOMAINE Produit de France

The 200-year-old 16-hectare (40-acre) Lequin-Roussot domaine includes just over 1 hectare (2½ acres) in the Passe-Temps *Premier Cru*. René and Louis Lequin take much care over every aspect of wine production and the result, in this case, is a cherry-scented, oak-aged red Burgundy.

DOMAINE PRIEUR-BRUNET PREMIER CRU MALADIÈRE

Santenay is divided into two parts, Haut-Santenay and Bas-Santenay; Maladière lies between the two. The site is not as favourable as those nearer Chassagne, and light, quick-maturing reds are often produced there. The Domaine Prieur-Brunet owns nearly 5 hectares (12 acres) of the vineyard, and its Maladière is lightly structured and supple, but with good earthy fruit and an attractive, bitter-cherry finish.

PROSPER MAUFOUX

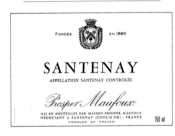

In the middle of Santenay are the premises of Prosper Maufoux, a *négociant* dealing in wines from every part of Burgundy. Local interests are not overlooked: Pierre Maufoux runs the large Domaine Saint-Michel with local grower Michel Gutrin. "Village" Santenay appearing under the Maufoux label will exhibit the strength and structure that is this *négociant*'s hallmark.

ROUX PÈRE ET FILS PREMIER CRU

When a wine is made from a number of different *premier cru* sites, then it will have no mention of any vineyard name on its label. This red wine, from the Saint-Aubin-based domaine of Marcel Roux, comes from parcels in Comme, Beauregard and Beaurepaire. It is full of the light, fresh, raspberry fruit charm of so many Santenay reds.

CÔTE DE BEAUNE-VILLAGES & HAUTES-CÔTES DE BEAUNE

These two appellations can be excellent sources of inexpensive Burgundy, better in each case than their Côte de Nuits counterparts. The exclusively red wines of Côte de Beaune-Villages (whites are sold as simple Bourgogne Blanc) may come from vineyard sites in any of 17 Côte de Beaune communes; note that there is a separate Côte de Beaune appellation for red and white wines from around Beaune itself. Scattered vineyards, many owned by domaines based in the Côte d'Or, are sited in the pretty hills that lie above and to the west of the Côte d'Or. These produce good red, white and rosé wines with the appellation Hautes-Côtes de Beaune. Much of it comes from the important *coopérative* Les Caves des Hautes-Côtes, which oversees around a quarter of production of both Hautes-Côtes de Nuits and Hautes-Côtes de Beaune, the latter producing the greater quantity.

ROGER BELLAND CÔTE DE BEAUNE-VILLAGES

LOUIS CARILLON ET FILS CÔTE DE BEAUNE-VILLAGES

LES CAVES DES HAUTES-CÔTES HAUTES-CÔTES DE BEAUNE

DOMAINE LUCIEN JACOB HAUTES-CÔTES DE BEAUNE

JEAN JOLIOT & FILS HAUTES-CÔTES DE BEAUNE

DOMAINE ANDRÉ ET BERNARD LABRY HAUTES-CÔTES DE BEAUNE

DOMAINE LEQUIN-ROUSSOT CÔTE DE BEAUNE-VILLAGES

DOMAINE MAZILLY PÈRE ET FILS HAUTES-CÔTES DE BEAUNE

CÔTE CHALONNAISE

T HE CÔTE CHALONNAISE takes its name from the town of Chalon-sur-Saône. There are no vineyards adjacent to the town itself, for the Saône, like any large river, has created a flat and fertile flood plain along its banks, and such soils do not yield fine wines. Chalon's Côte, with its attendant relief, lies some distance west of the town, and runs in a discontinuous chain from Bouzeron in the north, through Rully, Mercurey and Givry to Buxy and Montagny-lès-Buxy in the south. The district was traditionally known as the *région de Mercurey*, borrowing the name, in classic Burgundian style, of its best-known village and leading production centre. This term is not widely used at present.

Finding an identity

Despite a long history of vine growing, the region has had identity problems in the past, and these persist today. Wine laws are a recent invention, and prior to their installation it was commonplace and inevitable to pass off the wines of a small region like the Côte Chalonnaise as those of its larger and better-known neighbour. Much Mercurey will have been drunk as Beaune; historically, perhaps more than has been drunk as Mercurey. Today the region has its own appellations, but production is still tiny (only a seventh of the comparatively modest Côte d'Or total), and

the broken chain of villages and vineyards has no large focal point, like Nuits or Beaune, to act as a regional centre and shop window.

For consumers, however, the Côte Chalonnaise has much to offer, particularly to those who would otherwise be excluded from the pleasures of Burgundy by its high price. Nearly 70 per cent of the wines here are Pinot Noir reds, with Chardonnay, Aligoté and Gamay making up the balance. At best, they more than match many "village" wines of the Côte d'Or - at as little as half the price.

The style of the wines

Bouzeron is the most northerly of the Côte Chalonnaise villages, but its name may only be used in combination with Aligoté; excellent Chardonnay and Pinot Noir wines are also produced there, under the Bourgogne Blanc and Rouge appellations. The emphasis is on red wines in Rully, although the whites do not lag far behind, and the gap seems likely to close as demand for white Burgundy increases. Mercurey's vineyards are almost pure Pinot; indeed, this is the biggest Pinot Noir appellation in Burgundy. Givry, too, is overwhelmingly red in colour; but a measure of balance is restored with Montagny, as this appellation may only be claimed by white wines. Red wines from Montagny producers, as in the Bouzeron area, will go to market as Bourgogne Rouge.

BOUCHARD PÈRE ET FILS
ANCIEN DOMAINE CARNOT
BOURGOGNE ALIGOTÉ

Bouzeron, the most northerly of the Côte Chalonnaise villages, finally received an appellation of its own in 1979, when the quality of its Aligoté (but only its Aligoté) won it this distinction. Bouchard Père et Fils is the leading producer, with 34,000 bottles of Aligoté from the Ancien Domaine Carnot going to market every year. The wine is true to the variety: slender, sharp and lemony.

A. ET P. DE VILLAINE
BOURGOGNE LES CLOUS

From vineyards near Bouzeron on the Côte Chalonnaise comes this superb Chardonnay les Clous, made by the same hand that makes the wines of the Domaine de la Romanée-Conti - that of Aubert de Villaine. Bouzeron only enjoys appellation status for its Aligoté, so the wine is marketed as a modest Bourgogne. Would that all Bourgogne Blanc had the same honeyed, nutty aromas and complex, structured flavours as does this one.

RULLY

DOMAINE BELLEVILLE
PREMIER CRU "LES CLOUX"

Rully, together with nearby Bouzeron, marks the start of the Côte Chalonnaise. The village has a generous handful of *premiers crus*, of which Les Cloux, also known as Les Clouds, is one of the best. The white wine produced by Domaine Belleville from its holding there is always attractively aromatic, but can be disappointing on the palate. Disappointment may lessen as the vines age.

RAYMOND BÊTES
LA BERGERIE

Raymond Bêtes has only recently begun to bottle and market his own wines; their fresh fruit flavours and clean finish augur well for the future.

PIERRE COGNY
REMENOT

The red and white Rully wines of Bouzeron-based Pierre Cogny exemplify the rustic style of Burgundy, for better or for worse. They are full of unexpected suggestions; they mirror the characteristics of each passing vintage faithfully; they convince more fully in drinking at table than in tasting, when they can seem a little rough-edged. The red Remenot, from an unclassified *lieu-dit*, is typical in each respect.

DOMAINE DE LA FOLIE
NOËL-BOUTON
CLOS DE BELLECROIX

The Domaine de la Folie takes its name from the Montagne de la Folie, a 400-metre (1,312-foot) hill on whose slopes many of the best Rully vineyards are sited. Most of the 5 hectares (12 acres) cultivated by Xavier Noël-Bouton in the Clos de Bellecroix are planted with Pinot Noir, and he vinifies this fruit into an earthily satisfying red wine, one that acquires gamey, animal overtones after a few years in bottle.

DOMAINE DE LA FOLIE
NOËL-BOUTON
CLOS ST. JACQUES

The unclassified Clos de Bellecroix yields the leading red wine of the Domaine de la Folie; the unclassified Clos St. Jacques yields its leading white. Nearly 5 hectares (12 acres) of carefully tended Chardonnay produce a delicate, honeysuckle-scented white wine with lemony fruit flavours.

H. ET P. JACQUESON
PREMIER CRU "GRÉSIGNY"

The 11-hectare (27-acre) Jacqueson domaine is one of the most scrupulously run in Rully. Three-quarters of a hectare (2 acres) are cultivated by Henri and his son Paul in the *premier cru* Grésigny. Six times as much red as white wine is produced, and traditional vinification is followed by oak ageing, with 30 per cent new oak each year. These are wines of more finesse than is usual in Rully.

H. ET P. JACQUESON
"LES CHAPONNIÈRES"

This medal-winning red wine from the fine Jacqueson domaine is as handsome in the glass (full of sombre ruby glints) as the label is on the bottle. Les Chaponnières, where the Jacquesons have a 1.5-hectare (4-acre) holding, is not officially a *premier cru*, but the wine is certainly of comparable standing: deep, peppery and textured.

DOMAINE DE LA RENARDE
ANDRÉ DELORME, VAROT

This impressive 60-hectare (150-acre) estate is based in Rully but has vineyards throughout the Côte Chalonnaise. The Varot site alone occupies 18 hectares (45 acres) and is mainly planted with Chardonnay to give a supple white wine, full of fresh straw aromas, and with a palate that combines lime and spice.

CHÂTEAU DE RULLY
ANTONIN RODET

Since 1986 this estate has been overseen by the Mercurey-based domaine of Antonin Rodet, and 15 hectares (37 acres) are now planted with 80 per cent Chardonnay, 20 per cent Pinot Noir. The wines already show Rodet's careful craftsmanship and look set to improve in elegance and richness as the plantations age.

MERCUREY

BOUCHARD AÎNÉ & FILS
CLOS LA MARCHE

Bouchard Aîné is based in Beaune, but most of its 22 hectares (52 acres) of vineyards are in the Côte Chalonnaise. The Clos La Marche occupies 3 hectares (7¹/₂ acres); its Pinot Noir vines yield a raspberry-scented wine that is rounded and full on the palate.

CHÂTEAU DE CHAMIREY MARQUIS DE JOUENNES D'HERVILLE

The 25-hectare (62-acre) domaine of the Marquis de Jouennes d'Herville is another aristocratic estate under the wing of Antonin Rodet; both red and white Mercurey are produced, the red spending up to 18 months in oak (a third new annually) and the white up to a year. The red is an elegant and lively wine, with currant scents, structured and full on the palate; the white is nutty, sappy and stylish.

J. FAIVELEY CLOS DES MYGLANDS

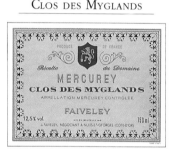

The Faiveley Domaine includes about 70 hectares (173 acres) in Mercurey, including a portfolio of well-placed *clos* such as the 9-hectare (22-acre) Clos des Myglands, making it the most important name in the village. The wine has a deep crimson colour, a forthcoming, blackcurrant-and-wood aroma and long, fruity flavours.

MICHEL JUILLOT "CLOS TONNERRE"

Twelve of the 600 hectares (1,483 acres) planted in Mercurey are in Michel Juillot's hands, including three in the *monopole* Clos Tonnerre. Monsieur Juillot has a sure touch with Pinot Noir, and his reds are among the most consistently good in the village - ripe and rich. The whites can be a little too weighty for their fruit.

YVES DE LAUNAY DOMAINE DU MEIX-FOULOT

At least half of the vineyard area in Mercurey is in the hands of half-a-dozen large *négociants*. Small growers such as Yves de Launay have to fight for a market presence; the tightly structured reds and fresh, almondy whites produced at the Domaine du Meix-Foulot do justice to their cause.

JEAN MARÉCHAL CUVÉE PRESTIGE

With under 10 hectares (25 acres) of vines, Jean Maréchal is not one of Mercurey's larger producers, but the quality of his red wines is as good as any. The Cuvée Prestige has a deep colour, rich berry scents, and wide-ranging flavours, in which pungent Pinot fruit is given allure by spice and leather notes.

DOMAINE MAURICE PROTHEAU & FILS PREMIER CRU CLOS L'EVÊQUE

The wines of the Domaine Maurice Protheau are marketed by the *négociant* firm of François Protheau, and most originate in the Côte Chalonnaise. The 6-hectare (15-acre) Clos l'Evêque yields perhaps the finest of the range: long vatting and new oak make for a firm, tannic structure and a certain somnolence in youth; they wake after seven or eight years and prove their mettle in the glass, with meaty aromas and earthy fruit.

FABIEN ET LOUIS SAIER LES CHENELOTS

Red Mercurey outnumbers white by around 20 bottles to 1, reflecting local tradition as much as the marl and limestone soils, for many vineyards - such as Les Chenelots - produce both types, both of which are good. The Saier's Mercurey Blanc is a fine example of the mid-weight, slightly toasty wine that Chardonnay gives here.

YVES DE SUREMAIN

Yves de Suremain and Hugues de Suremain are two of the more important local growers, and reliable alternatives to the big *négociants'* Mercureys are often to be found under these names. Excitement, too, is evident in the peppery Pinot flavours of this Domaine de Suremain wine, as well as in Yves de Suremain's Clos Voyen and Les Crets.

GIVRY

JEAN CHOFFLET

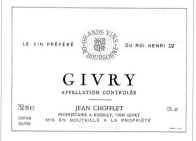

The Chofflet family has been making wine in Givry since the eighteenth century, and Jean Chofflet's lightly coloured, earthily characterful red Givry bears the stamp of local tradition very clearly. Givry's reds are in general less weighty, more zestful and spritely than those of Mercurey.

MICHEL DERAIN

Michel Derain is one of only a handful of growers in Givry to produce a white as well as a red wine. The white is marked by attractive floral aromas and a fresh, zestful flavour; the red is full and frank, with clear, cleanly realized Pinot fruit.

DOMAINE DU GARDIN
PREMIER CRU CLOS SALOMON

Givry, unlike the other villages of the Côte Chalonnaise, had no official *premiers crus* until recently. A few have now been classified, among them the 6-hectare (15-acre) Clos Salomon, a *monopole* of the du Gardin family. The red wine produced there combines fruit and spice in a most attractive manner, ageing gracefully across a decade.

DOMAINE JOBLOT
PREMIER CRU
CLOS DE LA SERVOISINE

This small, 6-hectare (15-acre) domaine includes two 2-hectare (5-acre) *clos*: the Clos du Cellier aux Moines (planted with Pinot Noir) and the Clos de la Servoisine (planted with Chardonnay). The Servoisine is full, lightly buttery and very supple and smooth on the tongue, finishing with delicate hazelnut notes.

DOMAINE RAGOT
CHAMP POUROT

Domaine Ragot has had a good record of prize-winning in the Concours Général at Paris and elsewhere in recent years. White Givry is a particular strength of this domaine, combining floral aromas with long, carefully balanced fruit flavours. The reds are almost as good, with their redcurrant fruit and sparely jointed structure.

REMOISSENET PÈRE & FILS
DOMAINE THÉNARD

One quarter of Givry's vineyards is in the hands of the Domaine du Baron Thénard, and one of the domaine's largest customers is the *négociant* firm of Remoissenet - which also markets the Thénard Montrachet. This is good Givry, its fruit a mixture of raspberry and bilberry. Its label, like everyone else's, bears the almost obligatory and almost meaningless *le préféré du roi Henri IV* - the favourite [wine] of Henri IV.

DOMAINE TATRAUX JUILLET

Bernard Tatraux's Givry is a pleasingly gamey red Burgundy of simple excellence, labelled without the delusions of grandeur that Henri IV inspires in other Givry growers, and sold without the high prices that they sometimes inflict on their customers as a consequence. Enjoy its youthful vibrancy as soon as you can.

MONTAGNY

CAVE DES VIGNERONS DE BUXY
PREMIER CRU, CUVÉE SPÉCIALE

"Premier cru" has a specific meaning in the Montagny context: it signifies that the must had a potential alcohol content of 11.5° before chaptalization. Only white wines are produced here, many of them by this cooperative; its top *cuvées*, like Cuvée Spéciale, are examples of the sinewy Chardonnay that the appellation can unveil.

CHÂTEAU DE LA SAULE
ALAIN ROY-THEVENIN
PREMIER CRU

Alain Roy-Thevenin produces some of the most attractively labelled and attractively flavoured Montagny at the Château de la Saule. Lowish yields, oak ageing and minimum pre-bottling treatments result in a golden-yellow wine of fresh, vanilla-and-butter aromas and deep fruit.

VEUVE STEINMAIER & FILS
PREMIER CRU MONT-CUCHOT

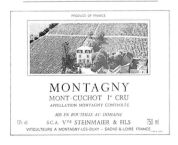

The Steinmaier family domaine is reputed for its freshly flavoured, nutty, sometimes floral white Burgundies from Montagny vineyards; that from the *lieu-dit* of Mont-Cuchot (*premier cru* only in terms of its alcohol content) is one of the best.

MÂCONNAIS

MÂCON OCCUPIES THE SAME position in relation to the region of which it is the capital as London does to the British Isles: it sits in the south-eastern corner, well away from the heart of things. But, as in Britain, much of the region's economic strength is concentrated around this capital, for Pouilly-Fuissé, -Loché and -Vinzelles, and the St Véran group of superior "-Villages", lie at Mâcon's doorstep. The further one gets from Mâcon - out towards Sennecey-le-Grand in the north, or St Gengoux-le-National or Cluny in the west - the more uniform and featureless the wines become.

White, Chardonnay-based wines are as dominant here as red Pinot Noir wines are in the Côte Chalonnaise. The Mâconnais does produce red wines, mainly from Gamay, but the pockets of clay and sandy soils selected by growers for red-wine production fail to yield wines of anything but local interest. Interest in the white wines, by contrast, is universal: they are broad, solid, structured Chardonnays, with a harmonious balance between lemony fruit and sinewy vinosity, generally fresh in style, rarely expensive.

The region can offer white Burgundies of complexity, too, from the better Mâcon-Villages and from the *crus* of the south-east, particularly Pouilly-Fuissé. Here limestone soils and beautifully exposed slopes produce wines that can approach Meursault in buttery richness and Puligny in aromatic finesse.

POUILLY-FUISSÉ

DOMAINE DE L'ARILLIÈRE
VINCENT-SOURICE

Pouilly-Fuissé can be produced in the villages of Pouilly, Fuissé (as this one is), Solutré, Vergisson and Chaintré: a belt of communes lying south-west of Mâcon. The elegant wine of the Domaine de l'Arillière has brisk, lemony scents and supple, lively fruit.

CHÂTEAU FUISSÉ
M. VINCENT ET FILS

With Château Fuissé's Vieilles Vignes, Pouilly-Fuissé gets as good as it can get. Intensity of flavour is the hallmark of this wine, with nuts, vanilla, pineapple, papaya and citrus all fighting, creatively, for expression.

ROGER LUQUET
CLOS DU BOURG

Roger Luquet's Clos du Bourg lies in the middle of the small village of Fuissé and produces full, rich, solidly built Pouilly-Fuissé. Monsieur Luquet has used oak increasingly in recent years, and this can occasionally dominate the fruit. A fine St Véran Les Grandes Bruyères also emerges from this cellar.

DOMAINE MANCIAT-PONCET

Much of the production of Pouilly-Fuissé is controlled by large Burgundy *négociants*, who export particularly to the USA. Small, quality producers, like Domaine Manciat-Poncet, have been squeezed out of this process in the past; today, though, a ready market can be found for their lightly coloured, densely flavoured Pouilly-Fuissé.

M. VINCENT ET FILS

Marcel Vincent and his son Jean-Jacques are perfectionists at every stage of production: only the best vats are allowed the Château Fuissé label. The rest bear the Vincent name - adequate assurance of a balanced, flavoury, oak-informed Chardonnay.

POUILLY-VINZELLES

DOMAINE MATHIAS

The little villages of Loché and Vinzelles, lying south-east of Pouilly and Fuissé, have won the right to separate appellations, prefixed by the magic name "Pouilly". The Pouilly-Vinzelles of Jean Mathias is an excellent white Burgundy in the Mâcon style, with plenty of sound, solid and satisfying lemony fruit.

POUILLY-LOCHÉ

CAVES DES CRUS BLANCS

GRAND VIN DE BOURGOGNE

POUILLY-LOCHÉ
Appellation Pouilly-Loché Contrôlée
Mis en bouteille à la propriété
CAVE DES CRUS BLANCS 71145 VINZELLES - France
Société Coopérative Vinicole
PRODUCT OF FRANCE
13% vol.   750 ml

Most of the production of Pouilly-Vinzelles and Pouilly-Loché emerges from the Caves des Crus Blancs at Vinzelles. Not all of this coopérative's cuvées are as attractive as they should be, but the Pouilly-Loché is full of supple fruit, finishing rich and earthy.

SAINT-VÉRAN

ROGER TISSIER
DOMAINE DES CRAIS

VIN DE BOURGOGNE
ROGER TISSIER

SAINT-VÉRAN
APPELLATION SAINT-VÉRAN CONTRÔLÉE
DOMAINE DES CRAIS
PRODUIT EN FRANCE
ROGER TISSIER, PROPRIÉTAIRE-RÉCOLTANT, LEYNES 71
Alc. 12,5% by vol.   e 750 ml

Saint-Véran is a convenience appellation for villages on each side of the ribbon occupied by Pouilly-Fuissé, Pouilly-Vinzelles and Pouilly-Loché. Its wines are as good as the best Mâcon-Villages. Roger Tissier's Domaine des Crais produces wines with leafy, honeyed aromas and tightly packed flavour.

M. VINCENT ET FILS

GRAND VIN
DE BOURGOGNE   MISE
                                    AU DOMAINE

SAINT-VERAN
APPELLATION SAINT-VÉRAN CONTRÔLÉE
M. Vincent et Fils Château de Fuissé (71)
PROPRIÉTAIRES-VITICULTEURS
750 ml

Some of the best Saint-Véran comes from Pouilly-Fuissé producers who, like the Vincent family, tease quality by hard pruning, careful vinification and intelligent use of the oak cask. This rich, mouth-filling wine is unlikely to disappoint.

MÂCON AND MÂCON-VILLAGES

The Mâcon area is huge; it is one of only two parts of Burgundy that justify such an epithet (Beaujolais being the other). Red, white and rosé Mâcon, and Mâcon Supérieur, are excellent only occasionally, by dint of individual effort. Excitement grows with geographical specificity: Mâcon-Villages, or Mâcon plus the name of a village (almost 50 are eligible), is often excellent, especially from growers of the intelligence of Jean Thévenet, or merchants of the consistency of Louis Latour. Nearly all Mâcon-Villages is white, and a soothing lake of wine is pressed and fermented yearly - by comparison, the Côte d'Or and Chablis between them manage only a third of the Mâconnais total.

ERIC ARCELIN
MÂCON LA ROCHE-VINEUSE

DOMAINE ARCELIN

MACON La Roche-Vineuse
APPELLATION MÂCON CONTRÔLÉE
MIS EN BOUTEILLES À LA PROPRIÉTÉ   75cl
Eric ARCELIN, propriétaire-viticulteur, La Roche-Vineuse (S-&-L)

DOMAINE DE LA BON GRAN
JEAN THÉVENET
MÂCON-VILLAGES

37,5 cl

DOMAINE
de la
BON GRAN
MACON-VILLAGES
Appellation Mâcon-Villages Contrôlée

Mis en bouteille au Domaine par
Jean THÉVENET
Propriétaire-Viticulteur à Quintaine - Clessé, par Lugny (S.-à-L.)
PRODUCE OF FRANCE

CAVE DE CHARDONNAY
MÂCON-CHARDONNAY

GRAND VIN DE   BOURGOGNE

Mâcon-Chardonnay
APPELLATION MÂCON-CHARDONNAY CONTRÔLÉE
12,5% vol.   750 ml
Cave de Chardonnay - 71700 CHARDONNAY - FRANCE
PRODUCE OF FRANCE

DOMAINE DE CHERVIN
ALBERT GOYARD
MÂCON BURGY

GRAND VIN DE BOURGOGNE

Mâcon Burgy
Domaine de Chervin
Appellation Mâcon Contrôlée   PRODUCE
Mis en bouteilles à la Propriété   OF FRANCE
750 ml
Albert Goyard, Propriétaire-Viticulteur
à Burgy (Saône-et-Loire) France

LOUIS LATOUR
MÂCON-LUGNY
LES GENIÈVRES

Mâcon-Lugny
LES Genièvres
APPELLATION MÂCON-VILLAGES CONTRÔLÉE
MIS EN BOUTEILLE PAR
LOUIS LATOUR, Négociant à Beaune (Côte-d'Or)

DOMAINE MANCIAT-PONCET
MÂCON CHARNAY

VINS DE   BOURGOGNE
élevé en fût
de chêne

Mâcon Charnay
Appellation Mâcon-Villages Contrôlée
13% vol.   LES CRAYS
Mis en bouteille au Domaine   e 750 ml
Domaine MANCIAT-PONCET
SÉLECTION GAEC DES CRAYS
Propriétaire Récoltant à Lévigny - 71850 Charnay-les-Mâcon

JEAN-PAUL THIBERT
MÂCON-FUISSÉ

Mâcon-Fuissé
Appellation Contrôlée   75 cl
Jean-Paul Thibert
Viticulteur à Fuissé (Saône-et-Loire)
Tél. (85) 35.63.86
MIS EN BOUTEILLE À LA PROPRIÉTÉ

CHÂTEAU DE VIRÉ
HUBERT DESBOIS
MÂCON-VIRÉ

CHATEAU DE VIRÉ
APPELLATION MÂCON-VIRÉ CONTRÔLÉE
HUBERT DESBOIS
PROPRIÉTAIRE À VIRÉ SAONE-&-LOIRE
Produce of France   Bottled in France
Sélectionné et mis en bouteilles par
MAISON PROSPER MAUFOUX
12,5% alc./vol. NÉGOCIANT EN VINS A SANTENAY COTE-D'OR 750 ml

BEAUJOLAIS

GEOLOGICALLY, BEAUJOLAIS IS not Burgundy at all. Its climate is different, and the prolific scale of production is notably un-Burgundian. Its chief grape variety is considered a pariah further north, and its methods of viticulture and vinification stand in contrast to those used everywhere else in Burgundy. Beaujolais is part of Burgundy because it is not part of anywhere else; it is a geographical convenience. The siliceous, granite-based soils of the northern Beaujolais make an unusual winegrowing medium, but one that the Gamay - a grape viewed with contempt on the Côte d'Or - loves. The granite is broken down into clays and pebbly soils, often with mineral admixtures (Moulin-à-Vent's manganese, for example).

Soil and climate

These soils are distributed over a bewildering variety of rounded hill slopes, shone on by a hot summer sun and occasionally drenched by some of France's most exciting thunderstorms. The Gamay vines are pruned into low, free-standing bushes *en gobelet* (in goblets) rather than along the trellis systems used everywhere else in Burgundy. Once harvested, the fruit is then vinified uncrushed for betweeen three and four days in a version of *macération carbonique*, before proceeding as elsewhere.

The northern Beaujolais is the part of the region that produces the finest wines: it is here that the 10 Beaujolais *crus* are found, and here that the superior Beaujolais-Villages zone is located. The differences between the *crus* are not so marked as to produce a tiered system of the *grand cru/ premier cru* type. The extremes are represented by Chiroubles (for lightness and delicacy) and Moulin-à-Vent (for depth), with Régnié and Brouilly producing the least expensive and often least exciting wines. Wine from small growers rather than large *négociants* reveals the difference between the *crus* most clearly - Beaujolais has this, at least, in common with the rest of Burgundy.

Beaujolais Nouveau

The best-known wines of Beaujolais are not its finest wines, the wines of the *crus*, but its least interesting wines, the wines of the Bas-Beaujolais or southern Beaujolais. Their fame is due to their being drunk in early infancy, as Beaujolais Nouveau. Such interest as they have is most pronounced when they are a few weeks old and singing with fruit; from the moment of purchase, they are on a downward slope. (A possible exception are those Beaujolais-Villages sold as Nouveau, though even they will have been vinified for pre-Christmas drinking: in this particular case, quality may hold but is unlikely to improve.) The reason that Beaujolais from vineyards between Villefranche and Lyon is less interesting than Beaujolais from further north is the change of soil: light, stony, golden-hued calcareous soils gradually replace granite. The bedrock of these *pierres dorées* (golden stones) makes for beautiful houses, but rather plain wines.

SAINT-AMOUR

DOMAINE DES BILLARDS
HÉRITIERS LORON

This domaine, owned by the Pontena-vaux-based *négociant* Loron & Fils, produces one of the best, most consistent wines of Saint-Amour. It is well-coloured, with supple aromas and juicy fruit. The potential offered by the village name has not been wasted on the label's designer.

DOMAINE DES DUC

At Saint-Amour-Bellevue, the Mâconnais meets Beaujolais: the white wine of the village is called Saint-Véran; the red Saint-Amour. Village style is for a very light and delicate Beaujolais, full of supple, tasty fruit, which is exactly what Jacques Duc supplies. It is hard to leave bottles of Saint-Amour unopened, but two or three years will serve to accentuate the charm of Duc's version.

CHÂTEAU DE SAINT-AMOUR
PIERRE SIRAUDIN

Pierre Siraudin has 7 hectares (17 acres) of vines in Saint-Amour, and from them he makes a *cru* Beaujolais as deep as the village's lightish sandstone and granite soils permit. Part of the harvest is sold to Piat; the rest goes into this fragrant yet full-bodied red wine, characterized by rich, slightly roasted fruit flavours, drawn out over a 7- to 10-day fermentation period in the presence of the grape skins.

JULIÉNAS

DOMAINE CLAUDE ET MICHELLE JOUBERT

Claude and Michelle Joubert's wine has all the pungency of Juliénas's best: its colour varies from purple in youth to blood red in maturity, while the aromas and flavours change from vivid, youthful fruit to spicy harmony after five years in bottle.

CHÂTEAU DE JULIÉNAS CONDEMINE

This property sells only its top wine under the Château de Juliénas label. It is strongly coloured with purple glints, and powerfully aromatic with a heady Beaujolais mixture of plums and blackcurrants, often needing a few years in bottle to unwind.

DOMAINE ANDRÉ PELLETIER LES FOUILLOUSES

André Pelletier is a member of the Éventail de Vignerons Producteurs, a group of producers who combine forces to bottle and market their wines. Both Les Fouillouses and Les Envaux are excellent examples of the palpitating fruit of Juliénas - as well as of the individuality that the Éventail seeks to foster.

CHÉNAS

CHÂTEAU DE CHÉNAS

Chénas is the smallest of the Beaujolais *crus*. The large cooperative that owns Château de Chénas produces almost half of all the wines of the appellation; its best *cuvées* are labelled with the château name and are rich and persistent, with a delicious depth of fruit.

HUBERT LAPIERRE

Hubert Lapierre is based at La Chapelle-de-Guinchay, outside the appellation zone, but produces a fine *cru* Beaujolais from his Chénas vineyards. Its dizzying aromas combine with the texture and muted power often found in this central portion of the *cru* area.

MOULIN-À-VENT

CHÂTEAU DES JACQUES

The wines of Moulin-à-Vent are the most majestic in Beaujolais: the best vintages, after years in bottle, resemble old Burgundian Pinot Noir. The Château des Jacques wines, vinified for the long term, can seem cumbersome early on; this is super-rich Beaujolais for a winter's night.

DOMAINE LÉMONON E. LORON & FILS

The wine of this 8-hectare (20-acre) domaine is one of the best marketed by Loron. Like the wine of Thorin's Château des Jacques, it excels in depth and breadth, though the fruit perhaps emerges a little more clearly here and the tannins are lighter.

CHÂTEAU DU MOULIN-À-VENT BLOUD

The Château du Moulin-à-Vent has almost as much vineyard land as the Château des Jacques. Jean-Pierre Bloud produces a fine, oak-aged Beaujolais of richness and depth from its Gamay vines. After half a decade of cellaring, the wine is a brilliant ox-blood red with spicy, gamey aromas, a meaty flavour and a velvety texture. It is one of the best wines of the *cru* - and of the region.

DOMAINE DE LA TOUR DU BIEF COMTE DE SPARRE

The label suggests vinous grandeur; the Domaine de la Tour du Bief suggests an exercise in the massive and the meaty; and the Comte de Sparre's name suggests a wine of antique and noble lineage. Combine the suggestions and you have something not far from reality: a big, sound, traditional Moulin-à-Vent to satisfy the heartiest of drinkers.

FLEURIE

CAVE COOP. DE FLEURIE-EN-BEAUJOLAIS

This *coopérative* dominates production in Fleurie. Standards - under Marguerite Chabert, president for over three decades - have been high, the special *cuvées* embodying the charm for which Fleurie is known. The *coopérative*'s basic Fleurie is unlikely to disappoint either, with its balance, delicacy and lingering raspberry perfume.

DOMAINE DE MONTGENAS

Maurice Bruone's, at the Domaine de Montgenas, is another member of the Éventail de Vignerons Producteurs, based at Corcelles. His Fleurie is scented and full of spritely fruit, but balanced by the depth and extract one would expect to find in a commune adjacent to Moulin-à-Vent.

DOMAINE DES QUATRE VENTS GEORGES DUBŒUF

Georges Dubœuf is unquestionably the most important *négociant* in Beaujolais, and his success has been built not only on his own fine bottlings, but also on his selection of domaine wines - such as this Fleurie, from Dr Darroze, full of succulent fruit and vivacity.

CHIROUBLES

DOMAINE DE LA GROSSE PIERRE ALAIN PASSOT

The beautiful names of Fleurie and Saint-Amour are often noted, while the subtler mellifluousness of Chiroubles passes unremarked. But its wines do not: their accessibility and spriteliness guarantee popularity. This Chiroubles, with its pretty aroma and refreshing cherry fruit, is exemplary.

CHÂTEAU DE RAOUSSET GEORGES DUBŒUF

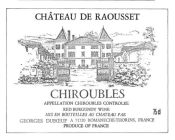

One of the more important producers of Chiroubles. The vines are old, so quality is high: Raousset wines have pungency and depth of fruit. Georges Dubœuf's bottlings ensure nothing is lost *en route* to the consumer.

MORGON

DOMAINE NOËL AUCŒUR

Morgon is the second largest and one of the most variable of the Beaujolais *crus*; Noël Aucœur's Morgon has a fine garnet colour, a rich aromatic profile and good depth of flavour. Like the best Morgon, it improves and fills out excitingly with age, acquiring seductive, chocolate and cherry notes.

DOMAINE DE COLONAT BERNARD COLLONGE LES CHARMES

Les Charmes is one of the two main hills in Morgon, the other being the higher Mont du Py, and a number of growers own vineyard sites within its 100 or so hectares (250 acres). One such is Bernard Collonge, who produces a vibrantly fruity wine, with the potential to age well for five or six years, from his parcel of vines there.

DOMAINE PIERRE SAVOYE CÔTE DU PY

Certain superior Morgon *climats* have distinguished themselves over the years, and the Côte de Py - on the slopes of the Mont du Py - is one of these. Savoye's wine is a Morgon first growth: deeply coloured, generously aromatic and appealingly fleshy.

RÉGNIÉ

DOMAINE NOËL AUCŒUR

This is the tenth *cru* of Beaujolais, decreed in December 1988. Its recognition marked the end of a long struggle by growers inside the commune, and those, like Noël Aucœur, based elsewhere but with vineyards in Régnié. The Aucœur example is supple and flavoury.

CHÂTEAU DU BASTY
M. PERROUD

Régnié is around the same size as Moulin-à-Vent, but it is its location (between Morgon and Brouilly) that indicates its character most clearly. Monsieur Perroud's Château du Basty is perhaps more Brouilly than Morgon, with its fine flowery fragrance and lightly structured, elegant flavours.

CÔTE DE BROUILLY

CHÂTEAU THIVIN
CL. GEOFFRAY

The 20-hectare (50-acre) estate of Château Thivin is run by Yvonne Geoffray, the widow of Claude Geoffray, and includes land in both Brouilly and Côte de Brouilly. Geoffray wines from the Côte de Brouilly vineyards are always among the best of the appellation: they have a luminous ruby colour, charmingly fruity aroma and are full, balanced and harmonious, with an appetizing mix of meaty fruit.

LUCIEN ET ROBERT VERGER
VIGNOBLE DE L'ECLUSE

Aromatic, comparatively slender for Beaujolais, but full of stylish fruit, this wine is made from Gamay grown on the slopes of Mont Brouilly, a retired volcano, in the l'Ecluse vineyard.

BEAUJOLAIS-VILLAGES

The 10 *crus* are not the only source of good Beaujolais. Villages such as Lantignié, Jullié, Lancié and Quincié may conceivably follow Régnié into the circle of the elect one day; meanwhile, they are simply Beaujolais-Villages, and their wines often give excellent value. Dedicated growers, such as Claude and Michelle Joubert, regularly produce Villages wines of higher quality than those Morgons or Fleuries bought as cheaply as possible by *négociants* from further north, struggling to offer a full portfolio to a supermarket client. If you do buy a *négociant*'s wines, always look for a Beaujolais address.

CHANUT FRÈRES
BEAUJOLAIS-VILLAGES

GEORGES DUBŒUF
BEAUJOLAIS-VILLAGES

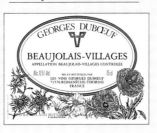

DOMAINE CLAUDE ET
MICHELLE JOUBERT
BEAUJOLAIS LANTIGNIÉ

CHÂTEAU DE LACARELLE
BEAUJOLAIS-VILLAGES

BROUILLY

CHÂTEAU DE LA CHAIZE
ROUSSY DE SALES

With nearly 150 hectares (370 acres) of vineyard, the Marquis de Roussy de Sales owns the largest single estate in Beaujolais. Opinions vary as to the quality of the wines, with the enthusiastic stressing the rich, stylish fruit and the less enthusiastic querying depth and concentration. But few would deny that Château de la Chaize is among Brouilly's best.

ANDRÉ LARGE

André Large, another member of the Éventail de Vignerons Producteurs in Corcelles, produces a Brouilly of luscious, ripe, heady fruit. Six villages can claim this appellation, by some measure the largest of the 10 *crus*, and the Large *caves* are sited in the most southerly of them, Odenas, not far from the Château de la Chaize.

CHAMPAGNE

CHAMPAGNE IS A celebratory wine *par excellence* for which there seems to be a never-ending demand. Such has been the popularity of the wine in the 1980s - export shipments have increased by three-quarters in five years - that the harvest, unless it is an extremely large one, can hardly keep pace with consumer requirements. The area permitted for planting has a finite limit of 31,050 hectares (76,727 acres) which is expected to be reached by the end of the century.

There are some 14,000 growers in Champagne, many thousands of whom own less than 1 hectare (2.5 acres), which looks at first sight like a recipe for chaos. The position is redeemed principally by two things: the structure of the industry, and the nature of the product.

The structure of the industry

The majority of small growers sell their grapes either to the Champagne houses or to cooperatives. 70 per cent of output - of the order of 250 million bottles in a good year - is handled by 150 shippers. Since they own only one-eighth of the 27,500 hectares (68,500 acres) presently planted, the additional grapes they need have to be bought in from other growers, thus giving them a flexibility and choice which they would not otherwise have. The main exceptions to this pattern are Louis Roederer, which takes pride in the fact that at least 80 per cent of its grapes come from its own 185 hectares (457 acres) of vineyards, and Bollinger, whose 140 hectares (346 acres) supply 70 per cent of its needs.

The product

The essence of Champagne lies not so much in the Champagne method, but in the superlative skill - based on nearly three centuries of experience - with which the winemaker blends the constituent wines. Non-vintage Champagne, which accounts for some 75 per cent of the total output, is always an assemblage of different *cuvées* from different vineyards and also wines from previous years, blended to produce a consistent and recognizable house style from year to year. Prestige *cuvées* are assembled in the same manner and can be drawn from over 30 different vats. Vintage wines, while from a single year, are also a blend from different vineyards, unless specifically declared as a single vineyard such as Krug's Clos du Mesnil Blanc de Blancs or Philipponat's Clos des Goisses Brut.

Quality and style

As the selection of the individual wines in this section illustrates, there is a wide range of excellent Champagnes, which differ not so much in quality - because at this level of wine-making such easy distinctions are simply not feasible - as in style. All

Maintaining consistency in the blend The unique combination of soil, grape variety and micro-climate is crucial for the quality and consistency of the blend. For that reason, the larger houses draw the grapes for their cuvées from villages situated all over the Champagne region, but mainly from the three most important, the Côtes des Blancs (devoted to the Chardonnay grape), the Montagne de Reims (predominantly Pinot Noir),and the Vallée de la Marne (Pinot Meunier).

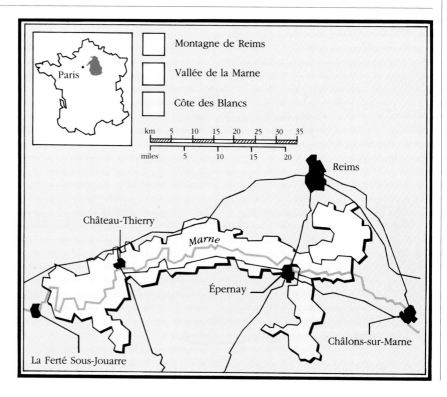

houses - particularly the *Grandes Marques* - set out to make their own distinctive impact. Style is determined by the quality of the grapes and the proportions in which they are blended. The best wines come from the best grapes, and the best grapes come from the 17 *grand cru* villages situated in the three main growing areas. When the price of grapes per kilo is fixed each year, it is these vineyards that can command 100 per cent of the price. Other vineyards - the *premier crus* (rated 90-99 per cent), and below down to 80 per cent - are entitled to the appropriate pro-rata payment. With vineyards scattered widely across the region, the berries are pressed on the spot to avoid any deterioration. There are reputedly nearly 2,000 press-houses in Champagne.

Grape varieties

Overall 39 per cent of vines in the Champagne vineyard are Pinot Meunier, 33 per cent are Pinot Noir, and 28 per cent Chardonnay. Of these three permitted grape varieties, the Pinot Noir and the Chardonnay have an affinity for the chalk sub-soil of the Montagne de Reims and the Côtes des Blancs. The Pinot Meunier is hardier and can thrive in the Vallée de la Marne which is subject to greater frost. There is no obligation to use all three grapes in the blend. Only Chardonnay is used in *blanc de blancs*, and often only Pinot Noir in *blanc de noirs*. Often in the better quality and vintage wines only Pinot Noir and Chardonnay are used. Notable exceptions are Krug and Pol Roger where a relatively high proportion of Pinot Meunier is specifically employed for the character it gives to the wines.

Styles of wine

Much champagne is made in the "British style", or - in labelling terms - *brut*. Some wines are even finished *extra brut*, ie bone dry like the Laurent Perrier Ultra Brut. Moving up the sweetness scale, extra dry is a little less than dry; *sec*, perversely, is medium sweet; *demi-sec* sweet, and *doux* very sweet (and also very rare). The base wines, the *vins clairs*, are fermented dry in the normal way.

Quality control *Harvesters sort out the ripe grapes.*

CHAMPAGNE VINTAGES

YEAR	CHARACTER	HARVEST
1989	Exceptional year, generous harvest, most houses will declare	247m bottles
1988	Very good year. Some declarations	224m bottles
1987	Good blending wines	264m bottles
1986	Good quality; a few declarations	259m bottles
1985	Small harvest; generally declared as a vintage	152m bottles
1984	Worst since 1972; blending wines	199m bottles
1983	Bumper year, quality to rival 1982, with consequent vintage declarations	302m bottles
1982	Splendid harvest, superb wines whose true excellence still being debated	295m bottles
1981	Small harvest, high quality, some vintage, but stocks needed to boost NV blends	92m bottles
1980	Modest year, few declarations	113m bottles
1979	Most houses declared, many fine wines	228m bottles

The degree of sweetness or lack of it is determined by the ultimate dosage applied after the secondary fermentation in bottle. In some cases the wine may be left in the bottle on its yeast deposit for later disgorging, to add a special flavour and bouquet. Wines treated in this way bear the mark RD - *récemment dégorgé* - (see Bollinger RD Extra Brut). *Crémant* Champagne, a lighter, creamier style, is being phased out. Rosé Champagne, however, once thought of as an amusing novelty, is now a feature of all serious lists. It has surely come of age when Moët & Chandon make a Dom Pérignon Vintage Rosé.

Youth or maturity

Champagne can be sold after a minimum ageing of one year for non-vintage and three years for vintage. In practice wines are cellared for a further two years before sale. Even then, the qualities of colour and complexity, honey, creamy richness, the subtle variations of nut and biscuit flavours, and all those other attributes of really matured Champagne will be forfeited by early drinking. The wines which follow lean very much towards culling the benefits of judicious ageing.

THE 25 HOUSES

The industry has traditionally been dominated by the 25 leading Champagne houses that belong to the *Syndicat des Grandes Marques de Champagne*, which was set up in 1964. However, the rising price of Champagne has led to a growing tendency for the smaller houses and cooperatives to sell direct abroad - this is a process that has opened up a much greater choice in the market.

The houses that belong to the *Syndicat* are:

Ayala-Montebello	Moët & Chandon
Billecart-Salmon	G H Mumm & Co
J Bollinger	Perrier-Jouët
Canard-Duchêne	Joseph Perrier Fils
Veuve Clicquot Pon-	Piper Heidsieck
sardin	Pol Roger
Deutz & Geldermann	Pommery & Greno
Heidsieck Monopole	Ch A Prieur (Champagne
Charles Heidsieck	Napoléon)
Henriot	Louis Roederer
Krug	Ruinart
Lanson/Massé	A Salon & Co
Laurent-Perrier	Taittinger/Irroy
Mercier	

THE CHAMPAGNE LABEL

Labelling requirements for Champagne are now very specific. The term *Appellation Contrôlée* need not appear; the word Champagne covers both the AOC and the term *méthode champenoise*. EC regulations also require indication of the source of production:

NM	négociant-manipulant	Champagne house
CM	coopérative de manipulation	cooperative
RM	récoltant-manipulant	grower making his own Champagne
RC	récoltant-coopérateur	grower selling wine made in a cooperative
SR	société de récoltant	family company of growers
MA	marque acheteur	buyer's own brand

Other mandatory information:
net volume
alcoholic content (between 10% and 13% by volume)
identity or code of producer
brand name
sweetness category
town and country of origin

AYALA
BRUT

GM - One of the most underrated Champagnes on the market, Ayala's vintage is always classic. Although much richer than its non-vintage, it still retains the elegant, ethereal and flowery qualities that are trademarks of Ayala's style.
🍾*PN 75%, CH 25%*

BARANCOURT
BRUT ROSÉ

One of the deeper-coloured pink Champagnes, this non-vintage wine has a powerful Pinot aroma that belies the small proportion of the grape used in the blend. This stylish Champagne is brimming with red-fruit flavours and has great finesse.
🍾*CH 85%, PN 15%*

BESSERAT DE BELLEFON
CUVÉE DES MOINES
ROSÉ BRUT

Originally called Crémant des Moines, this fine, non-vintage, pink Champagne is produced by a house that has built a reputation for producing true *crémants*. It is best drunk young when it is fresh, flowery and fragrant.
🍾*PN 50%, CH 40%, PM 10%*

BILLECART-SALMON
BRUT ROSÉ

A little-known firm that is fastidious about quality and consistency. Its *blanc de blancs* and Cuvée N.F. Billecart are both long-lived and classic, but above all else Billecart-Salmon prides itself on this ultra-light, non-vintage pink Champagne.
🍾*PN 60%, CH 40%*

BOLLINGER
ANNÉE RARE R.D.
EXTRA BRUT

GM - This takes the RD concept (see below) a little further. The wine is the same as both the vintage and the RD, but its contact with the yeast is even longer and released several years after the RD.
🍾*PN 65-70%, CH 20-25%, PM 5%*

BOLLINGER
COTEAUX CHAMPENOIS
AŸ ROUGE
LA CÔTE AUX ENFANTS

GM - This vintage wine has established itself as the most consistent red Coteaux Champenois produced, although Bollinger still consider its production experimental and are always striving to improve it.
🍾*PN 100%*

BOLLINGER
GRANDE ANNÉE BRUT

GM - Bollinger's vintage Champagnes are all cask-fermented, not filtered, and malolactic is not encouraged. Only truly great years are declared, hence the name and why, for example, you will not find a Bollinger 1980 or 1978.
PN 65-70%, CH 20-25%, PM 5%

BOLLINGER
GRANDE ANNÉE BRUT ROSÉ

GM - When Madame Bollinger was alive, she was adamant that Champagne was only white. Coming late into this fashionable sector of the market, Bollinger's pink, vintage Champagne is one of the five best wines of its type.
PN 65-70%, CH 20-25%, PM 5%, plus red wine

BOLLINGER
R.D. EXTRA BRUT

GM - RD is a trademark that stands for *Récemment Dégorgé*. The wine is exactly the same as the vintage, except that it has spent a longer time in contact with the yeast and is thus released a few years later. Great complexity.
PN 65-70%, CH 20-25%, PM 5%

BOLLINGER
VIEILLES VIGNES FRANÇAISES
BLANC DE NOIRS BRUT

GM - A massively rich wine made from ungrafted vines grown in Aÿ and Bouzy. Although it is unlike any other Champagne that is produced today, it is probably similar to how most Champagnes tasted in the nineteenth century.
PN 100%

CATTIER
CLOS DU MOULIN BRUT

This wine comes from a small vineyard that was once the site of a windmill and still has traces of a low wall, but is no longer a true *clos*. A very fine blend of three vintages, each of which are indicated on a back label, thereby identifying different *cuvées*.
PN 50%, CH 50%

CHARBAUT
CERTIFICATE
BLANC DE BLANCS BRUT

Possibly the most underrated *blanc de blancs* in Champagne, this rich, ripe and stylish vintage wine regularly retains a remarkable freshness for up to two decades.
CH 100%

CHARBAUT
CERTIFICATE ROSÉ BRUT

With help from Sainsbury's, Charbaut's pink Champagne created the vogue for this style in the UK. Even before this, the firm had something of a rosé reputation and this recent addition to the firm's prestige *cuvée* line is top class indeed.
PN 50-70%, CH 30-50%

DEUTZ
CUVÉE WILLIAM DEUTZ

GM - The ultimate Champagne from an Aÿ-based house, well-known for the grace, delicacy and breeding of its wines. It is not fined or filtered prior to the second fermentation and most vintages begin to peak at eight years.
PN 60%, CH 30%, PM 10%

GOSSET
GRANDE RÉSERVE BRUT

Like Bollinger, Gosset ferments its fullest wines in cask and avoids malolactic to produce long-lived Champagnes that remain fresh. This smooth, classy and complex non-vintage Champagne would put many so-called prestige *cuvées* to shame.
PN 65%, CH 35%

GOSSET
GRAND MILLÉSIME BRUT

One of the finest vintage Champagnes, from the flagship *cuvée* of the oldest house in the region. It has great depth and finesse and ages gracefully for 30 years or more, when its complex aromas stun the senses.
PN 60%, CH 40%

GOSSET
GRAND MILLÉSIME BRUT ROSÉ

This superb vintage pink Champagne contains wines from 15 of the region's 17 *grands crus,* impeccably blended with red wine from Bouzy. The result is delicately coloured, bursting with voluptuous Pinot flavours.
PN 54%, CH 46%

ALFRED GRATIEN
BRUT

This vintage Champagne is fermented in cask, where the malolactic is avoided, and undergoes a second fermentation sealed with a cork, not a crown-cap. After 10 years, the wine has a rich, ultra-clean, toasty flavour that assumes a broader, biscuity character over the next two decades.
PN/PM 60-70%, CH 30-40%

HEIDSIECK & CO
MONOPOLE
DIAMANT BLEU

GM - This deluxe vintage Champagne is undersold at about two-thirds the price of the other prestige *cuvées,* yet its smooth texture, minuscule bubbles and great finesse regularly make it one of the greatest wines of its kind.
PN 50%, CH 50%

CHARLES HEIDSIECK
CUVÉE "CHAMPAGNE CHARLIE"
BRUT

GM - Named after Charles-Camille Heidsieck, whose flamboyant lifestyle on trips to the USA in the mid-nineteenth century earned him the nickname of "Champagne Charlie". An enchanting, elegant Champagne.
PN 50%, CH 50%

HENRIOT
CUVÉE BACCARAT BRUT

GM - An undersung prestige *cuvée,* this vintage Champagne is made entirely from the firm's own vineyards and consistently represents the classical combination of finesse and complexity that it is possible to achieve by blending.
CH 60%, PN 40%

HENRIOT
BRUT SOUVERAIN

GM - Now one of the most consistent non-vintage Champagnes on the market, the gently effervescing Henriot Brut Souverain is full, satisfying and mellow at the time it is released for sale, yet slowly improves if kept for a few years.
CH 50-60%, PN/PM 40-50%

JACQUART
LA CUVÉE RENOMMÉE DE
JACQUART ROSÉ

Jacquart cosmetically changed its status from *coopérative* to *négociant* in 1989, when the members became shareholders. The overall quality is very good, but this non-vintage prestige pink Champagne is truly exceptional and can be compared to Roederer. The base wine is as for Renommé (*blanc*), to which 15-20% red wine from Bouzy, Cumière and Ambonnay has been added.

JACQUESSON

These lavishly labelled Champagnes conform to no set style, having ranged from *blanc de blancs* to traditional blends, yet they all share a certain complexity derived from at least 15 years of yeast-contact and the freshness of being late-disgorged.
Variable

JACQUESSON BB BLANC DE BLANCS

Nearly all the wines from this small, quality-conscious house are superb, but Jacquesson's reputation rests firmly on its ability to produce one of the lightest and most delicious of *blanc de blancs* Champagnes that is available.
CH 100%

KRUG COLLECTION BRUT

GM - This label is used on "re-releases" of older vintages that have been kept in contact with the yeast. The real pleasure is to drink these majestic wines side by side with the same, normally disgorged, vintage.
PN 50%, CH 30%, PM 20%

KRUG GRANDE CUVÉE BRUT

GM - A blend of 40-50 different, cask-fermented wines from seven or eight vintages, Grande Cuvée is aged six years before being sold, yet requires a further four years to appreciate its classic oxidative character.
PN 50%, CH 35%, PM 15%

KRUG CLOS DU MESNIL BRUT BLANC DE BLANCS

GM - The style of this wine falls somewhere between that of Salon and Taittinger's Comtes de Champagne. It is an intensely flavoured, sometimes exotic, cask-fermented Champagne, and has a sort of strange finesse.
CH 100%

KRUG ROSÉ BRUT

GM - Krug produces a non-vintage pink Champagne, rather than a vintage, but the pale *blanc de noirs* colour reveals why, because it is a mature blend with an exquisite and immaculately preserved flavour.
PN 52%, CH 24%, PM 24%

KRUG VINTAGE BRUT

GM - Some Krug vintages are easier to drink earlier than others, but none has ever been near ready until at least 12 years old. They are all textbook wines, but the 1964 was a bit special.
PN 50%, CH 30%, PM 20%

LANSON BRUT

GM - Lanson vintages are often slow and unremarkable starters, but most manage, however, to develop a wonderful, discreetly-biscuity style: patience is always needed with any Champagne that does not go through malolactic fermentation.
PN 45%, CH 45%, PM 10%

LANSON 225TH ANNIVERSARY CUVÉE

GM - Launched in 1985 to celebrate Lanson's 225th anniversary, this vintage Champagne is one of the firm's two prestige *cuvées*. A deeply flavoured, yet elegant wine, it is made entirely from Lanson's vineyards.
CH 55%, PN 45%

LAURENT-PERRIER CUVÉE GRAND SIÈCLE BRUT

GM - This is a non-vintage blend of three years, except in the USA where it is a vintage. Both are delicious, but the blend has a biscuity finesse, while the vintage is less complex, with an exotic, tropical fruitiness.
PN 50%, CH 50%

LAURENT-PERRIER CUVÉE GRAND SIÈCLE ALEXANDRA BRUT ROSÉ

GM - Grand Siècle's pink sister was launched simultaneously with the 1982 vintage; it is a pale-coloured, ultra-refined classic that is made by skin-contact.
CH 75% (min.), PN 25% (max.)

LAURENT-PERRIER CUVÉE ULTRA BRUT

GM - The ultimate *cuvée* of this bone-dry style of Champagne, Ultra Brut has a generous five years' bottle-age, but needs another five years' cellarage to mellow out and show its class.
PN 55-65%, CH 35-45%

MOËT & CHANDON
BRUT IMPÉRIAL

GM - One hardly dares to imagine just how much Moët vintage is produced by this giant of the Champagne trade, yet - amazingly - the quality is consistently excellent. This is a wine that can be purchased without a worry anywhere at all.
PM 40-50%, PN 30-40%, CH 20-30%

MOËT & CHANDON
COTEAUX CHAMPENOIS
SARAN
BLANC DE BLANCS

GM - Grapes used for this still white wine come from the same vineyards as those of Dom Pérignon. Although non-vintage, the style does vary from soft and buttery to firm and fruity in a similar way to a vintage.
CH 100%

MOËT ET CHANDON
CUVÉE DOM PÉRIGNON
BRUT

GM - The name of the most prestigious Champagne in the world once belonged to Mercier, but was purchased by Moët in 1930 and used, even years later, on Champagne's first commercial prestige *cuvée* - Dom Pérignon 1921.
PN 50%, CH 50%

MOËT ET CHANDON
CUVÉE DOM PÉRIGNON
ROSÉ BRUT

GM - The first vintage was 1959 and it was produced exclusively for the Shah of Iran to celebrate 2,000 years of the Persian Empire. It was not until 1970 that the 1962, the first commercial *cuvée*, was released.
PN 60%, CH 40%

MUMM DE CRAMANT
BLANC DE BLANCS
BRUT

GM - This non-vintage *cuvée* (formerly known as Crémant de Cramant) can occasionally disappoint, but when it is on form it is one of the most deliciously fresh and creamy, early-drinking *blanc de blancs* Champagnes available.
CH 100%

MUMM DE MUMM
BRUT

GM - Mumm's first prestige vintage *cuvée*, René Lalou, was perceived to be out of step with modern trends, although excellent and gracefully rich in quality, so the firm launched this lighter and more refined version.
PN 50%, CH 50%

BRUNO PAILLARD
BRUT

Bruno Paillard was the first new house in Champagne since the rise of Salon in the 1920s. The 1985 is Bruno Paillard's first true vintage, although he offers a remarkable range of older Champagnes that are produced by others under his own label.
CH 100%

BRUNO PAILLARD
PREMIÈRE CUVÉE BRUT

Not only is young Bruno Paillard passionate about quality, he is also a very sharp businessman. No sooner had Moët dropped the name Première Cuvée from their UK non-vintage brand, than Paillard adopted it worldwide for his.
PM 45%, PN 35%, CH 25%

JOSEPH PERRIER
CUVÉE ROYALE

GM - Some vintages of this *cuvée*, such as the 1982, start out deceptively lacklustre, but they fill out after a couple of years in bottle, when they begin to attain their true class. They all age gracefully.
PN 60%, CH 40%

PERRIER-JOUËT

PERRIER-JOUËT BELLE EPOQUE

PERRIER-JOUËT BELLE EPOQUE ROSÉ

GM - Some critics say that more effort goes into the production of this ornately-enamelled bottle than the vintage Champagne itself, but this is classic stuff, although it takes at least 10 years before it shows its true colours.
PN 60%, CH 40%

GM - There can be no presentation that is more stunning than this, with the late-nineteenth-century enamel design fired into clear glass, enhanced by the pink wine inside. The lingering flavour of this vintage pink Champagne is unique.
PN 60%, CH 40%

PERRIER-JOUËT BLASON DE FRANCE

GM - This consistently superior non-vintage Champagne is fresh, exciting, easy-to-drink and not lacking in finesse. Like all Perrier-Jouët wines, the Chardonnay grape dominates far more than its content in the blend would suggest.
PN 40%, CH 40%, PM 20%

PERRIER-JOUËT RÉSERVE CUVÉE BRUT

GM - This great house was founded by the uncle of Joseph Perrier, who combined his name with that of this wife. The vintage Champagnes of the house are always impeccable reflections of the character of the year, yet very Perrier-Jouët.
PN/PM 70%, CH 30%

PHILIPPONNAT CLOS DES GOISSES BRUT

A so-called south-south facing vineyard capable of producing vintage wine in years as miserable as 1951. Because of its sun-trap aspect, it is 1 per cent higher in alcohol than most other Champagnes and takes at least 10 years to mature.
PN 70%, CH 30%

PHILIPPONNAT RÉSERVE ROSÉ BRUT

This skin-contact, non-vintage pink Champagne is Philipponnat's basic non-vintage Réserve Brut to which a little red wine from the Clos des Goisses vineyard has been added, turning something very decent into pure hedonistic delight.
PN 42%, PM 36%, CH 22%

PHILIPPONNAT ROYALE RÉSERVE BRUT

The soft-styled mousse of all Philipponnat Champagnes is justifiably well-known and the fine, seductive flavour of this basic non-vintage is an indication of the unsung heights to which its upmarket wines aspire.
Fine quality, great value.
PM 40%, PN 35%, CH 25%

PIPER-HEIDSIECK BRUT EXTRA

GM - Piper's non-vintage is classic, but because it does not go through malolactic, it can seem a bit pedestrian when first released. If kept for a couple of years, however, the breeding and finesse become evident.
PN 40%, CH 30%, PM 30%

PIPER-HEIDSIECK RARE

GM - The 1976 vintage was the first of this prestige *cuvée*, which was launched in 1985 to celebrate the 200th anniversary of the founding of Piper-Heidsieck. Made entirely from *grand cru* wines, it is the epitome of finesse and elegance.
CH 60%, PN 40%

POL ROGER BRUT

GM - The fine fruity flavour of this vintage wine is a joy to drink as soon as it is released, yet will gradually develop over many decades a sublime and lingering complexity.
PN 40-50%, CH 40-50%, PM 0-20%

POL ROGER CHARDONNAY

GM - Perversely, a house that is so famous for its Pinot-dominated *cuvées* also produces one of the finest *blanc de blancs* vintage Champagnes; 1975 and 1982 were particularly special.
CH 100%

POL ROGER RÉSERVE SPÉCIALE PR

GM - Quietly undersold by Pol Roger, while it concentrates on promoting its Cuvée Sir Winston Churchill, this richer, more Pinot-influenced vintage wine is, however, one of the finest Champagnes produced.
PN 50%, CH 50%

POL ROGER CUVÉE SIR WINSTON CHURCHILL

GM - This remarkable wine is the finest prestige *cuvée* launched in recent times. The first vintage was 1975 and was produced only in magnums. As the great man himself once said, "I am easily satified with the best".

POMMERY LOUISE POMMERY ROSÉ

GM - The pink Louise Pommery was launched in 1988 and quickly established itself as one of the five best Champagnes of this type available. The pale colour of this delicate and delicious wine is obtained by skin-contact.
CH 54%, PN 46%

POMMERY CUVÉE SPÉCIALE LOUISE POMMERY

GM - This prestige vintage *cuvée* has a low dosage, but the exquisite quality and finesse of the wine from Pommery's *grand cru* vineyards provides the "sweetness" of ripe fruit, that belies the fact that it is actually very dry, as are all the wines from this house.
PN 60%, CH 40%

LOUIS ROEDERER BLANC DE BLANCS BRUT

GM - Not one of Roederer's most frequently-encountered *cuvées*, this pure Chardonnay vintage Champagne is, however, one of its most successful. Made entirely from *grand cru* wines, the style is that of a gentle *crémant*.
CH 100%

LOUIS ROEDERER BRUT PREMIER

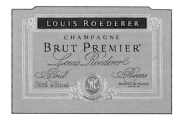

GM - This is the most consistent of the finest non-vintage Champagnes available. It has a ripe and voluptous bouquet and a succulent, not too dry flavour, with an unmistakable touch of class.
PN 66%, CH 34%

LOUIS ROEDERER
CRISTAL BRUT

GM - Made originally in 1876 for Tsar Alexander II, this vintage Champagne is produced almost every year, although the poorer the year the more rigorous the selection - thus even in 1974 and 1977 Cristal is great.
PN 55-60%, CH 40-45%

LOUIS ROEDERER
CRISTAL BRUT ROSÉ

GM - This very fine, skin-contact wine is an admirable pink partner to Louis Roederer's original prestige *cuvée*. It is a refined wine that has compact fruit and excellent potential longevity, it also looks stunning in Cristal's clear bottle.
PN 70%, CH 30%

DOM RUINART
BLANC DE BLANCS

GM - The quality difference between Ruinart and Dom Ruinart is so vast that it is almost as if the wines come from two houses. This *cuvée* ranks as one of the finest *blanc de blancs*.
CH 100%

DOM RUINART
BRUT ROSÉ

GM - Although the original Dom Ruinart is classic, it is arguable that this beautifully balanced, vintage pink Champagne, which is made by blending in a little red wine from Bouzy, is relatively superior for its type.
PN 50%, CH 50%

A. SALON
BRUT S
BLANC DE BLANCS

GM - Only made three or four times every 10 years from Chardonnay grown at Le Mesnil. No malolactic is allowed in this very special wine, which requires at least 10 years to start drinking and may take up to 50 years to peak.
CH 100%

TAITTINGER
COMTES DE CHAMPAGNE
BLANC DE BLANCS BRUT

GM - One of the three best *blanc de blancs* Champagnes of the *vin de garde* style, this wine sometimes has the creamy-vanilla undertones of new oak, lending an exotic character to its intense Chardonnay flavour.
CH 100%

TAITTINGER
COMTES DE CHAMPAGNE
ROSÉ BRUT

GM - This fine pink Champagne needs at least eight years to blossom, which explains why it may seem one-dimensional when it is first released. The dosage is rather noticeable in its youth, but eventually it marries perfectly.
PN 100%

DE VENOGE
BRUT VINTAGE

The blue *cordon* indicates the Swiss origins of this house, representing the de Venoge river in that country. All the wines made by this house represent good value, but the vintage is not simply a bargain, it is also extremely fine in quality.
CH 60%, PN 40%

DE VENOGE
ROSÉ BRUT CRÉMANT

This wine is just as delightful as its *belle époque* poster-inspired label. It was introduced when de Venoge was under the helm of Paul Bergeot, who used to be in charge of Besserat de Bellefon (which built its reputation on *crémant*) - hence the success of this particular wine.
CH 85%, PN 15%

VEUVE CLICQUOT
LA GRANDE DAME

GM - The top Champagne of this great house is made entirely from those vineyards that originally belonged to Madame Clicquot. Although often forgotten when prestige *cuvées* are discussed, it ranks with the very best.
CPN 60-70%, CH 30-40%

ALSACE

WINES HAVE BEEN MADE in Alsace since the Roman times and exported down the Rhine since the sixteenth century. But they are not wines that make any concessions to changes in popular taste: they are wines for the discerning and as such fit very suitably into a compilation of classic wines.

Style of the wines

With one exception, all Alsace wines are offered under the varietal name of the grapes used - the noble varieties - Riesling, Gewürztraminer, Tokay Pinot Gris, Muscat, Sylvaner, Pinot Blanc and Pinot Noir. Except for the derivatives of the Pinot Noir all the wines are white and dry. The grape varieties are principally German, the style of wine-making is undoubtedly French. It is perhaps understandable if many non-French wine-lovers fail to be immediately attracted by a dry Riesling, let alone a Gewürztraminer or Muscat, which sound as if they should be German and sweet. The French themselves have no problem. Alsace supplies them with approaching half of the white AC wine they consume.

Emergence of the appellation

Appellation Controlée status for the region was only acquired in 1962, and it was not until the 1980s that the important further step of selecting the 50 of the better sites as *grands crus* could be completed and formally promulgated. The late evolution to AOC status provided the opportunity for the Alsace wine industry to establish a strict code of rules for its wine production. A single Alsace appellation covers the whole of the region. Where wines come from a *grand cru* vineyard that name is incorporated in the appellation. So a Riesling wine from the great Schoenenburg vineyard at Riquewihr can announce itself as "Appellation Alsace Schoenenburg Controlée" or "Appellation Grand Cru Controlée" (with the name of the vineyard elsewhere on the label). All Alsace wines have to be bottled in the region, and must be 100 per cent of the wine of the year on the label.

Climatic influences The vineyards lie on the eastern slopes of the Vosges mountains and form a natural barrier against the wet Atlantic weather, making the hinterland of Colmar, the heartland of the Alsace vineyard, the driest area in Central Europe. The combination of sunshine and mists in late autumn can induce a botrytis condition that lends its superb lusciousness and flavour to the Sélection de Grains Nobles wines, and sometimes to the Vendange Tardive.

The most remarkable feature of development in the Alsace vineyard over the last 50 years has been the dramatic increase in the plantings of the noble varieties, which, from being less than 5 per cent, now account for some 85 per cent of the total. As always, some varieties are more equal than others, and the star of the galaxy is undoubtedly the Riesling, which is closely followed by Tokay and Gwürztraminer. These varieties are superbly suited to the remarkable *Vendange Tardive* and *Sélection de Grains Nobles* wines (see the table of wine

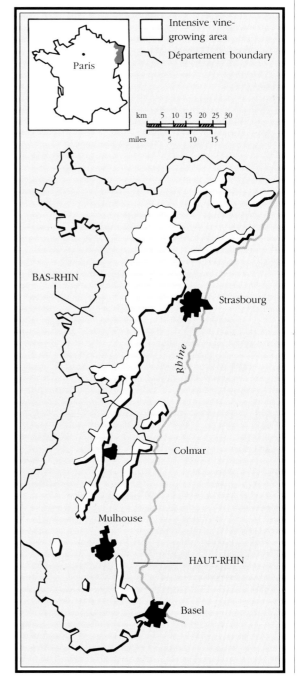

styles below) that are made in exceptional years. Together with Muscat, they make up the four varieties that are currently allowed to be sold as *grand cru* wines.

Development potential

Sylvaner and Pinot Blanc are normally vinified for early drinking as fresh young wines. Riesling and Gewürztraminer too can appear on reputable wine merchants' lists for immediate drinking within 12 months of the harvest. But more usually they will be two-year-old wines. It is clear however that all the better wines are designed to take somewhat longer than that to mature and develop. Riesling is the obvious candidate for ageing, but Tokay often demands even more time than Riesling. Even the humble Edelzwicker - see Cave Coopérative Ribeauvillé Clos du Zahnacker - can have a surprising development potential. The capacity for ageing derives from the character and robustness of the wines, and is not dependent on the assistance of lengthy barrel maturing in oak. Often the ripeness of the fruit can produce potential alcohol levels of as much as 16 per cent to 17 per cent and higher. The finest wines can have a normal life expectancy of up to 20 years, or more.

Structure of the industry

The wines selected here as classic examples come mostly from two dozen or so houses, from the large and prestigious like Dopff & Irion, Hugel and Schlumberger, and from small but impressive firms like André Kientzler and Marc Kreydenweiss. In fact, 6,300 proprietors own and work 12,000 or so hectares (31,000 acres) of the Alsace vineyard. Their output is either bought by the larger houses under contract or vinified in a cooperative; the latter being particularly important in Alsace.

VINTAGES

YEAR	CHARACTER
1988	A fine vintage in which some excellent late-harvest wines were made.
1987	A reasonable-sized harvest of AC and Grand Cru wines of just under 1 million hectolitres. Some very good quality *Vendange Tardive* wines in small amounts, but very little *Sélection de Grains Nobles*.
1986	The ideal combination of mists and sun in the late autumn made possible some excellent botrytized late-harvest wines, both *Vendange Tardive* and *Sélection de Grains Nobles*. A big harvest of easy-to-drink, early maturing AC wines.
1985	A smaller than usual harvest, but well balanced wines of good concentration, and extremely high overall quality. A good year for Gewürztraminer from a smaller crop, for Riesling and Tokay and for unbotrytized late-harvest wines.
1984	On the whole a year to drink young. Few wines for longer keeping.
1983	A superb vintage producing grapes of excellent ripeness and big, powerful, full-of-fruit wines that will need time to age. A feast of late-picked *Vendange Tardive* and *Sélection de Grains Nobles* offerings in a profusion not seen since 1976. Good botrytis. Riesling, Gewürztraminer and Tokay particularly successful.
1982	A permitted increased *rendement* of up to 130 hectolitres per hectare, nearly one third up on the norm, produced a very large vintage with many wines lacking sufficient concentration. Some good Rieslings and *Vendange Tardive* wines from better producers.

WINE STYLES

Crémant d'Alsace AOC	A separate appellation for sparkling wines made by the traditional method - as used in Champagne - mainly from Pinot Blanc, although Chardonnay, Riesling and Tokay Pinot Gris can also be used.
Edelzwicker	A blended wine, intended to be solely from noble grape varieties, made for drinking young. Usually principally composed of Pinot Blanc or Sylvaner, with perhaps a little Riesling to give character, and a little Gewürztraminer to give perfume.
Sélection de Grains Nobles	An extension of the Alsace appellation brought about in 1983, with the *Vendange Tardive*, for the wines produced in botrytis-affected years, from ripe, late-harvested berries. *Sélection de Grains Nobles* must have a minimum potential alcohol level of 14.3 per cent for Riesling and Muscat and 16.4 per cent for Gewürztraminer and Tokay Pinot Gris. The natural sugar levels in the ripe grapes in a good year can easily exceed these figures. Chaptalization is not allowed. Such wines are capable of lasting 100 years.
Vendange Tardive	Literally, late-harvested grapes. The wine, as with *Sélection de Grains Nobles*, can be made from one of four noble varieties. It must have a minimum potential alcohol level of 12.9 per cent for Riesling and Muscat and 14.3 per cent for Gewürztraminer and Tokay. The resulting wine, depending on the ripeness of the fruit, can be off-dry or sweet.

ADAM
RIESLING KAEFFERKOPF CUVÉE JEAN-BAPTISTE

Kaefferkopf is a vineyard that is traditionally famous for its blend of Gewürztraminer and one or two other grapes, usually Riesling. This wine, however, is pure Riesling and the 1983 vintage was one of 17 Alsace wines selected by *Institut National des Appellations d'Origine* in 1985 to celebrate its 50th anniversary.

JEAN BECKER
MUSCAT FROEHN

GC - Froehn is a south-south-west-facing slope that belongs to the hilltop village of Zellenberg and is reputed for its rich, long-lived Muscats. Since the late 1980s, Jean Becker has dramatically reduced his yields, concentrating the flavour and raising the quality of his wines. They are also sold under the Gaston Beck label on some markets.

LÉON BEYER
GEWÜRZTRAMINER CUVÉE DES COMTES D'EGUISHEIM

The wine sold under this evocatively rich label is the best Gewürztraminer produced by Beyer, one of the greatest houses of Alsace. Although not mentioned, the wine is made exclusively from the firm's *grand cru* Eichberg vineyards.

LÉON BEYER
RIESLING CUVÉE PARTICULIÈRE

This house does not share the *grand cru* philosophy, believing that the skill of the grower and winemaker is more relevant to the current quality of a wine. Thus there is no clue that the ripe flavours, great length and supreme finesse of this, Beyer's top Riesling, are unadulterated *grand cru* Pfersigberg.

LÉON BEYER
TOKAY PINOT GRIS
SÉLECTION DE GRAINS NOBLES

The consistent quality of this wine illustrates that Beyer has a profound understanding of the dessert-wine style, especially for a house with a reputation for totally dry wines. The enormous acidity in the 1986 vintage promises to keep it fresh for at least 20 years.

BLANCK
GEWÜRZTRAMINER FURSTENTUM

GC - Vines have been cultivated on the fairly steep, south-south-east-facing slope of Furstentum, which extends from Kientzheim into Sigolsheim, since at least 1330. Blanck owns more than 20 per cent of this *grand cru* and his Gewürztraminer is fabulously rich as well as beautifully balanced.

BLANCK
GEWÜRZTRAMINER FURSTENTUM
VENDANGES TARDIVES

GC - Furstentum's heat-retaining, stony-structure makes it ideal for late harvesting, while the calcareous nature of its soil encourages relatively higher acidity levels. Blanck harnesses these factors to produce wines of great finesse and concentration.

BLANCK
RIESLING FURSTENTUM
VIEILLES VIGNES

GC - Despite the huge success of Gewürztraminer, this *grand cru* is best suited to Riesling, provided the vines are mature. Blanck's Vieilles Vignes is typically complete and concentrated, with lots of acidity and often a slight *pétillance*.

BLANCK RIESLING SCHLOSSBERG

GC - Initially fatter and more aromatic than Furstentum, Blanck's Riesling from the south-east facing Schlossberg, a vineyard that covers part of Kaysersberg and Kientzheim, acquires firmness with age and always shows great finesse and complexity, even in generally poor years.

BLANCK
TOKAY PINOT GRIS
ALTENBOURG

Tokay Pinot Gris and Blanck are both well-known for the richness of their wines, yet none of Blanck's Tokay Pinot Gris are so rich as to lack finesse. Given five to eight years, Blanck's Altenbourg mellows into a perfection of honeyed fruit.

BOECKEL
SYLVANER ZOTZENBERG

The gently sloping, basin-shaped Zotzenberg vineyard in Mittel-bergheim has been famous for its Sylvaner for more than 600 years. True *grand cru* quality, but the system refuses to recognize Sylvaner, thus it cannot claim this status while other less traditional varieties can.

DOMAINE MARCEL DEISS
RIESLING
ALTENBERG DE BERGHEIM

GC - Of the three Altenberg *grands crus*, this one is fully south-facing with a great viticultural potential that has been exploited since the twelfth century. On its marly-limestone soil, Jean-Michel Deiss achieves Rieslings with concentrated and tangy fruit.

DOMAINE MARCEL DEISS
RIESLING
BERGHEIM ENGELGARTEN

Jean-Michel Deiss is one of the most passionate winemakers in the region. Totally dedicated to producing wines that express their *terroir*, Jean-Michel achieves an exuberance of aroma and elegance from this Riesling, which is grown on Bergheim's marly-clay soil.

DOPFF "AU MOULIN"
CRÉMANT D'ALSACE BRUT
CUVÉE BARTHOLDI

From the master of *crémant* this *cuvée* was launched in 1986 to celebrate the Statue of Liberty (sculpted by Alsace-born Auguste Bartholdi 100 years earlier). It is Champagne-like in structure yet utterly Alsatian in style.
PB 100%

DOPFF "AU MOULIN"
CRÉMANT D'ALSACE BRUT
BLANC DE NOIRS

Although the Crémant d'Alsace AOC was introduced as recently as 1976, Dopff "Au Moulin" made a commercial success of this style of wine as long ago as 1900. This is its top-of-the-range *crémant*. Rich and complex, it has fine autolytic character and an underlying hint of mint.
PN 100%

DOPFF "AU MOULIN"
GEWÜRZTRAMINER
BRAND DE TURCKHEIM

GC - Although perceived as a sparkling wine specialist, there is always a twinkle in Pierre-Etienne Dopff's eye whenever anyone discovers just how good Dopff domaine varietal wines are. Because Brand is a sun-trap, this wine can approach a *Vendange Tardive* style in some years.

DOPFF "AU MOULIN"
RIESLING SCHOENENBURG

GC - The fully south-facing slope of Riquewihr's Schoenenburg is fairly steep and stony, with high limestone content. It has been famous for Riesling since the Middle Ages. Dopff's own domaine Riesling from this vineyard has a deep and sustained flavour and a fine, racy style.

DOPFF & IRION
MUSCAT "LES AMANDIERS"

This firm shares the same origins as that of its cousins Dopff "Au Moulin" just down the road, but differs on the issue of *grands crus*, which is why there is no indication that this is 100 per cent pure Schoenenburg. The delicate and graceful features of this wine are best appreciated with food, especially fresh asparagus.

DOPFF & IRION
RIESLING "LES MURAILLES"

The grapes for this wine come partly from the Schoenenburg vineyard and partly from neighbouring Zellenberg; *les murailles* refer to the defensive walls that surrounded the fortified town of Riquewihr. The fine, flowery elegance of the wine is a perfect statement of Dopff and Irion's philosophy to seek finesse, rather than weight or size.

DOPFF & IRION
GEWÜRZTRAMINER
"LES SORCIÈRES"

This picturesque vineyard is a far cry from the gory origins of the name of the wine, which refers to witches being burnt at the stake. The wine is the richest of all Dopff and Irion wines, but never blowzy - not even in a year like 1976, when the pepper and liquorice intensity developed into delicious, sweet-spice flavours.

HUGEL
PINOT NOIR JUBILÉE HUGEL
RÉSERVE PERSONNELLE

The Jubilée Hugel range was introduced in 1989 to mark the 350th anniversary of this remarkable family firm. Only the ripest years are used for this wine, making it one of the darkest Pinot Noirs in Alsace. The wine is matured in small oak barrels - contrary to usual Hugel philosophy.

HUGEL
RIESLING
VENDANGE TARDIVE

It was Jean Hugel that made late-harvest wines famous in Alsace and eventually persuaded the authorities to introduce legislation to control its production. This particular wine is produced in only the best vintages, some four to six weeks after the start of the normal harvest. Its complex flavours require at least 10 years to achieve an exquisite harmony.

HUGEL
GEWÜRZTRAMINER
SÉLECTION DE GRAINS NOBLES

Late-harvested at about the same time as Hugel's *Vendange Tardive*, but from selected botrytized grapes, this is a succulent, concentrated and impeccably balanced wine with an almost unlimited lifespan.

HUGEL
TOKAY PINOT GRIS
VENDANGE TARDIVE

One of the most classic renditions of late-harvested Tokay Pinot Gris. Given eight years in bottle, its honeyed, nutty richness makes an ideal companion to the local *foie gras*.

CAVE COOP. DE KIENTZHEIM-
KAYSERSBERG
CRÉMANT D'ALSACE

This *coopérative* has a reputation for selling mature vintage *crémant*. The wines are given between four and five years yeast-contact and have a full, rich and ripe autolytic character.
PB 100%

ANDRÉ KIENTZLER
AUXERROIS
ELEVÉ EN FÛTS DE CHÊNE

It was with this wine that André Kientzler became the first winemaker in Alsace to achieve a good balance between fruit and wood. While wines aged in new oak will never challenge the pure varietal characteristics that have built this region's reputation, there should always be experiments and room for the Kientzlers of this world.

ANDRÉ KIENTZLER
RIESLING OSTERBERG
VIN DE GLACE

GC - The steep, east-south-east-facing slope of this *grand cru* in Ribeauvillé was once the property of the Seigneurs de Ribeaupierre. Its stony-clay soil has long been famous for producing long-lived Riesling that develop the classic "petrolly" bouquet, but Kientzler's *vin de glâce*, a sort of *Eiswein* equivalent, is a unique phenomenon in France.

DOMAINES KLIPFEL
GEWÜRZTRAMINER CLOS ZISSER

GC - Totally owned by Klipfel, Clos Zisser is part of the Kirchberg de Barr, a steep, south-east facing *grand cru* slope that has been renowned since 1760. The marly-limestone soil of Clos Zisser is ideal for Gewürztraminer, the wines of which are delicate and fruity.

MARC KREYDENWEISS
KRITT SYLVANER
ELEVÉ EN FUTS DE CHÊNE

At about the same time as André Kientzler perfected the marriage between the fruit of Alsace wines and wood, Marc Kreydenweiss was not far behind with this oak-aged Sylvaner. This grape may be one of the least likely with which to conduct oak-ageing experiments, yet its somewhat neutral character lends itself surprisingly well.

MARC KREYDENWEISS
MUSCAT CLOS REBGARTEN

This wine is 100 per cent pure Muscat Ottonel, grown on a slope overlooking Andlau. Its floral, apricot-skin aroma is followed through on the palate with fragrant, apricot-flavoured fruit and fine acidity.

KUEHN TOKAY PINOT GRIS

Kuehn prides itself on its three top wines: the Kaefferkopf, its St Hubert Gewürztraminer (which can have a most incredible bouquet in ripe years, such as 1983), and Baron de Schiélé Riesling, yet it is its generic Tokay that consistently deserves plaudits.

KUENTZ-BAS
CRÉMANT D'ALSACE
BRUT DE CHARDONNAY

One of only two pure Chardonnay sparkling wines in Alsace and easily the best. It would not be good for the character of Alsace wines if the Chardonnay became too popular, but the right to make such a rich, ripe and tangy oddity should be defended.

KUENTZ-BAS
GEWÜRZTRAMINER
CUVÉE JÉRÉMY
SÉLECTION DE GRAINS NOBLES

Only produced in exceptional years, the quantity of this botrytis wine is minute - never more than 100 cases.
The 1983 vintage was almost Californian in its rich pie-juice flavours and will need 20 years to peak.

KUENTZ-BAS
MUSCAT D'ALSACE
RÉSERVE PERSONNELLE

The instant appeal of this wine comes from the easy drinking, fresh and floral fruit of the Muscat Ottonel - 80 per cent of the blend. The balance is Vieux Muscat à Grains Rouges, which contributes complexity and finesse.

KUENTZ-BAS
TOKAY PINOT GRIS
CUVÉE CAROLINE
VENDANGE TARDIVE

Unlike some producers, who harvest *Vendange Tardive* no later than normal, Kuentz-Bas always leave it until mid- to late-November. The style may be off-dry or medium-sweet, depending on the vintage, but the wine is always a stunning balance between intensity and finesse.

LAUGEL
PINOT NOIR DE MARLENHEIM

Laugel is not one of the classic producers of Alsace, but it does hide some very well-made wines behind its value-for-money reputation and is the largest producer of Pinot Noir de Marlenheim, a wine that has been famous since the sixteenth century.

GUSTAVE LORENTZ
RIESLING
ALTENBERG DE BERGHEIM

GC - This wine comes from the same south-facing, marly-limestone slope as the Riesling of Marcel Deiss. It always seems riper, richer and more mellow, yet it has the same elegance and vibrancy. The 1976 was one of the finest Alsace Rieslings of that hot vintage, yet it was rejected by the tasting committee and refused its AOC. It scraped through only after it had been entered a second time.

GUSTAVE LORENTZ
TOKAY-PINOT GRIS
CUVÉE PARTICULIÈRE

Tokay-Pinot Gris is a wine that suits the rich style of Gustave Lorentz wines, but the Cuvée Particulière has more of everything - especially acidity, length and finesse.

JOS MEYER
GEWÜRZTRAMINER "HENGST"

GC - The Hengst is a fairly steep, south-east facing slope in Wintzen-heim with a dark calcareous scree over limey-marl. It produces one of the most fascinating Gewürztraminers in Alsace. Jos Meyer is a classic example - a wine that combines this grape's accepted character with the orange zest and rose-petal nuances that are reminiscent of the Muscat.

JOS MEYER
PINOT D'ALSACE
LES LUTINS

The fine, delicate lines of this elegant pure Pinot Blanc wine are accentu-ated by superb acidity, good fruit and a slight *pétillance*. A minor classic.

JOS MEYER
PINOT AUXERROIS "H"
VIEILLES VIGNES

This is, in fact, pure Hengst, but as the Auxerrois is not recognized as a *grand cru* variety, the wine cannot carry this status. If it was recognized, then the Hengst would be the greatest of Auxerrois *grands crus*, as this citrussy, racy wine testifies.

JOS MEYER
TOKAY PINOT GRIS
CUVÉE DU CENTENAIRE
VIEILLES VIGNES

The age of these vines is what gives the wine its intense varietal flavour and great acidity. If you want a textbook example of top quality Tokay Pinot Gris, this is it.

MURÉ
MUSCAT CLOS ST LANDELIN
VORBOURG

GC - Although the first mention of the Vorbourg, which extends from Rouf-fach into Westhalten, was more than 1,200 years ago, it is more of a *premier cru* than a *grand cru* and, within this context, it is the Riesling and Tokay Pinot Gris that fare best. This wine is, however, the exception - it is a true *grand cru* and Muscat. In the finest vintages this Muscat really does have the peach, apricot, mint and hazelnut complexity that all Vorbourg wines are supposed to possess.

MURÉ
PINOT-NOIR CLOS ST LANDELIN
VIEILLI EN PIÈCES DE CHÊNE

Chalky soil, low yields, 15 days' maceration on its skins and 11 months' maturation in small casks give this wine its dark colour, creamy-rich vanilla bouquet, excellent varietal character, soft, summer-fruit flavours and supple tannin structure.

MURÉ
GEWÜRZTRAMINER
ZINNKOEPFLÉ

GC - This vineyard covers parts of Westhalten and Soultzmatt and is so sun-blessed that it was the site of sun-worshippers in pagan times. Today it produces Gewürztraminer wines that are strong, spicy and fiery-flavoured.

DOMAINE OSTERTAG
PINOT BLANC

André Ostertag is busy getting to grips with many different styles - it is hard to predict which ones will be his forte. However, this deliciously fresh, ripe and tangy wine, with its attractive *pétillance,* is undeniably classic.

CAVE COOP. DE PFAFFENHEIM
HARTENBERGER PINOT GRIS
CRÉMANT D'ALSACE

This *coopérative* makes a large range of Crémant d'Alsace, every single one of which can be heartily recommended, although it is the Tokay Pinot Gris that excels because of the superb acidity that balances its intrinsic richness of fruit. Top quality.

CAVE COOP. DE PFAFFENHEIM
EDELZWICKER
MESSAGE D'ALSACE

Until the late 1980s, this wine was called Gentil d'Alsace, which was an old and noble name for Edelzwicker, a wine that has been devalued since the banning of Zwicker. The 1983 vintage was extraordinarily good - a truly great, blended wine. Recent vintages under the Message label have contained less Gewürztraminer and Tokay Pinot Gris and been much lighter in body, yet no less delicious.

PREISS-HENNY
GEWÜRZTRAMINER
CUVÉE CAMILLE PREISS

Preiss-Henny has been taken over by Léon Beyer, but some of its wines at least are still independently made by Hubert Preiss. The most precious possession of this house has always been its 2 hectares (5 acres) of *Grand Cru* Mandelberg in Mittelwihr, which has been famous since Gallo-Roman times and is where this delicate yet long-lived wine comes from.

CAVE COOP. DE RIBEAUVILLÉ
CLOS DU ZAHNACKER

Clos du Zahnacker is a single-site planted with equal quantities of Tokay Pinot Gris, Riesling and Gewürztraminer. It is technically an Edelzwicker, but a true *vin de garde,* capable of lasting 20 years or more. Proof that Edelzwicker can still be what it once was - a noble blend.

ROLLY GASSMANN
AUXERROIS MOENCHREBEN

If any two words can sum up the house-style of Rolly Gassmann, they are "supremely rich". Nearly all the wines are from its own domaine and are produced from relatively modest yields. In some years this wine can be almost Tokay Pinot Gris in its richness, but with an exotic, sometimes pineapply flavour.

ROLLY GASSMANN
GEWÜRZTRAMINER KAPPELWEG

This single-vineyard wine comes from Rorschwihr. It retains its youthful banana aroma for several years, yet an almost *Vendange Tardive* richness of sweet, ripe fruit on the palate is revealed from an early age.

ROLLY GASSMANN
MUSCAT D'ALSACE
MOENCHREBEN

Even in great years, Rolly Gassmann manages to achieve a nice balance between the richness of its house style and the fresh, floral fragrance of the Muscat's true varietal character. Drink very young.
  MBPG 67%, MO 33%

ROLLY GASSMANN
SYLVANER

A touch of *pétillance* lifts the balance of this surprisingly full and delicious wine. Given four or five years, Rolly Gassmann proves that Sylvaner can be a stylish wine in great vintages.

ROLLY GASSMANN
TOKAY PINOT GRIS

Take the richness of Rolly Gass-mann's house-style and apply it to the voluptuously concentrated fruit found naturally in the Tokay Pinot Gris and the result is outstanding. In a big year such as 1983, their *réserve* wine was almost Sauternes-like.

DOMAINES SCHLUMBERGER
GEWÜRZTRAMINER
CUVÉE ANNE SCHLUMBERGER

Made in exceptional years, when an Oechsle level of 125° or more can be achieved, this *cuvée* always has an extraordinarily elegant balance for such a big and concentrated wine. Great finesse and complexity. By 1989 only four vintages had been produced: 1964, 1971, 1976 and 1988.

DOMAINES SCHLUMBERGER
GEWÜRZTRAMINER
CUVÉE CHRISTINE
SCHLUMBERGER

The top of Schlumberger's range in all years except those rare vintages when Cuvée Anne is produced, this late-harvest wine has an Oechsle of around 115°. It has a very full, smooth and spicy flavour that is often lifted by a slight *pétillance*.

DOMAINES SCHLUMBERGER
RIESLING KITTERLÉ

GC - Kitterlé is a very steep, south, south-east and south-west facing slope in Guebwiller, in the south of the region. One of the truly famous *grands crus* of Alsace, although, ironically, renowned for its Clevner or Pinot Blanc wines, which are not allowed this status. Domaine Schlumberger's Riesling, however, shows great finesse.

DOMAINES SCHLUMBERGER
PINOT BLANC

The ripe, almost exotic Auxerrois flavour is beautifully balanced by the acidity of the Pinot Blanc, which itself is enhanced by a slight *pétillance*, making this about as classic as can be achieved with this style of wine.
PB 50%, AUX 50%

DOMAINES SCHLUMBERGER
RIESLING SAERING

GC - Situated beneath Kessler and Kitterlé (Guebwiller's other two *grands crus),* its softly-sloping vineyard, with its stony siliceous soil over calcareous-marl, has been well regarded since the mid-thirteenth century. Schlumberger's Saering Riesling is fine, floral and fruity.

PIERRE SPARR
GEWÜRZTRAMINER
TÊTE DE CUVÉE
SPARR PRESTIGE

This decadently rich wine is the result of a superb blend of two *grands crus*, Brand of Turckheim and Mambourg of Sigolsheim. Despite the immediacy of its attraction, this wine is one that is built to last.

PIERRE SPARR
PINOT BLANC RÉSERVE
DIAMANT D'ALSACE

A rich, off-dry, classy Pinot Blanc with a good length of true varietal character and an elegant finish.

TRIMBACH
GEWÜRZTRAMINER
CUVÉE DES SEIGNEURS DE
RIBEAUPIERRE

The style of this house is an uncom-promising one. Production techniques involve the prevention of the malolactic, which often results in wines that appear hard, lean and acidic in their youth, but invariably produce wines designed to last. The Gewürztraminer is a deep, powerfully constructed, full and pungently spicy wine that gradually develops a citrussy, terpene-rich finish.

TRIMBACH RIESLING CUVÉE FRÉDÉRIC ÉMILE

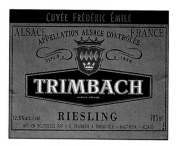

Because Trimbach's number two Riesling would be a great top-of-the-range Riesling at any other house, it makes better sense to view it as the second-best Riesling of Alsace, rather than of this house. It is similar in style to Clos Ste Hune, but broader in character and quicker to develop, although it will improve for 25 years or more.

TRIMBACH RIESLING CLOS STE HUNE

Named after a small plot located within the *grand cru* vineyard of Rosacker - Hunawihr - Clos Ste Hune is the greatest Riesling produced in Alsace. Occasionally another Riesling may, due to exceptional circumstances, approach its giddy heights of quality, but none ever surpass it. The wine takes at least eight years for even a hint of its incomparable class and breeding to show through.

CAVE COOP. DE TURCKHEIM GEWÜRZTRAMINER BRAND

GC - Brand is a sun-trap in Turckheim where, so legend goes, a battle took place between the sun and a local dragon. The sun burnt the dragon to the ground and the brand remains to this day. Brand Gewürztraminer is one of the most powerful wines of Alsace - full-blown yet fine flavoured.

CAVE COOP. DE TURCKHEIM PINOT NOIR D'ALSACE CUVÉE À L'ANCIENNE

This village was once famous for a red wine known as "Turksblood". It also has one of the three finest *coopératives* in Alsace and this special *cuvée* is consistently one of the region's most delicate, fine and utterly pure renditions of Pinot Noir.

DOMAINE WEINBACH MUSCAT

Since the death of her well-loved husband, Théo, the amazing Colette Faller has run this property. Truly a *grande dame* like the great widows of Champagne, Madame Faller's magical touch has brought Domaine Weinbach an unprecedented reputation and this classic, flowery Muscat is a particular favourite of hers.
MBPG 35%, MRPG 35%, MO 30%

DOMAINE WEINBACH RIESLING CUVÉE STE CATHERINE

Picked on or about Ste Cathérine's day - 25 November - this is always a true late-harvest wine, although, technically, the sugar level of its grapes might not qualify for *Vengange Tardive* status. A wine of great intensity and finesse.

DOMAINE WEINBACH RIESLING SCHLOSSBERG

GC - The south-east facing Schlossberg is a steep, terraced vineyard with a mineral-rich soil that covers part of Kaysersberg and Kientzheim. Compare Faller's wine with Blanck's to discover two entirely different styles, although they share the same concentration, complexity and finesse, plus the ability to excel even in poor years.

DOMAINE WEINBACH TOKAY PINOT GRIS QUINTESSENCE DE GRAINS NOBLES, CUVÉE D'OR

Sélection de Grains Noble is one of the most amazing categories of wines produced in the world, but Madame Faller's Quintessence is a class apart. The 1983 vintage of this Quintessence is one of the greatest Alsace wines ever made. Sublime now, its age, origin and potential longevity will still confound experts in the middle of the twenty-first century.

DOMAINE WEINBACH TOKAY PINOT GRIS VENDANGES TARDIVES

Rich and honeyed, with a little smoky complexity, this has some residual sweetness, although it is so overwhelmed by the high extract and fine acidity that it is almost unnoticeable.

DOMAINE WILLM
GEWÜRZTRAMINER
CLOS GAENSBROENNEL WILLM

GC - This is to Willm what Clos Zisser is to Klipfel. Both are totally owned sites within the Kirchberg de Barr, a *grand cru* renowned for the delicacy of its Gewürztraminer. Clos Gaensbroennel produces wine that is noted for the creamy elegance of its fruit.

WOLFBERGER
RIESLING CUVÉE ARMOURÉE

Wolfberger is the brand name for the *coopérative* at Eguisheim, the largest producer in Alsace. Cuvée Armourée is beautifully presented in the taller-sized bottles that were once traditional for this region, and the wines are skilfully chosen to portray the classic characteristics of their variety.

WOLFBERGER
ROUGE D'ALSACE

Noak's cartoon may seem somewhat frivolous for what is consistently one of the best red Pinot Noir wines this region produces, but Noak the artist is as revered in Alsace as the wine should be everywhere else.

WOLFBERGER
LA LOUVE DE WOLFBERGER

Another specially selected product that illustrates how this *coopérative* is concerned about more than quantity. Louve de Wolfberger was launched in 1989; the first vintage, 1985, was made from very ripe Tokay Pinot Gris grapes and aged in small oak barrels.

DOMAINE ZIND HUMBRECHT
GEWÜRZTRAMINER
HEIMBOURG TURCKHEIM

This domaine has pioneered reduced yields in Alsace. Heimbourg is a single vineyard in Turckheim, where Gewürztraminer vines grow on a calcareous soil and produce a very round, soft and delicately spicy wine, full of pithy, fleshy, fruit flavours.

DOMAINE ZIND HUMBRECHT
RIESLING CLOS HAÜSERER

This wine is made from a small vineyard in Wintzenheim where Riesling vines grow in heavy, calcareous-clay soil and produce an intensely aromatic wine that is full, round and powerful to taste, yet almost delicate in its balance. A profound wine that develops the terpene-rich, petrolly-complexity of a classic Riesling.

DOMAINE ZIND HUMBRECHT
RIESLING
HERRENWEG TURCKHEIM

Also in Wintzenheim, the Herrenweg vineyard is situated beneath Clos Haüserer, on a gravelly, alluvial and colluvial soil at the bottom of the slope. The wine is less rich than Clos Haüserer, but equally classic and long-living.

DOMAINE ZIND HUMBRECHT
RIESLING RANGEN DE THANN
CLOS SAINT URBAIN

GC - The fully south-facing Rangen vineyard consists of very steep slopes with a hard, dark, stony soil of volcanic origin, the character of which seems to be reflected in the very intense flavour and strong constitution of this Riesling wine.

DOMAINE ZIND HUMBRECHT
TOKAY PINOT GRIS ROTENBERG
SÉLECTION DE GRAINS NOBLES

The Rotenberg vineyard is situated close to the Hengst in Wintzenheim. In 1986 this wine achieved an incredible 182° Oechsle, but the acidity was even more amazing - 11.5 grams per litre (expressed as tartaric) in the finished wine, converting its enormous 230 grams per litre of residual sugar into piquant, tangy flavour that is unlike any other wine except the greatest German *Eiswein*.

JURA

THIS SMALL WINE REGION lies at the foot of the Jura mountains in the ancient province of Franche-Comté. A relatively unknown area, it produces the simply-labelled Arbois or Côtes du Jura reds, whites and rosés, but also two great - and expensive - specialities with great life expectancy.

The first - its *vin de paille* ("straw wine") - is a succulently sweet dessert wine unique to the Jura, so-named because the grapes were originally laid on straw mats to concentrate the sugar content before being vinified. The second is the dry *vin jaune* ("yellow wine"), not unlike a *fino* Sherry. After the alcoholic fermentation the wine is racked and sealed in thick oak barrels to age for a minimum six years. During that time, a yeast *flor* similar to that found in Jerez, forms on the surface of the wine, which slowly oxidizes. When it emerges it has acquired the deep yellow colour that gives it its name, and *fino*-like character. Unlike Sherry, it is not a fortified wine. The Savagnin grape from which the wine is made is a natural late-ripener and is deliberately harvested, as late as December when the first snow has come, to achieve a maximum sugar concentration. The resulting wine can age up to 100 years. The *vin de paille* can age up to 50.

Château-Chalon, one of the four separate AOCs in the region, is particularly famed for its *vins jaunes*. The other three areas are Arbois, Côtes du Jura, and L'Etoile. Together they account for a total vineyard area of some 1,000 hectares (2,500 acres) with about 1,000 growers.

VIN JAUNE

JEAN BOURDY
CHÂTEAU-CHALON

Jean Bourdy is one of the top growers of Château-Chalon (which is a commune, not a single estate). The village is perched upon a hill, overlooking the commune's 30 hectares (74 acres) of black marl vineyards.

CHÂTEAU L'ETOILE

L'Etoile is a small appellation southwest of Château-Chalon. The wines also come from the adjacent communes of Plainoiseau and Saint-Didier. The elegant, rich and nutty Château l'Etoile is best drunk when 15 to 20 years old.

FRUITIÈRE VINICOLE D'ARBOIS

When the Frutière Vinicole was established in 1906, it was only the second cooperative to be founded in France and had just 26 members. Now it has 140 members with 210 hectares of vineyards and produces some of the best wines in the Jura. Its *vin jaune* is particularly soft and mellow, making it easy to drink as soon as it is released, but will, like all its peers, last almost for ever.

ANDRÉ & MIREILLE TISSOT

The superb and sumptuous *vin jaune* of André et Mireille Tissot is from the AOC Arbois in the northern Côtes du Jura. It is presented in a traditional 62 cl bottle, called a *clavelin*.

VIN DE PAILLE

JEAN-MARIE COURBET
VICHOT-GIROD

Vichot-Girod is the brand name used for the rare and expensive *vin de paille* from Jean-Marie Courbet. After up to four years in wood and some bottle age, the wines have a golden colour, a complex bouquet and a powerfully rich, raisiny flavour.

ROLET PÈRE ET FILS

The Rolet Estate at Montigny-Les-Arsures is one of the finest in the Arbois appellation. The Rolet Style inclines to the more oxidative, typically showing a deep amber-gold colour, a powerful and rich bouquet with herby undertones and a deep flavour with a long, nutty finish.

THE LOIRE VALLEY

THE LOIRE, WITH ITS tributaries, plays host to some 60 different AOC areas along 400 kilometres (250 miles) of river bank. The river runs in an east-west direction through four major wine-producing districts, from Sancerre and the Central Vineyards, through Touraine and Anjou-Saumur, on to the Pays Nantais and the sea at the Bay of Biscay. The sheer size of the vineyard means that it includes a wide variety of climatic and soil conditions and a diversity of wine styles. Red and rosé wines are found in abundance, though outnumbered by dry and sweet whites; all are found in sparkling form.

The table of *Appellations Contrôlées* opposite shows how the overall output in the Loire is dominated by a handful of vineyards that produce very large quantities of drinkable, everyday wines. They are interspersed with individual areas that produce wines of unusual and exquisite quality.

The structure of the industry

The typical producer in the Loire valley is the small grower. There is a scattering of cooperatives, with a handful of larger ones that account for up to 2 million cases a year. The wine is not particularly distinguished, with the exception of the impressive wines of the Cave Coopérative du Haut Poitou, just north of Poitiers. A number of big merchant houses handle vast quantities of wine, either in bulk under various brand names, or under the all-embracing title of "Vin de Pays du Jardin de la France", which is the table wine category that embraces the entire region.

For classic wines, look particularly for names of family growers - Jean Baumard, Charles Joguet, Gaston Huet, Yves Soulez. To visit their small farms or establishments and to explore their cellars - occasionally beneath the very vineyard where the grapes grew - can be as intriguing as a trip to one of their grander neighbours, the lovely châteaux in the Loire valley.

The grape varieties

The region is principally dependent on three white wine grapes and two red. The whites are Muscadet in the Pays Nantais, Sauvignon Blanc in the Central Vineyards, and Chenin Blanc in Anjou-Saumur and Touraine. For the reds, the Cabernet Franc is a source of lighter red wines and is often blended with a little Cabernet Sauvignon to form the basis of some excellent, more serious wines from Chinon, Bourgueil and the improving and expanded red wine area of Saumur-Champigny. Among the indigenous grape varieties, along with

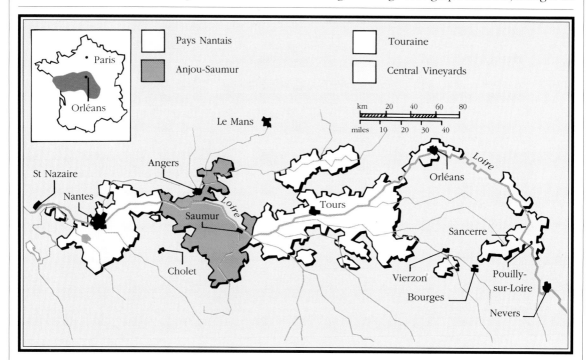

| Pays Nantais | Touraine |
| Anjou-Saumur | Central Vineyards |

The abundance of the Loire *The Loire, once France's most important waterway, rises in the Ardèche region of the Massif Central and ends its journey at Nantes and the Bay of Biscay, 1,000 kilometres (620 miles) away. Along the banks of the Loire lie not only the numerous beautiful châteaux, built by the nobility, but also the long-established vineyards which provide this region with its kaleidoscope of wines.*

Gros Plant, Chasselas and Pinot d'Aunis, is the red Grolleau, which is the mainstay of the huge rosé industry and allows financially for the long cellaring of many fine sweet Vouvrays. Gamay has acquired its own AC, and Chardonnay - another later introduction - has become more important: increased planting of Chardonnay now contributes not only to the blend of still white wines (occasionally surfacing as a varietal in its own right), but also to the sparkling wines of Saumur, where 20 per cent of Chardonnay and Sauvignon may now be added to the Chenin Blanc base. More unexpectedly, a major infusion is also permitted for sparkling wine from the red grape varieties, mainly Cabernet Franc.

The Chenin Blanc grape

The Chenin Blanc - also called the Pineau de la Loire - is a grape of classic proportions, perverse and highly complex, and cultivated in Anjou for 1,100 years. As a late-ripener in a northern climate, it has a high propensity to acidity that renders the young wine quite disagreeable, even in the best of summers. However, its acidity, great extract and complexity of flavour gives its wines - particularly the luscious, sweeter wines of Coteaux du Layon, Quarts de Chaume, Bonnezeaux and Vouvray - a phenomenal capacity to age in bottle for an extremely long period of time.

APPELLATIONS CONTRÔLÉES

■ Output approaching or in excess of 1 million cases
● Output over 250,000 cases

MUSCADET

Muscadet Sèvre et Maine ■
Muscadet des Coteaux de la Loire ●
Muscadet ●

ANJOU-SAUMUR

Anjou ■
Anjou Coteaux de la Loire
Anjou Gamay
Anjou Mousseux
Anjou/Rosé d'Anjou Pétillant
Rosé d'Anjou ■
Bonnezeaux
Cabernet d'Anjou ■
Cabernet de Saumur
Coteaux de l'Aubance
Coteaux du Layon ●
Coteaux du Layon Chaume
Coteaux du Layon Villages
Coteaux de Saumur
Quarts de Chaume
Saumur ■
Saumur Champigny ●
Saumur Pétillant
Saumur Mousseux ■
Savennières (and Coulée de Sérrant and La Roche aux Moines)

TOURAINE

Bourgueil ●
Chinon ●
Coteaux du Loir
Jasnières
Montlouis
Montlouis Mousseux
Montlouis Pétillant
St Nicolas de Bourgueil ●
Touraine ■
Touraine Amboise
Touraine Azay-le-Rideau
Touraine Mesland
Touraine Mousseux
Touraine Pétillant
Vouvray ● / ■
Vouvray Mousseux ●
Vouvray Pétillant

CENTRAL VINEYARDS

Menetou Salon
Pouilly Fumé ●
Pouilly-sur-Loire
Quincy
Reuilly
Sancerre ●
Vins de L'Orléannais

GENERAL APPELLATIONS

Rosé de Loire
Crémant de Loire

LOIRE VINTAGES

YEAR	DRY WHITES	SWEET WHITES	REDS
1989	Perfect harvest, with wines of great quality	Exceptionally fine wines, with plenty of noble rot	Fine reds for both early drinking and longer ageing
1988	Excellent for both Muscadet and Sancerre regions	A marvellous year, with good noble rot and potential for ageing	Good year; average yield
1987	Good for Muscadet and Sancerre; less successful elsewhere	Not particularly good; Touraine fared better than Anjou	Wet, cool year; acidic wines
1986	Splendid year for Sancerre; good for Muscadet	Excellent for Anjou, and noble rot. Not so good in Touraine	Quite successful for Chinon, Bourgueil and other reds
1985	Large, excellent Muscadet crop; Sauvignon full-bodied and forward	Exceptionally fine wines with noble rot in both Anjou and Touraine	Fine ripe harvest; excellent Touraine reds
1984	Under-ripe; high acidity in Muscadets, but lacking in Sancerre	Light wines for early drinking	Poor; reds light in style
1983	Quantity rather than quality; Muscadet generally flabby	Great depth and richness in Chenin wines	Good vintage; wines will age
1982	Large, less concentrated vintage	Generally short-lived wines, through late rains; Sancerre and Pouilly richer	Fruity, elegant reds; some Chinon and Bourgueil still drinking well
1981	Good for dry whites	Light, drinkable wines	Perhaps some Chinon and Bourgueil still available

MUSCADET & ANJOU-SAUMUR

USCADET, EITHER STRAIGHT or *sur lie,* is a popular wine, with an annual production of over 5 million cases. It has a cheap and plentiful image - a white equivalent to generic red Beaujolais - but the better producers are constantly seeking to upgrade its quality and image.

Sur lie wines from the better Sèvre et Maine area (identified as such on the label) are one step in this search for improved quality. These wines are retained on the lees, until 30 June of the year following the harvest at latest, and bottled without racking when needed. The process gives the wines greater freshness and flavour and a slight prickle from the residual carbonic gas. The best examples come from meticulous producers, whether a small grower or a forward-looking *négociant* like Sauvion. Sauvion is at the forefront of moves to offer Muscadets of superior quality, using single-vineyard and single-domaine wines, or selective wines under exclusive brand names.

Anjou-Saumur

The extensive vineyards of Anjou-Saumur produce some 9 million cases of wine a year. Of these, 85 per cent are either straight forward rosés, reds and whites for early drinking, or sparkling wines from Saumur. The remaining "quality" 15 per cent is attractive, predominantly Cabernet Franc reds from Saumur-Champigny; superb sweet wines for longer maturing from Coteaux du Layon, Quarts de Chaume and Bonnezeaux; and some remarkable dry whites from Savennières.

The latter, immediately south-west of Angers, contains two small vineyards of great repute, both *grands crus* - La Roche aux Moines and La Coulée de Serrant - and two other highly renowned south-facing slopes - Le Clos de Papillon and Epiré. The young wines from these vineyards are fiercely acidic and bitter - Chenin Blanc at its most arrogant. The wines can be drunk early with food, but if left for at least five years they achieve a wonderful metamorphosis and a further capacity to mellow and age for several decades.

Chenin Blanc can achieve the same magical transformation in the *moelleux* wines of the Coteaux du Layon, the Coteaux de l'Aubance and the oustanding growths on the Layon hillsides at Bonnezeaux and Quarts de Chaume, which have their own appellations. These wines can be distinctly longer-lived than their dry counterparts.

MUSCADET DE SÈVRE ET MAINE

MARQUIS DE GOULAINE
LA CUVÉE DU MILLÉNAIRE

A deep, full, rich-flavoured *sur lie* wine that keeps well and belies its Atlantic coast origins. Produced in small quantities, this is the top *cuvée* of Château de Goulaine, a large and splendid property owned and run by the 11th Marquis, Robert de Goulaine.

SAUVION FILS
CHÂTEAU DU CLÉRAY

Owned by the very large and friendly Sauvion family, Château du Cléray *sur lie* is consistently one of the finest Muscadets made. Look out, also, for the Découverte series of single-domaine wines bottled by the Sauvions, and Cardinal Richard, which is possibly the greatest Muscadet produced.

SAVENNIÈRES

DOMAINE DE LA BIZOLIÈRE,
PIERRE ET YVES SOULEZ

GC - The Soulez family took over Domaine de la Bizolière in 1982, to add to their existing Savennières holdings in Clos de Papillon and Château de Chamboureau. The parcel included part of the *Grand Cru* Roche aux Moines vineyard, which they now market under the Château de Chamboureau label. The wines have a clean and correct style with a certain hard-edged complexity.

DOMAINE DU CLOSEL
MME DE JESSEY

Owned by Madame Michèle Bazin-de-Jessey, this small domaine has 12 hectares (30 acres) of vineyards and produces a fine, elegant style of Savennières, partly from fermentation in cask. A crisp and potentially complex wine, Madame Jessey is having to rely more and more on stainless-steel tanks for fermentation.

CLOS DE LA
COULÉE DE SERRANT
MME A. JOLY

GC - This is *the* wine of Savennières in many people's eyes. The property was purchased by Madame Denise Joly in 1960. Since 1985 the tiny quantities of this wine are made utilizing the "biodynamic" system developed by Rudolph Steiner.

CLOS DU PAPILLON
DOMAINE DES BAUMARD

Made by Jean Baumard and his son, this is the ripest, gentlest, fruitiest and most elegant wine of the entire appellation. Without a hint of the traditional austere character of so much Savennières, this soft and seductive wine caresses the palate from an early age, yet also ages well.

ANJOU ROUGE

CLOS DE COULAINE
CÉPAGE CABERNET
FRANÇOIS ROUSSIER

The dark colour and the considerable depth of fruit found in François Roussier's wine is indicative of the sun-drenched, heat-retaining slopes of his vineyard, which is located in Savennières, but can only claim the Anjou appellation for red wine.

LOGIS DE LA GIRAUDIÈRE
ROUGE DE CÉPAGE CABERNET
JEAN BAUMARD

From the same stable as the Clos du Papillon above, the full, ripe, lush and velvety flavours consistently found in this well-coloured wine are a further testament to the wine-making capabilities of Jean Baumard.

COTEAUX DU LAYON

LE LOGIS DU PRIEURÉ
JOUSSET ET FILS

The careful production techniques of Louis Jousset and his son ensure that this is a classic Chenin Blanc wine. A wine that shows a richness worthy of higher appellations, even in 1988 when the vines were just five years old and the yield as high as 40 hl/ha.

MOULIN TOUCHAIS

Once dubbed the most well-known secret of the Loire Valley, the Touchais cellars seem to be bottomless. They are famous for holding back the wines until the family considers they are ready for drinking; various vintages such as 1964, 1959, 1955 and the glorious 1947 are still available commercially, albeit in small quantities.

CHÂTEAU DES ROCHETTES
J.L. DOUET

With its lovely botrytis nose and pimento-flavoured fruit, the 1982 *Sélection de Grains Nobles* is a rarity in the Coteaux du Layon. Non-botrytis wine is by far the norm and no less a *vin de garde*, as an 18-year-old 1971 "ordinary" Château des Rochettes demonstrated. Not a hint of botrytis, but complex flavours of toast, honey, vanilla, caramel, toffee and cream.

CLOS DE SAINTE CATHERINE
JEAN BAUMARD

You have to taste Jean Baumard's Bonnezeaux and Quarts de Chaume before you can accept that this beautifully balanced, silky-flavoured, elegant, ripe and fruity wine is actually not the very top of this range, despite its obvious finesse.

COTEAUX DU LAYON VILLAGES

The right to mention the name of the village is reserved for six of the best-situated villages in the north-east of the Coteaux du Layon appellation: Beaulieu, Faye, Rablay, Rochefort, Saint-Aubin and Saint-Lambert. The maximum yield is the same as the basic appellation, but the grapes must be riper, having at least 221 g/l of sugar, rather than 204. Technically, Coteaux du Layon-Chaume is a separate appellation with a lower yield of 25 hl/ha, but the growers do not regard its status as any different from the other six.

DOMAINE D'AMBINOS (BEAULIEU)
CLOS DES MULONNIÈRES
JEAN-PIERRE CHÉNÉ

CHÂTEAU DU FRESNE (FAYE)
ROBIN-BRETAULT

CHÂTEAU DE LA GUIMONIÈRE (CHAUME)
DOUCET

CHÂTEAU MONTBENAULT (FAYE)
CLOS DE LA HERSE, LEDUC

DOMAINE DE LA SOUCHERIE (CHAUME)
P.Y. TIJOU

DOMAINE DE TERREBRUNE

The initial succulence, potential longevity and sheer finesse of this classy wine make it a bright new hope for Bonnezeaux's long-neglected appellation. It is the result of a relatively new joint-venture of three young winegrowers, who are intent on seeing the popularity of these wines increase.

QUARTS DE CHAUME

DOMAINE DES BAUMARD

More evidence of Jean Baumard's wine wizardry, this elegantly rich and mellifluous wine has the silky texture and ripe-melon and pineapple aromas that can only come from Chenin Blanc that has been harvested at a low-yield and fermented to technical perfection. Easy to drink when young, but it will live as long as any Quarts de Chaume.

CHÂTEAU DE SURONDE
VIEILLES VIGNES
LAFFOURCADE

Firmer in style than Domaine Baumard, Monsieur Laffourcade's Quarts de Chaume is made from old vines and is powerful, concentrated and needs at least 10 years to mature before drinking and will continue to improve for a further 30 or more.

BONNEZEAUX

CHÂTEAU DE FESLES
"LA CHAPPELLE", J. BOIVIN

Jacques Boivin is the most famous producer in Bonnezeaux, exporting his wines all around the world. This *cuvée* is made only in exceptional years and is a selection of the best wines from the third and richest *trie*.

DOMAINE DU PETIT VAL
DENIS GOIZIL

From Vincent Goizil's tiny 2-hectare (5-acre) vineyard comes this delightful nectar of a wine that, contrary to the traditional practices of this rustic appellation, is not fermented in cask, but in a temperature-controlled vat, which might help to explain its ultra-clean, fine floral aromas.

SAUMUR-CHAMPIGNY

DOMAINE FILLIATREAU
VIEILLES VIGNES

With almost 30 hectares (74 acres) in Saumur-Champigny, Paul Filliatreau is the largest producer of this style of wine. Vieilles Vignes comes from vines of between 50 and 100 years of age and is a wine of exceptional concentration and colour. His Jeaune Vignes is not, incidentally, all that young, coming from vines of between 10 and 50 years of age.

DOMAINE DE NERLEUX
R. NEAU

Robert Neau and his son Régis make a wide variety of wines from this domaine, but their Saumur-Champigny represents the most important part of the volume produced. A fine-coloured wine made in the *vin de garde* style, Neau also produces an even richer wine called Cuvée de Chatain.

CLOS ROUGEARD
"LES POYEAUX"
FOURCAULT ET FILS

Two brothers, Jean-Louis and Bernard Fourcault, make wines that are the yardsticks for others. Deep, dense and powerful, Clos Rougeard is not unlike an old-fashioned claret and the best vintages will last just as long.

CHÂTEAU DE TARGÉ
EDOUARD PISANI-FERRY

Young Edouard Pisani-Ferry is the second generation to cultivate the 15 hecatres (37 acres) belonging to this property and his oak-aged wine is a precisely made wine of fine colour, rich creamy-vanilla fruit, with well-balanced tannin. A wine of some complexity and finesse.

DOMAINE DES VARINELLES
DAHEUILLER

Famous locally for producing the Saumur-Champigny that has graced the table of Pope John Paul II, Claude Daheuiller is very adept at producing Saumur-Champigny that is supple and easy to drink when young, but that gains complexity with age, thus appealing to everyone - a very catholic wine indeed!

SPARKLING SAUMUR

ACKERMAN
CUVÉE JEAN-BAPTISTE
ACKERMAN-LAURANCE

Owned by Monsieur Pannier, *the* man of Saumur, Ackerman-Laurance is best known for the excellent quality of its 1811 Brut that has a succulent, strawberry-scented rosé sister wine, but the finest quality of this house is to be found in the rich and flavourful Cuvée Jean Baptiste.
CB 75%, CH 15%, CF 10%

BOUVET LADUBAY TRESOR

Bouvet is owned by Taittinger, the famous *Grande Marque,* and this special *cuvée,* which has a short maturation in small oak casks and the extended ageing on its yeast, is the first Saumur to approach the finesse and complexity of a fine Champagne.
CB 80%, CH 20%

GRATIEN & MEYER
CUVÉE FLAMME

Alain Sedoux, who runs the company today, insists that this is not a prestige *cuvée.* Whatever he likes to call it, such is the quality of this smooth, full, rich and mature wine that it certainly brings prestige to the name of Gratien and Meyer.
CB 70%, CF 30%

CRÉMANT DE LOIRE

LANGLOIS
LANGLOIS-CHÂTEAU

Originally known as Langlois-Château - although it never has been a single domaine product - this wine once contained no less than 95 per cent Chenin Blanc and was sold under the Saumur appellation, when it had an ungenerous flavour with a distinctive metallic edge. Despite the supposedly lower AOC, this is now a far softer, finer and fruitier wine.
CB 60%, CF 25%, G 15%

TOURAINE

THE LARGER PART OF the output from the Touraine vineyards is of light- to medium-bodied reds from Gamay and Cabernet Franc grapes, and a growing industry in attractive, ready to drink, light whites from Sauvignon Blanc. The vineyards begin half-way between Saumur and Tours, with the first of two pairs of smaller, select areas: Chinon on the south bank, and Bourgueil opposite on the north; in addition there is the village of St Nicolas-de-Bourgueil, which has its own appellation. All three areas produce red wines (Chinon also has a little white and rosé), in relatively small quantities from Cabernet Franc, with an allowable content of up to 10 per cent Cabernet Sauvignon. They are wines which would not disgrace Bordeaux in quality.

Vouvray and Montlouis

The second pair of vineyards, facing each other across the Loire north and south, is Vouvray and its less well-known shadow, Montlouis. This is an area where the tufa sub-soil (chalk boiled by volcanic action), typical of the Loire, is especially common. Both of these vineyards are entirely white wine producers from the Chenin Blanc grape variety, which offers an extraordinary range: from dry to demi-sec (off-dry), to *moelleux* (covering a wide range of sweetness and intensity without being heavy or cloying). Bottle fermented sparkling wines (using the traditional method as practised in Champagne) are also made, since the high acidity of the Chenin grape makes it a most suitable sparkling wine base.

The superbly ripe quality of the sweeter wines is achieved by a practice of *triage*. The ripest grapes only are gathered each time, in a series of pickings made at intervals of a week or so. In exceptional years grapes from the best vineyards, or only some part of them, are affected by botrytis.

Chenin Blanc also endows sweet Vouvray wines in the good years with their amazing capacity to age without the specific assistance of noble rot. Youngsters at 10 years, 50 is no problem. Enormous cellars, tunnelled out from the tufa, house the thousands of bottles of finished wine, allowing them to age quietly and gracefully.

Historic wines *Wines have been made since 1513 at the beautiful Château de Chenonceau on the river Cher (a tributary of the river Loire).*

BOURGUEIL AND ST NICOLAS-DE-BOURGUEIL

AUDEBERT ET FILS
DOMAINE DU GRAND CLOS

Audebert et Fils is one of the biggest *négociants* in Bourgueil, but this is one of its own domaine wines from the 9-hectare (22-acre) Domaine du Grand Clos, which is located on the highest slopes just north of the town. The wine is fermented in temperature-controlled stainless-steel vats and matured in wood.

PIERRE CASLOT
VIEILLES VIGNES

Despite the fact that Pierre Caslot-Jamet utilizes some modern methods, his full, dense, muscular, purple-coloured wine is very much in the same style as the Bourgueil his father used to make, which is in keeping with a wine-making family that stretches back to 1650.

CASLOT-GALBRUN
DOMAINE HUBERT

Madame Caslot-Galbrun not only runs this 15-hectare (37-acre) domaine, but as Mayor of Benais she also runs the local village. Her small production of Bourgueil is all matured for at least one year in chestnut casks. It is always classic and correct, requiring a few years to round out.

COULY-DUTHEIL
LES CLOSIERS

Although better known for its range of excellent Chinon wines, Couly-Dutheil also market a superb Bourgueil under this label. It is typically ripe and agreeable, with an attractively perfumed nose and a fine ruby colour.

PAUL GAMBIER
"DOMAINE DES OUCHES"

A small domaine at Fontenay near Ingrandes-de-Touraine that consistently produces flavour-packed wines of the highest quality - rich in bouquet and colour.

LAMÉ-DELILLE-BOUCARD
DOMAINE DES CHESNAIES

The small amount of Cabernet Sauvignon in this St Nicolas-de-Bourgueil, which is always fermented and matured in wood, helps to explain its distinct style. The credit for its stunning quality - rich, soft-fruit bouquet, and the dense, creamy-rich fruit that is full of spicy-vanilla complexity - must be shared between the supreme skill of its vineyard worker and the natural properties of the *terroir*.
CF 90%, CS 10%

P. JAMET ET FILS

The sandy soil of this 20-hectare (50-acre) vineyard dictates the more delicate, elegant style of Pierre Jamet's wine, compared to that of Lamé-Delille's, even though it, too, has a small percentage of Cabernet Sauvignon and the wine does see some time in wood, after a year in vat.
CF 95%, CS 5%

CHINON

DOMAINE DE LA CHAPELLERIE
JEAN-FRANÇOIS OLEK

Akin to Bordeaux in style, Jean-François Olek's fulsome wine is matured in wood to provide an underlying spicy complexity and supple tannin structure.

COULY-DUTHEIL
CLOS DE L'ECHO

This is one of Couly-Dutheil's top wines. It is made from a vineyard that is situated on a steep, south-facing, calcareous-clay slope where an echo bounces off the walls of Château de Chinon. The wine, which spends about six months in cask, is always rich and smooth, with plenty of fruit and a generous bouquet. La Baronnie Madeleine is another top wine, which is very rich, but perhaps more elegant and often displays a smoky, spicy complexity.

CHARLES JOGUET
CUVÉE DU CLOS DE LA DIOTERIE
VIEILLES VIGNES

Another producer whose wines are on a par with - and not dissimilar from - a classy Bordeaux from the right bank. This wine seems to be filled with so much fruit that it is almost brimming over on the palate. A voluptuous, beautifully balanced wine, as is Charles Joguet's irrestistible Chinon Rosé.

MANZAGOL-BILLARD
DOMAINE DE LA NOBLAIE

Pierre Manzagol-Billard produces classic Chinon, which is honestly earthy and not without a tannic edge, but with plenty of solid Cabernet France fruit underneath. He also makes an interesting white Chinon.

DOMAINE OLGA RAFFAULT

Not be be confused with Raymond or Jean-Maurice Raffault (two other excellent producers of bigger-styled wines that are also based in Savigny-en-Véron), Domaine Olga Raffault is all lace and grace. A fine and delicately balanced wine that is best appreciated when young.

VOUVRAY AND SPARKLING VOUVRAY

DOMAINE BOURILLON-DORLÉANS

The wines produced by Frédéric Bourillon-Dorléans are always top-class and quite often the *demi-secs* are undersold, such as the 1985, which was such a big, beautiful and complex wine that it would have been a *moelleux* under almost any other label.

MARC BRÉDIF, PÉTILLANT

This firm, which was purchased by Patrick de Ladoucette of Château du Nozet in 1980, is particularly famous for the potential longevity of its sparkling Vouvray.

GILES CHAMPION VALLÉE DE COUSSE

Giles and his son are third and fourth generations to champion the cause at Vallée de Cousse. Their *demi-sec* has a deliciously delicate style, with vibrant, sherbetty fruit; while the *moelleux* is much bigger, taken from several *tries* and in years such as 1986 can contain as much as 80 per cent botrytized grapes.

PHILIPPE FOREAU CLOS NAUDIN MOELLEUX

One of the greatest growers of Vouvray, Philippe Foreau's *moelleux* wines are extremely stylish and elegant, yet require at least 10 years to show their true potential, and will benefit from another 20.

PHILIPPE FOREAU CLOS NAUDIN BRUT

As Foreau is one of the few growers who is able to make an attractive Vouvray *sec*, it is probably little wonder that he also excels at producing the sparkling version. Both the gently moussing *pétillant* and fully sparkling *brut* are best drunk young, yet remain fresh for up to 30 years or more.

RÉGIS FORTINEAU MOELLEUX

A careful producer of the bigger and richer style of *moelleux*, Régis Fortineau fares best in classic years, such as 1985.

BENOÎT GAUTIER CLOS CHÂTEAU-CHEVRIER

The Gautiers, who have been wine-makers since 1669, make various products, specializing in sparkling Vouvray, but it is the *moelleux* wines that are far and away the best. Their 1986 *moelleux* was made from 70 per cent botrytized grapes and had immense finesse.

LIONEL GAUTHIER-LHOMME

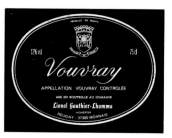

Although the 1985 *moelleux* has a slightly unclean nose, the 1986 is arguably the best wine of the vintage. A full, rich and youthfully honeyed wine that literally oozes with a fabulous concentration of fruit.

HUET LE MONT MOELLEUX

If Gaston Huet has been greatly respected in his long-established position as Mayor of Vouvray, he is now the local hero, having forced the long-awaited TGV route to go under the appellation's vineyards rather than through them. He owns three of the finest sites: Clos du Bourg, Le Haut-Lieu and Le Mont, and his wines are amongst the most vivacious and long-lived of all Vouvrays.

HUET BRUT

Gaston Huet's winemaker, who also happens to be his son-in-law, Noël Pinguet, is one of the best exponents of the art of fizzy Vouvray, making a supremely clean, elegant and refreshing wine that is best when drunk young.

JEAN PIERRE LAISEMENT
MOELLEUX

An architect of the fine and delicately poised school of crafting Vouvray wines, Jean-Pierre Laisement manages to extract elegance from even the most awkward of years.

PRINCE PONIATOWSKI
AIGLE BLANC

Although this is indeed a sweet wine, it is, relatively speaking, one of the drier versions of *demi-sec* available, but the rich depth of peachy flavour that is always apparent offers perhaps an object lesson. Why stretch the grapes to make an ordinary quality of sweet Vouvray in cooler years, when you can make an extraordinary quality of somewhat drier wine?

MONTLOUIS AND SPARKLING MONTLOUIS

BERGER FRÈRES
DOMAINE DES LIARDS
MOELLEUX

Perhaps best known for their sparkling Montlouis business, the Berger family also make fabulous still wines from their own vineyards. Ripe, creamy, extrovert peach flavours are the hallmark of this rare *moelleux* wine.

CHAPUT THIERRY
MOELLEUX

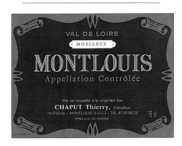

Even in 1987, Chaput Thierry's *moelleux* was a class apart. A surprisingly rich and ripe wine, which is full of juicy strawberry, peach and apricot flavours.

FRANÇOIS CHIDAINE

Chidaine is a fastidious winemaker whose 1986 is a fine example of the unusual toasty quality that he imparts into his succulently sweet and concentrated style of wine.

DANIEL MOSNY

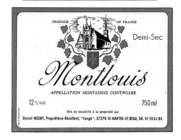

On Daniel Mosney's 12-hectare (30-acre) vineyard at Cang, near St Martin-le-Beau, he produces fine *demi-sec* and *moelleux* by using a combination of modern and traditional methods.

DOMINIQUE MOYER
MOELLEUX

This modest man produces some of the finest wine in Montlouis. The 1959 and 1947 are two of the greatest sweet wines ever made, even including Yquem. Thirty years on, the 1959 still had a hint of green to its pale, ageless colour, and is refreshing and juicy. More than 40 years on, the 1947 remains the palest example of this extraordinary vintage. The bouquet is as fresh as ripe strawberries and the balance in the wine between alcohol, residual sugar and its ripe acidity is as remarkable as it is long on the finish.

DOMINIQUE MOYER
PÉTILLANT

This has the quality of eternal youth: a 20-year-old *cuvée* in 1989 had a perfumed bouquet, rich peach and liquorice fruit on the palate, and no sign of oxidation or maderization.

CENTRAL VINEYARDS

THE SMALL GROUP OF villages at the eastern end of the Loire Valley, the so-called Central Vineyards, led by Sancerre, has set the standard for what the world now perceives as good quality white Sauvignon Blanc.

Sancerre is a vineyard of small growers: some 450, who farm an area of 1,600 hectares (4,000 acres) that embraces 14 villages. The best villages include Bué, Chavignol and Verdigny (look for the small print on the label). Sancerre is a white wine that needs selecting with care, for variations occur from maker to maker, and from site to site with the same maker. It is affected even more by vintage: an under-ripe year will unduly accentuate the greennesss and aggression of the Sauvignon; an over-ripe year can render it overblown, with a loss of finesse.

In a return to an earlier tradition - in pre-phylloxera days the Sancerrois made only red wines - a good quarter of today's Sancerre vineyard is devoted to Pinot Noir for the rosé and red wines that are back in vogue. Among leading growers, there are at least half a dozen - like Vacheron and Dezat - whose red Sancerre can be enthusiastically recommended.

Pouilly-sur-Loire

In terms of their finesse and the complex, flowery depth that emerges with a minimum of ageing, the Sauvignon Blanc wines of Pouilly-sur-Loire have the edge on Sancerre. The Sauvignon grape is known as the Blanc Fumé in Pouilly: the term *fumé* is thought to derive from the smoke-coloured skin of the grape. The wines have a certain roundness and need a year to 18 months in bottle to be at their best.

Menetou-Quincy-Reuilly

Apart from Pouilly-sur-Loire, the other villages - Quincy, Menetou-Salon and Reuilly - remain in comparative obscurity. But they supply wines of quality and individuality. Menetou-Salon, to the south-west of Sancerre, makes white, red and rosé wines in the same way as Sancerre. The typically Sauvignon whites are more rounded in character and the reds bear very favourable comparison. Quincy, which makes only white wine from the Sauvignon Blanc, is a name that deserves to be better known. Its AOC was granted before that of Sancerre, but most of its vineyards are very small and little wine is exported. Reuilly is even more obscure than Quincy, being not on the Loire but on a tributary of a tributary.

The wines of these villages may not reach the heights of Sancerre at its best, but then they are not so expensive. The wines are often very reliable: Menetou-Salon has a certain softness and Quincy an elegance which seem somehow to protect them from extremes. They are all wines best drunk young, and vintages do make a difference.

SANCERRE

B. BAILLY-REVERDY
CLOS DU CHÊNE MARCHAND

One of the most repected producers in Sancerre, Monsieur Bailly (he married a Reverdy) owns some 15 hectares (37 acres) of vines in Sancerre, two-thirds of which are planted with Sauvignon Blanc, one-third with Pinot. His red and rosé are both fine wines, but he is best known for the correctly assertive, but richly flavoured, Clos du Chêne Marchand.

HENRI BOURGEOIS
CÔTES DES MONTS DAMNÉS

Now run by Jean-Marie Bourgeois, this domaine continues to produce different Sancerres according to the site and soil of their origin, as established by Jean-Marie's late father, Henri. It is from the incredible Côtes des Monts Damnés that the biggest and the best wine comes, although the one characteristic does not necessarily follow the other.

LUCIEN CROCHET
CLOS DU CHÊNE MARCHAND

With some 7 hectares (17 acres) on this famous vineyard, Lucien Crochet has plenty of flexibility when it comes to selecting and blending. This shows in the wine, which has all the richness of the Bailly-Reverdy, but is more expressive and with greater pace and vitality.

VINCENT DELAPORTE

If these wines have a certain mid-Atlantic appeal, it might be because Vincent Delaporte spends almost as much time traipsing the vineyards of California, where he is a consultant, as he does those of the Loire.

ANDRÉ DEZAT ET FILS

The mayor of his village, Verdigny, André Dezat is proud of the fact that more than a third of his vines are Pinot Noir because, as he points out, Sancerre was a red wine until phylloxera destroyed its vineyards. All of his Sancerres - red, white and rosé - are elegant and stylish.

GITTON PÈRE ET FILS
LES BELLES DAMES SILEX

Just like Henri Bourgeois, Pascal Gitton makes and sells a great many different Sancerres, according to their soil and situation. This wine is rich, smooth and seductive, seldom showing the greener side of Sancerres, yet it is still admirably fresh and vital.

COMTE LAFOND
DE LADOUCETTE

Made by Ladoucette of Château du Nozet - of Pouilly-Fumé fame - this is usually a refined and well-balanced wine.

ALPHONSE MELLOT
DOMAINE LA MOUSSIÈRE

This is the largest *négociant* and most extensive vineyard owner in Sancerre, not to mention important producers of Pouilly-Fumé, Reuilly, Quincy and Menetou-Salon. There are two top wines: La Moussière, which is the biggest vineyard in Sancerre, and Cuvée EAM, which is a *tête de cuvée* selected from his best vats. Both wines are classic.

JEAN REVERDY
DOMAINE DES VILLOTS

Based in Verdigny, Jean Reverdy produces this Sancerre of great class, finesse and complexity. There is also a Clos de la Reine Blanche that is a product of even greater perfection.

DOMAINE JEAN-MAX ROGER
LE CLOS DERVEAU

A large *négociant* and vineyard owner based in Bué, Jean-Max Roger is able to select and bottle some really top Sancerres, as the results of some blind tastings have demonstrated. Their own domaine Le Grand Chemarin and Clos du Chêne Marchand are the top wines.

LUCIEN THOMAS
CLOS DE LA CRÊLE

This small property consists of 8 hectares (20 acres) situated just north of Chavignol, in the village of Verdigny, which is one of the largest communes of Sancerre. The finest wine of Domain Lucien Thomas is this Clos de la Crêle, which has a seering Sauvignon bouquet, backed up by the rich flavours of well-ripened fruit.

VACHERON
DOMAINE LES ROMAINS

The late Jean-Louis Vacheron was the first grower in Sancerre to be serious about red wine. In the rush to meet the demand for Sauvignon Blanc, those who did care to plant Pinot Noir relegated this vine to north-facing slopes, hence all the pale-coloured, insipid-tasting Sancerre Rouge. Vacheron's sons maintain the good colour, fine bouquet and pure Pinot flavour in these red wines; their whites are impressive, too.

POUILLY-FUME

BARON DE LADOUCETTE

The creation of Baron Patrick de Ladoucette in 1973 and since then produced only in good to exceptional years, this wine is exclusively from the vineyards of Château du Nozet. It is, in fact, a blend of five specific plots: La Belle Vue, Les Bleus, La Croix, Le Désert and La Fontaine. A soft and refined wine, it has a restrained but refreshing bouquet, gentle pear-flavoured fruit and a soft finish.

JEAN-CLAUDE CHÂTELAIN CHÂTELAIN PRESTIGE

Jean-Claude Châtelain is responsible for this exquisitely made, delightfully aromatic wine. It teems with deliciously ripe fruit, which is lifted by soft but lively acidity. Unfortunately for the French, this wine is rarely seen on the domestic market, because virtually the entire production is exported.

DIDIER DAGUENEAU SILEX

For this wine, Didier Dagueneau crushes the grapes and allows the juice to macerate on the skins before fermentation; he also puts a part of the wine into new oak for a while. The result is an unusually full, aromatic and complex wine for Pouilly-Fumé.

ANDRÉ DEZAT ET FILS DOMAINE THIBAULT

The Mayor of Sancerre Village - Verdigny - also makes fine Pouilly-Fumé in a somewhat more delicate style than his other wines.

GITTON PÈRE ET FILS CLOS JOANNE D'ORION

A passionate believer in the *terroir*, Pascal Gitton produces expressive Pouilly-Fumé, in addition to his several domaine Sancerres. His Les Foltières is an attractive rendition of this appellation, but the extremely refined and delightful style of Clos Joanne d'Orion is much the best.

DE LADOUCETTE

The original Château du Nozet is in fact a blend of Nozet grapes and selected purchased grapes or juice. It is a wine of great refinement - perhaps a little more austere than Baron de L, and certainly capable of much more complexity.

MICHEL REDDE ET FILS CUVÉE MAJORUM

The Michel Redde style is one of richness and ripeness, with effective balancing acidity and freshness. This particular example is a sort of Redde version of Baron de L with a look-alike bottle. It is made in exceptional years only, from old vines and in a limited quantity.

GUY SAGET LES ROCHES

A very large *négociant* that can usually be relied on to offer wines that are both good value and good quality. The style is soft, fresh and easy, yet never lacking in depth and length. Les Roches is its best Pouilly-Fumé.

CHÂTEAU DE TRACY COMTESSE A. D'ESTUTT D'ASSAY

This property has been in the Scottish-descended d'Estutt d'Assay family since 1586. Some still consider that the wine, which comes exclusively from the château's 23-hectare (57-acre) vineyard, rivals de Ladoucette and Baron de L, but it has a far fatter and heavier style.

MENETOU-SALON

GEORGES CHAVET ROSÉ

A well-established family of producers with a good repuation, especially for this truly delightful rosé - a deliciously dry wine bursting with fresh and pure Pinot Noir fruit aromas.

ALPHONSE MELLOT

The largest *négociant* and most extensive vineyard owner in Sancerre also makes one of the finest wines of Menetou-Salon. In fact it is quite similar to some of Mellot's Sancerres, though perhaps a touch crisper.

DOMAINE HENRY PELLÉ
CLOS DES BLANCHAIS
MOROGUES

Henry Pellé's top-of-the-range white Menetou Salon shows extra finesse, length and spicy complexity compared to his main blended *cuvée*, but not more weight - just extra class.

QUINCY

DENIS JAUMIER

Since the retirement of Raymond Pipet, who now intends to devote his attention to *la chasse*, Denis Jaumier - a young Bordeaux-trained *vigneron* - has stepped into the breach. He has a great reputation to keep up and seems to be coping well.

DOMAINE DE MAISON BLANCHE

Owned by Albert Bescombes, the family *négociant* of Moc-Baril in Saumur, this is the largest producer in what is really a very small appellation. The wines are consistently good in quality, with the purity of Sauvignon flavour expected from Quincy.

PIERRE ET JEAN MARDON

This domaine extends to some 10 hectares (25 acres) and produces a fine Quincy, typically tart, but with lots of pure gooseberry fruit and tasting fresh and crisp, rather than seeringly dry, thin and mean. There is also an attractive dry rosé with a delicate fruit flavour.

REUILLY

HENRI BEURDIN

Typical for Reuilly, this grower produces all three wines allowed by the appellation. The red is a well-coloured, old-fashioned wine; the rosé sometimes a little disappointing; but it is the white - a fine, floral wine with a soft, grassy complexity - that truly reflects Reuilly's *terroir*.

GÉRARD CORDIER

Gérard Cordier makes a fine, racy style of Reuilly blanc and an equally delightful, elegantly fresh and fruity rosé that is made from the Pinot Gris.

C. LAFOND
LA RAIE

Claude Lafond owns some 6 hectares (15 acres) of vines in Reuilly, where he produces this citrussy-fresh and floral-scented wine that is totally dry without being assertive. La Grande Pièce is a medium-sweet rosé made from the Pinot Gris, while Les Grands Vignes is a crisp, red Pinot Noir wine.

THE RHÔNE VALLEY

THE VINEYARDS OF THE Rhône Valley really form two quite separate areas, although the generic Côtes-du-Rhône AC embraces them both. Over 33,340 hectares (82,385 acres) are planted to vines, almost all in the Southern Rhône.

The quality north

The Northern Rhône produces wines of great quality. The area begins a few kilometres south of Vienne with the remarkable red wines of Côte Rôtie, closely followed by the two equally remarkable white wines of Condrieu and Château Grillet. Fifty kilometres (30 miles) further south, the celebrated hill of Hermitage - a granite outcrop of the Massif Central - looms out of a bend in the river and gives its name to the most distinguished red wine of the Rhône (and one of the best wines in the world). On the less favoured slopes of the hill, and in eleven surrounding villages, are the vineyards of Crozes-Hermitage; across the river lie the hillsides of Cornas, St Joseph and St Péray.

The effect of terrain

The wines of the Northern Rhône are individualistic wines, quite different in character from those of the south, since they are made from different grapes and grown on a markedly different terrain. In the north the vines are planted in the granitic and sandy soil of ribbon-like terraces, which are precariously placed on some of the steepest hillsides in France. The total output of these northern vineyards is minute, when compared to the massive annual outpouring of red, white and rosé wines of all quality levels from the vineyards of the Southern Rhône (see the tables on vineyard sizes on pages 172 and 179).

The abundant south

The Southern Rhône starts south of Montelimar and extends across the three *départements* of Drome, Gard and Vaucluse. The area is best known for the very plentiful Châteauneuf-du-Pape, a chameleon-like wine with a variety of styles. Next in importance are the powerful and long-lived wines of Gigondas (until 1971 one of the Côtes-du-Rhône Villages wines). Gigondas,

like Châteauneuf-du-Pape, is a wine for medium-term ageing. So too are the better examples of its neighbour, Vacqueyras, an area that was recently accorded its own appellation. There are another 16 villages in the Southern Rhône that remain

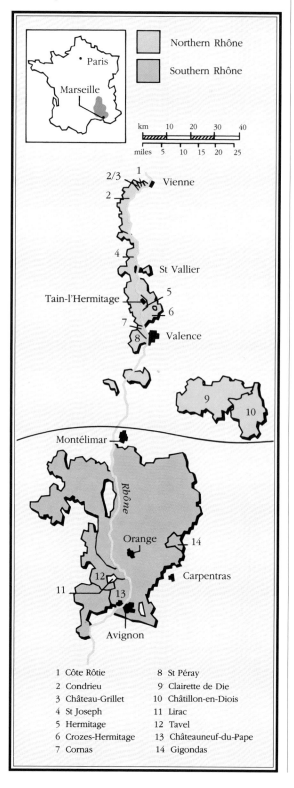

1	Côte Rôtie	8	St Péray
2	Condrieu	9	Clairette de Die
3	Château-Grillet	10	Châtillon-en-Diois
4	St Joseph	11	Lirac
5	Hermitage	12	Tavel
6	Crozes-Hermitage	13	Châteauneuf-du-Pape
7	Cornas	14	Gigondas

Regional variations The vineyards of the north are strung out along the river valley, covering never more than a few hundred metres in width. By contrast, the broad, southern vineyards - with their milder climate - can be many kilometres across, interspersed with fruit trees, melon fields and olive trees.

within the Côtes-du-Rhône Villages AOC, producing wines of greater depth, character and higher alcoholic strength than the generic Côtes-du-Rhône AC. On the south-west bank of the river are the distinguished rosé wines of Tavel, with their own appellation, and the reds and rosés of Lirac.

Separate AOCs have been granted to two Côtes-du-Rhône Villages for their *vins doux naturels* (sweet and partly fortified wines), to the white Muscat of Beaumes de Venise and the less well regarded red from Rasteau.

Away from the immediate confines of the river is the large appellation of Côtes du Ventoux, producing ever-improving red, white and rosé wines from vines on the slopes of the imposing Mont Ventoux. The other area beginning to make its quality mark is the Coteaux du Tricastin AOC, particularly successful with its reds, with little to distinguish them from Côtes du Rhône.

The soils of the south

The vineyards in the Southern Rhône fan out on either side of the river Rhône, forming an ever-widening pear shape which has its base at Avignon. The slopes of the landscape here are shallower than in the north, with limestone outcrops on clay soils and alluvial deposits, and stony or sandy top-soils, typified by the potato-sized pebbles (*galets*) at Châteauneuf-du-Pape and the sandier soils of Tavel and Lirac.

Grape varieties

In the north, reliance is placed on single grape varieties. Syrah is the key consitituent for reds of Côte Rôtie, Hermitage, Crozes-Hermitage, Cornas and St Joseph. Viognier is used for the whites of Condrieu and Château Grillet. At Hermitage, Crozes-Hermitage, St Joseph and St Péray (Cornas does not make any white wine) the whites are based principally on a typical Rhône valley grape, Marsanne. Since Marsanne does not have good ageing capability, Roussanne is also used - particularly in white Hermitage.

In the Southern Rhône a plethora of grape varieties is available. Thirteen different grapes can be grown legally by Châteauneuf-du-Pape winemakers, although most use about half that number or less: eight red, of which Grenache, Syrah, Mourvèdre and Cinsault are the most prominent (with Counoise, Vaccarèse, Terret Noir and Muscardin as runners-up); and five white, principally Clairette, Bourboulenc and Roussanne (plus Picpoul and Picardan).

At least 20 other varieties can be used in other wines in the south, but reds are most commonly a combination of Grenache, Mourvèdre, Syrah and Cinsault, and whites use Bourboulenc, Clairette, Grenache Blanc and Roussanne.

RHÔNE VINTAGES

YEAR	NORTH	SOUTH
1989	Exceptionally good, little short on quantity	Plentiful vintage; exceptional wines in Gigondas, Châteauneuf and Lirac
1988	Small vintage; huge wines with great maturing potential	Fruity wines of good quality
1987	An "off" year; light wines for early drinking	Lighter wines for early drinking
1986	Light wines but good quality	Châteauneuf and Gigondas very good in selective vinyards
1985	Hot, dry summer; big wines needing ten rather than five years' ageing	Plentiful and fruity harvest; Gigondas and Châteauneuf for medium term
1984	Modest wines now accessible; keep Hermitage and Côte Rôtie	Modest vintage; early drinking
1983	Exceptional and powerful wines needing time	Generally light wines; keep Châteauneuf
1982	Very good vintage, can now be drunk	Heat caused difficulties; some wines very good
1981	Small; better for whites. Best of reds still for keeping	Châteauneuf and Gigondas which survived a difficult year now drinkable
1978	Fantastic vintage; Hermitage and Côte Rôtie still need time to mature	The best Châteauneuf only just ready for drinking; Gigondas need more time

Sampling the vintage *Wines of the Côtes-du-Rhône are known in France as* vins du soleil *(wines of the sun).*

THE NORTHERN RHÔNE

AT CÔTE RÔTIE, HERMITAGE and Cornas, the Syrah grape produces red wines of great fruit and body and alcoholic strength, with a robust capacity for long development and evolution, placing them in the best years among the greatest red wines in the world. The wines of St Joseph, like Crozes-Hermitage are also from Syrah, but are usually lighter and for earlier drinking.

In some of the northern reds a small addition of white grapes in the vinification is permitted. Small amounts of Viognier are included by some growers in Côte Rôtie to soften the wine and elaborate the bouquet. Similarly, up to 15 per cent of Marsanne and Roussanne can be vinified with Hermitage and Crozes-Hermitage, and up to 10 per cent may be used with St Joseph.

Ageing potential of northern reds

Côte Rôtie and Hermitage are classic *vins de garde*, with a reasonable life expectancy of anything up to 25 years - even longer for an Hermitage of an outstanding year like 1978. Cornas can require a decade to allow its deep, complex, tannic character to evolve and soften, and in good years it can last as long again. Only the very best Crozes-Hermitage can compete with that, and - like St Joseph - it is normally drinkable earlier.

The style of white wines

The whites of the Northern Rhône fall into two types - white Hermitage for keeping and the rest for early drinking. About a quarter of the output of Hermitage is white, and this is produced from Roussanne and Marsanne, which is planted in patches among the Syrah vines. The leading traditional-style Hermitage is Chapoutier's Chante-Alouette, with a medium-term ageing capacity of 10 to 12 years. Best savoured in their first youth are the two wines regarded as the finest white wines of the Rhône valley - Condrieu and Château Grillet. Their lingering perfume comes from the Viognier, which is virtually unique to this part of France. Also for early drinking are the whites of Crozes-Hermitage and St Joseph, and the dry, still wines of St Péray. St Péray is perhaps better known for its sparkling wine, made by the traditional method as used in Champagne, and fruitier and heavier than most.

VINEYARD SIZES

VINEYARD	SIZE
Côte Rôtie	102 hectares (252 acres)
Condrieu	14 hectares (35 acres)
Château Grillet	3 hectares (7^1/$_2$ acres)
Hermitage	123 hectares (304 acres)
Crozes-Hermitage	903 hectares (2,231 acres)
St Joseph	245 hectares (605 acres)
Cornas	67 hectares (165 acres)
St Péray	48 hectares (118 acres)

CÔTE RÔTIE

PIERRE BARGE

Now run by Pierre's son Gilles, whose deep-coloured, intense, flavour-packed wines have a remarkably fine balance for their concentration. In classic years the bouquet has the dense, smoky, cassis-rich character of unfiltered Syrah, with sometimes a hint of spicy vanilla underneath.
SYR 95%, VIO 5%

BERNARD BURGAUD

These vineyards occupy both the plateau at Le Champin and its slopes, which are well-favoured but more laborious to work. The wine is aged for up to two years in small oak casks and not filtered prior to bottling; consequently it is well-coloured, with a supple tannin structure and a graceful style.

EMILE CHAMPET

His nimble build, nervy manner and pixie-like hat have caused people to liken Emile Champet to a goblin or gremlin, but nobody would ever apply a similar description to the warm, firm and spicily elegant wine produced from his steep, 2-hectare (5-acre) vineyard.

CHOL & FILS, DE BOISSEYT CÔTE BLONDE

This is a classic example of the elegance found in the best Côte Blonde wine. It is made from 2 hectares (5 acres) of vines growing on calcareous-sandy soil, which originally belonged to Joseph Duplessy, but is now part of Domaine de Boisseyt, whose vineyards were first established in 1797.

DÉLAS SEIGNEUR DE MAUGIRON

Owned by Deutz of Champagne fame, this old firm produces a traditional blend of the two *côtes*, *brune* and *blonde*, under its Seigneur de Maugiron label. It is aged in small oak casks, which give the wine its unmistakable vanilla characteristics and make it accessible when young.

A. DERVIEUX-THAIZE LA VIAILLÈRE

As Albert Dervieux has been president of the local Syndicat des Vignerons since 1953, it is perhaps no surprise that he produces some of the most fantastic, traditional wines of the appellation. His Frongent is simply stunning, although La Garde is infinitely superior, but it is the La Viaillère, from old vines on the iron-rich soil of the Côte Brune, that steals the show with every vintage.
🍇 *SYR 95-100%, VIO 0-5%*

GENTAZ-DERVIEUX "CÔTE BRUNE"

Marius Gentaz-Dervieux is the brother-in-law of Albert Dervieux and he, too, makes exceptional wine. This Côte Brune is a lush, plummy and elegant wine that is capable of ageing well, but drinks very well after less than 10 years.

PAUL JABOULET AÎNÉ LES JUMELLES

The Jaboulet syle is one of cassis-rich fruit with an underlying smoky-spicy complexity. Of the many great wines from this firm, none demonstrates these qualities with quite so much finesse as its Les Jumelles Côte Rôtie.

E. GUIGAL

Founded as recently as 1946, the firm of Guigal has become the largest player in the Côte Rôtie market and now owns Vidal-Fleury. Do not let its size put you off: this firm is one of the greatest producers of these wines, although its use of new oak is a rarely-practised technique in the Rhône valley. A third of Guigal's even most basic blends are treated to this luxury, while the entire *cuvée* of single-vineyard Côte Rôtie will spend at least three years in new wood.

CÔTES BRUNE ET BLONDE

This is the traditional, basic, blended Côte Rôtie, yet its deep, luscious flavour with creamy, smoky and spicy complexity outshines the top wines from many other producers.

LA LANDONNE

This single-vineyard Côte Rôtie is made from young vines growing on the Côte Brune. The first vintage was 1978; neither it, nor any of the vintages that have followed, are ready to drink. The wine assails the mouth with flavours that will require 20 or 30 years to tame.

LA MOULINE

Although from the intrinsically lighter Côte Blonde, the great age of the vines (which average 75 years) on this small patch of vineyard endow this wine with a deep, richer, smoother flavour than La Landonne. A wine of great finesse and intensity.

LA TURQUE CÔTE BRUNE

The new child of Guigal, the first vintage released was 1985 and barely more than 300 cases were produced. It is considered to be the firm's greatest wine so far.

173

JEAN-PAUL ET JEAN-LUC JAMET

This wine is classic, traditional Côte Rôtie. Not fat, but a big, firm wine with a full and sturdy tannin structure that requires many years to round out into the fine, floral finesse that less overtly fruity renditions of Syrah only achieve with sufficient bottle-age.

JASMIN

The ultimate producer of the elegant, fleshy, yet classy style of Côte Rôtie, Robert Jasmin finds a silky texture and a purity of fruit in the Syrah that few of his peers ever discover. The wine is aged in small, two-year-old oak casks that come from Burgundy.

R. ROSTAING
CÔTE BLONDE

René Rostaing produces these black-coloured monsters in his spare time, treating his Syrah wines to three years in small oak casks, with up to a third new barrels each year. The result is a fabulously rich wine, full of plump, lush and often exotic fruit flavours. His superb La Landonne Côte Rôtie is comparable to the extraordinary Guigal version.

DOMAINE J. VIDAL-FLEURY
LA CHATILLONNE
CÔTE BLONDE

The quality of the wines from this old firm, which dates back to 1781, went through a difficult period in the late 1970s and early 1980s, but has been on the up-and-up since the company was purchased by Guigal in 1985. Of its various single-vineyard wines, La Chatillonne is often judged to be best, although even the basic Côte Brune et Blonde blend is now on top form.

CHÂTEAU-GRILLET AND CONDRIEU

VIN BLANC DE
CHÂTEAU-GRILLET
NEYRET-GACHET

This is one of the smallest, single-domaine appellations in France. It has a pale colour, an entrancing floral bouquet and a lingering, delicate flavour with an elegant, peachy aftertaste. A wine of finesse and complexity, but also one that has yet to achieve its full potential, despite its great name and fame.

DÉLAS
VIOGNIER

One of the most underrated producers of Condrieu, the firm of Délas owns 2 hectares (5 acres) of prime vineyards in this appellation. The ultra-clean lines of this wine emphasize its elegance and floral qualities.

PIERRE DUMAZET
CÉPAGE VIOGNIER

At Limony, the Dumazet family have been making wine from the tiniest and steepest vineyard in the appellation for well over 100 years. The present incumbent, Pierre Dumazet, continues his father's practice of harvesting early in the morning, when the grapes are coolest, and produces some of the most memorable, flavour-packed and complex Condrieu it is possible to find.

E. GUIGAL
VIOGNIER

This wine is fermented in stainless-steel, to retain its purity of fruit, then up to 40 per cent is aged in oak for three months. The result is a wine of great clarity and richness, with the typical peach-blossom character of the Viognier, supported by creamy undertones of exotic fruit.

CHÂTEAU DU ROZAY
J.-Y. MULTIER

This vineyard is for the most part situated on the Coteau de Chéry, its château on the plain behind. The Multiers have owned the property since 1898 - although only as a secondary residence, their home being at Lyon, where the family manufactured military and church garments. There is a basic blended Condrieu, but the Château du Rozay, which has the classic peach-kernel character of fine Viognier, is well worth the extra price.

NIERO-PINCHON
COTEAU CHERI

Robert Niero took over this reputable property in 1985, but his father-in-law, Jean Pinchon, is still a consultant. Niero also owns a small vineyard in the basic Côtes-du-Rhône appellation, from which he makes a red wine under the Saint Agathe label. In 1990 he will produce his first Côte Rôtie.

GEORGES VERNAY

It was Georges Vernay who taught Jean-Yves Multier's father how to make wine. In fact, until 1978, Vernay used to make Château du Rozay for the Multiers. His own vineyards dominate the appellation, producing more than half of its wines. His basic Condrieu is excellent indeed, but his Coteaux de Vernon, which spends several months in new oak casks, is in another class. Quite possibly, the best Condrieu of all.

SAINT-JOSEPH

J.L. CHAVE

The king of Hermitage produces a tiny quantity of marvellous Saint-Joseph, a vibrantly fruity wine, full of spicy, raspberry flavours. A wine of no great complexity, but one that is a delight to drink when young and fruity, if you can find it.

BERNARD GRIPA

From some 5 hectares (12 acres) of vines on the slopes behind Mauves, on the opposite bank to Hermitage, in the south of this long, straggly appellation, Bernard Gripa produces a soft-textured, ripe and fruity wine that is ready for drinking between two and five years of age.

J.-L. GRIPPAT
White Saint-Joseph

This grower's vineyards are located on the slopes of Tournon and extend south into Mauves. Although the white wines of Saint-Joseph are all too often flabby and lacklustre, this one of Grippat's is one of the two best wines of the appellation. This is an exciting wine, with a fresh, flowery aroma, a clean, fruity flavour and youthful-honey undertones; it is best drunk within two years.

J.-L. GRIPPAT
VIGNES DE L'HOSPICE

Jean-Louis Grippat's regular Saint-Joseph is fresh, light and elegant, but his Vignes de l'Hospice is altogether different. Fatter, softer, richer and immediately seductive on the palate, it does, however, improve in the bottle for up to eight years.

J. MARSANNE & FILS

Jean Marsanne is another grower situated in Mauves making a superior Saint-Joseph, but in a much more serious, though not necessarily better, *vin de garde* style than those above. Indeed, Marsanne's firm-structured, sturdy-flavoured wine, with its intense, smoky character, is more like a rustic Hermitage.

ALAIN PARET

Situated at Saint-Pierre-de-Boeuf, this young grower and *négociant* produces some fine examples of Saint-Joseph, notably the excellent, medium-bodied Les Pieds Dendés, with its penetrating, smoky-raspberry flavour, and also the excellent Larmes du Père.

RAYMOND TROLLAT

The highly prized wines of this winemaker are made from over 3 hectares (8 acres) of vines at Saint-Jean-de-Muzols (just north of Tournon in the south of the Saint-Joseph appellation). The reds are made for keeping, although their full, ripe, vibrantly fruity flavours can be all too easy to succumb to in their youth. The white is a silky, seductive and elegant wine; with that of Jean-Louis Grippat, it is one of the two best white wines of the appellation. It has less overt character than Grippat, but a touch more finesse.

M. CHAPOUTIER

Chapoutier was founded in the heart of Tain l'Hermitage in 1808 and is today run by the exuberant Max Chapoutier. This firm is one of the largest owners of prime sites in Hermitage and Châteauneuf-du-Pape, in addition to which it has substantial holdings in other appellations and augments its own production by purchasing grapes from other producers.

HERMITAGE CHANTE-ALOUETTE

Traditionally the fullest-flavoured and longest-living white Hermitage produced, Chante-Alouette may seem overweight and unbalanced in its youth, but it will slowly rise to the boil. The vivid fruit flavours found in some vintages from the early 1980s onwards have also given this great wine an immediate as well as long-lasting appeal.

HERMITAGE MONIER DE LA SIZERANNE

La Sizeranne is the oldest known red Hermitage and is a wine of finesse and finely tuned flavour, rather than one of sheer weight or clout. Since 1985 this wine has taken on deeper, more intense colour.

HERMITAGE "LA CUVÉE DE L'ORÉE"

Max Chapoutier's theory of blending non-vintage Hermitage, most of which is sold under his Grande Cuvée label, has its critics, but few dispute that his very top-of-the-range blends are anything less than sensational, as this white wine demonstrates. In terms of pure quality, it is the Rhône's equivalent of a Montrachet.

HERMITAGE "LE PAVILLON"

Released by Max Chapoutier's father in 1956, this red Hermitage is the firm's original super-luxury, non-vintage blend. Much darker in colour than Chapoutier's regular Hermitage, it has a remarkably complex structure and deep flavour.

CROZES-HERMITAGE LES MEYSONNIERS

In truly great years, such as 1983, when it has both colour and fruit, this can be one of the best buys in the region, but it is not a wine to be bought in off-years or without tasting first.

CROZES-HERMITAGE

CAVE DES CLAIRMONTS

A partnership of three families with an enormous estate of vineyards located in five different communes spread throughout the appellation, Cave des Clairmonts has in recent years produced one of the most complete and satisfying Crozes-Hermitage around.

LES GAMETS FAYOLLE FILS LES PONTAIX

Established in 1870, this estate is situated at Gervans, just north of Tain, and is now run by Jean-Paul and Jean-Claude Fayolle, who make full, opaque-coloured wines that have an intensity of flavour and a true, smoky complexity that is seldom seen in Crozes-Hermitage.

FERRATON PÈRE & FILS LA MATINIÈRE

This vies with Jaboulet's Domaine Thalabert as the best and most consistent Crozes-Hermitage. Its deep, dark colour and rich, ripe-berry bouquet is backed up with vibrant, velvety fruit, which can have a penetrating smoky-cassis complexity. Yet despite this concentrated character, this is distinctly a wine of finesse, rather than size.

CHARLES TARDY ET BERNARD ANGE
DOMAINE DES ENTREFAUX

Based at Chanos-Curson, Charles Tardy and Bernard Ange have 15 hectares (37 acres) of vineyards, from which they produce a fine quality of Crozes-Hermitage in an elegant, aromatic style that quickly reveals its soft, seductive, blackcurrant and raspberry flavours.

HERMITAGE

JEAN-LOUIS CHAVE

The wine-making philosophy of Gérard Chave has been passed down to him by his father, just as it was passed down to him by his, a process that has gone on for more than 400 years. Uncompromising in his style, his red wine is built to last 20 years in even mediocre vintages, yet it has a beautifully stylish balance. His white is rich, glorious and sometimes exotic.

DÉLAS
CUVÉE MARQUISE DE LA TOURETTE

The red wine is quite superb - a rich, ripe-berry bouquet and classic smoky-cassis flavour, with a smooth, spicy complexity and hints of heather and dried flowers. The white is less successful, although some vintages - such as the 1985 - can be sensational.

FERRATON PÈRE & FILS
"LA CUVÉE DES MIAUX"

This label is used for Michel Ferraton's red Hermitage, which is a blend of two vineyards - Le Méal, which is shared by Paul Jaboulet Ainé and forms a major part of their famous La Chapelle blend, and Les Beaumes. In great years this is a deep-coloured, intensely flavoured wine in which the dense, smoke-filled fruit is packed tightly with a significant amount of tannin.

J.-L. GRIPPAT

If nothing else, Jean-Louis Grippat is a genius at producing surprisingly fresh and vivacious white wines in the Rhône's hot and sunny southern valley. His opulent, often exotic, white Hermitage is the greatest testament to this. Grippat's red Hermitage is not a blockbuster, but is an elegant and stylish wine of obvious class.

E. GUIGAL

Etienne and Marcel Guigal are not as consistent with their Hermitage as they are with their Côte Rôtie, but in great years - such as 1978, 1983 and 1985 - they manage to produce something quite exceptional. These big, dark, voluptuous wines are often a match for the very best wines of this appellation.

H. SORREL
LE GRÉAL

Since Henri Sorrel died in 1982, his son Marc has taken over. After an uncertain start, he quickly demonstrated his skills. This superb *cuvée* is a blend of two vineyards, Le Méal and Les Greffieux. The best vintages are deep-coloured, with a *pot-pourri* for a bouquet and dense, flavour-packed fruit on the palate. Velvety textured, they have a supple tannin structure and cassis-rich, smoky complexity.

H. SORREL
LES ROCOULES

Sorrel's white Hermitage has undergone a transformation since 1985. It now ranks as one of the finest of its type - a creamy-rich, deliciously fruity wine, with exotic vanilla overtones.

CORNAS

GUY DE BARJAC

This dark purple wine, with its deep, intense, smoky fruit-bush flavour and full, tannic structure, is the product of very old vines, between 50 and 70 years old, situated on steep, sun-soaked slopes. Like Hermitage, most Cornas leaves a fine, black sediment in the bottle, but Barjac's is heavier than most because he does not fine or filter his wine.

PAUL JABOULET AÎNÉ

Whereas many small growers eventually impose their own name on the label of their wines, rather than that of their father's, the name of Paul Jaboulet, who established this firm in in Tain L'Hermitage in 1834, lives on.

No other firm has managed to achieve such a high level of quality across so many Rhône appellations for so many generations and the consistency of this reputation is maintained and reflected in the name.

CORNAS

Not the best Jaboulet wine and certainly not the greatest Cornas, but this is consistently excellent and probably represents the best value wine throughout the entire Rhône valley.

CROZES HERMITAGE
DOMAINE DE THALABERT

Considering how large this vineyard is, the quality of Domaine Thalabert is extraordinary. This is the finest Crozes-Hermitage produced; Jaboulet seems to squeeze extra concentration out of the vines - only Ferraton's La Martinière can rival it.

HERMITAGE LA CHAPELLE

Not from one vineyard, but a blend of two called Le Méal and Les Bessards, this is consistently the greatest Hermitage produced. If a list of the top 10 wines in the world were drawn up, vintages of La Chapelle - such as 1983, 1978 and the legendary 1961 - would have to be seriously considered.

A. CLAPE

Auguste Clape makes the finest Cornas. He believes in fining his wines the traditional way - with egg white - but does not filter them. They are black, massive and impeccable, with plenty of supple tannin, intense fruit, great finesse and smoky-spicy complexity.

MARCEL JUGE
CUVÉE S C

Marcel Juge is another winemaker who does not fine or filter his wine. His basic Cornas is very good: an elegant, stylish wine, full of delicious, soft-fruit flavours. His Cuvée S C shows the same finesse, but with bigger, deeper, smokier characteristics.

JEAN LIONNET

It is perhaps no surprise to find that the most traditional, black and tannic Cornas is produced by the Lionnats, who have been making wine here-abouts for more than 400 years.

ROBERT MICHEL
"LA GEYNALE"

With 6 hectares (15 acres) of vine-yards in Cornas, five on steep terraces, Robert Michel makes a tough, black-coloured wine that requires considerable bottle-age to round out. His vines are old, averaging 40 years of age overall; in his tiny vineyard called La Geynale they are 80 years old.

NOËL VERSET

Verset's yield per hectare is the lowest in the appellation, which explains the enormous concentration of flavour in his black-tinged wines. His very best Cornas, such as 1983 and 1985, is seldom surpassed.

ALAIN VOGE

This grower has 5 hectares (12 acres) of prime hillside vineyard. His wine, which spends up to two years in a combination of stainless-steel and wooden vats, is deep and dense, with rich, fat, spicy Syrah flavours. It is full of voluptuous fruit and under-pinned by fleshy tannin and a smoky complexity. A wine of great finesse that is always beautifully balanced.

THE SOUTHERN RHÔNE

CHÂTEAUNEUF-DU-PAPE, the leading appellation of the Southern Rhône, is a well-known name, but the wine itself is difficult to classify. There is a surprisingly big output - over a million cases a year - and it is mostly red. Over 50 producers all employ differing methods of vinification - for instance the use of *macération carbonique* to achieve softer, more forward wines for earlier drinking. They also use different combinations of grapes, always with the emphasis on Grenache. Most of the wines have a capacity for ageing, whether they are big and tannic in style, or lighter and with greater finesse.

Other Southern Rhône appellations

In Gigondas the choice is more limited. Athough the total output is relatively large, approaching one third of that of Châteauneuf-du-Pape, the appellation boasts only about 30 private growers. In contrast to its illustrious neighbour, it is a name that has yet to be discovered.

A similar relationship exists between Tavel and Lirac. Tavel has established a much wider reputation than Lirac for its rosé wines. In their attempts to compete, the *vignerons* of Lirac have also developed a very attractive red wine.

Away to the east, on the river Drôme, a straight *méthode champenoise* is made at Die, but also - unusually - here they still vinify their sparkling Clairette de Die Tradition by the local method that involves a single fermentation process.

VINEYARD SIZES

VINEYARD	SIZE
Châteauneuf-du-Pape	3,077 hectares (7,600 acres)
Gigondas	1,153 hectares (2,850 acres)
Tavel	759 hectares (1,875 acres)
Lirac	617 hectares (1,525 acres)
Coteaux du Tricastin	1,417 hectares (3,500 acres)
Côtes du Ventoux	8,097 hectares (20,008 acres)
Beaumes-de-Venise	233 hectares (576 acres)
Rasteau	111 hectares (274 acres)
Vacqueyras	500 hectares (1,235 acres)
Côtes du Rhône Villages	3,198 hectares (7,902 acres)
Côtes du Rhône	33,340 hectares (82,385 acres)
Clairette de Die	1,040 hectares (2570 acres)

CHÂTEAUNEUF-DU-PAPE

CHÂTEAU DE BEAUCASTEL

One of three estates that utilizes all 13 grape varieties allowed by the regulations. Its vines are old, treated organically and have a very small yield of highly concentrated fruit. The wines are deep-coloured and juicy, with plummy-ripe, spicy-blackcurrant fruit, capable of great complexity when mature. This property also produces the finest white wine in Châteauneuf, a wonderfully exotic wine, part of which is aged in new oak.
Red GR 30%, MV 30%, SYR 10%, CN 5%, VAR 25%
White ROUS 80%, VAR 20%

DOMAINE DE BEAURENARD

Owner Paul Coulon is the seventh generation to make Châteauneuf-du-Pape on this property. He uses a combination of *macération carbonique* and traditionally fermented juice to produce a well-coloured, elegant style of wine that is intrinsically low in tannin and makes for easy drinking. Paul Coulon's white wine is one of the most vibrantly fruity wines of the appellation.
Red GR 70%, SYR 10%, MV 10%, CN 10%
White CL 90%, BLC 10%

CUVÉE DE BELVEDÈRE LE BOUCOU

Rarely seen outside the locality, this deeply coloured wine has an extravagant character, a rich, warming flavour that is full of summer fruits and a swirling, smoky complexity. Best drunk between 8 and 20 years of age, depending on the vintage.
GR 80%, CO 15%, SYR 5%

BOSQUET DES PAPES

A seldom encountered, but consistently fine-quality property that produces well-coloured, richly flavoured and very expressive wines that are easily accessible when young, but repay keeping.
GR 70%, VAR 30%

DOMAINE DE CABRIÈRES

A large and well-known estate to the north of Châteauneuf-du-Pape, these wines are precocious and fruity, yet have finesse and polish.
GR 55%, SYR 10%, MV 10%, CN 10%, VAR 15%

DOMAINE LES CAILLOUX

Run by the talented André Brunel, whose name is also one of the few worth looking out for on supermarket *cuvées*, this property produces big wines that are full of colour and flavour, yet not without finesse. They have a lovely plumminess and lots of smoky Syrah complexity.
GR 70%, MV 15%, SYR 10%, CN 5%

CHANTE CIGALE

The wines of this property are very traditional and are given longer ageing than usual in large wooden *foudres* prior to bottling. The wines are nicely coloured, with a rich and opulent, spicy flavour and a hint of smoky complexity.
GR 80%, SYR 10%, MV 5%, CN 5%

DOMAINE CHANTE PERDRIX

Owned by Nicolet Frères, this domaine produces a sensational, vibrant, velvety wine that is full of lush, almost exotic fruit flavours, hinting first of blackberries, then raspberries, blackcurrants, and even apricots.
GR 80%, MCD 20%

LES CLES D'OR

Jean Deydier owns a fine vineyard of 25 hectares (62 acres) between Mont Redon and Vieux Télégraphe and produces superb Châteauneuf-du-Pape, utilizing two-thirds traditional vinification, one-third *macération carbonique*. He also makes a fine white wine.
Red GR 80%, VAR 20%
White BLC 34%, GRB 33%, CL 33%

DOMAINE DURIEU

Paul Durieu has a well-planned vineyard, conscientiously rotated to afford a spread of maturity between 10 years for vigour and 70 for concentration. His Châteauneuf-du-Pape, which is a 50/50 blend of *macération carbonique* and traditionally vinified juice, is a medal-winning, entrancing, delectable, juicy wine that is almost ready to drink as soon as it is bottled.
GR 70%, MV 20%, SYR 10%

CHÂTEAU DES FINES ROCHES

This famous property belongs to the *négociant* firm of Mousset. Although the quality of the wine suffered in the 1970s, it has rapidly improved since 1981, regaining its past reputation. Today it is a fine-coloured wine that aims more for finesse rather than intensity of fruit.
GR 65%, SYR 15%, VAR 20%

CHÂTEAU DE LA FONT DU LOUP

This up-and-coming domaine is making a fine, traditional style of Châteauneauf-du-Pape. It is well-coloured and mellow in bouquet, with a flavour of cherries, blackcurrants and raspberries.
GR 70%, VAR 30%

DOMAINE FONT DE MICHELLE

This property is run by two nephews of Henri Brunier, the owner of the star-performing Domaine du Vieux Télégraphe. It produces a well-coloured, rich-flavoured wine, with a deep, spicy-*cassis* bouquet.
🍷 *GR 70%, SYR 10%, MV 10%, CN 10%*

CHÂTEAU FORTIA TÊTE DE CRU

This was the property of Baron le Roy, who was responsible for establishing the strict quality-control regulations of Châteauneuf-du-Pape in 1923. It is now run by his son, who makes a deep-coloured wine that is marked by its concentration of ripe berry-fruit flavours and clean spicy aftertaste. He also produces a fine Châteauneuf *blanc*.
🍷 *GR 80%, SYR 10%, MV 8%, CO 2%*

CHÂTEAU DE LA GARDINE

Produced by Gaston Brunel, one-third of the wine undergoes *macération carbonique*, two-thirds are traditionally vinified. This is a very correct style of Châteauneuf-du-Pape, if not always an exciting one, and is occasionally something special.
🍷 *GR 60%, SYR 23%, VAR 17%*

CHÂTEAU DE LA GARDINE
White Châteauneuf-du-Pape

The white wine is a deliciously dry, early-drinking wine, with a light richness and a fresh finish.
🍷 *ROUS 34%, BLC 33%, GRB 33%*

DOMAINE DU GRAND TINEL

A vast estate by Châteauneuf-du-Pape standards - 75 hectares (185 acres) - containing many old vines. The wine is full, lush and concentrated, with rich, nutty flavours, that can in great vintages improve for up to 20 years.
🍷 *GR 80%, VAR 20%*

PAUL JABOULET AÎNÉ LES CÈDRES

More than one *cuvée* of Jaboulet's Châteauneuf-du-Pape can be encountered, but this excellent, warm wine - usually full of spicy-*cassis* fruit, with a silky finish - is the most consistent.

DOMAINE DE MARCOUX

An up-and-coming wine on the export markets, the red wine is a full, deep, solidly constructed wine with lots of spicy fruit.
🍷 *GR 70%, CN 15%, MV 15%*

DOMAINE DE MARCOUX
White Châteauneuf-du-Pape

In recent years, this white wine has found favour amongst other growers in Châteauneuf-du-Pape itself as one of the finest in the appellation.
🍷 *CL 60%, BLC 40%*

CLOS DU MONT-OLIVET

Most of these traditionally produced wines are beautifully coloured with an extravagantly fruity bouquet and lots of elegant, ripe, cedary-sweet fruit flavours. They are always good to very good, but there is a feeling that they could be even better.
🍷 *GR 80%, SYR 10%, CN 5%, VAR 5%*

CHÂTEAU MONT-REDON

This property makes wine of a consistent quality even in so-called off years. They are typically nicely coloured, have good fruit, firmness and finesse and can also possess a fine, spicy, peppery, herbal complexity in great years.
🍷 *GR 65%, SYR 15%, CN 10%, MV 5%, VAR 5%*

DOMAINE DE NALYS

An overrated property that produced a quaffing wine until 1985, when it began to make wines of a much better quality. The new style is richer and more attractive, with an underlying softness.
GR 60%, SYR 12%, CN 6%, VAR 22%

CHÂTEAU LA NERTHE

Since this famous château was purchased by the Rhône *négociant* David and Foillard in 1985, its vineyard and winery have undergone considerable renovation. These wines are huge, dark and brooding, with a deep and tannic flavour and are capable of great complexity.
GR 60%, MV 30%, VAR 10%

CLOS DE L'ORATOIRE DES PAPES

Once one of the greatest Châteauneuf-du-Papes, the wine from this vineyard rarely excites, but it still has a potentially exciting *terroir* and should no more be written off than Château Margaux when it, too, was going through a bad patch.

CLOS DES PAPES

The traditional methods used by this property produce some of the finest wines of its appellation. Deep, dark and delicious, they are wines that are rich, ripe and spicy with lots of voluptuous, velvety fruit flavours.
GR 70%, MV 20%, SYR 8%, VAR 2%

PIGNAN

It is unclear whether this is always the second label of Château Rayas or occasionally a totally different wine. In any case, it certainly has an uncanny resemblance to its famous stable-mate in certain years.

CHÂTEAU RAYAS

Many consider this to be the finest Châteauneuf-du-Pape and, when it excels, it justifies this fame. However, it has always been dogged by a somewhat inconsistent performance, although when successful it can be devastatingly good. The unique character of Rayas is attributed not merely to its 100 per cent Grenache content, but also to its very old vines that produce concentrated fruit. A great Rayas has a uniquely rich flavour and a luscious, velvety texture. It bulges with ripe, spicy, berry fruit and has a remarkable, sweet herby-cedary complexity.
GR 100%

DOMAINE DES SÉNÉCHAUX

Wines have been made at Domaine des Sénéchaux for some 600 years. This 30-hectare (74-acre) estate is one of the few properties to utilize the full number of 13 grape varieties allowable by the regulations and produces an outstanding, expressive and well-coloured wine.
GR 70%, CN 10%, SYR 5%, MV 5%, VAR 10%

CUVÉE DU VATICAN

This *cuvée* is used for both Diffonty's Châteauneuf-du-Pape and Côtes-du-Rhône production. The wine has a very deep colour and lots of tannin. Vins de Pays and Côtes-du-Rhône are also produced.

LE VIEUX DONJON

This is a rarely encoutered, but truly exiting wine from a small domaine. It is full, rich and warm, with plenty of ripe blackcurrant flavour and a delicious smoky, toasty complexity.
GR 80%, SYR 10%, VAR 10%

DOMAINE DU VIEUX TÉLÉGRAPHE

The style of Vieux Télégraphe has changed somewhat over the years, but its quality remains at the very highest level. Its wines are warm and mellow, with the spicy glow of classic Châteauneuf's loyal Grenache grape.
GR 70%, SYR 15%, MV 10%, CN 5%

GIGONDAS

DOMAINE LES GOUBERT CUVÉE FLORENCE

The regular wine of Domaine les Goubert is amongst the very cream of Gigondas' production, but this wine is a class apart. In 1985 Jean-Pierre Cartier produced the domaine's first Cuvée Florence from selected wines aged in new oak casks; this ruddy-coloured, decadently fruity wine, with its oaky character, is the result.
GR 88%, SYR 10%, MV 2%

DOMAINE DE LONGUE-TOQUE

This wine once had an almost black colour and a dense, smoky flavour. Now it is partly made by *macération carbonique* and given a light filtration. Although of a much lighter character, its exuberantly fruity style still makes it one of the finest Gigondas.
GR 65%, SYR 20%, CN 10%, MV 5%

DOMAINE LES PALLIÈRES

Pierre and Christian are sons of Hilarion Roux, the first person to sell domaine-bottled Gigondas. Most of the vines growing on this 25-hectare (62-acre) estate are very old, endowing the wine with its dark, opaque colour and the concentration and complexity of its flavour.
GR 60%, MV 25%, SYR 10%, CN 5%

DOMAINE RASPAIL AY

Not to be confused with Château Raspail, which has been owned by Gabriel Meffre since 1979, this part of the old property is owned by the Ay family, with Dominique - the son of François - now in charge. His wine is deep-coloured, with a mouth-watering floral-raspberry bouquet and lots of fruit on the palate.

DOMAINE SAINT-GAYAN

Roger Meffre, whose family has farmed this property for almost 500 years, produces a wine of extraordinary complexity, length and finesse. This man's passionate pursuit of perfection obliged him to cut away no less than one-fifth of the crop two weeks prior to the harvest in 1986, when a humid summer led to rampant rot.
GR 80%, SYR 15%, MV 5%

TAVEL

DOMAINE DE LA GENESTIÈRE

Madame Andrée Bernard runs this model 25-hectare (62-acre) estate and produces a Tavel Rosé *par excellence*. A maceration that varies between 12 and 24 hours, depending on the vintage, gives a fairly deep-coloured wine that is fresh, crisp and totally dry in flavour, yet bursting with fruit and finesse. Red and white wine are also produced from 10 hectares (25 acres) in Lirac.
GR 50%, CN 20%, VAR 30%

DOMAINE MABY LA FORCADIÈRE

From their large domaine of 40 hectares (100 acres), the Maby family produces a fine, full, delightfully clean, dry and fruity rosé.
GR 70%, CN 15%, MV 15%

LIRAC

DOMAINE DE CASTEL OUALOU

A lightish wine with soft, raspberry-flavoured fruit in most years. It comes into its own in big years - such as 1978 and 1983 - when the smoky-cassis of Syrah dominates. "Oualou" in Algerian means "there is none", hence the cross through the castle.
GR 70%, SYR 15%, MV 15%

DOMAINE MABY
LA FERMADE

The Maby family owns some 30 hectares (75 acres) in Lirac, where they produce a rosé and a fine, fresh, dry white. But it is the superb red Lirac that is the best: a deep-coloured wine with a billowing bouquet of summer fruits and plenty of tannin.

GR 70%, CN 15%, MV 15%

CHÂTEAU SAINT-ROCH
CUVÉE ANCIENNE VIGUERIE

Every year the best wines are set aside by Jean-Jacques Verda for this wine, which represents less than 10 per cent of the red wine production of Château Saint-Roch. It spends two years in wooden vats and a further two years in bottle before it is sold.

GR 55%, SYR 15%, MV 15%, CN 15%

COTEAUX DU TRICASTIN

DOMAINE TOUR D'ELYSSAS
VIN DE SYRAH

This estate was established by the late Pierre Labeye. The red and rosé wines produced from a blend of Grenache, Cinsault, Carignan and Syrah are excellent, particularly from the single-vineyard Cru de Meynas, but it is the small amount of dark and dense, pure Syrah wine, both oak-aged and straight, that has long been the very finest Tricastin available.

MUSCAT DE BEAUMES-DE-VENISE

DOMAINE DES BERNARDINS

Under the uncompromising charge of Pierre Castaud, this was such a distinctive, big, almost assertive wine that people loved or hated it. Now that Domaine de Bernardins is run by Castaud's brother-in-law, Monsieur Maurin, the wine is very much lighter and more elegant - a style that appeals to more people.

CAVE COOP. DE
BEAUMES-DE-VENISE
MUSCAT DES PAPES

This is not necessarily the cheapest Muscat de Beaumes-de-Venise by the time it filters on to the shelf, cunningly disguised in a screwtop, look-alike whisky bottle, but discerning drinkers will know that quality definitely lurks beneath.

DOMAINE DE COYEUX

The fastest rising star on the firmament of Muscat de Beaumes-de-Venise, Domaine de Coyeux seems to have quickly established itself in every quarter of the trade, from supermarkets to the very best restaurants. Do not let the former dissuade you from trying this most elegant and fragrant of nectars.

DOMAINE DE DURBAN

Bernard Leydier's Domaine Durban staggers the senses by its impossible concentration and sumptuous sweetness, which seems to be in direct contradiction to its light colour. This is the most exotic Muscat de Beaumes-de-Venise.

CLAIRETTE DE DIE

ACHARD-VINCENT
TRADITION

Situated at Saint-Croix, this firm has been producing fine *Tradition* using organic methods since 1983. The wine has a strong, flowery Muscat aroma, retains it *mousse* particularly well and finishes with a well-balanced sweetness.

MUSC 70%, CL 30%

BUFFARDEL FRÈRES
CARTE BLANCHE

This firm is generally considered the best house in Clairette de Die, although with equal amounts of Clairette and Muscat in this wine the style is more restrained. Buffardel is also the foremost promoter of the *brut* style of Clairette de Die made from 100 per cent Clairette grapes.

CL 50%, MUSC 50%

CÔTES-DU-RHÔNE-VILLAGES

The wines of the Côtes-du-Rhône-Villages are usually a distinct step up from regular Côtes-du-Rhône. The vast majority of the production for these wines comes from the southern Rhône, although, theoretically, it can come from either the north or the south. Gigondas, Cairanne, Chusclan and Laudun were the original four villages that formed this appellation. Gigondas achieved its own AOC in 1971, but other villages have been added from time to time and there are now no less than 16. One less, in fact, than there used to be - the village of Vacqueras followed the example set by Gigondas, gaining its own appellation from the 1988 vintage. Although there are some improving whites and some excellent rosés, it is the reds for which this appellation is deservedly renowned. The reds are made from a blend of grapes, including a maximum of 65 per cent Grenache plus up to 25 per cent Syrah, Mourvèdre and Cinsault, with a further permitted 10 per cent from a range of different varieties. The labels below represent one important producer from each of the 12 major villages.

BEAUMES-DE-VENISE
CHÂTEAU REDORTIER

RASTEAU
DOMAINE LA SOUMADE

VACQUEYRAS
DOMAINE LA FOURMONE

CAIRANNE
DOMAINE RABASSE CHARAVIN

SABLET
CHÂTEAU DU TRIGNON

VALRÉAS
JEAN-PIERRE BROTTE

CHUSCLAN
CAVE DES VIGNERONS
DE CHUSCLAN
CUVÉE DES MONTICAUD

SAINT-GERVAIS
DOMAINE SAINTE-ANNE

VINSOBRES
DOMAINE DU CORIANÇON

SÉGURET
JEAN-PIERRE BROTTE

VISAN
DOMAINE DE LA CANTHARIDE
CUVÉE DE VISAN L'HERMITE

LAUDUN
DOMAINE PELAQUIÉ

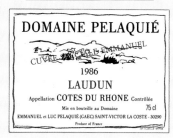

SOUTHERN FRANCE

SOUTHERN AND SOUTH-WESTERN France are well known as producers of vast quantities of everyday wines, but they are also building a reputation for exciting wines of the highest quality.

The diversity of South-West France

South-West France has 30 AOC areas in a broad expanse of country that starts east of Bordeaux in the Dordogne and runs south through Gascony, the Armagnac country and the Basque lands to the Pyrenees. It includes one of France's largest and most successful *vin de pays* zones, Vin de Pays de Côtes de Gascogne. Although the wine-growing districts are so scattered, there are some common wine styles and grape varieties, mainly influenced by the close proximity of Bordeaux.

Bergerac, with its claret-style reds and sweet whites of Monbazillac, is the largest of the quality regions. Its reds are vinified from the four main Bordeaux grapes of Cabernet Sauvignon, Cabernet Franc, Merlot and Malbec; as are the reds from Côtes de Buzet, Côtes de Duras and Pécharmant.

Greater regional individuality is displayed in Cahors, where the principal constituent is Malbec. Tannat is the local grape which dominates in Madiran, the Côtes de St Mont, Irouléguy and Béarn. Jurançon, in the foothills of the Pyrenees, makes a range of dry, sweet, even sparkling white wines from local grapes. Local grapes are also still used in Gaillac and for the sparkling wines of Blanquette de Limoux.

Languedoc and Roussillon

The provinces of Languedoc and Roussillon - the Midi - form France's largest wine region. It stretches across four *départements*, following the Mediterranean coastline westward from Arles and the mouth of the Rhône to the Spanish border. The vineyards cover 35 per cent of France's planted area and account for almost half its total output.

The grape varieties derive from Spain in the south-west and Rhône in the north-east; Carignan being the mainstay in Roussillon, Minervois in Languedoc and Fitou. Although from 1990 new AOC rules require a bigger input of the more interesting Syrah and Mourvèdre, more adventurous growers are disregarding the AOC and labelling their wines simply *vin de pays*.

Improvements in quality

Traditionally a source of workaday wines, quality in Languedoc-Rousillon has significantly improved recently. The region now has a collection of AOC and VDQS designations. Those that have achieved most prominence are Côtes du Roussillon and Coteaux du Languedoc, with their Villages extension, closely followed by Corbières, Costières du Gard (now known as Costières de Nîmes), Fitou, Minervois and St Chinian.

Viticulture in Provence

In comparison to the Midi or South-West, Provence is a small wine region. It is really the hinterland of Marseille and Toulon, on the southern rim of the Côtes du Rhône region. Nonetheless, it produces some 45 million cases of wine each year, 60 per cent of it dry rosé, although the growing reputation of the area is based on its reds.

Provence enjoys a climate that is as amenable as anywhere in France with high levels of sunshine and more dependable vintages than its northern neighbour in the Rhône Valley. A range of soil conditions and a variety of favourable micro-climates allow a growing number of enterprising winemakers to experiment with combinations of local grapes and others from the nearby Rhône or Bordeaux.

Among the seven AOCs of Provence are four smaller ones of long standing in Cassis, Bandol, Palette and Bellet. The much larger area of Côtes de Provence was elevated from VDQS status as recently as 1977, and Coteaux d'Aix en Provence was upgraded, with Coteaux les Baux, in 1984.

The Bandol *vins de garde* based on Mourvèdre, Grenache, Cinsault and Syrah have long been the flagship for Provençal quality. The little appellation of Palette on the edge of Aix-en-Provence produces full-bodied reds of a similar blend, and whites - of Clairette and Ugni Blanc - that are matured in wood. The aromatic white wine of Cassis has a similar *cépage*. Bellet, to the north of Nice, relies for its whites on Rolle, a native, supported by Chardonnay and Ugni Blanc. For its red wines, the local Braquet grape is the most dominant variety.

Experimenting with grape varieties

Côtes de Provence winemakers are often ready to disregard the restrictions of the appellation in their search for better quality and grape types. For instance, Carignan is prescribed for reds with up to 30 per cent of Syrah. The reality is different, with anything up to 90 per cent Syrah or Cabernet Sauvignon. Similarly with the whites, Sauvignon Blanc is a favourite introduction, to enhance crispness and acidity, but it is not an official variety.

SOUTH WEST

BARON D'ARDEUIL, BUZET

The Vignerons Réunis produces some of the finest wines in Côtes de Buzet. They use over 3,000 oak *barriques*, many of which are new. This silky-smooth Baron d'Ardeuil is made from older vines and matured in new oak.

CHÂTEAU LA BASTIDE
CÔTES DU MARMANDAIS

This property in the Côtes du Marmandais is owned by Jean-André Laffitte, who is a member of Univitis, an organization of some 500 growers in the south-west of France. Château la Bastide is a full, fruity red wine that consistently rates as one of the finest Marmandais.

CHÂTEAU DE CAIX, CAHORS

This Château is owned by Prince Henrick, husband of the Queen of Denmark, both members of "Les Côtes d'Olt" *coopérative*. The wine is dark in colour and deep in flavour, with classic style and silky finesse.

LES CÔTES D'OLT
CAHORS IMPERIAL

This is one wine that does hark back to the famous old "black wine" of Cahors. Through strict selection in the cellar of their finest wines and no expense spared in the use of new oak, Les Côtes d'Olt produces a 100 per cent Malbec wine that is regularly comparable in quality, though not character, to a top Bourgeois growth of the Médoc.

CHÂTEAU FONTAINE
CAHORS

Formerly sold as Vin de Cahors Jean Galbert, this excellent Cahors is now produced by Pierre Johnstone, who purchased Monsieur Galbert's property in May 1989. This wine is typically well-coloured, but possesses an exceptional depth of flavour and rare finesse for a Cahors.
MB 85%, TAN 8%, M 5%, JUR 2%

CHÂTEAU DE GUEYZE
BUZET

This estate was established in 1973 and now produces one of the darkest and most densely flavoured wines in the district. The wine is very full-bodied and has a firm tannic structure, yet is elegant, with rich vanilla and violet overtones.

JURANÇON
PRESTIGE D'AUTOMNE
VENDANGES TARDIVES

The sweet and seductive, late-harvested wine of Jurançon was used at the Christening of Henri de Navarre in 1553. Today, when the climatic conditions are right, this is by far the best wine of its type, with a honeyed richness that hints of pineapples and peaches, candied peel and cinnamon.

DOMAINE DE LAULAN
CÔTES DE DURAS

The red wines of the Côtes de Duras are not *vins de garde*, but when produced with the quality of Domaine de Laulan, they can be one of the most delicious early-drinking wines in the world. This property also produces an excellent dry Sauvignon wine.

DOMAINE DE MIGNABERRY IROULÉGUY

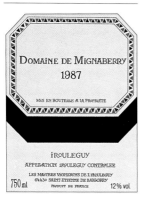

Produced by the local *coopérative* which has a virtual monopoly over the production of Irouléguy. The *coopérative* uses Tannat and Cabernet grapes grown on vineyards in Basque country, producing a deep, dark and tannic wine, with a rich and mellow flavour and an earthy-spicy aftertaste.

CHÂTEAU MONTUS, MADIRAN

The high percentage of Tannat in this Madiran gives it a fantastically deep colour, great concentration of fruit and a firm tannic construction. The wine is matured in new oak *barriques,* an expensive operation that is becoming a trend in this appellation.

CHÂTEAU PIERRON, BUZET

This independently owned property in Buzet has almost 15 hectares (37 acres) under vine and produces a very regular quality of wine, with lots of round *cassis* fruit, enhanced by creamy-vanilla oak complexity and firmly underpinned with ripe tannins.

COLLECTION PLAIMONT CÔTES DE SAINT MONT

Plaimont's oak-aged, predominantly Tannat wine called Collection is an intensely flavoured wine of extraordinary complexity that puts many a fine AOC in Armagnac to shame.

ROBERT BRUT, CINQUANTENAIR BLANC DE BLANCS BLANQUETTE DE LIMOUX

Blanquette de Limoux has an older history than Champagne and today makes a sparkling wine that is exceptional, considering the sunny clime of its southern vineyards. The Robert family is one of its best producers, although their label is tautologous because only white grapes are allowed: every bottle of Limoux must be a *blanc de blancs*.

DOMAINE DES TRES CANTOUS LE MOELLEUX DE ROBERT PLAGEOLES, GAILLAC

The Plageoles have grown grapes in Gaillac for over 500 years. If Gaillac Moelleux is less exotic than Jurançon *Vendange Tardive,* the sultry sweetness of its spicy, apple and quince flavour is no less seductive.

CHÂTEAU DU TREUIL DE NAILHAC, MONBAZILLAC

This fine wine comes from north-facing slopes near Sigoulès. Its great concentration and intense sweetness is delicious young, but has a honeyed complexity after 10 years in bottle.

LANGUEDOC-ROUSSILLON

DOMAINE DU BOSC CABERNET SAUVIGNON

Pierre Bésinet produces *vins de pays* of exceptional quality. The Cabernet Sauvignon is a round and stylish wine with fine varietal character.

DOMAINE DU BOSC CÉPAGE SYRAH

This rich and powerful Cépage Syrah is this domaine's real claim to fame. Bésinet also produces a range of white wines, including an aromatic Muscat Sec, a flavourful Marsanne and a fresh, fragrant Grenache Blanc.

CHÂTEAU CAP DE FOUSTE
CÔTES DU ROUSSILLON

Under the auspices of Les Vignerons Catalans, this estate pioneered the restrained use of *macération carbonique* and new oak for its red wines. The fresh and fleshy wine that resulted has a deliciously soft flavour, with hints of red-fruit and vanilla.

DOMAINE CAZES
CÉPAGE MUSCAT BLANC
MOELLEUX

From their 85 hectare (210-acre) estate at Rivesaltes, Cazes Frères produce a varied range, including still red Côtes du Roussillon Villages, but it is Muscat, particularly fortified Muscat, that this family firm has justly become famous for. Perhaps the most underrated wine is its unfortified Cépage Muscat Blanc Moelleux, which is an elegant wine full of sumptuous, semi-sweet, zesty fruit.

DOMAINE CAZES
MUSCAT DE RIVESALTES

Cazes Frères is best known for its Domaine Cazes Muscat de Rivesaltes: a succulent wine with a deliciously tangy flavour. The production of this wine is 10 times greater than the Cépage Muscat Blanc Moelleux.

DOMAINE CAZES
VINTAGE RIVESALTES

Produced on a relatively small scale is the Domaine Cazes Vintage Rivesaltes, an ultra-clean, early-bottled, ripe, fruity red wine that will open the eyes of anyone who thinks that all Rivesaltes are rancid and oxidized.

CELLIER DES COMTES
CUVÉE CAVEAU DU PRESBYTÈRE
CARAMANY

Caramany is the best of the Côtes du Roussillon's 25 *villages* appellations and Cellier des Comtes is one of the labels used for wines made by Les Vignerons Catalans. This special *cuvée* is an overtly fruity red wine. It is a *macération carbonique* wine, but has hints of vanilla and spice from maturation in oak.

DOMAINE DE FONSALADE
SAINT-CHINIAN

This estate, lying north-east of Béziers, consists of 30 hectares (74 acres), two-thirds of which are on schistous hillsides within the Saint-Chinian appellation. It produces a fine red wine, plus a delightful rosé.

CHÂTEAU GREZAN
CUVÉE ARNAUD LUBAC
FAUGÈRES

This 46-hectare (114-acre) vineyard borders the village of Laurena, west of Béziers, in the foothills of the Cévennes mountains. Its proprietor, Michel Lubac-Lanson, produces red and rosé AOC Faugères from vines grown on a schistous soil, including the exceptionally fine Cuvée Arnaud Lubac. Matured in oak *barriques,* this wine has a voluptuous vanilla and violet flavour, with a certain spicy complexity.

CHÂTEAU DE JAU
CÔTES DU ROUSSILLON

Bernard and Jean Dauré run this 42-hectare (104-acre) estate in the Côtes du Roussillon, where they make this château-bottled red wine. It is a well-balanced wine of some finesse, with elegant, silky-spicy fruit.

CHÂTEAU DE JAU
MUSCAT DE RIVESALTES

This Muscat de Rivesaltes, produced by the Daurés, is an aromatic and sumptuous sweet wine that begs to be drunk as young as possible. They also produce a good Banyuls and a delicious *nouveau*-style Vin de Pays des Côtes Catalanes, which is bottled three weeks after the harvest.

LES MAÎTRES VIGNERONS DE CASCASTEL
FITOU, CUVÉE SPECIALE

With 80 members owning just over 1,000 hectares (2,470 acres), this is not one of the largest *coopératives* in the area, but it is one of the best. Its top wine - Cuvée Speciale - is consistently one of finest Fitou produced.

The Carignan provides its great concentration and complexity, while the mellow warmth of Grenache softens the wine in the mouth.

DOMAINE DU MAS BLANC
COLLIOURE "LES PILOUMS"

This is one of the greatest wines from the Collioure, an appellation that is reserved for the early-harvested wines of Banyuls. The wine is deep-coloured, with a full, intense flavour and soft, spicy aftertaste.

MAS CHICHET
CABERNET

Jacques Chichet is the largest cultivator of Cabernet in Roussillon - it thrives on his calcareous-clay soil. The wine illustrated is a very fine blend of both Cabernets. Chichet also produces a rosé, which is sold as a Vin de Pays Pyrénées-Orientales.
CS 60%, CF 40%

MAS DE DAUMAS GASSAC

Situated 48 kilometres (30 miles) north-west of Montpellier at Aniane, this property has been dubbed "the Lafite of the Languedoc". When Aimé and Véronique Guibert purchased Daumas Gassac in 1970, wine was the last thing on their minds. But then they were visited by Professor Enjalbert, the Bordeaux geologist and author, who found the Guiberts had a fine volcanic soil that was an astonishing 20 metres (65 feet) deep. Enjalbert predicted that it would yield a world-class wine if cultivated as a *Grand Cru,* and that is exactly what Aimé Guibert set out to achieve. The red is a world-class wine in almost true Médocian style, yet with a touch of warm Mediterranean spice. As with all fine wines, it is different from year to year, but maintains its own very distinctive style. A wine of great longevity, the red Daumas Gassac may be compared to the top *cru classé* of Pauillac or St Estèphe. The white is in the same class, but far more exotic, with the Muscat giving a ripeness of perfume to the oak, not unlike a New World wine.
Red CS 80%, MB, SYR, CF, PN & TAN 20%
White CH 40%, VIO 40%, PMG 10%, MUSC 5%, BLC 5%

DOMAINE DE MAYRANNE
CUVÉE PAULA, MINERVOIS

Minervois is a vast appellation encompassing no less than 61 different communes. Its wines tend to be modest rather than exceptional, but this small domaine has built up a considerable reputation for its elegant wine, which hints of creamy-oak and peppery-cherry fruit.

CHÂTEAU VAL JOANIS
CÔTES DU LUBÉRON

The determination of the owner of this property, Jean-Louis Chancel, has been largely responsible for the recent elevation of this appellation from VDQS to AOC: Val Joanis is now the jewel in Lubéron's crown.

CHÂTEAU LA VOULTE-GASPARETS, CUVÉE ROMAIN PAUC, CORBIÈRES

Reverdy's wines have good colour, soft, spicy-fruit on the nose and lots of berry-fruit flavour on the palate. His special *cuvées* are more intense, with creamy oak tannins.

PROVENCE

CHÂTEAU BARBEYROLLES
CÔTES DE PROVENCE

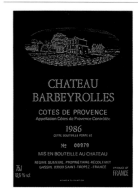

This old property was acquired by Régine Sumeire in 1982, who has revived its long-lost reputation. The superb red has a bouquet of freshly picked blackberries.

CHÂTEAU DE CALISSANNE CUVÉE PRESTIGE COTEAUX D'AIX EN PROVENCE

A 20-hectare (50-acre) vineyard surrounds this historical château and produces a quality of wine that stands out in the Coteaux d'Aix en Provence appellation. Its Cuvée Prestige is produced in red, white and rosé. They are all beautifully made, but the oak-aged red is the most serious.

CHÂTEAU DE CRÉMAT BELLET

Bellet is a tiny appellation in the hills north of Nice that is cooled by Alpine winds. Château de Crémat produces a sublime rosé and a well perfumed red of surprising finesse. However, it is this fine, firm yet fragrant white wine that truly excels.

LA LAIDIÈRE BANDOL

Bandol probably produces Provence's greatest red wines and this property at Saint-Ann d'Evenos on the eastern edge of the appellation makes one of the darkest and most striking red Bandols. Do not, however, overlook La Laidière's stunning rosé, a serious, complex and utterly beguiling wine.

MAS DE LA DAME COTEAUX D'AIX EN PROVENCE LES BAUX

This property is situated in Les Baux, a picturesque hill-top village in the east of the appellation, just 13 kilometres (8 miles) from the Rhône. The wines are vinified in stainless-steel and its Réserve du Mas ranks as one of the best Coteaux d'Aix en Provence currently produced.

MOULIN DES COSTES BANDOL

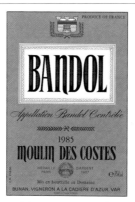

The Bandol rosé is nice and attractive, but the least interesting Moulin des Costes wine. The white can be extraordinarily rich and fresh, but varies from vintage to vintage. Red Bandol is what Paul Bunan is best at and this rubs off on his pure Cabernet Sauvignon Bunan which has to be sold as a Vin de Pays Mont Caume, but is equal to his great Bandols.

CHÂTEAU DE PIBARNON BANDOL

This 30-hectare (74-acre) property at La Cadière produces one of the most remarkable red Bandol wines. It has a lovely deep colour and is absolutely full of lush, velvety fruit flavours beautifully underpinned with supple tannins and creamy oak.

DOMAINE DE SAINT BAILLON CUVÉE DU ROUDAI

Situated in the heart of the Côtes de Provence, the grapes of this property are picked by hand and vinified in a modern winery. They make an exciting rosé with exceptionally fresh acidity. The Cuvée du Roudai is a big, blackcurranty red wine with delicious hints of vanilla.
CS 65%, SYR 35%

CHÂTEAU SIMONE, PALETTE

Despite the fact that more than 30 grape varieties are permitted for this appellation, Palette is one of the most definitive wines of the Provence. Château Simone encompasses three-quarters of the district and its red wines are legendary; the rarely encountered, rich and powerful, oak-aged whites can also be sensational.

DOMAINE TEMPIER, BANDOL

This property in Le Plan du Castellet includes some of Bandol's finest vineyards. Winemaking is an entirely natural process without fertilizers or chemicals. The pale rosé is aromatic, elegant and refreshing; the fine reds have deep colour, a bouquet of ripe berries and herbs and concentrated fruit flavours with firm tannins. They continue to evolve for many years.

~ G E R M A N Y ~

GERMANY EXPORTS ABOUT a third of its harvest, something approaching 3 million hectolitres (33.3 million cases) annually, of which more than two-thirds is destined for the UK and the USA. The bulk of exported wine is Liebfraumilch and other generic *Bereich* and *Grosslage* wines, such as Piesporter Michelsberg, Niersteiner Gutes Domtal and Bernkasteler Kurfürstlay. These all quite legitimately fall under the heading of *Qualitätswein* (in its *QbA* variant: see table opposite) - literally quality wine from one of the 11 specified German wine regions - but in reality they are mass-produced wines.

At the other end of the scale are the world-famous wines of great estates like Schloss Johannisberg and Schloss Vollrads or of many marvellous single vineyards, such as Bernkasteler Doctor and Steinberg. These wines come from the better-known areas of Germany: the Mosel-Saar-Ruwer, Rheingau, Nahe, Rheinhessen and Rheinpfalz (the Palatinate). The list of 11 designated regions in which quality wines can be made is completed by Baden, Württemberg, Franken, Ahr, Hessische-Bergstrasse and Mittelrhein. In size and output Rheinhessen and Rheinpfalz are by far the largest regions, containing 25 per cent and 23 per cent

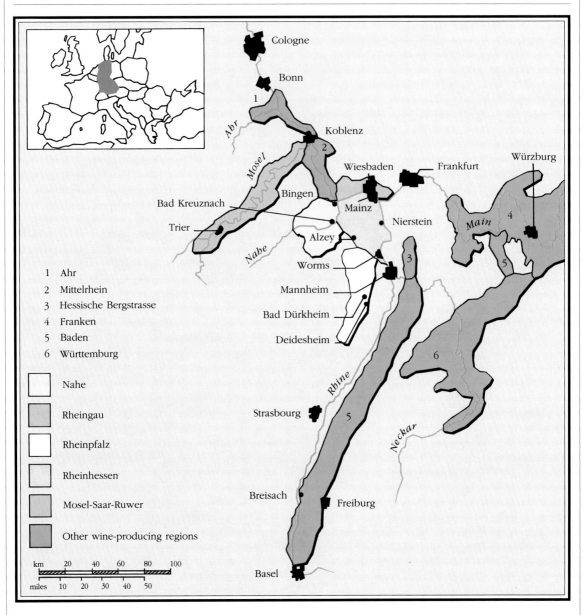

1   Ahr
2   Mittelrhein
3   Hessische Bergstrasse
4   Franken
5   Baden
6   Württemburg

Nahe

Rheingau

Rheinpfalz

Rheinhessen

Mosel-Saar-Ruwer

Other wine-producing regions

Physical factors *Fine German wines chiefly derive their character from the climate of Germany's* *northerly geographical position, modified by a network of unique micro-climates, created by the rivers* *Rhine, Mosel, Saar, Ruwer, Nahe, Neckar and Main, which cause the grapes to ripen to such perfection.*

192

respectively of Germany's vineyards. They effectively supply between them the whole of the vast annual production of Liebfraumilch, although the wine can also be made in Rheingau and Nahe.

The hierarchy of the vineyards
There are 90,000 individual growers working in the 96,000 hectares (227,230 acres) of vineyards in Germany. Since the institution of the German wine law in 1971, their holdings are concentrated into 2,600 individual vineyard sites (*Einzellagen*), which are the source for the whole of the country's output. The best wines will invariably carry the name of the vineyard of origin on the label, preceded by the name of the village in which the vineyard is situated. The less fine wines will in general be grouped with those of other adjoining

Mosel landscape *A typical view of the river Mosel as it runs through Germany conveys the steepness of its banks.*

THE OECHSLE SCALE

The 1971 German wine law placed the quality emphasis on the degree of sweetness of the grape juice from which the wine is made. This principle runs through the quality structure for each level of German wine, from *Tafelwein* to *Trockenbeerenauslese*. The degree of sweetness, which determines the quality category of the wine, is measured in degrees Oechsle. Minimum Oechsle levels vary between regions and grape varieties.

QUALITY CATEGORY	CHARACTER OF THE WINE	MINIMUM OECHSLE
Deutscher Tafelwein	The lowest grade of wine; has to be entirely German in origin. At present this category represents 3 to 5 per cent of total production.	44 - 50°
Landwein	A new category in 1982; a table wine from a Landwein district, of which there are 15. Also a small contributor to total quantity.	47 - 55°
Qualitätswein bestimmter Anbaugebiete (QbA)	Quality wine that comes from any one of the 11 wine regions (*Anbaugebiete*). Liebfraumilch is included in this category.	51 - 72°
Qualitätswein mit Prädikat (QmP):	Quality wines made from grapes that have achieved the prescribed degree of natural ripeness, without chaptalization. The *Prädikaten* are set out below:	
Kabinett	Lightest, most delicate, and driest in style, of the *Prädikat* wines.	67 - 85°
Spätlese	Literally made from "late-picked" grapes (late being relative to the picking of the Kabinett grapes); the wines achieve a marvellous balance between a light, firm sweetness or alcohol and a racy acidity.	76 - 95°
Auslese	A richer style from genuinely late-harvested and selected bunches; usually made only in good vintages.	83 - 105°
Beerenauslese	A very rich, sweet wine made with individually picked, super-ripe berries, which have become shrivelled on the vine through the effect of noble rot (*Edelfäule*); achieved very infrequently.	110 - 128°
Eiswein	A wine made from healthy grapes that are left on the vine until December or even January, and are pressed in their frozen state. The water is frozen, but not the sugars and acids, thus making a very concentrated juice that gives an intensely sweet, but at the same time delicate and finely acidic wine. Very rare and expensive.	110 - 128°
Trockenbeerenauslese	The sweetest category of wine, made from dried, individually selected berries affected by noble rot; with a potential alcoholic strength of 21-2 per cent, it may only achieve 5.5 per cent alcohol, thus endowing the wine with an intense concentration of residual honeyed sweetness. Possible only in the finest years.	150 - 154°

vineyards within the larger boundary of a *Grosslage*, of which there are 152 in all. The *Grosslagen* are in turn contained within 35 districts (*Bereiche*) which form part of the 11 designated regions. A sub-regional wine such as Bereich Bernkastel is easily identifiable by the appearance of the word "Bereich" on the label. Unfortunately, however, it is not always so easy to distinguish between a *Grosslage* wine (such as Klüsserather St Michael) and a single-vineyard wine (such as Klüsserather Brüderschaft) without being familiar with all the *Grosslagen* names in current use. This difficulty highlights a major flaw evident in the German wine law of 1971.

Chaptalization and Süssreserve

Where there is a need to compensate for the lack of ripeness of the grapes in lesser years - which tends to mean most of them - the addition of sugar in various forms is permitted in order to build up the potential alcoholic strength of the grape juice. This process, known as chaptalization, is allowed for all wines up to and including *Qualitätswein bestimmter Anbaugebiete (QbA)*. Chaptalization is never allowed for *Qualitätswein mit Prädikat (QmP)* because they are expected to have enough natural sweetness to achieve the alcoholic and residual sugar levels appropriate to the style of wine. The German term for chaptalization, *Anreicherung* (literally, "enrichment") underlines the intention of the process, which is to improve the wine by obtaining a proper balance between alcohol, acidity and sugar content.

Süssreserve is a sweetening agent composed of unfermented grape juice. It is added at the end of the vinification process before bottling to adjust the final sweetness of the wine. It may be used with any German wine but its use is subject to strict provisions that cover grape variety, quality and source of origin. These rules ensure that the

Historic label *This label adorned a Neroberger from the Rheingau State cellars. The word "Cabinet" (literally, "treasure store") on the label refers to a room in Kloster Eberbach where casks were stored by monks that made wine there. The* Kabinett *category derives from this term.*

Süssreserve is similar in kind to the wine to which it is added. *Süssreserve* may be added to *QmP* categories and is widely used up to *Spätlese* level.

Growth of interest in drier wines

The past decade or so has seen a preference among the Germans themselves for drier styles of wine that can be served as a suitable accompaniment to food. *Trocken* (dry) and *Halbtrocken* (medium dry) wines are now made in the best vineyards alongside the sweeter styles at both *QbA* and *QmP* levels. A *Trocken* wine can have up to 9 grams per litre (g/l) of sugar as long as the required balance of acidity is preserved. *Halbtrocken*, which is often preferred because its additional touch of sweetness seems to give more body to the wine, is allowed a sugar content not more than 10 g/l greater than the overall acid content (expressed as tartaric acid), with a maximum limit of 18 g/l.

In the Rheingau there has been a move towards higher quality dry Riesling wines, inspired by a group of leading growers called the Charta Association - a name that occasionally appears on the label. The lead has been followed by others and the practice is now quite widespread. The drier wines have a refinement that enables them to age gracefully in bottle quite as well as their sweeter

GERMAN VINTAGES	
YEAR	**VINTAGE**
1989	A fine vintage - bigger than 1988; a lot of wines of *Prädikat* level and *Trockenbeerenauslesen* in Mosel.
1988	Outstandingly good vintage, with excellent wines in Mosel and Saar, Rheinhessen and Rheinpfalz; much *Kabinett* and *Spätlesen* made and some higher categories. Variable in the Rheingau.
1987	Good quality vintage, with a lot of fresh, lively wines at *Kabinett* level.
1986	A variable year with good Riesling *Kabinett* and *Spätlese* wines if carefully selected.
1985	A smaller harvest, but a year when some very good wines were made; fine Riesling *Spätlese* and *Auslese* wines in the Mosel and in Rheinpfalz, and a high proportion of *Kabinett*.
1984	Particularly attractive at *QbA* level.
1983	Very fine year of large quantity with top quality; ripe, fruity wines producing excellent *Spätlesen* and *Auslesen*, with the occasional *Trockenbeerenauslese* and *Eiswein*.
1982	Very large vintage; generally unexciting wines.

counterparts. *Trocken* and *Halbtrocken* wines up to *Spätlese* or even *Auslese* level can now be encountered in export markets, and the terms are also used for red wines.

Grape varieties

Despite the appearance of Scheurebe, Kerner, Rieslaner, Optima, Bacchus and other new grape varieties from research centres over the years, the Riesling retains its pre-eminence as the top German quality grape. The classic Riesling is widely grown on all the better sites, and most notably in Mosel-Saar-Ruwer, Rheingau, Nahe and Rheinpfalz. The Müller-Thurgau grape (currently thought to be the crossing of two Riesling clones) nonetheless remains the most widely planted variety, occupying about 25 per cent of the area under vine. Silvaner, once the most prolifically grown variety, now takes third position after Riesling, followed fairly closely by Kerner and Scheurebe. Spätburgunder (Pinot Noir) and Portugieser, which are the principal red wine grapes, each have less than a 5 per cent share of the vineyards and are mostly concentrated in Baden, Württemberg and Ahr.

The quality pattern of German wines

In Germany the base of its production pyramid is not table wine, as it is in France and Italy, but quality wine, albeit of the lowest *Qualitätswein* category, QbA. The proportions of *Tafelwein* and *Landwein* in a German harvest are incredibly small. New regulations affecting wine production, passed by the German national parliament in July 1989, encourage growers to provide lower quantities but higher quality wine at realistic prices. The effect of this may well be to declassify quantities of QbA, so increasing the amount of *Tafelwein* available, which in world terms would offer a more realistic approach to quality.

Typically, in a normal year, the bulk of the German harvest will comprise QbA. For example, in 1987, which was generally regarded as a mediocre year, 82 per cent of output was QbA, with only a slim 14 per cent of wine produced reaching above that level. In 1985, a much better vintage, 51 per cent of the harvest was QbA, with 49 per cent being of higher quality, or *Qualitätswein mit Prädikat* (QmP). In a very ripe harvest, such as that of 1983, the proportion of fine *Spätlese* wines might be as high as 30 per cent of the harvest, with a significant addition of outstandingly good wines at the higher *Auslese* to *Trockenbeerenauslese* levels. Such harvests are very infrequent, although there are, quite exceptionally, just a few microclimates where, more often than not, it is possible to make a higher-quality *Prädikat* wine each year. Ironically, the consequence of a very ripe harvest

is the depletion of the crop at QbA and *Kabinett* level because a greater number of the better grapes would already have been creamed off.

However, since the QbA category is currently all-embracing, it contains superbly made individual-vineyard wines from leading growers in otherwise poor years as well as large quantities of cheap Liebfraumilch. What the law will not often allow as *Qualitätswein* are the new-wave wines from those growers who since the early 1970s have been experimenting with ageing their wines in new oak, Bordeaux-style *barriques*. Such wines are often refused an AP number (*Amtliche Prüfungsnummer*), and have to be content with a *Deutscher Tafelwein* designation. All QbA and QmP wine labels are required to display an AP number as proof that they have been tasted, analyzed and considered typical for their variety, origin and status. The last two digits of the AP number generally indicate the year of bottling, which is a useful clue to the age of a wine when its vintage has not been stated on the label.

GERMAN TERMS	
Anbaugebiet	A designated German wine region; there are 11 quality regions in all.
Bereich	The sub-region or district within an *Anbaugebiet;* there are 35 within the 11 regions.
Domäne	A domaine or estate. If the term appears on the label, the wine must have come exclusively from that estate.
Edelfäule	Noble rot; botrytized grapes shrivel to give a highly concentrated juice and a distinctive, superb honeyed flavour to the wine.
Einzellage	An individual vineyard site; there are 2,600 by law.
Grosslage	A group of individual sites producing quality wines of similar style, sold under the *Grosslage* name; there are 152, but only a few are well known.
Süssreserve	Sweet, unfermented grape juice.
Trocken	Dry; the English word is also beginning to be used on labels. (*Halbtrocken* means half-dry).
Weinbaudomäne	Wine domaine or estate.
Weingut	Wine-producing estate.
Winzergenossenschaft	Winegrowers' cooperative cellar.

MOSEL-SAAR-RUWER

WITH ITS DRAMATIC VINEYARD sites, exclusive planting areas and fabled winegrowers, the Mosel-Saar-Ruwer is ideally placed as a producer of fine wines. At the heart of the region, the Bernkasteler Doctor vineyard overlooks the picturesque town of Bernkastel, with south to south-south-west-facing slate slopes rising up at an angle of 60 to 70°. These dramatic vineyards directly catch every ray of sun and receive the reflected heat not only from the river below but also, it is believed, from the roofs of Bernkastel.

Exploiting the micro-climates

The diligence of the owners here - who include Wegeler-Deinhard and Dr H. Thanisch - is typical of winegrowers in the Mosel, who have to seek out the critically important micro-climates at every bend in the river in order to ripen their grapes in this most northerly European winemaking area. The majority of vineyards, out of a total coverage of 11,650 hectares (28,800 acres), are to be found in the heart of the region, the Middle Mosel. The Saar wines are produced from a few hundred hectares and the Ruwer even less. There are some 13,750 growers in the region, most having very small holdings. A large part of the wine produced is handled by merchants and shippers.

Grape varieties

Riesling is the principal grape, and used in all the leading estates, giving the wines the elegant, flowery, racy character typical of the region. Müller-Thurgau is also planted, as well as small amounts of Kerner and Elbling.

The Ahr

North of the Mosel is the small region of the Ahr, situated in a deep river valley, which produces red wines and Weissherbst (a single-variety rosé from black grapes only), and a few whites.

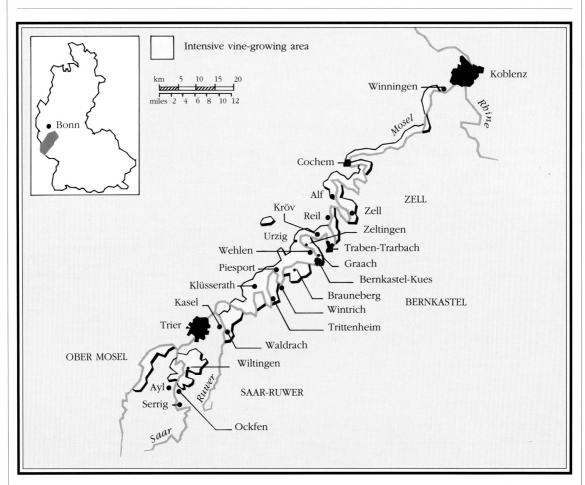

The path of the Mosel *The Mosel starts its journey in the Vosges mountains and joins the Rhine at Koblenz.* *Further upstream, it is joined first by the river Saar and then, near to Trier, by the Ruwer. The snake-like progress* *of each of these waterways through steep, difficult terrain creates the micro-climates for the vineyard sites.*

AHR

STAATLICHE WEINBAUDOMÄNE MARIENTHAL

AHR
1987er
Marienthaler Klostergarten
Spätburgunder · Spätlese
trocken
QUALITÄTSWEIN MIT PRÄDIKAT
A. P. Nr. 1 791 295 26 88
Erzeugerabfüllung
Landes- Lehr- und Versuchsanstalt für
Landwirtschaft, Weinbau und Gartenbau
Staatliche Weinbaudomäne Marienthal/Ahr
alc.
10,5 vol % D-5483 Bad Neuenahr-Ahrweiler 0,7l

*Marienthaler Klostergarten
Spätburgunder Spätlese Trocken*

Only red wines are made on this vineyard's loamy, south-facing slopes and the classic Spätburgunder, or Pinot Noir, accounts for 60 per cent of the vines grown.

BISCHÖFLICHES PRIESTERSEMINAR

Kanzemer Altenberg Riesling Spätlese

In 1966 this property became part of the Verwaltung der Bischöflichen Weingüter, a triumvirate of ecclesiastical estates in Trier. This fine, spicy wine comes from the Altenberg vineyard on the Upper Mosel.

WEINGUT ELISABETH CHRISTOFFEL-BERRES

Uerziger Würzgarten Riesling Spätlese

The Christoffel and Berres families have made wine for over 400 years. Only Riesling is grown here; this wine is from part of the Uerzige Würzgarten vineyard once called Kranklay.

WEGELER-DEINHARD

Bernkasteler Doctor Riesling Spätlese

Bernkasteler Doctor is the most famous vineyard in Germany and Wegeler-Deinhard is arguably its best-known producer. Deinhard only produces wine under the Doctor's label in years when the grapes ripen to the upper limits of *Kabinett*, otherwise it is blended into wider appellations such as its superb *Grosslage* Badstube.

FRIEDRICH-WILHELM-GYMNASIUM

*Trittenheimer Apotheke
Riesling Kabinett*

Originally established by Jesuits in 1561, this producer's cellars are situated in the centre of Trier. One of the largest estates in the Mosel-Saar-Ruwer, the vineyards that produce this fine Riesling are located at Graach, Trittenheim and Mehring on the Mosel, and Ockfen, Oberemmel and Falkenstein on the Saar.

FORSTMEISTER GELTZ ZILLIKEN

Saarburger Rausch Riesling Auslese

Once divided into three separate estates, this Saar-based estate was brought together again as recently as 1976 and is now in the hands of the Zilliken family. This typically racy wine comes from very steep, south-facing slopes of Devon slate and red quartz-rich loam.

FRITZ HAAG

*Brauneberger Juffer-Sonnenuhr
Riesling Spätlese*

The cellars of Fritz Haag, whose family has been growing wine since 1605, are situated in Brauneberg, close to the famous Juffer and Juffer-Sonnenuhr. This wine comes from the latter slope, which is very steep, south-south-west facing and has a deep slaty soil that gives a powerfully rich, yet classic, steely flavour.

VON HÖVEL

Oberemmeler Hütte Riesling Spätlese

Together with three other vineyards, von Hövel owns the entire *Einzellage* of Oberemmeler Hütte and its 800-year-old cellars. It is situated on classic Devon-slate soils and produces a well-flavoured wine that is capable of great complexity.

WEINGUT KANZEMER BERG

Kanzemer Altenberg Riesling Spätlese

The estate of Maximilian von Othegraven is situated in the centre of the Kanzemer Altenberg. The vines are located on extremely steep slopes of thin slaty soil where the yield is particularly low indeed, just 330-440 cases, and the wine possesses a characteristic intensity of flavour.

LEO KAPPES

*Zeltinger Sonnenuhr Riesling
Trocken Auslese*

Joachim Kappes, the present incumbent of this Zeltingen-based estate, is as fastidious about quality as any winemaker could be. His wines, which are, of course, vinified in traditional wooden casks and never fined, are all made in an uncompromising dry style, as this classic Auslese Trocken illustrates.

REICHSGRAF VON KESSELSTATT

Graach Josephshöfer Riesling Auslese

The Reh family took over this great Trier-based estate in 1978. In 1983 Annegret Reh-Gartner was appointed managing director and winemaker and, in 1989 was named "Winegrower of the Year" for producing wines as outstanding as this Riesling.

HEINRICH LENZ-DAHM

*Pündericher Marienburg
Riesling Auslese*

Lenz-Dahm's fourteenth-century estate consists of three vineyards in Pünderich, which are steep, slaty, and planted entirely with Riesling. They are the Marienburg, which produces an elegant, fine-featured Auslese, and the Nonnengarten and Rosenberg.

*Pündericher Marienburg
Riesling Auslese Trocken*

Günther Lenz is a great believer in the *Trocken* or dry style, which he pioneered in the Mosel and to which he hopes one day to devote his entire production. Currently, more than 80 per cent of his wines are dry.

EGON MÜLLER ZU SCHARZHOF

Scharzhofberger Riesling Auslese

The vines of this estate in Wiltingen grow on steep, south and south-east-facing slopes, covered with a thin layer of stony slate soil that yields just 55 hectolitres per hectare. The wine is exquisitely perfumed, with an intense, racy flavour and fine acidity.

CHRISTOPH VON NELL

*Waldracher Kurfurstenberg
Riesling Auslese Trocken*

In the heart of the Ruwer valley, this estate owns vineyards in two *Einzellagen*: the south-facing, slaty Dominikanerberg and the south-east facing loamy-slate Paulinsberg. Von Nell also makes fine wine from grapes grown outside his own domaine, such as this dry Auslese from Waldrach.

*Kaseler Dominikanerberg
Riesling Auslese*

This traditional Riesling Auslese comes from the pride of Christophe von Nell's Kaseler estate, the exclusively owned 6-hectare (15-acre) Dominikanerberg *Einzellage*. Some 95 per cent of his wines are fermented and matured in tank, not cask.

DR. PAULY-BERGWEILER

Wehlener Sonnenuhr Riesling Auslese

Descended from two of the Mosel's most famous dynasties, the Bergweilers and Prüms, this is one of the few German estates to enjoy widespread distribution in the USA. The Wehlener Sonnenuhr is a flowery, silky wine.

JOH.JOS.PRÜM

*Wehlener Sonnenuhr
Riesling Beerenauslese*

The Prüms are the most famous winemaking family on the Mosel. The name is prolific amongst the wine estates, but it is the wines of Johann Joseph Prüm, situated on the Sonnenuhr slope on the opposite bank to Wehlen itself, that are far and away the greatest. Only *Prädikat* wines from Prüm's own vineyards are sold under the Joh.Jos. name. The estate's *Qualitätswein* are labelled as Manfred Prüm.

S.A. Prüm

*Graacher Himmelreich
Riesling Auslese*

The only other Prüm to approach the great reputation of Joh. Jos. is S.A., which is named after Sebastian Aloys. Situated in Bernkastel-Wehlen, with steeply sloping, weathered-slate vineyards that stretch across 10 *Einzellagen* in Graach, Bernkastel and Wehlen, the estate is planted only with Riesling. The wines produced are classic for their appellations.

Weingut Edmund Reverchon

Filzener Herrenberg Riesling Auslese

This substantial estate, situated at the confluence of the Saar and Ruwer rivers, has only been planted with vines since the beginning of the twentieth century, but its south and south-west-facing slaty slopes produce Riesling of great finesse.

Weingut Max Ferd. Richter

*Mülheimer Helenenkloster
Riesling Eiswein*

This family-owned estate, based in Mülheim, has been in continuous operation since 1680. The wines are supremely elegant and can be remarkably good value, but above all Dr Dirk Richter is regarded as the Mosel's leading *Eiswein* specialist.

St. Nikolaus-Hospital

Bernkasteler Lay Riesling Spätlese

Situated in Bernkastel-Kues, this estate owns 7 hectares (17 acres) of Riesling-only vineyards in splendid sites such as Brauneberger Juffer, Wehlener Sonnenuhr and Bernkasteler Lay. All the wines are made in traditional 1,000-litre wooden *Füder*.

Weingut Schloss Lieser

Lieserer Schlossberg Riesling Auslese

This famous property encompasses the *Einzellagen* of Lieserer Schlossberg, Lieserer Süssenberg and Lieserer Niederberg-Helden and is part of Freiherr von Schorlermer Gutsverwaltung (one of the largest wine estates on the Mosel). Entirely planted with Riesling, the vineyards are on steep slopes of slaty soil and produce typical Mosel. The classic honeyed Auslese is particularly successful.

C. von Schubert'schen Schlosskellerei

*Maximin Grünhäuser Abtsberg
Riesling Auslese*

The oldest documented mention of this great estate, situated in Grünhaus, dates from 966. Of von Schubert's three *Einzellagen* it is the stunning quality of its Abtsberg that has made this estate's worldwide reputation.

Staatlichen Weinbaudomänen

*Avelsbacher Hammerstein
Riesling Spätlese*

All the wines from this estate are made in traditional 1,000-litre *Füder*, which are located in the Staatsdomäne's vaulted cellars in Trier. This *Spätlese* from the Ruwer is balanced and delicately flowery.

Wwe. Dr.H.Thanisch

Berncasteler Doctor Riesling Auslese

At one time, the Thanisch family was the largest vineyard owner in Bernkastel. It still owns the largest section of the Doctor and good sites in other famous Bernkastel vineyards such as Lay, Graben and Schlossberg, plus parts of the equally great *Einzellagen* Wehlener Sonnenuhr and Brauneberger Juffer-Sonnenuhr.

Vereinigte Hospitien

Serriger Vogelsang Riesling Auslese

This charitable organization boasts the oldest cellars in Germany and is composed of seven separate estates, with 55 hectares (136 acres) of vineyard scattered over 10 villages strung out across the Mosel and Saar.

RHEINGAU

THE RHEINGAU OBTAINS its unique micro-climate from the south-facing promontory thrown up by the Rhine as it turns westwards at Mainz, at the foot of the wooded hills flanking the Taunus mountains. The broad sweep of water and above-average hours of sunshine during the growing period combine in the best years, rather like the Garonne does in Sauternes, to provide a favourable climate for the perfect maturation of grapes. The reputation of the region rests firmly on the Riesling grape, which occupies 80 per cent of the 2,759 hectares (6,800 acres) planted. In complete contrast to the rest of the region, the State Domaine at Assmannshausen, just downstream of Rüdesheim, makes entirely red and pink wines from 100 per cent Spätburgunder (Pinot Noir). The pink Weissherbst can attain *Eiswein* and *Beerenauslese* quality levels.

The white wine of the Rheingau

The wines of the Rheingau are often talked about in the same breath as those of the Mosel as being the world's finest whites. However, Rheingau wines achieve more body and depth of flavour than the wines produced by their much larger rival, while displaying a comparable elegance. The more favourable climatic conditions enjoyed in the Rheingau are reflected in the Oeschle requirements for the region. Minimum Oeschle levels anticipated for *QbA* and *QmP* wines are about 10 per cent higher than those for the Mosel. Both sweet and dry *Prädikat* quality wines are made, and there is a return towards drier styles.

The Association of Charta Estates

Many leading estates are members of the Association of Charta Estates, which aims to produce Rheingau Riesling of the highest quality and of a balanced dryness to accompany food. Charta requirements are more stringent than those of the 1971 German Wine Law. The regulations require that the wine must be 100 per cent Riesling made entirely from a single estate, and the approval process insists upon blind tasting of samples. Charta wines are sold in bottles embossed with the double-arch symbol of the organization.

The Mittelrhein

The Mittelrhein, to the north of the Rheingau, is mainly planted with Riesling vines. These have a more steely character than the wines of the Rheingau, and most are drunk locally.

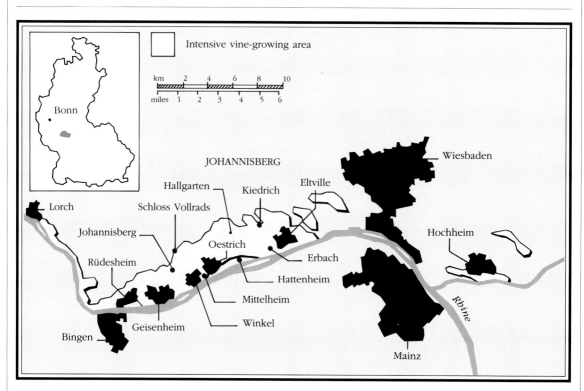

Intensive vine-growing area

JOHANNISBERG

The richness of the Rheingau
The north bank of the river Rhine is a treasury of famous village names and aristocratic private estates.
The Rheingau has 500 independent estates, most of which bottle their own wine. Most of the remaining 2,000 small private growers are members of 10 regional cooperatives.

MITTELRHEIN

WEINGUT TONI JOST

*Bacharacher Hahn
Riesling Spätlese*

The Riesling and Spätburgunder account for almost 80 per cent of this estate's total production and are consistently the finest wines made in the Mittelrhein.

J.B. BECKER

*Wallufer Walkenberg Riesling
Spätlese Trocken*

With five *Einzellagen* located in Eltville, Rauenthal and Walluf itself, the Becker family produces an excellent range of Rheingau wines, particularly those made in the *Trocken* or dry style, such as the Walkenberg Riesling Spätlese illustrated here.

BARON VON BRENTANO'SCHE

*Winkeler Hasensprung Riesling
Spätlese Halbtrocken*

The first Hasensprung Goethewein was produced in 1949 to commemorate the 200th birthday of Goethe of *Faust* fame, who described the 1811 vintage of this wine in *Westöstlichen Diwan* as "unforgettable".

GEORG BREUER

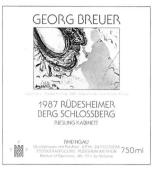

*Rüdesheimer Berg Schlossberg
Riesling Kabinett*

This estate is run by the indefatigable Bernard Breuer, whose enthusiasm and winemaking philosophy is reflected in the *avant-garde* label he uses for his *Kabinett* wines. The elegance of this naturally light and dry style of wine perfectly expresses his concept of a classic Rheingau.

WEINGUT AUGUST ESER

Oestricher Doosberg Riesling Spätlese

Established in Oestrich-Winkel in 1759, this family *Weingut* owns just 4.5 hectares (11 acres) of vines in Oestrich, Winkel, Mittelheim, Hallgarten, Hattenheim, Rauenthal and Rüdesheim. The majority of Eser's wine is made in *Trocken* and *Halbtrocken* styles.

WEINGUT GRAF VON KANITZ

Lorcher Pfaffenwies Riesling Kabinett

Located down-river from Assmannshausen and far from classic Riesling slopes, this estate produces excellent wine, such as the supple Rieslings from the Pfaffenwies vineyard, and does so using only organic methods.

LANDGRÄFLICH HESSISCHES WEINGUT

*Geisenheimer Kläuserweg
Riesling Kabinett*

Considerably expanded, this modern winery, owned by the ancient house of the princes of Hessen, extends into Winkel, Geisenheim - from where this earthy Riesling comes - Eltville and Rüdesheim, covering some 40 hectares (100 acres) in 18 *Einzellagen*.

WEINGUT FREIHERR ZU KNYPHAUSEN

*Erbacher Steinmorgen
Riesling Eiswein*

Built by monks in 1141, this estate was purchased by the von Knyphausen family in 1818. Most of its 16.5-hectare (40-acre) vineyard is situated on south and south-west facing slopes of loess-loam soil. The wines are bottled within a year of the harvest and retain great fruitiness.

FREIHERR LANGWERTH VON SIMMERN

*Hattenheimer Mannberg
Riesling Spätlese*

Freiherr Langwerth von Simmern
CONT.

*Hattenheimer Nussbrunnen
Riesling Eiswein*

Since 1464, when Johann Langwerth von Simmern was presented with the Hattenheimer Mannberg vineyard, this estate has acquired some of the finest sites in the Rheingau and makes some of the region's greatest wines. The fabulously rich and racy Riesling *Eiswein* is from Hattenheim's famous Nussbrunnen vineyard, of which the Freiherr Langwerth von Simmern owns almost half. It has a south-south-east facing slope and a varied soil of loess, loam and marl.

FÜRST LÖWENSTEIN

*Hallgartener Schönhell
Riesling Kabinett*

Owned by Graf Matushka, whose winemaker at Schloss Vollrads, Georg Senft, is also responsible for making these wines. The two styles of comparable *Prädikaten* are quite different, with Fürst Löwenstein showing a fatter, less aristocratic character.

WEINGUT G.H. VON MUMM

*Johannisberger Mittelhölle
Riesling Kabinett*

*Johannisberger Hannsberg
Riesling Trocken*

The origins of this estate go back to 1811, when a Frankfurt wine merchant purchased the entire crop of Schloss Johannisberg. It was the profits from that legendary vintage that enabled Peter Arnold Mumm to buy his first vineyards. He went on to establish P.A. Mumm, Geisler and Co. (the beginnings of Champagne G.H. Mumm, the *Grand Marque*). In 1957 the von Mumm estate was purchased by Rudolf August Oetker, since when the emphasis has been on the production of drier styles of wine.

DR. HEINRICH NÄGLER

*Rüdesheimer Magdalenenkreuz
Riesling Kabinett*

This small family-run, quality-conscious estate in Rüdesheim was established in the nineteenth century. The wines are classic, dryish Rheingau, with good concentration.

BALTHASAR RESS

*Hattenheimer Nussbrunnen
Riesling Spätlese*

Thirty-five vineyards make up this medium-sized estate, but despite the variety of character and style, the quality is always uncompromising.

WEINGUT SCHLOSS GROENESTEYN

*Rüdesheimer Berg Rottland
Riesling Spätlese*

This illustrious estate dates from the fourteenth century and has been in the hands of the Groenesteyn family since 1640. There are 33 hectares (81 acres) in production and most of the vines are grown on gentle to steep slopes. The wines are always impeccably made.

SCHLOSS JOHANNISBERGER

*Schloss Johannisberger
Riesling Spätlese*

The most famous estate in the Rheingau, vying with nearby Schloss Vollrads as the producer of this region's greatest wines. All Schloss Johannisberg wines have an extraordinary concentration and complexity, combined with great acidity and immeasurable finesse, but perhaps the most classic wine is its Spätlese, which, after all, was "invented" here.

SCHLOSS REINHARTSHAUSEN

*Erbacher Marcobrunn Riesling
Trockenbeerenauslese*

*Erbacher Siegelsberg
Riesling Kabinett Halbtrocken*

This substantial 70-hectare (173-acre) estate dates back to the twelfth century. The wines are marked by their time in cask and a higher than usual alcoholic content, which confirms their classic, relatively dry Rheingau style. The *Trockenbeerenauslese* is from the Erbacher Marcobrunnen, the estate's most famous site. The Erbacher Siegelsberg label was designed by W. Mühlum-Pyrápheros and is an expression of "sidereal" art, which he invented in 1963.

WEINGUT EBERHARD RITTER UND EDLER VON OETINGER

Erbacher Hohenrain Riesling Kabinett

The von Oetingers produce wines of great individual character, quality and complexity. The wines are powerful, with high levels of acidity, but also highly concentrated in fruit.

DOMÄNENWEINGUT SCHLOSS SCHÖNBORN

*Erbacher Marcobrunn
Riesling Spätlese*

Over 80 per cent of this estate is Riesling, scattered over some 30 *Einzellagen* in the Rheingau.

SCHLOSS VOLLRADS

Schloss Vollrads Riesling Kabinett

Owned and run by Germany's greatest ambassador of fine wine, Erwein Graf Matushka-Greiffenclau, whose family has owned vineyards on the Rheingau since the eleventh century. Some connoisseurs rate the elegant, stylish Schloss Vollrads wines as the finest in the Rheingau; certainly, this estate is one of the four great growths of the Rheingau.

VERWALTUNG DER STAATSWEINGÜTER

Rauenthaler Baiken Riesling Eiswein

Steinberger Riesling Eiswein

Seven state-owned wine estates, totalling 136 hectares (335 acres) of prime Rheingau sites, are administered by Dr Hans Ambrosi from Eltville, although Kloster Eberbach, the Cistercian abbey, is better known as the Staatsweingüter's headquarters. It is at this splendid Cistercian abbey that the famous annual wine auctions are held: the exceptionally high prices regularly bid for the Staatsweingüter's *Eiswein* and *Trockenbeerenauslese* wines are largely responsible for the financial success of this state-owned combine of vineyards.

WEINGUT TROITZSCH

*Lorcher Schlossberg
Riesling Kabinett Trocken*

This small estate was one of the first to dedicate its production to fully fermented, bone-dry wines. By maintaining modest yields per hectare, it achieves a depth and concentration that is often lacking in *Trocken* wines.

WEINGUT ROBERT WEIL

*Kiedricher Gräfenberg
Riesling Spätlese*

This fine Rheingau estate is now owned 75/25 by Suntory and Graf Matushka. It could well be that the Graf was attracted by the style of Weil's wine, which has always fallen somewhere between the elegance of Schloss Vollrads and the fatness of Fürst Löwenstein.

DOMDECHANT WERNER'SCHES WEINGUT

*Hochheimer Domdechaney
Riesling Spätlese*

This 12-hectare (30-acre) estate in Hochheim produces some of the finest wines in the Rheingau. All of its vines grow on south-facing slopes of calcareous clay and produce wines of great purity, finesse and elegance.

NAHE

THE REGION OF NAHE takes its name from the river Nahe, which flows into the Rhine at Bingen. With its 4,300 hectares (10,620 acres), it is one-fifth of the size of Rheinhessen (its immediate neighbour to the east) and unlike it in character. There is a relatively small number of growers, many of whom seem willing to sell their wines directly to passing customers. The cooperatives account for only 20 per cent of the harvest.

Nahe is principally a white wine region, with a tremendous reputation for the quality of its Riesling wines. Nevertheless, Riesling is not actually the predominant grape variety: with 30 per cent of planting, Müller-Thurgau has now replaced Silvaner as the most widely planted variety. Kerner, Scheurebe and Bacchus grapes are also grown.

The dominance of Riesling

Riesling remains, however, the principal variety for all the leading estates, and *Prädikat* wines are made from it in both sweet and drier versions.

Nahe Rieslings have a fine combination of fruit and lively acidity, and the best have excellent ageing potential. The better wines of the region come from the south and west, upstream of Bad Kreuznach, a pleasant spa town that forms a centre for the region. The weathered clay and sandstone soil in and around Bad Kreuznach - which contains the fine Narrenkappe vineyard and others within the *Grosslage* of Kronenberg - is particularly suited to the production of fine Riesling wines. South and west of Bad Kreuznach, the terrain becomes more rocky and steep, at times almost to the point of being vertical. It includes some excellent vineyard sites, among them the well-known Kupfergrube, Hermannsberg and Hermannshöhle, which are located near Niederhausen-Schlossböckelheim, where the pace-setting State Domaine is situated.

Steep site *The Ehrenfels stands among the vines on the Rüdesheimer Berg where the Nahe and Rhine rivers meet.*

WEINGUT OKONOMIERAT
AUGUST E. ANHEUSER

Kreuznacher Brückes Riesling Spätlese

This large estate originated in 1869 as part of Anheuser & Fehrs, the wine merchants. Its 60 hectares (148 acres) of vines are located between Bad Kreuznach and Schlossböckelheim.

The *Spätlese* produced in Bad Kreuznach's Brückes vineyard is fine and full, with a slightly spicy edge.

PAUL ANHEUSER

Kreuznacher Krötenpfuhl Riesling Spätlese Halbtrocken

Kreuznacher Kahlenberg Riesling Spätlese

The origins of this estate are the same as those for August E. Anheuser, but the estate was split in two 19 years after it was established. Its 75 hectares (185 acres) are scattered across 27 *Einzellagen* in seven villages, and its wine ranks with that of Schlossgut Diel as the finest Nahe produced. There is a tendency to drier styles on this estate, although not to the same degree as when Paul took over from his father, who had never made a sweet wine in his life apart from the occasional *Auslese*. To Rudolf Anheuser, *Kabinett* and *Spätlese* merely meant higher initial must-weight levels, never greater residual sweetness. Today, Paul Anheuser has loosened up in the sweet wine direction, although he retains his father's love of the drier style. The yield in his vineyards is modest, and he macerates the juice with the grapeskins prior to pressing and fermentation, which is carried out in wood at very low temperatures. This results in an amazingly light balance for wines of such depth of flavour.

Weingut Hans Crusius & Sohn

Traiser Rotenfels Spätburgunder Spätlese Roseewein Trocken

Traiser Rotenfels Riesling Kabinett

Hans Crusius's estate dates back to the sixteenth century. The Traiser Rotenfels vineyard has steepish slopes with southerly exposures and weathered porphyry soil (coloured igneous rock with a high pH).

The Spätburgunder Spätlese Roseewein *Trocken* has a deliciously soft and pure Pinot flavour, while the Riesling Kabinett is well perfumed, with an elegant balance.

Schlossgut Diel

Dorsheimer Pittermänchen Riesling Trocken

Grauburgunder Trocken

Since the mid-1980s, Schlossgut Diel has established itself as the Nahe's finest wine estate. Changes began in the late 1970s, when Dr Ingo Diel's son, Armin, started to influence his father away from new crosses and sweeter styles to more traditional varieties and bone-dry wines. The yield is low, and a good proportion of Diel's production is aged in new oak. The varietal character of these wines is affected by the presence of this oak, so they have been refused *AP* numbers, but, as Diel manages to sell all this wine to top restaurants and private customers at twice the price, he initially did not mind labelling it *Deutscher Tafelwein* and now positively prefers it.

Weingut Carl Finkenauer

Winzenheimer Rosenbeck Riesling Eiswein

The Finkenauer family has owned this estate in Bad Kreuznach since 1792. The soils range from clay-loam to red sandstone and fine sand. Much of the production is *Trocken* or *Halbtrocken*, although succulent specialities such as this *Eiswein* are occasionally made.

Weingut Reichsgraf von Plettenberg

Kreuznacher Kahlenberg Riesling Spätlese

Winzenheimer Rosenbeck Riesling Auslese

This 40-hectare (100-acre) estate has been in existence since the eighteenth century, but the von Plettenberg connection has occurred as recently as 1912. The vineyards owned by this old family are to be found in 17 *Einzellagen*, most of which are centred in and around Bad Kreuznach. They produce fine wines that age well and are often reasonably priced.

Prinz zu Salm-Dalberg'sches Weingut

Wallhäuser Mühlenberg Riesling Spätlese Trocken

Originally the property of the knights of von Dalberg, this 10-hectare (25-acre) estate has been in continuous family ownership since 1200, with control passing through the grandparents of the current owner to the Princes zu Salm. The wines are fine and fruity with a lively character.

Verwaltung der Staatlichen-Weinbaudomänen

Schlossböckelheimer Kupfergrube Riesling Beerenauslese

In 1902 this estate was established at Niederhausen-Schlossböckelheim by the royal Prussian court. It consisted of 26 hectares (65 acres) of very steep vineyards that had long been abandoned. Since then the Nahe wine industry has improved enormously: the vineyards have almost doubled, and the wines have served as models to growers throughout the region. This Beerenauslese is from one of the region's finest vineyards, the supersteep Kupfergrube, and is a dazzlingly concentrated, vivacious wine, even in its third or fourth decade.

RHEINHESSEN

RHEINHESSEN, WITH ITS 23,000 hectares (56,830 acres) under vine and 24 *Grosslagen* vineyard sites, is comfortably the largest of the German wine-producing regions. It is a large supplier of bulk wines, including at least 50 per cent of all Liebfraumilch. Liebfraumilch, by definition, is a *Qualitätswein (QbA)* from any of the four Rhineland regions (Rheingau, Rheinhessen, Nahe or Rheinpfalz) and made from Riesling, Müller-Thurgau, Silvaner or Kerner grapes. But, in practice, none comes from Rheingau and little from Nahe.

The Rhein Terrasse

Rheinhessen's image also suffers through the hijacking of the good name of Nierstein, the village at the quality heart of the Rheinhessen. All too often it is used to sell great quantities of bland and blended wines from the region as Niersteiner Gutes Domtal (a *Grosslage* wine) or Bereich Nierstein, blended wine from the Nierstien subregion rather than from the best sites.

To counteract this effect, Nierstein and eight adjoining villages on the slopes of the Rhine between Worms and Mainz, at one time called the Rheinfront, have formed the "Rhein Terrasse" association to protect the reputation of the wines from the river-front vineyards. Bodenheim, Nackenheim, Oppenheim, Dienheim, Guntersblum,

Ludwigshöhe, Mettenheim and Alsheim are the other villages involved. Their vineyards exploit their proximity to the river, and south-east-facing slopes, to make the best Rheinhessen Riesling and Silvaner wines. At their best, these wines, produced in a wide variety of individual styles, bear favourable comparison with those of the Rheingau, in contrast to the cheap Müller-Thurgau-dominated blends from the undulating hinterland.

Quality improvements

The trend towards drier wines in the Rheingau is mirrored in Rheinhessen. The Rheinhessen wine development organization monitors the production by some 200 growers of a quality-conscious varietal Silvaner Trocken sold under a common label as RS Rheinhessen Silvaner. Other initiatives like the Weingut Louis Guntrum Classic and the classic dry Rieslings of Heinrich Braun and Geschwister Schuch aim to enhance the quality standards of the better wines of the region.

Rheinhessen reds

The small amount of production of red wine in the region - about 6 per cent of total output - is centred on the small town of Ingelheim in the north of the area facing across the river to the Rheingau. It has traditionally been made from Spätburgunder.

WEINGUT BÜRGERMEISTER
ANTON BALBACH ERBEN

Niersteiner Pettenthal Riesling Spätlese

Niersteiner Hipping Riesling Spätlese

The Balbachs have been winemakers based in Nierstein since 1654, when the family received its coat of arms, shown on the label as three palms over a brook, a graphic interpretation of "Palms-brook" or Balbach. There are 18 hectares (44 acres) of vineyards in six *Einzellagen* situated within the boundaries of Nierstein. The vines grow on steep and very steep Rheinterrasse slopes of red schist and loess. The wines combine a fatness of fruit with good acidity to provide a certain nervy finesse.

WEINGUT HEINRICH BRAUN

Niersteiner Rosenberg Riesling Spätlese

A family-owned estate since 1690, Weingut Braun now comprises 18 hectares (44 acres) of gently sloping vineyards with slate, loam and loess soils. Peter Braun, current owner, is a devotee of fully fermented dry Riesling and, since 1985, has begun to use new oak, sometimes rather forcefully, on a number of his wines.

CHRISTIAN BRENNER

Bechtheimer Geisersberg
Weisser Burgunder Auslese

Dornfelder mit Trollinger
Spätlese Trocken

Unluckily for Christian Brenner, his grandfather happened to establish this family estate at Bechtheim in 1877, which made it impossible to produce a special centennial wine as 1977 was one of the worst vintages on record. So the estate decided to celebrate its 111th birthday with this Weiser Burgunder from the excellent 1988 vintage. All Brenner's wines are fully fermented and bone-dry.

DR. DAHLEM ERBEN KG

Oppenheimer Sackträger
Riesling Spätlese

Although this Oppenheim estate dates from 1923, when it was separated from the Dahlem's other farming concerns, the family has cultivated vines on most of its 25 hectares (62 acres) for many generations. Few of the wines here are made in the dry style. This *Spätlese*, from the fine Sackträger vineyard just above Oppenheim, demonstrates all the fragrance and subtlety that the best Rheinhessen sites can achieve.

WEINGUT GUNDERLOCH-USINGER

Nackenheimer Rothenberg
Riesling Auslese

This is part of the original Carl Gunderloch estate, which was immortalized by Carl Zuckmeier in his play *Fröhlichen Weinberg*. It is now owned by Carl Otto Usinger and managed admirably by Fritz and Agnes Hasselbach, who make some of the best wines in Nackenheim.

WEINGUT LOUIS GUNTRUM

Oppenheimer Herrenberg
Silvaner Eiswein

Niersteiner Oelberg
Riesling Kabinett Trocken

Based on the wine-merchant business established by Louis Philipp Guntrum in 1824, this estate is run by Hajo Guntrum, who has no time for the cheap wines that have tarnished Germany's image. The quality of wine is very high, especially the dry Guntrum Classic. This is bottled in a traditional Rhine *flûte* and is Hajo's answer to the Rheingau Charta wines, which he admires for their quality-control and commercial success.

FREIHERR HEYL ZU HERRNSHEIM

Niersteiner Ölberg Riesling Spätlese

Niersteiner Brudersberg
Riesling Auslese

Niersteiner Pettental
Riesling Kabinett Trocken

Situated in the centre of Nierstein, surrounded by a wall-enclosed park and formal gardens that were originally planted in the sixteenth century, this 26-hectare (62-acre) estate is widely judged to be one of the very best in the Rheinhessen. The barons Heyl of Herrnsheim have been making wine here since at least 1893, when the distinctive blue label seen here on the Niersteiner Olberg Riesling *Spätlese* was first used. It was designed by J. Sattler, a well-known nineteenth-century book designer, and depicts a cellarmaster in a robe bearing the *Fleur de Lys* of the Heylschen coat of arms and clutching the family's heraldic key. All wines from Heyl zu Herrnsheim of Auslese upwards utilize a label with the combined coat of arms of the Heyl and Ysenburg families. Since the mid-1970s, part of the Heyl zu Herrnsheim has been farmed organically, and these wines - such as the *Kabinett* Trocken shown here - have their own special label. The Trocken wines produced by Peter von Weymann are of unusual fullness and depth.

Weingut Oberstleutnant Liebrecht

Bodenheimer Hoch Kerner Spätlese

Established by First Lieutenant Liebrecht in 1904, three generations of Liebrechts have built up a solid reputation for the quality and style of these wines, which come from 12.5 hectares (30 acres). This *Spätlese* shows the generously spicy fruit of the Kerner grape variety.

J. Neus

*Ingelheimer Pares
Spätburgunder Kabinett*

Also known as Weingut Sonnenberg, this estate is renowned for its dry red wines, particularly its soft Spätburgunder. All of its 10 hectares (25 acres) of vines are in Ingelheim, such as this Pares, but it is most famous for Ingelheimer Sonnenberg itself, an *Einzellage* that Neus owns in its entirety.

Weingut Rappenhof

Rappenhof Chardonnay Trocken

Owned by the Muth family since the eighteenth century, Weingut Rappenhof is now run by Dr Rheinhard Muth, President of the German Winegrowers Association and Mayor of Alsheim, where the estate is based. The quality here is exceptionally high, especially for the Chardonnay which is aged in new oak, but without swamping the bright, fruit character.

Weingut Schales

Dalsheimer Steig Huxelrebe Eiswein

The 1983 vintage of this *Eiswein* celebrated 200 years' ownership of this estate by the Schales family - the property has had a reputation for this rare style of wine ever since Heinrich Schales took over in 1930. Unusually for a fine German estate, only 10 per cent of the vines grown are Riesling.

Franz Karl Schmitt

Niersteiner Orbel Riesling Spätlese

Originally called Weingut Franz Karl Schmitt-Hermannshof, when it was established at Nierstein in 1549, the name Hermannshof remained until as recently as 1976, when the estate was divided. It was from this estate that the first Rheinhessen *Trockenbeerenauslese* was made in 1900.

Gustav Adolf Schmitt'sches Weingut

*Niersteiner Oelberg
Silvaner & Riesling Eiswein*

This is an enormous estate which includes excellent sites in Dienheim, Dexheim, Oppenheim and Nierstein itself. Although most of its production goes into blended products, it also produces some truly fine individual wines, such as this *Eiswein*.

Weingut Geschwister Schuch

*Niersteiner Rehbach
Riesling Spätlese Trocken*

The Niersteiner Rehback Riesling Spätlese *Trocken* is a typical example of this house's classic dry Rheinhessen, a style that accounts for at least 25 per cent of its production.

Weingut Reinhold Senfter

*Niersteiner Auflangen
Scheurebe Auslese*

Most of the vineyards of this estate are situated in Nierstein on the Hipping, Oelberg, Paterberg, Orbel and Pettenthal *Einzellagen* where the soils are red and sedimentary. Only *Prädikat* wines are made, although some are produced in a dry style.

Weingut Villa Sachsen

*Binger Scharlachberg
Riesling Beerenauslese*

Villa Sachsen is famous for its firm but fine Binger Scharlachberg, which is often brightened by a little naturally residual carbon dioxide. This Nestlé-owned producer's Beerenauslese is succulently sweet and concentrated, thanks to low-yielding vines.

RHEINPFALZ

THE RHEINPFALZ VINEYARDS run from Rhein-hessen, along the west bank of the Rhine, and southwards towards Alsace. Like Alsace, the Rheinpfalz is flanked on the west by mountains (the vineyards lie on flat or gently sloping land at the foot of the wooded hills) and the area enjoys a dry and sunny climate.

With its 20,800 hectares (50,400 acres) under vines, the Rheinpfalz (or Palatinate) is Germany's second largest region, but its huge output makes it the biggest producer. Half of the region's output from its 25,000 growers is Liebfraumilch. The work-horse for these wines is the Müller-Thurgau, which accounts for about a quarter of the plantings in the region, the principal area being in the southern Rheinpfalz in the Südliche Weinstrasse.

The better wines of the region come from the central Rheinpfalz. Here, on light, sandy soil the Riesling reasserts itself to produce ripe, full-bodied, bone-dry wines of outstanding quality. Fine dry wines are also made from Gewürztraminer, Weissburgunder, Silvaner and Muskateller; sweeter styles from Kerner and Scheurebe; and reds from Spätburgunder and Portugieser.

WEINGUT ANNABERG

*Kallstadter Annaberg
Riesling Spätlese Trocken*

*Kallstadter Annaberg Scheurebe
Spätlese Trocken*

Situated in Bad Durkheim-Leistadt, the Annaberg estate is one of the oldest in this part of the Pfalz. It was at Weingut Annaberg that exceptional Sheurebe wines were made in the immediate post-war era for the very first time. It was these wines that persuaded various viticultural research stations to persevere with their work on this new cross. Since it had been created by Dr Sheu in 1916, experimental wines had been disappointing and the Sheurebe was nearly abandoned, but Annaberg's success turned the tables and it is now the fifth most important variety planted.

WEINGUT GEHEIMER RAT DR. V. BASSERMANN-JORDAN

*Ruppertsberger Nussbien Riesling
Kabinett Trocken*

Established in the sixteenth century, there is a substantial 50 hectares (123 acres) of vineyards around this estate's cellar in Deidesheim. Drier styles are a speciality, such as this lively Kabinett from the village of Ruppertsberg, south of Deidesheim.

JOSEF BIFFAR

*Deidesheimer Mäushöhle
Riesling Auslese*

Some 70 per cent of the vines cultivated on this small family-run Deidesheim estate are Riesling. There are 12 hectares (30 acres) of vineyard with mostly loam and/or sand soils. Some 40 per cent of the harvest is sold in bulk as grape must, allowing Biffar to concentrate his production on the fuller, more concentrated wines for which he is known.

DR. BÜRKLIN-WOLF

*Wachenheimer Gerümpel
Riesling Eiswein*

Between 1777 and 1846 John Ludwig Wolf developed and extended this property into one of largest wine estates in Germany. In 1846 his granddaughter married Dr Albert Bürklin, so creating the name of one of Germany's greatest wine estates.

WEGELER-DEINHARD

*Deidesheimer Herrgottsacker
Riesling Kabinett*

This part of the Wegeler-Deinhard estate was established in 1843 by Freidrich Deinhard. This Riesling *Kabinett* from Deidesheim's largest *Einzellage*, Herrgottsacker, is fragrant and finely balanced, but with the rich finish characteristic of the Rheinpfalz.

K. FITZ-RITTER

*Dürkheimer Feuerberg
Gewürztraminer Spätlese*

This family estate has some 23 hectares (57 acres), 6 per cent of which are planted with Gewürztraminer to produce a range of softly aromatic wines. White wines are fermented in stainless-steel and red wines in wooden casks.

WEINGUT KOEHLER-RUPRECHT

*Kallstadter Saumagen
Riesling Spätlese*

Koehler-Ruprecht's 8.5 hectares (20 acres) of vineyard are so sun-blessed that they always produce *Prädikaten*, even in so-called off years. Now in the hands of the great Bernd Philippi, the estate continues its tradition of producing classic styles, such as the Kallstadter Saumagen Spätlese illustrated here.

*Kallstadter Feuerberg
Spätburgunder Eiswein*

Bernd Philippi also makes esoteric wines, such as a *Trockenbeerenauslese* made from a blend of grape varieties and aged in new oak, or this Kallstadter Feuerberg Spätburgunder Eiswein, which has a *clairet* colour, a rich, succulent bouquet and a sumptuous soft-fruit flavour.

WEINGUT LINGENFELDER

*Freinsheimer Goldberg
Riesling Spätlese*

Rainer Lingenfelder was chief oenologist at Sichel Söhne before taking over his father's estate. His Goldberg Riesling is one of the best in the Palatinate, and his experiments with dry Spätburgunder are legendary.

MÜLLER-CATOIR

*Gimmeldinger Meerspinne
Grauburgunder Auslese Trocken*

Situated at the foot of the Haardter Schlossberg, this well-reputed estate has been family-owned since 1744. The use of sulphur is minimal - some wines receive none whatsoever.

WEINGUT PFEFFINGEN

*Ungsteiner Herrenberg Scheurebe
Trockenbeerenauslese*

*Ungsteiner Honigsäckel
Riesling Auslese*

Karl Fuhrmann has presided over this old-established estate for 35 years. He is the President of the Rheinpfalz Winegrowers Association, and Weingut Pfeffingen has long been regarded as a model estate by his colleagues. He owns vineyards in Ungstein, Herrenberg, where this Scheurebe *Trockenbeerenauslese* hails from, and Nussriegel. Both of these *Einzellagen* are situated within the wider Honigsäckel *Grosslage*, the appellation used for the Riesling *Auslese*. His wines typically have the Pfalz fatness and flavour one expects, yet possess a surprisingly delicate balance.

WEINGUT ÖKONOMIERAT REBHOLZ

*Siebeldinger Königsgarten
Gewürztraminer Auslese Trocken*

This 9-hectare (22-acre) wine estate has been in the Rebholz family for over 300 years. It was here that the first Müller-Thurgau *Trockenbeerenauslese* was made in 1949. All the wines from this Siebeldingen property are *Naturwein* - they are not chaptalized nor subjected to the addition of *Süssreserve* - but the term has sadly been defunct since the 1971 laws.

WEINGUT GEORG SIBEN ERBEN

*Deidesheimer Grainhübel
Riesling Spätlese*

No less than 95 per cent of the vines grown on this estate are Riesling, an extraordinarily high proportion for the Rheinpfalz region. The vineyards cover just under 13 hectares (32 acres) and are situated in 14 different *Einzellagen* in Deidesheim, Forst and Ruppertsberg. The estate sells wines from its *monopole* Odinsthal in Wachenheim, under the Hofgut Odinsthal name.

FRANKEN

FRANKEN (FRANCONIA) IN northern Bavaria is no further north than the Mosel or Rheingau, but it does not enjoy the same favoured micro-climates: it can suffer from severe spring frosts and a shorter ripening season. The 4,700 hectares (11,614 acres) of vineyard are scattered over 125 villages among some 6,000 growers. About half of their output is handled by cooperatives.

Grape varieties

Frankenwein is traditionally made in dry or semi-dry fashion. Frankische Trocken is in fact very dry, meaning less than 4 grams/litre of residual sugar. Despite the climatic problems of this region, some of the better estates in the vicinity of Würzburg grow a fair amount of Riesling on the lighter limestone soils and produce assertive, racy wines in good vintages. The Bürgerspital zum Heiligen Geist, one of three large charitable estates in the area, and one of the largest estates in Germany, grows more Riesling than anything else.

Silvaner, which has traditionally provided the sturdier performance in this area, retains its importance, giving a wine that has an attractive and, for the Silvaner, an unusually robust style. At the same time - exaggerating the trend elsewhere in Germany - plantings of Müller-Thurgau have very nearly doubled over the last 20 years and now account for over half the total output of Franken. Other white varieties include Scheurebe, Kerner, Traminer, Rieslaner (a Riesling-Silvaner cross), Ruländer, Weissburgunder and Bacchus. The small amount of red wine comes from limited plantings of Spätburgunder and Schwarzriesling.

The Hessiche-Bergstrasse

West of Franken is the tiny area of the Hessische-Bergstrasse, which is almost entirely devoted to white wines, predominantly Riesling, with some Müller-Thurgau, Silvaner and Gewürztraminer.

Distinctive bottle shape *Quality wines from Franken are exported in the traditional dumpy-shaped* Bocksbeutel.

THE HESSISCHE BERGSTRASSE

STAATSWEINGUT BERGSTRASSE

Situated in Bensheim, where vineyards have flourished since 765, this Staatsweingut developed out of an experimental vineyard owned by the grand duke of Hessen-Darmstadt. Since 1904 it has been run by the Hillenbrand family. The estate's 31.5 hectares (78 acres) include two exclusively owned *Einzellagen* - Schönberger Herrnwinger and Heppenheimer Centgericht - which produce the finest wines in the Hessische Berg-strasse. This Riesling *Spätlese* from the Steinkopf vineyard is full and balanced, with a lively fruit finish.

Heppenheimer Steinkopf Riesling Spätlese Trocken

Heppenheimer Centgericht Riesling Eiswein

BAYERISCHE LANDESANSTALT FÜR WEIN UND GARTENBAU

Würzburger Stein Rieslaner Kabinett

This 120-hectare (296-acre) state-owned wine estate has its wine cellars at the Staatliche Hofkellerei in Würzburg, a rococo-styled edifice of such splendour that it once prompted Napoleon to describe it as "the most beautiful rectory in Europe". Reislaner is a variety with its origins in Franken, and on the steep slopes of the superb Stein vineyard it produces a pungent and earthy wine.

BÜRGERSPITAL ZUM HL. GEIST

Würzburger Abtsleite Riesling Spätlese

Würzburger Stein Gewürztraminer Kabinett Trocken

Established in 1319 and today encompassing 140 hectares (346 acres) of vineyard, this is one of the largest and oldest wine estates in Germany. From its cellars, which are also in Würzburg, Bürgerspital produces some of Franconia's greatest wines. Made in either tanks or oak casks, some of which are always new, the high prices these wines fetch enable this charity to look after 300 old and infirm people in its two homes.

FÜRSTLICH CASTELL'SCHES DOMÄNENAMT

Casteller Bausch Silvaner Eiswein

The almost 60 hectares (148 acres) of Fürstlich Castell'sches make it the largest privately owned wine estate in Franconia. It has been owned by the family of Prince Albrecht of Castell-Castell since at least the sixteenth century, and the spread of *Einzell-agen* it encompasses includes eight that are exclusively owned. This *Eiswein* from Silvaner vines grown in the Bausch *Einzellage* combines impact and intensity with spicy charm.

JULIUSSPITAL-WEINGUT

Würzburger Stein Silvaner Spätlese Trocken

This vast estate of 160 hectares (395 acres) includes the *monopole* of Iphöfer Domherr. The first Franconian estate to be awarded the Gold Prize of the National Ministry of Agriculture. Most of its wines are made in the dry style, yet this Silvaner *Spätlese* from Stein has the rich, earthy character the region is famed for.

FÜRSTLICH LÖWENSTEIN-WERTHEIM-ROSENBERG'SCHES WEINGUT

Homburger Kallmuth Silvaner Kabinett Trocken

This Cistercian estate with its 25 hectares (62 acres) of widely scattered vineyards, including five exclusively owned *Einzellagen*, dates from the twelfth century but came into the possession of the Löwenstein family as recently as the beginning of the nineteenth century.

WEINBAU ERNST POPP KG

Iphöfer Julius-Echter-Berg Riesling Kabinett Trocken

The 14 hectares (34 acres) of south-south-west facing slopes of *Keuper* (a coloured sandy clay), which have belonged to the Popp family since 1878, include some of the finest sites of the Steigerwald. Most of the wines, including this one, are fully fermented and totally dry.

PAUL SCHMITT

Randersackerer Pfülben Silvaner Kabinett Trocken

This small family-run wine estate, founded in 1860, has just over 6 hectares (15 acres) and is based in Randersacker, 5 kilometres (3 miles) east of Würzburg. Virtually all the vines grow on fairly steep slopes with a limestone soil. The wines are never chaptalized; they are fully fermented and have a natural elegance.

ROBERT SCHMITT

Randersackerer Sonnenstuhl Silvaner Spätlese Trocken

Also in Randersacker, but established much earlier than Paul Schmitt's estate, this seventeenth-century property encompasses 7 hectares (17 acres) of steeply sloping vineyards. This Randersackerer Sonnenstuhl Spätlese Trocken shows the finesse to which the Silvaner can aspire when it comes from a favourable *terroir* and is made by a gifted winemaker.

HANS WIRSCHING

Iphöfer Julius-Echter-Berg Riesling Kabinett

The Wirsching family has been making wine in Iphofen since the early seventeenth century. Today, Hans Wirsching owns a large estate of 45 hectares (111 acres), some 80 per cent of which is south-facing. The wines produced have a particularly fresh and fruity style.

WÜRTTEMBERG

THE VINEYARDS IN Württemberg cover 9,600 hectares (23,722 acres) and are widely scattered among the farmlands and on the slopes of the River Neckar to the north of the large industrial city of Stuttgart. The region has a warm growing season and a wide range of grape varieties.

The pattern of growers

Although Württemberg is Germany's main red wine region, its reputation outside the area is limited, since most of the wine is consumed locally. The 16,500 growers have small holdings: for them, winegrowing is more a simple hobby to supply their own needs. Most of the output in the region is handled by cooperatives. The leading private estates are small, although some are well established with aristocratic antecedents.

Grape varieties

Slightly more than half the grapes grown in the region are red, principally Trollinger, Lemberger, Portugieser, Spätburgunder and Pinot Meunier (known here as Schwarzriesling or Müllerrebe). The local speciality, Schillerwein, is made from red and white grapes in various shades of pink. White wines come mainly from Riesling, Müller-Thurgau and Kerner, but Sylvaner, Ruländer and, notably, Traminer are also used.

WEINGUT GRAF ADELMANN

Kleinbottwarer Traminer Kabinett Trocken

The previous owners of this top estate were the Barons von Brüssele; their name remains on the label even though the present owners are the counts of Adelmann. The best wines are sold as Brüssele'r Spitze.

WEINGUT ROBERT BAUER

Flein Sonnenberg Riesling

This small estate has vineyards located in Flein and Weinsberg with south-facing slopes of *Keuper* and loam soils. With the exception of *Eiswein*, all of Robert Bauer's wines are fully fermented and have less than one gram per litre of residual sugar.

FÜRST ZU HOHENLOHE-OEHRINGEN'SCHE WEINGUT

Verrenberger Verrenberg Spätburgunder Kabinett Trocken

This 20-hectare (50-acre) estate includes the exclusively owned Verrenberger Verrenberg vineyard. Its wines are much sought after by top German restaurants.

SCHLOSSKELLEREI GRAF V. NEIPPERG

Neipperger Schlossberg Traminer Auslese

The Counts of von Neipperg have owned vineyards here since the twelfth century. Cask-ageing gives a gently spicy, softly contoured Traminer from the estate's home vineyards at Neipperg.

STAATL. LEHR- UND VERSUCHSANSTALT FUR WEIN- UND OBSTBAU

Weinsberger Schemelsberg Lemberger Spätlese Trocken

Founded in 1868, this Staatsweingut is the oldest viticultural research station in Germany. The depth of colour in its red wines, such as this dry Lemberger *Spätlese*, results from a short, hot, pre-fermentation maceration.

WÜRTT. HOFKAMMER-KELLEREI STUTTGART

Stettener Brotwasser Riesling Spätlese Trocken

The Stettener Brotwasser is one of four exclusively owned *Einzellagen* that account for almost half of this estate's 45 hectares (111 acres).

BADEN

BADEN, WITH ITS 14,900 hectares (36,800 acres) of vineyard, contributes 15 per cent to the total German wine harvest. Its vineyards extend in a narrow strip, for 400 kilometres (250 miles) through the foothills of the Black Forest mountains from Baden-Baden to Basle, and enjoy a warm climate similar to Alsace's.

The more distinguished of its seven *Bereiche*, or sub-regions, are Ortenau, producing quality *Prädikat* Rieslings and Spätburgunder reds; Kaiserstuhl and Tuniberg, with its powerful reds from volcanic soils; Markgräflerland, where Gutedel (Chasselas) comes into its own; and Bodensee (Lake Constance), where the pink Weissherbst is made. Müller-Thurgau is the principal white grape variety, but a wide range of other grape varieties is used to create a diversity of styles. The output of the region is dominated by the cooperatives, particularly a huge installation at Breisach in south Baden, the Zentralkellerei Badischer Winzergenossenschaften (ZBW). A few private estates make some excellent varietal wines, mainly reds from Spätburgunder and whites from Weissburgunder and Gewürztraminer.

WEINGUT BLANKENHORN

Schliengener Sonnenstück Gewürztraminer Spätlese

The Blankenhorn family is one of the most respected producers of Gutedel; its other varieties include Gewürztraminer, such as this softly spicy example from the loamy slopes of Schliengener Sonnenstück.

VERSUCHS-U. LEHRGUT BLANKENHORNSBERGER

Blankenhornsberger Doktorgarten Ruländer Spätlese Trocken

Founded in 1842-4, this 25-hectare (62-acre) estate has been managed by the Freiburg Wine Institute since 1954. The estate today comprises the Doctorgarten *monopole*.

WEINGUT HERMANN DÖRFLINGER

Müllheimer Sonnhalde Grauer Burgunder Spätlese Trocken

The Dörflingers fully ferment their wines to bone-dryness, and this *Trocken* exemplifies the house style.

FREIHERR V. GLEICHENSTEIN

Oberrotweiler Eichberg Weisser Burgunder Kabinett Trocken

Freiburger Schlossberg Spätburgunder Weissherbst Kabinett

Founded in 1634, this estate's 18 hectares (44 acres) are all within the Vulkanfelson *Grosslage* on the superior sites of the Kaiserstuhl. The Weiser Burgunder comes from the Eichberg, where the volcanic soil mixes with loam and clay to produce a solidly fruity, dry white wine. The Spätburgunder has been made as a *Weissherbst*, a lightly coloured style of wine that originated from black grapes attacked by *Edelfäule*, but is now made as a normal rosé and is a speciality in Germany's warmer regions. It is gently flavoured, with hints of strawberry fruit.

WEINGUT DR. HEGER

Ihringer Winkleberg Silvaner Spätlese Trocken

This small estate was established in Ihringen in 1953 by Dr Max Heger, a *Hobbywinzer*. Now run by his grandsons, who maintain the exceptionally low yield that made the quality and reputation of these wines. Nearly all are fully fermented, and the Silvaner is the Hegers' particular speciality.

FRANZ KELLER SCHWARZER ADLER

*Oberrotweiler Eichberg
Grauburgunder Spätlese Trocken*

This tiny 4-hectare (10-acre) estate
situated in Vogtsburg-Oberbergen
makes the finest wines in Baden.
Wines for early drinking are
fermented in tanks, while those
for ageing are made in wood, some
of which are small *barriques*.

WEINGUT EMIL MARGET

*Hügelheimer Gottesacker
Gutedel Kabinett*

The Marget family has been making
wine on this 7.5-hectare (18-acre)
estate in Hügelheim since 1771. All
the wines are fully fermented in oak
casks to bone-dryness on principle,
and no *Süssreserve* is used.

MAX MARKGRAF VON BADEN

*Durbacher Schloss Staufenberg
Müller-Thurgau Kabinett Trocken*

Founded in 1173, the huge monastic
complex at Schoss Salem and its vineyards came into the ownership of the
Margraves of Baden in 1803, after the
secularization. Schloss Salem is the
Bodensee residence of Max von
Baden, the current Margrave, and the
linchpin to his four wine estates:
Weingut Bermatingen, Weingut
Birnau, Schloss Kirchberg and, as
illustrated here, Schloss Staufenberg.

GRÄFLICH WOLFF METTERNICH'SCHES WEINGUT

*Durbacher Schlossberg
Clevner Traminer Beerenauslese*

The harvest is generally held back
here, so that a greater than normal
proportion of the wines attain high
Prädikat levels, such as this
Durbacher Schlossberg Clevner
Traminer Beerenauslese.

FREIHERR V. NEVEU'SCHE GUTSVERWALTUNG

*Durbacher Josephsberg
Klingelberger (Riesling) Spätlese*

This 12-hectare (30-acre) estate on the
outskirts of Durbach is owned by the
family of Prince-Bishop Franz Xaver
von Neveu. The wines are made in
the estate's own cellars, but they are
bottled and marketed by the vast
Badischer Winzerkeller, formerly
known as ZBW.

WEINGUT SALWEY

*Oberrotweiler Kirchberg Spätburgun-
der Weissherbst Spätlese Trocken*

The 10 hectares (25 acres) of vineyard
in this Oberrotweiler estate are
sloping or steeply sloping, and
90 per cent are south facing. This fine
Spätburgunder is a particularly full
and well-flavoured *Weissherbst* and
comes from the volcanic soils of
Oberrotweil's Kirchberg.

WEINGUT RUDOLF STIGLER

*Ihringer Winkler Berg
Riesling Spätlese Trocken*

Situated at Ihringen, this estate was
founded by Rudolf Stigler's grandfather in 1870, when he purchased
5 hectares (12 acres) of the famous
Ihringer Winkler Berg vineyard.
Because of its sunny exposure,
between 90 and 95 per cent of
production is of *Prädikat* level. Both
red and white wines are fermented on
their skins, giving them a perfume
unusual in the wines of Baden.

WINZERGENOSSENSCHAFT BÜHL EG

*Affentaler Spätburgunder
Rotwein Kabinett*

This cooperative was established at
Bühl-Eisenthal in 1908 and currently
has almost 1,000 members, producing
an average of 4.5 million bottles each
year. Its most famous medal-winning
wine is Affentaler, which means
"Monkey Valley". It is a light red wine
from the Spätburgunder grape and
comes in a monkey-embossed bottle.

WINZERGENOSSENSCHAFT NEUWEIER-BÜHLERTAL

*Neuweierer Mauerberg
Riesling Kabinett*

Situated in Baden-Baden, this
cooperative was set up in 1922 and
has 300 members with just over 200
hectares (495 acres) of vineyard. This
Riesling *Kabinett* is typical of the
soft-edged style of the Ortenau.

~ ITALY ~

ITALY STILL PRODUCES more wine than any other country in the world, even though its total output, and that of other major European wine-producing countries, is currently tending to fall. In 1988 Italy produced 76.8 million hectolitres, equivalent to some 850 million cases of wine, which was roughly one third of all European and a quarter of world production. In the same year France, usually a close rival, came a poor second. Only some 12 per cent of Italy's huge output is DOC wine, that is to say wine from a defined area of origin (*Denominazione di Origine Controllata*) as recognized by the country's wine law which came into being in 1963. Even within the select DOC category, the number of wines of real interest to the connoisseur of classic wines is very limited. A range of interesting and individually outstanding wines has been developed outside the DOC regulations, as *Vini da Tavola*, by producers concerned for excellence, regardless of the restrictions of legislation.

Geography of the vineyards

Italy is favourably situated between latitudes 35°N and 45°N. Wine is produced in each of its 20 regions, in a variety of geological, topographical and micro-climatic conditions - from the Alps in the north to the southern tip of Calabria, across the Mediterranean to Sicily and Sardinia, and to Pantelleria off the coast of Tunis. Winegrowing is mostly small-scale and the industry very fragmented. The average size of the 1.25 million viticultural estates in Italy is 1 hectare (2.47 acres).

Most of the notable wine regions lie in the northern half of the country, starting in the North-West with Piedmont, which boasts a longer list of DOCs than any other Italian wine region, and produces, in Barolo and Barbaresco, some of the most distinguished red wines in Italy. Lombardy, produces one or two good reds and fine sparkling

The Piazza del Campo, Siena Al fresco *wine-drinking is a relaxing and integral part of the Italian lifestyle.*

wines, but the other two regions in this area, Valle d'Aosta and Liguria, are less significant.

The three regions in the North-East, Trentino-Alto Adige, Friuli-Venezia Giulia and Veneto, are all of increasing importance, particularly as areas where French grape varieties have been successfully introduced. Many now take precedence over native white varieties, including Chardonnay which is rapidly growing in popularity in each of the three regions. Cabernet and Merlot are also well established, particularly in Friuli and Veneto.

Central Italy covers the seven wine regions of Tuscany, Emilia-Romagna, Marches, Umbria, Abruzzi, Molise, and Latium. Emilia-Romagna is home to Lambrusco, and the first white wine to acquire DOCG status, Albana di Romagna. The Marches is principally known for white Verdicchio, but also for individual reds. Abruzzi's fame relies on the Montepulciano grape that gives its name to the wine, while the few reds of any real quality in Latium depend on French rather than Italian varieties. In terms of classic wines, however, the principal focus of attention in Central Italy is on Tuscany, with Umbria in its wake.

In Southern Italy, the Italian Midi or *Mezzogiorno* produces vast quantities of bulk wine but a few classic wines are emerging. Apulia and Sicily account for over a quarter of all Italian wines, whereas Basilicata, Calabria, Campania and Sardinia contribute about 8 per cent in all.

Grape varieties

There are over 1,000 different *vitis vinifera* varieties grown in Italy, of which over 350 can be used under EC regulations. In practice, the Italian wine industry relies for its better known wines on a couple of dozen of them. The most important indigenous grapes used in quality red wines are Nebbiolo (for Barolo, Barbaresco and related Piedmont wines like Gattinara and Ghemme), Sangiovese in its various clonal forms (for Chianti, Brunello di Montalcino, Vino Nobile di Montepulciano) and Corvina, Molinara and Rondinella (for Valpolicella). The whites include Garganega (for Soave), Moscato (for Asti Spumante principally), Cortese (for Gavi) and Trebbiano and Malvasia (for Orvieto, Frascati and others). Use is also being made of foreign varieties: Cabernet Sauvignon, Cabernet Franc, Merlot and Pinot Nero (Pinot Noir) among the reds, and Chardonnay, Sauvignon Blanc, Pinot Grigio (Pinot Gris), Sylvaner, Riesling and Müller-Thurgau for whites, most often as varietal wines. Chardonnay is now widely planted in Lombardy, where it is used with Pinot

Nero to supply the burgeoning sparkling wine industry; it is also used experimentally in parts of Tuscany, as well as in Piedmont, Emilia-Romagna, Apulia, and extensively in the North-East.

Italian wine laws

Italian wines fall into three categories. Most basic is the *vino da tavola,* a category that effectively (with the *vini tipici*) covers all wines which do not qualify as *Denominazione di Origine* *Controllata* (DOC). The idiosyncratic attitudes of Italian winemakers and law-makers are such that this catch-all category today includes a very large number of the finest wines made in Italy, not on account of their quality, but because their makers are using grapes (for instance Cabernet Sauvignon or Chardonnay) or vinification/maturation methods that are not permitted by the DOC regulations. Some 230 delimited geographic areas are classified within the DOC. The law defines not only the

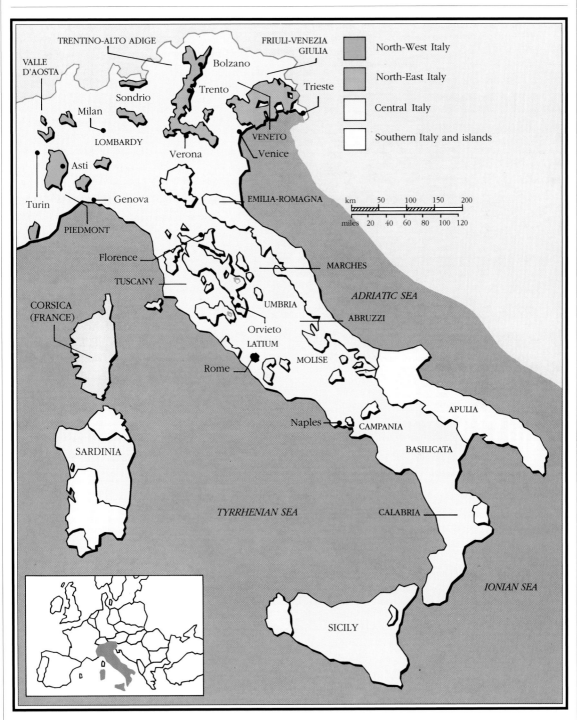

The land of wine *Italy has been famed for its wine as far back as the time of the Ancient Greeks. Today,* *Italy still makes more wine and exports more than any other country in the world. Vines are grown* *throughout the length of the penin- sula: from the high Alps in the north to the Calabrian "toe" in the south.*

area of origin but also specifies the grape varieties to be used and sometimes the vinification methods, but it has never become any more of a guarantee of quality than the French AOC has done. The quality still has to be judged by the level of excellence achieved by the winemaker.

In an attempt to improve matters, a higher classification entitled *Denominazione di Origine Controllata e Garantita* (DOCG) was introduced in the 1980s. The *garantita* (guaranteed) element of the DOCG covers the authenticity and quality of the wine, as established by analytic and organoleptic tests. When these tests are successful, a seal of approval is bestowed by a national committee, guaranteeing the quality of the wine in the bottle at the point at which it leaves the producer.

Five red wines (Barolo, Barbaresco, Brunello di Montalcino, Vino Nobile di Montepulciano and Chianti) and one white (the little-known and not very highly regarded Albana di Romagna) have so far been accorded this élite status. However, the real test of the workability of this new and ambitious higher category listing comes with the inclusion of Chianti.

The Chianti *denominazione* takes up a substantial part of Tuscany and has an enormous output to be monitored. Chianti Classico alone has some 70,000 hectares (190,000 acres), and from a classic wine viewpoint it is the most important of the seven Chianti zones. The more stringent of the new DOGC requirements have been applied, however, only to three of the zones, Chianti Classico, Chianti Rufina and Chianti Colli Fiorentini, in reducing permitted yields in the vineyard and banning the use of blending wines from the south (up to 15 per cent is still allowed for the other four regions). The confusion is ironic in that the motivation for the country-wide DOC laws in 1963 came through the good sense of the Chianti Classico growers. Time will tell.

Room for improvement

New technology and experimentation are part of a general move to improve the quality of Italian wines. The move is being spearheaded by a number of outstanding individuals like Antinori or Frescobaldi in Chianti, Ezio Rivella at Villa Banfi in southern Tuscany, or Angelo Gaja in Barbaresco. Research is being conducted into clonal selection and the *uvaggio* (mix of grapes) when vineyards are replanted. In Tuscany the *Consorzio* (trade organization) of Chianti Classico growers has initiated a 10-year project to improve the quality and marketability of its wines. This will tackle not only clonal selection, but choice of root stocks, grape quality, growing, pruning and harvesting techniques, site suitability and density of cultivation. However, techniques such as the re-introduction

of the use of *ripasso* in Veneto - the process by which the red wines are refermented on the lees of more powerful *recioto* wines to give them greater body and character - have to be conducted outside the DOC rules, thus depriving the resulting wine of DOC status.

Current trends

A current trend in Italy is to individualize wines and elevate them above the generally perceived level of the DOC by the production of single-vineyard wines. These are no longer referred to, as they once were, by the term *cru*, but by *vigna* or *località*. The practice may mark the beginning of a movement towards a hierarchy of Italian wines comparable to the French *grands crus*.

ITALIAN TERMS

Abboccato	Slightly sweet
Amabile	Gently sweet
Amaro	Bitter; very dry
Annata	Vintage year
Asciutto	Bone dry
Azienda Agricola	Estate bottling own wines
Barrique	Small 225l oak barrel
Botte	Very large oak vat
Cantina Sociale	Growers' cooperative
Casa Vinicola	Wine firm
Cerasuolo	Cherry pink
Chiaretto	Pale red, almost pink
Classico	Heart of a DOC area
Consorzio	Growers' association
Cru	Vineyard site
DOC	Denominazione di Origine Controllata
DOCG	DOC Garantita
Dolce	Very sweet
Fiore	White wine fermented from must of very lightly pressed grapes
Frizzante	Lightly sparkling
Imbottigliato	Bottled
Liquoroso	Sweet, usually fortified
Località	Single vineyard site
Passito	Wine from dried grapes
Recioto	Rich wine, from passito grapes
Riserva	Specially selected wine aged for longer in wood or bottle according to DOC regulations
Ronco (pl. Ronchi)	Single vineyard site
Rosato	Pink, rose
Rosso	Red
Secco	Dry
Spumante	Fully sparkling
Stravecchio	Very old; rarely used on label
Superiore	Higher standard/higher alcohol content/combination of these
Uvaggio	Wine from mix of grapes
Vecchio	Old; may indicate prescribed period of ageing
Vigna, Vigneto	Single vineyard site
Vin Santo	Wine from Passito grapes, often sweet
Vino da Tavola	Table wine category

ITALIAN VINTAGES

YEAR	NORTH-WEST	NORTH-EAST	CENTRAL	SOUTHERN
1989 Widespread rain and hail in the northern half of Italy caused a very uneven vintage	Excellent Barolo and Barbaresco, but patchy elsewhere in the region	Uneven vintage. Trentino and Friuli fine, but lower quality in Veneto	Chianti affected by rain and hail; good Chianti Classicos because of their "heartland" sites	Drought; grapes down in quantity, but very ripe fruit
1988 A substantially reduced harvest, comparable to 1985, although many wines of fine quality	Asti exellent; good quality Piedmont and Lombardy reds; whites well structured; small harvest	High-quality wines, but small harvest; very good Soave and Valpolicella	Excellent wines but quantity much reduced; fine year for Chianti Classico Riservas	Quality and quantity both suffered through drought
1987 Adverse weather conditions widespread; good quality overall; production down	Asti excellent; high quality reds in Piedmont; Valtellina hit by freak storms	Good but not exceptional for the region; qualities down for Veneto and Trentino whites	Good Brunellos; Chiantis fair, though Classicos uneven; balanced whites and reds in Umbria	Production severely curtailed by weather conditions
1986 A late summer produced wines for drinking not keeping	Some good, forward reds in Piedmont, but little Barolo	Reds forward, good for early drinking; some good whites and *ripasso* wines	Fruity, forward reds, a few wines suitable for ageing; whites patchy	Big output; individual wines need selecting with care
1985 An exceptional year, but very small vintage throughout Italy	Superb year, very small vintage; fine Barbarescos and Barolos for keeping	Good whites; fine Amarone in Veneto	Excellent reds in Tuscany, especially Riservas; wines for long keeping	A number of good individual wines
1984 A wet and disappointing year, resulting in mediocre vintage	Generally poor in Piedmont, with the occasional good Barbaresco	Whites better than reds, but overall poor quality	A few good Tuscan reds, but very poor Brunello and Chianti Classico	Reds in Sardinia and Sicily fared better than the rest of the country
1983 An abundant year, but mixed quality	Large harvest; many wines below par in Piedmont	Reds for early drinking in Veneto; whites short on acidity	Some very good wines in Tuscany for ageing	Drought caused extensive damage; quality better than 1982
1982 Very good to excellent year, and a big vintage	Notably good reds in Piedmont	Veneto reds and whites above average; rich Amarones; fine wines in northern regions	Fine Chianti Classicos and Brunellos for long keeping	Drought hit harvest, but some good wines from higher sites

If the ferment elsewhere in Italy is over grape varieties and consequent wine styles, in Piedmont the debate is over vinification methods. On the one side are the traditionalist advocates of long barrel-ageing of Barolo and Barbaresco in large, old, wooden *botti* to allow the natural secondary flavours of the Nebbiolo grape to emerge; on the other are the modernists who support a shorter fermentation period in stainless steel followed by a brief period in small *barriques* of new oak, to produce more forward wines that display the primary fruit flavours of the grape. Giacomo Conterno, whose magisterial Barolo, Montfortino, can spend at least 10 years in wood, and another 10 in the bottle before it begins to be ready, is an extreme example, but generally traditionaliusts seek long fermentation on the skins, giving tannic wines that need long ageing. Marcello Ceretto, who makes both Barolo and Barbaresco, is typical of those who believe firmly in the new style of forward, fruity wines with less aggressive tannin, which is achieved by a much shorter maceration (7 to 21 days on the skins as against 30 to 50 days). The Barbaresco wines of Gaja, another modernist, are normally made to be sold soon after completion of the obligatory two years's ageing. Whatever the method employed, the aim in Piedmont today is wines of the highest possible quality.

NORTH-WEST ITALY

PIEDMONT, BORDERING FRANCE and Switzerland, is the home of two of Italy's greatest classic red wines - Barolo and Barbaresco. It also produces large quantities of an inimitable, sweet sparkling wine called Asti Spumante. The contrast between the two could not be more marked.

Barolo and Barbaresco are wines made by small growers, stamped with the character of their makers and commanding premium prices. The Nebbiolo grapes from which they are made are grown in the two villages that give their names to the wines, and seven neighbouring communes. Nebbiolo accounts for only 10 per cent of Piedmont's total, which includes not only Barolo and Barbaresco but also other Nebbiolo-based wines, such as Gattinara, Spanna, Ghemme, Carema, Sizzano and Nebbiolo d'Alba.

Ageing requirements

The wines are very tannic when young, so invariably need long ageing. They are also naturally high in alcohol - Barolo is normally 13 per cent or more - which is acquired without added sugar since chaptalization is prohibited. The minimum legal ageing before sale is one year in wood for Barbaresco and two for Barolo, then followed by a year in bottle. Barolo, with not less than five years' ageing, can be described as *Riserva*. A Barbaresco *Riserva* needs only four years' ageing.

The outmoded term *Riserva Speciale* is still sometimes used, but has no force. The best vintages will develop in bottle for a decade or more.

Moscato grapes are grown in 49 villages south of Asti and supply a booming industry with upwards of 100 million bottles a year of Asti Spumante and the semi-sparkling or still Moscato d'Asti wines. Pressurized tanks called *autoclavi* are used for a single fermentation in a version of the *cuve close* or tank method, ideal to retain the naturally sweet, aromatic flavour of the Moscato.

Other white grapes of significance in Piedmont are the Cortese, the grape for Gavi, and the Arneis which is making something of a comeback. Angelo Gaja is amongst several growers experimenting with Chardonnay. The red Barbera and Dolcetto grapes complete the list of important Piedmont varieties, both of which can produce quality wines from the very best producers.

Lombardy wines

The neighbouring region of Lombardy principally makes white wine. The largest plantings are of Chardonnay and Pinot Nero (vinified into white and sparkling wines), with support from Pinot Bianco and Riesling Italico. Nebbiolo, known locally as Chiavennasca, is the basis of reds in Valtellina, and Cabernet and Merlot are used in some *vino da tavola* wines.

PIEDMONT

ARNEIS

CASTELLO DI NEIVE

This wine is the Latin equivalent of the finest Condrieu: dry and lightly rich, it has a creamy fragrance that is best enjoyed young.

BRUNO GIACOSA

This top Barbaresco producer makes a slightly fuller style of Arneis. It is a fine quality wine, with a certain nutty complexity, although it lacks the same degree of finesse as the Castello di Neive.

ASTI SPUMANTE

GIUSEPPE CONTRATTO

Contratto was one of the last houses to ferment its Asti Spumante in bottle; today, it ferments in *autoclavi* but still there is no denying the finesse of this fresh, grapey, luscious wine, with its long sweet finish and its intriguing hint of ripe peaches.

TOSTI

Few Asti Spumantes can match the richness and vivacious, creamy peach and orange-peel flavours that mingle seductively with the luxuriously fine *mousse* of this Tosti wine. The tiny bubbles are proof positive that *cuve close* is not an inferior method.

BARBARESCO

CASTELLO DI NEIVE
SANTO STEFANO

Santo Stefano is not just Castello di Neive's top Barolo, it is its greatest wine, amid a range that includes the finest Arneis produced and some memorable *cuvées* of Dolcetto d'Alba.

CERETTO ASIJ

Barbaresco-based Marcello Ceretto is one of this *denominazione*'s most gifted winemakers. The purity of fruit and spicy-complexity of his rich, well-coloured Asij challenge Francophiles to take Italian wine seriously.

CERETTO
BRICCO ASILI

This has even greater richness than the Asij, yet - astonishingly - a lighter balance, making a fragrantly expansive, velvety-textured wine on the palate. The epitome of finesse.

PIO CESARE

Very much considered to be in the traditional mould, the firm of Pio Cesare - established in 1881 by one Cesare Pio - does in fact ferment its wine in temperature-controlled stainless-steel vats, after which it is aged in wood for three or more years. This produces a wine that is neither beefcake, nor ultra-elegant, but something in between.

GIUSEPPE CORTESE
VIGNA IN RABAJÀ

This grower used to work for the Marchesi di Gresy when he began to make this wine from his own vineyard, but his success at producing a delicious, overtly fruity and forward style of Barbaresco now means that he need only work for himself.

GAJA

This wine is simply labelled Gaja, which is all that is necessary if you are one of the cognoscenti. Gaja, who is the undisputed champion of this *denominazione*, is that rare type of innovative winemaker whose genius is recognized by even the most traditionalist of his competitors. All Gaja Barbaresco is superb, but his single-vineyard wines - Costa Russi, Sori Tildin and Sori San Lorenzo - are in a different class. They are huge, darkly-coloured wines, full of mouth-swelling, concentrated fruit and absolutely staggering in their richness, complexity and finesse.

BRUNO GIACOSA
SANTO STEFANO DI NEIVE

The fact that Bruno Giacosa has just one small Barolo vineyard is testament to the fact that buying in grapes does not necessarily mean the wine produced will be inferior to that made from the winemaker's own vines. His fabulously rich and complex single-vineyard Barbarescos are all produced from purchased grapes, yet are consistently amongst the world's most exciting wines. The Gallina is superb, but his Santo Stefano di Neive is even better.

MARCHESI DI GRESY
CAMP GROS MARTINENGA

This important grower has 30 hectares (75 acres) of prime sites, including its highly rated Martinenga vineyard. Marchesi di Gresy's Camp Gros Martinenga has a sublime, heady bouquet and soft, voluptuous fruit. It is ripe and delicious to drink when young, but ages gracefully and attains great finesse after 10 years or so.

MARCHESI DI GRESY
GAIUN MARTINENGA

Although it is sometimes difficult to separate this from the Camp Gros Martinenga, the Gaiun Martinenga is capable of greater finesse and complexity, rather than more weight or depth.

PRODUTTORI DEL BARBARESCO
VIGNETI IN ASILI

This cooperative is generally considered to be the finest in Italy, specializing in producing Barbaresco: its single-vineyard Barbarescos are outstanding. It is fascinating to compare the size of this Asili with the supreme fragrance of Ceretto's: only the mouth-filling, never-ending length they share provides the taster with a link between the two.

PRODUTTORI DEL BARBARESCO
VIGNETI IN MONTESTEFANO

This deeply coloured and profoundly serious wine is an utterly satisfying Barbaresco, well known for the immense structure of its plummy-rich, spicy-complex fruit.

BARBERA D'ALBA

ELIO ALTARE

The ubiquitous Barbera grape usually provides a light, acidic and undistinguished red. In the hands of the fastidious Elio Altare, however, it makes an entirely different class of wine - brimming with seductive fruit.

BAROLO

BORGOGNO

Owned by the Boschis family, this firm is famous for its old stocks, regularly releasing wines up to 40 years old for commercial sale. It takes at least 10 years for the fruit to emerge through the mask of tannin, and 20 years or more for the wines to show their classic richness and finesse.

CERETTO
BRICCO ROCCHE

Bruno Ceretto makes several different Barolos. His Bricco Rocche is the fullest and firmest of these, although it is not to be compared with the most massive, tannin-ridden monsters of this *denominazione*. It has something of the beautifully crafted style Ceretto expresses in his Barbaresco.

CERETTO
ZONCHERA

Of all Ceretto's Barolos, it is the elegantly perfumed Zonchera that comes closest to his best Barbaresco.

CLERICO

One of the most talented of the new breed of Barolo producers, Domenico Clerico keeps the amount of time his wine spends in wood to the bare minimum. The result is all freshness and purity of fruit. His Barolo is immediately attractive and demonstrates great vitality on the palate, yet possesses the balance and finesse to improve with age.

ALDO CONTERNO
GRANBUSSIA

One of the top producers in this *denominazione* is Aldo Conterno. His Bussia Soprano is a wonderfully rich wine, with dark, dense fruit and lots of smoky-spicy complexity, yet this is his basic Barolo. The flagship of Aldo Conterno's range is Granbussia, a wine that few Barolos can touch for its sheer size-to-finesse ratio.

GIACOMO CONTERNO
MONFORTINO

The old Conterno family firm of some five generations goes under the name of Giacomo Conterno and is run by Aldo's brother Giovanni. The top-of-the-range Barolo here is the near-legendary Monfortino, which is possibly the most backward and traditional wine of the *denominazione*, but after 20 or 30 years it has incomparable depth and complexity.

FONTANAFREDDA

Although the basic Barolo of this firm, which was founded in 1878 by the son of King Victor Emmanuel II, can be inconsistent, its single-vineyard Barolos (made only in great years) are classic examples of the modern, fruit-laden style. Of the half-dozen or so of this style, the Lazzarito and La Rosa are the most outstanding.

BRUNO GIACOSA
BUSSIA DI MONFORTE

With wines such as this, and his outstanding Rocche di Castiglione Falletto, ultra-traditionalist Bruno Giacosa proves some wines do have the fruit to stand up to long maturation in wood.

GIUSEPPE MASCARELLO
MONPRIVATO
IN CASTIGLIONE FALLETTO

Old-style Barolo from the house of Giuseppe Mascarello, which experimented briefly with modern methods when Mauro Mascarello took over. The Monprivato deserves its heavyweight reputatation, but has such a clarity of concentrated fruit that one can forgive the huge tannic structure that will take decades to soften.

ODDERO

Only generic wines are produced by this firm, which was founded in 1878 (the same year as Fontanafredda), but their unrivalled premium quality is assured by the fact that no single-vineyard Barolos are produced.

RENATO RATTI
MARCENASCO

The death of Renato Ratti in 1988 was a great loss to Barolo. He believed that the tannins must be ripe, which means they are hydrolyzed and the grip in the mouth is a supple one, allowing the fruit to penetrate the tactile impression of the tannin. Ratti's nephew, Massimo Martinelli, continues to make great Barolo in this style.

VIETTI
DELLA LOCALITA' ROCCHE

This wine is made by Alfredo Currado (son-in-law of the founder, Mario Vietti) by a combination of modern and traditional techniques. It is one of the most powerful Barolos, but its backward characteristics do often need to be nursed out by swirling the glass in the warmth of one's hands.

DOLCETTO D'ALBA

RENATO RATTI

Renato Ratti's nephew, Massimo Martinelli, makes a delicious, vivid, purple-coloured Dolcetto that absolutely gushes with soft, ripe, up-front fruit flavours.

GATTINARA

DESSILANI

Founded in 1924 by Luigi Dessilani and Figlio, this firm has the greatest reputation in the Gattinara *denominazione* and produces full-bodied wines in an unashamed rustic style.

GAVI

CASTELLO DI TASSAROLO

Owned by the Marchesi Spinola, the Castello di Tassarolo in Alessandria makes a fine, dry Gavi that has a soft style, cut by crisp acidity and a slightly nutty aftertaste. It is best drunk as soon as it is bottled, when the acidity is at its most refreshing.

LA SCOLCA
GAVI DEI GAVI

La Scolca in Alessandria was the first wine to establish international interest in the Cortese grape and the Gavi appellation. It should be drunk young, when it can be a bit *frizzantino*, although it does gain a charming honey-rich flavour if kept in bottle for a couple of years.

GHEMME

ANTICHI VIGNETI DI CANTALUPO

The resinous smells of tar and earth that typify the wines of this appellation are due to its *terroir*, but they mar the quality of a wine when allowed to dominate. This is something that does not affect even the basic Ghemme of Antichi Vigneti di Cantalupo, a wine that has an abundance of ripe, elegant fruit and fine floral finesse. This producer's top wines, the Collis Carellae and Collis Breclemae, have the added bonus of some amusing back labels, which recommend the wines for "meditation" and "bringing cheer to meetings among friends".

MOSCATO D'ASTI

FONTANAFREDDA

Moscato d'Asti is normally still - or has only the barest hint of a prickle - thus the smallest defect shows up, so the finest of Piedmont's Muscat grapes are reserved for this wine. It is a deliciously soft, delicately rich wine with peach and orange flavours. The purity of these flavours is perfectly captured by the high-tech production methods of Fontanafredda.

OTHERS

ROCCHE DEI MANZONI
BRICCO MANZONI

This is made from a judicious blend of Nebbiolo and Barbera grown by Valentino Magliorini, an ex-restaurateur, at Monforte on the southern border of the Barolo district. After a spell in small oak *barriques*, the deep-coloured, rich and generously balanced wine is almost ready to drink, but it will be at its best between five and ten years from the date of harvest.

VALLANA
SPANNA DEL PIEMONTE

Spanna is the local name for the Nebbiolo grape, so theoretically this *vino da tavola* should represent Piedmont's most basic wine from this variety. Vallana's Spanna, however, is a fat, fruity, dense-flavoured wine that can develop great complexity over 10 years or more and is superior to many a Barolo or Barbaresco.

LOMBARDY

FRANCIACORTA

CUVÉE BELLAVISTA BRUT

One of Italy's few truly classic sparkling wine producers, Bellavista produces a fine fizzy Franciacorta at its splendid estate in Erbusco. Made by the *metodo tradizionale*, with fermentation in bottle, this wine has a depth of flavour that is so often lacking in Italian sparkling wines.

CÀ DEL BOSCO BRUT

The sparkling wines of Cà del Bosco will be most appreciated by wine drinkers with a distinct Francophile bias. The firm's basic *brut* has good bottle-age and shows well as soon as it is sold, although it will improve for a further 18 months or more.

CÀ DEL BOSCO PINOT

Produced mostly from Pinot Bianco (Blanc), but with the addition of a small percentage of Pinot Nero (Noir) and Pinot Grigio (Gris), this wine is the fruitiest of all the Cà del Bosco's sparkling Franciacorta *cuvées*. There is also a superb Pas Dose that is much drier and requires a year or two of extra age in bottle for the flavour to fill out.

LONGHI-DE CARLI ROSSO

Made primarily from Cabernet Franc, to which some Barbera and Merlot has been added, this medium-bodied wine is best drunk between three and five years after the vintage.

VALTELLINA

ENOLOGICA VALTELLINESE SFORZATO TRE LEGHE

The Enologica Valtellinese's single *cru* Paradiso is one of the finest Valtellina Sassella wines, but Tre Leghe Sforzato is perhaps its most outstanding wine. *Sforzato*, or "strained", is a term that may only be used of a distinctly dry and concentrated Valtellina made from sun-dried grapes.

TONA SASSELLA

Sassella must be made from at least 95 per cent Chiavennasca, a local Nebbiolo clone. The soft Il Terziere is one of the finest Sassellas made.

OTHERS

ANGELO BALLABIO NARBUSTO

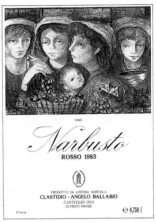

The first non-Italian to discover this wine was Master of Wine Clive Coates, who was so impressed by its quality that he purchased some for the Malmaison Wine Club in the 1970s, despite the fact that he had to sell it at a much higher price than his most expensive Barolo at the time. In style, Narbusto comes between Barolo and a fine Châteauneuf-du-Pape, with hints of old-style Rioja. It has an extraordinary depth and richness of fruit for a wine that has spent eight years in wood.

CÀ DEL BOSCO MAURIZIO ZANELLA

Named after the owner of Cà del Bosco, Maurizio Zanella is a full, rich, deeply-coloured wine. Its delicious, soft, juicy-fruitiness comes from a small proportion of *macération carbonique* wine in the blend and its supple tannic structure from one year in small oak *barriques*.

🥂 *CS 40%, CF 30%, M 30%*

NORTH-EAST ITALY

THE THREE REGIONS of North-East Italy have rapidly become a second home for French varietals. Chardonnay in particular has achieved prominence, but not entirely at the expense of native varieties. In Trentino-Alto Adige, Trentino, the southern half, is Italian; Alto Adige (or Südtirol), in the north, is German-speaking. The Alto Adige wines, which make up 30 per cent of the region's DOC output, can therefore carry either the Germanic *QbA* or the Italian DOC designation on the label.

Trentino-Alto Adige

Trentino and Alto Adige DOCs are umbrella denominations for a considerable range of single varietal wines, which include Cabernet, Merlot and the native Schiava (Vernatsch) among the red wines, and Traminer Aromatica (Gewürztraminer), Chardonnay and Moscato Giallo (Goldmuskateller) among the white wines. All the bottle-fermented, dry, sparkling wines in the region are outside the DOC system.

Veneto

The third largest of the wine-producing regions of Italy, Veneto boasts the highest output of DOC wines, of which Valpolicella, Bardolino and Soave are the most popular. The principal grapes that are used for these wines are unique to Veneto: Garganega (di Soave) for the Soave, and Corvina, Rondinella and Molinara for the reds. Veneto also has some unusual sweeter wines. Two of these are derivatives of Valpolicella and Soave: the sweet white Recioto di Soave and the red Recioto di Valpolicella. The latter can also be vinified dry, when it will be called Amarone.

The *recioto* process uses carefully selected grapes, which after picking are spread out on straw matting. After a few months, the grapes become dried out and raisined, enabling highly concentrated wines to be made. This method is employed by Maculan, in Breganze, to make another of Italy's maverick, non-DOC wines, the succulently sweet Torcolato, which is made with both Tocai and Vespaiolo grapes.

Friuli-Venezia Giulia

This region is one of the country's smaller producers, but it also happens to be the source of some of its finest wines. Like Trentino-Alto Adige, the DOCs embrace an extremely wide variety of single-grape wines. Fine quality wines are made in the region both as DOC and as *vino da tavola*. Red DOC varietals come from Merlot, Cabernet (Sauvignon and Franc), Pinot Nero and Refosco. There is a wide choice of whites that includes the widely grown, local Tocai Friulano, as well as Pinot Bianco, Riesling, Chardonnay and Sauvignon. Some of the finest reds, however, are non-DOC Cabernet blends.

TRENTINO-ALTO ADIGE

ALTO ADIGE (SÜD-TIROL)

ALOIS LAGEDER CABERNET SAUVIGNON LÖWENGANG

The prominent old Alto Adige firm Alois Lageder owns 20 hectares (50 acres) of vineyards, which account for less than 5 per cent of its total production. The quality is consistently high. This *barrique*-aged wine has deep colour and full, *cassis* fruit laced with smoky-herbaceous complexity.

ALOIS LAGEDER CHARDONNAY BUCHHOLZ

This excellent wine is made by Alois Lageder's talented winemaker, Louis Dellman, from Chardonnay vines grown on the hillside village of Buchholz in the Südtiroler DOC. It is a lightly rich wine, with a buttery flavour and a complex biscuity character. The newly released, oaked Löwengang Chardonnay is also well worth trying.

ALOIS LAGEDER ST MAGDALENER CLASSICO

St Magdalener is a full-bodied, smooth red wine, made from the Vernatsch or Black Hamburg grape; it had the dubious honour of being ranked by Mussolini as one of Italy's greatest wines.

J. TIEFENBRUNNER CHARDONNAY

Herbert Tiefenbrunner makes a much lighter style of Chardonnay than Lageder, but it is not without substance and displays more true varietal character than many of the somewhat heavier styles. This is a racy wine, full of zingy fruit flavour and inclined to a slight spritz.

J. TIEFENBRUNNER GOLDMUSKATELLER

In this wine Herbert Tiefenbrunner produces one of the most fragrant, elegant and finely tuned Muscat-type wines in Italy. It is a light-bodied wine, with deliciously tangy fruit.

TRENTINO

CONTI BOSSI FEDRIGOTTI CABERNET

The Fedrigotti family has been growing Cabernet and Merlot vines since the last century. Their Cabernet, a blend of Cabernet Franc and Cabernet Sauvignon, has an intensity of flavour that is hard to obtain from grapes in Italy's North-East.

OTHERS

CASTEL S. MICHELE

This fine blend of Cabernet Franc, Cabernet Sauvignon and Merlot is the Istituto Agrario's greatest wine, with greater longevity than its pure varietal red wines. The grassiness of the Cabernet Franc is skilfully fleshed out with the Cabernet Sauvignon and the Merlot adds a juicy fatness.

EQUIPE 5 BRUT RISERVA

This sparkling-wine house produces five different *cuvées*: Brut, Extra Brut, Sec, Brut Rosé, and the wine here, Brut Riserva. This is made from a blend of Pinot grapes and always displays fine autolytic character, suggesting good bottle-age and sufficient yeast-contact.

CONTI BOSSI FEDRIGOTTI FOIANEGHE ROSSO

This Merlot-dominated Cabernet blend is only a *vino da tavola*, yet its combination of fruity Merlot and intense Cabernet has the edge on Fedrigotti's pure Merlot and blended Cabernet. Fedrigotti also makes a delightful Chardonnay-Traminer white.

GIULIO FERRARI RISERVA DEL FONDATORE

This *riserva* is named after Giulio Ferrari, who founded Italy's longest-established and most consistent producer of classic dry sparkling wines. Giulio Ferrari, Riserva del Fondatore is a Chardonnay-Pinot blend of great depth, with fine fruit and a firm, yeasty flavour.

POJER E SANDRI CHARDONNAY

From their steep hillside vineyards at Faedo, Mario Pojer and Fiorentino Sandri produce some of the finest wines in Trentino-Alto Adige but, such is the Italian system, they have the status of *vino da tavola*. This particular wine is made in a surprisingly aromatic style. However, after a year or two in bottle, the flavour broadens out and acquires its classic varietal character.

POJER E SANDRI MÜLLER THURGAU

This finely structured, highly aromatic, penetratingly flavoured, dry white wine is one of only a tiny number of truly classic renditions of Müller-Thurgau in the world.

Zeni
Chardonnay di S. Michele

This sensational wine is bursting with ripe, vibrant fruit flavours and has gained in richness, quality and stature in recent years. The Zeni brothers also make a superb Pinot Blanc from a single vineyard called Sorti.

Zeni
Teroldego Rotaliano

Grown on the gravelly Campo Rotaliano plain, the only place where the indigenous Teroldego grape can thrive, the Zenis produce one of the most stunning red Italian DOC wines. It is bottled early to retain its fruit.

FRIULI-VENEZIA GIULIA

COLLI GORIZIANO

Borgo Conventi
Collio Merlot

Lighter and less plump than Fedrigotti's rendition of the same varietal from the Alto Adige, the great quality of this wine is its superb elegance and the silky finesse of its fruit.

Borgo Conventi
Collio Sauvignon

Gianni Vescovo produces fine domaine-bottled wine at this former walled convent at Farra d'Isonzo. This elegant, crisp, grassy-varietal Sauvignon is considered to be the best of them all, although his Tocai Friulano can sometimes rival it.

Schiopetto

Established as recently as the late 1960s by Mario Schiopetto, whose white wines have since achieved a reputation of legendary proportions. His Pinot Bianco (Blanc) and Riesling are fine wines by any standards, and his Tocai Friulano is one of the finest dry white wines made in Italy.

COLLI ORIENTALI DEL FRIULI

Abbazia di Rosazzo

This small state-of-the-art winery at Corno di Rosazzo was established as recently as 1981 by jet-setting, multi-talented Walter Filiputti. No one makes better DOC Colli Orientali wines than Filiputti, although his best wines are all *vino da tavola*.

OTHERS

Abbazia di Rosazzo
Ronco delle Acacie

This is Walter Filiputti's brilliant *barrique*-aged blend of Pinot Bianco (Blanc), Ribolla, Malvasia and Tocai Friulano. It has an exotic bouquet that is combined with mouth-watering fruit flavours and beautifully understated creamy new oak on the finish.

Abbazia di Rosazzo
Ronco dei Roseti

This curious Franco-Prussian blend of Cabernet Franc, Cabernet Sauvignon, Merlot, Limberger, Refosco and Tazzelenghe is the brainchild of Walter Filiputti. Aged for one year in *barriques*, it requires several more to knit together into one homogeneous whole. When it does, it is sensational.

Jermann
Pinot Bianco

If all Italian white wines were made to the standards of Angelo Jermann, Italy would have a national reputation to match the regional one of Burgundy. Jermann's Pinot Bianco is remarkably rich for what is normally such a light variety, yet it cannot match the exotic excitements of either his Chardonnay or Pinot Grigio.

JERMANN
VINTAGE TUNINA

Jermann's top-of-the-range wine, Vintage Tunina is a super-luxury blend of Chardonnay, Pinot Bianco, Sauvignon Blanc and Picolit. An unctuous, sensuous wine, full of the ripest and most exotic flavours, it is so sensational that it simply has to be tasted to be believed.

RONCO DEL GNEMIZ

This property produces very good whites, especially Pinot Grigio, Chardonnay and Tocai Friulano under the Colli Orientali DOC, but it is its classic Bordeaux *vino da tavola* blend of Cabernet Sauvignon, Cabernet Franc, Merlot and Malbec for which it is best known.

VIGNE DEL LEON
SCHIOPPETTINO

The Schioppettino is an ancient Friulian grape variety that was nearly extinct until its wines became fashionable in the 1980s. The Vigne del Leon is a very ripe and well-rounded wine with a spicy-scented bouquet and a rich fruit flavour that only attains finesse after five years or more from the date of its harvest.

VENETO

BREGANZE

MACULAN
BRENTINO

Founded in 1937, this family-run operation is now under the control of Fausto Maculan, one of Italy's most inspired young winemakers. His Brentino Rosso is a Merlot-dominated Bordeaux blend that spends one year in *barriques* and oozes fruit. It has a wonderfully supple tannic structure that requires just three years or so to peak, yet the wine will remain at its apogee for a good 10 years or more.

MACULAN
CABERNET FRATTA

This half-and-half Cabernet Sauvignon and Cabernet Franc is made from over-ripe grapes and is one of the two superstar wines that have established Maculan's reputation. It spends at least one year in new oak *barriques* and can be compared to a second-growth claret in terms of quality, if not style.

MACULAN
PRATO DI CANZIO

The only white wine that stands out in the Breganze DOC. Comprising 70 per cent fulsome Tocai, with Pinot Bianco (Blanc) and Riesling to give a light touch to the blend, the wine spends six months in new *barriques*. This gives a rich, tangy flavour, with a hint of spice, an excellent balance of fruit and acidity, and just a suggestion of sweet-creamy oak underneath.

LISON-PRAMAGGIORE

TENUTA SANT' ANNA
CABERNET SAUVIGNON

Owned by Agricola Rus SpA, this concern owns and cultivates 250 hectares (618 acres) of vineyards in Veneto and Friuli. This Cabernet Sauvignon is grown on a clay soil mixed with sand and lime, which produces a very classy wine.

SANTA MARGHERITA
CABERNET SAUVIGNON

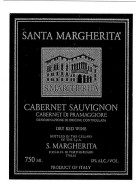

A high-tech operation owned and run by the Marzotto family. This wine has good colour, a fine bouquet and rich chocolatey fruit that begins to mellow after three years in bottle and attains a significant degree of finesse after another two or three.

SANTA MARGHERITA
SELVA MAGGIORE MERLOT

In the Pramaggiore DOC the Merlot has always been more serious than Cabernet and this Selva Maggiore is an outstanding example of the heights this grape variety can reach.

SOAVE

ANSELMI
CAPITEL CROCE MONTEFORTE

Anselmi is the saviour of Soave, although his fabulously rich and oaky Croce Monteforte is not an example for others wines to follow. It is over-powered by its creamy toast and vanilla overtones when first released, but its class is confirmed when the fruit eventually dominates.

ANSELMI
CAPITEL FOSCARINO

This great Soave sees no new oak. Only from the DOC's *Classico* zone can a wine of such abundant fruit be produced and only then if as much as 25 per cent of the potential crop is pruned away during the summer to concentrate the vines' efforts.

ANSELMI
RECIOTO DEI CAPITELLI

This wine is a revelation. It has a glorious golden colour, a sumptuous bouquet of honey, flowers, nuts and molasses, and a sweet and complex flavour of honeyed-spicy fruit. The finish is long and concentrated, with a smoky-creamy oak aftertaste.

VALPOLICELLA RIPASSO

ALLEGRINI
LA GROLA

The Allegrini family has established an extraordinary reputation for the quality of its Valpolicella, especially under the auspices of the latest generation, Franco Allegrini. His La Grola is a silky-smooth non-DOC Valpolicella of great finesse, which is made by the *ripasso* method.

TEDESCHI
CAPITEL SAN ROCCO

From Tedeschi's Capitel San Rocco vineyard, this wine is another example of how the *ripasso* can enrich the basic wines of Valpolicella. It is a beautifully coloured wine, well endowed with rich fruit flavours, and can age well for up to 10 years.

OTHERS

CONTE LOREDAN-GASPARINI
VENEGAZZÚ DELLA CASA

One of the first *vino da tavola* to establish a worldwide reputation, this classic Bordeaux blend of Cabernet Sauvignon, Cabernet Franc, Merlot and Malbec from the Montello Hills can be variable according to the vintage and sometimes has a touch too much *pétillance,* but great vintages, such as the 1977, are classic wines and improve for 10 or 15 years.

MACULAN
TORCOLATO

If Fausto Maculan were responsible for just this one wine, he would go down in the history of Italian wine as one of its greatest and most innovative figures. This sensationally rich and sumptuous dessert wine is made from *passito* grapes, but has no hint of bitterness and is strangely close in style and quality to a great Sauternes.

FATTORIA DI OGLIANO
CAPO DEL MONTE

Winemaker Gianni Spinazzé produces this unique wine by blending Cabernet Franc with Marzemino, a rare grape these days. The resulting wine can take five years to mature.

CENTRAL ITALY

I T IS IN CENTRAL ITALY that most of the new thinking about winemaking techniques, clonal development and new wine styles is taking place. This thinking has been led by Antinori and Frescobaldi, old-established concerns, and the more recent estate of Villa Banfi in Montalcino; all are organizations with great resources behind them. Cabernet Sauvignon and Chardonnay grapes, alongside or in place of native varieties, coupled with Bordeaux-style ageing in new oak *barriques* instead of the more traditional large Slavonian oak *botti*, have set new standards of excellence that the rigidity of the DOC regulations cannot contain. Tuscany today offers a cornucopia of new wines ranging from pure Sangiovese and pure Cabernet Sauvignon, to Sangiovese-dominated or Cabernet-dominated reds, and pure Chardonnay whites. They command a price well above most DOC prices, despite being categorized as *vini da tavola*.

Traditional Tuscan wines of excellence

Tuscany lays claim to three of the five red wine DOCGs approved for the whole country in Brunello di Montalcino, Vino Nobile di Montepulciano and Chianti. The Sangiovese grape is the basic constituent of each, as indeed it is the dominant grape throughout the whole of Central Italy in one or other of its clonal disguises. In Chianti wines it is joined by Canaiolo Nero, Trebbiano, Malvasia and up to 10 per cent of other grape varieties (often Cabernet Sauvignon). A great part of the top-class wines of Chianti come from the Chianti Classico zone, which contain the older, better situated hill sites in the "heartland" of the region. The whole Chianti denomination, which is one of the biggest in the country, is divided into six further zones, Colli Fiorentini, Colli Senesi, Colli Aretni, Colline Pisane, Montalbano and Rufina. Producers within any of these six zones can become members of the Chianti Putto *Consorzio*; the best wines tend to come from the Rufina or occasionally the Colli Fiorentini or Colli Senesi.

Wines from Umbria

Of the other central Italy regions, Marches, Abruzzi, Molise, Latium and Umbria, it is the last which provides the best quality. Umbria, where Antinori also have a presence through their Castello della Sala vineyard - has two notable DOC wine areas, both named after small hill towns, Orvieto and Torgiano. Orvieto produces only white wines in dry and sweet (*abboccato*) forms, that can be superb, especially if they have been affected by noble rot. The Torgiano DOC is effectively the output of one large estate. Owned by Dr Giorgio Lungarotti, a long-time standard-bearer for fine Italian wine, it provides the springboard for a number of remarkable new non-DOC wines.

TUSCANY

In the hands of the two talented oenologists Pierro and Angelo Soci, this old estate has foresaken the heavily tannic style for a more *avant garde* approach. Its wine remains full-bodied, but the tannin is supple and the fruit rich and concentrated.

BIONDI-SANTI

If any wine is guaranteed to excite both extremes of like and dislike, it is Biondi-Santi, the most famous and wincingly expensive of all Brunello di Montalcino. Those who love it have to wait 20 years or more before its outer defences of tannin begin to budge, while those who hate it cannot find any fruit at all by the time this has happened.

TENUTA CAPARZO LA CASA

This property is another in the new-wave vein of Altesino, where the aim is to pack as much fruit into the bottle as possible, but not at the expense of quality. The fruit in this wine has a distinctly oaky character, finished with lots of finesse and complexity.

CASTELGIOCONDO

Tenuta di Castelgiocondo's 175 hectares (432 acres) make it one of the largest wine estates in Brunello di Montalcino. Perhaps because of its size, the wine has been underrated, but it is a serious wine of exceptional value and toasty-complexity.

PODERI EMILIO COSTANTI

Although made with the time-honoured mask of tannin, Costanti packs so much fruit behind this phenolic fence that when it comes down, a magnificent wine is revealed.

TENUTA IL POGGIONE

This property is one of the largest Brunello di Montalcino estates. Owned by the Franceschi family, it was founded in 1890. The wines, which are made by Piero Talenti, are deliciously fruity in their youth, but have the body and build to last and improve for 10 years or more.

TALENTI
PODERE PIAN DI CONTE

Piero Talenti also has his own small estate. He does not have Tenuta il Poggione's same flexibility to pick, choose and blend from a variety of vineyard sites, but through strict controls in both vineyard and cellar, he produces wines that always rival, and may surpass, other Brunellos.

CARMIGNANO

CONTE CONTINI BONACOSSI
VILLA DI TREFIANO

Cuttings of Cabernet Sauvignon from Château Lafite-Rothschild were planted at Conte Ugo Contini Bonacossi's fifteenth-century Tenuta di Capezzana in the late 1960s. It was from this, and on the basis of Brando di Cosimo III de Medici's delimitation in 1716, that Carmignano became the first DOC in Tuscany to permit the use of French grape varieties. Although the Villa di Capezzana Riserva is the best-known wine from this appellation and consistently one of its finest, it is Villa di Trefiano, first made by Count Ugo's son, that is considered to be the greatest Carmignano from Bonacossi.

CHIANTI

MARCHESE L. E P. ANTINORI
VILLA ANTINORI RISERVA

Like Ruffino, Antinori is best known for their easy-to-drink, round and supple basic Chianti and, like Ruffino, Antinori also makes exceptional, characterful wines. Its Villa Antinori Chianti Classico Riserva is one of the most consistent wines in the region.

BADIA A COLTIBUONO

Badia a Coltibuono dates from the late eighth century, when the Firidolfi family built a private chapel, which became a monastery in 1053. The monks planted vines and made the first wine on this Classico estate.

CASTELLARE DI CASTELLINA

Paolo Panerai is the editor of Italy's *Capital* magazine and owner of Castellare and the wines all bear his famous bird motifs. Made by Maurizo Castelli, one of Tuscany's most innovative winemakers, Castellare's Chianti Classico is fine and stylish.

CASTELLO DI NIPOZZANO

The noble house of Frescobaldi has owned vineyards in the Chianti region since the late thirteenth century. This wine, Montesodi and Remole are its best Chiantis today. The Castello di Nipozzano comes from the Rufina district and is a *riserva* bottled only in the best years. It is a rich, yet elegant wine, full of ripe fruit and has a complex cedary aftertaste.

CASTELLO DEI RAMPOLLA

This property, owned by the Napoli Rampolla family, produces some of the greatest Chianti Classicos. They are deep-coloured, packed with rich and concentrated fruit, and remain vital and fresh into old age, when they gain extraordinary complexity.

CASTELLO VICCHIOMAGGIO
VIGNETO PRIMA VIGNA

This superb single-vineyard, *barrique*-aged Chianti Classico, with its power-packed, sensational Sangiovese flavour, is by far Anglo-Italian John Matta's best wine.

FONTODI

Domiziano and Dino Manetti produce a style of Chianti Classico that even Francophiles cannot resist. It oozes velvety, ripe berry and seductive fruit flavours, all gently underpinned with supple tannin, a hint of *barrique* ageing and lots of finesse.

ISOLE E OLENA

Since Paolo de Marchi took over the winemaking on this estate in the late 1970s, the quality has gone from good to excellent and is approaching great. This is another wine that emphasizes plump fruit flavours more than dried-out tannic tradition.

MONSANTO
RISERVA DEL POGGIO

Monsanto's top Chianti, the Riserva del Poggio, has masses of fruit, even if it is pretty dense during the first decade or so of its life, but this multi-dimensional wine eventually achieves great class and a generous style.

MONTESODI

This Chianti Rufina, which is from a micro-*cru*, an individually named site within the Nipozzano vineyard, is the greatest single wine produced by the Marchesi de Frescobaldi. It is a blend of Sangiovese and Cabernet Sauvignon with great concentration and beautiful, creamy-smoky complexity which comes from ageing in *barriques,* some of which are new.

PODERE IL PALAZZINO

This substantial but sumptuous wine has encouraged some critics to name Alessandro and Andrea Sderci's property the "Pétrus of Chianti". Be that as it may, its deliciously rich flavour and distinctive oak-complexity make it one of the greatest wines of this appellation.

REMOLE

The Marchesi de Frescobaldi owns eight estates in the Chianti region with a combined total of more than 500 hectares (1,235 acres) of vineyards. Remole comes from Tenuta di Poggio a Remole, 24 kilometres (15 miles) north-east of Florence, and is hall-marked by its silky elegance.

BARONE RICASOLI
BROLIO RISERVA

The Brolio estate was acquired by the Ricasoli family in 1141 and seven centuries later Bettino Ricasoli laid down the recipe for Chianti. Brolio was once a first growth of Chianti. It has not declined; others have merely improved, and Brolio Riserva is as good as it has ever been.

ROCCA DELLE MACIE
RISERVA DI FIZZANO

With its appealing hint of oak, the basic "black label" Rocca delle Macie ranks as one of Chianti Classico's greatest wine bargains and the rich, intensely flavoured, *barrique*-aged Riserva di Fizzano is a fine wine by any standards.

RUFFINO
RISERVA DUCALE

Not to be confused with the Rufina district north-east of the Classico area, Ruffino is one of the largest producers of fresh and fruity generic Chianti. It also makes some fine *cuvées*, like this Riserva Ducale, which has sumptuous fruit and cedary complexity.

ROSSO DI MONTALCINO

TENUTA IL POGGIONE

Bursting with ripe, intense fruit in virtually every vintage, this concentrated but supple wine has a spicy-complexity that makes it the best Rosso di Montalcino in the appellation.

TALENTI
PODERE PIAN DI CONTE

Unlike other traditional wines of this area, which are hard and mean, the Podere Pian di Conte produced by Talenti has both fruit and power.

VINO NOBILE DI
MONTEPULCIANO

AVIGNONESI

This deeply coloured, richly flavoured Vino Nobile has a fine structure of ripe tannins that takes several years to round out and is one of the few truly noble wines of this DOC.

PODERI BOSCARELLI

The Marchesi de Ferrari-Corradi owns this small, relatively young property, the wines of which vie with those of Avignonesi as the very finest Vino Nobile di Montepulciano.

OTHERS

BALIFICO
CASTELLO DI VOLPAIA

This blend of Sangiovese and Cabernet comes from Castello di Volpaia in the Chianti region. It is a true Tuscan superstar and the greatest of Giovannella Stianti Mascheroni's wines. Very rich and oaky, with velvety fruit, lots of concentration and great complexity. It is fascinating to compare this with the Coltassala, another excellent *vino da tavola* from Castello di Volpaia, but in a more ethnic-Italian, less classy, style.
SGV 70%, CAB 30%

BRUNO DI ROCCA
VECCHIE TERRE DI MONTEFILI

The first vintage, in 1983, caused excitement when launched in 1986. The 1985 was even more sensational. A huge wine with lots of oak but also plenty of fruit, flavour and complexity to back it up. Lots of ripeness and chocolatey-spicy complexity.
SGV 70%, CAB 30%

CÀ DEL PAZZO
TENUTA CAPARZO

Packed solid with concentrated sweet fruit and underpinned with a hint of oak, this beautifully balanced wine comes from the Brunello di Montalcino district, but because it contains a large proportion of Cabernet it cannot claim that DOCG nor even the Rosso di Montalcino DOC.
SGV 50%, CAB 50%

CAPANNELLE
DI RAFFAELA ROSSETTI

A pure Sangiovese of obviously high quality, but a more ethnic-Italian style, with the traditional hardness of the grape showing through a somewhat rustic *barrique*-ageing.
SGV 100%

CEPPARELLO
ISOLE E OLENA

This pure Sangiovese is a blend of reserve wines that have been given long ageing in *barrique*. It has a fine, concentrated, fruity bouquet, lots of fruit and flavour and a cedary, cigar-box complexity.
SGV 100%

COLTASSALA
CASTELLO DI VOLPAIA

The elegant and well-refined bouquet on this Sangiovese-dominated wine comes from its small proportion of Mammolo grape and the vanillin from the Limousin oak used to mature Coltassala. It does not have the exciting quality of Castello di Volpaia's Balifico and, except for the supple, sumptuous 1985 vintage, it is somewhat hard and reserved, but nonetheless it is a true *vin de garde*.
SGV 95%, MAM 5%

GHIAIE DELLA FURBA
TENUTA DI CAPEZZANA

The Bordeaux vines used for this excellent *vino da tavola* are grown on a gravelly part of Tenuta di Capezzana, in the Carmignano DOC. Ghiaie della Furba's classic *cassis* concentration is underlined by the spicy-cedary overtones of its *terroir*.
CAB 60-70% , MER 30-40%

LE GRANCE
TENUTA CAPARZO

From the innovative producer of La Casa, the outstanding Brunello, the deep, rich pure varietal flavour of this Chardonnay wine is already superb, but gets better with each vintage.
CH 100%

GRIFI
AVIGNONESI

The first vintage of this wine came as recently as 1981. It has a substantial build, but its fruit is rich and voluptuous, with cherry-chocolate complexity and creamy-oak finesse. One of the finest *vino da tavola* currently produced in Tuscany.
SGV 80%, CF 20%

GROSSO SANESE
PODERE IL PALAZZINO

Alessandro and Andrea Sderci's pure Sangiovese is a truly sumptuous affair, considering the mineral-hardness that is normally the hallmark of this grape. The Grosso Sanese is a well-structured wine with a great intensity of fruit and a spicy-cedary-oak complexity.

IL MARZOCCO
AVIGNONESI

A pure Chardonnay of potentially tremendous quality, packed solid with rich, ripe fruit and dominated by more than an injudicious amount of oak, but it is a flavoursome mouthful all the same.

MONTE VERTINE RISERVA

To say this is Chianti Classico in all but name would be to insult Sergio Manetti: his Monte Vertine used to sell under this appellation until he rejected the DOCG, because of its tarnished image; instead, he sold it on his own, bright reputation.
SGV 90%, CAN 10%

NEMO
CASTELLO DI MONSANTO

A powerful, pure Cabernet Sauvignon wine from the single-vineyard of Il Mulino in Mulino di Scanni. It is made by the producer of Monsanto Riserva del Poggio and, like that wine, it has masses of dense fruit and benefits from at least 10 years' maturation.
CS 100%

PALAZZO ALTESI
ALTESINO

The grapes of this stunningly success-ful wine are grown at Montosoli, an exceptional single vineyard with *tufa* soil. About 20 per cent of the wine is fermented by *macération carbonique*.
SGV 100%

LE PERGOLE TORTE
MONTE VERTINE

This wine is as ripe and voluptuous as any pure Sangiovese could possibly be, proving how great Chianti could be with a much reduced yield and a talented wine-maker. Full and velvety rich, it gushes with lush, concentrated fruit.
SGV 100%

QUERCIAGRANDE
PODERE CAPACCIA

A pure Sangiovese, this outstanding wine has a soft, inviting bouquet with lovely understated oak, which asserts itself more on the palate.
SGV 100%

SAMMARCO
CASTELLO DEI RAMPOLLA

The first vintage has not yet reached peak maturity, but Sammarco is already dubbed the Mouton-Rothschild of Tuscany. Power-packed, intensely flavoured, full of ripe and concentrated fruit, and overflowing with plummy-oaky-spicy finesse.
CAB 75%, SGV 25%

SASSICAIA
TENUTA SAN GUIDO

The origins of Sassicaia, which means "hill of stones", stretch back to 1948, when Mida Incisa della Rochetta planted the first Cabernet Sauvignon vines on a hill of stony ground called Castiglioncello. It was Mida's son Mario Incisa who made the first wine, but his family was not impressed and suggested he was better suited to horse breeding. The project to produce a pure Cabernet Sauvignon wine was abandoned. Then, in 1959, Incisa remembered his experiment and dug out a few bottles. He was surprised how well they had devel-oped and purchased new French *barriques* in which to continue his experiment, but it was not until 1968, when Mario's uncle - none other than Piero Antinori - stepped in, that the first commercial vintage of Sassicaia was produced. Since then it has become a legend.
CS 100%

SASSOLATO
VILLA CILNIA

Giovanni Bianchi's amazing Sau-ternes-like Sassolato is produced from *passito* grapes of Malvasia, Trebbiano and Chardonnay and matured in *barriques* of new French oak. Only Fausto Maculan's Torcolato in Veneto can compare with it.

I SODI DI S. NICCOLO
CASTELLARE DI CASTELLINA

This blend of Sangiovese and black Malvasia is loaded with fruit and very quickly shows great finesse, although it has the potential to age very well. The 1985 vintage was ranked by the *Wine Spectator* as the sixth best wine in the world.

TIGNANELLO
MARCHESI L. E P. ANTINORI

Intrigued by the success of Sassicaia, Piero Antinori brought out its own up-market *vino da tavola* called Tignanello. The first vintage was 1971, but unlike Sassicaia, this wine was a compromise between Bordeaux and Tuscany, using Sangiovese as the base and blending in some 20 per cent of Cabernet Sauvignon. Until that moment, nobody truly appreciated the harmony that could be achieved between these two grapes, which is akin to the natural balance of Cabernet and Merlot, but with a different permutation of checks and balances. It was Tignanello, therefore, that sparked off the new-wave of so-called super-Tuscan wines, although, of course, Sassicaia was the catalyst by which Tignanello came about.
🍷 *SGV 80-90%, CS 10-20%*

UMBRIA

ORVIETO

BARBERANI
CALCAIA

While Luigi Barberani's Le Corone is acknowledged as one of the best single-vineyard wines of Orvieto, Calcaia is in an entirely different class. It is a delicious dessert wine made from botrytized grapes.

BIGI
VIGNETO TORRICELLA

Bigi decided to select the best wine from its Torricella vineyard and bottle it separately; many people consider it to be the finest Orvieto available.

OTHERS

LUNGAROTTI
RUBESCO TORGIANO RISERVA

One of the great names of Umbria is Lungarotti and the fame of his Rubesco Torgiano has been such that it has been given its own DOC and is set to become DOCG soon.

LATIUM

TORRE ERCOLANA

This interesting Franco-Italian blend has been made since the early 1960s and relies heavily on the great grapes of Bordeaux giving a much needed boost to the local, rather undistinguished Cesanese to produce Latium's finest wine. Some vintages positively burst with bouquet and fruit; others are more pedestrian.
🍷 *CAB 36%, M 32%, CES 32%*

EMILIA-ROMAGNA

RONCO DEI CILIEGI
BALDI DI CASTELLUCCIO

This is the best of Gian Matteo Baldi's three single-vineyard, pure Sangiovese wines. It has good colour, an elegant bouquet, supple tannic structure and rich, silky fruit. Its restrained use of oak helps to polish a wine of obvious finesse.

E. VALLANIA VIGNETO TERRE ROSSE CHARDONNAY

This wine is finer than Emilia Romagna's best Albana di Romagna, the *vin ordinaire* that became Italy's first white DOCG. With its fine depth of flavour, it gives the perfect balance between true varietal character and authentic Italian style.

ABRUZZI

MONTEPULCIANO D'ABRUZZO

ILLUMINATI

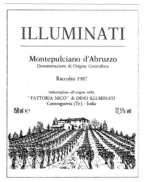

This wine is very stylish, leaning more towards Valentini than Colle Secco, yet very accessible in its youth. Illuminati's Invecchiato is a *riserva* version of greater complexity.

CANTINA TOLLO COLLE SECCO

There are two different styles of Montepulciano d'Abruzzo, one is soft and fruity, the other firm and tannic. The wealth of soft, fat fruit in this densely coloured wine makes it an outstanding example of the former.

VALENTINI VECCHIO

Widely acclaimed as the greatest producer of Montepulciano d'Abruzzi, Edoardo Valentini makes a firm style of wine with a good tannic grip but with an elegant silky-violet aftertaste. It needs eight years to mellow and improves for 20 or more.

MARCHES

ROSSO CONERO

GAROFOLI VIGNA PIANCARDA

The basic Rosso Conero of Garofoli ranks with some of the best in this DOC; it is a soft and easy wine with a slightly bitter aftertaste. The deeper, darker, richer Vigna Piancarda is a single-vineyard version of classier and more complex quality.

MARIO MARCHETTI

The most famous producer of Rosso Conero, Dr Mario Marchetti makes deep-coloured wines that are fine but muscular, rich in plummy fruit and that need over six years to mellow.

ROSSO PICENA

VILLA PIGNA

This is the best producer of Rosso Picena, a fast-improving full, firm red wine from just south of the Rosso Conero area. Villa Pigna reflects the typical Rosso Piceno character, being somewhat smoother and juicier than Rosso Conero. It is a wine that requires less time to mature.

OTHERS

FATTORIA DI MONTESECCO TRISTO DI MONTESECCO

This wine has an unusual, high-quality blend of Malvasia, Pinot Grigio (Pinot Gris), Riesling Italico and Trebbiano Toscano. It is a delightfully dry white wine, with vivacious, well-balanced fruit and a soft, creamy-oak aftertaste.

VAL DI NEVOLA ROSSO DI CORINALDO

A consistently well-made, pure Merlot wine that has more exuberance of fruit than most of its more northerly Latin cousins. It retains its fresh, juicy-spicy varietal character for between four and eight years, when it is at its peak and drinking well.

SOUTHERN ITALY

S OUTHERN ITALY, KNOWN AS THE *Mezzogiorno* (meaning midday, as in France's Midi), comprises the four regions Campania, Apulia, Basilicata and Calabria. It has only just begun to produce wines recognised as classics. The topography of Apulia (Puglia) suggests anything but a promising wine-producing area. It is a vast, sundrenched plain, seared by the hot wind from Africa (the *favonio*), with no mountains to give relief or provide cooler, hilly sites. Nonetheless, it is among the most innovative and forward-looking of Italy's wine regions. Chardonnay, Sauvignon Blanc and Pinot Bianco (Pinot Blanc) have all been introduced. Cabernet Franc and Pinot Noir reds are successful because of the system of training vines on high wires, pioneered in particular by Simonini. Rivera are more traditionalist, using the indigenous Uva di Troia grape.

The traditional grape of Greek origin, Aglianico, planted in both Basilicata and Campania, is making a comeback to produce some of the best reds of the South. Basilicata produces the fine Aglianico del Vulture, a dry red that can also be sweet and sparkling. Calabria, mountainous and volcanic, makes robust reds and dry whites from local grapes, including the quality white, Greco.

D'ANGELO
AGLIANICO DEL VULTURE
BASILICATA

The finest Aglianico wine in Italy, this has a deep colour and a big build, yet it is well-balanced, with a rich, chocolate-cherry flavour and a firm tannin structure. Slightly rustic in its youth, it develops a silky finesse with age.

UMBERTO CERATTI
GRECO DI BIANCO, CALABRIA

In the hands of Umberto Ceratti, this *passito* is one of Italy's greatest wines. Small and overripe grapes make a deceptively strong, yet succulently sweet and smooth, *liquoroso* wine.

ROSA DEL GOLFO, APULIA

This is one of Italy's finest rosés. It is made by the *lacryma* or "teardrop" system, whereby the grapes softly crush under their own weight. There is a minimal amount of maceration with the skins, yielding a fragrantly scented, light-bodied, delightfully dry, delicately coloured wine with a fresh and gently fruity flavour.

RIVERA ANDRIA
CASTEL DEL MONTE RISERVA
IL FALCONE, APULIA

This is Apulia's greatest red wine. Not a great boast, but Il Falcone is certainly a fine wine by any standards. It is a full-bodied, flavoursome red wine with a very fine, scented bouquet.

ATTILIO SIMONINI FAVONIO
CABERNET FRANC, APULIA

East of Foggia, in northern Apulia, this estate was established by Attilio Simonini from Veneto, who had the idea that native French varieties would grow well here, despite the flat, dry land. The Cabernet Franc is produced in both straight and oak-aged versions, the latter being especially good.

ATTILIO SIMONINI FAVONIO
CHARDONNAY, APULIA

This estate's Chardonnay is sometimes aged in oak and is improving with each vintage. A crisp and fruity Pinot Bianco (Blanc) is also made.

~ S P A I N ~

SOMETHING OF THE LUSTRE of a country's finest wines will always brighten its cheapest wines, as the French have known for a long time and the Italians are now discovering. Before the mid-1970s when the world began to appreciate the wines of Rioja, Spanish wine meant no more than cheap - and often poor - wine, with a cheap and always poor image. The impetus for change came with the introduction of a wine law in 1970. Since then, Spain has experienced a significant, if gradual, improvement in the image and quality of its wines, without exhibiting quite the fervour of experimentation that is being shown in Italy at the present time. But there has been an increased investment in new technology and more attention paid to new plantings of more suita'le grape varieties in the vineyards. The progress towards high quality continues.

It is a measure of Spain's recent progress that a wide range of its wines can now be included in a collection of classic wines. Spain in the early 1990s is no longer a country at the crossroads. Entry into the European Community (EC) in January 1986 clarified the need for Spanish producers to offer wines of quality in order to compete with those of their European rivals.

Leading quality of Rioja and Penedés

Spain is well placed to produce competitive quality wines. The standards have already been set by the excellence and range of styles developed to a classic - and now widely admired - level in Rioja for both red and white wines from native grape varieties. In Penedés the successful introduction of imported grape varieties by Miguel Torres has given a sure lead which is beginning to be more widely followed by other producers. Although foreign varieties are not authorized in

Old Jerez scene *A horse-drawn cart transports casks of Sherry from the vineyard to the* bodega - *the wine company that will store and sell this fortified wine.*

Rioja, experimental plantings are being made by a number of *bodegas* there, with a range of red and white French grapes. In Rioja, just as in Penedés, the benefits of capital investment and the installation of modern technical processes have been well demonstrated. At the same time, both areas retain the best of established tradition.

The country's vast physical resources

Spain also has the physical resources to establish a great wine industry. It has a greater area under vine than any other European country - 1.6 million hectares (4 million acres) - and its potential for development, even within that total, is enormous. Its overall production - 400 million cases in 1988 - huge as that seems, is not nearly as large as Italy or France. This apparent anomaly has a number of causes. First of all, there is the problem of drought, a recurrent feature in the Spanish climate that afflicts at least two-thirds of the country. The effect of drought is to reduce the annual yield dramatically. The northern part of Spain, which embraces Rioja, Navarra and Penedés, is fortunate enough to enjoy a temperate climate and a good amount of rainfall. The centre, taking in New Castile, Valencia, La Mancha, Valdepeñas, Alicante and Extremadura, is generally sunny and dry. The hot weather is even more in evidence in the south of Spain with its relentless, scorching summer heat and desperately low rainfall.

Problems to overcome

Coupled with the drought is the high incidence of older, spaciously planted, low-bearing vines and inappropriate grape varieties. These factors necessitate considerable capital investment for replanting. There has been resistance to this chiefly because of the ultra-traditional mentality of many of the growers; the generally conservative attitude of cooperatives (65 per cent of the wine is made in cooperatives); and the general expense involved. As a result the yield for each unit area under vine is extremely low in Spain, a third or even a fifth of what it is in parts of France, Italy and Germany. If, for instance, temperature-controlled fermentation spread in a big way through La Mancha (where it has already been introduced), coupled with the possibility of irrigation (at present forbidden by Spanish law), it would not be difficult to imagine the effect on the export market. Since La Mancha produces one-third of all Spanish wine, mostly white, the balance of favour in export markets could swing very markedly in Spain's direction. Finance for improved viticulture and vinification processes is in hand with grants now available from the EC and loans from national and regional government sources.

Spain's wine laws

The *Denominación de Origen* (DO), the Spanish system of *Appellation Contrôlée*, came into being in 1970. Through the agency of the local *Consejos Reguladores* (the regulating councils for demarcated regions), a central institute (INDO) lays down the boundaries for each region, the authorized grape varieties, the yield, methods of vinification, alcoholic content and the rules for ageing. The 32 regions include over 60 per cent of the country's vineyards. The more familiar names are Rioja, Penedés, Navarra, Valdepeñas, Ribera del Duero, La Mancha, Jerez, and Tarragona, together with Cava, which has its own DO and is the designation used for traditional champagne-method sparkling wines from any region. Other less well-known DO names are beginning to appear on wine merchants' lists, such as Priorato, Rueda, Toro, Jumilla, Alella, Valdeorras and Costers del Segre. These regions have emerged to wider notice invariably because of the activities of a particularly innovative individual or company within the region. The development by Codorníu of the 1,000-hectare (2,470-acre) vineyard at Raimat, near Lérida in western Penedés, has been almost solely responsible for bringing the new DO of Costers del Segre into being, and will undoubtedly make it better known. In Rueda, the name of the

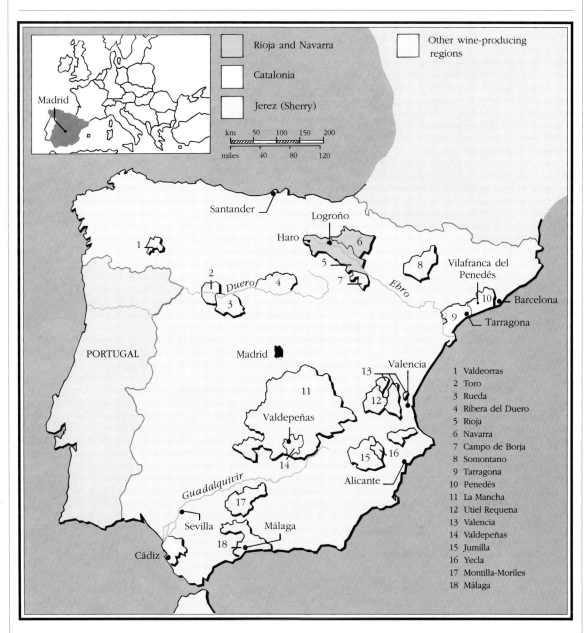

Rioja and Navarra

Catalonia

Jerez (Sherry)

Other wine-producing regions

1	Valdeorras
2	Toro
3	Rueda
4	Ribera del Duero
5	Rioja
6	Navarra
7	Campo de Borja
8	Somontano
9	Tarragona
10	Penedés
11	La Mancha
12	Utiel Requena
13	Valencia
14	Valdepeñas
15	Jumilla
16	Yecla
17	Montilla-Moriles
18	Málaga

Variety of climates Spain's potential as a wine producer lies in its diversity of climates. Whilst the north has a temperate climate and plenty of rainfall, the centre, and more particularly the south, are hot and dry. Such extremes produce a variety of wine styles, from slender whites to massive reds and fortified wines.

Marqués de Griñon is almost synonymous with this previously little-known DO; ironically, this is as much through the reputation of the red *vino de mesa* that the *bodega* makes from outside the region, as for its aromatic white wine, which is made from the Verdejo grapes of Rueda itself. The Rioja *bodega*, Marqués de Riscal, also makes its white wines from grapes grown in the Rueda DO.

Recent changes

The gap between DO level wines and everyday *vinos de mesa* was filled in 1986, when Spain joined the EC and introduced a new category (equivalent to *vin de pays*) called the *vinos de la tierra*. These wines must contain 60 per cent of the grapes authorized for the region, and conform to rules on alcohol level and use of sulphur dioxide. By early 1990 no *vinos de la tierra* had appeared on export markets. Provision has also been made for a higher DO category (similar to Italy's DOCG): this would enable existing DOs (Rioja would be one of the prime contenders) to apply for a higher *Calificada* or "qualified" status. So far none has been announced.

Grape varieties

Spain is reputed to have over 600 grape varieties. By far the largest growing area is devoted to the white wine grape, Airén, with 476,300 hectares (1,176,960 acres). Otherwise known as Lairén, it is the principal (indeed, to all intents and purposes,

the only) white grape in its home region, the vast central plain south of Madrid embracing La Mancha and Valdepeñas. Airén has traditionally produced a dull white wine with a high alcohol content, and is also used to lighten the heavy reds from the local Tempranillo (known here as Cencibel). The advent of modern technology and the practice of early picking among more forward-looking producers in the region has already transformed it into a much more attractive, lighter, fresher, medium-bodied varietal.

Garnacha Tinta, Monastrell and Bobal, the leading red varieties, come a long way behind the white Airén in volume. Garnacha Tinta is used in Rioja Baja, Navarra and Penedés, where it yields a highly alcoholic, dark-coloured wine. The colour is prone to fade, and the wines do not age well, except in rare instances, such as in Priorato.

Monastrell makes deep-coloured, beefy red wines that age well in Penedés, Levante (Jumilla and Yecla) and Valencia, and is also used for *rosados*. Bobal is the main grape of Utiel-Requena, deep-coloured, relatively low in alcohol and high in acidity. Tempranillo, the classic Spanish variety, with its fine colour and good acidic balance, is the mainstay of red Riojas but occupies only 33,633 hectares (83,107 acres), although it is on the increase in Rioja and other parts of northern Spain.

The white Palomino and Pedro Ximénez are grown in Jerez, while the white grape of Catalonia is Xarel-lo. Among other whites are Viura (the

SPANISH VINTAGES

YEAR	RIOJA	NAVARRA	PENEDÉS	RIBERA DEL DUERO
1989	Good	Good	Good	Average
1988	Good	Good	Good	Average
1987	Very good: low yield	Good	Average	Good
1986	Good	Good	Average: in selected cases	Very good
1985	Good: largest crop ever	Good	Very good: low yield	Very good: Castile reds very tannic
1984	Average	Very good	Very good	Average
1983	Good	Very good	Good	Very good
1982	Excellent	Excellent	Very good	Very good
1981	Very good	Excellent	Very good	Excellent

grape of white Rioja and Navarra, alias Macabeo in Penedés) and two lesser-known, quality grapes, Verdejo and Parellada.

Spain has been remarkably slow - perhaps advisedly - to adopt French grape varieties. However, in one notable case, at Vega Sicilia in Ribera del Duero, Cabernet Sauvignon, Merlot and Malbec have been grown for a century, and the Cabernet is now officially accepted there. Elsewhere Cabernet and Merlot receive tentative approval, and Pinot Noir and Gamay are also being tried out. The whites can be best evaluated by examining the list successfully planted by Torres in selected cooler sites in Penedés - namely Gewürztraminer, Muscat, Riesling, Sauvignon Blanc and Chardonnay. Marqués de Riscal is also experimenting with Chardonnay and Riesling in Rueda, and with Pinot Gris, and has already produced some marketable Sauvignon Blanc wines there.

Sparkling wines

Spain's sparkling wine industry is firmly founded on the *méthode champenoise* (a term that will not be legal in the EC after 1994 for any wines that have not actually been produced in Champagne). Six out of every seven bottles of Spanish sparkling wine are fermented in this traditional fashion, and those bottles add up to some 120 million every year. Cava, the name generally adopted for these traditionally bottle-fermented sparkling wines, has its own *denominación* (not formally established until 1986), but unlike other DOs it does not relate to a single identifiable area. About 90 per cent is produced in Penedés, in and around the town of San Sadurní di Noya, south-west of Barcelona - 85 companies in San Sadurní make three-quarters of all Spanish Cava. The *denominación* is also scattered in isolated pockets elsewhere in Catalonia and across north-eastern Spain, including some villages in Rioja. Companies range in size from Codorníu, which is the world's largest single producer of *méthode champenoise* wine, down to small family concerns such as Mont-Marçal.

The principal grapes authorized for Cava are the white Macabeo, Parellada and Xarel-lo, which are all native Catalan varieties, plus Chardonnay (Codorníu and Mont-Marçal both now produce a pure Chardonnay Cava). The red Garnacha and Monastrell are also allowed, in order to tint the small amount of rosé Cava that is being produced. The decision to allow the inclusion of Chardonnay in the blend, so long as the proportion is not allowed to change the fundamentally Spanish nature of the wine, could well benefit both the quality and stability of the wine. The native grape varieties do not have particularly good ageing capability, so it is considered advisable to drink Cava when it is young and fresh.

SPANISH TERMS

Abocado	Medium sweet
Alto	High; upper
Año	Year
Bajo	Low; lower
Blanco	White
Bodega	Winery
Brut	Dry
Cava	Spanish sparkling wine made by the Champagne method
Clarete	Light red wine
Consejo Regulador	Regulating body for each DO
Contra etiqueta	Back label
Cosecha	Vintage
Crianza	Ageing
Denominación de Origen (DO)	Guaranteed name of origin
Dulce	Sweet
Elaborado por	Made, blended or matured by
Embotellado por	Bottled by
Espumoso	Sparkling
Etiqueta	Label
Fino	Very dry, pale sherry
Flor	Layer of yeast that provides the distinctive flavour of *fino* sherry
Gran Reserva	Red wine aged at least two years in cask and three in bottle; white or rosé aged at least four years, of which six months are spent in cask
Joven	Young
Reserva	Red wine aged at least three years, of which one is spent in cask; white or rosé aged at least two years, of which six months is spent in cask
Rosado	Rosé
Seco	Dry
Sin crianza	Without any wood ageing
Solera	System of ageing sherry by replenishing the oldest butt from a series of younger ones
Tinto	Red
Vendimia	Harvest
Viejo	Old
Vino de la Tierra	Table wine of specified area
Vino de mesa	Table wine

Stringent efforts are always being made to ensure that Cava reaches a consistently high quality. Yields are restricted in the vineyards, vinification is carried out with the most modern equipment, and only the free-run juice is used for the must. Like Champagne, Cava is blended as a non-vintage wine, or produced as a single-year vintage. The former is aged for a minimum of nine months, and the latter is aged for three years. Cava, like Champagne, is made in a wide range of styles from very dry to sweet. At the extremes, Brut Natur and Extra Brut are the driest forms of the wine and Dulce is the sweetest. The Cava that is most widespread and likely to be encountered is the dry Brut.

RIOJA & NAVARRA

RIOJA'S WINES CAN NOW be said to have come of age. The excitement caused by the heavily oaked, vanilla-flavoured reds has subsided, and a choice range of both red and white wines is now presented to the consumer, including aged wines (*con crianza*) or lighter, younger wines (*sin crianza*). The region is blessed with a temperate climate, a mild spring, short hot summers and long warm autumns. The heat is modulated by the Atlantic: the same sea that gives Bordeaux its mild climate. However, vintage years do not assume such great importance as they do in Bordeaux. The average output from the region's 37,500 hectares (92,665 acres) of vineyard has been rising over the last decade, with an expected average harvest now of about 12 million cases of wine.

The Rioja wine region stretches for 100 kilometres (62 miles) along the valley of the river Ebro, with Logroño, the provincial capital at its centre. Two of its three wine districts, Rioja Alta and Rioja Alavesa, lie upstream to the north-west of Logroño, while the third, Rioja Baja, lies to the south-east of Logroño. The calcareous clay soils of the Alta and Alavesa districts, their higher and cooler situation on the first foothills of the Sierra de Cantabria mountains, and their greater exposure to Atlantic influences (the Rioja Baja has a more Mediterranean climate) combine to produce finer quality wines. All three areas, however, make their contributions, since Rioja reds are often based on grapes from the three districts. Great fruitiness is the main characteristic of wines made from grapes from Rioja Alta, finesse from Alavesa, while the Baja wines offer coarser, more full-bodied flavours.

Grape varieties

The seven approved grape varieties of Rioja are all indigenous, with Tempranillo - otherwise called Tinto Fino, Cencibel or Ull de Llebre - being by far the most important. The other reds are Garnacha Tinta (or Garnacho), Graciano and Mazuelo (known elsewhere in Spain as Cariñena). The main white grape is Viura (or Macabeo), supported by Malvasía, and sometimes a little Garnacha Blanca.

Rioja producers today are a mixture of long-established traditional concerns and modern, newly built *bodegas* into which, in many cases, massive outside investment has been funnelled. The Marqués de Riscal *bodega,* established in the 1860s, is still there, along with five very distinguished producers of the late nineteenth century: Marqués de

Murrieta, La Rioja Alta, López de Heredia Viña Tondonia, CVNE and Bodegas Bilbaínas. Marqués de Cáceres and El Coto are products of the 1970s that have quickly carved out for themselves a reputation for wines of excellent quality.

Navarra

Rioja's immediate northern neighbour, Navarra, has as yet very little to show in the context of classic wines. The reputation of the area was built on rosé wines, made as well as any in Spain from the Garnacha Tinta grape, but, in terms of quantity, red wines (also mostly from Garnacha) have overtaken them with over half the annual production. The best of the reds come from the (as yet) small plantings of Tempranillo, or Tempranillo and Graciano, and are centred in the north of the region in the Tierra Estella and Valdizarbe districts. Such reds as are exported come mainly from a few private estates, although the vast bulk of production is in the hands of cooperatives. A very small amount (about 5 per cent) of white wine is produced. The Viura and Malvasía varieties are beginning to be used to produce better-quality, fresh, fruity whites.

In contrast to Rioja, research is being pursued into the use of a range of imported varieties at a viticultural research station in Olite, the Estación de Viticultura y Enología de Navarra (EVENA). Thirty-four different grape varieties from France, Italy, California and elsewhere have been planted by EVENA in experimental vineyards all over the region. These include Cabernet Sauvignon, which is already authorized in the region, Chardonnay, Merlot, Pinot Noir, Gamay, Syrah, Chenin Blanc, Gewürztraminer, Sangiovese, Barbera, Rhine Riesling and Ruby Cabernet (from California).

Marqués de Riscal *One of Rioja's oldest bodegas.*

RIOJA

CONTINO GRAN RESERVA

This single-vineyard Rioja is partly owned by CVNE and run like a Bordeaux château. Unusually for Rioja, Contino uses only estate-grown grapes and ages only in French oak, replacing casks about every three years. The *Gran Reserva* has immediate appeal, complexity and finesse.

CONTINO RESERVA

This full-bodied wine has a deep colour, an aromatic bouquet and powerful plummy fruit that subdues the creamy, vanilla notes of the oak. It normally requires some bottle-age.

BODEGAS EL COTO
COTO DE IMAZ

The elegant, graceful *tintos* have made El Coto's reputation, and their style is as immaculate as the winery itself, especially the El Coto *Reserva* and Coto de Imaz *Reserva*.

CVNE
IMPERIAL GRAN RESERVA

CVNE is one of the most traditional *bodegas* of Rioja, and its Imperial *Gran Reserva* has remarkable finesse for one of the most substantially built wines of the region. It has a dense colour and a bouquet of sweet oaky-fruit with caramel complexity. This serious, well-fleshed wine has a fine tannic structure that enables it to last a long time.

CVNE
MONOPOLE BLANCO SECO

If traditional Rioja *blanco* is over-oaked and dried-out, then CVNE Monopole Blanco is not traditional. It has plenty of oak, but it is creamy and new, rather than old and oxidized. The fruit is crisp, fresh and, although light, in no way dried-out.

CVNE
VIÑA REAL GRAN RESERVA

The Viña Real *Gran Reserva* is full-bodied and complex, but has a more voluptuous style than the Imperial, with its creamy-rich fruit providing immediate appeal. Its fine balance of acidity and a supple tannin structure endows Viña Real with immense finesse and length.

BODEGAS LAN
GRAN RESERVA LANDER

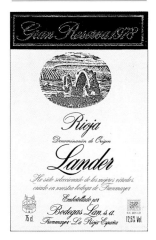

The basic *tinto* has a ripe-fruit bouquet and palate, hinting of raspberry and sweet tobacco. Lander has the same weight and style, but is more intense; released at the height of its maturity, it will last for years.

MARQUÉS DE CÁCERES
BLANCO

This *bodega* belongs to the French Fornier family, so it is not surprising that this *blanco* is the leader in the new-wave of dry whites, and that it looks and tastes more like a Sauvignon Blanc than a Spanish Viura.

MARQUÉS DE CÁCERES
GRAN RESERVA

It is only at *Gran Reserva* level that the finesse, quality and sweet-fruit complexity of Marqués de Cáceres reveals itself. Yet the basic *tinto* and *Reserva* do develop in bottle and can prove a match for a traditional Rioja.

BODEGAS MARQUÉS DE MURRIETA

Murrieta's Reserva *blanco* is sought out by those who adore Rioja's extreme traditional style. They consider it Spain's finest white wine; others simply believe it to be oxidized. The *crianza blanco* has a different style; one that has recently shown more fruit and freshness. The wine style at which this *bodega* excels is *tinto*, and its normal *tinto* and Reserva *tinto* are consistently amongst the best Riojas. The outstanding late-released Castillo Ygay Gran Reserva is the finest *tinto* produced from Murrieta's Ygay vineyard. It represents a tiny production of selected vintages - the 1934 was available until 1983, when it was replaced by 1942. The release of the relatively youthful 1968 at the request of the Spanish Royal House makes it truly a wine of kings and king of wines.

YGAY

YGAY RESERVA

CASTILLO YGAY GRAN RESERVA

MARQUÉS DE CÁCERES TINTO

The basic *tinto* style is quite light, yet firm and not dissimilar to an unpretentious claret.

MARQUÉS DE RISCAL RESERVA

Once the top Rioja *bodega*, Marqués de Riscal began to go downhill in the early 1970s. This decline was due to bad cooperage, which meant that the wines often reeked of an unpleasant, musty-mushrooms smell. In the late 1980s this problem was recognized, and the *bodega* began disposing of its bad barrels and buying brand new ones. As from the excellent 1988 vintage and the even better 1989, the great quality of Marqués de Riscal has re-emerged from the ashes of its own barrels.

BODEGAS MARTINEZ BUJANDA VALDEMAR VINO BLANCO

This high-tech winery makes an oaky, medium-bodied *tinto* with strong vanilla, peppery-oak overtones; the *blanco* shown here is a new-wave wine, with pure, fresh fruit notes.

BODEGAS MUGA PRADO ENEA RESERVA

This top wine has a classy, ripe-berry and creamy-oak nose, and rich, chewy fruit and tannic grip. Delicious to drink when released, it does not achieve its full potential until after another five years or so bottle age.

BODEGAS OLARRA CERRO AÑON RESERVA

This ultra-modern, "Y"-shaped *bodega* houses a state-of-the-art winemaking capability and produces two basic ranges, Añares and Cerro Añon (the Reserva of which is illustrated here). Typical for Rioja *tinto*, both ranges are esentially Tempranillo-dominated, but the Cerro Añon is even more so.

REMELLURI

The exquisite balance, elegance and finesse of this single-vineyard Rioja Alavesa belies its great richness of fruit and long, oaky finish. It has an extraordinary fine floral-oak bouquet hinting of violets and lovely soft, ripe, creamy-sweet fruit, with enough supple-tannin grip to age gracefully.

LA RIOJA ALTA
RESERVA 890

The rarest of La Rioja Alta's two best and most famous *Reserva* wines, the 890 is named after the year 1890, not simply because it was an exceptional vintage, but because that is the date that this *bodega* was founded.

LA RIOJA ALTA
RESERVA 904

Named after the excellent 1904 vintage, which coincided with the date this *bodega* became a limited company, the 904 spends slightly less time in wood than the 890 and is produced more often and in greater quantity. Nevertheless, this does not dilute its quality: the 904 is a very classy wine with a rich and warm spicy-oak complexity.

LA RIOJA ALTA
VIÑA ARDANZA RESERVA

This is a traditional oaky *Reserva* that has some finesse and is full in both body and colour. There is often a ground white pepperyness on the nose and lots of very rich plummy-peppery fruit.

BODEGAS RIOJANAS
MONTE REAL

This family-owned *bodega* owns 200 hectares (495 acres) of vineyards and has a reputation for the high ratio of quality to value, especially for its *tinto*. The Monte Real is medium to full-bodied wine made in a less oaky style but, with an interesting plummy nose that shows some mineral-complexity and fat-sweet plummy fruit on the palate, Bodegas Riojanas Monte Real is usually good value.

BODEGAS RIOJANAS
VIÑA ALBINA GRAN RESERVA

The Viña Albina has more intensity of flavour and shows greater influence of oak than this *bodega's* Monte Real.

R. LOPEZ DE HEREDIA
VIÑA TONDONIA

This extremely high-quality *bodega* is situated in Haro. The style was once the most traditional in Rioja, but while younger wines are becoming a bit schizophrenic, seemingly unable to make up their minds whether to be full and oaky or light and fruity, the rich and oaky Tondonia *Reserva* and *Gran Reserva* remain very traditional wines capable of great longevity.

R. LOPEZ DE HEREDIA
VIÑA TONDONIA
BOSCONIA

The Bosconia *tinto* is fatter, riper and plumper than the more jammy Tondonia *tinto*.

NAVARRA

BODEGAS JULIAN CHIVITE
125 ANIVERSARIO

The 1981 vintage was used to launch this wine in 1985 to celebrate the 125th Anniversary of this *bodega*. Made entirely of Tempranillo, kept six months on its lees and aged for two years in *barriques*, this very rich, deliciously soft and oaky *tinto* is the best wine in Navarra.

PRINCIPE DE VIANA

This is the premium wine of Bodegas Cenalsa, an ultra-modern winery established in 1983. The Principe de Viana is *barrique*-aged and has a very fine and elegant style for a pure Garnacha (Grenache) wine.

CATALONIA

THE PROVINCE OF Catalonia in the north-east corner of Spain adjoins the French border and runs down the Mediterranean coast to Barcelona, its capital, and on to Tarragona. It embraces seven areas with DO status (Ampurdán-Costa Brava, Alella, Priorato, Terra Alta, Costers del Segre, Tarragona and, most prominently, Penedés), the most notable of which have only recently emerged on to the world scene.

Penedés

Penedés in a few short years has established itself as the region that makes the widest range of quality wines in Spain. It enjoys a combination of calcareous soil, a temperate climate with the right level of rainfall and proximity to the Mediterranean. The Alto or Superior Penedés is the coolest and farthest inland, where the Parellada vines grow on chalky hillsides and provide new-style, light, aromatic whites that have revolutionized thinking about Spanish whites. Here, too, is where the newly introduced Pinot Noir is cultivated.

About 60 per cent of Penedés's output comes from the Medio Penedés, including an enormous production of Cava sparkling wine from Xarel-lo and Macabeo, and the best of the new, lighter style reds - younger, softer, fruitier and only lightly oaked. The Bajo Penedés is the hot, rugged country of the coastal strip, a traditional area for the production of fuller-bodied reds.

The recent emergence of Penedés has been largely due to the initiatives launched by two long-established local families. Over the last 20 years Bodegas Torres has transformed Spanish winemaking, with the successful introduction of iported grape varieties and the use of temperature-controlled cold fermentation techniques in stainless steel. Codorníu, the world's largest single supplier of traditionally produced sparkling wine, is the most innovative of the Cava producers and owns a huge modern installation at San Sadurní de Noya.

Other areas

North of Barcelona is Alella, the smallest *denominación* in Spain. It has one go-ahead private *bodega*, Marqués de Alella, and an old-established cooperative, which handles the wine of some 150 local growers - and little else. Wines are mostly white and are produced mainly from the Xarel-lo grape. The Priorato area is 10 times Alella's size and makes its classic reds from Garnacha Tinta and Cariñena, and whites from Garnacha Blanca, while experimenting with imported varieties. Costers del Segre is a recent DO area, virtually created for the Codorníu estate at Raimat near Lérida, where, in 1988, the company first opened its impressive, new winery - a spectacular modern building. Terra Alta, inland from Tarragona, produces predominantly white wines from both Garnacha Blanca and Macabeo vines.

ALELLA

MARQUÉS DE ALELLA
CHARDONNAY

The largest privately-owned *bodega* in the area, Marqués de Alella boasts an immaculate, state-of-the-art stainless-steel winery that produces the finest wines in Alella. Of these, the fresh, light and vibrantly fruity Chardonnay is the best of all.

PRIORATO

SCALA DEI CARTOIXA

This spotless stainless-steel winery is the best and most famous in Priorato and is located in the village of Scala Dei, with its ruins of the twelfth-century Carthusian monastery that gave its name to the region and its wine. The amazingly deep, dark and densely flavoured Cartoixa is Scala Dei's deluxe oak-aged wine.

SCALA DEI NEGRE

All Scala Dei's wines are produced from its own vineyards, and the grapes are picked as early as the regulations will allow. The fresh and fruity Negre is the youngest *tinto* produced by Scala Dei.

PENEDES

JEAN LEON
CABERNET SAUVIGNON

Established in 1962 by Jean Leon (a Spanish-born American who lives in California and sells his wines in his Los Angeles restaurant), it is not surprising that these full-flavoured wines have a Californian style. The Cabernet is good, though not as great or as consistent as the Chardonnay.

JEAN LEON
CHARDONNAY

Jean Leon's Chardonnay is a rich, oaky wine that falls in style between Napa and Puligny-Montrachet.

TERRA ALTA

PEDRO ROVIRA
ALTA MAR

From the best producer in Terra Alta, Alta Mar is a fresh, fruity and aromatic semi-sweet white wine which is made from Garnacha Blanca and Macabeo.

MIGUEL TORRES

Although the Torres wine-business in Penedes has been handed down from father to son since 1870, it has been the innovative image of Miguel Torres Jnr that has boosted the firm's reputation. Initially Miguel was a reluctant student of oenology and viticulture - his father had to force him to take his first course in France. Miguel Torres was the first to grow classic French and German grapes in the Penedes and introduced cool-fermentation techniques to Spain. He created the black-label version of Gran Coronas and won the prestigious "Gault-Millau" Wine Olympics in 1979 with his first vintage (1970), against stiff opposition from Château Latour 1970 and Château La Mission Haut-Brion 1961. More recently, Miguel Torres reclassified his best wines by their *prago* (single-vineyard name). The black-label Gran Coronas comes from Mas La Plana, while the green-label Gran Vina Sol comes from the Fransola vineyard.

GRAN CORONAS RESERVA

A rich and boldly flavoured red wine, heavily influenced by 18 months ageing in American oak.
CS 70%, TEMP 30%

GRAN CORONAS RESERVA
MAS LA PLANA

The black-label Gran Coronas is consistently the best Spanish red wine. Its concentration of Cabernet fruit is supported by supple tannin and creamy oak.
CS 90%, CF 10%

GRAN VIÑA SOL

Ever since the recent increase in the proportion of Chardonnay in this blend (which receives a subtle ageing for three months in new *Limousin* oak), the quality of Gran Viña Sol has improved and become quite serious indeed.
CH 52%, PAR 48%

GRAN VIÑA SOL RESERVA

A wine for those who love traditional oaky Spanish whites, but prefer to have fresh fruit, as opposed to oxidized cold tea, beneath the vanilla.
PAR 70%, SB 30%

MILMANDA

The most recent and most extraordinary addition to the Torres portfolio, Milmanda is a superb, single-vineyard Chardonnay, fermented and aged in new French oak *barriques*. An expensive wine, but worth the price.
CH 100%

COSTERS DEL SEGRE

RAIMAT
ABADIA

Owned by Codorníu, the giant Cava company, the great success and quality of this elaborately restored estate was instrumental in creating the recent Costers de Segre DO. It was the smooth and classy Raimat Abadia that first caught media attention.

RAIMAT
CABERNET SAUVIGNON

The Raimat Cabernet Sauvignon is even richer than the Abadia, but matures more rapidly.

RAIMAT
TEMPRANILLO

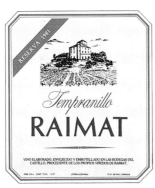

A small production of very impressive pure Tempranillo has maintained the international respect for, and interest in, the progress of Raimat, one of Spain's most innovative wineries.

OTHERS

CELLER HISENDA MIRET
VIÑA TOÑA XAREL-LO

Ramon Balada is the talented young winemaker who produces pure varietal wines from three traditional Catalan grapes at the family-owned Celler Hisenda Miret. Sold under the Viña Toña label, his Parellada, Macabeo and Xarel-lo are strikingly fresh and vibrant.

MAS RABASSA
XAREL-LO

The small *bodega* and vineyards of Mas Rabassa belong to Josep María Torres i Blanco, cousin of the famous Miguel Torres. Its medal-winning white wines have scintillating freshness and tangy fruit acidity. The 1985 Xarel-lo was voted best white wine in Spain by the "Club de Gourmets".

CELLERS J. ROBERT
SITGES RESERVA ESPECIAL

This small family *bodega* is one of the few remaining producers of Sitges, a rich and honeyed wine made from sun-shrivelled Malvasia grapes which are grown just south of Barcelona.

CAVA

CASTELLBLANCH
BRUT ZERO

This one-million-case firm was established in 1908 by Jeronimo Parera Figueras and now belongs to Freixenet, one of Spain's two giant Cava groups. The Brut Zero, in its distinctive bottle and red seal, is its best-known wine and is produced to a very good standard. It has a true biscuity-apple flavour and is very dry, but has good fruit and is never tart.

CASTELLBLANCH
LUSTROS BRUT

Of Castellblanch's two prestige *cuvées* Gran Castell and Lustros, this wine is both better and cheaper.

CODORNÍU CHARDONNAY

It was Codorníu's Raimat operation that first produced a Chardonnay Cava, and later the parent company brought out its own version. These two wines are a class apart from even the greatest of traditional Cavas.

FREIXENET BRUT BARROCO

This firm was established in 1889 and currently produces the most famous of all Cavas, Freixenet Cordon Negro, which is easily recognizable by its matt-black bottle. However, this wine is grossly overrated, and a vastly superior wine is to be found in its smooth and stylish prestige *cuvée*, Brut Barroco.

JUVÉ Y CAMPS EXTRA BRUT RESERVA DE LA FAMILIA

Established in 1921, this firm produces several Cavas from its estate of 150 hectares (370 acres), but without doubt the best is its Reserva de la Familia, or "family reserve". This high-quality wine combines richness and acidity with good bottle age and a fine autolytic character.

ANTONIO MESTRES

The Mestres family have owned these vineyards and produced wine since 1312. There are several good-quality Cavas made here, but it is the Clos Nostre Senyor, with its five years' yeast-contact, that is its most astonishing product overall. This is not simply a wine of superb richness, it is also one of great autolytic complexity.

MONT-MARCAL BRUT

This small house belongs to the Sancho E Hijas family and produces an excellent generic Cava, illustrated here; a Gran Reserva, which can be excellent but is not consistent; and a pure Chardonnay sparkler.

RAIMAT CHARDONNAY BRUT

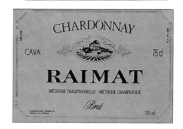

Spain's first sparkling Chardonnay, this wine proved that top-quality Cava was possible. Although it is a consistently delicious wine by any standards, pure Chardonnay is generally not the right direction for Cava wines. Chardonnay should be used to boost the ethnic character of indigenous Spanish varieties if Cava is to achieve its own identity.

SEGURA VIUDAS

Now part of the huge Freixenet group, this is the best Cava house in the Penedés and thereby Spain. Other Freixenet wines made in the Segura Viudas cellars include those marketed under the labels of René Barbier, Conde de Caralt and Jean Perico. Segura Viudas wines all have the true biscuity character of fine, mature Cava.

BLANC DE BLANCS

The Blanc de Blancs is a truly delicious selection of high-quality wines, but as all of this firm's Cavas are produced exclusively from white grapes, the "Blanc de Blancs" name, although shown only on a slip label, is nevertheless unnecessary and somewhat confusing.

BRUT RESERVA

The rich, biscuity Brut Reserva has a tremendous record of consistency and is far and away the best generic non-vintage Cava produced.

BRUT VINTAGE

The basic Brut Vintage can be a quite stunning wine. The fact that it is inexpensive makes it exceptionally good value.

RESERVA HEREDAD BRUT

The Reserva Heredad has all the autolytic character expected from a wine that has had up to six years' yeast-contact.

RIBERA DEL DUERO

THE RIVER DUERO, on its way west through the province of Castilla-León to Portugal, links three wine areas in north-western Spain, the names of which are becoming more familiar in export markets: Ribera del Duero, Rueda and Toro (see pages 253-4). The reputation of each is being built on the wines of one or two outstanding and resourceful producers. Due north of Madrid, in 5,800 hectares (14,325 acres) of the dry plateau that envelops Burgos, Valladolid and Segovia, is the Ribera del Duero DO. About 60 per cent of the grapes are Tinto del Pais (a local variant of Tempranillo, the Rioja grape). Other authorized varieties are Garnacha Tinta, Cabernet Sauvignon, Merlot and Malbec. If the classification of three imported varieties is surprising in this situation, it is because of the influence of a single *bodega*, Vega-Sicilia - for over a century, the exponent of outstanding quality in the area. Its vineyards were planted in 1864 with pre-phylloxera Cabernet Sauvignon, Malbec and Merlot grapes from Bordeaux, and Tinto del Pais. Simultaneously, Alejandro Fernandez has achieved great acclaim for a red made from local Tempranillo. Wines of quality, from Tempranillo and aged in new oak, are also made at the Bodega Ribera Duero at Peñafiel.

ALEJANDRO FERNANDEZ
TINTO PESQUERA

Since Robert Parker suggested that Tinto Pesquera might be the Pétrus of Spain, its price has soared. Pétrus it is not, but Fernandez makes a fine, oak-dominated, smooth wine.
TEMP 100%

BODEGAS MAURO

Produced from prime-quality grapes, immaculately fermented in temperature-controlled stainless-steel vats and aged in oak for up to 30 months, these big, concentrated and complex wines are well-balanced and have great potential longevity, but are largely underrated.
TEMP 60%, GR 20%, ALB 10%, VRA 10%

BODEGAS HNOS. PÉREZ PASCUAS
VIÑA PEDROSA

The small, well-equipped and well-run family-owned *bodega* of Hermanos Pérez Pascuas produces an elegant style of wine, wonderfully aromatic and full of silky-rich fruit.
TEMP 100%

BODEGA RIBERA DUERO
PROTOS

The Ribera Duero Sociedad Cooperativa at Peñafiel is an efficient producer of above-average wines, but its special Protos *cuvée* stands out as one of the very best wines of the DO. This is a rich, mellow oaky wine with a deep fruity flavour. The Protos *Gran Reserva* is not always superior.
TEMP 100%

BODEGAS VEGA-SICILIA
"UNICO"

Vega-Sicilia "Unico" is generally regarded as Spain's greatest wine, but it spends too long in wood and could be even better. Some vintages have spent 25 years or more in wood. This has been reduced to a maximum of 10 or so under the current management, yet this is still too long. As the wine goes through such a bewildering array of wooden vessels of varying size and age, any rationale behind this practice would seem to be more logistical than philosophical. That some vintages of "Unico" so successfully survive this treatment is a testament to the great potential quality of Vega-Sicilia's *terroir*. The *bodega's* second wine carries the village appellation of Valbuena. There used to be two versions of Valbuena, one aged in wood for three years and another for five years. Now there is just the one *cuvée* and this is bottled after just two or three years, exactly when depending on the character of the vintage.
TEMP 60-80%, CS 15-25%, M & MB 0-15%

LESSER-KNOWN SPAIN

AMONG THE MORE OBSCURE winegrowing areas of Spain are many regions that are beginning to achieve greater prominence. Two of these areas - Campo de Borja and Somontano - are in the large north-eastern province of Aragón (the third Aragónese DO is Cariñena). Campo de Borja lies south of the river Ebro at the south-eastern end of the Rioja Baja. It produces reds that are full, robust and alcoholic, and *rosados*, using 90 per cent Garnacha, with up to 10 per cent Macabeo or Garnacha Blanca. The problem is insufficient acidity, and experiments are being carried on with Tempranillo and Mazuelo.

The Levante

Jumilla, Yecla and Utiel-Requena are DOs in the Levante. In Jumilla, wines made from the Monastrell grape as 100 per cent varietal take the alternative *denomiación*, Jumilla Monastrell. The vineyards of Yecla, at the highest point of inland Alicante, are planted with Garnacha and Monastrell on chalky, stony soil. Two producers here effectively control output between them - Bodegas Ochoa and the Cooperative La Purisma.

Utiel-Requena, which is also mountainous, uses Bobal grapes for its *rosados* and for reds. The reds do not age very well, and plantings are gradually giving way to Tempranillo and Garnacha grapes. The colour and alcoholic strength of the wines in these areas are enhanced by the *doble pasta* method, whereby must is fermented on a double quantity of grape skins and pulp.

Quality in Rueda and Toro

Rueda and Toro are small DOs downstream of Ribera del Duero. Scattered vineyards, planted with Verdejo and some Viura grapes, surround Rueda. The arrival of cold fermentation, introduced locally by Marqués de Riscal, gave new life to the Verdejo, making a wine in the lighter style, without traditional oak ageing. Riscal is the largest producer in the region, but the quality accolade for white Verdejo is now claimed by Marqués de Griñon wine. In Toro, Tinto de Toro (Tempranillo) and Garnacha Tinta are the red grapes, and Malvasía and Verdejo, the whites. Toro reds are traditionally full-bodied, but modern vinification and earlier picking are giving softer results.

Difficult viticultural conditions and the indifferent quality of Garnacha wine have discouraged private *bodegas* in Valdeorras; the whole production is handled by three cooperatives. Valdepeñas is a large DO that produces attractive, light red wines from Tempranillo (called here Cencibel), in spite of the arid climate. However, 85 per cent of the output is white wine, from the Airén grape, which is also blended with Cencibel. *Reservas* and *Gran Reservas* tend to be 100 per cent Cencibel.

BORDEJÉ GRAN RESERVA
DON PABLO
CAMPO DE BORJA

Small family-run *bodega* producing Campo de Borja, an appellation that derives its name from the notorious Borgia family, who used to run things in this part of Spain at the height of their power in the late fifteenth century. The wines range from the light, Beaujolais-style Tinto Joven to the fuller, more serious *Gran Reserva* Don Pablo, illustrated here.

ASENSIO CARCELEN
SOL Y LUNA
JUMILLA

Phylloxera has not been able to penetrate the hilly vineyards of Jumilla, and, as a result, 90 per cent of the vines remain ungrafted. The Sol y Luna ("Sun and Moon") label illustrated here is from a sumptuous sweet red wine of some complexity that is produced from the Monastrell grape variety.

BODEGAS CASTAÑO
VIÑA LAS GRUESAS
YECLA

This dark, deep, intense-coloured wine is made from Garnacha (Grenache) and Monastrell grapes and has the full, concentrated character that typifies the *doble pasta* style, where fermentation takes place in the presence of twice the normal volume of grape skins.

BODEGAS C. AUGUSTO EGLI
CASA LO ALTO
UTIEL-REQUENA

This Swiss-owned *bodega* makes a big and beefy wine, a traditional blend of Cencibel and Garnacha (Grenache).

BODEGAS FARIÑA
COLEGIATA TINTO
TORO

One of the cleanest, most modern wineries in Spain, this *bodega* sold its wines under the Colegiata label until 1986. Bottles with the Farina name contain 50 per cent Cabernet Sauvignon, endowing the wine with quality and longevity.

BODEGAS LALANNE
LAURA LALANNE
SOMONTANO

As the family of Francisco Lalanne has French origins and current connections in Bordeaux, it is perhaps not surprising when one discovers that they grow Cabernet Sauvignon and Merlot and merely use Tempranillo to prop-up some sort of ethnic identity.

MARQUES DE GRIÑON

Bodegas de Crianza Castilla La Vieja is located in Rueda, which is the DO claimed by the soft and gentle dry white Marques de Grinon. It is, however, the red Marques de Grinon that has made this *bodega's* name, with its smooth, rich oaky flavour, although it is merely a non-DO *vino de mesa* from Toledo.

COOP. O BARCO
MENCIÑO, VALDEORRAS

The cooperative in Orense makes this fruity wine with broad flavours and an agreeably modest alcohol level.

ENRIQUES OCHOA PALAO
YECLA, CUVÉE PRESTIGE

This privately owned *bodega* was established in 1978, and its reputation has risen steadily. Made from 100 per cent Monastrell, the Tinto Ochoa is a delightful, ripe, rich and succulent red wine that is full of oaky-soft-fruit flavour, while the Cuvée Prestige has a deeper, denser, more serious style.

SEÑORIO DE LOS LLANOS
VINO GRAN RESERVA
VALDEPEÑAS

This is the top wine from Bodegas los Llanos, the best producer in Valdepeñas, La Mancha's solitary fine-wine area. The *Gran Reserva* is made from 80 per cent Tempranillo blended with 20 per cent of the white Airén grape and has a full aroma, rich fruit and a long, smooth aftertaste.

COOP. SOMONTANO DE
SOBRARBE
MACABEO SELECCION
MONTESIERRA

Somontano is the smallest DO in Aragón, and this cooperative is its largest producer. The Macabeo Seleccion Montesierra is sensational: full of fresh, vital, varietal fruit and underscored by creamy-vanilla oak - the style is almost New World.

COOP. SOMONTANO DE
SOBRARBE
SEÑORIO DE LAZÁN
RESERVA MONTESIERRA

The Señorio de Lazán Reserva Montesierra is a very classy wine: a delicious, Tempranillo-dominated *tinto* that is full of lush red-fruit and subtle, creamy new oak flavour.

SHERRY & THE SOUTH

THE SOURCE OF THIS WORLD-FAMOUS wine is a comparatively small vineyard area of 15,000 hectares (37,000 acres) on the extreme south-west corner of the Spanish coast. Sherry must be matured in Sanlúcar de Barrameda to be sold as Manzanilla, a wine with a characteristic salty tang. Situated just around the coast, east of Gibraltar, is the DO of Málaga and, inland to Málaga's north, lies the DO of Montilla-Moriles.

Climatic effects

The unique qualities of Sherry derive from the peculiarities of its climate - an ideal one for grapevines - and its soil. Hot, dry summers are preceded by mild winters. With its exposed position, rainfall is relatively high, and so is the general humidity. The best vineyards - classified as Jerez Superior - that produce grapes for the most elegant *finos*, are on a friable, chalky white soil called *albariza* , high in calcium carbonate and organic material. The spongy *albariza* absorbs the rain and traps it below the surface for the benefit of the vines. The less chalky *barro* and sandy *arena* soils produce coarser wines. Vineyards sited in the latter are gradually disappearing.

The wines of Jerez also depend on another unusual factor - the influence of two prevailing winds. The *pontete* is a warm, wet, west wind from the Atlantic. It provides the level of humidity that permits the growth on the Palomino grape of the micro-organisms to produce *flor* - a special yeast - essential to the development of *fino* sherry. The *levante*, a hot, arid easterly wind dries the vines and "cooks" the grapes to give them their peculiar metabolic balance.

Sherry

The five main categories of Sherry, that is to say, *manzanilla, fino, amontillado, palo cortado* and *oloroso*, are all naturally dry wines. *Manzanilla* and *fino* are the lightest and most delicate. *Amontillado* is strictly a *fino* that has been matured for more than six to ten years, so that its *flor* has died and it begins oxidative ageing. *Olorosos* are sherries that developed little or no *flor* and, with a high degree of fortification, have matured in contact with the air to develop a darker colour and a richer flavour. *Palo cortado* is a delightful odd-ball, somewhere between an *amontillado* and an *oloroso*, having the nutty bite of the one and the rich oxidized fragrance of the other. Once the character of the wine has been established, it is fortified, blended and matured using the *solera* method: wine drawn off from the end of a series of casks (or *solera*) is replenished with wine from the previous cask, which, in turn, is replenished from the next oldest and so on, back through the series. As a result of this, the style of the house is constantly maintained.

The sweetening of sherries is achieved through grape-based agents, especially very sweet wine made from the Pedro Ximénez grape, or PX. Pedro Ximénez and Moscatel are also used to make dark, intensely sweet Sherries more suitable, some think, for pouring over ice cream than drinking.

Málaga

The sweet, fortified dessert wine of Málaga was favoured by the Romans, and extremely popular in nineteenth-century Europe, but is somewhat neglected today. The little coastal town of Málaga lies, like Jerez de la Frontera, in the south-east corner of Spain, just to the east of Gibraltar. The vines for its wines grow on the mountain slopes to the north of the town. Málaga wine comes, or came, in an even wider range of styles than Sherry, from dry, Seco or Blanco Seco, to sweet, Dulce Color, Pedro Ximénez and Moscatel, to lusciously sweet Lágrima in its various forms. The *denominación* stipulates the colour of the wines, ranging from white through golden to black, and these terms, together with the degrees of sweetness, can be incorporated in the name - for example, Dulce Negro. Dulce Color, sweetened with *arrope* (a concentration of juice obtained by boiling it down to one-third of its original volume), is the most popular style locally. Lágrima, made from free-run juices - the "tears" of the fruit - is the finest of the sweet and aromatic styles. Málaga, like Sherry, is a blended wine aged in *solera*.

Montilla-Moriles

North of Málaga is the small hill-town of Montilla, which combines its name with that of the neighbouring village of Moriles to form a separate *denominación* for the lighter style, Sherry-lookalike wines of Montilla-Moriles. The main grape used is the secondary grape of Jerez, Pedro Ximénez. The wines are generally vinified today in stainless steel, instead of the old-fashioned, earthenware *tinajas* (although, in some places, *tinajas* are still in use). The wines naturally reach an alcohol level of about 15 per cent. *Finos* are not fortified, whereas *olorosos* may be. The better wines are aged in *solera*. Montilla is sold abroad in dry, semi-sweet and sweet forms.

MÁLAGA

SCHOLTZ HERMANOS

Dulce Negro

Lagrima 10 Años

Solera 1885

Founded in 1807, this wine company was acquired by a German family in 1885, when it assumed its present title. Scholtz Hermanos, the most famous name in Málaga, produces many excellent *cuvées*. Dulce Negro, a dark-coloured wine that has been sweetened with *arrope*, has a dense structure of rich, raisiny, intensely sweet flavour. The Lagrima 10 Años, which is made entirely from free-run juice, is the most luscious of all Scholtz Hermanos styles, but it is the Solera 1885 that has the most finesse, depth and length of all - it is a wine of great complexity as well as lusciousness. The first casks for this *solera* were laid down in the year that control of this company was taken over by the Scholtz Hermanos family. A part of that wine is still found in every bottle produced today, although the amount would be so miniscule that it would have to be measured in molecules!

MONTILLA-MORILES

GRACIA HERMANOS

Pale Dry

This family-owned *bodega* produces a large range of superior Montilla, from the light Kiki *fino* to its sweet and nutty Pedro Ximénez Dulce Viejo, a 15-year-old *oloroso*. The standard wine is equally acceptable.

SHERRY

BARBADILLO

Manzanilla Fina

Sanlucar Cream

The *bodega* of Antonio Barbadillo at Sanlucar de Barrameda, founded in 1831, owns 1,000 hectares (2,470 acres) of vineyards. With its modern facilities, it produces 70 per cent of all Manzanilla. Although the entire range is recommended, the fragrant Manzanilla Fina and the super-concentrated Sanlucar Cream are outstanding.

DELGADO ZULETA

Manzanilla Pasada "La Goya"

Also situated in Sanlucar de Barrameda is Delgado Zuleta. Established in 1744, it is one of the region's oldest *bodegas* and is best known for this light, crisp Manzanilla Pasada "La Goya".

DIEZ-MERITO

Don Zoilo Very Old Fino

Victoria Regina Dry Oloroso

With its 200-hectare (495-acre) estate, which comprises seven separate vineyards, all located within the Jerez Superior district, Diez-Merito has been one of the five largest producers of Sherry since the beginning of the twentieth century. In 1985, this company and Bodegas Internacionales were brought together under the ownership of Marcos Eguizabal. The two *bodegas* currently own 800 hectares (1,980 acres) of vineyards and vinify their wines together. The Don Zoilo range of Diez-Merito provides well-aged wines of excellent value, particularly the deeply flavoured *fino*. However, this *bodega's* greatest wine is the Victoria Regina, a genuinely dry and well-aged *oloroso* produced from a *solera* of special reserve wines.

PEDRO DOMECQ

Botaina Amontillado Viejo

La Ina Fino

Venerable Pedro Ximenez

Established in 1730 by Patrick Murphy, an Irish farmer, the Domecqs did not arrive on the scene until 1816. Today, this great house is the oldest of the large firms that dominate the Sherry business. The Botaina is a well-aged *amontillado* of great finesse, made only from Palomino grapes. Domecq's classic Palomino La Ina Fino is widely acknowledged to be one of the best *finos*, despite the vast size of its production. Another Sherry of similar finesse, but from Pedro Ximénez, not Palomino grapes, is the genuinely old, deep, concentrated and succulently sweet Venerable. It is, however, quite expensive, although Pedro Domecq produces even greater rarities with wines such as Nelson, Napoleon and Bolivar. These are released very occasionally, only in minute quantities, and are greatly sought after by connoisseurs.

DUFF GORDON

El Cid

Established in 1768 by the British Consul in Cadiz, Duff Gordon was taken over by the house of Osborne in 1872. Duff Gordon is known for its sweetness, but, as the El Cid brand typifies, the style is light and elegant.

GARVEY

Tio Guillermo Amontillado

Pedro Ximenez

This historic firm, founded in 1780, came under the infamous Rumassa group in the 1970s, which increased production at the expense of quality. Since then, Garvey has been subjected to strict quality control, which has continued under the German cooperative AG - the owners since 1985. San Patricio, its high-volume *fino*, has been returned to its former excellence. Tio Guillermo has a nutty-rich flavour. However, no Garvey wine is more satisfying than the succulent, spicy-sweet Pedro Ximenez.

GONZALEZ BYASS

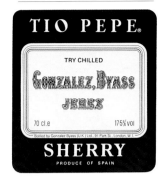

Tio Pepe Fino

Amontillado Del Duque

Matusalem Oloroso Dulce

One of the great names of Jerez, Gonzalez Byass was established in 1870 by Manuel Maria Gonzalez and is currently run by Mauricio Gonzalez-Gordon, the Marquis of Bonanza. With more than 2,000 hectares (4,940 acres) of vineyards and an annual production of 25 million bottles, Gonzalez Byass is the largest Sherry house in business today and produces many super-quality wines in its range. Few people cannot have heard of Tio Pepe Fino, the world's top-selling *fino* sherry, which is considered by many to be the bench-mark for *fino* Sherry and to show classic *flor* characteristics. Perhaps the two most exciting wines from Gonzalez Byass are Amontillado del Duque - a genuine old *amontillado* of great finesse - and Matusalem, which is a fabulously rich *oloroso* with great raisiny complexity and a long, gracefully sweet aftertaste.

EMILIO LUSTAU

Although this firm was established at Jerez de la Frontera by José Berdejo y Veyan in 1896, it was merely on a hobby basis, and it was only later that the founder's son-in-law, Emilio Lustau, put the firm on its commercial footing. The quality of the Lustau Sherry range is very consistent, ranging from a hugely important own-label business, through its excellent standard range, to its quite exceptional Almacenista range. These authentic, unblended Sherries are only available in limited quantities, and Lustau issue a list every six months. Their Almacenista wines are of such an extraordinary quality that Master of Wine, Jancis Robinson, was prompted to say "Very special... this is to Sherry what your langostinos are to fish-fingers".

Almacenista

Dry Oloroso

Palo Cortado

JOHN HARVEY

1796 Palo Cortado

Although this house was established in Jerez de la Fontera as recently as 1970, its history in connection with Sherry really stems back as far as 1796, when the British-based John Harvey & Sons was established. This explains the origins of Harveys 1796 range, which was launched in the mid-1980s.

MARQUÉS DEL REAL TESORO

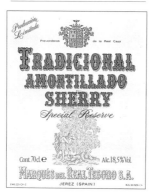

Tradicional Amontillado
Special Reserve

Established at Jerez de la Frontera in 1904 by Don Juan Jácome y Pareja, the grandson of the first Marqués del Real Tesoro or Marquis of the "Royal Treasure". The latter acquired his title from a grateful King Carlos III, after he melted down his own silver to forge cannon balls to arm the Spanish fleet. The label illustrated is of a dry, nutty, traditional Amontillado.

OSBORNE

Pedro Ximenez 1827

Bailen Oloroso Dry

The origins of Osborne stem from the friendship between Thomas Osborne Mann and Sir James Duff, the head of the historic house this firm was destined to acquire in 1872. The Pedro Ximenez 1827 is rich and treacly with a complex, raisiny aftertaste. Bailen is Osborne's finest product, and its polished-mahogany hue, profoundly rich flavour and wonderfully mellow complexity make it a contender of the greatest dry oloroso made today.

LA RIVA

Tres Palmas Fino

This historic old firm of Jerez de la Frontera was established in 1776 and is now owned by Pedro Domecq, but the great reputation of this small house is such that it is still run by the de la Riva family as a separate *bodega* with its own individual style.

SANDEMAN

Bone Dry Old Amontillado

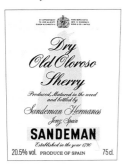

Dry Old Oloroso

Dry Old Palo Cortado

VALDESPINO

This family-run *bodega*, established in 1430, is the oldest one in Jerez. Valdespino is comprised of 200 hectares (495 acres) of vineyards and immaculate vinification facilities, using a combination of modern and traditional methods to produce some of the most respected wines in the entire region. Although blending takes place in spotless stainless-steel vats, some 85 per cent of the wines are fermented in cask. The result is a classic style of Sherry so rare these days that most people would not recognize it for what it is. The Don Gonzalo is full of fat, juicy, broad flavours, but is a totally dry *oloroso*. The Don Tomas Amontillado is as dry as it is intense and yet so delicate and fine. The Pedro Ximenez is a gloriously decadent dessert wine with a dense and deliciously sweet, raisiny complexity. The *solera* Sherry is one of the most fascinatingly complex wines you are likely to encounter.

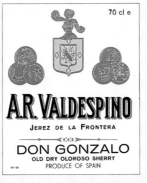

Don Gonzalo Old Dry Oloroso

Don Tomas Amontillado

Pedro Ximenez Solera Superior

*Solera 1842
Oloroso Viejo Dulce*

Although more famous for its Ports, the house of Sandeman was established in 1790, not in Vila Nova de Gaia, nor in Jerez de la Fontera, but in London by George Sandeman, who set up an import business specializing in both Port and Sherry. Eventually Sandeman decided to make a stake in both regions as a producer: the move to Jerez took place in 1879, some 38 years after the firm had acquired a lodge in Oporto. Sandeman have always produced a well-appreciated range of Sherries, and its finest products include the intensely flavoured yet fragrant and fine Bone Dry Old Amontillado, the super-concentrated, well-polished Dry Old Oloroso and the extraordinary, complex Dry Old Palo Cortado.

WILLIAMS & HUMBERT

Dos Cortados

Although known as the producer of Dry Sack (the name derives from a sixteenth-century British term for "dry" Spanish wine) this winery's finest wine is its Dos Cortados.

~ PORTUGAL ~

P ORTUGAL IS A COUNTRY that has great promise as a producer of fine table wines. It has a
highly suitable climate, with plenty of sunshine
and ample rain crossing its coastline from the
Atlantic; substantially under-used vineyard resources; and a good selection of local grape
varieties of individuality and character, which do
not need bolstering with imported varieties.

Portugal is also a land of striking contrasts. It is
the world's seventh largest wine producer, with a
production of some 100 million cases. Exports,
however, account for only 15 million cases, and
little of that can, as yet, be thought of as classic
wine. Other than Port, the bulk of its exports are
the semi-sparkling rosé wines from Mateus and
Lancers and the white wine from the northern
Vinho Verde region. Port, on which the reputation
of the country has traditionally rested, represents
less than 7.5 per cent of its total output. Exports of
white Vinho Verde from the rugged terrain north
of Porto are more often than not commercial,
sweetened versions of the crisp, dry white wines
consumed at home. The output of Dão, often
thought of as Portugal's classic red table wine
region, is only some three million cases, 10 per
cent of which is white, and it rarely lives up to its

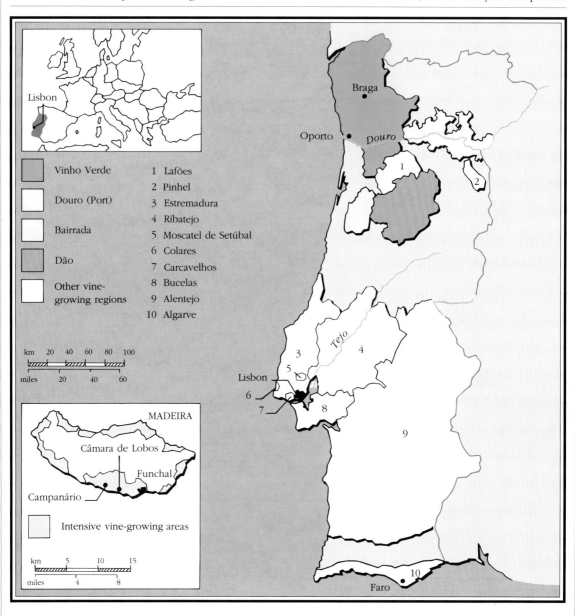

Main wine areas *The northern half
of Portugal has always been an
important winemaking area: Port,*

*Vinho Verde, Dão and Bairrada all
come from the north. But the future
may see the development of regions*

*around the river Tejo, in Ribatejo and
Alentejo, both of which have the
potential to make exciting table wines.*

reputation. Twice as much wine is produced from the smaller adjoining area of Bairrada (again 90 per cent red) but quality, so far, is apparent only in the efforts of one or two individual producers. The area with the greatest output, Oeste - producing, with a few notable exceptions, bulk wines - is a name unknown to most people.

Demarcated regions

Portugal took its first steps to regulate the content and standards of its wines as long ago as 1756, with provisions for Port. Seven quality regions were already demarcated in the early 1900s, but by 1990 Portugal was still struggling to evolve a system that will accord with European Community regulations. There now exist 11 demarcated areas with the top, quality status of *Região Demarcada*. Wines from these regions, bottled under the jurisdiction of the national regulating body, now the *Instituto da Vinha e do Vinho*, carry a *Selo de Origem* (Seal of Origin). Douro has Região Demarcada status for both Port and table wines, and the others areas are Vinho Verde, Dão, Bairrada, Algarve, Bucelas, Colares, Carcavelhos, Moscatel de Setúbal and Madeira. The reputations of Port, Vinho Verde and Madeira are already well established. Dão, an inland mountainous area lying south of the Douro, and Bairrada, between Dão and the Atlantic coast, are both regions that are becoming better known for red wines and, in the case of Dão, for its small production of whites. Bucelas, Colares, Carcavelhos and Moscatel de Setúbal, all near Lisbon, are less important today, with the exception of the fortified dessert wine of Moscatel de Setúbal.

Two of the largest undemarcated regions are potential sources for many interesting new wines - Ribatejo in central Portugal, and Alentejo, south of the Tejo river. Several areas within both these provinces were named in 1979 as "determinate areas" - an intermediate step to full demarcation. Ribatejo, up to now a source for bulk wines, has six new demarcated areas - Tomar, Chamusca, Santarem, Almeirim, Cartaxo and Coruche. A further 15, in the country's north and east, are looking for official recognition by 1991.

Grape varieties

Portugal, surprisingly, does not share many grape varieties with its neighbour, Spain. The Tinta Roriz, or Aragonez, is the Tempranillo of Spain; and Loureiro and Trajadura appear both in Vinho Verde and in Galicia, Spain. There has been no widespread attempt to introduce classic French varieties. Cabernet Sauvignon is used, most notably for the Quinta da Bacalhôa, and experimental quantities of Sauvignon, Chardonnay and Gewürztraminer have been planted in the Douro. But the trend, no doubt to the long-term benefit of the Portuguese wine industry, is to persist with native varieties. Touriga Nacional, the leading Port wine grape, is an important ingredient in Dão, and Tina Roriz, another Port variety, is used elsewhere, but producers usually use a traditional mix of local grapes that are specific to each area.

Chief producers

A large part of the vinification and distribution of table wines is in the hands of cooperatives (there are over 100 of them) and large merchants like Sogrape, J.M. da Fonseca Internacional, Caves Velhas, Borges & Irmão, and Carvalho, Ribeiro & Ferreira. When looking for examples of classic Portuguese wines the range is often limited to the best wines of these merchants and of a handful of individual, usually small, producers.

PORTUGUESE TERMS

Adega	Wine-producing cellar
Aguardente	Brandy
Branco	White
Colheita	Vintage
Doce	Sweet
Engarrafado na origem	Estate-bottled
Espumante	Sparkling
Garrafeira	High-quality with long ageing requirement
Instituto da Vinha e do Vinho	National controlling body
Licorosa	Sweet fortified wine
Maduro	Matured
Quinta	Single estate or farm
Região Demarcada	Legally demarcated wine region
Reserva	High-quality wine from a demarcated region
Rosado	Rosé
Seco	Dry
Selo de Origem	Seal of Origin
Tinto	Red
Vinha	Vineyard
Vinho da Mesa	Table wine
Velho	Old
Verde	Young, unaged

Dramatic vineyards *The terraced, vine-covered slopes of the river Douro are some of the most spectacular in Europe.*

TABLE WINES

VINHO VERDE, PORTUGAL'S most northerly demarcated table wine region, is one of its largest. It is also one of its best-known regions, largely through the export of popular brands of white Vinho Verde by large concerns such as Sogrape and Borges & Irmão. The Vinho Verde that is chosen for export is invariably white, as are all the examples included in our selection of classic wines. Yet in the region itself, some 70 per cent of production is actually red Vinho Verde, a fairly brutish drink that does not commend itself to the more sophisticated European palate.

With reputedly well in excess of 60,000 small-holders growing grapes, most of the production is handled either by the large, commercial companies, the 21 cooperatives, or is for home consumption. An association of single-estate owners (APEVV) has been formed with the aim of raising standards, and their efforts are beginning to have an effect. White Vinho Verde at its best is a dry, light, fragrant and delicate drink, aromatic and refreshing and relatively low in alcohol. It still retains a slight sparkle from residual carbon dioxide. The grapes used vary from maker to maker; the main ones, Alvarinho, Avesso, Loureiro, Pedernã, Trajadura and Azal Branco, can be vinified as single varietals or used as a blend.

It is ironic that more table wine - both red and white - is normally made in the Douro than Port wine, for which the area is famous. The river that runs through the region is the Duero of Spain, home to the vineyards that produce the famous Spanish Vega Sicilia wine and to those of Portugal's most expensive red wine, Barca Velha. Reds display a range of styles; exceptionally for Portugal, whites include the use of foreign varieties.

Dão and Bairrada

Dão, a mountainous, inland area around Viseu, produces less exciting red wines than the Douro region, from a 20 per cent minimum of Touriga Nacional, and whites from a minimum of 20 per cent Encruzado grapes. Red *garrafeiras* have two years minimum in vat and one year in bottle. Bairrada reds are single variety wines based on the Baga grape. The success of two particular makers, Luis Pato and the Caves São João, points the way for other growers in the region. Most of the white goes to produce high-quality sparkling wine.

The large provinces of Ribatejo in central Portugal and Alentejo in southern Portugal are benefiting from improvements in vinicultural techniques. Both provinces have already produced some attractive new table wines that will help to establish them as important wine regions of the future. Some of the inner districts in both regions have been elevated to demarcated status and they all look ready to assume increasing importance as top sources of high-quality, readily drinkable table wines.

VINHO VERDE

CASA DE COMPOSTELA

A fine, light, fresh and fruity, cool-fermented wine made mostly from the Pedernão grape, blended with Loureiro and Trajadura, grown at Requião, near Famalicão. The 36 hectares (90 acres) at Casa Agricola de Compostela make it one of the largest Vinho Verde estates.

CASA DE SEZIM

This wine is made at Nespereira, near Guimarães on an estate that has been in the same hands since 1375. It is made mainly from the Loureiro grape and blended with Trajadura, Pedernão and a little Azal branco. Its full aroma and considerable weight make it the second best Vinho Verde after Palácio da Brejoeira.

CÊPA VÉLHA
ALVARINHO

Produced from the Alvarinho grape grown at Monção on the Spanish border, this wine is somewhat richer and firmer than most Vinhos Verdes, with a stronger, almost fat, fruit flavour that retains freshness for up to two years in bottle.

PALÁCIO DA BREJOEIRA "ALVARINHO"

The facade of the neo-classical Palácio da Brejoeira is also used for the label of Mateus Rosé, but the makers of Portugal's most ubiquitous pink fizz have nothing to do with the owners of this property, whose pure Alvarinho wine is the finest and most prestigious Vinho Verde produced.

PASSO DE TEIXEIRÓ

This wine comes from the Quinta do Passo near Teixeró, a property that has belonged to Champalimaud family of Quinta do Côtto since the thirteenth century. Made from predominantly Avesso grapes, it has a distinctive, soft flavour, due to the schist soil on which it is grown.

QUINTA DA AVELEDA BRANCO SECO

Better known for its sweetish, bulk-produced Aveleda and its equally large selling but far more classic Casal Garcia, it is, however, the single-vineyard Quinta da Aveleda, with its fine, fresh flavour and barely discernible *pétillance*, that made the name of Aveleda famous.

QUINTA DO CRASTO

A traditionally produced Vinho Verde with a delicate and aromatic character, this is made from predominantly Pedernão, Azal and Avesso grapes grown on the slopes of the river Paiva at Travanca, near Cinfães.

QUINTA DA LIVRAÇÃO

This light, fragrant Vinho Verde has a most attractive delicate character that remains fresh and vital for up to a year or two in bottle. It is produced from a blend of various grape varieties that are grown on 10 hectares (25 acres) of contiguous granitic slopes of the river Tâmega, at Livração, near Marcos de Canaveses.

QUINTA DO TAMARIZ

Quinta de Santa Maria has produced this fine, fresh and well-balanced single-vineyard Vinho Verde since 1939. This label shows a pure Loureiro wine; there is also a Loureiro and Trajadura blend. The grapes are grown on the south-facing, granitic slopes of Quinta do Tamariz estate at Carreira, near Barcelos.

SOLAR DAS BOUÇAS

This pure Loureiro varietal wine is made on a small, well-equipped estate at Prozelo, near Amares. It has a characteristically light aroma, a correctly crisp flavour, a very slight *pétillance* and an aftertaste that is reminiscent of orange flower water.

DOURO

FERREIRINHA BARCA VELHA TINTO

Made by Fernando de Almeida of the famous Port house of Ferreira at its Quinta do Vale de Meão near the Spanish border, the silky-textured Barca Velha is in many ways Portugal's answer to Spain's Vega Sicilia, but it is matured in bottle, rather than over-aged in cask, and this gives the wine more finesse.
TR 60%, TB 15%, TF 15%, TA 10%

FERREIRINHA RESERVA ESPECIAL TINTO

It takes up to 10 years for Fernando to make up his mind whether a vintage is good enough to be sold as Barca Velha. If it is not, it is sold as Reserva Especial, which is usually softer, with broader fruit flavours, but is not considered of any lesser quality by non-Portuguese palates.

PLANALTO RESERVA BRANCO SECO

This tangy, rich, dry white wine is not from a single vineyard, nor are the grapes (Malvasia, Gouveio and Viosinho) grown by Sogrape, but the quality demanded effectively doubles the grapes' price and makes this the Douro's finest white wine.

QUINTA DO CÔTTO GRANDE ESCOLHA TINTO

This blend of grapes is virtually the same as the base wine of Champalimaud's Quinta do Côtto Port, but fully-fermented, rather than fortified, and aged in new oak. It has creamy-rich fruit and a voluptuous flavour.
TR 30%, TF 20%, BO 20%, TN 20%, VAR 10%

QUINTA DA PACHECA TINTO

Serpa Pimentel produces various pure varietal white wines, but he has far more success with the fruity finesse of this traditional red Portuguese blend, with its fillip of Cabernet Sauvignon.
TN, TB, TR & TC 95%, CS 5%

BAIRRADA

FREI JOÃO RESERVA TINTO

The wines sold under the Caves São João label are usually purchased from local cooperatives, but they always have more accessible fruit than most other Bairradas. Frei João has a deep purple colour, intense plummy fruit and a fine supple tannin structure.

LUIS PATO TINTO

This small family-owned winery is run by ex-pharmacist Luis Pato, a radical winemaker who gives great emphasis to the *terroir*. He produces soft, fruit flavours in his wine, and uses new oak for their maturation.

DÃO

CONDE DE SANTAR TINTO

The mansion Conde de Santar belongs to A. A. Calem & Filho of Oporto, the largest family-owned Port house, who make this *cru* Dão from a vineyard near the house. It is made, aged and bottled on the property.

OTHERS

ADEGA COOP. DE BORBA C.R.L. TINTO

Like many cooperatives on the Iberian peninsular, this cooperative in Alentejo ferments at a very high temperature and leaves its wines too long in cement before bottling. Like few Iberian cooperatives, however, it produces fresh red wines with excellent concentration of luscious fruit.

BUÇACO TINTO RESERVA

This incredible red wine is produced by the legendary Palace Hotel at Bussaco, near Coimbra. It is made from Baga, Tinta Pinheira, Bastardo and Trincadeira grapes and aged for 36 months in oak, chestnut or mahogany. It ages remarkably well, as is shown by the long list of old vintages on the hotel's wine list.

COLARES CHITAS

This wine from Antonio Bernadino Paula da Silva is the best Colares available. It is typically tough and austere for the first 20 years, due to traditional practices such as retaining all the stalks during the fermentation and incorporating all the harsh press-wine in the final *cuvée*, but it has an intense, rasping quality of fruit that is as indestructable as the tannin.
RAM 80%, VAR 20%

MARGARIDE'S CASAL DO CONVENTO DA SERRA

From one of the two vineyards of the Casa Agricola Herdeiros de Dom Luís de Margaride, this soft red wine owes its juicy-rich flavour to the Merlot, which is supported by the Cabernet Franc and Portugese varieties.

QUINTA DO CARMO GARRAFEIRA

The old Tricadeira, Periquita and Alicante vines here produce a modest yield of grapes. The wine has a good colour, strong bouquet and full, silky-textured, fruit-packed flavour.

JOSÉ MARIA DA FONSECA SUCCS

A separate company from J.M. da Fonseca Internacional, the bulk-branded wine firm that is also located in Azeitão, this family-owned firm is Portugal's greatest producer of table wines.

GARRAFEIRA TE

Fonseca label Quinta de Camarate's reserve wine simply as Garrafeira TE, but it is a concentrated and characterful wine that benefits from two years' maturation in wood.

MOSCATEL DE SETÚBAL 20 YEAR OLD

This firm also produces fortified Moscatel from Setúbal. Young vintage wines are produced, yet the 20 Year Old retains a certain grapiness, as well as a creamy-caramel flavour and a spicy-raisiny complexity.

PASMADOS

This rich red wine is made from Touriga Nacional, Perequita, Moreto and Alforcheiro grapes.

QUINTA DE CAMARATE

The Periquita, Espaldeiro and Cabernet Sauvignon vines of Quinta de Camarate produce a rich *vinho tinto* that shows its class after five years in bottle.

JOÃO PIRES

Harnessing the latest technology and under the artful eye of Australian winemaker Peter Bright, João Pires has become the only firm to rival J.M. de Fonseca Succs as Portugal's most sucessful table wine producers, with a range of diverse wines. Confusingly, though, the company is owned by J.M. da Fonseca Internacional.

QUINTA DA BACALHÔA

This Cabernet Sauvignon wine is softened with a little Merlot and aged in new oak. It has a deep colour and blackcurrant flavour, with supple tannin, and is capable of considerable development in bottle.

TINTO DA ANFORA

The Tinto da Anfora is a full-bodied red of some complexity. It is aged in new oak, which gives it coconutty undertones, and in chestnut, which contributes to its dry, spicy-cedary character.

WHITE PALMELA WINE

This exuberantly fruity Muscat, although labelled "dry", does have some residual sweetness, but this is beautifully balanced by its exciting, lively, sherbetty acidity.

PORT

WITH ITS STYLE, reputation and longevity, Port is a wine of classic proportions. Unlike Sherry, Port is nearly always sweet. The fortifying Brandy is added during the fermentation process when about half the natural grape sugar has already been fermented into alcohol, leaving a residual sweetness level of about 90 grams per litre. The spirit arrests the fermentation, creating the desired balance between alcohol and sweetness. The clear, flavourless grape spirit used for fortification is known as *aguardente*. It has an alcoholic strength of 77 per cent and is added in a proportion of approximately one-fifth spirit to four-fifths wine must. The wines at this stage are still unblended, and are left to rest at the *quinta* (farm), high up on the steep, terraced slopes of the Douro, 130 kilometres (80 miles) from the Port lodges. In the new year, about four months after the harvest, the young wine for the major Port houses is transported in *pipes*, which are casks holding 550 litres (121 gallons), to the lodges at Vila Nova de Gaia, on the south bank of the river at Oporto. While the hot, sunny climate of the middle Douro at Pinhão is regarded as ideal for the vines, the more moderate, and damper, climate of Vila Nova de Gaia is more suitable for ageing the wine, once the blending has been carried out.

The average annual production of base wine is around 200,000 *pipes*, but the amount the Government allows to be fortified and made into Port each year depends on a number of factors, and is always less than the amount produced, except in years of very restricted harvest. In 1988, 140,000 *pipes* were permitted (although, in the event, fewer were produced).

Two basic styles of Port

The style of Port is determined by the method of ageing - in wood or in bottle. Wood Port is bottled when ready for drinking, and is intended for consumption within the following two years. The best are sold as Tawny Ports with an indication of age (10, 20, 30 or 40 years). With time, these Tawnies acquire an exquisite elegance and silkiness.

Vintage Port (a blend of the finest wines available to the shipper, declared only in the best years) develops its powerful fruity complexity from age in the bottle, after an initial two years in cask. To preserve the full vigour of the wine, it is bottled without being filtered, and as a result will throw a deposit in the bottle and require decanting. Vintage Ports can take anything up to 15 or 20 years to reach maturity and remain at a peak for many years thereafter.

Late-bottled Vintage (LBV) falls between the two styles. Wine of a single year of good but not outstanding quality, normally from the better part of the Douro valley, is matured in cask for up to six years. LBV Ports do not need decanting.

Vintage-dated Single Quinta wines have become more popular recently. They are top-quality single-vineyard products (usually from the best *quinta* of the shipper) from a year when a normal vintage is not declared. They are produced, and should be treated, like normal Vintage Ports but tend to mature a few years earlier.

PORT VINTAGES

Vintages are declared only three or four times a decade, and need not be declared by every shipper. The best years see the largest number of declarations. The declared wine represents only some two to three per cent of the total harvest. A shipper makes his declaration two or three years after the harvest.

YEAR	DECLARED PORT VINTAGES
1985	A superb vintage, which all shippers decided to declare. The best wines have a long life; but many will be for early drinking.
1983	Very fine vintage declared by many shippers. Wines have good tannin and fruit, maturing about 15 years from the harvest.
1982	Soft, ripe-flavoured wines declared by a few houses (who subsequently chose not to declare in 1983); available for early drinking, 10 years of age onwards.
1980	Attractive wines of medium depth, drinkable after a 15-year maturation, from 1995 onwards.
1977	The best year since 1963; powerful wines of great depth and flavour, needing 20 years to mature; generally declared.
1975	Widely declared vintage of light, elegant wines, available for early drinking.
1970	Big, well-structured, rounded wines, full of flavour, that will manage to provide superb drinking into the 1990s.
1966	Excellent (initially underrated) vintage of firm, full-flavoured wines, already set for drinking.
1963	Generally considered to be the greatest of the post-war vintages; wines of great depth and structure, just approaching maturity, but will last into the twenty-first century.

CÁLEM

Quinta da Foz Vintage

Although established in 1859, Cálem's initial business was to sell table wine in bulk to Brazil, and it was not until later than it entered the Port trade via a cooperage business. Now it is the largest of the family-owned Port houses. Its Quinta da Foz has the Cálem soft and juicy style, with more depth and character than its regular Vintage Port.

CHAMPALIMAUD

Quinta do Côtto Vintage

Quinta do Côtto Tawny Velho Doce

The Quinta do Côtto property at Régua has been in the Montez family for some 700 years, the French connection occurring as recently as that country's revolution, when a Champalimaud married António de Aranjo Cabral Montez. It must be an amusing irony to this ancient family that its single-*quinta* wines are the fastest rising stars on the international Port firmament, but it has only been possible since the Gaia maturation laws have been relaxed. The Vintage is fruity and full of finesse, while the Tawny Velho Doce is seductively soft and mellow, with a deliciously rich coffee-nutty complexity.

CHURCHILL'S

Finest Vintage Character

Vintage

Quinta da Água Alta Vintage

The first independent Port house to be established in more than 50 years, Churchill Graham was founded in 1981 by Johnny Graham, who used to work for Cockburn's, and his wife Caroline, *née* Churchill. It has three excellent properties, two in the Pinhão valley and, most important of all, Quinta da Agua Alta in the Douro itself, which produces a magnificent wine and is sold as a single-*quinta* Port in some vintages. This house is determined to keep its quickly earned reputation; all of its Ports have an excellent deep colour, intense fruit, great finesse and classic structure.

COCKBURN'S

Vintage

Founded in 1815 by Robert Cockburn, who married Mary Duff, a lady much admired by Lord Byron, this house was purchased by Harveys of Bristol, which has since come under the auspices of Allied-Lyons. Its vintage Ports have good colour and depth, with fine fruit, silky texture and a chocolatey complexity.

CROFT

Quinta da Roéda Vintage

To many people Croft is best known for its Sherries, yet it is one of the oldest Port houses. In all but a few years, its Vintage Ports are not as weighty as most. Two exceptions have been 1975 and 1985, when its great concentration made Croft one of the top wines of the vintage. Its Quinta da Roéda is consistently fine.

DELAFORCE

His Eminence's Choice
Superior Old Tawny

Although owned by IDV (International Distillers and Vintners) since 1968, and thus a sister company to Croft and to Morgan, this is still very much a family-run firm, with fifth-generation David Delaforce in day to day control. Its style is very much on the lighter-bodied side, which particularly suits His Eminence's Choice, an exquisite old Tawny with a succulent balance and a lingering fragrance.

DOW'S

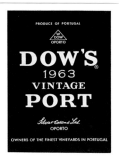

Vintage

Dow's is not a house, but a label used by Silva & Cosens, which itself is one of many brands of the Symington family, but a Dow's Vintage Port is a very individual wine. Big, black and backward, it is concentrated and drier in style than most, with a great depth of spicy-chocolatey fruit.

FERREIRA

Duque de Bragança 20 Years Old

Superior White

This famous firm was established in 1761, although it did not achieve its great reputation until the mid-nineteenth century, when it was under the helm of Dona Antonia Adelaide Ferreira, the Veuve Clicquot of Oporto. Ferreira has for some time been the brand-leader in Portugal and was taken over in 1988 by European Cellars. Tawny Port is very much its forte and its warm, mellow Duque de Bragança is one of the finest 20 Year Old Ports on the market. The smooth, rich, slightly sweet Superior White is the best white Port available.

FONSECA GUIMARAENS

Vintage

Fonseca, Monteiro & Co changed its name when purchased by Manuel Pedro Guimaràens in 1822, and has been part of Taylor's since 1948. Its vintage Port, although not quite as massive as Taylors, is very much of the same deep-coloured style, with a rich, ripe flavour and a sensual chocolatey-raisiny complexity.

GRAHAM'S

Vintage

Graham's was founded in 1820 as a textile business and only got into the Port trade when its Oporto office accepted wine in payment of a debt six years later. Now it is another piece of the Symington Port empire. It is the big, black and beautifully sweet Graham's Vintage Port that has earned this house its great reputation.

QUINTA DO NOVAL

Nacional Vintage

Vintage

Over 40 Year Old Tawny

This beautiful 85-hectare (210-acre) estate, set high above Pinhão in the Upper Corgo district, was founded by Antonio José da Silva in 1813, but it has been controlled by the van Zeller family for four generations. This property's most famous wine is Quinta do Noval Nacional, a dense coloured, powerfully structured, super-concentrated wine made exclusively from the 5,000 ungrafted vines that grow on the terrace just beneath the house. The Nacional might be sensational, but the regular Vintage is also a Port of the highest order and is highly sought after by connoisseurs for its inimitable grace and finesse. The 40 Year Old retains the mellow warmth of a true tawny, whereas so many others are more like liqueurs than Ports.

RAMOS-PINTO

Old Vintage-Dated Tawny

Quinta do Bom-Retiro 20 Years

Adriano Ramos-Pinto was just 20 years old when he started this firm in 1880, but he laid very firm foundations for what is now one of the most respected Portugese-owned, family-run Port houses. It specializes in late releases of old vintage-dated tawnies, of which the spectacularly youthful 1937 illustrated here is perhaps its greatest ever. The Quinta da Urtiga is an excellent single-*quinta* Port of "Vintage Character" and represents superb value, while its famous Quinta do Bom-Retiro is a 20-year-old Tawny of absolute classic quality.

ROYAL OPORTO WINE CO.

Quinta das Carvalhas Fine Aged Tawny

Quinta do Sibio Fine Mellow Tawny

Founded by the Marquis de Pombal in 1756 to regulate the Port trade, this company is now privately owned and a source of inexpensive vintage Port. It owns eight *quintas* and produces single-*quinta* wines from Quinta das Carvalhas and Quinta do Sibio. Its reserves of old wines are used for late-released, vintage-dated Tawnies.

SMITH WOODHOUSE

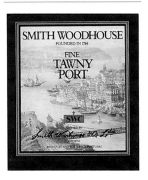

Fine Tawny

For some reason, the wines from this old British-founded Port house (now owned by the Symingtons) are not as highly thought of in Portugal as they are on export markets. The quality across the entire range is very respectable, but it truly excels with its Fine Old Tawny Ports.

WARRE'S

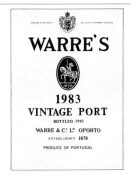

Vintage

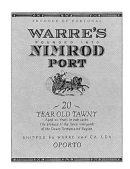

Nimrod 20 Year Old Tawny

Established in 1670, only the German-founded house of C. N. Kopke can claim to be older than Warre & Co., although this firm only assumed its present name when William Warre entered the business in 1729. Of all the Ports produced, it is those of Warre's and Graham's, both Symington family brands, that compete as the most concentrated and darkest Vintage Port after that of Taylor's itself. In contrast, Warre's Nimrod is one of the most elegant of 20-year-old Tawny Ports.

TAYLOR'S

Established in 1692 by Job Bearsley, Taylor's underwent no less than 21 changes of title before adopting its present one, which derives from the names of various partners: Joseph Taylor in 1816, John Fladgate in 1837, and Morgan Yeatman in 1844. In 1774 Taylor's became the first shipper to buy a property in the Douro valley and 100 years later purchased Quinta de Vargellas, the firm's flagship vineyard. The fragrant, complex wine of Quinta de Vargellas was the first single-*quinta* Port to be commercialized. The entire range of this firm's wines is of a consistently high quality, but it is its Vintage Port that comes to mind as soon as the name Taylor's is mentioned. It is the darkest and most massive of all vintage Ports and regularly achieves the highest prices at auction.

10 Years Old Tawny

Quinta de Vargellas Vintage

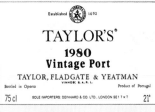

Vintage

MADEIRA

Madeira is a volcanic island where cultivable land is at a premium, so the vineyards, which have to compete with other crops, are split into thousands of smallholdings. The island is subject to generous Atlantic rainfall, with hot summers and warm winters. It lies in the Atlantic 600 kilometres (about 400 miles) off the coast of Morocco, and is even further from Portugal. True Madeiras - those made exclusively from the grapes that give the wines their names - are relatively scarce. About a quarter of the grapes currently grown on the island are Tinta Negra Mole, used in the past to produce large quantities of noble-variety "lookalikes". Under the terms of Portugal's entry into the European Community this is no longer permitted: 85 per cent of the wine in the bottle must be from the grape variety named - from Malvasia, Bual, Verdelho and Sercial. Malmsey (from the Malvasia grape) is the sweetest, with great fruit and fragrance; Bual, usually a little less sweet, is dark in colour, elegant and fragrant; Verdelho is golden, nutty and medium-dry; Sercial is the lightest and driest. The best and most intensively grown areas are on the south slopes of the island around the capital Funchal, where the classic grapes are planted in increasing quantity, as a result of the stricter provisions since 1986. Cheaper Madeira will have to be sold as Sercial-style, for instance, or simply labelled "dry", "medium-dry" and so on.

Unique winemaking methods

One factor that gives Madeira its character, and its fabled longevity, is the unique process of "baking" the young wine (the *vinho claro*) for several months. The present-day process imitates the heating and cooling effects of the long sea-journeys that casks of Madeira enjoyed when bound for export markets in the eighteenth century. Special ovens or *estufas* raise the temperature of the wine to 45°C (113°F) for a period of four months, or 50°C (122°F) for three months. The higher-quality wines are fortified before the process, and the cheaper ones afterwards, with grape spirit of 99.6 per cent alcoholic strength. Thereafter the better wines are matured in cask for anything up to 25 years. Madeira, like Sherry and Port, is blended (produced from several harvests), but only with rare vintage declarations. The terms Reserve, Special Reserve and Exceptional Reserve may be applied to wines of respectively at least five, 10 or 15 years old. A vintage wine will have been aged for at least 20 years in wood and two years in bottle. These wines have been known to last for 200 years and more.

Traditional transport *On the island, local men carry fat goatskins, bulging full with Madeira wine, on their backs.*

BLANDY'S

This house was established in 1811 by John Blandy, who had been posted to the island four years earlier as part of the British garrison, which was there to protect Madeira during Napoleon's invasion of the Iberian peninsula. Blandy's basic range of the four Madeira grapes is named after four dukes; it is most famous for its deliciously soft and sweet Duke of Clarence Malmsey. When sentenced to death and asked how he would like to be executed, the Duke made the immortal reply "I should like to be drowned in a butt of Malmsey, sir". It is a fine wine, but the toffee-rich 10 Year Old with its clean, creamy-sweet fruit, is Blandy's greatest non-vintage Malmsey.

Duke of Sussex Dry Sercial

Duke of Clarence Rich Malmsey

10 Year Old Malmsey

COSSARTS

Cossart Gordon & Co was founded in 1745, making it one of the oldest trading names in Madeira. The entire range is exemplary, including the generics, but true individual quality commences with the Finest Reserve (formerly Finest Old Reserve) wines, which are blends that utilize wines that have matured in wood for at least five years. The wines sold under Cossarts Special Reserve label have an even smoother, more luxurious richness and are matured in wood for at least 10 years, although the label does not boast the fact. But it is the Duo Centenary Celebration Sercial and Bual that not only represent the finest wines of Cossarts, but are consistently two of the greatest Madeiras. With wines matured in wood for between 15 and 60 years or more, the Sercial attains a stylish succulence so rarely experienced at the driest end of the Madeira spectrum and the Bual is so fabulously rich that it tastes like a marvellous old vintage Malmsey.

Finest Malmsey Reserve Over 5 Years

Duo Centenary Celebration Sercial

Special Reserve Malmsey

Duo Centenary Celebration Bual

POWER DRURY

Special Reserve Malmsey

Founded in 1888, Power Drury was taken over by the Madeira Wine Company in 1925 but, unlike Blandy's, Cossarts *et al*, its name sank slowly out of sight. It was revived in the 1980s by the release of such sumptuous wines as its Special Reserve Malmsey and tiny amounts of pure vintage delights like 1954 Malmsey, 1952 Verdelho and 1910 Bual.

RUTHERFORD & MILES

Reserve Bual Over 5 Years Old

Special Reserve Malmsey Over 10 Years Old

This famous brand has a distinctive style that sets its wines apart from the other fine wines produced by the Madeira Wine Company. The Reserve Bual is smooth, mellow and fruity, with a toasty-nutty complexity. The luscious Special Reserve Malmsey has the true concentration of a blend containing wines of at least 10 years maturation in wood, with a great raisiny-sweetness and spicy-finesse.

HARVEYS

Medium Rich Malmsey

The famous Bristol-based firm of Harveys, with its almost 200-year-old association with fortified Iberian wines, has a long held tradition of shipping and bottling its own brand of Madeira. This full and voluptuous, yet fine and fragrant Malmsey is pro-·duced by Henriques & Henriques, which is one of the few independent Madeira houses.

LEACOCK'S

Full Rich Malmsey

Established in 1741 by John Leacock, an orphan who had been raised by a weaver in London, this brand has gained the reputation of producing some of the most traditional and flavourful wines in Madeira, as graphically illustrated by this Full Rich Malmsey, a huge wine with great extract and lots of coffee-caramel complexity.

~ EASTERN ~ MEDITERRANEAN

THE COUNTRIES THAT LIE on the eastern shores of the Mediterranean were probably the earliest home for the vine. Today, grapes are grown in Turkey, Israel and Lebanon, but mostly - because of strong Islamic influences - they are grown for eating rather than for wine. The warm climate here, and in Greece and Cyprus, makes it hard to produce quality wines, but there are successful vineyards in isolated micro-climates.

The legendary Commanderie St John

Although Cyprus produces table wines and so-called "Cyprus Sherry", it is best known for its fabled, sweet red dessert wine, Commanderie St John, formally known as Commandaria. It is made from indigenous, ungrafted vines, grown mostly in the south-facing foothills of the Troodos mountains, where rainfall is sufficiently high.

Classic wines of Greece

The largest wine production in Greece is of Retsina, the table wine that is flavoured with pine resin; however, this is a wine better drunk *in situ* than exported. The traditional products that maintain a good reputation are the sweet dessert wines, the Muscats of Samos, the Malvasia of Crete and the sweet red wines of the Peloponnese, particularly the Mavrodaphne of Patras. Following the lead of Château Carras in Thessalonika, Greek wines have been coaxed into the twentieth century. French grapes (sometimes blended with indigeous varieties) and modern vinification methods, combined with *barrique* ageing for fine reds, provide an increasing number of good wines. Further west, in Macedonia, Naoussa reds are produced entirely from Xynomavro.

Israel and Lebanon

Israel's wines make little impact on export markets, except for the Jewish Kosher market. New vineyards were established at the end of the nineteenth century, with a winery that was financed by Edmond de Rothschild. Today, the best results come from vineyards with French varieties, planted on the cooler Golan Heights in the North-East.

Political turmoil in Lebanon has not deterred one man, Serge Hochar at Château Musar, from producing excellent wines. Trained in Bordeaux, he has been the most prominent producer in the Bekaa valley, Lebanon's main winegrowing area.

CYPRUS	GREECE	J. BOUTARI & SONS GRANDE RÉSERVE

COMMANDERIE ST. JOHN

"ACHAIA" CLAUSS MAVRODAPHNE OF PATRAS

This sweet, *solera*-made, unfortified dessert wine was first made in the twelfth century when the Knights of the Order of St John administered it to injured knights returning from the Crusades who were recuperating in Cyprus. It is produced from a blend of black and white grapes that have been left to shrivel in the sun for 10-15 days after the harvest.

"Achaia" Clauss make the finest Mavrodaphne of Patras, which is the best wine in their range. It is a rich, sweet, red liqueur or dessert wine with a smooth, sweet-oak finish that can be enjoyed either when young and fruity or smooth and mature.

The firm of Boutari is one of the most reliable producers in Greece. Boutari's Grande Reserve is produced entirely from the best Xynomavro grapes grown on the firm's own vineyards in Naoussa. It is even bigger and darker than Boutari's basic Naoussa, with noticeably higher acidity, lots of tannin and very rich and spicy fruit. It can improve in the bottle for 15 years or more.

ANDREW P. CAMBAS
LION OF NEMEA

The deep, dark spicy red wine of Nemea has been produced for over 2,500 years and is known locally as the "Blood of Hercules" because his blood was shed when he fought and killed the Nemean lion. The Lion of Nemea, made from the Agiorgitiko grape, is now produced by Andrew P. Cambas and is one of the best two or three Nemea produced.

CHÂTEAU CARRAS

From the Côtes de Meliton appellation in Sithonia, the middle of Halkadiki's three peninsulas, this wine is from equal amounts of Cabernet Sauvignon and Cabernet Franc. It is the brainchild of the late John Carras, a multi-millionaire who set out to produce the greatest wine in Greece and achieved it with a little help from Professor Peynaud.

GENTILINI

Young Nicholas Cosmetatos is fastidious about quality and produces an ultra-clean, fresh, light and delicious dry white wine from the Tssaoussi and Robola grapes grown on his 2.5-hectare (6-acre) vineyard at Minies on Cephalonia, one of the Ionian Islands.

CHÂTEAU PEGASUS NAOUSSA

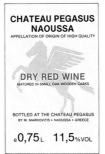

This fine wine is produced in limited quantities from the best grapes grown on Chateau Pegasus, the most respected estate in the Naoussa region. The wine, which is matured in oak *barriques* for nine months, is deep in colour, rich in fruit and has some finesse.

COOP. VINICOLE DE SAMOS
SAMOS SWEET MUSCAT WINE

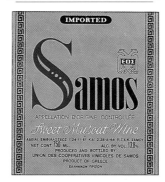

The Union des Coopératives Vinicoles de Samos consistently produces some of the finest Muscat wine of Samos, which is one of the world's greatest dessert wines. The wine is superbly rich and raisiny, with a perfect balance and a long mellifluous finish. Also look out for the cooperative's fabulous Samos Nectar.

TSANTALI AGIORITIKOS

This fine wine is made from a blend of Cabernet Sauvignon and Limnio grapes grown on Mount Athos or Agioritokos, the third peninsula of Halkidiki, where no female (human or animal) has been allowed to set foot since the edict issued by Emperor Constantine Monomachos of Byzantium in 1060.

ISRAEL

YARDEN VINEYARDS
SAUVIGNON BLANC

Vines used to grow on the Golan Heights beneath Mount Hermon in antiquity, but had been abandoned for hundreds of years when they were reclaimed by a kibbutz in 1983. Prior to this, the best Israeli wines were very poor quality. The wines from the Yarden and Gamla vineyards, which are run jointly, quickly caught the attention of wine enthusiasts. The Gamla Cabernet Sauvignon is ridiculously cheap for such a rich, clean and blackcurranty wine. Even better than the Gamla Cabernet Sauvignon is this crisp, dry and elegant Yarden Sauvignon Blanc from Galilee. (Both wines are kosher.)

LEBANON

CHÂTEAU MUSAR

Serge Hochar regularly performs a minor red wine miracle in his war-torn Bekaa Valley vineyard. He was once prevented from making wine as the various militia shunted his grapes around until they went sour, but he has never produced a wine that was anything less than enjoyable. By blending Cinsaut and a little Syrah into a predominantly Cabernet Sauvignon wine, and ageing for a year in oak *barriques*, he manages to create something comparable to a top Bordeaux or Rhône. From good vintages, Château Musar can develop in bottle for 15 years or more.

E A S T E R N
~ E U R O P E ~

WINES ARE PRODUCED ALL over Eastern Europe, including the USSR, but so far classic wines are available only from a few countries.

Austria's wine areas are clustered together on its border with Czechoslovakia and Hungary. Some 75 per cent of the wines are white, produced from, among others, the native Grüner Veltliner grape and Riesling. Quality wine categories are comparable to those of Germany, but with higher must-weights and the extra *Ausbruch* category.

Bulgaria exports 85 per cent of its production, with Cabernet Sauvignon, Riesling and Chardonnay grapes accounting for 40 per cent of plantings, though native varieties still thrive. Their wine law defines 20 *Controliran* regions of origin.

Hungary has a range of indigenous grapes and a potential for some attractive table wines, both white and red. Its claim to fame rests entirely on its unique white dessert wine, Tokay, made from the native Furmint and Hárslevelü grapes.

AUSTRIA

BURGENLANDISCHER WINZERVERBAND RUSTER BEERENAUSLESE

The Burgenlandischer Winzerverband is a collective established in 1959. In a range of some 40 wines, the Ruster Beernauslese, typically full and fat, is considered to be one of the best.

WEINGUT ELFENHOF RUSTER TROCKENBEERENAUSLESE

This luscious *Trockenbeerenauslese* comes from the Neusiedler See, a vast and shallow lake with a unique micro-climate that induces botrytis virtually every year. Weissburgunder is one of the most important varieties at Weingut Elfenhof.

WEINGUT FEILER-ARTINGER RUSTER AUSBRUCH WEISSBURGUNDER

Ausbruch is an ancient style of wine that harks back to the days of the Austro-Hungarian Empire and is a speciality of the town of Rust. It has the super-concentrated botrytis character of a *Trockenbeerenauslese*, but with the lighter, more elegant balance of a *Beerenauslese*.

DOMÄNE BARON GEYMÜLLER RHEINRIESLING KABINETT

Baron Rudolf von Geymüller runs a 24-hectare (59-acre) vineyard in the Krems-Hollenburg area of Kamtal-Donauland. This wine comes from a small site on the Goldberg *Einzellage*. Good Austrian Rheinrieslings such as this are elegant and ripe, yet racy; other fine Rieslings come from Durnstein in the Wachau.

WINZER KREMS RHEINRIESLING SPÄTLESE

The Riesling produces Austria's most classic, but least exploited, wine. An Austrian *Spätlese* must have a much higher must-weight than the German equivalent. The greatest Riesling *Spätlesen*, produced at Krems in the Kamtal-Donauland district, are comparable to great German *Spätlesen*.

SCHLOSSWEINGUT MALTESER RITTERORDEN GRÜNER VELTLINER

The finest Grüner Veltliner wines have a fiery flavour: a style that is far removed from the bland *vin ordinaire* generally available in Austria. This 40-hectare (99-acre) estate, half planted with Grüner Veltliner, is run by the innovative winemaker, Laurenz Moser. Its wines are marketed through the firm of Lenz Moser.

WEINGUT MOORHOF BOUVIER TROCKENBEERENAUSLESE

BOUVIER
Trockenbeerenauslese
Apetlon — Neusiedler See
1983

Owned and run by Alexander Ugner, this 13-hectare (32-acre) estate grows five grape varieties (Welschriesling, Gewürztraminer, Rheinriesling, Cabernet Sauvignon and Bouvier). The Bouvier is an early-ripening variety that often reaches *Trocken-beerenauslese* level within the influence of the Neusiedler See.

SCHLUMBERGER BLANC DE BLANCS BRUT

Established in 1842 by Robert Schlum-berger, who, after working for Ruinart, took the Champagne process to Austria. The fresh, flowery and aromatic Riesling *blanc de blancs* is ideal for those who like the *sekt* style, but want something drier.

BULGARIA

SVISCHTOV CABERNET SAUVIGNON

This is the *Controliran* version of Bulgarian Cabernet Sauvignon, the minor classic from Suhindol that put this country on the wine map. Svischtov is located north of Suhindol, close to the Romanian border, and this wine can be so rich in some vintages that it smells and tastes like an essence of *cassis*.

HUNGARY - TOKAJI

Royal Tokaji, or Tokaji Essencia, was legendary. It was an elixir so prized by the Tsars of Russia that they maintained a detachment of Cossacks to escort convoys of it from Hungary to the royal cellars at St Petersburg. Tokaji owes its character to shrivelled-up, heavily botrytized Furmint and Hárslevelü grapes, which are collectively called Aszú. This rotten mass is put into a wooden tub called a *putton* for six to eight days, during which time a highly concentrated juice - pure Essencia - collects at the bottom of the container. Only a quarter of a pint of this precious liquid is yielded. After it is removed, the *putton* of Aszú is kneaded into a paste and added to a dry base wine. The base wine is kept in a 140-litre cask called a *gönc*. It is deliberately not filled up, a significant air-space being left to encourage the oxidized side of Tokaji's character. The sweetness of Tokaji Aszú depends on how many *puttonyon* (plural of *putton*) are added: a two is allowed but never made; the normal grades are three, four and five *puttonyos*, although six is sometimes produced.

ASZÚ 5 PUTTONYOS

This wine combines the sweetness of a Bual Madeira and the oxidative complexity of a *vin jaune*.

ASZÚ ESSZENCIA

Although Essencia is no longer a pure Aszú, it is the richest, sweetest and most complex Tokaji currently produced and a great wine in its own right. Its intense botrytis character does not begin to charm until 30 years old or so and will live for 100 or more.

FURMINT

Made only from the Furmint grape, this is a fiery, full-flavoured wine with a distinctive, dry, oxidative-appley character.

HÁRSLEVELÜ

Aslo a pure varietal wine, the Hárslevelü is softer and spicier than the Furmint.

MUSKOTÁLYOS ASZÚ 5 PUTTONYOS

Only occasionally encountered, this luscious, raisiny wine is one of the world's great Muscat dessert wines.

SZAMORODNI ÉDES/SWEET

Szamorodni is a non-botrytized blend of Furmint and Hárslevelü. It can be produced dry (*száraz*) or in this sweet (*édes*) version, which is effectively the basic sweet wine of the region.

~ E N G L A N D ~

THE CULTIVATION OF wine grapes in the northern hemisphere is most successful between the latitudes 30° to 50° north of the equator. The 50th parallel runs along the English Channel, leaving the British Isles beleaguered to the north of it. The emergence of a wine industry in Southern England and Wales over the past few decades is a minor miracle made possible by the Gulf Stream - perhaps now assisted by global warming.

The quality of English wines has continued to improve since the 1970s and the number of vineyards has grown to over 300. There are now about 900 hectares (2,225 acres) planted with vines, an area sufficiently large to prompt the European Community to insist on an official Vineyard Register, although only a few English vineyards are sizeable in commercial terms.

Geographic location of vineyards

The greatest concentration of English vineyards is in the south and the south-east of the country. The "Garden of England", Kent, formerly famed for its hop plantations, together with neighbouring Sussex, is the most popular location. The home counties of Surrey, Berkshire and Buckinghamshire all have vineyards, and several sites in the Thames Valley and Oxfordshire have proved successful. Hampshire (including the Isle of Wight), Dorset, Devon and Cornwall all have increasing numbers of vineyards, where there is sufficient shelter from strong winds. Other vineyards have been established in the low-lying lands of East Anglia and there are also some sizeable plantings in Somerset, Avon and Gloucestershire, as well as a few in South Wales and Hereford.

In EC terms, English wines are defined only as "table wines". With the aim of improving on this, the English Vineyards Association (EVA), issues its Seal of Quality each year to wines that have passed the double hurdle of a laboratory analysis and an organoleptic test by a panel from the Institue of Masters of Wine. The aim of English winemakers is to create high-quality wines, since it will never be possible to produce wines in bulk.

Grape varieties and style of wine

A surprisingly wide range of 50 or so grape varieties is planted, reflecting the need to discover vines that will produce better fruit and bigger yields in uncertain climatic conditions. Of the 10 most popular vine varieties, taking up 80 per cent of the planted area, the most widely grown is Müller-Thurgau. In diminishing order, the others, mainly German crossings, are Reichensteiner, Seyval Blanc, Schönburger, Bacchus, Huxelrebe, Madeleine Angevine, Pinot Noir, Kerner and Ortega. Classic varieties such as Cabernet Sauvignon, Chardonnay and Riesling, are grown, but in experimental quantities.

Since there are fewer red wine grape varieties that ripen well in a cool climate, it is hardly surprising that the majority of English wines are white. Mostly dry or medium-dry with, in the best examples, a pleasing aromatic character, English wines have developed a personality that is truly English, rather than a copy of any other country's wines. Some producers have experimented successfully with Champagne-method sparkling wine production, and a few palatable light reds and rosés are made.

BARTON MANOR

Barton Manor, in the Isle of Wight, was mentioned in the Doomsday Book. The present owners, Anthony and Alix Goddard, have produced a string of medal-winning wines. The wines are good blends and are sometimes slightly spritzy.

BIDDENDEN ROSÉ

Since the early 1980s this Kent vineyard has consistently produced some of England's finest wines, from the basic but spicy Müller-Thurgau, through its attractive Rosé, which is made exclusively from Pinot Noir, to the Ortega, its top-performing, medal-winning style.

BRUISYARD ST PETER

Ian and Eleanor Berwick own one of East Anglia's best-run vineyards. Their 4-hectare (10-acre) site is planted entirely with Müller-Thurgau and is susceptible to a small amount of "noble rot", which may account for the very fat and distinctive style of their wines.

CARR TAYLOR REICHENSTEINER

David Carr Taylor is probably the most enterprising of England's vineyard owners. He takes his Kent wines to France, where they regularly win medals, and has even promoted his wines in the top stores in Texas. The Reichensteiner is one of his most successful medium-dry Germanic-style wines and is excellent value. His range also includes more than one *méthode champenoise* sparkling wine.

CHALKHILL BACCHUS

These wines range from sweetish everyday blends, such as Special Selection, to top-quality varietals, the finest being very dry and aromatic. The winemaker is Mark Thompson, who is also consultant to the ambitious Wellow Vineyard project. He made his reputation with this seering, slightly spritzy, gooseberry-flavoured Chalkhill Bacchus.

CHILFORD HUNDRED

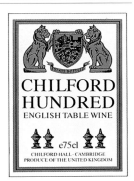

This Cambridgeshire vineyard derives its name from the royal ford where the jurors of the Hundred met in the eleventh century. Chilford Hundred's dry and medium-dry wines are made from a blend of German varieties and are of a consistently high quality.

ELMHAM PARK DRY

Situated at North Elmham in Norfolk, this is the only English Vineyard to be run by a Master of Wine and the quality of Elmham Park's attractively packaged, fresh, fragrant and elegant wine is such that owner Robin Don has even been able to sell it to French wine merchants. It has also been served at the British Embassy in Paris and in Washington.

LAMBERHURST KERNER

With more than 20 hectares (50 acres) planted in Kent, this is one of the largest and best vineyards in England. The aromatic Kerner is one of more than nine varieties grown on this estate. Winemaker Stephen Skelton, who once owned Tenterden Vineyard, also vinifies and bottles wine for up to 30 other English vineyards.

PULHAM MAGDALEN

Pulham has always sold its wines under the Magdalen label, ever since its very first vintage won the coveted Gore-Browne Trophy. From its vineyard in Diss in Norfolk, it has made a number of medal-winning wines, including an interesting Auxerrois, which tastes like crisp, smoky Chardonnay.

TENTERDEN

Lamberhurst's winemaker Stephen Skelton used to own this vineyard in Kent, and he is still retained as consultant. His Seyval Blanc drew a myriad of superlatives from wine writers when it won the Gore-Browne Trophy in 1981, since when other varieties have also proved successful.

WELLOW MEDIUM DRY

In 1985 Andy Vining purchased Wellow in Romsey, Hampshire, which has an exceptionally favourable micro-climate. Once fully in production by the mid 1990s, Vining aims to have 40 hectares (100 acres) under vine. Although it is still too early to assess the quality of the wines, Wellow stands a good chance of being not only the largest English wine producer, but one of the best too.

WOOTTON MÜLLER-THURGAU

Owned and run by Major Colin Gillespie, who has been Chairman of the English Vineyards Association since 1981, this Kent vineyard has consistently produced fresh, clean, attractive medal-winning wines, especially from Müller-Thurgau, Schönburger and Seyval Blanc grapes.

~ N O R T H ~
A M E R I C A

THE AREAS IN NORTH AMERICA that are suitable for winegrowing range from the Canadian vineyards in British Columbia and Ontario (the northernmost of which lie along the 50th parallel North) to those of Mexico (as far south as latitude 25° North). In between, there are 40 wine-producing states, the most important being California.

The principal style of winemaking for quality wines in North America is based on the modern concept of the *varietal*, a wine made from a single grape variety and sold under the grape name. The idea was originally encouraged in California by the late Frank Schoonmaker and has since been widely adopted elsewhere across the world.

Canada

The two grape-growing provinces of Canada, British Columbia and Ontario, are separated from one another by over 3,000 kilometres (1,860 miles) and a range of mountains. Over 90 per cent of Canadian wine comes from the Ontario vineyards that are clustered around the Niagara Falls. The grapes grown in British Columbia, on the other side of the Rocky Mountains, come from the Okanogan Valley, 200 kilometres (125 miles) east of Vancouver. *Labrusca*, French-hybrid and *vinifera* varieties are all grown.

The United States

The wines of the United States today present themselves as rivals to the best of Europe. They are in fact relative newcomers to the world scene, despite a history going back 400 years. The modern style of American wines has only been developed since the repeal of Prohibition in 1933 and the country's recovery from the effects of the Second World War. Many of the leading wineries in California are the products of private investment and enthusiasm in the 1960s and later, either through the acquisition and planting of entirely new sites or the resuscitation of earlier enterprises that had fallen on hard times.

In California and in the states of Washington, Oregon and Idaho (bracketed together as the Pacific Northwest), the industry is firmly based on classic European *vitis vinifera* vines. Cabernet Sauvignon, Chardonnay, Sauvignon Blanc and Rhine Riesling, among others, all flourish there in the welcoming climates and congenial soil conditions. Varieties of the native grape of North America, *vitis labrusca*, are still widely grown in many of the other states of the Union, although the strong, exotic flavour of its wines, described as "foxy", is not popular outside its areas of origin. The *vitis vinifera* (or in the north eastern states an occasional French-American hybrid vine) is used in preference to the indigenous *labrusca* vine for all wines of international standing.

Mexico

Although it pre-dates any other on the North American continent, the modern Mexican wine industry has been developed only since the mid-1950s. The most important areas are in the north; there are wineries near Mexico City, but they depend on grapes and wines produced further north. Most of the output is of grapes for the table, or to supply the country's brandy industry.

The introduction of European grapes

The European *vitis vinifera* vine was first introduced to the Americas in the form of the Mission grape by the Spanish conquerors of Mexico. They were commanded by the fabled Hernando Cortés who became its first Governor at the beginning of the sixteenth century. From Mexico, cuttings were subsequently taken to California by the Franciscan missionaries nearly 200 years later, and are popularly thought to have been planted in San Diego, just north of what is now the Mexican border, in the first of a chain of mission stations that spread northwards along the Californian coast, taking the Mission grape with it. (California at that stage was still part of Mexico.)

Developments in the US wine industry

By the time California seceded from Mexico to join the United States in 1848, winegrowing on a commercial scale with *vinifera* grapes had begun in southern California. One of the more significant initiatives of the period was that of Jean Louis Vignes, a Frenchman who established, with vines from his home country, a 162-hectare (400-acre) vineyard in Los Angeles, and extended his trade as far north as the Central Coast area of Monterey.

Further north, the influx of population to San Francisco, brought about by the 1849 gold rush, was followed by financial encouragement from the state to plant new vineyards, and the introduction of fresh *vinifera* varieties from France and

Germany. This led to a rapid expansion of the California vineyard area, with the result that by 1870 California had taken its place as the leading winegrowing state in the Union. This was the period during which the remarkable Hungarian immigrant, Agoston Haraszthy, had such a brief and seminal influence on Californian winegrowing. Appointed by the Governor of California to carry out a study of winegrowing methods in Europe, he is credited with bringing back with him 100,000 cuttings of 300 different vine varieties.

Meanwhile, winegrowing in other states of the Union continued to be based on native *labrusca* plantings. French Huguenots had made wine in Florida from the native Scuppernong grape as early as 1562. Many subsequent attempts had

California

Pacific Northwest

Canadian wine-producing regions

Other wine-producing regions

High quality North America is now one of the world's top wine producers, in quality as well as quantity. At least 40 states of the US produce wines, although only a few are made from vinifera vines. It is the west coast that produces by far the most important quality wines. Canada also has a small but growing wine industry.

SIMI
Since 1876

1935
SONOMA
ZINFANDEL

ALCOHOL 12½ % BY VOLUME

PRODUCED AND BOTTLED BY
SIMI WINERY, INC.
HEALDSBURG, SONOMA CO., CAL.

Post-Probibition *Maintaining a long tradition, the Californian Simi winery still produce high quality wines today.*

been made in the East and Midwest to plant European varieties, but these failed through cold winters or vine pests (a foretaste of phylloxera which later ravaged vineyards in northern California between 1873 and 1900). The cultivation of *labrusca* grapes on a commercial scale was happening in Pennsylvania by the turn of the nineteenth century, and spread to Washington DC, South Carolina, New York, Massachusetts and Missouri in the next 50 years.

Phylloxera and Prohibition

By 1890, California with the Atlantic Northeast States of New York, Ohio, Missouri and New Jersey were leading winegrowing states with products considered capable of competing internationally with European wines. This emerging industry was all but ruined by Prohibition, coming as it did in the wake of phylloxera and succeeded shortly afterwards by American involvement in the Second World War. The conclusion of hostilities, however, brought with it a renewed interest

among Americans in better quality wines, because Americans fighting in Europe had been introduced to European wine there, and had developed a taste for it. By the 1960s, extensive new plantings had begun to take place in California, fuelled in the 1970s by the phenomenon of "boutique wineries" - small-scale undertakings in the Napa and Sonoma Valleys and elsewhere by enthusiastic individuals from other walks of life, more often than not with the most spectacular results. By the middle 1970s new-style, high quality, California "premium" wines began to appear in international markets.

Rivals in the Pacific Northwest

California has now achieved such a dominant position in the US as a wine producer, that it is difficult to imagine it ever being seriously challenged. Some 90 per cent of the wine made in the US is made in California. California's historical concentration on *vinifera* grapes, when other states have persevered with *labrusca* varieties, coupled with its superb climate, has given it a commanding lead over Eastern and Midwest states. Any challenge to it comes in terms of quality rather than quantity from the Pacific Northwest states of Washington, Oregon and Idaho.

The second largest *vitis vinifera* and, therefore quality, wine-producing region of the US is Washington State, a recent upstart with a mere six per cent of California's vineyard area but second only to California in its output of quality *vinifera* wines. Washington has a potential area suitable for winegrowing that is thought to be about 15 times that presently in use - an area that would be three times the size of Napa and Sonoma.

Most of Washington's vineyards lie to the east of the Cascade Mountains, which shield them from the worst of the heavy rains carried in from the Pacific Ocean. These vineyards are dry to the point of being arid, despite Washington's reputation for being a wet state. Annual rainfall to the

HEAT-SUMMATION SYSTEM

Devised by the University of California at Davis, this is a system of dividing climates into zones by calculating the mean temperature over the growing period (1 April - 31 October) and adding up the number of degrees each day over 50° Fahrenheit. Devised early in the development of

US viticulture, this pioneering work was used to help growers setting up in California, where climate varies widely, to plant grape varieties suitable to their particular climate. The system, though only an approximate guide, is still used widely throughout America and elsewhere.

REGION	NUMBER OF DEGREE DAYS	EQUIVALENT WINE REGIONS	SUITABLE GRAPE VARIETIES
I	2,500 or less	Germany; Champagne; Burgundy	Pinot Noir; Chardonnay; Rhine Riesling; Cabernet Sauvignon; Sauvignon Blanc
II	2,501 - 3,000	Bordeaux; Piedmont	Grapes as above
III	3,001 - 3,500	Tuscany; Rhône Valley	Sauvignon Blanc; Sémillon; Zinfandel; Syrah; Chenin Blanc
IV	3,501 - 4,000	S. Spain; parts of Cape S. Africa	Carignan; Touriga; Barbera; Muscat; Palomino
V	4,000 or more	N. Africa	Cinsault; Sousão; Grenache; Verdelho

east of the mountains is only 18-20 cm (7-8 inches) a year. This situation is compensated by the large-scale irrigation system in the Yakima Valley.

Vinifera vines were planted in Oregon during the nineteenth century, but languished during Prohibition, and a fresh start had to be made in the 1960s, spearheaded by viticultural graduates of the University of California at Davis. Since then, the number of vineyards has multiplied. Most are relatively small, family-run concerns.

The Atlantic Northeast

On the Atlantic Northeast coast, it was not so long ago that New York State vied for the title of being second to California in output. The output was based to a large extent on *labrusca* varieties, but with increasing use of French-American hybrids - the crossing of *vitis vinifera* with native American species - and the occasional intrusion of individual growers who have achieved a reputation for some fine quality *vinifera* wines.

Approved viticultural areas

Consumers of American wines both at home and abroad have become accustomed to selecting them, rather as they might a claret from Bordeaux, on the strength of the fame of an individual maker, like Robert Mondavi or Heitz or, failing that, a reliance on the general reputation of a growing area such as Napa or Sonoma in California, or Finger Lakes in New York State. Behind those individuals and areas, however, there is a body of American wine law, administered by the Bureau of Alcohol, Tobacco and Firearms (BATF), which is changing shape as time goes on.

American appellation system

The American system of appellation starts with a country-wide category for wines of table wine level. In general, when an appellation appears on a label, 75 per cent of the wine must come from grapes grown in that region. The same applies for each state appellation and each county within the state. Complication sets in with the provision for multi-state appellations in which wine from any two or three contiguous states can be blended and bottled. Since 1978, the BATF has been seeking greater clarification by designating areas within each of the states as Approved Viticultural Areas (AVAs). The intention is to establish precise geographical boundaries for areas that have distinctive viticultural features and have already won a measure of recognition at home or abroad. The number of AVAs designated now approaches 100, but their effectiveness has still to be seen. To the extent that differences in geography, climate and soil will create for the wines of each area their own characteristics, the AVAs will prove a valuable

step forward. The fact that some quite famous areas are already included in the list of AVAs (as well as some anomalous omissions) does not as yet help the consumer, since there is no provision for the term AVA to be declared on the label. The obvious follow-up is to establish specific vineyard appellations within the viticultural areas: an idea that has already been mooted in California.

NORTH AMERICAN VINTAGES

YEAR	CALIFORNIA	PACIFIC NORTH-WEST
1989	Rain during harvest spoilt promising vintage; Pinot Noir and Chardonnay did better than others	Washington: record harvest of superb quality; Oregon: average size, very good quality
1988	Another small, troublesome vintage of average quality, except for Chardonnay which did better	Washington: very fine vintage, already showing great complexity; Oregon: good, but uneven
1987	Smallest harvest for five years produced high quality and intensely flavoured red and white wines	Washington: excellent whites, even finer, dense reds; Oregon: small crop, clean fruit
1986	A successful, fine vintage for both reds and whites	Washington: a better year for whites; reds soft and luscious; Oregon: large crop of very good quality
1985	Vintage of the decade with rich, balanced whites, and powerful reds	Washington: very good, complex reds, very good whites; Oregon: excellent
1984	Undue heat caused harvest of mixed quality for whites, full-bodied Cabernet Sauvignons and poor Pinot Noir	Washington: light, uneven whites, medium to full-bodied reds; Oregon: disappointing and short-lived
1983	Warm, damp year with rain at harvest time gave unremarkable wines of mixed quality	Washington: record harvest, whites medium-bodied, complex reds; Oregon: great vintage
1982	Big harvest, generally producing medium quality, fairly short-lived wines	Washington: average whites, better reds, complex Cabernets; Oregon: huge harvest, good but light
1981	Short, hot growing season produced small yield. Good early-picked whites, with unspectacular, short-lived reds	Washington: good whites, reds very closed and slow to emerge; Oregon: tiny harvest, disappointing

CALIFORNIA

THE KEY FACTOR FOR winegrowers in California is climate. Soil conditions, and the suitability of one grape variety rather than another in a particular area, have not in the past been regarded as important as climate, although this may change as the concept of Approved Viticultural Areas (AVAs - see page 281) develops.

Mendocino

Although Mendocino lies to the north of the Napa and Sonoma Valleys and is the most northerly of the California wine areas, the coastal range protects the vineyards providing a warm, dry climate, with some parts too hot even for fine wine production. The largest quality area, around Ukiah on the upper reaches of the Russian River, is climatic Region III, according to the heat-summation scale of the University of California at Davis (see page 280), as are the Redwood and Potter Valley areas, immediately to the north of it. Fetzer and Parducci are among the better-known vineyards. Nearer the coast is the up-and-coming, Anderson Valley AVA, in climatic Region I, where the Champagne house of Roederer has established its base for North American sparkling wine.

Sonoma

Sonoma had a slight headstart on Napa as a wine region, but has taken longer to establish itself as a source of quality wines. It now has a string of outstanding wineries, among them Chateau St Jean, Clos du Bois, Dry Creek, Iron Horse, Jordan, Kenwood and Simi. The influence of the Pacific, and the geographical structure of the county with its three main valleys - Alexander, Sonoma and Dry Creek - create a pattern of micro-climates that vary between heat-summation Regions I, II and III. The warmest tend to be in the north of the county and the coolest in the south. Sonoma lies on the ocean side of the Mayacamas Mountains, and this creates a cooling effect in the more westerly Russian River and Dry Creek Valleys. Varietal wines are made from a range of grapes that includes Cabernet Sauvignon, Chardonnay, Chenin Blanc, Gewürztraminer, Merlot, Petite Sirah, Pinot Noir, Pinot Blanc, Sauvignon Blanc, Rhine Riesling and Zinfandel.

Napa Valley

Smaller than its competitor Sonoma in size, Napa still retains its world-wide prestige as California's (and thus America's) leading fine wine region. The Napa Valley is situated 80 kilometres (50 miles) north-east of San Francisco. The vineyard area is 40 kilometres (25 miles) long and is sheltered on both the east and west sides by mountains. The route from Napa at the southern end of the Valley, through Yountville, Oakville, Rutherford and St Helena to Calistoga, is peppered with famous, and up-and-coming, names (some 150 in all). At the heart of the area, Region II on the heat-summation scale, is the so-called Rutherford Bench where Cabernet Sauvignon prospers and a clutch of famous names is gathered - Heitz (at St Helena), Beaulieu (at Rutherford), Mondavi (at Oakville) and Joseph Phelps (at St Helena). The heat-summation scale indicates the northern end of the valley as the warmer Region III (more suitable for Zinfandel and Petite Sirah) and the southern end as the cooler Region I (an area for Chardonnay and Pinot Noir).

Climatic anomalies

Generalizations can be misleading because there are individual micro-climates throughout the valley that differ from the surrounding area. This curious climatic anomoly is due to coastal fogs coming in from the Pacific. As the entries in the following pages indicate, Cabernet Sauvignon and Chardonnay are successfully grown in suitable micro-climates all over the region, and Riesling and Gewürztraminer (cool-climate varieties) are produced by Stony Hill Vineyard in Region III just south of Calistoga. In the Region I vineyards of Carneros, cooler conditions caused by offshore breezes and sea mists from San Francisco Bay are suited to the growth of Chardonnay and Pinot Noir, as the reputations of Acacia, Carneros Creek and Saintsbury wineries testify.

North-Central and South-Central Coasts

The winegrowing regions hugging the coastline from San Francisco southwards to Monterey, taking in Livermore Valley, Santa Clara and Santa Cruz, are bracketed as North-Central coast, and the newer areas occupied by small estate wineries in San Luis Obispo and Santa Barbara as South-Central. Livermore, Santa Clara and Monterey support large-scale producers, some old-established like Almaden and Paul Masson (1852), as well as more recent ones, such as Taylors Californian Cellars (1979). At the same time they are also host to a number of small wineries which are devoted to the highest standards of winemaking. Smaller-scale enterprises are also established in the South-Central counties of San Luis Obispo (with its up-and-coming areas of Paso Robles and Edna Valley) and in Santa Barbara (the Santa Ynez Valley). In the main, through the moderating influence of the Pacific, cool micro-climates favour the Burgundian varieties of Chardonnay and Pinot Noir, but fine examples are also produced of Cabernet Sauvignon, Zinfandel, Sauvignon Blanc and Rhine Riesling. Heat-summation zones range from Region I to Region III in these two areas.

Sierra Foothills

The Sierra Nevada mountains flank California's great Central Valley to the east and separate California from the state of Nevada. The vineyards that are established in the Sierra Foothills could not be more different in style from the giant installations producing enormous quantities of everyday wines in the Central Valley. The counties of El Dorado and its three neighbours, Placer, Amador and Calaveras, were the locations of California's gold-rush in the mid-nineteenth century. Sites suitable for small winegrowing estates in the Foothills were vacated at the time of Prohibition, but since the 1970s there has been a renewed rush to open up wineries there. In contrast to the bulk wines of the Central Valley, the wines produced in the Foothills are extremely high quality, premium varietals, particularly from Zinfandel and Sauvignon Blanc, but also from Chardonnay, Cabernet Sauvignon and Muscat.

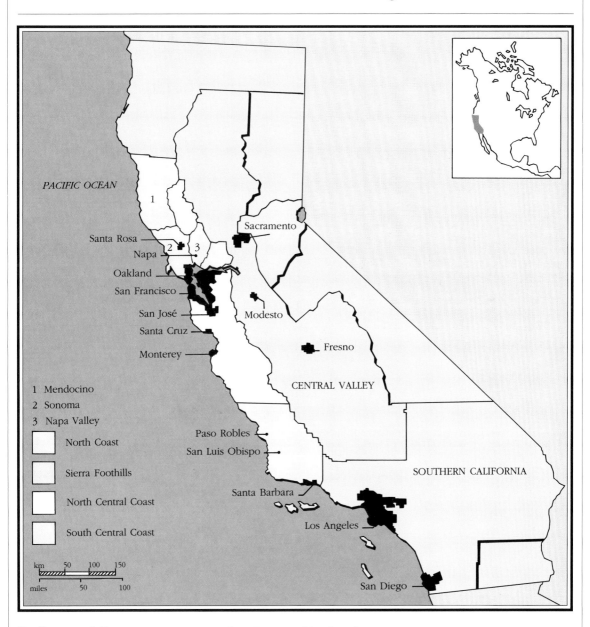

Quality control Temperature variation across California is tremendous: in some places, such as southern Sonoma, it is as cool as northern Europe and in others, for example Central Valley, it is as hot as North Africa. Higher quality wines are produced in the areas that are cooled by sea and bay winds and the great coastal fog bank. The very hot Central Valley produces the majority of California's table wine.

MENDOCINO

FETZER VINEYARDS

Barrel Select Chardonnay

Special Reserve Zinfandel

This family firm, established in 1968, has built up a reputation for exceptional value-for-money wines. It is best known for Cabernet Sauvignon, Zinfandel and Chardonnay. Most of the latter are not oaked, but they have a purity and intensity of fruit; it is this that dominates the toasty richness of the Barrel Select oak-matured Chardonnay. The Special Reserve Zinfandel is opaque, fat and fruity, and requires five years to mature.

HUSCH

Anderson Valley Gewürztraminer

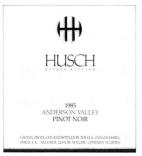

Anderson Valley Pinot Noir

Tony Husch built this winery near Philo in 1971, three years after he had planted a vineyard in the Anderson Valley. In 1979 Husch sold out to Hugo Oswald, the owner of a winery and vineyard in the Ukiah Valley, who combined the properties and set about winning a string of medals. Two of the most successful are the Gewürztraminer and Pinot Noir illustrated here. They have a fine, if restrained, style and come from the original Anderson Valley property.

JEPSON VINEYARDS

Vintage Reserve Chardonnay

Sauvignon Blanc

Situated just outside Ukiah and originally called the William Baccala Estate, this vineyard produces excellent Chardonnay, a reputation maintained under the Jepson label, whose first vintage was 1985. The Vintage Reserve Chardonnay has a deep, full flavour and excellent acid balance; while the soft, seductive Sauvignon Blanc has a fine varietal character.

McDOWELL VALLEY VINEYARDS

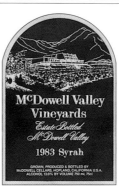

Syrah

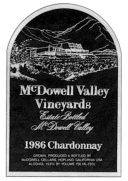

Chardonnay

It was the wines of the McDowell Valley estate, an ambitious enterprise owned and managed by Richard and Karen Keehn, that gave birth to the McDowell Valley AVA. Twelve different varieties of grape produce a large range of high-quality wines. By far the best is the Syrah, a big, rich, full-flavoured wine with ripe fruit and oaky-pimento complexity. The Chardonnay is less consistent, but when it is successful (1987, for example), its fine tangy acidity is backed up by bright, ripe, pineapple flavours.

MILANO WINERY

Chardonnay

Although this winery's vineyards go back to the turn of the century, the first wine launched under the Milano label was from the 1977 vintage. Of Milano's many interesting, well-flavoured wines, it has been the earliest vintages of Chardonnay that have turned out to be the best value.

NAVARRO VINEYARDS

Chardonnay

Edward Bennet and Deborah Cahn established this vineyard, just north of Philo, in 1975. Of the various wines which they make here, it is the whites that are notably excellent, particularly Gewürztraminer. Navarro Chardonnay has gone from good to great, the turning point being the 1986 vintage, which has lots of rich, ripe, luscious fruit, deftly underpinned with creamy-toasty oak.

PARSONS CREEK WINERY

Brut Reserve

Carneros Chardonnay

Founded at Ukiah in 1979, this up-and-coming winery has no vineyards, but owner and winemaker Jesse Tidwell produces some of the best wines in the area. His Brut Reserve is a fine *méthode champenoise* with a good acidity balance and some evidence of autolytic character on the finish. The Chardonnay is from the Sonoma section of the Carneros AVA. It is an oak-matured wine with plenty of butterscotch and cinnamon fruit.

ROEDERER ESTATE

Anderson Valley Brut

The French Champagne house of Louis Roederer sunk $15 million into 200 hectares (500 acres) of prime vineyards in the Anderson Valley, then sunk the winery into the ground to keep the wines cool with minimum air-conditioning. There is no mistaking the ripeness of fruit in the Brut Sparkling Wine, but its resemblance to the real thing is one of the closest in any California wine.

SONOMA

BELLEROSE VINEYARD

Cuvée Bellerose

This small winery on the West Dry Creek Road, Healdsburg, has built a reputation on its Cuvée Bellerose, a Bordeaux-type blend of (mostly) Cabernet Sauvignon, with Cabernet Franc, Merlot, Petit Verdot and Malbec. Excellent Merlot and Sauvignon Blanc varietals are also produced.

BELVEDERE WINERY

Russian River Valley Chardonnay Reserve

Discovery Cabernet Sauvignon

This winery specializes in producing single-vineyard wines from bought-in grapes. Of particular note is its Cabernet Sauvignon from the Robert Young vineyard in Sonoma. Belvedere produces a big, oaky Chardonnay with lots of butterscotch fruit from the Russian River Valley and a lighter, more exotic version from Carneros, but is generally less consistent with this grape. Basic wines of good quality are sold under its Discovery Series label.

CARMENET VINEYARD

Cabernet Sauvignon/Merlot/ Cabernet Franc

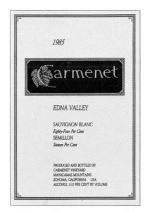

Edna Valley Sauvignon Blanc/ Semillon

This Bordeaux-influenced operation is the brilliant offspring of the Burgundy-oriented Chalone Vineyard. The red blend is simply sensational. True to Bordeaux traditions, each vintage is different and yet, as befits a great *cru classé*, it consistently ranks as one of the finest California wines produced. The white blend is wonderfully rich and fruity and would shame all but the best Graves.

CHATEAU ST JEAN

*Alexander Valley Chardonnay
Robert Young Vineyards*

Russian River Valley Fumé Blanc

All wines here are high-quality, but the Robert Young Vineyards Chardonnay has to be singled out for its distinctive style and finesse. The Fumé Blanc La Petite Etoile from the Russian River Valley has been a tremendous success, combining intense varietal flavour with depth and style.

CLOS DU BOIS WINERY

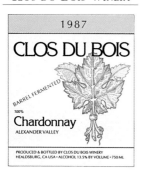

*Barrel Fermented Chardonnay
Alexander Valley*

Merlot

With more than 400 hectares (1,000 acres) of vineyards and more medals than any other Californian winery, Clos du Bois produces a vast quantity of truly impressive quality wine. The Barrel Fermented Chardonnay from the Alexander Valley is rich, oaky and reliable, but it is the two single-vineyard versions of this grape, Calcaire and Flintwood, that are the most fascinating, particularly the latter. The juicy, flavoured Merlot benefits from a good proportion of Cabernet Sauvignon.

B.R. COHN

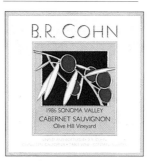

*Cabernet Sauvignon
Olive Hill Vineyard*

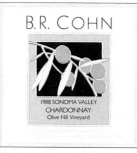

Chardonnay Olive Hill Vineyard

This tiny winery produces stunning wines that were initially underpriced. These wines offer the rare combination of hedonistic pleasure and profound complexity. The Cabernet Sauvignon Olive Hill Vineyard is rich and ripe, with voluptuous fruit and a dazzling toasty-oak complexity. The Chardonnay Olive Hill Vineyard is beautifully balanced and packed with buttery, creamy Chardonnay flavour.

DEHLINGER WINERY

*Cabernet Sauvignon
Russian River Valley*

Chardonnay Russian River Valley

This small winery was established by Tom Dehlinger at Sebastopol in 1976. Since that time he has managed to produce a consistent stream of high-quality wines that show both true finesse and excellent style. The Cabernet Sauvignon displays extraordinary elegance for a wine of such weight and intensity. The Chardonnay Russian River Valley is utterly beguiling. It brims with ripe, seductive, buttery fruit, yet is totally perplexing in its nutty-butterscotch, honeyed-toffee complexity.

DE LOACH VINEYARDS

*Russian River Valley
Chardonnay O.F.S.*

Russian River Valley Fumé Blanc

When Cecil and Christine De Loach set up this winery in the late 1970s, they hit gold with their big, rich Zinfandel. The winery is best known today for its rich, buttery, lemony Chardonnay. The O.F.S. Chardonnay is something special; an intriguing wine that is so complex it is almost possible to taste any exotic fruit suggested. The Fumé Blanc is as aristocratic a rendition of the Sauvignon Blanc as California can produce.

DRY CREEK VINEYARD

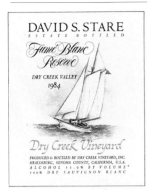

David S. Stare Fumé Blanc Reserve

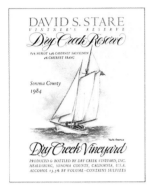

David S. Stare Dry Creek Reserve

It is nothing short of amazing that the David S. Stare Fumé Blanc Reserve can represent no less than two-thirds of Dry Creek's formidable 60,000 case production and yet consistently rank as one of the best and most serious Sauvignon Blancs produced in California. The other top wine here is the David S. Stare Dry Creek Reserve, a Merlot-dominated blend of Bordeaux grapes that is fat and juicy, with a touch of pimento complexity.

FIELD STONE WINERY

Petite Sirah Alexander Valley

Late Harvest Johannisberg Riesling Alexander Valley

This winery was established at Healdsburg in 1977 by the late Wallace Johnson. It remains a family-run affair that continues to produce some first-rate wines. The Petite Sirah is, of course, no relation to the great Syrah of the Rhône, but is from Field Stone's Alexander Valley vineyard; this variety can produce a deep-coloured, intensely flavoured wine with enough rich curranty-spicy fruit to shame many a Cornas. The Late Harvest Johannisberg Riesling is elegantly ripe and succulently sweet, with intriguing nuances of peach, pineapple and pear.

GRAND CRU VINEYARDS

Alexander Valley Gewürztraminer

Collector's Reserve Alexander Valley Cabernet Sauvignon

This was established in 1970 on the site of the original pre-Prohibition winery La Moine. Its sole aim was to sell only Zinfandel in a multiplicity of styles, but when the Zinfandel boom faded, the variety was dug up and others planted. The vineyard and winery were subsequently sold and it is the current owners, Walt and Bettina Dreyer, who built up Grand

Cru's reputation. They achieved this, for the most part, through their Gewürztraminer, which is a slightly sweet wine, crisply balanced with concentrated, rich, ripe fruit. The Cabernet Sauvignon has a deft balance and is made for elegance rather than power.

GUNDLACH BUNDSCHU WINERY

Rhinefarm Vineyards Gewürztraminer

Rhinefarm Vineyards Cabernet Sauvignon

The best wines of this high-quality winery come from the 45-hectare (110-acre) estate called Rhinefarm Vineyards. The Gewürztraminer is highly thought of, but it is the Cabernet Sauvignon that is Gundlach Bundschu's best and most consistent wine. This has a deep, dark colour and is full of fat, intense, juicy flavours and rich toasty-oak complexity.

HACIENDA WINERY

Chardonnay Clair de Lune

Hacienda Winery CONTD

Selected Reserve Cabernet Sauvignon

When Frank Bartholomew sold Argoston Harazthy's Buena Vista winery in 1973, he kept this part of the original property called Hacienda, which he later sold to Crawford Cooley, the current owner. The crisp, clean and elegantly under-stated Chardonnay Claire de Lune is the finest of Hacienda's wines, although it is building a reputation for its Cabernet Sauvignon Selected Reserve.

HANZELL VINEYARDS

Chardonnay

Pinot Noir

This highly individual winery was a trend-setter in the 1950s, when it began to produce big, buttery, barrel-fermented Chardonnay with lots of oaky-complexity. This grape still makes Hanzell's finest wines today. The Pinot Noir is a serious wine made to last. It does not have the immediate appeal expected from this variety, but it does have finesse and shows best with food.

IRON HORSE VINEYARDS

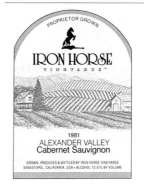

Alexander Valley Cabernet Sauvignon

Brut

This winery produces one of the world's great sparkling wines. Iron Horse also produces a still Chardonnay that can be recommended and Cabernet Sauvignon that is better still. However, it is the finesse, balance and autolytic elegance of its *méthode champenoise* that makes this winery so important: from the excellence of its Brut, which is the winery's basic vintage product, through the complexity of its Late Disgorged wines, to its recent introduction, the succulent, soft-fruit delights of the Brut Rosé.

JORDAN VINEYARD & WINERY

Cabernet Sauvignon Alexander Valley

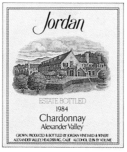

Chardonnay Alexander Valley

Since this spectacular winery was established in the mid-1970s, it has become as famous for its architecture as it has for the wine it produces. The soft, stylish and deeply flavoured Cabernet Sauvignon gained almost instant admiration from the day its first vintage, 1976, was released, but the Chardonnay also has its admirers.

KENWOOD VINEYARDS

Cabernet Sauvignon

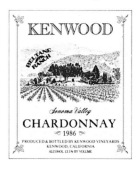

Beltane Ranch Chardonnay

This winery, originally built in 1905, was purchased in 1970 by Martin and Michael Lee, who built its reputation for making a concentrated style of wine. Cabernet Sauvignon is Kenwood's top varietal and its plummy-curranty richness is well integrated with spicy-oak complexity, especially in its Artist Series selection. Of the Chardonnays, which have great attack, it is the Beltane Ranch that has achieved the greatest reputation.

KISTLER VINEYARDS

Dutton Ranch Chardonnay
Russian River Valley

*Kistler Estate Vineyard
Cabernet Sauvignon*

Established in the late-1970s by Stephen Kistler and Mark Bixler, this rapidly improving winery has 16 hectares (40 acres) of mountainside vineyards. Many famous California wineries would be proud of even the poorest Kistler wines. The Dutton Ranch Chardonnay, from the Russian River Valley, is a wine of great finesse: rich, full and complex, with layer after layer of toasty-oaky fruit. The Kistler Estate Vineyard from Sonoma Valley produces a Chardonnay with more obvious, but lush and seductive fruit, as well as a truly tremendous Cabernet Sauvignon.

LAUREL GLEN VINEYARD

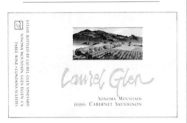

*Sonoma Mountain
Cabernet Sauvignon*

Laurel Glen is another mountainside location with an impressive reputation. From its 15 hectares (35 acres) of Sonoma Mountain AVA vines, owner and winemaker Patrick Campbell produces one of the county's most succulent and beautifully balanced Cabernet Sauvignons. Well-coloured and deliciously ripe, it has excellent natural acidity and ages gracefully.

LYETH ESTATE

Alexander Valley Table Wine

Alexander Valley Red Wine

One of California's most exciting new wineries, Lyeth Estate concentrates on producing red and white wines that are typical Bordeaux blends. The white wine is a delicious and classy blend of 80 per cent Sauvignon and 20 per cent Sémillon that falls between the best new-wave Graves and Daumas-Gassac. The red wine is an elegantly soft and juicy blend that is dominated by the Cabernet Sauvignon, but that is also full of velvety Merlot flavours.

LYTTON SPRINGS WINERY

Zinfandel Private Reserve

Situated between the Alexander and Dry Creek Valleys, Lytton Springs was established as recently as 1976, yet probably has the greatest reputation for the big, old-fashioned style of Zinfandel of any winery in California. Since the end of the Zinfandel boom, Lytton Springs has begun to produce Sauvignon Blanc and Chardonnay, but it continues to make Zinfandel in its original, blockbusting style.

MATANZAS CREEK WINERY

Merlot

Sauvignon Blanc

They say that the British turned first growth Château Latour into a dairy when they installed stainless-steel vats. Bill and Sandra MacIver turned a dairy into one of Sonoma's first growths. They began in 1978, producing overblown wines of unpretentious quality, but since 1985 there has been a new winery and, with it, a new winemaker, David Ramey (a former Simi winemaker). Ramey has proved to be particularly adept at producing fine, rich, wines with superb fruit-acidity balance, and this has transformed the rustic renditions of Matanzas formative years into the great growths of today. The Merlot has creamy fruit and displays astonishing finesse, while the Sauvignon Blanc is the epitome of elegance.

MILL CREEK VINEYARDS

Dry Creek Valley Chardonnay

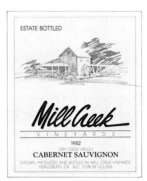

Dry Creek Valley Cabernet Sauvignon

Mill Creek Vineyards CONTD

Mill Creek's Chardonnay is exquisitely balanced, made from hand-harvest grapes that are crushed and macerated prior to fermentation, initially in stainless-steel, but ending up in small French oak barrels, which contribute to the creamy, toasty-oaky complexity of the wine. The Cabernet Sauvignon has some oaky-complexity, but is more forward in style.

PIPER SONOMA

Brut

Tête de Cuvée

Piper Sonoma is a wholly-owned subsidiary of Piper Heidsieck. Although these wines have unmistakably non-Champagne flavours that hint of spices and exotic fruits, the malotartaric balance and the autolytic character are consistent with the real thing, so the wine needs time to develop in the bottle. The Vintage 1985 Brut, for example, will not begin to fill out until 1993. On the other hand, the Tête de Cuvée lags one or more vintages behind and should be ready when it is sold.

RAVENSWOOD

Zinfandel

Joel Peterson is the master when it comes to Zinfandel. His basic Sonoma County Zinfandel is packed with rich, ripe, berry-like fruit: a wine of great concentration and character. The Old Hill Vineyard is a massive monster and the Dickerson Vineyard a textbook lesson in how to combine size with finesse. Ravenswood produces other excellent wines, including a stunning Merlot.

ST FRANCIS WINERY

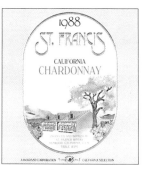

Chardonnay

Merlot

This winery was built in 1979, six years after Joe Martin had purchased the 40-hectare (100-acre) property on which it stands. The reputation of his vineyard was such that winemakers were willing to pay a substantial premium for his grapes. This gave Martin the confidence to build his own winery. The entire St Francis range can be recommended, but the giants are its Chardonnay and Merlot.

SIMI WINERY

Chardonnay

Reserve Cabernet Sauvignon Alexander Valley

Founded by Giusepe and Pietro Simi in 1876, this winery was originally called Montepulciano, after the brothers' hometown in Italy. It was not until almost a century later that this winery began to establish its reputation under the auspices of Mary Ann Graf (who was America's first female qualified oenologist), and more recently Zelma Long. Considering the huge size of Simi's production, Long produces some stunning wines, especially her power-packed, ripe, toasty-oaky Chardonnays. The Rosé of Cabernet Sauvignon is a delicious, quaffing wine; even more special is the complex, oaky Cabernet Sauvignon Reserve, which over a recent number of years has progressed from strength to strength.

SONOMA-CUTRER VINEYARDS

Chardonnay Cutrer Vineyard

Chardonnay Les Pierres Vineyard

Brice Jones established Sonoma-Cutrer vineyards in 1981, building with it one of California's most technically advanced wineries to specialize exclusively in the production of Chardonnay wines. Perfectionist Bill Bonetti is the winemaker, and his three Chardonnays are totally different, yet individually stunning.

The basic wine, if such a thing exists at Sonoma-Cutrer, is the Russian River Ranches, which is an exotic and exuberant, fruity blend from three properties. The greatest wines are, however, the toasty rich Cutrer Vineyard and silky, elegant Les Pierres Vineyard.

TRENTADUE WINERY

Petite Sirah

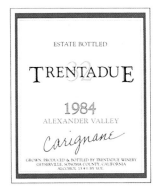

Alexander Valley Carignane

Leo Trentadue owned a vineyard in the Santa Cruz Mountains in the early 1960s, but moved to Geyserville in 1969 and planted this 81-hectare (200-acre) vineyard in the Alexander Valley. He produces a characterful selection of varietal wines that are rarely, if ever, filtered. The Petite Sirah is dark, fat and plummy, while the Carignane has higher acidity and requires several years more bottle-age to mellow.

WILLIAM WHEELER

Dry Creek Valley Cabernet Sauvignon

William Wheeler produces some fine wines from his 71 hectares (175 acres) of Dry Creek Valley vineyards. He is capable of producing a rich, fiery and yet, soft and buttery Chardonnay, but it is his big Cabernet Sauvignon that has made Wheeler's name, although some vintages can be dogged by a vegetal character.

NAPA

ACACIA WINERY

Pinot Noir Carneros Iund Vineyard

Chardonnay Carneros Marina Vineyard

This winery was established in the Carneros district in 1979 and produces fine Chardonnay and Pinot Noir wines. The Carneros Pinot Noir is a light-bodied, cherry flavoured wine for early drinking; the single-vineyard selections (Iund, St Clair and Madonna) are more complex, with a smoky-spicy elegance. The Marina Vineyard Chardonnay has well-focused varietal flavour and a good balance between oak and acidity.

BEAULIEU VINEYARD

Georges de Latour Private Reserve Cabernet Sauvignon

Dry Sauvignon Blanc

This once-great winery came to prominence as the centre of Californian innovation under the legendary André Tchelistcheff. It still maintains the highest standards for its highly prized, utterly Californian Georges de Latour Private Reserve Cabernet Sauvignon. Recent vintages of the Dry Sauvignon Blanc have shown a rare class for this grape.

BERINGER

Private Reserve Chardonnay

Private Reserve Cabernet Sauvignon

Founded in 1881, this is one of the oldest wineries in the Napa Valley, but was in a depressed state when purchased by the Nestlé company in 1970. Since then production has soared to almost one million cases per year. The Hudson Ranch Chardonnay has a superb ratio of acidity to oak, ensuring that the mature toasty flavours will never be flabby. Beringer's Private Reserve Cabernet Sauvignon is best between eight and ten years after the harvest, when its toasty oak has begun to integrate with the rich spicy-*cassis* fruit and it develops a smoky-cedary complexity.

CARNEROS CREEK WINERY

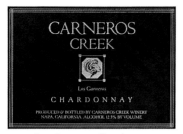

Los Carneros Chardonnay

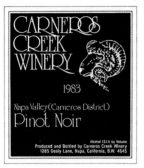

Carneros Pinot Noir

Established in 1972, this winery went through a dull patch in the early 1980s, but is now back on course. The Chardonnay is made in a buttery-lemon style with toasty oak and a good acidity. The Pinot Noir shot to fame with the 1977 vintage, after which its flavours became very attenuated, but since the 1986, the style has been delicately rich, with a spicy raspberry and cherry character.

CAYMUS VINEYARDS

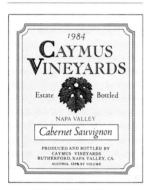

Cabernet Sauvignon

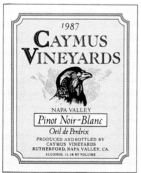

Pinot Noir-Blanc Oeil de Perdrix

Two Charles Wagners make up the father-and-son team that has run this high-quality winery since its inception in 1968. Caymus is known especially for the stunning quality and range of wines produced from Cabernet Sauvignon. The Pinot Noir is much less successful, with the exception of the Oeil de Perdrix - a delightful *blanc de noirs* that bursts with delicately perfumed fruit.

CHAPPELLET VINEYARD

Cabernet Sauvignon

Johannisberg Riesling

A string of sensational wines have been produced here since Chappellet's first vintage in 1969. The Cabernet Sauvignon is particularly successful, combining intense fruit, firm structure and great finesse, but other excellent wines include the Johannisberg Riesling, which is soft and sensual, with lots of ripe, peachy fruit flavour.

CHATEAU CHEVRE

Merlot Reserve

Sauvignon Blanc

This vineyard was originally a goat farm, which explains why ex-pilot Gerald Hazen called it Chevre when he founded the winery in 1979. Its magnificent Merlot is world class: a big, rich, juicy and fat wine with soft, spicy oak. The Sauvignon Blanc is a distinctive wine and usually excellent, but it can be inconsistent.

CHATEAU MONTELENA

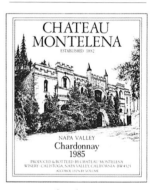

Chardonnay

Zinfandel

This property was founded by Senator Tubbs in 1882 and named Chateau Montelena in honour of Bordeaux. The prominence of the Chardonnay was established in the mid-1970s by Miljenko Grgich, and it is still one of the few Californian Chardonnays that can age well. The Cabernet Sauvignon is an intense wine with a rich, spicy-mint complexity, while the Zinfandel is less profound, but more dashing, with its big, bold and vivid ripe-berry flavours.

CLOS DU VAL

Zinfandel

Merlot

Clos du Val has benefited from the French influence of Bernard Portet, who has been the winemaker here since 1972. Portet has even taken to Zinfandel, the all-American grape, from which he produces a wine with a rich, blackberry fruit, backed-up with firm tannin structure. The Merlot is typically fat and juicy.

CONN CREEK

Barrel Select Cabernet Sauvignon

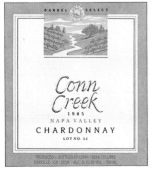

Barrel Select Chardonnay

Bill Collins founded this 50-hectare (120-acre) vineyard and its essentially Mediterranean-style winery on the Silverado Trail in 1974. Conn Creek soon became known for its intense, stylish, well-focused Cabernet Sauvignon. Although the wines from this variety went through a somewhat dull patch, it seems they are now back to their previous form. The Chardonnay wines are very firm in style, yet have great extract and plenty of underlying fruit.

CUVAISON VINEYARD

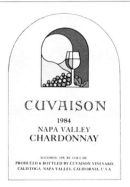

Chardonnay

With a large 100-hectare (250-acre) vineyard in the Carneros district, the assertive style of this Swiss-owned, Spanish-style winery lends itself best to the Chardonnay, which develops a fine toasty flavour in the bottle.

DIAMOND CREEK VINEYARDS

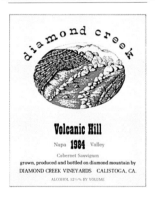

Volcanic Hill Cabernet Sauvignon

Gravelly Meadow Cabernet Sauvignon

Al Brounstein has been making outstanding wines from this 8-hectare (20-acre) vineyard since 1972. He specializes in one grape, the Cabernet Sauvignon; restricts production to allow the influence of the soil to emerge; ages the wines in Nevers oak for less than two years; and never filters. The two labels here represent the two most contrasting styles of Diamond Creek's three Cabernet Sauvignons: the overtly rich and vibrant Volcanic Hill, and the Gravelly Meadow, which is easiest to drink initially, yet develops the most finesse.

DOMAINE CHANDON

Brut Reserve

Blanc de Noirs Brut

Established by Moët & Chandon as long ago as 1968, the success of Domaine Chandon is an indication of the forward-thinking policy of this *Grande Marque* giant of Champagne. The winery houses one of the finest restaurants in the Napa Valley: so where better to taste the rich Chandon Brut Réserve or the chocolaty Chandon Blanc de Noirs?

DOMINUS ESTATE

Dominus

The first vintage of Dominus was the 1983, and it was released as recently as 1988. However, this and the following vintages suggest it may be one of the potential *grands crus* of the Napa Valley. Its great concentration and complexity is the combined effort of Robin Lail and Marcia Smith, daughter of the late John Daniel of Inglenook fame, and Christian Moueix of Château Pétrus. A wine to watch.

DUCKHORN VINEYARDS

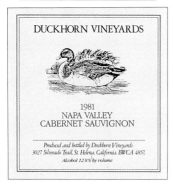

Cabernet Sauvignon

Merlot Three Palms Vineyard

Dan Duckhorn launched the first wines from his tiny vineyard with the 1978 vintage. Fermentation in stainless-steel and ageing in French oak give Duckhorn wines their supremely clean lines and refined, oaky uplift. The Cabernet Sauvignon is one of California's classics, with smoky-complex cherry, plum and vanilla flavours, but it is the superb Merlot Three Palms Vineyard that has not only established Duckhorn's prestigious reputation but has, almost single-handedly, given rise to California's cult following for this varietal.

DUNN VINEYARDS

Cabernet Sauvignon Howell Mountain

Randy Dunn makes a tiny quantity of world-class Cabernet Sauvignon from his small, 2.5-hectare (6-acre) holding in Howell Mountain vineyard. This great wine typically has huge extract, with supporting tannin structure, a super-concentrated, spicy-*cassis* flavour and a powerful, complex finish. It is a wine that takes at least 10 years to peak. Dunn also produces a more accessible, but equally high quality, Cabernet Sauvignon under the wider Napa Valley AVA.

FAR NIENTE WINERY

Chardonnay

This 50-hectare (120-acre) vineyard and revitalized pre-Prohibition winery near Oakville was originally established in 1885. Gil Nickel, the current owner, has been determined to make his mark with fine Chardonnay, which has been hugely successful, but the quality is sometimes dogged by a heavy-handed use of vanilla-oak. The Cabernet Sauvignon improves with each vintage.

FOLIE À DEUX WINERY

Chardonnay

This tiny winery and its 6 hectares (15 acres) of vineyards just north of St Helena got its name because when Larry and Eve Dizmang started out in 1981, they were well aware that owning a winery was not the way to get-rich-quick. The limited quantity of Cabernet Sauvignon, Chenin Blanc and Chardonnay has, however, become much sought after, and the latter variety is particularly successful.

FORMAN VINEYARD

Cabernet Sauvignon

Chardonnay

This operation was launched with the 1983 vintage by Rick Forman, who had made his name at Sterling Vineyards in the mid 1970s and worked at several wineries in between. The Forman philosophy is the perfect harmony between French tradition and Californian sunshine, always allowing the character of the vintage to shine through. His Cabernet Sauvignon and Chardonnay are classic and complex in structure, yet opulent and fruity in style. They also promise exceptional longevity.

FREEMARK ABBEY WINERY

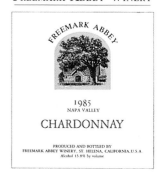

Chardonnay

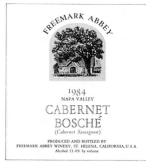

Cabernet Bosché

Established as a winery and vineyard in 1895, Freemark Abbey is a fantasy name derived from the three original owners: Charles *Freeman*, *Mark* Foster and Albert "*Abbey*" Ahern. Although the winery fell into disuse during the Prohibition, it was resurrected in 1967. The wines are snapped up by knowledgeable buyers, particularly the creamy, tropical-fruit flavoured Chardonnay and the Cabernet Bosché, which is the richest and most toasty of Freemark's Cabernet Sauvignons.

FROG'S LEAP

Chardonnay Carneros

Cabernet Sauvignon

Not a French-owned rival to Stag's Leap: this winery is owned by John and Judy Williams, who built their winery on the site of an old frog farm. The Carneros Chardonnay has excellent acidity and shows real finesse after a year or two in the bottle. The Napa Valley Cabernet Sauvignon is full and solidly made, with well-focused fruit and a cedary-spicy *cassis* complexity.

GIRARD WINERY

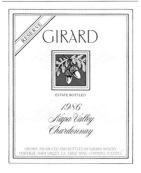

Chardonnay Reserve

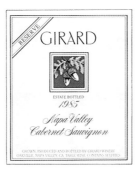

Cabernet Sauvignon Reserve

A typically Californian tale, Stephen Girard planted his first vineyard in 1970 and built up a reputation for the quality of his grapes before he took the gamble and set up his own winery in 1980. All of Girard's wines show a rare ability to balance, but those marked "Reserve" have a distinct qualitative edge, an even greater concentration, and age gracefully into stunningly stylish wines. The Chardonnay Reserve is overflowing with rich, buttery fruit and is beautifully underscored by toasty-oak complexity. The Cabernet Sauvignon Reserve is a deep, dark, brooding wine in its formative years, but bursts with fabulous, smoky *cassis* fruit after five or six years from the harvest.

GRGICH HILLS CELLAR

Chardonnay

Late Harvest Johannisberg Riesling

This winery is owned and run by Miljenko Grgich, who was the winemaker at Chateau Montelena, where he was responsible for its great reputation for Chardonnay. At Grgich Hills, Miljenko produces the sort of blockbusting Chardonnay that explodes with fruit years after its peers are dead and gone. The secret is in the balance and Miljenko knows intuitively exactly what that should be. His Alexander Valley Zinfandel has the same rich and exuberant style, and his Fumé Blanc, one of the most delicious and exotic renditions of the Sauvignon Blanc found anywhere in the world. Even more impressive is the succulent Late Harvest Johannisberg Riesling, which is perfect with a fresh, juicy peach.

GROTH VINEYARDS

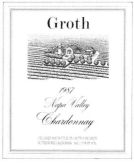

Cabernet Sauvignon

Chardonnay

Dennis Groth established this small winery and vineyard in the hills south of Yountville a few years before his first vintage of 1982. His winemaker, Nils Venge, was responsible for a string of first class Cabernet Sauvignons at Villa Mount Eden in the 1970s. At Groth, Venge has continued his success with this grape, producing powerfully flavoured but beautifully balanced wines with a rich, chocolate and raisin fruit flavour, firm tannin structure and lots of spicy-herbal complexity. The deliciously rich and oaky Chardonnay gains in finesse and style with each vintage.

HEITZ CELLARS

Martha's Vineyard
Cabernet Sauvignon

Bella Oaks Vineyard
Cabernet Sauvignon

The first Heitz winery was established in 1961. It was the almost perfect 1968 vintage of Martha's Vineyard that created the Heitz's legendary reputation for Cabernet Sauvignon. Martha's Vineyard did not receive its name until 1966, when it was bought by Tom and Martha May from Belle and Barney Rhodes, two financial backers of the Heitz venture from its earliest days. Heitz also has its own vineyards, which now total 284 hectares (700 acres). Martha's Vineyard Cabernet Sauvignon is famous for its deep, distinctive, spicy-minty-curranty character and requires 10 to 15 years to peak, while the Bella Oaks Vineyard Cabernet Sauvignon has a spicy-minty-cherry flavour that is slightly more accessible in its youth.

LONG VINEYARDS

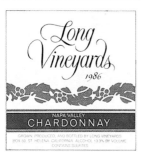

Chardonnay

Sonoma County Sauvignon Blanc

Bob Long and his Simi winemaker wife, Zelma, started this tiny winery on Pritchard Hill above Lake Henessy in 1977. He built up a reputation for white wines, particularly Chardonnay, which is full, rich and flavoursome with a fine nutty-buttery complexity and an acid balance that guarantees good longevity. His Sauvignon Blanc has a growing reputation as wine of more depth of interest, class and complexity than is usually found in this varietal.

MAYACAMAS VINEYARDS

Cabernet Sauvignon

Chardonnay

The original stone winery of Mayacamas was built in 1889. It fell into disuse during the Prohibition era, but was resurrected by British-born chemist Jacy Taylor in 1941, who replanted the vineyards. Taylor remained for almost 30 years before he was bought out by Bob Travers, a Stanford University-educated investment banker. Mayacamas is the highest vineyard in Napa, with almost 20 hectares (50 acres) of terraced hillside vineyards that yield high quality grapes with exceptionally high acidity levels. It is this acidity that gives the wines their great longevity, and it is the guiding hand of Travers, not Taylor, that has made them some of the finest that the Napa Valley has ever produced. The Cabernet Sauvignon is a deep, dense, brooding wine that takes time to develop, but is well worth the wait. The Chardonnay is a rich and intense wine, with lots of extract and a beautiful balance.

MONTICELLO CELLARS

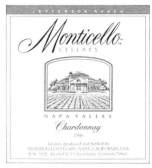

Jefferson Ranch Chardonnay

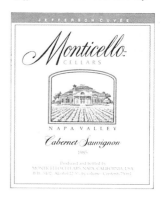

Jefferson Cuvée Cabernet Sauvignon

Jay Corley purchased this vineyard, which now encompasses 80 hectares (200 acres), in 1971 and sold his grapes to other wineries before building his own, which he modelled on Thomas Jefferson's home in Virginia. Monticello's first vintage was 1980 and its reputation is better for whites than reds, although recent releases of Cabernet Sauvignon have been exciting. A Monticello Chardonnay typically has a fragrant bouquet that belies its rich buttered-toast flavour, with the Jefferson Cuvée having a slight edge over the Corley Reserve in most vintages. Monticello's Cabernet Sauvignons have been stunning of late. Both the Jefferson Ranch and Corley Reserve are big, densely flavoured, complex wines that are bursting with creamy-spicy *cassis* fruit; the decision of which is best is more a matter of personal taste than intrinsic quality.

ROBERT MONDAVI WINERY

It was Italian-born Cesare Mondavi who began the Mondavi interest in wine, and by the time of his death in 1959 both his sons, Robert and Peter, were in the wine business, running the Charles Krug winery that their father had purchased. Robert was the innovator who was prepared to double the prices they were charging in order to fund more sophisticated production facilities. Peter was more conservative and did not want to price themselves out of the market. As a consequence, Robert left and set up his own winery in 1966. It was the first to be built in the Napa Valley since the Prohibition and its mission-style architecture has made it one of the most instantly recognized wineries in the world. He immediately launched the most intensive research programme ever attempted by any Californian winery. The costs were met, as he had intended, by setting new price levels for Napa Valley wines, but even Mondavi's new-found friends and customers thought he had gone a little far when in 1979 he released the 1974 Reserve Cabernet Sauvignon at $30 a bottle. To this day, however, that particular vintage proved to be one of the greatest Californian Cabernet Sauvignons ever made, and in most years the Reserve Cabernet Sauvignon does justice to its legendary reputation. The difference between the basic and Reserve Cabernet Sauvignons is like chalk and cheese, but there is less of a contrast between the Pinot Noir wines. The Reserve is the finer of the two, but the basic version has improved at a faster rate, and this has narrowed the gap in quality. The Fumé Blanc is rich, serious and oaky; the Moscato d'Oro is fragrant, sweet, heavenly wine. The list of wines produced by Robert Mondavi and its 400-plus hectares (1,000 acres) of vineyards goes on and on.

Reserve Cabernet Sauvignon

Fumé Blanc

Reserve Pinot Noir

Moscato D'Oro

OPUS ONE

Opus One

In 1980 Robert Mondavi collaborated with the late Baron Philippe de Rothschild of Château Mouton-Rothschild to make Opus One. Its opening price made the Robert Mondavi 1974 Reserve Cabernet Sauvignon seem a pauper by comparison. After a somewhat uncertain start, this Cabernet-Merlot blend has begun to achieve the sort of quality that one expects from its stratospheric price. The turning point was the superb 1985 vintage, and with its very own winery in operation since 1990, there is no reason why Opus One cannot maintain this sort of world class quality year in, year out.

ROBERT PECOTA WINERY

Muscato di Andrea

Gamay Beaujolais

NIEBAUM-COPPOLA ESTATE

Rubicon

This 45-hectare (110-acre) venture is owned by Hollywood movie director Francis Ford Coppola, who in 1978 purchased the Victorian home of Captain Gustave Ferdinand Niebaum, founder of the neighbouring Inglenook winery. A perfectionist of the silver screen, Coppola has proved no less meticulous about the quality of the wine he makes and is just as adamant about how it should finally be presented to the public. His powerfully constructed Rubicon not only has undeniable class, quality and finesse, but is always approaching full maturity when released.

Robert Pecota CONTD

When Robert Pecota purchased this 16-hectare (40-acre) vineyard on the foot of Mount St Helena at the cooler, northern end of the Napa Valley, the first thing he did was to dig up the vines and plant such *vin ordinaire* oddities as Flora, Gray Riesling and Saint Macaire. Since then, however, owner-winemaker Pecota has planted more classic varieties. This is now a grossly underrated winery that produces some ravishing white wines, especially Chardonnay and Muscato di Andrea, one of the most heady and succulent renditions of the Muscat grape currently produced in California. The reds are less successful, but the Gamay Beaujolais is delightfully fruity and unpretentious.

PINE RIDGE WINERY

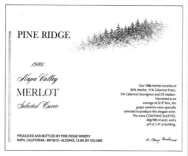

Merlot Selected Cuvée

Cabernet Sauvignon Andrus Reserve Cuvée Duet

In 1978 Gary Andrus established Pine Ridge on the site of the old Luigi Domeniconi winery on the Silverado Trail. Using a combination of the best of both French and Californian philosophies, Andrus has slowly chiselled out a growing reputation for his wines. Blended from more than one variety grown in various locations to create a more complete and complex wine, Andrus nevertheless sells his Pine Ridge products as essentially varietal wines to appease the demands of the American market. The Merlot Selected Cuvée is a seductive superstar, full of lush, velvet-soft fruit. Of all the excellent, elegant, beautifully balanced Cabernet Sauvignons, the Andrus Reserve Cuvée Duet is the most stylish.

RAYMOND

Cabernet Sauvignon

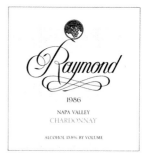

Chardonnay

Roy Raymond and his three sons worked for Beringer before establishing this vineyard in 1971. With such a pedigree, their wines are of the highest quality: the Cabernet Sauvignon is full and concentrated, with a fine smoky-toasty oak complexity; and the Chardonnay is made in a similar rich, ripe smoky-toasty style.

JOSEPH PHELPS VINEYARDS

Joseph Phelps bought his vineyard as recently as 1973 and hired Walter Schug as his winemaker. Schug trained in Germany, but had been making wine in California since 1961. One of his earliest wines at Joseph Phelps, the 1974 Insignia, probably stands side-by-side with Mondavi's 1974 Reserve as one of the two greatest red wines California has ever produced. It certainly made the reputation of both Phelps and Schug. Of Phelps's top Cabernet Sauvignons, the Insignia and the Bachus Cabernet Sauvignon-based wines are typically minty-eucalyptus; the former, perhaps, more opulent. Another Cabernet Sauvignon, the Eisele, is a dense, compact wine that seems to brood in its youth, but is explosive with fruit, flavour and complexity at its peak. The Délice du Semillon is an exotic Sauternes-like, oak-aged wine of stunning style and quality, but this is a relatively new wine and, over the years, Phelps has become more famous for its Germanic, rather than French, style of dessert wine. At the top of this range is the Special Select Late Harvest Johannisberg Riesling, which is technically the same standard as a German *Trockenbeerenauslese*, but has an even more elegant balance.

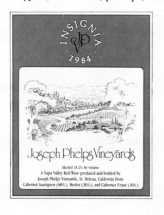

Insignia

Délice du Semillon

Special Select Lake Harvest Johannisberg Riesling

SAINTSBURY

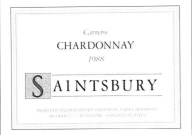

Carneros Chardonnay

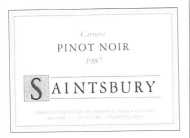

Carneros Pinot Noir

When David Graves and Richard Ward established this winery in the Carneros district, they named it after Professor George Saintsbury as a mark of their uncompromising dedication to quality. Had Saintsbury tasted the Burgundian varietals they have since produced, he would no doubt have included them in his *Notes on a Cellar Book*. The Chardonnay is very rich and concentrated, with delicious lemony fruit, and is amazingly inexpensive, while the Pinot Noir is supremely elegant, with a delightfully fragrant varietal aroma and delicately rich fruit on the palate.

SCHRAMSBERG VINEYARDS

Cuvée de Pinot

This winery, with its ageing caves cut deep into the side of Diamond Mountain was built by Joseph Schram in the 1890s, but had long been inactive when Jack and Jamie Davies acquired the property in 1964. They expanded the tunnel system, which they saw as ideal for the production of sparkling wines. Schramsberg's elegant, flowery Blanc de Blancs has always been the most consistent of these wines, but in vintages like 1985, when the Cuvée de Pinot has an excellent acidity level, it is this wine that truly excels.

SCHUG CELLARS

Heinemann Vineyard Pinot Noir

Beckstoffer Vineyard
Carneros Chardonnay

Founded in 1981 by Walter Schug, the Geisenheim-trained winemaker who made his reputation at Joseph Phelps. The first wines were released in 1983 and since 1985 they have begun to establish some consistency. The Heinemann Vineyard Pinot Noir is light-delicate, rather than light-thin. The Beckstoffer Vineyard Chardonnay is a barrel-fermented blockbuster with a deep, malty complexity.

SILVER OAK CELLARS

Cabernet Sauvignon

Alexander Valley Cabernet Sauvignon

The joint founders of Silver Oak Cellars are Justin Meyer and Raymond Duncan, former owners of Franciscan Vineyards. It is no coincidence that the impressive stone cellar is reminiscent of the Christian Brothers' Greystone Cellar, since Justin Meyer began his wine career as a Christian Brother. Meyer's ambition to make nothing but Cabernet Sauvignon has been pursued with an almost religious fervour and the results verge on the miraculous. Certainly no other winery has managed to produce three different Cabernet Sauvignons of such stunning quality as Silver Oak's rich, ripe and cedary Napa Valley, with its wonderful mellow accessibility; the exotic, blackberry-plummy fruit and ever-unfolding, spicy-chocolatey finesse of the Alexander Valley; and the Bonny's Vineyard's huge flavour, smouldering sensuality and almost mind-blowing complexity.

SMITH-MADRONE

Riesling

Chardonnay

Stuart and Charles Smith bought part of the old Madrone vineyard on Spring Mountain in 1971, where they have reclaimed the neglected ground and now some 16 hectares (40 acres) of vines. The overriding characteristic of even the best Smith-Madrone wines is an acidity balance that is almost awkward in its youth, but eventually harmonizes. The Riesling has an attractive honeysuckle nose, crisp, floral fruit and a well-balanced aftertaste. The Chardonnay is rich and flavoursome, with a fine acidity balance, but the wine requires a little bottle-age to come together.

STAG'S LEAP WINE CELLARS

The first vintage from this most prestigious winery was the 1972, but it was the 1973 that made Stag's Leap and its owner-winemaker Warren Winiarski world famous. In 1976, the wine came top in a Franco-American tasting in Paris, rudely pushing no less a wine than Château Mouton-Rothschild 1970 into second place. There are some good, ordinary and excellent Cabernet Sauvignon and other wines produced here, but it is essentially the 1973 that made this winery's fame, and one special bottling of Cabernet Sauvignon, the sensational Cask 23, that has maintained it. This wine has an immense concentration of dense *cassis* fruit that has such a powerful, undeveloped extract in its youth that it attacks every facet of the palate with its distinctive earthy-leather spicy bite, but, given 10 or more years in bottle, this evolves into a chocolatey-textured, minty-eucalyptus finesse and is enriched by toasty-coffee complexity of new oak. And this is just one of the wines from this fine winery. The White Riesling and Chardonnay are both produced from grapes that are bought in, as these varieties are not grown in Stag's Leap's own vineyard. Nothing can compare to the Cask 23, but the raw material for these two varietals is obviously well selected because the Riesling always has great finesse, while the Chardonnay is consistently rich and buttery, and gains complexity with the handling of each new vintage.

Cask 23

White Riesling

Chardonnay

SPOTTSWOODE

Cabernet Sauvignon

Sauvignon Blanc

The great house, garden and vineyard of Spottswoode are well-known and date back to the late eighteenth century, but the winery was built as recently as 1982 by the current owners, Harmon and Mary Brown. In this short time, the Brown's winemaker, Tony Soter, has firmly established Spottswoode as one of the true *grands crus* of California. In the style of a Bordeaux *grand vin* - selected from only the finest barrels and made entirely from grapes grown on the surrounding vineyard - the tiny quantity of Spottswoode Cabernet Sauvignon each year since 1982 has been powerful in construction and great in extract, with masses of spicy-*cassis* fruit and lots of smoky-toasty oak complexity. It is definitely a wine made for keeping, as is the excellent Sauvignon Blanc, which would shame many a top Graves.

STONY HILL VINEYARD

Chardonnay

Sémillon de Soleil

When Fred and Eleanor McCrea planted their steeply sloping vineyard in the West Hills in 1943, they were virtually on their own. Even by the time the McCreas built their winery in the early 1950s, the only other hillside competitor was still Mayacamas. Prior to his death in 1977, Fred McCrea had established a reputation for producing rich, firm, well-proportioned Chardonnay that retains a remarkable freshness in the bottle over several years, a style and a quality that Eleanor McCrea has been able to maintain. Stony Hill has also produced a fine White Riesling and Gewürztraminer, both of which have been underrated, and, more recently, Sémillon de Soleil, a delicious and decadently rich wine made in the Sauternes style.

TREFETHEN VINEYARDS

Chardonnay

Cabernet Sauvignon

This famous winery and vineyard was established in 1886 and named Eschol; its Cabernet Sauvignon won a gold medal at the San Francisco Viticultural Fair in 1890. After the Prohibition, the winery was used as a storage facility for Beringer until 1968, when it was purchased by Gene Trefethen. The first estate-bottled wine from Trefethen's 240-hectare (600-acre) vineyard was a 1974 White Riesling released in 1977, but it was not until the 1974 Chardonnay had been released a year later than Trefethen's quality potential was truly recognized. The reputation of successive vintages of this Chardonnay is for a wine that requires time in bottle to develop. Trefethen Cabernet Sauvignon combines opulent, cherry-plum and berry fruit flavours with a solid tannin structure.

TULOCAY WINERY

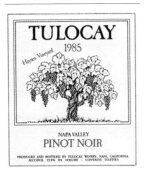

Haynes Vineyard Pinot Noir

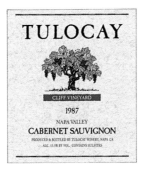

Cliff Vineyard Cabernet Sauvignon

The Tulocay winery, which owns no vineyards, was set up by Bill Cadman. The cherry and spicy-vanilla flavours that have typified its Pinot Noir have brought Cadman a certain fame. His Chardonnay is rich and oaky and his Cabernet Sauvignon is generally a fine, expressive wine full of vibrant fruit, with cedary-spicy-oak overtones.

VILLA MOUNT EDEN WINERY

Reserve Cabernet Sauvignon

Dry Chenin Blanc

This winery was bought by James and Anne McWilliams in 1969. They hired winemaker Nils Venge, who was responsible for a string of first-class Cabernet Sauvignons in the 1970s. Since the winery was purchased by Washington State's Ste Michelle in 1986, the Cabernet Sauvignons have been released earlier, but the quality is still very high. The Chenin Blanc is so deliciously dry and ripe as to make the offerings from the Loire look mean by comparison.

OTHER NORTH COAST

KALIN

Cabernet Sauvignon

Established in 1977, this family-owned winery has no vineyards of its own, but produces high-quality wines from fastidiously well-selected grapes. The Cabernet Sauvignon is very elegant and stylish, yet can outlive and outperform weightier California Cabernets. The various cuvées of Chardonnay all have great extract, exceptional longevity and mind-blowing, smoky-toasty complexity. The pure Sauvignon Blanc is made in the most delightful of dry styles and is packed with vibrant juicy, exotic, creamy fruit.

KENDALL-JACKSON VINEYARDS

The Proprietor's Cabernet Sauvignon

The Proprietor's Chardonnay

The Kendall-Jackson label has only been in existence since 1983, but the wines have rapidly gained excellent reputations. Chardonnay is widely agreed to be the best varietal and its greatest Chardonnay is the exotically rich The Proprietor's Chardonnay, with its buttery-toasty oak complexity.

The Cabernet Sauvignon is less consistent, yet the Proprietor's Cabernet Sauvignon is at least the equal of its white sister wine, as the stunning 1985, with its concentration of lush, stylish fruit flavours and deep toasty oak finesse dramatically demonstrates.

KONOCTI WINERY

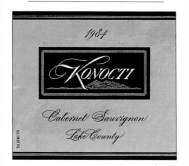

Cabernet Sauvignon Lake County

Fumé Blanc Lake County

Pronounced "Ka-nock'tie", this firm was established by a cooperative of 27 Lake County growers in 1974, and a winery was built five years later. In 1983, Parducci Wine Cellars of Ukiah in Mendocino was impressed enough by the wines to take a 50 per cent shareholding in Konocti. Considering how inexpensive these wines are, the quality achieved is extraordinary. The Cabernet Sauvignon has a rich varietal flavour, lots of mellow fruit, with well integrated oak and a supple tannin structure. The Fumé Blanc has lashings of ripe, deliciously dry fruit.

SIERRA FOOTHILLS

KARLY WINES

Amador County Zinfandel

Buck and Karly Cobb planted a small vineyard and built this winery in Amador County in 1979. This underrated winery makes high-quality Zinfandel wines that are quietly packed with flavour and show extraordinary finesse.

MONTEVIÑA WINES

Shenandoah Valley Zinfandel Montino

Shenandoah Valley Fumé Blanc

This winery just east of Shenandoah was built in 1970 to capitalize on the growing market for Zinfandel and quickly established itself as one of the best specialists in this variety. The Zinfandel Montino is somewhat light and definitely ready to drink when sold, while the Winemaker's Choice has big, bold flavours. Rarely encountered is the excellent, rich and lush Fumé Blanc.

SHENANDOAH VINEYARDS

Sobon Amador County Zinfandel

Sobon Amador County Zinfandel Port

This 4-hectare (10-acre) vineyard was established in 1977 by Leon Sobon. Sold under the Sobon label, Shenandoah's Zinfandel is a dashing, strikingly fresh wine, blazing with ripe and ready berry flavours. There is also an excellent Zinfandel Port: not what Europeans expect from any genuine Port, but taken entirely on its own, as a fortified varietal wine, it is absolutely delicious.

SIERRA VISTA WINERY

El Dorado Cabernet Sauvignon Special Reserve

El Dorado Fumé Blanc

John and Barbara MacCready settled in this spectacular location in 1977. The Cabernet Sauvignon Special Reserve is riper and fuller than most examples of this varietal from El Dorado and has a firm structure, with a fine, spicy-oak complexity. The Fumé Blanc is soft and gentle, with delicately rich, fruit-salad flavours.

STEVENOT WINERY

Calaveros County Chardonnay Grand Reserve

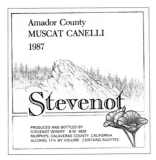

Amador County Muscat Canelli

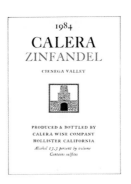

Zinfandel Cienega Valley

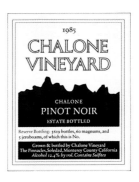

Chalone Pinot Noir

This winery was established in the late-1970s. Stevenot's basic California Chardonnay has attractive tropical aromas, firm fruit and a certain spicy-butterscotch complexity from its oak maturation. The Grande Reserve is bigger and finer. But it is the glorious Muscat Canelli, with its exotic, peach and orange fruit flavours, tangy acidity and sweet aftertaste, that excels.

NORTH CENTRAL COAST

This company is one of California's premier pioneers in the continuing quest for perfect Pinot Noir. Potentially, its top *cuvées* are probably the best, although Calera's pursuit of elegance can produce a certain "prettiness" of style. The best Calera's of *cru* Pinot Noirs is its ripe and rich, cherry and plum flavoured Jensen, but their Reed and Selleck Pinot Noirs also rank amongst the very best of California's renditions of this grape. Calera's Zinfandels are also very fine.

The Chalone winery, which owns 63 hectares (155 acres) of vineyard, was established in 1965 and the first estate wines were released four years later. Concentrating on Chardonnay, Pinot Blanc and Pinot Noir, Chalone has produced a remarkable string of fabulously fine, rich and complex wines from these varietals. Their extraordinary, exquisite style consistently place this winery at the forefront of California's "Burgundian" specialists.

CALERA WINE COMPANY

CHALONE VINEYARD

CONGRESS SPRINGS VINEYARDS

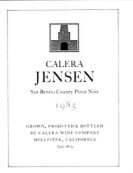

Jensen San Benito County Pinot Noir

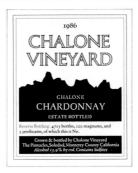

Chalone Chardonnay

Montmartre Santa Cruz Mountains Chardonnay

BONNY DOON VINEYARD

Winemaker Randall Graham specializes in "Rhône" varieties, makes sublime Pinot Noir, and even produces a *vin de paille*. The Syrah comes from Estrella River's Paso Robles vineyard, but Graham always manages to obtain a greater intensity and vibrancy of flavour than Estrella. As a tribute to one of his favourite Châteauneuf-du-Papes, Vieux Télégraphe, Graham produced the first vintage of Bonny Doon Old Telegram in 1985, a stunning pure

varietal Mourvèdre wine full of spicy-complex aromas and concentrated plum and currant flavours. Le Cigare Volant, or Flying Cigar, celebrates the ordinance passed by Châteauneuf-du-Pape's village council in 1954, banning flying cigars, saucers and other UFOs, which would be liable to impounding if they landed. A Californian adaption of a Châteauneuf-du-Pâpe blend, this is a gloriously rich blend of Mourvèdre, Grenache and Syrah.

Syrah Paso Robles

Old Telegram

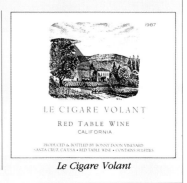

Le Cigare Volant

Congress Springs Vineyard CONTD

Santa Clara County Pinot Noir
San Ysidro Vineyard

This winery's basic Santa Clara Chardonnay is very good, but more impressive are its top *cuvées*, such as the vibrant Montmartre or Reserve, with barrel-fermented, toasty-oak flavours. The Pinot Noir from the San Ysidro is soft and spicy, with cherry and redcurrant varietal flavours.

JEKEL VINEYARD

Arroyo Seco
White Johannisberg Riesling

Arroyo Seco Pinot Blanc

Bill Jekel was one of the pioneers of Monterey County winemaking, establishing this vineyard in 1972 and building a winery six years later, since when his views - some would say controversial views - on soil have often overshadowed his wines. The quality of Jekel's white wines has been consistently high, and his succulently sweet White Johannisberg Riesling, with its exotic fruits and elegant style is widely regarded as the most impressive of these, although he can produce a classy Pinot Blanc that should not be overlooked.

MOUNT EDEN VINEYARDS

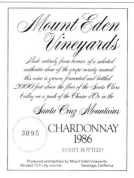

Santa Cruz Mountains Chardonnay

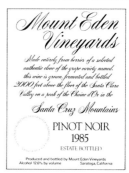

Santa Cruz Mountains Pinot Noir

Mount Eden Vineyard produces just three varietals, all of which are fine in quality. Best of all is the stylish Chardonnay with its ripe, buttery aromas and rich, tropical fruit flavours, beautifully highlighted by lots of creamy-toasty-vanilla oak. The number two wine is Mount Eden's Pinot Noir, and in good vintages, when its soft, lush flavours are concentrated, it can vie with the Chardonnay.

RIDGE VINEYARDS

This enterprise began in 1959 and was soon producing wines to baffle those who questioned the potential longevity of California wines. The Cabernet Sauvignon, in particular, has become famous for its great ageing capability. Ridge Monte Bello Cabernet Sauvignon typically has a deep, dark, opaque colour, great intensity of flavour, huge extract and firm tannin structure. It is not drinkable for at least 10 years, but, after 15 or more,

it is totally stunning. Generally, Ridge Zinfandels are relatively soft and fruity, yet have broad, expansive flavours that never seem to be wanting, but there are several vineyards (Geyserville, Lytton Spring, Park-Muscatine) and each one produces a dramatically different style. The York Creek Petite Sirah is a hedonist's dream come true, a voluptuous wine, full of rich summer-fruit flavours, gently underpinned by a little toasty-oak.

Cabernet Sauvignon Monte Bello

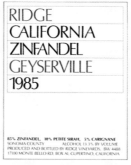

Zinfandel Geyserville

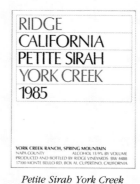

Petite Sirah York Creek

SOUTH CENTRAL COAST

AU BON CLIMAT

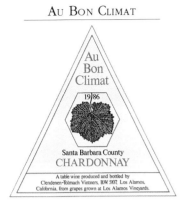

Santa Barbara County Chardonnay

This small winery is the brainchild of Jim Clendenen and Adam Tolmach, whose winemaking experience from Australia and Burgundy, as well as California, influences the classic style and tremendous quality of Au Bon Climat's Pinot Noir and Chardonnay wines. The Chardonnay ranges from the deliciously rich and elegant basic label, with its opulent, often exotic, fruit, through the smoky-toasty intensity of the Reserve, to the Benedict Vineyard, which in 1987 yielded just 1.5 hectolitres per hectare. The basic Santa Barbara Pinot Noir has all the class, quality and fruit-acidity balance of a good village Burgundy, and the better bottlings are like finer Burgundies.

EDNA VALLEY VINEYARD

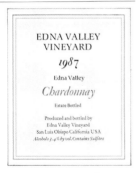

Edna Valley Chardonnay

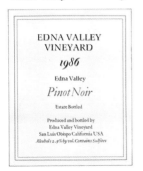

Edna Valley Pinot Noir

This winery in San Luis Obispo was built in time for the 1980 vintage as a joint venture between the vineyard owner Jack Niven and Chalone Vineyards of Monterey County. Like Chalone, Edna Valley is a Burgundian varietal specialist and has built up a splendid reputation for its superb toasty Chardonnays and very rich and jammy Pinot Noirs.

ESTRELLA RIVER WINERY

Johannisberg Riesling Paso Robles

Chardonnay Paso Robles

Although Paso Robles is an old wine-growing district, Estrella River, built in 1977, was the first new winery in the area for many years and was responsible for broadening the spectrum of its wines from the once all-pervading Zinfandel. Estrella does make various red wines and the Syrah is particularly successful, but the emphasis is now on white. The Johannisberg Riesling is remarkably light, crisp and fresh for a southern California wine; the Chardonnay is also crisp and fresh, but supported by rich, fat, exotic fruit.

MAISON DEUTZ

Brut Cuvée

The Aÿ-based Champagne house of Deutz and Geldermann chose the chalky hills south of Arroyo Grande (not to be confused with the Arroyo Seco AVA, the soil of which has a low lime content) to plant its 160-hectare (400-acre) vineyard and produce a Champagne-style wine. The wines are generally fruitier than their original French counterparts, but have a good balance and are beginning to develop an autolytic complexity.

ZACA MESA WINERY

*Reserve Pinot Noir
Santa Barbara County*

Chardonnay Santa Barbara County

Established in 1978 during the hiatus between the first and second wave of wineries to encroach upon the Santa Ynez Valley, Zaca Mesa is now second only in size to Firestone Vineyards and produces some very fine wines from the ungrafted vines in its phylloxera-free vineyards. The Pinot Noir has, since the 1985 vintage, been one of the best in California, with its earthy-plum and spicy-cherry flavours and an amazingly long finish, considering the lightness and elegance of its balance. The Chardonnay is a wonderfully rich and voluptuous wine, with a veritable fruit salad of flavour, deliciously underscored by ripe, creamy oak.

PACIFIC NORTHWEST

DESPITE A HISTORY OF winemaking that predates the Prohibition, *vinifera* grapes are a recent enterprise in the Pacific Northwest.

Washington

Washington's vineyards are situated mainly east of the Cascade Mountains, with three designated wine districts: Columbia Valley, Yakima Valley and Walla Walla Valley. White varietal wines are made from Chardonnay, Sauvignon Blanc, Sémillon, Rhine Riesling, Muscat and Gewürztraminer. Red varieties include Cabernet Sauvignon, Merlot, Pinot Noir, Lemberger and Grenache.

Oregon

The three regional appellations in Oregon are Willamette Valley and Umpqua Valley, both AVAs, and Rogue River. Strict regulations have been in force since 1977: the label must state the appellation of origin; the wine must be made entirely from grapes grown in that area; and the wine must contain not less than 90 per cent of the grape name stated (75 per cent for Cabernet Sauvignon to allow a Bordeaux-style blend with other red Bordeaux grapes). White wines are made from Sauvignon Blanc, Gewürztraminer, Chardonnay, Riesling, Sémillon, Pinot Gris and Muscat Ottonel; reds from Pinot Noir, Zinfandel, Pinot Meunier, Merlot and Cabernet Sauvignon.

Idaho

Inland of Oregon, Idaho has a warmer climate in which Riesling and Chardonnay grow well on the slopes between Caldwell and Wilder. Winter temperatures are a problem, but one or two growers are succeeding with *vinifera* varieties.

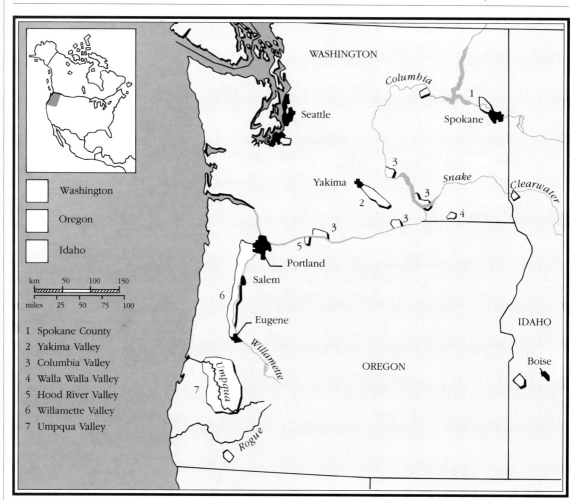

Washington

Oregon

Idaho

| km | 50 | 100 | 150 |
| miles | 25 | 50 | 75 | 100 |

1 Spokane County
2 Yakima Valley
3 Columbia Valley
4 Walla Walla Valley
5 Hood River Valley
6 Willamette Valley
7 Umpqua Valley

Vineyards in the three states

Washington has an equivalent of just 6 per cent of California's vineyards, but it is second only to California in its output of quality vinifera wines. Oregon has a cooler climate than Washington, whilst inland Idaho is the smallest, as yet embryonic, winemaking state in the Pacific Northwest.

OREGON

ADAMS VINEYARD

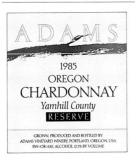

Chardonnay Yamhill County Reserve

Pinot Noir Yamhill County Reserve

Peter and Carol Adams planted their vineyard in the hills near Newberg in 1976 and produced their first vintage in 1981. Terrific Chardonnays, big, rich and oaky, and Pinot Noirs that show great strength, yet true elegance, Adams' wines are definitely "food wines", a term that is all too often abused in the USA, but meaningful here. It perhaps comes as no surprise to discover that Carol Adams is a respected food journalist.

ADELSHEIM VINEYARD

Polk County Pinot Noir

Marion and Polk Counties Chardonnay

David Adelsheim studied at the Lycée Viticole in Beaune before this hilltop winery was built in 1978. It overlooks the Willamette Valley vineyard he planted in 1972. David Adelsheim was responsible for having both the Willamette and Umpqua valleys recognized as AVAs in 1984. Adelsheim's Pinot Noir has a deep bouquet and flavour of ripe black cherries and the lingering taste of spicy-toasty oak. The Chardonnay, which comes from Marion and Polk Counties, needs time in bottle to fill out the promise of its well-integrated oak and fine acid balance.

ALPINE VINEYARDS

Willamette Valley Chardonnay

Willamette Valley White Riesling

This vineyard at Alpine, south of Corvallis in the Willamette Valley, was planted by Dan and Christine Jepson in 1976, who produced their first vintage in 1980. The tightness of style that often epitomizes these wines in their youth is due to the fact that the malolactic fermentation is not automatically encouraged for either Alpine's red wines, or its steely, Chablis-like Chardonnay. The off-dry White Riesling has steadily improved from a fine and lively wine with honeysuckle aromas and grapefruit flavours, to a riper, apricoty style.

AMITY VINEYARDS

Willamette Valley Pinot Noir

Myron Redford is both winemaker and owner of this well-known winery and vineyard. No-one could be more dedicated to this state's potential as a world-class winemaking region, yet Redford was originally planning to make wine from grapes grown in Washington's Columbia Valley and it was only when he heard that this hillside vineyard at Amity, just south of McMinnville, was for sale, that he opted for Oregon instead. Initially, Amity's reputation was for a light, ready-to-drink type of Pinot Noir, but the style soon became more serious and this winery's Pinot Noir is now one of the longest-lived in Oregon.

ARTERBERRY

Yamhill County Pinot Noir

Although the vineyards of owner and winemaker Fred Arterberry are located in the Red Hills east of Dundee, his winery is actually in the back streets of McMinnville. Essentially a sparkling wine specialist, he also produces a deliciously plump Pinot Noir red in various different *cuvées*.

BETHEL HEIGHTS VINEYARD

Willamette Valley Pinot Noir

Bethel Heights Vineyard CONTD

Willamette Valley Chardonnay

The vines of this vineyard are planted on the south-facing slope of an ancient volcano in the Willamette Valley AVA. It was first cultivated in 1977, although owners Ted and Terry Casteel did not produce their own wine until the vintage of 1984. The wines have steadily improved and the Pinot Noir and Chardonnay now rate amongst the very finest, flavourful and most elegant in Oregon.

CAMERON WINERY

Willamette Valley Pinot Noir

Willamette Valley Chardonnay

Marine biologist John Paul is the owner and winemaker at this small operation, which was launched with the 1986 vintage. The ex-assistant winemaker for Konocti and Carneros Creek wineries in California, Paul's primary passion has always been for red Burgundy. His Pinot Noir is ripe and voluptuous, with more than enough spicy-cherry varietal flavour to match the oak. The Chardonnay is a fabulously rich and lush wine, full of creamy-butterscotch complexity.

ELK COVE VINEYARDS

Willamette Valley Pinot Noir

Willamette Valley Chardonnay

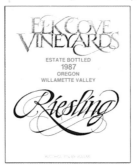

Willamette Valley Riesling

This winery is perched on the crest of a hill above Gaston and overlooks its vineyard, which has grown considerably since it was first planted in 1974. Since 1986, owners Pat and Joe Campbell have made an increasingly fine Pinot Noir in an elegant, early drinking style. Their Chardonnay is rich, with lots of toasty-butterscotchy oak influence. The Riesling shows true varietal flavour and pleasing acidity to balance its sweetness.

EVESHAM WOOD

Willamette Valley Pinot Noir

EVESHAM WOOD

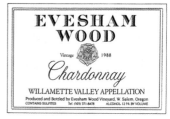

Willamette Valley Chardonnay

This new winery was established by Alsace-trained Russ Raney. A former winemaker for the Adams Vineyard, Raney purchased a vineyard in Polk County and planted it with Pinot Noir and Chardonnay. The first wines received rave reviews, especially the deep-flavoured, unfiltered Pinot Noir, a big, elegantly flavoursome wine packed with creamy, spicy-cherry complexity. The Chardonnay is deep-flavoured but needs bottle age to develop its toasty-oak richness.

THE EYRIE VINEYARDS

Willamette Valley Pinot Noir

Willamette Valley Chardonnay

Willamette Valley Pinot Gris

The Eyrie Vineyard is just outside Dundee in a most beautiful location. Owned and run by David Lett, its 1975 Pinot Noir was the first wine to put Oregon on the international wine map. Lett entered it into a blind tasting competition in Paris in 1979, which was run by Robert Drouhin, the head of one of the greatest houses in Burgundy. It was Drouhin's own superb 1959 Chambolle-Musigny that won, but Lett's Pinot Noir came second, demolishing the reputation of some prestigious Burgundies in the process. Lett also makes good Chardonnay, but, with the obvious exception of his velvety-rich Pinot Noir, it is the Pinot Gris that is his most exciting wine.

FORIS

Gewurztraminer

This is an absolutely stunning Gewürztraminer. Its heady spicy-floral aroma is intriguing, intermingled with delicate nuances of rose petals and verbena, which is reflected on the palate as a complex aftertaste to its fresh and vibrant fruit flavour.

HIDDEN SPRINGS WINERY

Pinot Noir

This vineyard in the Eola Hills between Salem and Yamhill was planted in 1972. The first commercial vintage was 1980 and the Pinot Noir won the only gold medal at Seattle's Enological Society Festival in 1983. The Pinot Noir has not been successful in every vintage, but when it is, the wine has a fine perfumed purity and almost textbook varietal flavour.

HILLCREST VINEYARD

Umpqua Valley Riesling

Owner Richard Sommer was the first person to reinstate *vinifera* vines in Oregon after the Prohibition, when he planted Riesling at this vineyard near Rosenburg in the Umpqua Valley in 1961. While Sommer remains one of the finest viticulturists in the state, others have left him behind as far as winemaking technique is concerned. That said, his Rieslings are sometimes sensational. Hillcrest's basic Riesling in 1983 and Late Harvest Riesling in 1978 were world class.

KNUDSEN ERATH WINERY

Willamette Valley Pinot Noir

Willamette Valley White Riesling

This famous winery originated in 1969, when neighbours Dick Erath and Cal Knudsen combined their vineyards. Since then, the reputation of Knudson Erath has soared, as has its production, and its firmly structured, long-living Pinot Noir is considered one of Oregon's classics. The Knudson Erath White Riesling is a bit erratic: the 1986 was one of the least successful examples of this grape produced in Oregon, yet the 1987 was one of the greatest.

OAK KNOLL WINERY

Willamette Valley Vintage Select Pinot Noir

Willamette Valley Vintage Select Chardonnay

This winery gained fame when André Tchelistcheff held aloft a glass of Oak Knoll 1980 Vintage Select Pinot Noir at the 1983 Oregon State Fair and told the panel of wine judges "I am prepared to defend this wine with the last breath in my body!" It won a gold medal and the Governor's Trophy. Oak Knoll's Pinot Noir has an intense redcurrant-and-cherry varietal flavour, with rich, spicy complexity, and the Vintage Select is probably the greatest Pinot Noir regularly produced in Oregon. Less well-known, but almost as exciting, is Oak Knoll's Vintage Select Chardonnay, which has a fine, perfumed aroma and delicately rich, buttered-apple flavour.

PANTHER CREEK CELLARS

Willamette Valley Pinot Noir

This new winery was established by Ken Wright. His experience from several Californian wineries has rubbed off on his well-focused Pinot Noir, which has the immediate appeal and lush flavours reminiscent of that state.

PONZI VINEYARDS

Dick and Nancy Ponzi are California expatriates who fled their home state for the peace of Oregon's outback. When Nancy Ponzi first planted the vineyard in 1974, the Oregon Department of Agriculture advised her that it was impossible to grow *vinifera* grapes in the Willamette Valley. She knew better. Ponzi is now one of the most consistent of Oregon's top-performing wineries. Its Pinot Gris is rich and ripe, with deep, fat, juicy flavours and a certain creamy finesse that puts this varietal in the same league as those produced by The Eyrie Vineyards and Tyee. On a similar quality level is Ponzi's Chardonnay, one of the best in Oregon, and the superb Dry White Riesling, with its spicy-melon aromas and concentrated apricot flavours. Yet it is the Pinot Noir that has made this winery's reputation: well-coloured and full-flavoured, it has soft, seductive, fruit and a velvety texture.

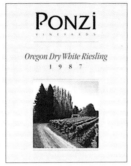

Willamette Valley Pinot Gris

Willamette Valley Dry White Riesling

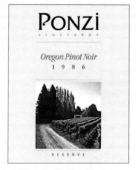

Willamette Valley Pinot Noir

REX HILL VINEYARDS

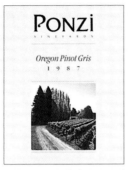

Willamette Valley Chardonnay

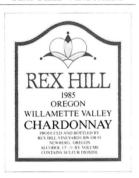

Dundee Hills Vineyards Pinot Noir

Established in 1982, the aim here is to produce well-focused wines and give them an upmarket price, which will stress their quality to consumers. Rex Hill has been making better Chardonnay with each passing vintage, but is best known for its various single-vineyard Pinot Noir wines: Archibald, Dundee Hills, Maresh, Medici, and Wirtz, as well as its basic Willamette Valley Pinot Noir.

SHAFER VINEYARD CELLARS

Willamette Valley Chardonnay

Willamette Valley Pinot Noir

Willamette Valley Sauvignon Blanc

Harvey Shafer was simply a farmer who was known as one of the finest sources for high-quality grapes in the Tualatin Valley, before he decided to take the plunge and build himself a winery. Each new vintage sees an increasing amount of buttered-apple fruit in his Chardonnay and the Pinot Noir shows great promise, but it is the Sauvignon Blanc that has fared best, although its herbaceous fruit and smoky-vanilla oak sometimes clash.

SISKIYOU VINEYARDS

Pinot Noir

When California expatriates Chuck and Suzi David decided to start up a vineyard in Oregon in 1974, they chose the Illinois Valley in the south-west of the state, where even then it was known that warm-climate varieties such as Cabernet Sauvignon and Zinfandel could be cultivated. Chuck David died in 1983, but Suzi carried on with the help of Donna Devine. This team is still finding its feet, but the Pinot Noir shows sweet-cherry promise in its varietal fruit.

SOKOL BLOSSER WINERY

Sokol Blosser is a romantic dream that quickly got out of hand. Bill Blosser and Susan Sokol purchased this 50-hectare (125-acre) orchard property in the Red Hills of Dundee in 1971, planning to spend their weekends there planting a vineyard, using the fruit trees to fund their hobby. But to make the vineyard pay, they had to build a winery and hire a winemaker, and this in turn dictated the minimum size of their production to cover his salary. Sokol Blosser soon became one of the largest wineries in Oregon, but since nothing is truly big in this state, it has remains staunchly quality-conscious. Chardonnay is its

best varietal, particularly the Reserve, which has delightful apple-blossom and ripe pear aromas, delicately rich buttered-apple fruit, with a beautifully integrated toasty-oak complexity. The Pinot Noirs have vibrant cherry-fruit flavours and good acidity, requiring a year or two in bottle to fill out. This particular vintage of White Riesling Select Harvest is one of Oregon's greatest sweet Rieslings. Its ripe dessert apple bouquet is edged with honeysuckle, following through on to a fruit-packed palate that has a fine balance between the richness of its fruit and acidity, with honeyed-botrytis complexity.

Yamhill County Chardonnay

Yamhill County Pinot Noir

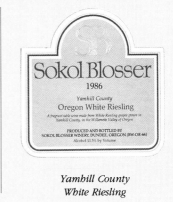
Yamhill County White Riesling

TUALATIN VINEYARDS

Willamette Valley Pinot Noir

Willamette Valley White Riesling

Formerly a chemist with the Louis Martini winery in California, Bill Fuller established this winery in 1973 with the help of Bill Malkmus, an investment advisor. Tualatin Vineyards is known to produce blockbusting Chardonnay and elegant Pinot Noir and has recently gained a reputation for its classic White Riesling.

TYEE WINE CELLARS

Willamette Valley Gewürztraminer

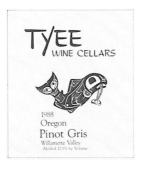
Willamette Valley Pinot Gris

Barney Watson was the winemaker for Oregon's experimental winery before he joined forces in 1983 with David Buchanan, a marine biologist. They planted a vineyard on Buchanan's 180-hectare (450-acre) property, near an Indian reservation at the confluence of Beaver and Muddy Creeks in the foothills of the

Coast Range. (A "tyee" is a Northwest Indian word for anything that is the biggest and best of a group.) Since its stunning 1986 Gewürztraminer, this winery has had a great reputation for this variety, but the grape is sensitive to vintages and cannot always perform well in Oregon. Tyee's Pinot Gris is, however, a consistent wine: its richness and finesse put it in the same class as The Eyrie Vineyards and Ponzi.

VALLEY VIEW VINEYARD

Barrel Fermented Chardonnay

The first vintage from this vineyard was 1976. But it was not until the mid-1980s that its true potential was gradually realized by its new winemaker, John Guerrero, who trained at the University of California, Davis. The Chardonnay is elegant, with apple-blossom aromas, buttered-apple fruit and a certain barrel-fermented complexity of creamy-smoky oak on the finish.

YAMHILL VALLEY VINEYARDS

Pinot Noir

Set up in 1982, this property now comprises 40 hectares (100 acres) of vines in the Willamette Valley. The Pinot Noir has lots of firm spicy-cherry and raspberry varietal fruit.

WASHINGTON

ARBOR CREST

Johannisberg Riesling Select Late Harvest

Columbia Valley Bacchus Vineyard Merlot

Owned by the Mielkes, Arbor Crest has 36 hectares (90 acres) of vineyard near Spokane. Its lush, honeyed Johannisberg Riesling Select Late Harvest with its tangy apricot fruit, botrytis complexity and perfumed finesse is rapidly becoming a legend. The 1986 Bacchus Vineyard Merlot has a deep, sweet, coffee-chocolate intensity of fruit and smoky-toasty oak: it is one of the best examples of this variety produced in Washington.

BARNARD GRIFFIN

Barrel Fermented Fumé Blanc

Each wine sold under this label is a personal statement by Griffin, who is the winemaker for the award-winning Hogue Cellars. His Barrel Fermented Chardonnay is nothing short of sensational. The Barrel Fermented Fumé Blanc is best drunk young when its verbena aroma and racy flavours are at their most bracing.

BLACKWOOD CANYON

Pinnacle Columbia Valley Botritized White Riesling

Built in 1982, two years before the vineyard was planted, this winery burned down in 1985 and was rebuilt on a much grander scale. The Pinnacle Botritized White Riesling is the star of the range. The 1986 vintage was the equivalent of a Trockenbeerenauslese: a wine of dazzling concentration and complexity with exquisite balance.

BOOKWALTER

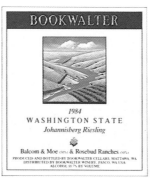

Johannisberg Riesling

This winery was established in 1984 by Jerry Bookwalter, who was the general manager of Sagemoor Farms, the largest group of vineyard holdings in the Pacific Northwest between 1976 and 1983. It produces various Rieslings with charming floral aromas and fresh, crisp fruit-salad flavours. The Late Harvest White Riesling can be quite exceptional.

CASCADE ESTATES WINERY

Yakima Valley Muscat Canelli

Originally established as a fruit-wine operation in Marysville, this winery was purchased by a group of investors from Tacoma, who moved the business to premises in Sunnyside. True grape wines are now made, and Muscat Canelli is the most sumptuous of these - a delicious wine with a sherbet and tangerine-peel flavour and fabulous acidity.

CHATEAU STE MICHELLE

Chateau Reserve Late Harvest White Riesling Hand-Selected Clusters

Limited Bottling Muscat Canelli

This is the largest wine producer in the Pacific Northwest. Its origins stretch back to the repeal of the Prohibition, but the first *vinifera* wines under the Ste Michelle label were produced in 1968. The *méthode champenoise* wines of the late 1970s showed great potential, although the current production is very ordinary. The wine Ste Michelle truly excels at is Riesling, particularly its Château Réserve Late Harvest White Riesling, Hand-Selected Clusters, which is a rich, honeyed, apricot- and lemon-flavoured nectar. Less well known, but just as delicious is the peach-and-pineapple, sherbetty Muscat Canelli.

COLUMBIA

Otis Vineyard Yakima Valley Cabernet Sauvignon

Red Willow Vineyard Yakima Valley Cabernet Sauvignon

Formerly Associated Vintners, this winery is run by Canadian-born Master of Wine David Lake, a man who has been instrumental in raising the standards of Washington's wine industry. The top Columbia wines are those that carry Lake's signature on the label and the best of these are the Cabernet Sauvignons. They are quite different in style. His Otis Vineyard is an elegant and supple wine, with sweet, ripe oak and is made for early drinking, but also ages well. His Red Willow Vineyard is one of hidden depth, needing several years bottle-age to fill out the fruit in mid-palate to match the smoky-cedary oak complexity on the finish.

COLUMBIA CREST

Columbia Valley Chardonnay

Often described as the second label of Chateau Ste Michelle, Columbia Crest is more than that: it is a separate winery, with state-of-the-art technology, its own winemaker, and a distinct, good-value reputation. Its Chardonnay is made in a delicious, ready-drinking, buttered-apple and vanilla-oak style, with fine lemony acidity.

COVEY RUN

Yakima Valley Chardonnay Partner's Reserve

Yakima Valley Botrytis Affected White Riesling

Yakima Valley White Riesling Ice Wine

When this winery and its 73-hectare (180-acre) vineyard was founded in 1982, it was called Quail Run, and it was under this name that its first wines were sold. However, there was a small winery in the Napa Valley called Quail Ridge, so the owners decided to change the name to Covey Run - a covey being a flock of quail. The basic Chardonnay fills the mouth with voluptuous fruit flavours, while the Chardonnay Partner's Reserve has a decadently rich, vanilla and caramel ice-cream flavour. Covey Run's top *cuvées* of White Riesling are always a bit special, but the Botrytis Affected and Ice Wine are simply sensational.

THE HOGUE CELLARS

Merlot

Markin Vineyard Late Harvest White Riesling

After rearing cattle and growing spearmint for chewing-gum, Warren Hogue turned to running this ambitiously-sized vineyard and winery. The quality is high and it deserves to succeed. The 1983 Merlot was one of this winery's great surprises: oaky, but with more than enough ripe fruit to match it, this 100 per cent pure Merlot is still gaining length and complexity. While the 1985 had just 75 per cent Merlot, the 1986 had 92 per cent, and was almost as good as the 1983. When it comes to Late Harvest White Riesling, only the vintage prevents this winery producing exceptional wine every year: the 1985 and 1988 were world class.

KIONA

Yakima Valley White Riesling Ice Wine

This small winery was estalished by Jim Holmes and John Williams in 1980, five years after they first planted the Kiona or "brown hills" vineyard on the lower slopes of Red Mountain. Kiona is known for its Riesling, particularly for its Late Harvest and Ice Wine, which are delicately rich and elegant.

LATAH CREEK WINE CELLARS

Merlot

Latah Creek was established in 1982 by Mike Conway, who worked for the Gallo winery. His Merlot has spicy-berry aromas, a concentrated flavour of plums, raspberries and peppers, and cedary-chocolate complexity.

LEONETTI CELLAR

Merlot

Leonetti's Gary Figgins has been winning medals for his Walla Walla wines since 1982. His Merlot is a vivacious wine with a mouth-tingling concentration of ripe berry flavours; it is best enjoyed four or five years old.

MOUNT BAKER VINEYARDS

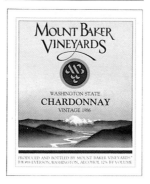

Chardonnay

Situated in the Nooksack Valley, Mount Baker Vineyards exploits the rare microclimate here that can ripen classic varieties such as Chardonnay. This 1986 vintage is an unusual, but absolutely delightful wine. Its aromas of buttered-apple and pineapple give an impression of light elegance, yet it is much richer on the palate, with very ripe fruit and a creamy-butter-scotch intensity on the finish.

PRESTON WINE CELLARS

White Riesling Ice Wine

Bill Preston was one of the first to be convinced of the potential of a Washington wine industry. He now runs the largest privately owned winery in the Pacific Northwest. The quantity is high, but so is the quality. The remarkable White Riesling 1986 Ice Wine has a Trockenbeere-nauslese-like toffee-botrytis richness.

QUARRY LAKE

Merlot

Although the Balcom family were amongst the first to cultivate *vinifera* grapes in Washington, this 40-hectare (100-acre) venture was established as recently as 1986. The Merlot is a soft, velvety wine with fat, juicy, red-fruit flavours, but few of this winery's other wines have shown any sign of quality or consistency. However, this is a high-tech business that is determined to succeed, so Quarry Lake might be a label to watch.

QUILCEDA CREEK VINTNERS

Cabernet Sauvignon

Owner and winemaker Alex Golitzin is the nephew of that dean of the Californian wine industry, André Tchelistcheff, and, in his own way, Golitzin is just as gifted. There is only one Quilceda Creek, and it is 100 per cent Cabernet Sauvignon. The most stunning red in the Pacific Northwest, it is big, black and tannic, but packed solid with flavour. It has the potential to achieve the finesse and complexity of a great Pauillac, given 15 to 20 years in bottle.

SNOQUALMIE WINERY

Columbia Valley Semillon

This winery was estalished in 1983 by Joel Klein, who was Chateau Ste Michelle's winemaker from 1974 to 1982. In addition, Klein purchased F.W. Langguth, Washington's second-largest winery, in 1987. The Chardonnay Reserve 1987 is better than previous vintages, though not special, but the 1988 Sémillon is a revelation.

WOODWARD CANYON WINERY

If the single greatest red wine is Quilceda Creek, then Woodward Canyon produces the greatest Northwest wines across the board. The Cabernet Sauvignon is ripe, oaky, plump and powerful, while the Charbonneau is an elegantly stylish Cabernet Merlot blend from Walla Walla. The Washington Chardonnay has a full-blown varietal character, great length and a firm finish. The Rozaberg Chardonnay is restrained, but has more finesse.

Columbia Valley Cabernet Sauvignon

Walla Walla County Charbonneau

Washington Chardonnay

STEWART VINEYARDS

Columbia Valley Late Harvest White Riesling

Dr George Stewart and his wife Martha grew grapes on two properties - on the Wahluke slope of the Columbia River and in the Yakima Valley near Sunnyside - throughout the 1960s and 1970s. Impressed by the quality of grapes they were selling to various Washington wineries, they eventually established this winery on top of Cherry Hill, near Granger, in 1983. The Late Harvest White Riesling has a refreshing, sherbetty nose and elegant, apricoty fruit.

PAUL THOMAS

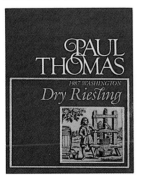

Dry Riesling

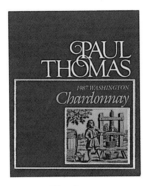

Chardonnay

A producer of fruit wines, this winery also makes "the real stuff". The Dry Riesling is fresh and sherbetty, with piquant fruit; the Chardonnay has a pineapple aroma, tropical fruit flavours and a fine fruit-acidity balance.

WORDEN

Dry Chenin Blanc

This winery was established in 1979 by Jack Worden, a former pharmaceuticals salesman turned orchardist. The 1988 Chenin Blanc has a delicate, crisp-apple aroma and flavour.

IDAHO

STE. CHAPELLE

Special Harvest Winery Hill Johannisberg Riesling

Symms Family Vineyard Chardonnay Reserve

Founded in 1976, this is Idaho's leading winery, now run by Dick Symms, with talented Mimi Mook as winemaker. The Johannisberg Riesling Winery Hill Special Harvest is a rich sweet wine, with an elegant, peach and creamy-vanilla flavour. Another elegant wine is the tropical fruit and floral-oak Chardonnay Symms Family Vineyard Reserve.

OTHER USA

MOST OF THE STATES IN the United States produce wine of some kind (AVAs have been established for at least 24 of them). Apart from California, and before the recent emergence of the states of the Pacific Northwest, the most impact has been made by New York State and its neighbouring states on the Atlantic coast - New Jersey, Maryland, Pennsylvania and Virginia.

New York State
Until the recent expansion of Washington State, New York State was second after California in wine output, largely resulting from the native American grapes with which it was originally planted. Vineyards in New York State today are a mixture of *labrusca*, French-American hybrids and *vinifera*. Whilst *labrusca* still holds sway, the hybrids are becoming increasingly important: in the 1980s many vineyards were still being newly planted with them.

Vinifera vines have their individual champions, most prominently Dr Konstantin Frank, who initiated their introduction to the state in the 1950s at Gold Seal vineyard, and who, since 1965, has produced Chardonnay and Riesling wines in his own Vinifera Wine Cellars at Hammondsport in the Finger Lakes area.

Finger Lakes is still the most important of the New York State wine districts, although Chautauqua on the east side of Lake Erie now has the larger vineyard area. The Hudson Valley and Niagara are the other districts (the former, like Finger Lakes, became an AVA in 1982), and there has been a return to grape growing on Long Island, where an AVA was established in 1985.

While a great deal of output is handled by large concerns like The Taylor Wine Company, with its interests in California and elsewhere, an increase in the number of small wineries was made possible by a change in the State law in 1976, which opened the way for enterprises like Glenora and Plane's Cayuga Vineyard.

Vinifera varieties principally in use are Chardonnay and Rhine Riesling, with some Gewürztraminer and Cabernet Sauvignon. French hybrids include Vidal Blanc, Seyval Blanc, Chelois, Baco Noir, Marechal Foch and Aurore.

Virginia
Virginia is the state where Thomas Jefferson strove unsuccessfully to raise *vinifera* vines in the 1770s. The first commercial *vinifera* vineyards did not come to Virginia until the 1970s, in the wake of a state law encouraging small growers to plant new vineyards and enabling them to sell the products from their wineries. However, Jefferson's successors have fared better and have succeeded in producing prize-winning wines ranging from varietal Cabernet Sauvignon to Bordeaux-style blends, Chardonnay and Riesling. Despite their efforts, however, and even after the inauguration of a Vinifera Winegrowers Association in Virginia, French hybrids are still far more commonly employed in the vineyards, in some cases by the successful *vinifera* growers.

Maryland
Cold winters are a serious threat to *vinifera* vines in Maryland. One solution was offered in the 1940s by Philip Wagner, who chose to put his faith in French hybrids and started a whole new style of winegrowing in the Atlantic Northeast. The establishment of three AVAs for districts in Maryland speak for the success of hybrids. There are, nonetheless, a few isolated brave efforts being made with *vinifera* grapes.

New Jersey
New Jersey has 400 hectares (990 acres) of *labrusca* vineyards. It processes much more wine than it produces from its own vineyards, either that imported from other states, or made from fruits other than grapes. Quality *vinifera* table wine is the exception rather than the rule.

Pennsylvania
Plenty of grapes are grown in Pennsylvania, but not many are used for wine. A determined campaign in the late 1960s against the restrictive State Liquor Laws led to the development of "farm" wineries (small private holdings entitled to sell their own wines), and the same happened in a number of other states similarly afflicted. Cabernet Sauvignon, Chardonnay and Rhine Riesling are the key *vinifera* grapes in use.

Texas
Wine was reputedly made in Texas by the Franciscan missionaries 130 years before they planted their vines in California. Over three centuries later, a leading French wine company, Cordier, has renewed that faith by investing in a large vineyard. Cordier have added Sauvignon Blanc to the, as yet, short list of *vinifera* vines already being grown in Texas, which includes Chardonnay and Gewürztraminer, Grenache and Carignan.

MARYLAND

BOORDY VINEYARDS

Seyval Blanc Sur Lie Reserve

Petit Cabernet, Cabernet Sauvignon

This is where journalist Philip Wagner introduced hybrids to the Atlantic Northeast: a turning point in America's viticultural history. Wagner retired in 1980, selling the vineyard to Rob Deford. The Seyval Blanc Sur Lie Reserve is a delicious, well-flavoured wine in its own right and much better than most of the Atlantic Northeast's *vinifera* wines when the harvest is a difficult one. The Petit Cabernet is made from young vines and is available from the vineyard only.

NEW JERSEY

TEWKSBURY WINE CELLARS

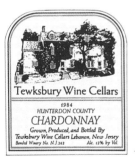

Hunterdon County Chardonnay

Veterinary surgeon Dr Daniel Vernon established this winery in the hilly north of Hunterdon County in 1979. The first *vinifera* wine to attract notice outside the Hunterdon itself was the dry Gewürztraminer, but the full, crisp, oak-aged Chardonnay is now its most successful wine.

NEW YORK

BANFI VINEYARDS

Old Brookville Nassau County Chardonnay

As the largest exporter of Italian wines to the USA, it is not surprising that Banfi decided to set up an estate-winery in America, although the choice of Long Island is less obvious. The well-focused Old Brookville Chardonnay has fine natural acidity and a subtle toasty oak aftertaste.

BENMARL

Estate Reserve Hudson River Region

One of New York's oldest wineries, the vineyards of Benmarl were re-planted in 1957. ("Benmarl" is Gaelic for the slaty-marl soil here.) Its dry white wines are made from Seyval Blanc and have a crisp, fruity flavour.

BULLY HILL VINEYARDS

Special Reserve Baco-Noir

Walter Taylor is a prolific artist and winemaker. The grandson of the founder of the Taylor Wine Company, he left that firm in 1970, then established this lakeside operation just north of Hemmondsport in 1958. He attacked nearly everybody in the Finger Lake wine industry for "watering down their wines". He is also on record as saying that hybrids are "the greatest innovation since the wine bottle". Certainly there cannot be a wider range of hybrid wines produced anywhere else in the galaxy and each wine has its own arty label, most of which change with each vintage. Hybrid wines can prove difficult to swallow, although this smoky-raspberry Baco-Noir (Folle Blanche x *riparia*) slips down easily enough.

CASA LARGA

Blanc de Blancs

This small Finger Lakes winery and vineyard was established in 1978 by Andrew Colaruotolo. The Blanc de Blancs is one of the most successful and stylish *méthode champenoise* produced in New York State.

GLENORA

Finger Lakes Chardonnay

*Johann Blanc
(Dry Johannisberg Riesling)*

Glenora CONTD

This award-winning Finger Lakes winery was established in 1977. Located south-east of Dundee on the western shore of Seneca Lake, Glenora is set within a private estate of 400 hectares (1,000 acres), more than half of which are planted with vines. The style of the Chardonnay is tart and tight, but full and fruity, resembling a decent Chablis in good years. The Johann Blanc is a fine, dry Johannisberg Riesling with an elegant peachy aftertaste.

GOLD SEAL

Charles Fournier Blanc de Blancs

Originally called the Imperial Winery and now part of the Taylor Winery group, this historic firm built up its reputation on New York "Champagne". The quality of these wines today is the result of over 100 years' expertise from various winemakers whom Gold Seal has lured away from the French Champagne industry. Charles Fournier was the most influential of these and the Charles Fournier Blanc de Blancs is the best of Gold Seal's sparkling wines.

HERON HILL

Finger Lakes Johannisberg Riesling Ingle Vineyard

This winery and its lakeside vineyard just north of Bully Hill Vineyards was founded in 1977 by John Ingle and Peter Johnstone. Its best wines are the flavoursome Otter Spring Chardonnay and the Finger Lakes Johannisberg Riesling Ingle Vineyard, which is ripe and tangy with delightful peachy fruit.

PLANE'S CAYUGA VINEYARD

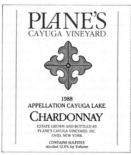

Cayuga Lake Chardonnay

Established in 1980 by Robert Plane, this small estate is a well-run, quality orientated operation just outside Ovid. It has quickly built up an extraordinary reputation for its Chardonnay, a wine that can be quite oaky, but gains weight in the bottle.

VINIFERA WINE CELLARS

Finger Lakes Chardonnay

Finger Lakes Johannisberg Riesling

Vinifera Wine Cellars was founded in the 1960s by Dr Konstantin Frank, the father of *vinifera* wines in the Atlantic Northeast. His Chardonnay and Johannisberg Riesling were hailed as the Northeast's first fine wines, setting an example for other small wineries.

WAGNER VINEYARDS

Finger Lakes Chardonnay Reserve

This 60-hectare (150-acre) vineyard on the eastern shore of Seneca Lake was established by Bill Wagner in 1978. Its Barrel Fermented Seyval Blanc is a revelation for those who reject hybrid wines on principle. However, the top wine here is the Barrel Fermented Chardonnay, which has lots of buttered-apple and tropical-fruit varietal flavour, a well-knit toasty-oak complexity and a certain creamy-spicy finesse.

HERMANN J. WIEMER

Finger Lakes Chardonnay

While working for a certain hybrid afficionado, Wiemer produced some outstanding *vinifera* wines from his own vineyard. They received rave reviews, he got the sack, and he has not looked back since. The house style is restrained and elegant, and the best wine is Wiemer's smooth, buttery Chardonnay.

PENNSYLVANIA

ALLEGRO VINEYARDS

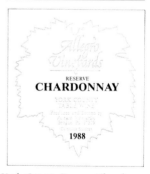

York County Reserve Chardonnay

This operation was founded in 1980 by the Crouch brothers, two young musicians who suddenly had the urge to run a winery and vineyard - hence the name. The favourite wines of winemaker John Crouch are Chardonnay and Cabernet Sauvignon. The Reserve Chardonnay is a rich, oaky wine, with good buttery varietal character.

NAYLOR

York County Chardonnay

This small wine estate on the Barrens plateau, Stewartstown, was established in 1978. It was York County's third winery, but the first one in more than 170 years! Naylor is best known for its elegant late-harvest Riesling and its citrussy-oaky Chardonnay.

TEXAS

DOMAINE CORDIER

Sauvignon Blanc

Originally a joint Franco-American venture, the French firm of Cordier took full control in 1987. Early indications are that the Sauvignon Blanc will be an immediate success for ready drinking, but the oak-aged Chardonnay may be the classiest product when the vines are older.

VIRGINIA

BARBOURSVILLE VINEYARDS

Monticello Cabernet Sauvignon

Monticello Riesling

Established by the Zonin family of Gambellara, who have been making wine in Italy since 1821, Barboursville was the first commercial *vinifera* vineyard in Virginia when it was planted in 1976. The standard of winemaking here is very high; the best are the full, fragrant, spicy-herbaceous Cabernet Sauvignon and the delicate, medium-dry Riesling.

INGLESIDE PLANTATION

Chardonnay

Cabernet Sauvignon

The Ingleside Plantation is a 900-hectare (2,250-acre) tract of land in the highlands of Northern Neck. It had belonged to the Flemer family for 130 years, when Carl Flemer decided to grow grapes there in the late 1970s. Ingleside's full-time winemaker is Jacque Recht, a former oenologist at Brussels University, and his technical expertise has been responsible for winning numerous medals and awards. The Chardonnay has the restrained, elegant style Europeans are accustomed to; the Cabernet Sauvignon is tempered with juicy Merlot and shows considerable finesse.

MEREDYTH

Cabernet Sauvignon

Archie Smith began planting grapes on his 87-hectare (215-acre) farm in 1972, when cattle-rearing became unprofitable. His Cabernet Sauvignon has a violety-minty aroma, a deep flavour and an herbaceous complexity.

MONTDOMAINE

Cabernet Sauvignon Private Reserve

This Cabernet Sauvignon is a Bordeaux-style blend, softened with 20 per cent Merlot, plus a little Cabernet Franc. Conversely, Montdomaine's excellent Merlot has been plumped up with 20 per cent Cabernet Sauvignon and a touch of Cabernet Franc. Also produced is a Chardonnay Barrel Select, with smoky, butterscotch complexity. These are medal-winning wines; the reds age particularly well.

PIEDMONT VINEYARDS

Chardonnay

Although vintages are variable, Piedmont Vineyards has earned wide praise for its rich, buttery, full-bodied Chardonnay, with its spicy-creamy finesse and toasty-oak complexity.

CANADA

CANADIAN VINEYARDS, as is the case with most North American vineyards, were originally planted with *labrusca* vines. The first two commercial wineries were opened by Barnes in 1873 and Bright's the following year. It is only since the 1930s that vineyards have been planted with French hybrids, and - by a handful of more ambitious growers - European *vinifera*.

The introduction of *vinifera* vines

A young Frenchman, Adhemar de Chaunac (who has since given his name, ironically, to a hybrid vine) is credited with introducing a collection of *vinifera* vines, including Chardonnay and Pinot Noir, to the country in 1946. He was 10 years ahead of the celebrated Dr Konstantin Frank, who successfully brought *vinifera* grapes to neighbouring New York State. De Chaunac's action enabled Bright's, where he was winemaker, to produce the first Canadian *vinifera* varietal wine, a Chardonnay, in 1956.

Canada's main growing areas

The most important growing area is the Niagara Peninsula in Ontario. Vineyards are planted on the escarpment north of the Falls, where a handful of producers account for three-quarters of the country's total output. On a latitude just south of that of Bordeaux, the micro-climate is assisted by the moderating effect of the waters of Lake Ontario and Lake Erie, and it is protected in winter by the steep northerly hills. The obstacles caused to intending winemakers by the Canadian Liquor Laws (restricting the outlets through which wine might be sold) have gradually been removed to allow a number of new small estate wineries to be developed, on which the growing reputation of Canada's wines now rests. Inniskillin, set up in 1974, was the first of these wineries. It now has 28 hectares (70 acres) and is one of the few Canadian vineyard names presently known abroad. The principal *vinifera* grape varieties that are used include Chardonnay, Gamay, Gewürztraminer, Johannisberg Riesling and Pinot Noir, and the hybrids Seyval Blanc, Seyve Villard, Vidal Blanc and Villard Noir.

British Columbian vineyards

In British Columbia, west of the Rocky Mountains, 1,620 hectares (4,000 acres) of vineyard, a sixth of the country's total, are situated in the Okanagan valley north of the Washington State border. Until the 1960s much of the wine in British Columbia was made from grapes grown in Washington State. A number of wineries in Ontario now have vineyards in British Columbia. Vineyards are also found in the provinces of Nova Scotia, Alberta and Quebec. So far, however, true classic wines are only produced in Ontario, but this may change as the other areas develop.

CHÂTEAU DES CHARMES

Founded in 1978 by Frenchman Paul Bosc, who studied oenology at Dijon University, this estate was named after "Charmes", his family's villa on the Algerian coast. The white wines include two styles of Chardonnay: the attractive, lighter white-label version, and the richer black label. Its best dry white wine, however, is its Gewürztraminer, a delicious wine with vibrant, mouthwatering, piquant fruit. The Cabernet is comprised of 40 per cent Cabernet Sauvignon, 40 per cent Cabernet Franc and 20 per cent Merlot, and has good colour and body, soft texture and herbaceous-tobacco complexity. The Riesling T.B.A. is a super-concentrated wine, intensely sweet and full-bodied, with an exuberant apricot, lemon and liquorice flavour and lashings of acidity. Almost Trockenbeerenauslese in style, "T.B.A." actually stands for "Totally Botrytis Affected".

Gewürztraminer

Cabernet

Riesling T.B.A.

INNISKILLIN

Niagara Peninsula Pinot Noir Reserve

Niagara Peninsula Chardonnay

Ontario Icewine

Inniskillin came into being when Austrian-born Karl Kaiser purchased vines from Don Ziraldo's nursery, made wine from the grapes, and gave Ziraldo a bottle. The two men struck up a friendship and the rest is history. Inniskillin produces the finest Pinot Noir in Canada. It is already comparable to some of Oregon's Pinot Noirs, and the varietal purity improves with each vintage. The Chardonnay lags behind, but since the 1986 vintage has shown almost equal promise. The bright lemon-yellow colour of the Icewine immediately attracts, and its bouquet is heady, rich and fabulously complex. It is intensely sweet, beautifully balanced and has ripe apricot and peachstone flavours.

KONZELMANN VINEYARDS

Late Harvest Gewürztraminer

Late Harvest Vidal Eiswein

From a family with a winemaking tradition extending back to 1893, Herbert Konzelmann made his first wine in his native Germany as long ago as 1959, but purchased this property as recently as 1982. His first Canadian vintage was 1986. Gewürztraminer is the wine that has very quickly made Konzelmann's name, but it is his Vidal Eiswein, one of Niagara district's specialities, that is by far the most outstanding wine he has produced to date. For his 1987 vintage, the grapes were so rich that he could have added a litre of water to every three of juice and it would still have qualified as a Trockenbeeren-nauslese back in Germany! The wine is full-bodied, intensely sweet with a complex, apricot-glaze flavour and lots of refreshing acidity.

PELEE ISLAND WINERY

Riesling Italico

This unique property with 40 hectares (100 acres) of *vinifera* vineyards on an island in Lake Erie is Canada's most southerly point. The Riesling Italico is a fine, fresh, elegant wine that does more justice to this grape than most European wines do.

REIF WINERY

Chardonnay

Kerner

Vidal Ice Wine

The Reif family were growers and winemakers the Rheinpfalz in Germany for well over 100 years before Ewald Reif emigrated to Canada in 1977. He purchased 55 hectares (135 acres) of land, much of which was planted with Labrusca vines, which he uprooted and replanted with hybrid and *vinifera* vines. Initially he supplied other wineries with his grapes, most notably Inniskillin, but from 1982 he also began to produce his own wines. In 1987 Ewald's nephew, Klaus Reif, took over. Ewald may turn out to be Ontario's greatest winemaker. His Vidal is fresh, aromatic and, although it has 11 grams per litre of residual sugar, tastes deliciously dry. The Chardonnay has an elegant aroma, with delicate, understated new oak. The Riesling Medium Dry has beautiful fruit-acidity balance, with a lovely Riesling perfume on the aftertaste. Kerner is very fresh and aromatic with juicy, piquant fruit, in a Spätlese style. Reif's Ice Wine is rich and sweet, with a deep, unctuous peachy flavour.

~ SOUTH ~
AMERICA

BY SOME FREAK OF CLIMATE, wine is made in South America as near the equator as Bolivia. However, the areas for quality wines at present, and those in line for future development, lie much further south, between latitudes 30 and 40° South, in Chile and Argentina.

Chile has already shown that it has the climatic conditions and grape varieties to produce high-quality wines of world standing. Argentina would appear to be similarly poised, and certainly has the necessary resources - 346,000 hectares (855,000 acres) of vineyard make Argentina one of the world's leading quantity wine producers. The vineyards of Chile occupy only one-third of that area - 116,000 hectares (287,000 acres). After Chile, the next largest producer is Brazil. Brazil's most successful areas are west and south of Rio de Janeiro in Rio Grande do Sul, and one or two wines from classic varieties are beginning to make their way onto the export market. A leading concern is the Palomas winery at Santona do Livramento, established in 1974, which has a holding of 22,000 hectares (54,000 acres) planted with *vinifera* grapes. The Companhia Vinicola Riograndese at Caxias do Sul on the other hand has grown *vinifera* grapes since its inception in 1934. The country has the potential, if the right level of competitive quality can be achieved. Brazil's southern neighbour, Uruguay, still manages to plant 22,000 hectares (54,000 acres), the output from which is usually consumed locally. Its three main growing areas are Salto, Colonia and Montevideo. Bolivia, Peru, Colombia and Paraguay have much smaller acreages and generally produce wines for local consumption.

Chile and Argentina

The better winegrowing areas of Chile and Argentina are found in the same latitudinal band, as are the more promising wine areas of Brazil on its Atlantic Coast. The prime Central Valley region of Chile lies on the 35th Parallel South on one side of the Andes, with the vineyards of Mendoza immediately opposite on the other. In each case, vineyards are planted in the foothills of the Andes and spread out into the adjoining plains.

South America's wine industry *Of the seven or eight wine-producing countries in South America, so far only Chile and Argentina have produced classic wines.*

Climatic conditions, however, considerably favour Chile. The area around and immediately south of Santiago is dry, but with a higher rainfall than Argentina and the benefit of moist and cooling winds from the Pacific Ocean. Chilean vineyards in the foothills of the Andes are not irrigated, although irrigation occurs elsewhere. Across the Andes, Argentina's highly cultivated Mendoza province is an arid, semi-desert region, and from the earliest days irrigation has been a necessity. It is achieved today by an advanced system of canals fed by the mountain rivers that flow down from the snow-covered Andes, and by thousands of deep, man-made wells. Because of the hot climate and the systematic use of irrigation, vintage differences for climatic reasons do not occur here in the way they do elsewhere.

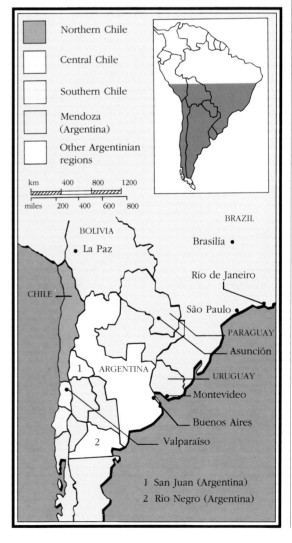

Northern Chile

Central Chile

Southern Chile

Mendoza (Argentina)

Other Argentinian regions

| km | 400 | 800 | 1200 |
| miles | 200 | 400 | 600 | 800 |

BRAZIL

BOLIVIA

Brasília •

• La Paz

Rio de Janeiro

CHILE

São Paulo

PARAGUAY

Asunción

1 ARGENTINA

URUGUAY

Montevideo

Buenos Aires

2 Valparaíso

1 San Juan (Argentina)
2 Rio Negro (Argentina)

CHILE

AMONG THE SOUTH AMERICAN countries, Chile is the best placed to produce quality wines of world standing. Deep limestone soils, low rainfall, the absence of spring frosts, continuous sunshine, and nights cooled by the Pacific Ocean and the Andes create conditions in its quality growing areas that are admirably suited to the development of classic grape varities. The country's other remarkable advantage is that all its vines are ungrafted - that is, they are grown on original French root stocks. Through the initiative (unintentional but, in the event, far-sighted) of a certain Sylvestre Ochagavia, classic Bordeaux vines were imported into the country for planting in 1851, 20 years ahead of the phylloxera scourge that swept through France from the 1870s. Ringed by mountains, desert and the Pacific Ocean, the vineyards of Chile were preserved from the dreaded aphid, making them collectively the most significant vineyards in the world that are still phylloxera-free. An added benefit is that ungrafted vines have a life-span almost three times that of plants grafted on to American root stocks. The Chilean wine-grower is therefore saved the considerable expense of replanting every 30 years, as would otherwise be necessary.

The local Pais grape, related to the Mission grape of the Spanish colonists, is grown in the arid North-Central region (making wines for distillation as Brandy) and elsewhere in the South-Central Valley, Southern Region, and Central and South-Central Secano. Grapes grown in the 37,150 hectares (91,800 acres) of Central Valley, the second largest of Chile's six winegrowing regions, include Cabernet Sauvignon, Merlot, Pinot Noir, Sauvignon Blanc, Sémillon and Chardonnay. Some of the most important quality wines are made in the Maipo Valley and Curicó.

The Spanish winemaker, Miguel Torres, established a vineyard in the Maule Valley, south of Curico in 1979, where he introduced cold fermentation in stainless steel. Coming hard on the heels of financial encouragement from the Chilean Government, these technical improvements have transformed the quality of white Chilean wines which had hitherto lagged behind the reds.

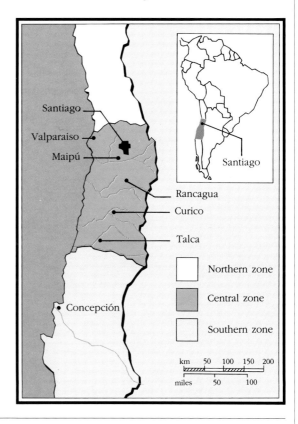

Chile's Central Valley *The best quality wines are produced from vineyards in Central Valley, which hovers on a latitude of 35° South, around and south of Santiago.*

CALITERRA

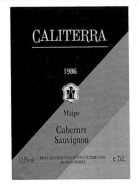

Maipo Cabernet Sauvignon

Curicó Chardonnay

These wines are produced by Viña Errázuriz-Panquehue in the Aconcagua Valley, but deserve their own mention because, while they might be second labels, they are definitely not second quality and claim to come from different areas. The Maipo Cabernet Sauvignon is a most elegant wine with brilliantly focused flavours; the most striking aspect of the Curicó Sauvignon Blanc is its freshness; while the Curicó Chardonnay has an excellent concentration of ripe, creamy-apple fruit and fine acidity.

JOSÉ CANEPA

Maipo Vino Blanco

Maipo Vino Tinto

This firm was established in 1930 and has 600 hectares (1,500 acres) to supply its high-tech winery. The Vino Blanco is a fresh white wine, with vibrant fruit flavour. It is more Sauvignon Blanc than the Canepa Sauvignon Blanc and, frankly, a more impressive wine. The Vino Tinto is delightful, with chocolatey fruit.

CASTILLO DE MOLINA

Lontue Cabernet Sauvignon

Lontue Sauvignon Blanc

This is the premium label of Viña San Pedro, which has a bewildering number of labels, including many single-vineyard wines from its holdings in the Maule area, south of Santiago. It is one of the so-called "big four" of Chile (San Pedro, Concha y Toro, Santa Rita and Santa Carolina dominate the domestic market and account for almost 70 per cent of all exports). The Castillo de Molina Cabernet Sauvignon is a classy Chilean wine with a mellow, oaky bouquet and a richly flavoured palate, hinting of black cherries, blackberries and plums, with cedary undertones. The Castillo de Molina Sauvignon Blanc is rich and creamy, with vanilla oak dominating the fruit.

CONCHA Y TORO

Maipo Cabernet Sauvignon

Cabernet Sauvignon Merlot

ERRAZURIZ PANQUEHUE

This is the only winery of significant size to base its operations in the Aconcagua Valley. Founded in 1879 by Don Maximiano Errazuriz Valdivieso, it is now run by the Chadwicks, an English family that had married into the maternal side of the Errázuriz family and at one time owned one-third of Viña San Pedro. Despite this, the quality and consistency of Errazuriz Panquehue have only recently been recognized on an international basis, making this firm the fastest rising star in the Chilean wine industry. The Sauvig-non Blanc is a crisp, fresh wine that develops an excellent depth of ripe, tangy fruit after two years in bottle, but the Chardonnay is delicious at an earlier stage, with lots of rich, creamy-apple fruit. The Cabernet Sauvignon is full and chocolatey, while the Cabernet Sauvignon Don Maximiano is richer, yet softer, with a luxurious feel and a fine, violety aftertaste.

Maule Sauvignon Blanc

Aconcagua Cabernet Sauvignon

Maule Chardonnay

Aconcagua Cabernet Sauvignon Don Maximiano

The largest and one of the best wineries in Chile with massive viticultural holdings in the Maipo Valley and extending southwards into the Bio Bio area. But Concha y Toro is best known for its Cabernet Sauvignon - always excellent, with vibrant fruit and a mouth-tingling acidity that gives the wine great length, and blended with Merlot the Concha y Toro Cabernet Sauvignon/Merlot is especially smooth and mellow.

COUSINO MACUL

Cabernet Sauvignon Antiguas Reservas

Chardonnay Gran Vino

This winery probably produces Chile's finest red wine, the Cabernet Sauvignon Antiguas Reservas, which is an extraordinarily classy wine of great richness and potential longevity. The Cousino Macul Chardonnay is the winery's most underrated wine - rich and bursting with fruit.

MONTES

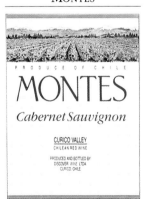

Curico Valley Cabernet Sauvignon

SANTA RITA

This winery at Buin in the Maipo Valley, just south of Santiago, is currently producing excellent wines and experimenting with even better ones. The excellent Cabernet Sauvignon 120 is so called because Bernado O'Higgins, the liberator of Chile, and 120 of his men hid in Santa Rita's cellars after the Battle of Rancagua. The basic Cabernet Sauvignon has a great deal of sweet, ripe blackcurranty fruit, while the Cabernet Sauvignon Reserva is rich in vanilla-oak, while having the weight of fruit to match. There is no obvious vanilla character to the Cabernet Sauvignon Medalla Real, which is significanlty more mellow, with ripe, tangy, mature fruit. The Chardonnay is a delicious, ready drinking wine made in a rich Mâcon style.

Maipo Valley Cabernet Sauvignon 120

Maipo Valley Cabernet Sauvignon Reserva

Medalla Real Maipo Valley Cabernet Sauvignon

Medalla Real Maipo Valley Chardonnay

Aurelio Montes joined up with three owners of some of the finest vineyards in Chile, to produce limited quantities of export-quality wines. The Montes Cabernet Sauvignon is a fine and stylish wine that has been aged in new Kentucky Bluegrass oak.

SAINT MORILLON

Cabernet Sauvignon

These wines are marketed for export by Licores Mitjans, which also makes Valdivieso sparkling wine. Of their Cabernet Sauvignon wines, the best is the excellent Cabernet Sauvignon Reserva which has lots of sweet, ripe fruit flavour and a soft, cedary finish.

SANTA EMILIANA

Chardonnay

Santa Emiliana CONTD

Cabernet Sauvignon Reserva Especial

Produced by Concha y Toro, these wines are named after Doña Emiliana, the daughter of the firm's founder, Don Ramón Subercaseaux Mercado. The Chardonnay is one of the best in Chile, with lots of rich, creamy-apple fruit and fine acidity and the Cabernet Sauvignon Reserva Especial is very rich and ripe, with a fine concentration of creamy-*cassis* fruit.

TORRES

Santa Digna Cabernet Sauvignon

*Santa Digna
Cabernet Sauvignon Rosé*

Bellaterra Sauvignon Blanc

Spain's most innovative winemaker, Miguel Torres Jnr, considers Chile to be a viticultural paradise. By having wine operations in both hemispheres, he has the luxury of two vintages a year with which to experiment and build his experience on. The Santa Digna Cabernet Sauvignon is an elegant, well-flavoured wine with a fine, spicy-oaky complexity, while the Santa Digna Cabernet Sauvignon Rosé is one of the most exciting, unpretentious, utterly delicious wines to come out of South America. The Bellaterra Sauvignon Blanc is a fresh and floral dry white wine with a subtle, creamy-spicy oak influence.

VIÑA CARMEN

Maipo Sauvignon Blanc Gran Reserva

*Maipo Cabernet Sauvignon
Gran Seleccion*

Founded in 1850, but recently revitalized under new ownership, these wines are today made by Ignacio Recabarren, the talented oenologist at Viña Linderos. The grapes come from Viña Carmen's own Maipo Valley vineyards. The Sauvignon Blanc is fresh, fruity and crisp, with a good varietal character. The Cabernet Sauvignon is soft and silky.

VIÑA LINDEROS

Cabernet Sauvignon

A reliable producer of some of Chile's most elegant Cabernet Sauvignon wines, Viña Linderos was established in 1865 by Don Alejandro Reyes Cotapos, a powerful politician who held several ministerial positions. The firm passed into the hands of the current owners, the Ortiz family, in the early part of this century and is technically Viñedos Ortiz SA, although it is still commonly known by its original name. The Cabernet Sauvignon is renowned for its classic aroma and delicately rich, *cassis* fruit flavour.

VIÑA LOS VASCOS

Cabernet Sauvignon Colchagua

One of Chile's oldest wineries, this was originally established by the Eyzaguirre family in 1772, but ceased production and the vineyards were seized during this century. The vineyards were purchased back by the Eyzaguirre family in 1975, and Viña Los Vascos recommenced production as recently as 1982. The Cabernet Sauvignon is made in an unpretentious fruity style for early drinking.

ARGENTINA

ARGENTINA IS THE FIFTH largest wine producer in the world, with a long winemaking history. The centrally placed (latitude 32° South), western province of Mendoza, in the foothills of the Andes, is its main viticultural region with 260,000 hectares (642,000 acres) of vineyard. Its output accounts for two-thirds of the country's total production. Mendoza is mainly a red-wine region where the native Criolla is still widely grown. Its most common European grape variety is Malbec, which is used effectively in blends with other varieties. Cabernet Sauvignon is growing in importance, particularly for export markets. Under the influence of immigrant Italian and Spanish growers, the range of red varieties extends to Barbera, Lambrusco and Tempranillo; Pinot Noir and Syrah are also grown. About one-fifth of the vineyard area is planted with white grapes, including, most importantly for quality wines, Chardonnay and Rhine Riesling. The long list of white varieties also includes Chenin Blanc, Muscat, Sémillon, Palomino and Pedro Ximénez.

North of Mendoza there are vineyards in San Juan, La Rioja, Catamarca, Salto and Jujuy, where hot-climate wines from non-classic grapes are produced. Rio Negro, south of Mendoza, is a more promising area for fine wines, its cooler climate already supporting a range of *vinifera* vines.

BIANCHI

Nuestro Borgoña Fino Tinto

Established in 1928 by Valentin Bianchi, this firm's top wine is the red Nuestro Borgoña. It is an unusual, but successful, blend of Barbera and Malbec; a full-bodied wine of true richness and real character.

BODEGAS ESMERALDA

Mendoza Cabernet-Malbec

This winery was established in 1939 at San Martin in the Mendoza region, where it has huge vineyard holdings. Its Chardonnay and Cabernet Sauvignon are better focused and more vibrantly flavoured than almost every other Argentinian wine. As well as its exciting Cabernet-Malbec, it also produces a superb Cabernet Merlot.

BODEGAS LA RURAL

Vina San Felipe Riesling Renano

This attractive, light, fresh and fruity Riesling Renano comes from the fertile Tupungato Valley in Mendoza. Renano is the true Rhine Riesling, not one of the many synonyms for the ubiquitous Welschriesling.

PASCUAL TOSO

Barrancas Maipu Cabernet Sauvignon

This small, family-run winery in San Jose produces one of Argentina's best known and best quality Cabernet Sauvignons, Barrancas, which is clean and fruity, with a fine concentration of *cassis* varietal flavour.

TRAPICHE

Fond de Cave Mendoza Cabernet Sauvignon

Medalla Vino Fino Tinto

Trapiche is part of Peñaflor, the largest winery in Argentina and the second largest in the world, with appropriately high standards of wine technology. The vast majority of Peñaflor's production is made from the local Criolla grape for domestic consumption only, and cheap export wines are sold under the Andean Vineyards label. However, some fine wines are made from classic grape varieties by Peñaflor's Bodegas Trapiche. The rich Cabernet Sauvignon and smooth Medella, another Cabernet wine, are by far the best wines in the Trapiche range, and they take their place amongst the very finest produced in Argentina.

~ S O U T H ~
A F R I C A

I N 1652 JAN VAN RIEBEECK established the first settlement in the Cape and in the same year planted the first vines. Some time later, Simon van der Stel, founder of Stellenbosch, planted vines at Constantia. However, it was not until the beginning of the last quarter of the eighteenth century that Hendrik Cloete began to make Constantia wines famous throughout Europe.

Today South Africa accounts for just over 2 per cent of total world wine production, of which just over half is consumed as wine, the balance either being converted into Brandy or put into store for future use. The responsibility for this latter category falls firmly on the KWV (*Ko-operatieve Wijnbouwers Vereniging van Zuid-Afrika*) which was established between 1917 and 1918. Uniquely

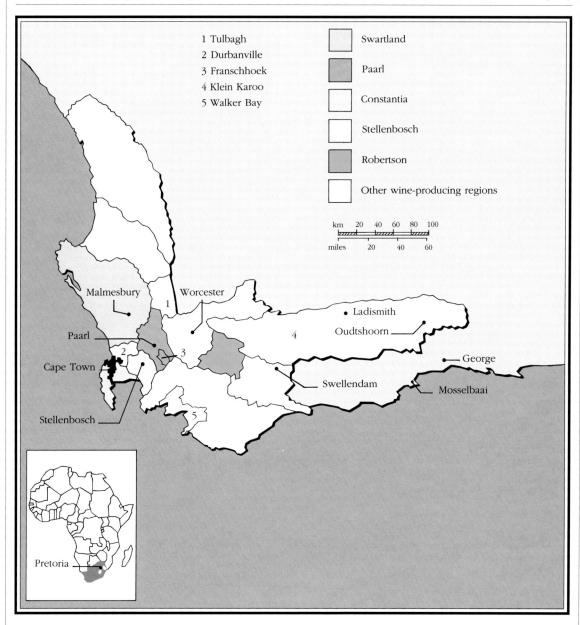

1 Tulbagh
2 Durbanville
3 Franschhoek
4 Klein Karoo
5 Walker Bay

Swartland

Paarl

Constantia

Stellenbosch

Robertson

Other wine-producing regions

km   20   40   60   80   100
miles   20   40   60

Malmesbury   Worcester

Paarl   • Ladismith

Cape Town   Oudtshoorn

Stellenbosch   Swellendam   George
    Mosselbaai

Pretoria

Climatic influences *Despite the hot and arid conditions, vines flourish in the Cape. Vineyards benefit from the modifying influences of two mighty oceans - Atlantic and Indian - and irrigation systems in the drier regions. Equally important is the unique soil structure that comes from some of the oldest mountains known to man.*

in the world of wine, the KWV has a quasi-legal role in both regulating the industry as well as representing the growers and producers it is meant to regulate.

Changes in direction

Between 1918 and as recently as 1980, the vast majority of the production of the Cape (and certainly its reputation) was based on fortified wines: Cape Sherries and Ports, dessert wines and, of course, Brandy. During the 1970s certain estates, and Stellenbosch Farmers' Winery in particular, were not only concentrating on light wines (table wines), but were also rapidly pioneering certain techniques that were to accelerate during the latter part of the decade into a veritable explosion of activity during the 1980s. These techniques comprised cold fermentation for white wines and small oak cask ageing for red wines.

In 1980 not a single "Bordeaux blend" had been released on the market, although today there are at least 25, together with a host of other red blends in which Cabernet Sauvignon plays a major role. The big, alcoholic, often intensely rich, porty wines of the late 1960s and 1970s have been transformed into some of the most individual and exciting red wines in the world. And they are being closely followed by another dramatic development, that of Chardonnay, a variety that had been prevented from entering the country by the rules of the over-regulated industry. Some of the Cape's Chardonnays, and indeed Sauvignon Blancs, can now compete with the finest from both the New and Old Worlds.

The situation today

Today, some 80 per cent of the South African industry is controlled by just one conglomerate, Cape Wine Distillers. Nevertheless, much of the rapid development in the quality of wine is the result of the dedication of the many young winemakers who are connected with the independent estates, some of whom are members of the Cape Independent Winemakers Guild. The rapid learning curve of the members of this Guild has helped propel the development of the industry forward at a speed that could not have been contemplated a few years ago. Further deregulation of the industry should increase competition and result in continued advancement.

The Cape has suffered badly from the lack of suitable plant material. Much of the vine stock in use during the 1960s and 1970s was not virus-free, and consequently the growers had difficulty ripening the grapes, even in some of the warmer areas. New virus-free stock is now rapidly coming into production, and one can expect to see substantial differences in the near future.

SOUTH AFRICAN VINTAGES

Until very recently South African vintages have consistently followed an interesting pattern of two-year cycles. In broad terms, since the beginning of the 1970s the even-numbered years (for example, 1970, 1972, 1974) have seen excellent red wine vintages while the odd-numbered years (for example, 1971, 1973, 1975) have provided favourable conditions only for white wines. This appears to be the result of a two-year climatic phenomenon in which a hot year is followed by a generally cooler and wetter one. Recently, the increasing ability of the South African winemakers to handle more difficult conditions has meant that exceptional wines have also been made in the "lesser" years, particularly since 1983. In any case, the weather cycle appears to have finally been broken in 1987.

As with all vintage chart assessments, allowance should be made for the substantial variation in climatic conditions and the local micro-climates that exist throughout this widely spread wine growing region.

YEAR	VINTAGE
1989	Generally good red wines with some of the best winemakers claiming exceptional results. Whites lack real character although there are several major exceptions.
1988	Great heat affected both reds and whites, but those estates with a high degree of control managed to make some good wines, especially Sauvignon Blanc and Chardonnay in the whites and Bordeaux blends in the reds.
1987	The vintage that broke the pattern with some excellent, well-coloured reds which have the potential for long life. Whites variable, some very good but others rather acid.
1986	Average white wines in this hot, almost drought, vintage. Some superb reds with great concentration and extract.
1985	Pleasant to good whites. Reds variable, often light and a little feeble although some fine, very elegant wines made, especially in the Bordeaux blends.
1984	A difficult year for whites because of extreme heat during harvest. Reds superb with excellent structure, fruit and balance.
1983	Rather average for both whites and reds because of high yields and the resultant low acidity levels. A few notable reds, mainly from the talented new winemakers.
1982	Above average whites, but few remain available. Exceptional reds, especially Cabernet and Cabernet blends.
1981	A lovely white wine year with outstanding fruit and acidity balance. Generally unexciting reds. Few of the "new" wines available.
	Whites probably past it. Some excellent, powerful long-lived reds, now hard to find.

ALLESVERLOREN CABERNET SAUVIGNON

Swartland - The hot, dry climate here has produced powerful and robust wines. The recent introduction of small oak barrels and new vinification techniques have brought additional finesse and greater complexity; wines for ageing. Also noted for Port and Shiraz, the latter winning one of the few trophies at Vinexpo in 1980.

ALTO, CABERNET SAUVIGNON

Stellenbosch - This estate on the slopes of Helderberg had a formidable reputation for its "old-style" vintages of the 1960s and 1970s. Its most recent release brings it "up-to-date" with a deeply fruity, concentrated oak-aged Cabernet Sauvignon, which will require up to 10 years to achieve maximum ripeness.

ALTYDGEDACHT, TINTORETTO

Durbanville - Perhaps better known for their fine Cabernet Sauvignon, this estate, close to Table Bay, produces an interesting blend of Barbera and Shiraz: a big, powerful, full-bodied earthy wine which requires several years ageing to soften and harmonize.

BACKSBERG, CHARDONNAY

Paarl - One of the most successful private estates in South Africa, noted for selling direct to the consumer rather than through the trade. Its Chardonnay is a great success; barrel-fermented and oak-aged, it has excellent structure, fruit and length. Extremely attractively priced.

BACKSBERG KLEIN BABYLONSTOREN

Paarl - This is an exciting oak-aged Cabernet and Merlot blend with good fruit, tannin and acidity balance, which promise longevity. Previous vintages have been more rounded and soft, although highly drinkable.
CS 40%, M 40%, CF 20%

BELLINGHAM, SHIRAZ

Franschhoek - A substantial range of wines is marketed by Union Wine who own Bellingham farm, although grapes are purchased from other sources. The Shiraz, which usually comes from the Bellingham vineyards, is an interesting wine of positive character; it is partly oak-aged, smoky and chocolatey, but relatively light in style.

BERTRAMS ROBERT FULLER RESERVE

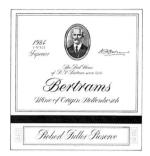

Stellenbosch - Bertrams Robert Fuller Reserve is already an outstanding Bordeaux blend with a full oaky richness, yet obvious Cabernet style mellowed by Merlot. One of only four estates to produce a Zinfandel.
CS 70-80%, M 30-20%

BLAAUWKLIPPEN CABERNET SAUVIGNON RESERVE

Stellenbosch - Probably the best wine of this important and well-known producer, and sold through the annual Guild auction. It is deeply coloured with significant structure helped by additional oak ageing. The soil here produces a very distinctive berry fruit flavour. Good availability.

BON COURAGE RED MUSCADEL JEREPIGO

Robertson - One of the finest examples of Cape Jerepigo's in the refined style. It has an attractive, light ruby colour with an intense, smooth, ripe fruit flavour and excellent length. Very sweet, but delicious.

LE BONHEUR
CABERNET SAUVIGNON

Stellenbosch - A specialist of only three wines, Cabernet Sauvignon, Blanc Fumé (Sauvignon) and Chardonnay, Mike Woodhead has been a leading producer during the 1980s. This wine is an example of the new-style, oak-aged, harmonious and refined Cabernets, having excellent fruit flavours. Recent Merlot plantings will presumably be included in future "blends".

BOPLAAS, PORT

Klein Karoo (Little Karoo) - A wide variety of wines is produced here by Carel Nel in what is a fairly hot region. However, he achieves surprising elegance in his "light" wines although his best wines to date are dessert or "Port" styles. This label is his finest "Port", made from 100 per cent Tinta Barocca. Excellent quality but available only from the estate.

BOSCHENDAL, CHARDONNAY

Paarl - A large estate in Groot Drakenstein with a substantial range of wines, Boschendal has the greatest plantings of Chardonnay in the Cape, which are also used for its excellent *méthode champenoise* sparkling wine. This highly attractive, barrel-fermented Chardonnay has a distinct European "Chablis" style. It is very drinkable and good value.

BOSCHENDAL
JEAN GARDÉ GEWÜRZTRAMINER

Paarl - This Gerwürztraminer marks Boschendal's first and highly successful attempt to produce and market a single-vineyard wine; it has a refined flavour and bouquet, just off-dry. The Jean Gardé vineyard is on the mountain slope, so benefits from a cool climate and excellent drainage.

BUITENVERWACHTING
BLANC FUMÉ

Constantia - A rare example of "organic" farming in the Cape, the wines produced here are carefully fashioned by Jean Daneel. This Sauvignon Blanc Fumé has a deep flavour, which reflects its oak fermentation. It has a good light colour, attractive gooseberry flavour and excellent acidity balance.

CLOS CABRIÈRE
PIERRE JOURDAN

Franschhoek - The first estate in the Cape to specialize in bottle-fermented sparkling wines from Pinot Noir and Chardonnay. Achim von Arnim and Pieter Fereira continue to make the finest in the Cape, although results have been a little inconsistent. Pierre Jourdan has a fine mousse, pale colour and much finesse.

DELAIRE, BLANC FUMÉ

Stellenbosch - Another new venture producing excellent results under the experienced hands of Mike Dobrovic. The vineyards are located in a cooler area, which appears to benefit the white wines most. This is a noticeably oaked wine with good depth and length and will require a couple of years to develop.

DELHEIM, GRAND RESERVE

Stellenbosch - This big estate produces a range of wines, but its reputation is firmly based on the Grand Reserve, a Cabernet Sauvignon-based blend with the addition of Merlot and Cabernet Franc. Under the expert hand of Kevin Arnold, now at Rust en Vrede, this was an impressive, richly concentrated yet well-balanced wine, one of the best in the Cape. The new winemaker, Philip Costandius, promises equally great results.

EIKENDAL, CLASSIQUE

Stellenbosch - Probably the best of a range of wines, this is an oak-matured Cabernet Merlot blend that displays the richness associated with some of the leading estates located between the Helderberg and Stellenkloof. It is well structured, with plenty of fruit and good cedar wood tones.

NEIL ELLIS
CABERNET SAUVIGNON

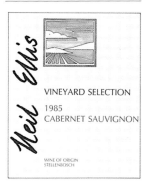

Stellenbosch - Four wines are produced by this talented winemaker who has recently left Zevenwacht to set up his own wine range. Best known for his white wines, Ellis has also produced some outstanding, very delicious Cabernet Sauvignons that show a marked fruit character and supreme oak-ageing elegance.

NEIL ELLIS, RHINE RIESLING

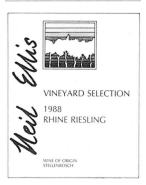

Stellenbosch - At present Neil Ellis buys his grapes from a number of estates. Whites include a superb Fumé Blanc, an oak-aged Sauvignon and this dry wine, with its classic Riesling bouquet and full, spicy palate.

FLEUR DU CAP, PINOTAGE

Coastal Region - A range of a dozen fine wines is made by the Bergkelder. Good rather than special, they can be relied upon to give consistent quality. The latest release of the Pinotage was a big, well-structured wine, deeply fruity, with noticeable oak overtones. The 1986 was quite exceptional.

GLEN CARLOU, CHARDONNAY

Paarl - Walter Findlayson, ex-winemaker and manager of Blaauwklippen, concentrates on the classic grapes of Bordeaux and Burgundy. His first release, a well-made Chardonnay, had immediate appeal, but his name may well be made with the outstanding Bordeaux blends that are currently in the pipeline.

GROOT CONSTANTIA
CABERNET SAUVIGNON

Constantia - This is the famous estate, founded in 1685, from which the legendary Constantia wines of the 1790s originated. Recently, its wines have lacked excitement, but under new direction they are rapidly regaining their former glory. An excellent Cabernet with blackcurrant overtones.

HAMILTON RUSSELL VINEYARDS
PINOT NOIR

Walker Bay - This estate is the leading exponent of the classic Burgundy grapes in the Cape. This wine has a true Pinot Noir flavour and enough body and balance for up to a decade of ageing.

HARTENBERG, SHIRAZ

Stellenbosch - As this estate only releases its wines about six years after each vintage, the most recent stocks available are still of the old style. However, the quality is very good, and this Shiraz is a classic example of its type. Matured in large oak vats, it is a substantial wine with plenty of fruit and good tannin grip.

JACOBSDAL, PINOTAGE

Stellenbosch - This is the only wine bottled by the estate, although it does grow other varieties. Produced on sandy soil on the Cape flats, it has classic berry flavours and an elegance that many lack. A regular success.

KANONKOP, PAUL SAUER

Stellenbosch - This is one of the Cape's leading estates, specializing only in red wines. Beyers Truter has made a succession of outstanding wines; the soil here makes a truly unique style. Paul Sauer is their finest wine; it is basically a Bordeaux blend with a very small percentage of Souzão as well as Malbec. A very fine, long-term wine, it has a big, distinctive flavour, complex fruit and great length.
CS 75%, CF 15%, M 10%

KANONKOP, PINOTAGE

Stellenbosch - This is simply the best Pinotage in the Cape: a wood-aged, complex wine with none of the frequently noticeable acetone character that so many wines possess. The 1985 won Truter the Diners Club "Winemaker of the Year" award, although all vintages up to the latest release are excellent.

KLEIN CONSTANTIA SAUVIGNON BLANC

Constantia - Perhaps the finest estate in all the Cape, this is a consistent producer of brilliant wines, even though it only started to operate with the 1986 vintage. Recent red wines have been outstanding, but it was the 1986 Sauvignon Blanc that won outright acclaim and would make an ideal sparring partner for Cloudy Bay's Sauvignon Blanc from New Zealand. Exciting wines.

K.W.V., LABORIE

Paarl - Laborie is the KWV's own estate, although they regularly buy from other well-known estates. The last release of their white from the Sauvignon Blanc grape was an outstanding wine of real varietal character. Just one of a vast range of wines sold mainly for export.

LANDSKROON, SHIRAZ

Paarl - The best wine of a range made by the de Villiers family, who have been in the business for over 300 years. This is an old-fashioned wine; its complex flavour is deeply fruity, with a noticeable touch of oak.

LEMBERG, AIMÉE

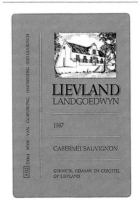

Tulbagh - This is the smallest wine estate in the Cape (production less than 1,500 cases), run by Janey Muller who is determined to produce top-quality wine in this arid region. Two grape varieties are grown, Sauvignon Blanc and Hárslevelü. This oak-aged Sauvignon Blanc is a full-bodied dry wine made in a style similar to the classic Graves of Bordeaux. Difficult to obtain, but worth it.

LIEVLAND CABERNET SAUVIGNON

Stellenbosch - A newcomer to the field of top-quality red wines, although well known for outstanding whites, like Weisser Riesling and Noble Late Harvest. From 1986 the Cabernet Sauvignons have shown great class with lovely ripe-berry flavours, good structure and the promise of excellent development and longevity. Good value.

MEERENDAL, SHIRAZ

Durbanville - A traditional, full-bodied, fruity style of Shiraz produced from wines that are over 50 years old. The estate is also noted for Pinotage, although it grows many of the more popular European varieties.

MEERLUST, RUBICON

Stellenbosch - First produced in 1980, this was *the* Cabernet-Merlot blend in the Cape. Still consistently fine with elegance rather than vigour, this is the style many are trying to emulate. The estate also produces outstanding varietal wines from Cabernet Sauvignon, Merlot and Pinot Noir.

MIDDELVLEI CABERNET SAUVIGNON

Stellenbosch - Middelvlei is best known for Pinotage and Cabernet Sauvignon, the latter being this estate's finest wine. In recent years it has been made in a classic tannic style that is built to last, but with sufficient fruit and oak-cask influence to prove worth the wait.

MONT BLOIS
MUSCADEL LIQUEUR WINE

Robertson - Until recent plantings, this was an estate that only made this one wine. It is a full-bodied, fortified white wine, a regular award winner and a gold medal winner at Vinexpo in 1989, and has a positive dried apricot nose and richly sweet palate.

LA MOTTE, SAUVIGNON BLANC

Franschhoek - Owned by the Rupert family of Bergkelder fame, this refurbished estate started with white wines and is now releasing reds. This wine is an excellent example of a full-bodied yet relatively elegant Sauvignon Blanc. Well worth looking for.

NEDERBURG
EDELKEUR AUCTION RESERVE

Paarl - It is difficult to choose just one wine from a regular range of over 40, excluding the famous Auction Reserve wines. Perhaps most remarkable is Edelkeur; Brözel developed this botrytized wine to perfection. Deep golden apricot colour, with a remarkable ripe, dried apricot flavour, it has an excellent honeyed style and balanced acidity. Exceptional.

NEETHLINGSHOF
CABERNET SAUVIGNON

Stellenbosch - Much money has been spent on this estate recently and the appointment of Günter Brözel promises dramatic results. To date, this has been its best wine: a classic Cabernet Sauvignon with good fruit and length and a strongly oaked character.

L'ORMARINS, BLANC FUMÉ

Franschhoek - This is an estate to watch. Its first great success was the Blanc Fumé, a substantial oak-aged Sauvignon Blanc with excellent balance of fruit and acidity. Recently also noted for Cabernet Sauvignon and an outstanding Chardonnay.

OVERGAAUW, TRIA CORDA

Stellenbosch - Braam van Velden produces many excellent wines. Tria Corda is one of the Cape's earliest Bordeaux blends, started in 1981. Elegant, with a subtle oak flavour, its key is balance rather than vigour.
CS 65%, CF 20%, M 15%

JOHN PLATTER RESERVE
CABERNET SAUVIGNON
(CLOS DE CIEL)

Stellenbosch - John Platter, the eminent writer and commentator on Cape wines made this wine, amongst others, at Delaire, his previous estate. Today, he is the proud owner of Clos de Ciel, and those wines should be appearing soon. This is a well coloured and structured Cabernet with excellent fruit and acidity for long cellerage. Its style is elegant rather than powerful.

RIETVALLEI, MUSKADEL

Robertson - This estate is a specialist in red Muskadel only, although new plantings will change this shortly. This is a big concentrated wine with plenty of richness and sugar. Extra depth and quality come from some very old vines planted in the first decade of the twentieth century.

J.C. LE ROUX
HERE XVII GRAND CUVÉE
MÉTHODE CHAMPENOISE

J.C. Le Roux is the name given to a range of sparkling wines made by the Bergkelder. The Here XVII is made exclusively from Pinot Noir and is disgorged after two years on the yeast. This is one of the Cape's finest sparkling wines.

ROZENDAL

Stellenbosch - A regular favourite at the annual Cape Independent Winemakers Guild auction, this is now a Bordeaux blend, although it used to contain a proportion of Cinsault. Old vines, supplemented by new plantings, make this a well-structured, deeply coloured, complex, barrel-matured Cape red.

RUITERBOSCH MOUNTAIN CUVÉE SAUVIGNON BLANC

Mossel Bay - This cool-climate region should produce some outstanding wines. The first vintage of this wine in 1989 hints at some of the elegance and finesse that may be looked forward to in the future.

RUSTENBERG

Stellenbosch - With a succession of brilliant wines, this is perhaps the leading estate of the Cape. The white wines were sold under the Schoongezicht label, an adjoining estate. This is a "Bordeaux blend" of great elegance yet substance; it is often at its best after 10 years or so. A must in any serious wine drinker's cellar.

RUSTENBERG VINTAGE PORT

Stellenbosch - One of the few Cape Ports that genuinely reflects the true Vintage Port style of Portugal. Highly sought after and, like the best of this great estate, often sold with obvious success at the annual Cape Independent Winemakers Guild auction.

RUST EN VREDE, SHIRAZ

Stellenbosch - Another of the Cape's most popular estates which, under the ownership of Jannie Engelbrecht and the recent appointment of the talented Kevin Arnold, ex-winemaker at Delheim, is sure to become even more in demand. The wines here have great vigour and a distinctive style that requires ageing. This Shiraz has a surprising elegance and great fruit. A real winner.

SIMONSIG, CHARDONNAY

Stellenbosch - A substantial estate owned by the Malan family. Of the more special wines, the Chardonnay has recently sky-rocketed to be one of the finest of the Cape. It has excellent citrus flavour and superb balance and grip, which are bound to make it a favourite amongst serious wine drinkers.

SPIER, PINOTAGE

Stellenbosch - Even bigger production than Simonsig, but not quite of the same overall quality. The Pinotage, however, is an excellent traditional wine made in the classic mould: big, full-bodied and full of fruit.

STELLENRYCK CABERNET SAUVIGNON

Stellenbosch - This is the up-market range from the Bergkelder, although the grapes often come from Durbanville. This wine is often one of the best in the Cape; it has excellent deep colour and multi-dimensional flavours, tempered by oak ageing for between one to two years. A wine made for longer-term cellaring.

TALANA HILL, CHARDONNAY

Stellenbosch - Talana Hill is a new venture with a currently minute level of production (some 300 cases or so) of excellent Chardonnay, which is made for the owners by the brilliant Jan Coetzee of neighbouring Vriesenhof. Although it is too early to tell what the future holds for this winery, its first vintage (1988) has already developed a beautiful, refined and elegant style.

THELEMA, CHARDONNAY

Stellenbosch - A serious new estate, beautifully located on the Simons-berg, which has already produced a series of excellent wines - mainly white, although new releases of Cabernet promise exceptional wines. The latest barrel-fermented and matured Chardonnay is superb.

THEUNISKRAAL GEWÜRZTRAMINER

Tulbagh - A semi-sweet wine produced in this relatively warm growing area. Yet it possesses a balance and fine Gewürztraminer flavour that makes it a very worthy example of its type.

TWEE JONGEGEZELLEN TJ SCHANDERL

Tulbagh - One of the Cape's early pace-setters, this estate was the first to employ cold-fermentation techniques, and did so with great success. Like all the wines made here now, this wine is a blend of several grape varieties. It is an off-dry, well-balanced wine with an attractive aroma from Gewürztraminer and Muscat, which are part of the blend.

UITKYK, CARLONET

Stellenbosch - Located on the Simonsberg for over 200 years, Uitkyk is a substantial estate. This oak-matured Cabernet of medium weight but good balance should last at least 10 years. Recent refurbishment should see even better wines.

VAN LOVEREN, RHINE RIESLING

Robertson - A wide variety of grape varieties is planted on this large estate, which produces alcoholic wines but with good varietal style. It is best known for its white wines; the 1987 Rhine Riesling was particularly successful, winning the South African Show award.

VERGENOEGD CABERNET SAUVIGNON

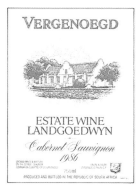

Stellenbosch - A mainly red wine estate, which until 1989 continued to make its wines in large wood. This is a medium-bodied Cabernet with good varietal character and, in recent years, increasing fruit. New vintages should be more exciting, with the benefit of small oak maturation.

VILLIERA, CRU MONRO

Paarl - Villiera is a large estate that in recent years has begun to produce some exciting wines under the able direction of the Grier brothers. The Cru Munro is an excellent Bordeaux blend with a distinct cedar wood flavour and plenty of rich fruit, which promises a long life.
CS 60%, M 40%

VILLIERA TRADITION DE CHARLES DE FÈRE, RESERVE BRUT

Paarl - This is the Cape's most popular bottle-fermented wine, made primarily from Chenin Blanc and Pinotage and some Pinot Noir, but it will include Chardonnay in future. Technically, the Reserve Brut is an excellent spark-ling wine made with the guidance of Jean-Louis Denois from Champagne. It has extra bottle-ageing on the yeast, resulting in great complexity and flavour.

VRIESENHOF, CHARDONNAY

Stellenbosch - One of the great winemakers of the Cape, Jan Coetzee makes consistently fine wines even in lesser vintages. A specialist in Chardonnay, and Cabernet Sauvignon and Cabernet blends, he has shown that elegance and balance are more important than sheer power. Both the 1988 and 1989 Chardonnays show excellent citrus and biscuit flavours.

VRIESENHOF, KALLISTA

Stellenbosch - A "Bordeaux blend" based mainly on Cabernet Sauvignon, but with increasing importance being given to Merlot and Cabernet Franc. A wine of refinement, elegance and balance. Increasing length and depth will make this wine one of the Cape's most sought after. Some of the best wines sold at the Guild auction.

WARWICK, TRILOGY

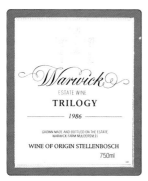

Stellenbosch - Triology is this estate's "Bordeaux blend"; it also makes an excellent straight Cabernet Sauvignon. Both have outstanding deep colour, are packed with fruit yet have substantial tannin and positive oaky character. A cellar to watch closely.

WELGEMEEND, DOUELLE

Paarl - Billy Hofmeyr was the prime force in forming the Cape Independent Winemakers Guild. His Estate wine is probably his best, but this excellent blend of mainly Malbec with Cabernet is unique to the Cape. Its deep colour with good fruit flavour and excellent tannin structure provide excellent value.

WELGEMEEND, AMADÉ

Paarl - This is a medium-weight, oaky, "Rhône" styled wine, with plenty of fruit and flavour. The Welgemeend Amadé is a blend of Shiraz, Grenache and Pinotage; the Shiraz tends to take the dominant role, contributing finesse and fine fruit to this highly individual wine.

WELTEVREDE, GEWÜRZTRAMINER

Bonnievale - With the exception of Red Muscadel, this is a white wine estate in the Bonnievale Ward of the Robertson district. The Gewürztraminer is an off-dry wine (although it has been made sweeter, even as a later harvest style), with a richly fruity character and an interesting scented bouquet.

DE WETSHOF, RHINE RIESLING

Robertson - A specialist in white wines only, Danie de Wet has been a leading pioneer in the region. This is a warm-region estate, yet the Rhine Riesling is consistently a lovely dry wine, with excellent, refined flavour and a fine bouquet, that ages well.

ZANDVLIET, SHIRAZ

Robertson - A red wine specialist, going very much against the trend in this area. The Shiraz is a medium-bodied dry wine, which is aged in both large and small wood. Its pleasant fruity style matures comparatively quickly and is best drunk relatively young.

ZEVENWACHT CABERNET SAUVIGNON

Stellenbosch - Also noted for both Riesling and Gewürztraminer, this Cabernet Sauvignon has been made by the brilliant winemaker Neil Ellis, who has recently left to work on his own venture. This is an attractive wine with ripe, intense summer fruit flavours. It has an almost exotic fruit intensity but sufficient tannin for long-term development.

ZONNEBLOEM SAUVIGNON BLANC NOBLE LATE HARVEST

Stellenbosch - Made by Stellenbosch Farmers' Winery, the extensive Zonnebloem range was a dependable, rather than special, group of wines which is now being substantially upgraded. There are exceptions, however, and this remarkable Sauvignon Blanc Noble Late Harvest displays a magnificent ripe-apricot flavour, which is tempered by an excellent, refreshing acidity.

~ AUSTRALIA ~

AUSTRALIAN WINES CAME of age in world markets in the 1980s. A late starter, the country is now one of the major producers of world-class wines, fully capable of competing in terms of quality with the best in California - its arch-rival in the New World - and Europe. Yet the quantity of wine produced by Australia, surprisingly enough, is not that great. Australia is an immense country (it could absorb the whole of western Europe), but its vineyard areas are relatively small by world standards. The four main winegrowing states, in descending order of productive capacity, are South Australia, New South Wales, Victoria and Western Australia, each producing roughly half as much as the preceeding one. The largest, South Australia, produces 60 per cent of all Australian wines. It has a vineyard area of 27,000 hectares (66,700 acres) in total, which is little bigger in size and output than the Rheinhessen in Germany. The premium quality wines that appear in foreign markets represent a very small percentage of that total output. Enthusiastic smallholders as far apart as the northerly Queensland interior and the southerly island of Tasmania re-established each of these areas as thriving local wine districts in the early 1970s and 1980s.

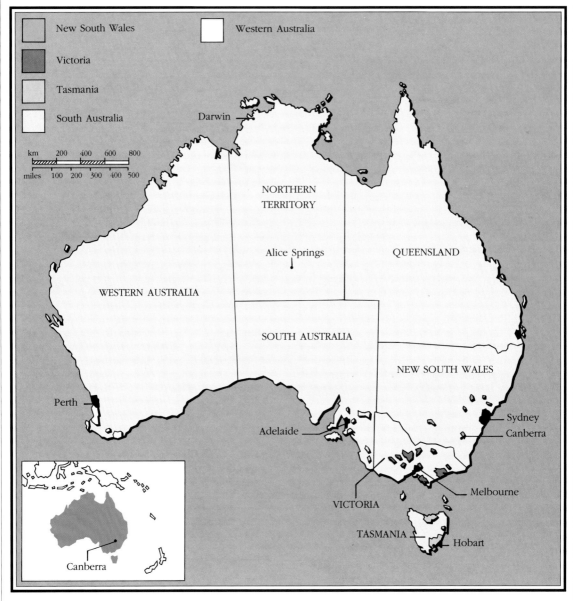

New South Wales

Victoria

Tasmania

South Australia

Western Australia

Darwin

NORTHERN TERRITORY

Alice Springs

QUEENSLAND

WESTERN AUSTRALIA

SOUTH AUSTRALIA

NEW SOUTH WALES

Perth

Adelaide

Sydney

Canberra

Melbourne

VICTORIA

TASMANIA

Hobart

Canberra

Australia's wine industry Despite its size, Australia does not as yet produce vast quantities of wine, but its best wines are rivalling California for quality in the New World. Its most productive and successful vine-growing areas are located between Sydney in New South Wales and Adelaide in South Australia.

The increasing stature abroad of Australian wines over the last two decades is in some ways the spin-off of a strong home market. For many years Australians had been producing, consuming and exporting large quantities of cheap, fortified wines. By the early 1970s they had discovered the delights of lighter, fresher white table wines. In the following decade the sales of lighter white wines tripled, most of which came from the consumption of basic-quality cask wine. It was the Australians who popularized the bag-in-the-box, a cardboard box with a plastic bag interior which collapses as the wine is used, thus reducing oxidation to a minimum. In the same period Australia's consumption *per capita* increased from 8 litres in 1970 to 17.3 litres in 1980. The stimulation of increased demand brought with it significant vinicultural advances, which then led to the introduction of the most advanced standards of technology in the world. Attracted by the opportunities, a new and enthusiastic breed of winemakers has come into the business, trained, among other places, in wine schools at Roseworthy Agricultural College in South Australia, or at Brian Croser's Riverina College of Advanced Education in New South Wales.

Meeting world demand

Increased wine production has gone hand in hand with improvements in quality, with the large companies like Penfolds, Lindemans, McWilliams, Orlando and Seppelts providing a large part of the better quality wines. In the quest for quality, new cooler growing areas have been cultivated in the Barossa Ranges, Western Australia, southern Victoria, Tasmania and elsewhere, and there have been continual improvements in the style of the wines. Wines are fresher, with more intense fruit flavours, better acidity levels, lower alcohol content and more distinguishable regional characteristics. Change in the wine industry in Australia is now endemic. Australian winemakers have responded superbly to world demand for new-style varietal wines from Chardonnay and Cabernet Sauvignon. At the same time they have retained the inimitable and typically Australian character of their Shiraz and Semillon wines, and created their own incomparable versions of Rhine Riesling.

Geography and climate

Most of the Australian land mass is quite unsuitable for winegrowing (although, against all the odds, Alice Springs in the hot Northern Territory boasts its own vineyard, Chateau Hornsby). The Australian continent lies squarely between latitudes 10° South and 40° South. In the search for suitable climatic conditions, its vineyards cling to the southern and south-eastern seaboards. The tropical and sub-tropical climate of the northern half of the country gives way to hot, continental conditions, which intrude into north-west Victoria around Mildura and the Swan Valley in Western Australia, then becomes more Mediterranean along the coast, shading to the cool, temperate climate of Tasmania. Within that broad structure exists a multiplicity of micro-climates for the production of quality wines, whether in the foothills of the Brokenback Range in the Lower Hunter Valley, or on the "flat patch" of Coonawarra, in the foothills of the Australian Alps at Milawa sheltering from the continental climate of north-east Victoria, or the cooler climes of Mount Barker and Frankland River in Western Australia. Melbourne is the most southerly mainland point (leaving aside the island of Tasmania, where some attractive, cool-climate wines are being made) and is on a latitude comparable to that of San Francisco.

First beginnings

The Hunter Valley in New South Wales has the country's longest vine-growing tradition, reaching back to the arrival of the British First Fleet in 1788, who planted vines there after the first cuttings failed to prosper in Sydney's Farm Cove, on the current site of the Opera House. A Hunter Valley Viticultural Association was formed in 1847, and by the 1860s the first vineyards had been laid out on the rich, volcanic soils around the towns of Cessnock and Pokolbin in the Lower Hunter Valley. Victoria's first vines were planted in 1838 in the Yarra Valley immediately to the east of Melbourne. The state was so badly ravaged by phylloxera that it is only now beginning to revive the production of good-quality table wines, and a number of small wineries have been started there in recent years. Yarra itself survived until 1921, and its revival began only 40 years later. Now a number of small growers have re-established themselves, among them being James Halliday, the eminent Australian wine writer, who set up as recently as 1985 at Coldstream Hills. Yarra is now very much looked upon as a "new wave", cool-climate region, where Pinot Noir may well go on to flourish in future.

The vine cuttings for South Australia were introduced in 1837, and a year later John Reynell planted his Reynella vineyard with vines which came from South Africa. The Reynella winery is still active in MacLaren Vale, just south of Adelaide, though no longer in family ownership. Tasmanian viticulture, which had made an earlier start in 1823, did not survive the end of the nineteenth century and was only re-established in the late 1950s. It now has five wine-producing areas, two of the best known properties being Marion's Vineyard and Pipers Brook. Cabernet

Sauvignon and other Bordeaux varieties are grown, in addition to Pinot Noir, Rhine Riesling, Chardonnay, Traminer and Müller-Thurgau.

The Western Australian industry is both old and new. The two leading companies in the region are Houghton, which first came to the area in 1836, followed four years later by Sandalford, both of them on original sites in Swan Valley. The new area in Western Australia, which has made such an electric impression with the sheer quality of its wines since its inception in the late 1960s, is at Margaret River, south of Perth on Australia's extreme south-western tip. Mount Barker and Frankland River are further to the south-east.

Significant developments

Probably the single most important development as far as the modern Australian wine industry is concerned was triggered by Gramps, the owners of Orlando, when in the early 1950s they introduced the process of cold fermentation in stainless steel. The effect, particularly on white wines, was remarkable, making possible lighter, fresher, more fragrant wines that retained much more of the grape flavour. Their lead was quickly followed, and thus they paved the way for the astonishing Australian white-wine boom of the 1970s and 1980s when, in a period of 10 years, sales of dry white wines soared from 30 million litres to an incredible 180 million litres.

The benefit of controlled temperature fermentation for red wines is just as important in the hot Australian climate as is the use of new wood for ageing potential. In 1952, Max Schubert of Penfolds, influenced by the method used in Bordeaux of maturing red wines in small, new oak barrels, had succeeded in producing the first vintage of the now fabled Grange Hermitage. His success was not immediately recognized, but Grange Hermitage has since been hailed as Australia's finest red wine, and the method is now essential to the production of high-quality Australian reds.

Boutique wineries

The growth in what are known as "boutique wineries" - small, usually family, undertakings - has also been significant. It has been estimated that there are some 500 wineries in Australia, 450 of which are small concerns, but they have only a 2 per cent share in the country's production. The rest is in the hands of the 50 or so largest companies. The tendency for these larger companies is to consolidate their interests across the country, buying vineyards in different states, trucking grapes in refrigerated containers thousands of miles, and vinifying the wine at a large, high-tech centre, usually in the Barossa Valley. This consolidation is likely to increase and it gives added importance to smaller, individually-owned concerns, where it is possible for the unexpected and the experimental to take place.

The Australian quality factor

Australia does not as yet possess a comprehensive national system for regulating wine quality. Some wine regions, including Margaret River in Western Australia and Mudgee in New South Wales, have attempted to introduce controlled appellations, but the idea has not caught on nationally. Two forces, however, are currently at work to encourage top-quality levels of winemaking in Australia. The first, unexpectedly perhaps in a world accustomed to the levelling-down effects in large production, is the increasing control of the Australian wine industry by a very small number of bigger concerns. In Australian wine terms, big can be beautiful. Lindemans, the largest winemaking concern in the country, and Penfolds, into which Lindemans has now been absorbed, have both earned reputations for the high standards of their wines. This is also true of the bigger firms like Orlando, Seppelts or McWilliams, and of a mass-production area like Riverina which, despite its bulk-wine image, creates some quality products.

Wine shows and awards

The second influence towards encouraging quality is the network of highly organized, competitive wine shows. Almost everywhere in the Australian wine belt seems to have its annual show, with awards for every conceivable class of wine. Within New South Wales alone there is the Hunter Valley Show, the Mudgee Show, the Pokolbin and District Winemakers' Show. All the leading conurbations have their distinguished annual occasions: the National Wine Show at Canberra, and shows at Hobart, Brisbane, Sydney, Adelaide, Perth and Melbourne. It is at Melbourne that the most coveted and prestigious of all Australian awards, the Jimmy Watson Trophy, is presented for the best one-year-old red wine in the show. The shows have a number of real benefits. Since they are so avidly supported, they tend to bring together the best wines of recent vintages and thereby enhance and encourage the attainment of still higher quality levels. While it is perhaps inevitable that the larger concerns scoop the pool, this is not always the case. The event can provide a platform and superb publicity for a completely unknown winemaker. When Cape Mentelle won the Jimmy Watson Trophy at the Melbourne Show in 1983, the first small winery to do so for 15 years, it not only projected itself onto the world stage, but also focused attention on the newly emerging wines areas of Margaret River and Mount Barker in Western Australia.

AUSTRALIAN VINTAGES

YEAR	NEW SOUTH WALES	VICTORIA	SOUTH AUSTRALIA	WESTERN AUSTRALIA
1989	Excellent early whites in Upper Hunter. Lighter wines in Lower Hunter. Mudgee yields lower; Murrumbidgee higher.	Lighter reds in Milawa in mixed harvest conditions; whites average in Great Western; diminished Yarra Valley crops.	Low yields and variable quality in Adelaide, Eden Valley and Clare. Good in Barossa. Good yields and quality in Coonawarra.	High-quality Chardonnay and Sémillon in cool season at Margaret River; promising reds. Generally good quality elsewhere.
1988	Earlier harvest in Upper Hunter; excellent whites and subtle reds. Late vintage in Lower Hunter: soft whites; some exceptional reds.	Successful vintage in Milawa. Good harvest in Great Western. Intense wines from Yarra, despite wet harvest. High quality in Mornington Peninsula.	Low yields in Adelaide Hills; soft reds. Good in Barossa. Fine harvest in Clare. Quantity hit by frost in Coonawarra/ Padthaway; good Cabernet Sauvignon.	Spring hail followed by hot harvest conditions in Margaret River. Good quality Pinot Noirs and Chardonnays produced.
1987	Excellent wines from Lower Hunter. Moderate crop in Upper Hunter; quality whites, average reds, but good Pinot Noir.	Deep-flavoured wines in Milawa. Low crop at Great Western, except Pinot Noir. Average yield at Yarra caused by cold weather.	Adelaide whites better than reds. Distinctive wines in Barossa, but lower yield. Quantity down in Clare; quality high in Coonawarra.	Good wines from Margaret River. Best Chardonnays and Chenin Blancs in Swan Valley. Good whites in Mount Barker/Frankland.
1986	Classic whites and fine reds in Hunter Valley. Late frost cut Mudgee yields, but produced promising white and red varieties; Shiraz exceptional.	Intense reds and fortified wines from late vintage at Milawa. Half average crop in Great Western. Good crop at Yarra; Pinot Noir and Cabernet outstanding.	Exceptional wines from Adelaide Hills. Outstanding vintage in Barossa. Good harvest in Clare. Exceptional wines in Coonawarra.	Good reds in Margaret River; lighter whites. Intense Shiraz and Cabernet at Mount Barker/Frankland. Good Chardonnay and Cabernet in Swan Valley.
1985	Hail reduced crop in Lower Hunter, wet harvest caused uneven ripening; good Sémillons, Chardonnays and Pinot Noir. Good quantity and quality in Upper Hunter.	Well-balanced wines in Great Western. Good quantity in Milawa; good varietal whites, excellent reds; luscious fortified wines. Top whites and Shiraz in Yarra Valley.	Good quantity and quality in Adelaide Hills. Extremes in Barossa affected output. Weather in Clare reduced yields, but good reds and whites. Fine harvest in Coonawarra/Padthaway.	Exceptional whites in Margaret River; lighter reds. Reds and whites of good quality in Mount Barker. Some very good early-picked wines in Swan Valley.
1984	Cool season, with fruity whites and lighter reds in Lower Hunter. Reduced yield in Upper Hunter, rain interrupting harvest. Excellent reds and whites produced in Mudgee.	One of the best of vintages in Milawa: crisp whites and stylish reds. Cool summer delayed harvest in Great Western; some outstanding reds. Good late harvest-wines in Yarra.	Above average yield and high quality in Adelaide Hills. Good vintage in Barossa. Balanced wines, with outstanding Rhine Rieslings from Clare. Mixed results in Coonawarra.	Quality whites and well-balanced reds in average Margaret Valley harvest. Yields down in Mount Barker/Frankland with mixed results. Improved quality in Swan Valley.
1983	Lower Hunter harvested fine reds and whites. Upper Hunter had its third successive drought, but the surviving wines were of very high quality.	Drought decimated Great Western crop. Short harvest in Milawa and Rutherglen. Irrigated Mildura vineyards better. Frost, hail, drought, wasps and rain in Yarra.	Crops devastated everywhere except for irrigated vineyards, which produced some wines of high quality.	Big harvest in Margaret Valley and excellent wines. Good results in Mount Barker/Frankland. Well-balanced wines in Swan Valley.
1982	Reduced harvest in Upper Hunter; good Chardonnay, Sauvignon Blanc and Semillon. Moderate season in Lower Hunter produced good quality whites and reds.	Big, good harvest in Great Western. Late, wet harvest in Milawa; Chardonnay and Traminer outstanding; average reds. Cool summer in Yarra produced classic reds and good whites.	Whites good and reds above average in Barossa. Lighter Rhine Rieslings from Clare Valley. A vintage year for Cabernet Sauvignon in Coonawarra and good quality whites.	Cool season in Margaret Valley, with good quality wines, especially Cabernet. Cool conditions in Swan Valley benefited whites. Improved good yields in Mount Barker/Frankland.
1981	Good wines from Lower Hunter, despite drought. Upper Hunter, with the same climate, produced some excellent, bigger style whites, but reds were mediocre.	Some good wines in Great Western. Ripe harvest in Milawa, good for liqueur Muscats. Frost affected yields in southern Victoria.	Hot, variable conditions caused unbalanced fruit in Barossa and low acid levels in Clare. Results better in Coonawarra.	Fine vintage whites and reds in Swan Valley. Lighter style Mount Barker wines. Lower yield but even-ripening, well-balanced wines in Margaret River.

NEW SOUTH WALES

THE FINE WINES OF New South Wales come principally from the Hunter Valley and from the little district of Mudgee on the slopes of the Great Dividing Range where Chardonnay was first introduced to Australia. The domestic cask-wine industry is supplied mainly from Riverina in the Murrumbidgee Irrigation Area, which is centred on Griffith - one of the largest wine-producing districts in Australia. Riverina also produces quality wines, including the reds from McWilliams and the luscious, botrytized De Bortoli whites, which have attracted world attention.

The Hunter Valley

The Lower and Upper Hunter Valley areas produce wines of fine quality and great style. The Hunter Valley's heat-summation figures are 50 per cent higher than for Coonawarra (which is similar to Bordeaux) and nearly double those for the "cool climate" Yarra Valley in Victoria. It has low overall rainfall, while the sub-tropical climate can bring hail and rain at harvest time in late January onwards, when it is least required for the purpose

of cultivating successful vines. The heat in the Lower Hunter is somewhat moderated by cloud and sea breezes; whereas the climate in the Upper Hunter, further inland, is hot, necessitating large-scale irrigation systems.

Grape varieties

The Lower Hunter's reputation is built on its splendid Sémillon whites and forceful Shiraz reds (the Syrah grape of the Rhône Valley, also known in Australia as Hermitage). Both wines have unusually fine ageing qualities. Famous names established in the Lower Hunter include Lindemans, Rothbury and Tyrrell's. Dr Max Lake of Lake's Folly encouraged plantings of Cabernet Sauvignon in the region, and this and Chardonnay appear in every good winemaker's portfolio. The Upper Hunter came to prominence with the re-establishment in 1969 of the Rosemount Estate and Arrowfield properties. It is particularly the superb Chardonnays of Rosemount that have been so instrumental in the development of the Upper Hunter as a quality white-wine area.

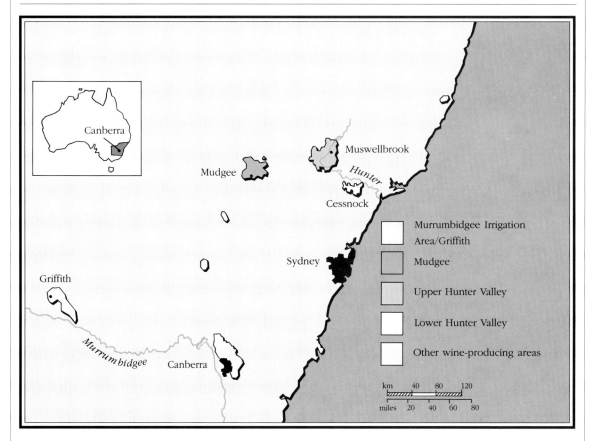

Canberra

Muswellbrook

Mudgee

Hunter

Cessnock

Sydney

Griffith

Murrumbidgee

Canberra

Murrumbidgee Irrigation Area/Griffith

Mudgee

Upper Hunter Valley

Lower Hunter Valley

Other wine-producing areas

| km | 40 | 80 | 120 |
| miles | 20 | 40 | 60 | 80 |

A tradition of wine *Wines have been made commercially in the Hunter Valley since the 1820s. The* *valley of the river Hunter provides two vine-growing areas, the Lower Hunter and the Upper Hunter. The Mudgee* *and Murrumbidgee Irrigation Areas complete the list of New South Wales' diverse wine-producing areas.*

ALLANDALE

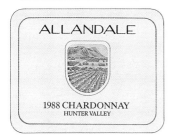

Hunter Valley Chardonnay

Hunter Valley Cabernet Sauvignon

This winery, founded at Pokolbin by Edward Joualt, has a 6-hectare (15-acre) vineyard of Chardonnay, Sémillon and Pinot Noir in the Lower Hunter Valley. Yet most of its production comes from grapes bought from selected growers. The current winemaker is Bill Sneddon, whose viticultural philosophy inclines to European attitudes. Both these wines have been matured in French Nevers oak, enhancing the Chardonnay's lemony fruit with a lovely buttered-toast richness and adding ample tannin support to the ripe berry fruit flavours in the Cabernet Sauvignon.

ARROWFIELD WINES

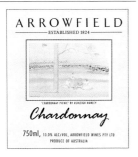

Chardonnay

Semillon

This estate dates back to 1824 when Governor Macquarie granted the land to one George Bowman, who named huge fields after variations of his surname, hence "Bowfield", "Archerfield" and "Arrowfield". In 1969 Arrowfield Wines was bought by a holding company, which extended the vineyards and installed an intricate drip-irrigation system. Unfortunately the bulk of its vines were Shiraz and the market was shifting to white wines, resulting in its vineyards being drastically cut back, although at 180 hectares (445 acres), this is still a significant operation. Chardonnay is this winery's claim to fame. With ripe, exotic fruit and supporting oak richness, this wine is always successful. The Semillon is a quick developer, with fine, rich fruit and excellent acidity.

BOTOBOLAR VINEYARD

Mudgee St. Gilbert

Mudgee Chardonnay

Established in 1971 by Gil Wahlquist, Botobolar comprises almost 30 hectares (75 acres) of Mudgee vineyards, an underrated wine area. Situated 260 kilometres (160 miles) north-west of Sydney, most Mudgee vines grow at a height of between 450 and 650 metres (1,475 and 2,130 feet) and benefit from a much cooler climate than those in the Hunter Valley. The vines of Botobolar - one of the highest Mudgee vineyards - undergo a longer growing season and the wines have a better natural acidity balance. These are organically produced wines of a fine and interesting quality. The St Gilbert is a Cabernet-Shiraz blend of uncommon quality and complexity. The Chardonnay is a finely scented, delicately rich wine with attractive tropical fruit flavours.

BROKENWOOD

Semillon

Graveyard Vineyard Cabernet Sauvignon

One of the original owners of this vineyard at Pokolbin in the Lower Hunter was wine author and winemaker James Halliday. Since he has moved on, Brokenwood's 20 hectares (50 acres), selectively planted with Cabernet Sauvignon, Shiraz and Chardonnay, continue to produce wines of the highest standard. Since 1983, the winemaker has been Iain Riggs, who has maintained this winery's reputation for producing medal-winning wines of individual and distinctive character. The Semillon is extraordinarily exotic for its variety, and the Graveyard Vineyard Cabernet Sauvignon is a complex wine with lots of smoky-*cassis*, capsicum and cedary flavour.

CASSEGRAIN VINEYARDS

Pokolbin Semillon

Coonawarra Cabernet Sauvignon

Cassegrain Vineyards CONTD

The Port Macquarie area supported vineyards in the 1860s, but no vines were in existence when, in 1980, John Cassegrain established this 16-hectare (40-acre) vineyard in Hastings Valley. Although he has home-grown Pinot Noir, Merlot, Chardonnay, Cabernet Sauvignon, Chambourcin, Sauvignon Blanc and Gewürztraminer, he still sources most of his wines from other vineyards. The new oak influence on the Semillon from the Lower Hunter is elegant and not overstated. His best wine is the fine, supple Coonawarra Cabernet Sauvignon, which has an herbaceous, berry-flavoured fruit and fine cedary complexity.

CHATEAU FRANCOIS

Pokolbin Mallee Semillon

This small 2.4-hectare (6-acre) vineyard in Pokolbin was established in 1969 by Don Francois. He cultivates Shiraz, Pinot Noir, Sémillon and Chardonnay, from which he produces 1,000 cases of high-quality wines. The Chateau Francois Pokolbin Mallee Semillon is a rich-flavoured wine with youthful honey in the fruit and a creamy-smoky complexity.

CRAIGMOOR WINES

Mudgee Semillon Chardonnay

Mudgee Cabernet Sauvignon

Since this old-established Mudgee winery and its 30 hectares (75 acres) of vineyard were purchased and revitalized by Montrose in the mid-1980s, the wines have shown increasing finesse. The Semillon Chardonnay, for example, has an entrancing spicy-oak dominated bouquet, with firm, creamy-fruit flavours on the palate. The Cabernet Sauvignon has a ripe and powerful *cassis* nose, vibrant berry fruit flavours on the palate and an herbaceous, cedary-spicy complexity on the finish.

DE BORTOLI WINES

Sauternes Botrytis Semillon

Rare Dry Botrytis Semillon

Founded in 1955, this winery near Griffith has 60 hectares (150 acres) of vineyard, which is not big by Australian standards, but production is huge. The quality is mostly modest, but De Bortoli can produce excellent wines (and in large quantities), particularly sweet whites. Europeans do not normally like New World producers using their classic wine names, but who could not be besotted by De Bortoli's so-called Sauternes: a huge, oaky-rich botrytis wine with lots of creamy, honeyed flavour? And there is the stunning Rare Dry Botrytis Semillon, with its scintillating concentration and complexity.

HUNGERFORD HILL VINEYARDS

Hunter Valley
Show Reserve Chardonnay

Hunter Valley Shiraz

Established in 1967, Hungerford Hill has some 145 hectares (360 acres) of vineyard in the Hunter Valley and Coonawarra. Some of its wines are the product of both vineyards: as they are 1,130 kilometres (700 miles) apart, it is a bit like blending Rioja with wine from the Great Hungarian plains, but the results are fine nevertheless. Of the more individual products, the Show Reserve Chardonnay is luxuriant, with exotic, buttery-peachy fruit and lovely toasty oak. The Shiraz is made in a lighter, more elegant style, yet retains the richness of its new American oak ageing.

HUNTINGTON ESTATE

Mudgee Semillon

Mudgee Cabernet Sauvignon

Bob Roberts entered the wine business in 1969 with a law degree, which was not much use, so he took a winemaking course by post with an institute in England. His clean, fleshy, well-balanced, stylish wines regularly beat those made by some of the most highly qualified professionals. The Huntington Estate Semillon is a young, fresh and flavoursome wine whose richness is enhanced by a little residual sugar. This is a common practice (not just in Australia, but throughout the New World) in most so-called dry whites, but the honesty of labelling it "Medium Dry", as Bob Roberts does, is rare. The Cabernet Sauvignon is ripe and rich, with a good dollop of spicy-toasty oak.

LAKE'S FOLLY

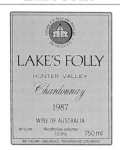

Hunter Valley Chardonnay

Hunter Valley Cabernet

This winery is the passion of Sydney surgeon Max Lake who pioneered Cabernet Sauvignon and Chardonnay in the Hunter Valley as far back as 1963, when it was entirely planted with Shiraz and Sémillon. He also introduced the use of new oak to the region. His Chardonnay is firmer than most, but has a great intensity and integrates beautifully with its subtle oaky character after a little bottle age. The Cabernet has a sweet, juicy, herbaceous character that is gently underpinned with sweet, ripe oak.

LILLYPILLY ESTATE

Spatlese Lexia

LINDEMANS WINES

The country's largest winery, Lindemans turns out nearly four million cases a year. Its range is vast and full of gems. Its most renowned wine is the Hunter Valley Semillon, which is sold either as Hunter River Riesling, Chablis or Burgundy. The 1965 Hunter Valley Semillon Bin 2755 was relaunched as part of Lindemans' Classic Range in 1989. The Padthaway Sauvignon Blanc is one of the crispest, most upfront versions of this varietal. The Pyrus Coonawarra Red Wine is a classic Bordeaux blend of Cabernet Sauvignon, Cabernet Franc, Merlot and Malbec, with the structure of a fine Médoc. One of Australia's greatest wines, the Limestone Ridge Shiraz Cabernet bursts with creamy-oaky blackcurrant fruit and is enjoyed for this concentrated fruit,when young, and for its profound flavour and complexity when 10 or 15 years old.

Lindemans Classic
Hunter Valley Semillon Bin 2755

Padthaway Sauvignon Blanc

Pyrus Coonawarra

Coonawarra Limestone Ridge
Vineyard Shiraz Cabernet

Chardonnay

This vineyard was first planted in 1972, the Year of the Tree, and was thus named after a native species of Australian tree, the lilly pilly. It is owned and run by Pasquale Fiumara, and his son Robert is the winemaker. The whites are better than the reds, especially the Spatlese Lexia, which is a sweet, rich and grapy wine made from late-harvested Lexia or Muscat d'Alexandrie grapes. The fresh, floral-buttery Chardonnay is improving all the time.

McWILLIAM'S WINES

Inheritance Collection
Traminer Riesling Bin 77

Mount Pleasant Elizabeth

McWilliam's Wines CONTD

*Show Series
Limited Release Vintage Port*

With purchases to supplement its 300 hectares (740 acres), this traditional firm has built up an annual production of over two million cases. The Inheritance Collection Traminer Riesling is a refreshing wine with a fine, spicy aroma and delicate, tangy fruit. The Mount Pleasant Elizabeth is a Sémillon wine that is sold as a Riesling in Australia. It has a smoky aroma with a honeyed-apple flavour that develops in the bottle. Best is the Mount Pleasant Show Series Vintage Port - an oak-matured Shiraz-based fortified wine of great character.

MIRAMAR WINES

Mudgee Semillon Chardonnay

Mudgee Cabernet Sauvignon

This 20-hectare (50-acre) vineyard and winery was established in 1977 by Ian McRae, who quickly started winning medals for the fine quality of his big, rich wines. The Mudgee Semillon Chardonnay has plenty of ripe, buttery-pineapple Chardonnay flavour to back up the Semillon's grassy-herbaceousness. It is a wine that will reward a little bottle-ageing. The Mudgee Cabernet Sauvignon tastes like a clever blend of herbaceous, early-picked fruit and big, meaty ripe grapes.

MONTROSE WINERY

Mudgee Special Reserve Chardonnay

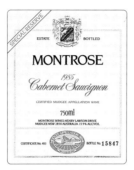

*Mudgee Special Reserve
Cabernet Sauvignon*

Established by two Italian engineers in 1974, but now part of Wyndham Estate, this high-quality 75-hectare (185-acre) vineyard produces wines that are already exciting and yet are constantly improving. The Special Reserve Chardonnay has a distinctive smoky-oak complexity overlaying masses of ripe, exotic, pineappley fruit. The Special Reserve Cabernet Sauvignon is a cedary classic that requires several years in bottle to show its full potential.

PETERSONS WINES

Hunter Valley Chardonnay

Hunter Valley Semillon

The Hunter Valley is not really suited to growing Chardonnay grapes, but Ian and Shirley Peterson's vineyards are tucked away in a little corner of Mount View that truly is. Judging from their new winery and tasting facility, the Petersons look set to expand. Their Chardonnay has fruit of such obvious class and finesse that the considerable creamy-spicy oak character hardly intrudes. The Cabernet Sauvignon is an intensely flavoured, compact wine with excellent acidity, but it is the whites that are their forté and the Semillon and "Sauternes" are both stunning.

MURRAY ROBSON WINES

Hunter Valley Traditional Semillon

Hunter Valley Cabernet Sauvignon

This operation was established in 1972, when teetotal Murray Robson bought a 90-hectare (220-acre) estate at Mount View. His intention was simply to build a holiday home there, but in 1974 he was gathering his first harvest. Since his second (medal-winning) vintage, Robson has not looked back. His Hunter Valley Traditional Semillon has fruit that is ripe, ample and ready to enjoy. The Cabernet Sauvignon is ripe and lush, full of soft-fruit flavours, and has an underlying minty finesse.

ROSEMOUNT ESTATE

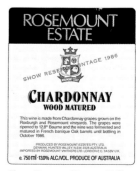

*Show Reserve Hunter Valley
Chardonnay*

White's Creek Vineyard
Hunter Valley Semillon

The original Rosemount winery dates back to 1864, but fell into disuse long before coffee- and cocoa-trader Bob Oatly revitalized it in 1969. From modest beginnings, it now has almost 500 hectares (1,235 acres) of vineyards and two ultra-modern wineries at Tumbarumba and Denman, where the level of winemaking is fastidiously high. Rosemount is a company that markets its products aggressively, both at home and abroad. It is the Chardonnay that has firmly established Rosemount on export markets, especially the rich, toasty-oaky Show Reserve and the Roxburgh (which is the Hunter Valley vineyard at the heart of the Show Reserve). The ripe and toasty Semillon, which comes from the adjoining White Creek vineyard, is so rich that it is best drunk on its own, without food, and in not too great a quantity. The best red is Kirri Billi Cabernet Sauvignon, whose creamy-minty fruit is soft and velvety, but has sufficient tannin and acidity to partner food well.

THE ROTHBURY ESTATE

Brokenback Vineyard
Hunter Valley Chardonnay

Brokenback Vineyard
Hunter Valley Semillon

This great Australian winery was founded in the late-1960s by Len Evans, the indefatigable publicist of Australian wine, when he and 10 other investors purchased some land from Murray Tyrrell that was surplus to his own winery's requirements. Between 1968 and 1971, some 300 hectares (740 acres) were planted with the Hunter Valley's traditional varieties: 65 per cent with Shiraz,

35 per cent with Sémillon. Just as Rothbury was getting under way, the red wine boom abruptly halted. It took a good 15 years to emerge from the downward-spiral effect of this slump, and it is good for the consumer that it has managed to do this because from the start, and throughout its difficulties, the exceptional standard of Rothbury wines has helped create Australia's high-quality winemaking image. One wine that has helped bridge the gap between Rothbury's hand-crafted quality and its commercial success is its Chardonnay, which seems to have an almost European acidity balance and the fruit of a well-focused California wine. Yet underneath there is an exotic, peachy character to the fruit and a ripe-sweetness to the oak that is distinctly Australian. Nevertheless, it is the ripe, honeyed fruit of the Hunter's traditional Semillon that still makes it Rothbury's greatest wine. And, indeed, one of Australia's greatest wines, too.

SAXONVALE WINES

Bin 1 Hunter Valley Chardonnay

TYRRELL'S VINEYARDS

This old-fashioned firm has a typical Hunter Valley winery built of corrugated iron and with an earth-floor. The range is huge and many of the wines can be of modest quality, yet the very best Tyrrell's wines are uncompromising in their richness, flavour and complexity, ranking with some of Australia's greatest wines. The serious, Shiraz-dominated Long Flat Red is Tyrrell's best-seller, and Vat 47 Pinot Chardonnay its top wine. A rich, elegant wine, this Chardonnay has masses of ripe pineappley fruit and acquires a toasty aristocracy when four

or five years old. The style of Pinot Noir has progressed over the years, although somewhat inconsistently. Murray Tyrrell has always favoured a wine of depth and grip, but this has led to somewhat hard wines that have lacked varietal elegance. His 1987 Pinot Noir Premier Selection was greatly improved by fermenting half the wine using *macération carbonique*, which gave the wine much better mid-palate fruit, but slightly reduced the varietal aromas. More experimentation along these lines could well give Tyrrell's a world-class Pinot Noir.

Long Flat Red

Vat 47 Pinot Chardonnay

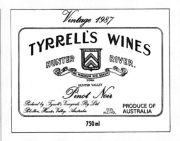

Hunter Valley Pinot Noir

Saxonvale Wines CONTD

Bin 1 Cabernet Sauvignon

This high-tech winery and its 120-hectare (295-acre) vineyard was established in 1970. In 1978 it was acquired by the Macdougall brothers, who did a good job of building up the sales image of Saxonvale until 1985, when it was taken over by the Wyndham Estate. The quality across the range is very good, but the whites are generally of a higher standard. The Chardonnay is especially fine, rich in extract, with zesty fruit and unobtrusive oak, and is capable of great improvement in bottle. One of the best red wines is the Cabernet Sauvignon, a deep-coloured, big, rich wine with a minty-cedary complexity.

J.Y. TULLOCH & SONS

Hunter Valley Chardonnay

Hunter Valley Cabernet Sauvignon

This old wine firm was founded as long ago as 1893, but is now part of Penfolds, although it is still managed by a Tulloch. The quality of these wines is generally good, with just the occasional real blockbuster. The straight Chardonnay is a spicy-toasty wine, with a light but rich, pineappley fruit. The Cabernet Sauvignon is a sturdy wine with good, solid fruit and an earthy-herbaceous character.

WYNDHAM ESTATE WINES

Bin 888 Cabernet Merlot

Show Reserve Verdelho

The original Hunter Valley property known as Wyndham Vineyard was established in 1830 by George Wyndham, but the sprawling estate of today dates from 1971, when Brian McGuigan formed a company to exploit the Wyndham name. Wyndham Estate now owns various other wineries, including Amberton, Craigmore, Hollydene, Montrose and Saxonvale. It also sells quality wines under the Richmond Grove and Hunter Estate labels. The Cabernet Merlot Bin 888 is a big wine with a smoky-*cassis* and cedary-capsicum bouquet, lots of ripe berry and cherry flavour, and a luscious toasty-oak uplift. Wyndham's Verdelho, which was first released with the 1985 vintage, is a fine, full-flavoured dry white wine with grapefruity aromas and a mellow, toasty-oak aftertaste.

QUEENSLAND

Queensland is one of the last places that one might expect to find a vineyard, yet there are a dozen or more wineries and a small industry has existed here since the 1850s. Surprisingly, the summers are cooler than Riverland in Southern Australia, and Mudgee and Hunter in New South Wales. The Semillon Sauvignon Blanc is one of the best wines under the Ballandean Estate label, which Sundown Valley Vineyards, a former table grape producer, uses for its top of the range wines. The Robinsons Family Vineyards was established in 1969 by John Robinson, who got his passion for wine when living in France close to the Beaujolais region. This is one of the best wineries in the region and the Chardonnay is one of its top wines. Stone Ridge was founded by Jim Lawrie and Anne Kennedy in 1981, since when they have steadily established this winery's reputation as one of the most innovative in Queensland. Bungawarra was originally founded in the 1920s by Angelo Barbagello, but was re-established in 1979 by Alan Dorr and Philip Christensen, who won a gold medal with their first wine.

Ballandean Estate Semillon Sauvignon Blanc

Robinsons Family Cool Climate Chardonnay

Stone Ridge Vineyards Shiraz

Bungawarra Wines Bents Road Chardonnay

VICTORIA

ALTHOUGH IT IS the smallest of the wine-producing states, Victoria provides 13 per cent of Australia's total output of wine from 6 per cent of the vineyard area. The explanation for this is the very heavy yields and quantities in the irrigated vineyard area along the Murray River in the northeast corner of the state. This region, like the Riverland of South Australia and the Murrumbidgee Irrigation Area of New South Wales, contributes great quantities to the cask-wine industry. Over three-quarters of the wine produced in Victoria comes from this source. The remaining fraction is small when compared even with Western Australian wine regions, but it includes many of Australia's more interesting wines.

The Muscat grape

The Milawa/Glenrowan region, in the foothills of the Australian Alps, makes a remarkable contribution to the reputation of Australian wines, even though there are relatively few wineries in the area. The principal producers are Baileys of Glenrowan and Brown Brothers of Milawa. This reputation rests especially on the Muscat grape which, through climatic and topographic variations and differing production methods, produces a range of wine styles throughout the region. Brown Brothers, in particular, produces a fine range of table wines in addition to the world-famous dessert liqueur wines of Milawa/Glenrowan and neighbouring Rutherglen.

Cooler climate areas

The dominant feature in western Victoria has been the sparkling wine industry centred around Seppelts Great Western, although still table wines of quality are also made. In the search for a cooler climate, and to expand the sparkling wine operation, vineyards have been established by Seppelts in the newer area of Drumborg, just north of Portland on the coast. Nearer to Melbourne are two other recently developed cooler climate areas in Yarra Valley (which has come back into its own after a long decline) and Mornington Peninsula.

Before phylloxera struck in the nineteenth century, Victoria was Australia's leading wine producer. Many vineyards were not replanted, but new wineries producing high-quality varietal wines are on the increase, so the potential to produce some of Australia's finest wines remains.

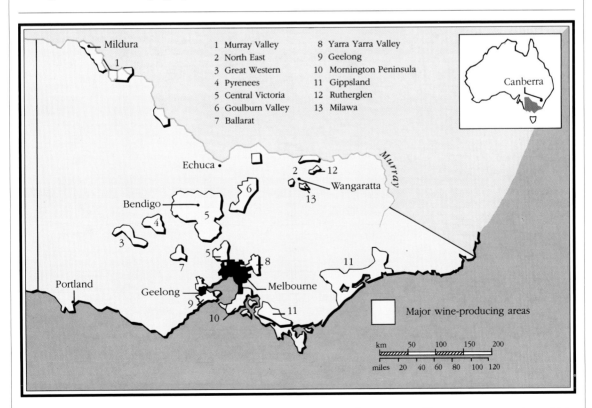

1 Murray Valley
2 North East
3 Great Western
4 Pyrenees
5 Central Victoria
6 Goulburn Valley
7 Ballarat
8 Yarra Yarra Valley
9 Geelong
10 Mornington Peninsula
11 Gippsland
12 Rutherglen
13 Milawa

Major wine-producing areas

Regional variations in Victoria

Despite being a relatively small area when compared with other Australian wine-producing states, Victoria boasts a great diversity of micro-climates, soils and altitudes. Such variety enables winegrowers to cultivate high-quality grapes and produce wines with distinctive regional styles.

BAILEYS OF GLENROWAN

When the goldrush hit Victoria, Richard Bailey opened a store in the small mining town of Glenrowan. After the gold ran out, the miners drifted away and Bailey bought the Bundarra property with his profits. The first vines were planted in 1870, and successive generations have built up a great reputation for the wines produced, particularly the rich, luxuriously sweet dessert wines. The aromatic, powerfully flavoured HJT Liqueur Muscat is one of Baileys' greatest wines, but all the liqueur Muscats are great. The Founder is amazing for the fragrance of its aroma and the lusciousness and complexity of its nutty, raisiny, caramelized flavour. The Winemakers Selection is even richer and nuttier, with concentrated flavour and a big toasty finish. The unfortified wines are less spectacular, although the reds can excel, and Classic Style Hermitage is a big, flavour-packed wine of class.

Founder Liqueur Muscat

*Winemakers Selection
Old Liqueur Muscat*

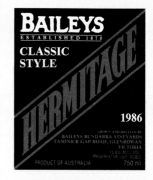

Classic Style Hermitage

BALGOWNIE VINEYARDS

Chardonnay

Estate Pinot Noir

This estate was established by the late Stuart Anderson, a pharmacist who switched career mid-stream when he decided to plant this vineyard in the Bendigo area in 1969. Although purchased by Mildara Wines in 1986, Balgownie Vineyards still continues to make the top-quality wines (particularly Burgundian varietals) that have earned this winery such a well-deserved reputation. The Chardonnay has well-focused lemony, buttered-apple notes that are reminiscent of a top Californian wine. The Estate Pinot Noir displays a fine, spicy-cherry varietal character, with an elegant juicy-fruit flavour.

BEST'S GREAT WESTERN

Bin No. 0. Chardonnay

Bin. No. 0. Hermitage

Established in 1866 by Henry Best (the brother of Joseph Best, founder of the Great Western champagne cellars), Best's is one of the least known of the old wineries. There are some interesting wines here. The Chardonnay Bin No. 0 has a smoky-oak aroma, with elegant, lime and tropical fruit flavours on the palate and bitterness of undeveloped extract (which can give a grapefruity hint on the aftertaste when the wine is young). The Hermitage Bin No. 0 has a oaky-fruit bouquet, a ripe berry fruit flavour and minty-cedary complexity.

CAMPBELLS

Old Rutherglen Muscat

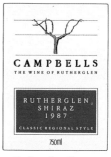

Rutherglen Shiraz

This 70-hectare (173-acre) vineyard was planted by Scottish-born John Campbell in 1870. This is one of the best fortified wine specialists, producing such sumptuous delights as its Old Rutherglen Muscat, a wickedly rich and raisiny nectar from a *solera* originally laid down in 1950. However, Campbells has now begun to branch out into varietal wines, one of the most successful of which is its well-concentrated Rutherglen Shiraz.

BROWN BROTHERS

Established in 1889 by Scottish-born John Graham Brown, this great Milawa winery and its 150 hectares (375 acres) of vineyard are firmly in the control of his descendants today. For many years this was the only winery trying to convince export markets of Australia's exciting potential in the quality wine sector. Without any doubt, the greatest Brown Brothers wine is its deep, dark, stunning creamy-*cassis* Koombahla Cabernet Sauvignon, yet such is the strength of this winery's large range that its basic Victorian Cabernet Sauvignon also has a splendid intensity of vivid black-fruit flavours. The basic Victorian Chardonnay is a delicious, soft, ripe, buttery wine, but better still is the almost European King Valley Chardonnay and the Family Reserve, which is wonderfully creamy, rich and spicy. The Orange Muscat and Flora is exotically perfumed and succulently sweet, with ripe, peachy flavours. The Very Old Tokay is a lusciously rich and complex dessert wine that hints of raisins, candied peel and molasses.

Koombahla Cabernet Sauvignon

King Valley Chardonnay

*Late Harvest
Orange Muscat and Flora*

Very Old Tokay

Royal Vintage

Established with the help of Rémy Martin in 1960 and totally owned by the French Cognac company since 1969, this winery is essentially known for Cuvée Spécial, its good and constantly improving *méthode champenoise*, which is made from Chardonnay and Ugni Blanc and blended from different years. Blue Pyrenees Estate is a superb Cabernet-based wine with an invigorating, fresh capsicum and cedarwood bouquet. The other great wine here, however, is another *méthode champenoise* wine, the Royal Vintage, which is a limited release of selected wine from a single vintage. Given four years on its lees prior to disgorgement, Royal Vintage shows fine autolytic character, which is enhanced by a rich toastiness when allowed to develop in the bottle for a year or two.

CHATEAU TAHBILK

Cabernet Sauvignon

Shiraz

CHATEAU LE AMON

*Big Hill Vineyards
Cabernet Sauvignon*

This small vineyard around Bendigo was planted by Ian Leamon in 1973, who named his "chateau" after a play on his surname. Its best wines are the fresh, elegant, peppery Marong Shiraz, the rich, minty-*cassis* Cabernet Sauvignon and the strong, characterful Hermitage-Cabernet Sauvignon.

CHATEAU REMY

Blue Pyrenees Estate

Chateau Tahbilk CONTD

Established in 1860, this is the oldest winery in Victoria and, appropriately, Chateau Tahbilk is very traditional in winemaking practices, always producing wines that improve over a long period in bottle. Cabernet Sauvignon is its greatest wine and can be very tannic, requiring a minimum of 10 years bottle-age. The Shiraz is almost in the same class and, although it is also a big, strapping wine, the tannins are more supple, making its rich, smoky-minty-cedary fruit more accessible when young.

COLDSTREAM HILLS

*Lilydale Chardonnay
Yarra Ridge Vineyard*

Pinot Noir Rising Vineyard

This young winery is the enterprise of James Halliday, the doyen of Australia's wine writers. He dabbled in the production end of wine in the 1970s, when he was a partner in Brokenwood in the Hunter Valley, but felt it best to sever that connection when his law firm moved from Sydney to Melbourne. He purchased this property in the hotly tipped Yarra Valley and successfully launched Coldstream Hills as a public company. Having spent his life criticizing other wines, he obviously takes extreme care with the quality of his own, because other producers would surely have a field day if he gave them the slightest chance. His elegant Lilydale Chardonnay has lovely apple-blossom aromas and tangy tropical fruit flavours, but it is the Pinot Noir that is Coldstream Hills' most exciting contribution to Australian wine so far. It has the real depth and backbone of a top Côte d'Or Burgundy as well as true varietal finesse.

CRAWFORD RIVER

Riesling (Beerenauslese Style)

The first vines were planted in this vineyard by cattle-rancher John Thompson in 1975, who took an external winemaking course with Riverina College before attempting to make his first vintage in 1981. This course has to be recommended if Crawford River's Riesling is anything to go by. The 1989 vintage illustrated here was made from grapes picked at 19.3 Baumé, which makes it borderline *Trockenbeerenauslese*, although it modestly claims to be only *Beerenauslese* in style. There is nothing meek about this marvellous wine, however: it has a powerful botrytis bouquet; a fabulously rich lime, pineapple and peach fruit; and an intensely sweet finish, with plenty of lively acidity.

DE BORTOLI YARRINYA ESTATE

Yarra Valley Cabernet Sauvignon

Yarra Valley Shiraz

This 18-hectare (44-acre) vineyard at Dixon Creek in the Yarra Valley was established under the name of Chateau Yarrinya by Graeme Miller in 1971. When he won the legendary Jimmy Watson Trophy for his 1977 Cabernet Sauvignon, Chateau Yarrinya became the first-ever small winery to win this most prestigious of Australia's wine awards. Since it was recently purchased by De Bortoli, it has lost its "chateau" designation and gained a restaurant but, more importantly, has kept the highest quality aspirations for its Cabernet Sauvignon, which retains its bold cherry and *cassis* fruit and creamy-spicy-vanilla complexity. The Shiraz has ripe berry fruit and spicy-plum flavours, with sweet vanilla-oak.

DELATITE

Gewürztraminer

Cabernet Sauvignon and Merlot

This 20-hectare (49-acre) vineyard near Mansfield, north of Melbourne, was planted by Robert and Vivienne Ritchie in 1968. The purpose was to sell grapes to other wineries, but in 1982 the Ritchies built a facility of their own. The spicy Gewürztraminer is quite fat, but definitely dry, and has excellent acidity. The Cabernet Sauvignon and Merlot has a distinctive minty-varietal aroma and plump, juicy fruit, with vivid *cassis* character.

DROMANA ESTATE

Cabernet Merlot

Chardonnay Schinus Molle

Gary and Margaret Crittenden planted this 5-hectare (12-acre) vineyard in 1981. The Cabernet Merlot has a classic, herbaceous-capsicum-*cassis* bouquet and tight, but intense, fruit that develops well in the bottle. On the other hand, the Schinus Molle, or peppercorn tree, is an elegant and tasty Chardonnay with ripe, tangy, pineappley fruit that begs to be drunk as young as possible.

ELGEE PARK

Rhine Riesling

Cabernet Merlot

Elgee Park was founded by Baillieu Myer in 1972 with the help of Ian Hickinbotham, at whose Anakie winery the wines were initially made. They have been estate-produced since 1980, and a new winemaking facility was constructed in 1984. The Riesling has a delightful honeysuckle aroma and elegant fruit on the palate. The Cabernet Merlot is a ripe fruity wine with a supple tannin structure and a spicy-cedary complexity. It comprises 70 per cent Cabernet Sauvignon and almost equal proportions of Cabernet Franc and Merlot.

THE HEATHCOTE WINERY

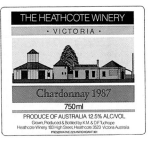

Chardonnay

Gewurztraminer

This 16-hectare (40-acre) vineyard and winery was established by Doris and Kenneth Tudhope in 1978. The red volcanic loam soil at Heathcote is considered to be suited to Shiraz, but all the wines are of excellent quality. The Chardonnay can be stunningly rich, with soft, supple, ripe grape-fruity notes. The Gewurztraminer has a full, spicy aroma, clean, lively fruit and a well-balanced dry flavour.

HICKINBOTHAM WINEMAKERS

Geelong Pinot Noir

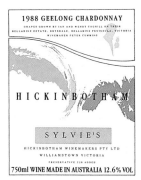

Sylvie's Geelong Chardonnay

Alan Hickinbotham was responsible for establishing the now-famous oenology course at the Roseworthy Agricultural College. His son Ian, a well-known wine columnist, was winemaker at Wynns Coonawarra estate, Kaiser Stuhl and Penfolds before taking over the Anakie vineyard to fulfil his ambition of making his own wine. After graduating from Bordeaux University, Ian's son Stephen was just making a reputation as one of the country's most talented winemakers when he was tragically killed in an air-crash. Stephen's brother Ian created a vineyard on the Bellarine Peninsula and, despite their untimely loss, the Hickinbotham family has gone from strength to strength. The Pinot Noir is a deeply coloured, impressive wine with a fine varietal intensity. The bright, intense, fruity Sylvie's Geelong Chardonnay is named after Sylvie Spielmann from Alsace, who "endeared herself" to the Hickenbothams during their 1988 vintage.

MAIN RIDGE ESTATE

Pinot Noir

Chardonnay

Main Ridge Estate CONTD

This tiny 3-hectare (7-acre) vineyard on Mornington Peninsula was planted in 1975 by Nat White, who built a winery - the first on the peninsula - in time to make his first commercial vintage in 1980. Not that a few hundred cases is really commercial. He merely has to put up a "Wine for Sale" sign on his front gate to take care of his marketing concerns. The Pinot Noir has an exceptional richness and fine varietal character, with ripe strawberry fruit. The Pinot Meunier is a delightful, early-drinking wine, with soft, juicy fruit and a gentle oak uplift. The Gewürztraminer has an excellent lychee flavour, and the Chardonnay, which is doubtless the best white wine here, is full of ripe, tight fruit, with creamy-spicy oak overtones.

MERRICKS

Cabernet Sauvignon

Chardonnay

There are two wine-making Merricks and both, confusingly, are in Thompson Lane, Merrick. This one is owned by Noel Brian Stonier, whose first vintage was in 1984. The wines used to be made by the Hickinbotham Winery, but are now made by Tod Dexter at Elgee Park, as the Stoniers have no winery of their own. Both wineries have done Merricks proud, producing wines of great quality, if tiny quantity. The Cabernet Sauvignon has a stunning colour and an intense bouquet of ripe berry fruits with fine herbaceous complexity and finesse. The Chardonnay is ripe and lush, with sweet-ripe pineappley fruit.

MERRICKS ESTATE

Shiraz

Cabernet Sauvignon

Established in 1978 by Geoff Kefford, the other one of the two Merricks is just as tiny and just as quality-conscious, albeit after a somewhat shaky start. This is one of those numerous New World ventures in which a totally unqualified person sets out to make world-class wine and succeeds. In this case, however, it was not before book-learned amateur Kefford poured some of his undrinkable mistakes down the drain. Since then the quality has skyrocketed, particularly as far as Shiraz is concerned. Few Shiraz can match those of Merricks Estate for fragrance and finesse. It is not a variety for which such adjectives readily spring to mind, but there must be something special about this vineyard because this sublime wine rates as one of Australia's finest. The Cabernet Sauvignon suffers by comparison, yet is an extremely fine wine in its own right.

MILDARA WINES

Church Hill Cabernet Merlot

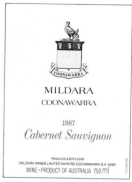

Coonawarra Cabernet Sauvignon

Established in 1888, Mildara currently has over 250 hectares (618 acres) of its own vineyards and controls various other wineries, such as Balgownie, Krondorf and Yellowglen, not to mention Morton in New Zealand. Since the late-1970s, this winery has proved that old dogs can learn new tricks by moving on from its old renowned tradition, which was based almost entirely on fortified wines, to develop a faithful following for its rather elegant style of varietal wines. Pitched at the same price as Mildara's Flower Series, but a distinct step-up in quality, is its Church Hill range, of which the delicious creamy Cabernet Merlot is the best wine.

Another step-up are Mildara's Coonawarra wines. The Coonawarra Cabernet Sauvignon is an elegant, well-perfumed wine that demonstrates an intelligent use of oak.

MITCHELTON VINTNERS

Cab Mac

Goulburn Valley Chardonnay Reserve

Semillon Chardonnay

Named after Major Thomas Mitchell, the first settler to cross the Goulburn river, this winery was established in 1969 at Mitchellstown. Superior selections from other areas are sold under the Winemakers Selection; the straight Mitchelton label is for wines from its own excellent Goulburn Valley vineyard. The mature Classic Release wines are always worth paying extra for, and wines under the Thomas Mitchell label, near the bottom of the range, represent good value. Best-known for its classy wood-matured Marsanne and Cab Mac (a Cabernet vinified by *macération carbonique*), there are many fine wines in the Mitchelton range. The wood-matured Reserve Chardonnay has a remarkably light balance for a wine with so much ripe, toasty fruit. With a little time in bottle, the fruit in the Victorian Semillon Chardonnay assumes a fabulous honeyed-richness.

MONTARA VINEYARD

Ondenc

Pinot Noir

This family-owned winery has 17 hectares (42 acres) of prime vineyards on the side of Mount Chalambar in the Great Western district. It was established in 1970 by Jack and Thelma McRae and is also known as McRae's Montara Vineyards. One of the best wines here is the Ondenc, a minor variety from south-west France that was once popular in Bergerac, but has long been out of fashion because of its naturally high acidity. This is its advantage in Australia, where it is also erroneously known as the Sercial grape. Ondenc has a vibrant, fruity taste, with creamy-spicy vanilla-oak uplift. The Pinot Noir has a strawberry varietal aroma and rich, spicy fruit.

MORRIS WINES

Liqueur Muscat

Established in 1859 by George Morris, this firm now belongs to Orlando, but is run by the founder's great-great-grandson, Mick Morris. Of all the sensational liqueur Muscats and Tokays made in Victoria, Morris's are probably the best. One could easily run out of superlatives describing the luscious, rich, raisiny Liqueur Muscat shown here, yet it is merely one wine in Morris's range.

MOUNT CHALAMBAR

Riesling

Chardonnay

This tiny vineyard at Ararat in the Great Western district was first planted in 1980 by Trevor Mast, a winemaking consultant. Yield is restricted and production small, enabling Mast to make a quick reputation with his intense, concentrated Mount Chalambar Riesling, a wine with a pungent, spicy-citrus aroma and super-rich, fruit-packed flavour. The Chardonnay - a rich, classy wine - suffers by comparison.

MOUNT LANGI GHIRAN

Shiraz

Riesling

Three brothers, Don, Gino and Sergio Fratin, first planted this 20-hectare (49-acre) vineyard on Mount Langi Ghiran in 1970, but did not build their own winery until 1980, when they hired Trevor Mast as consultant winemaker. There have been many fine wines made here over the last 10 years, but the Shiraz has probably showed the most dramatic improvement. From being a one-dimensional wine that lacked ripeness and mid-palate fruit, it now has lots of juicy-spicy fruit and a fine, peppery, cedary-herbaceous complexity. The Victoria Riesling is an elegant wine with vital, tangy, citrusy fruit.

REDBANK

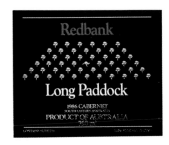

*Long Paddock Cabernet
Southeastern Australia*

Redbank CONTD

Sally's Paddock

First planted in 1973 by Neil and Sally Robb, this 16-hectare (40-acre) vineyard pioneered the new wave of winemakers in the area now called the Pyrenees district. The Long Paddock has suffered from the odd off-vintage, but is essentially a clever, Cabernet-dominated blend, with soft, attractive fruit, a cedary oak influence and a supple tannin structure. The Sally's Paddock is a full and creamy Cabernet-Shiraz-dominated wine, packed with minty-*cassis* fruit.

SEPPELT

Great Western Vintage Brut

Great Western Vineyards Chardonnay

Great Western Vineyards Hermitage

This firm has its heart in South Australia, but vineyards in other states, including Victoria, through its acquisition of the Great Western champagne cellars. The Great Western bubblies (the most medal-strewn of Australia's sparkling wines) are, for European tastes, too much like big, blowsy Chardonnay wines that happen to be fizzy. The still varietal wines are more attractive, especially the typically big, buttery Chardonnay and the densely flavoured rich and oaky Hermitage.

ST HUBERTS WINES

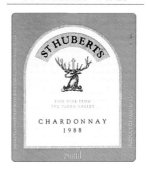

Yarra Valley Chardonnay

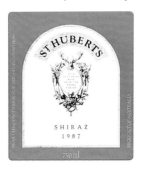

Yarra Valley Shiraz

The original St Hubert vineyard was planted by the Swiss immigrant Hubert de Casella in 1862, but production came to a gradual halt in 1912. The present-day operation began in 1966, when Tom Cester replanted the vineyard and produced wine in a converted chicken shed in a determined effort to resurrect the St Hubert name. The wines were sometimes brilliantly successful, but the quality was erratic. Under new ownership, this unevenness has now been smoothed out although, unfortunately, this has meant the disappearance of the extraordinary successes as well as the dismal failures. The Chardonnay has lots of ripe, upfront, tropical fruit character, with well-integrated, creamy-sweet oak. The Shiraz, which used to be disastrous, now has attractive spicy fruit, with some cedary complexity.

ST LEONARDS

Chardonnay

Late Harvest Sauvignon Blanc

James Scott first planted vines here back in 1866, when he named the estate after his hometown. He soon suffered from financial difficulties and sold up to Henry Ireland from New Zealand. By the turn of the century, St Leonards had some 40 hectares (100 acres) in full production, but this had dwindled to virtually nothing by the time it was sold in 1959. It was not until 1973, when the estate was sold once again, that the new owner, John Darbyshire, began replanting the vineyard. The first two vintages were made by Brown Brothers, and it was this firm that formed a syndicate to buy the property in 1980. These are excellent wines indeed. The St Leonards Chardonnay has a smoky-creamy oak bouquet, with ripe melon and peach fruit on the palate, with a grapefruit bitterness of undeveloped extract on the finish, which suggests that the wine has excellent ageing potential. The Late Harvest Sauvignon Blanc is an extraordinarily rich and complex wine full of exotic, tropical fruit flavours that no Sauternes could ever hope to capture.

SEVILLE ESTATE

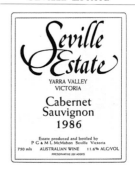

Yarra Valley Cabernet Sauvignon

Riesling Beerenauslese

This small vineyard of barely 4 hectares (10 acres) on north-facing slopes is owned by Dr Peter McMahon, one of the many medical doctors to practise winemaking in the Yarra Valley. The quality can slip, but so infrequently that one can rely on McMahon to produce something outstanding in every bottle. The Cabernet Sauvignon is a classic wine by any standards, and is reminiscent of fine St Julien. The Riesling Beerenauslese is a luscious wine of great concentration and power.

STANTON & KILLEEN

Rutherglen Liqueur Muscat

Rutherglen Moodemere Shiraz

Timothy Stanton and his son John Lewis Stanton first planted vines at Rutherglen in 1875. It was not until 1948 that a Killeen came on the scene, when Norman Killeen married Joan Stanton. Killeen was a Bachelor of Agricultural Science and the manager of Rutherglen Viticultural Research Station. He joined the firm in 1953, since when it has been known as Stanton & Killeen. The firm, which now has 22 hectares (55 acres) of vineyards, is still family owned and run. Its reputation is for great dessert wines such as the ripe, raisiny Liqueur Muscat, which has a lovely brick-red glow to the colour, but Stanton & Killeen also make excellent unfortified wines, the best of which are in the Moodemere range. Finest of these is the Moodemere Shiraz, which has rich berry flavours with a distinctive minty nuance.

TALTARNI VINEYARDS

French Syrah

Cabernet Sauvignon

Taltarni is Aboriginal for "red earth"; the soil in this vineyard is an iron-rich siliceous-clay and therefore red. The site here was selected on the basis of this soil and the climate. It was established by Bernard and Dominique Portet, the sons of André Portet, who was technical director at Château Lafite-Rothschild between 1955 and 1975. Bernard moved on to found his own winery, Clos du Val, in California. This blend of French, American and Australian influences is obviously magical. The wines have been excellent from the start and yet improve with each and every vintage. The French Syrah is one of Taltarni's most interesting wines, with its opulent bouquet, intense oak-enhanced ripe berry-fruit flavours and soft, silky tannins. The Cabernet Sauvignon is simply classic.

TISDALL WINERY

Victoria Chardonnay

Mount Helen Chardonnay

This ambitious but successful venture consists of 130 hectares (320 acres) of vineyard established by Peter and Diana Tisdall in 1979. The Victoria Chardonnay is a very rich and ripe wine that shows remarkable elegance. Earlier vintages were a bit too oaky, but the 1988 has more than a sufficient amount of fruit to balance the oak, which was well integrated as soon as it was released in 1989. The Mount Helen Chardonnay is almost sweet with ripe fruit, and is a much bigger wine that has obvious finesse and great complexity.

VIRGIN HILLS

Virgin Hills

The creation of Hungarian-born Melbourne restaurateur Tom Lazar, this one-wine-winery must be unique in Australia. It is labelled simply Virgin Hills, with no indication of varietal or generic character. The wine is, in fact, approximately 75 per cent Cabernet Sauvignon, blended with mostly Syrah and a little Malbec. Lazar did not even learn his winemaking from a correspondence course (as did Bob Roberts of Huntington Wine in New South Wales), he simply read a book, planted a vineyard and made his wine, and it was not long before Virgin Hills was being hailed as one of Australia's finest wines. That was in 1980, since when Lazar has retired. His successor Mark Sheppard continues to follow Lazar's methods, and the wine firmly remains one of the country's best. Chardonnay, Gewürztraminer and Rhine Riesling are also planted, so there may well be a great white Virgin Hills wine in the future.

WANTIRNA ESTATE

Pinot Noir

Cabernet Sauvignon & Merlot

This estate was founded in 1963 just outside Melbourne, by city solicitor Reg Egan, who manages to produce these early-drinking wines of supreme elegance and finesse in his spare time. The Pinot Noir has real Pinot flavour and feel, with sufficient fruit to match its creamy-smoky influence. The Cabernet Sauvignon and Merlot has an excellent, super-bright colour. It successfully combines soft, sumptuous, herbaceous fruit with fine, cedary complexity.

YARRA BURN

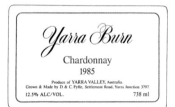

Yarra Valley Chardonnay

Pinot Noir

This small vineyard in the Yarra Valley was planted in 1976 by former wine-merchant David Fyffe. With some exception, the Chardonnay is usually a big, voluptuous wine with ripe, peachy fruit. The Pinot Noir shows excellent varietal character and well-focused fruit, with a spicy-creamy strawberry and cherry flavour.

YARRA YERING VINEYEARD

Dry Red Wine No 1 Cabernet Sauvignon

Dry Red Wine No 2 Shiraz

Dr Bailey Caradus was the first to pioneer vinegrowing in the Yarra Valley, establishing this vineyard in 1969. His basic blended wines excel. In the Dry Red No 1 the Cabernet Sauvignon is blended with Malbec and Merlot to make a stylish Bordeaux-type blend with serious fruit and a fine cedary complexity. The Dry Red Wine No 2, a Shiraz-dominated, Rhône-type blend, is a bigger wine, with compact, spicy-peppery fruit. These wines are made to age in bottle.

YELLOWGLEN VINEYARDS

Brut N.V.

Brut Crémant

This exciting little operation was established in 1971, when Ian Home planted the 18-hectare (45-acre) vineyard with the clear intention of making *méthode champenoise* wine, although some of his early vintages included still varietal wines. When Frenchman Dominique Landragin left Great Western to join Home in March 1982, it came as a great surprise to the Australian wine world. A lot of public attention was focused on Yellowglen, and consequently sales of the brand soared with its distribution seemingly finding its way into every nook and cranny of Australia's city and urban sprawl. Dominique Landragin now has his own winery at Mount Helen, having handed over the winemaking to Jeffrey Wilkinson, although his name still appears on the label next to Home's. These wines display some of the best sparkling wine potential in Australia, although they can be too buttery and do not yet have enough finesse. The Brut N.V. is stronger flavoured and more complex, while the Brut Crémant is lighter and more elegant.

YERINGBERG

Lilydale Pinot Noir

Lilydale Marsanne

This great old Australian vineyard was originally planted in 1862 by Swiss-born Baron Guillaume de Pury. Under his charge, the vineyard grew to some 30 hectares (75 acres). Today it covers barely 2 hectares (5 acres), although it is still in the hands of the de Pury family, and the entire estate covers a considerable 400 hectares (990 acres). Its small production today is of consistently fine quality. The Pinot Noir is exceptionally rich and flavoursome, yet retains the true elegance of its variety. The Marsanne has a fine honeysuckle aroma and shows great finesse on the palate.

TASMANIA

TASMANIA, OFF THE COAST OF Victoria, is on a latitude of 40 to 42° South, the equivalent latitude to Bordeaux. As an island, its cooler climate gives Tasmania a position of great potential importance in Australian viticulture. Already its white wines display distinct varietal character, while reds are lighter in style with greatly pronounced fruit flavours. Heemskerk and Pipers Brook are the two largest winery operations and lie in the northern coastal strip to the east of Devonport. Together with Moorilla Estates, south of the capital Hobart, Heemskerk and Pipers Brook played a leading part in establishing a reputation for Tasmanian wines that already goes far beyond the small total of wine produced.

Cabernet Sauvignon is the most planted grape variety, followed by Chardonnay, Pinot Noir, Rhine Riesling and Gewürztraminer. Success with the early-ripening Pinot Noir and Chardonnay prompted Louis Roederer to invest in the island.

HEEMSKERK

Cabernet Sauvignon

Heemskerk's successful cool-climate vineyards attracted the great Champagne house of Louis Roederer to this venture. One of its best wines is the Cabernet Sauvignon, which has a delicately rich, soft fruit flavour. Great things are expected from a Roederer-inspired *méthode champenoise*.

MARION'S VINEYARD

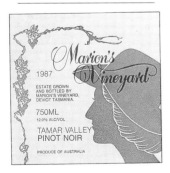

Tamar Valley Pinot Noir

Mark and Marion Semmens established this 5-hectare (12-acre) vineyard in the Tamar Valley in 1980. Their most serious wine is Pinot Noir, a wine of finesse and complexity. The typically strawberry slant is tinged by a distinctive note of mint.

MEADOWBANK VINEYARD

Cabernet Sauvignon

This delightful Derwent Valley vineyard was planted by Gerald Ellis in 1974. There are now 7 hectares (17 acres), mostly of Riesling and Cabernet Sauvignon. The latter is a wine of considerable finesse, with an herbaceous, berry-fruit bouquet and ripe, plummy-cedary palate.

MOORILLA ESTATE

Pinot Noir

Established as long ago as 1958, the Alcorso family's pioneering Tasmanian winery has firmly established that Tasmania is easily capable of producing great wines. There have been good Chardonnays, excellent Cabernet Sauvignons and sensational Botrytis Rieslings, but efforts are now being concentrated on Pinot Noir, which has a fine, juicy-strawberry and spicy complexity.

PIPERS BROOK VINEYARD

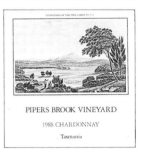

Chardonnay

After a nationwide study of conditions most favourable for viticulture, Andrew Pirie chose this site at Pipers Brook in Tasmania. Since establishing this vineyard in 1973, he has consistently produced delightful wines of the highest quality. One of his best wines is the Chardonnay, which has an almost European balance of fruit, acidity and extract.

POWERCOURT VINEYARDS

Pinot Noir

Founded by Ralph and Roslyn Power, this 2-hectare (5-acre) vineyard produces tiny quantities of Pinot Noir and Cabernet Sauvignon.

SOUTH AUSTRALIA

MANY OF SOUTH AUSTRALIA's premium wine areas are situated close to Adelaide, cooled by the sea breezes of the Great Australian Bight. The vineyard areas closest to the city are the Barossa and Eden Valleys to the east; the Adelaide plains, which include Penfold's Magill Vineyard, to the north; and McLaren Vale and Langhorne Creek to the south. Over 400 kilometres (250 miles) away to the south-east is Coonawarra, with its extension, Keppoch/Padthaway, *en route*. The most northerly district is the Clare/Watervale area, which has a correspondingly warmer climate, although not nearly as hot as the extensive Riverland area, which is South Australia's bulk wine-producing region (boosting South Australia's output to 60 per cent of the country's total).

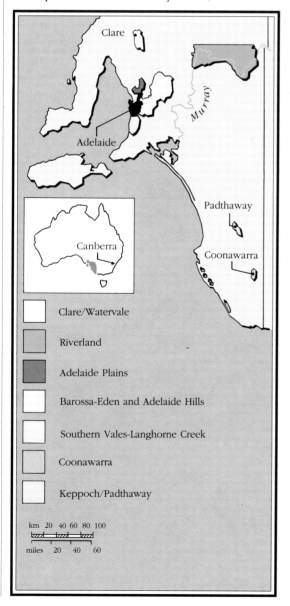

Clare

Adelaide

Murray

Padthaway

Canberra

Coonawarra

	Clare/Watervale
	Riverland
	Adelaide Plains
	Barossa-Eden and Adelaide Hills
	Southern Vales-Langhorne Creek
	Coonawarra
	Keppoch/Padthaway

km   20   40   60   80   100

miles   20   40   60

Vines were first planted in South Australia at Adelaide in 1837. Within a decade the Barossa Valley was opened up, and Clare Valley and McLaren Vale were established at about the same time. Coonawarra, originally settled in the 1880s, was re-opened in the 1950s when Wynns bought property there. Land in Coonawarra became scarce, so companies developed vineyards at Keppoch/Padthaway, 90 kilometres (55 miles) north.

The Barossa Valley

The Barossa Valley is not only a growing area, but also serves as a production centre for larger companies like Penfolds, Orlando, Seppelts, Yalumba and Wolf Blass. The better sites are found at higher altitudes in the Barossa Ranges, Eden Valley, Pewsey Vale and Adelaide Hills. More white grapes are grown than red: the white varieties are primarily Rhine Riesling, Sémillon and Gewürztraminer; the reds, Cabernet Sauvignon and Shiraz, with some Pinot Noir and Pinot Meunier.

Clare Valley/Watervale

Clare has a hot, dry climate, but many of its vineyards are high up and have cooler temperatures. Clare Valley's Rhine Rieslings are among the best in Australia. Chardonnay, Sémillon and Sauvignon Blanc are also successful. Cabernet Sauvignon is often blended with Malbec or Shiraz.

Coonawarra

The fame of Coonawarra rests on a small strip of red soil - Terra Rossa - 14.5 kilometres (9 miles) long and 1.6 kilometres (1 mile) wide, often thought of as the Médoc of Australia. A light covering of weathered limestone soil overlays a thick limestone belt, which sits on a water table that feeds the roots of the vines. By Australian standards, it is a cool climate region, with a heat-summation level similar to Bordeaux (see page 280). Spring frosts, wet harvests and diseases are hazards. Nonetheless, it is regarded as the single best area for fine quality table wines in Australia. Cabernet Sauvignon, Rhine Riesling, Shiraz and Chardonnay are the principal grapes. In recent years the development of Keppoch/Padthaway has extended the Coonawarra area.

Australia's largest wine region South Australia accounts for some 60 per cent of all Australian wines, most of which come from the irrigated vineyards of the Riverland area. Classic wines come from Coonawarra in the south and from several of the cooler wine-growing areas around Adelaide.

ANGOVE'S

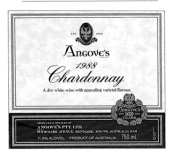

Chardonnay

Cabernet Sauvignon

Established by Dr William Angove in 1886, this winery is best known today for two wines: Tregrehan Claret (named after a Cornwall estate that once belonged to the Angove family) and Bookmark Riesling. These are good commercial wines, but there are better wines available, such as the full, complex, oaky Chardonnay, which has great grapefruity extract. The Cabernet Sauvignon is a super, deeply coloured, deeply flavoured wine, rich in sweet, creamy, *cassis* fruit, which drinks well four or five years after the harvest.

JIM BARRY WINES

Clare Valley Lodge Hill Riesling

Clare Valley Cabernet Sauvignon

This excellent winery was launched with the 1974 vintage by Jim Barry, who describes the winemaking techniques employed by himself and his two sons, Mark and Peter, as "an exciting blend of mature wisdom and the innovative enthusiasm of youth". Barry's wisdom dates back to 1947, when he graduated from Roseworthy College. The first qualified winemaker in Clare, Barry spent the next 22 years working for the Clare Cooperative before establishing Chateau Clare for the Taylor company. It was at about the same time that he purchased his own vineyard. As the vineyard required a lot of replanting, it was not until 1973 that Barry quit Taylors to work for himself. His slightly sweet, honeysuckle and passion-fruit Lodge Hill Riesling is a wine that bridges the gulf between popular taste and top quality. The Cabernet Sauvignon is a rich, oaky elegant wine with a cedary-capsicum complexity.

BASEDOWS

Cabernet Sauvignon

This small property boasts a great name in South Australia's viticulture. It was established in 1896 by Johann Basedow, who had owned a major share of Chateau Tanunda, and Martin Basedow, a former Minister for Education for South Australia and one of the founders of the University of Adelaide (which was later to become Roseworthy Agricultural College). In 1972, Basedows became a public company and the family lost control. Douglas Lehmann, the son of Peter Lehmann, has been the winemaker here since the mid-1970s. He makes a large number of excellent wines, including the soft, minty-spicy Cabernet Sauvignon.

BERRI ESTATES

Shiraz Cabernet

Barossa Valley Sauvignon Blanc

This huge combine of cooperatives, the first of which was established in 1922, has 2,100 hectares (5,189 acres) of vineyard and produces 4.5 million cases of wine each year. Many wines are surprisingly good quality, considering how inexpensive they are. The Cabernet Shiraz has a rich, jammy-blackcurrant flavour, while the Shiraz Cabernet is more black-peppery. The Cabernet Sauvignon is a rich, ripe and oaky with a powerful spicy-*cassis* flavour and some cedary complexity. It has triumphed in blind tastings against wines that are two or three times its price. As to the whites, the Fumé Blanc is a deliciously rich and tangy wine, while the Sauvignon Blanc is rather simple and unexciting.

WOLF BLASS WINES

Yellow Label Cabernet Sauvignon

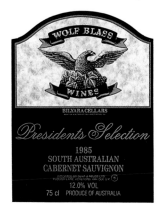

Presidents Selection Cabernet Sauvignon

Wolf Blass CONTD

Wolfgang Franz Otto Blass trained in Germany, gained Champagne experience in Reims and worked at Kaiser Stuhl Nuriootpa, South Australia, before branching out on his own in 1969. His huge range of aggressively marketed wines has notched up over 2,000 medals at wine shows. The style is rich and oaky and stands a better chance of impressing a judge with one small sip than it does of maintaining interest throughout a meal. Perhaps the best wine with food is the Yellow Label Cabernet Sauvignon, which has complex, tightly packed fruit and a firmer tannin structure than most Blass wines. The huge, rich, soft, almost sweet Presidents Selection has lots of hedonistic fruit, and is regarded by Blass himself as his greatest wine.

BLEASDALE VINEYARDS

Verdielho

Langhorne Creek Cabernet Sauvignon

This 50-hectare (124-acre) vineyard at Langhorne Creek was established in 1850. The labels feature HMS Buffalo, the ship on which Frank Potts, the firm's founder "1st arrived in 1836". Today's winemaker is a descendant, Michael Potts. His most famous wine is the *rancio*-styled Verdielho, which is aged just under the roof, where heat accumulates, for a decade or more to replicate the *estufagem* process employed in Madeira. He also makes a Burgundy-style table wine version. Best of Bleasdale's wines is the full, dark, dense Cabernet Sauvignon which has an intense, ripe berry-fruit flavour.

BOWEN ESTATE

Coonawarra Shiraz

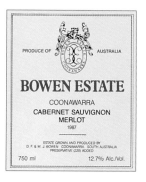

Coonawarra Cabernet Sauvignon Merlot

This 24-hectare (59-acre) vineyard at Penola, on the southern edge of the Coonawarra district was purchased in 1972 by Roseworthy graduate, Doug Bowen, while he was the winemaker for Lindeman's Rouge Homme winery. He left Rouge Homme in 1975, when he crushed his first commercial harvest. His wines have exceptional varietal character. The Coonawarra Shiraz has deliciously ripe, vibrant fruit flavours that would seduce any wine-lover, but Doug and Joy Bowen consider their rich, chocolatey, stylish Coonawarra Cabernet Sauvignon Merlot to be their very best wine.

BRANDS LAIRA

Coonawarra Cabernet Sauvignon

Eric Brand was a successful baker when he married Nancy Redman in 1950. The couple bought land from Nancy's brother Owen, the owner of the Rouge Homme vineyard. Two hectares (5 acres) consisted of vines and for 16 years the Brands sold their grapes to Lindemans. When Owen Redman sold Rouge Homme to Lindemans in 1966, he suggested to his brother-in-law that he should build a modest winery to supply Thomas Hardy with the Shiraz wine he had been providing from Rouge Homme. From this small beginning, Eric Brand has built up a nationwide reputation for the Coonawarra wine from his Laira vineyard. His Cabernet Sauvignon is classically structured, yet elegant.

BRIDGEWATER MILL

Rhine Riesling Dry

Cabernet Sauvignon Malbec

The idea of converting the Old Bridgewater Mill in the Adelaide Hills into a showpiece restaurant-winery for Petaluma came from Brian Croser. Several million dollars have been spent on renovating and refurbishing the restaurant to compliment its fine cuisine. Its sparkling wine cellars were dug out of solid rock. That these Bridgewater Mill wines are supposed to be a second-label range is due only to the exceptionally high quality of Petaluma's wines. Best of all are the Rhine Riesling, which is made in a dry, austere, almost Alsatian style, and the Cabernet Sauvignon Malbec, which has a classic bouquet, velvety soft texture, and a sweet, ripe berry-fruit flavour.

CHATEAU REYNELLA

Reynella Cabernet Sauvignon

McLaren Vale Chardonnay

This property, which includes Australia's oldest cellar, belongs to Thomas Hardy & Sons, who have panelled Chateau Reynella's interior with staves from wooden vats. An extremely rich, yet elegant wine, the Cabernet Sauvignon has a full-blown bouquet, with a tiny herbaceous hint and sweet-ripe, oaky, berry-fruit flavours on the palate. The Chardonnay has lots of flavour, but the fruit is unusually tightly packed and requires a few years in bottle to fill out and become toasty.

CORIOLE VINEYARDS

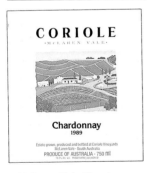

McLaren Vale Chardonnay

McLaren Vale Cabernet Sauvignon

This estate was called Chateau Bonne Santé until purchased in 1967 by Dr Hugh Lloyd of the Lloyd Aviation family. The property then comprised some 8 hectares (20 acres) of 60-year-old Shiraz vines, but now totals 22 hectares (54 acres) of mixed varieties. Since Lloyd made his first vintage in 1970, Coriole quickly established a reputation for producing some of the best red wines in McLaren Vale and is now building up a name for its whites. The wines are now made by his son Mark, who once worked for an English vineyard. The Chardonnay is rich, but tightly formed, with fine citrus-fruit and a spicy-oak uplift. The Cabernet Sauvignon is a rich, soft wine with nutty-toasty oak.

CROSER

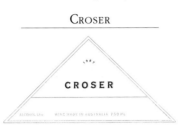

Croser

Named by Brian Croser of Petaluma, this Franco-Australian *méthode champenoise* venture is partly funded by Bollinger, the great Champagne house. The grapes grown in the Piccadilly Valley above Adelaide are thought to be particularly suited to sparkling wine production. Nevertheless the first effort, a pure Chardonnay from the 1984 vintage, was merely like a rich varietal wine with bubbles. Although superior for an Australian sparkling wine, it rightly disappointed Croser, who released it under the Bridgewater Mill label. The 1985 80/20 Chardonnay/Pinot (sold as the first Croser) was a bit better, although it was still dominated by too much varietal richness. The 1986 Croser (a 70/30 blend) was not bad, but it was the 1987 (a 65/35 blend) that gave Brian his first classic-quality Australian sparkling wine.

D'ARENBERG

McLaren Vale Old Vine Shiraz

White Muscat of Alexandria

The d'Arenberg vineyards, covering some 80 hectares (198 acres), were originally planted by the Milton family in the 1890s, but were purchased by Francis Osborn in 1912. He changed the name of the estate first to Bundarra and then to d'Arenberg just prior to his own first vintage (which was in 1928), and two years after the birth of his son, who was also named d'Arenberg. "D'Arry" Osborn, as he became known, took control in 1957 and built up its reputation. It is now run by his son, Chester, whose Old Vine Shiraz challenges Kays Amery Vineyard Block 6 Shiraz for its concentrated flavour. The White Muscat of Alexandria is extremely fresh, fragrant and grapey for such an intensely flavoured fortified wine.

ELDERTON

Hermitage

Pinot Noir HA

These Barossa vineyards have been in production since the turn of the century, but it was only in 1984 that current owners Neil and Lorraine Ashmead released their own wines. The Hermitage is a big, fat, soft wine, with voluptuous peppery-berry fruit and fine cedary-minty complexity. The Pinot Noir has ripe, elegant, strawberry-flavoured varietal fruit.

ANDREW GARRETT

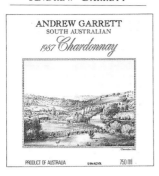

Chardonnay

After working for several wineries, whizz-kid winemaker Andrew Garrett set up his own very successful operation. There is no doubting the quality of the white wines he produces. The fresh, crisp, Sauvignon Semillon has upfront, grassy fruit. The deliciously soft and creamy Chardonnay has elegant, pineappley fruit and a refined vanilla-oak uplift. However, the reds are less successful.

RICHARD HAMILTON

Willunga Cabernet Sauvignon

Willunga Fumé Blanc

This 45-hectare (111-acre) vineyard was founded in 1971 by Dr Richard Hamilton, the great-great grandson of Richard Hamilton, whose Ewell vineyard was one of the first commercial vineyards in South Australia around 1837. Dr Hamilton makes an interesting, if somewhat eclectic, range of wines from his Willunga and Coonawarra vineyards. One of the best reds is the clean, lean, elegant Willunga Cabernet Sauvignon. The whites are, however, of a much higher quality and the soft, ripe Fumé Blanc, with its creamy-spicy oak influence is by far the best of all.

THOMAS HARDY & SONS

This very large company, which was established in 1853, now owns Houghton, Chateau Reynella and the Stanley Wine Company. Its vast range and enormous production covers the entire spectrum of styles and qualities. Of all the fine wines in the stylishly labelled Hardy Collection, the Padthaway Rhine Riesling Beerenauslese stands out. It is a consistently rich and concentrated wine, with an intense, luscious, exotic, raisiny bouquet and an immense, yet elegant, complex flavour. A dry wine on a more down-to-earth level is the Siegersdorf Rhine Riesling. Produced in a typically exotic Australian style, it can, however, develop a true petrolly-Riesling nose with elegant peachy-ripeness of fruit on

the palate, if given just an extra year in bottle. The Nottage Hill Claret is Hardy's most popular red wine and can taste firm, sweet and simple when purchased, yet given a year or two in bottle it is clearly capable of developing fat and complexity. The greatest dessert wine produced by Hardy's is its Reserve Bin Sauvignon Blanc. As the label states, this is a unique wine. No other winery in the world has decided to fortify a Sauvignon Blanc, although from the success of this wine, there is no reason why not. It has the colour of a Bual Madeira, with a khaki-hue on the meniscus. The bouquet falls between a Madeira and a genuine old Oloroso Sherry, with a fabulous toffee-coffee richness of fruit on the palate.

Padthaway Rhine Riesling Beerenauslese

Nottage Hill Claret

Siegersdorf Rhine Riesling

Reserve Bin Sauvignon Blanc

HENSCHKE

Mount Edelstone Vineyard

Hill of Grace Vineyard

This winery originated from the vineyard planted in 1868 by Johann Henschke. It now has 80 hectares (198 acres) of vines scattered over the higher, cooler areas of the Barossa Valley. Its famous vineyards, Mount Edelstone and Hill of Grace, produce this winery's greatest and most characterful wines from very old Shiraz vines. The Mount Edelstone is a smoky-oaky, complex wine with deep flavour of stone-fruits and black pepper. The Hill of Grace is particularly soft and lush, yet every bit as concentrated, with huge extract and smoky-toasty oak complexity.

KATNOOK ESTATE

Coonawarra Chardonnay

Coonawarra Sauvignon Blanc

Established in 1979, this firm has built up a vast estate of 560 hectares (1,384 acres). Only Wynns can claim to have more vineyards in South Australia, but the vast bulk of this production is sold to other wineries in the form of grapes, juice or wine. Less than 15,000 cases are sold under its Katnook Estate and Riddoch Estate labels. These wines range from good to excellent. The Chardonnay is extremely ripe, exotic and peachy, with lots of grapefruity extract. The Sauvignon Blanc has a deliciously rich gooseberry flavour.

KAY BROTHERS

Amery Vineyards Block 6 Shiraz

Amery Winery Liqueur Muscat

This small 7-hectare (17-acre) vineyard is one of the oldest in the McLaren Vale, having been originally founded by Herbert and Frederick Kay in 1890. The Amery Vineyards Block 6 Shiraz is in fact produced from a plot of vines planted just two years after this date. These old vines produce a small crop of highly concentrated grapes, making a big, fat, juicy-flavoured wine with a smoky-*cassis* complexity. The Amery Winery Liqueur Muscat is a luscious, raisiny wine made in a lighter, more delicate style than those from Rutherglen in Victoria.

TIM KNAPPSTEIN WINES

Clare Valley Cabernet Sauvignon

Clare Valley Rhine Riesling

This winery should not be confused with the Mick Knappstein label produced under the auspices of Hardy's. The venture is in fact the sole property of Mick Knappstein's nephew Tim, who was a Gold Medal graduate of Roseworthy College and who worked for the Stanley Wine Company when it was run by his uncle. Such was his natural talent,

Tim was only 20 years old when he became the winemaker at Stanley, where he created the now-famous Leasingham range and won no less than 500 awards with the wines he made under that label. The quality and character of his Tim Knappstein Enterprise Wines are every bit as high and interesting. The Cabernet Sauvignon, deceptively intense and well-structured, always shows finesse, and the Rhine Riesling maintains an almost European varietal style.

KRONDORF WINERY

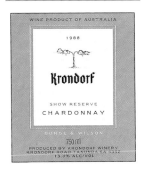

Show Reserve Burge & Wilson Chardonnay

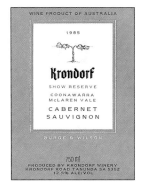

Show Reserve Burge & Wilson Coonawarra McLaren Vale Cabernet Sauvignon

Krondorf winery produces a large range of extremely fine wines, the very best of which are sold under the Burge & Wilson label. This series of labels is named after the two brilliant founders who rapidly established the fame and reputation of this winery and sold out in 1986, after just eight years. With such an extraordinarily successful combination of wine expertise and business acumen, Burge and Wilson deserve to spend the rest of their lives in luxury. The Show Reserve Chardonnay has lots of ripe peachy fruit and buttered-toast oak. The Show Reserve Coonawarra McLaren Vale Cabernet Sauvignon is fantastically rich, yet supremely elegant, with sweet-ripe mulberry fruit and toasty oak overtones.

MARIENBERG WINERY

*Winemaker's Selection Shiraz
Limited Release*

This 18-hectare (44-acre) vineyard was established by Ursula and Geoff Pridham in 1966, and produced wines two years later. Ursula Pridham, Australia's most prominent female winemaker, creates a range of distinction. Her delight is to make limited releases, like this Shiraz Limited Release, which has soft, sweet, ripe, peppery-berry-fruit notes.

GEOFF MERRILL

Coonawarra Cabernet Sauvignon

*Mount Hurtle McLaren Vale
Sauvignon Blanc*

Established in 1983 by Geoff Merrill, Hardy's former chief winemaker, this nineteenth-century winery on Mount Hurtle overlooks his small but expanding vineyard. The Cabernet Sauvignon is made from bought-in grapes and is full-to-bursting with rich, vibrant, cedary-*cassis* fruit. The Sauvignon Blanc from his own vineyard is very fresh and ripe, with elegant, grassy-asparagus fruit.

MOUNTADAM

Eden Valley Chardonnay

Eden Valley Pinot Noir

David Wynn established this 40-hectare (99-acre) vineyard in 1970. One of the first vines he planted was Chardonnay, a virtually unknown variety in Australia at the time. A rich, creamy wine with barrel-fermented smoky-toasty aromas, this remains one of his greatest wines and has exceptional potential longevity. His Pinot Noir is a delicately rich, typically strawberry-flavoured wine of fine varietal character.

NORMANS WINES

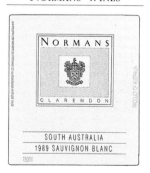

Clarendon Sauvignon Blanc

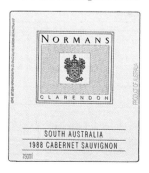

Clarendon Cabernet Sauvignon

With 60 hectares (148 acres) and a history extending back to 1851, this company has established a reputation for its large and traditional range of wines. The Sauvignon Blanc is fresh, light and herbaceous in style, with crisp, clean fruit. The Cabernet Sauvignon has a particularly elegant and stylish balance for such a deep-coloured wine.

ORLANDO WINES

*South Eastern Australia
St. Hilary Chardonnay*

*St. Hugo Coonawarra
Cabernet Sauvignon*

Several rapid changes of ownership have brought this company into the hands of the French-based Pernod-Ricard company. The recent successful takeover of New South Wales-based Wyndham Estate gives them 20 per cent of the Australian market. Significant producers of cask and flagon wine under the Coolabah label, the real joy of this company lies in the honest quality of the Jacob's Creek range, with the Saint series demonstrating the sort of huge step up in quality that they can offer. St. Hilary is a rich, melony, buttered Chardonnay and St. Hugo shows magnificent chocolatey-cherry, plum and truffle flavours.

PIRRAMIMMA

McLaren Vale Chardonnay

McLaren Vale Liqueur Port

A small part of the Pirramimma property was planted prior to its acquisition by A. C. Johnston in 1892, whose descendants run this 55-hectare (136-acre) estate today. The Chardonnay is firm and oaky, with good grapefruity extract and some smokey complexity. The McLaren Vale Liqueur Port is a smooth and mellow tawny style, with an attractive coffee-toffee intensity.

Primo Estate Winery

Botrytis Riesling Auslese

Joseph Double Pruned Cabernet Sauvignon

The first vines were planted in 1973 by Primo Grilli, but it was not until 1979 that Primo Estate wines appeared. This 21-hectare (52-acre) vineyard on the Adelaide Plains is now run by Primo's sons, Joe and Peter Grilli. Their speciality is an artificially induced Botrytis Riesling Auslese, which has a fragrant bouquet of over-ripe dessert apples and some delicate botrytis complexity. The double-pruning of Cabernet Sauvignon results in an extended *véraison* and, thus, a much later crop - usually late May. This provides grapes with higher levels of natural extract and acidity, which in turn creates a wine of greater finesse and complexity.

PENFOLDS WINES

Established in 1844 by Dr Christopher Penfold, this is a great winery in every respect. Owning wineries such as Wynns, Kaiser Stuhl, Tollana, Seaview and Tulloch, which between them operate an estate of some 2,000 hectares (4,942 acres), Penfolds is great in quantity. With wines such as the superb Grange, which is considered by many to be Australia's finest wine, Penfolds is equally great in quality. Theoretically, Grange should mean Magill, a small vineyard on the eastern outskirts of Adelaide, but the amount of Magill Shiraz used has varied between 15 and 70 per cent, the balance of the Shiraz coming from Kalimna, Clare and Koonunga. In 1982 a large part of the historic Magill was sold off for urban development. (The French equivalent of such madness would be if Château Haut-Brion sold part of its prized vineyards to a hypermarket so that it could be used as a car park.) The remainder of the Magill vineyard is no longer used for Grange, as it is now sold exclusively under The Magill Estate label. However, Grange remains one of Australia's greatest wines. It is historically a blend to which, in some years, even a little Cabernet Sauvignon has been added. The wine in fact tastes more like Cabernet Sauvignon than Shiraz. Its construction is a remarkable balancing act, providing a powerful punch of flavour, yet showing great finesse and the ability to age remarkably well in bottle over a number of years. It has size and power, but there is a certain restraint. The Magill Estate is a different style: as deep-coloured and as intensely flavoured as one would have expected from the one-time soul of Grange, its style is less traditional and more accessible. Other great Penfolds wines include the Kalimna Bin 28 Shiraz, which has a smoky-peppery elegance, but is far more full-bodied than the label suggests, as is the big, ripe-berry-flavoured Bin 128 Coonawarra Shiraz, although there is no denying its feminine elegance. The South Australian Chardonnay is an attractive wine with a certain richness and a creamy-sweet-spice oak complexity, but Penfolds is not so fortunate with its white wines, although some limited release Chardonnay can reach the same tremendous levels of success as its red wines.

Kalimna Bin 28 Shiraz

Bin 128 Coonawarra Shiraz

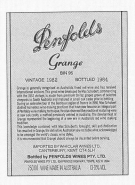

Grange Bin 95

The Magill Estate

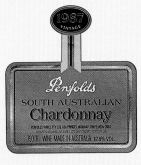

Chardonnay

PETALUMA

The standards set by globe-trotting winemaking consultant Brian Croser, the founder of Petaluma, have had a profound effect on the Australian wine industry. After a Bachelor of Agricultural Science from Adelaide University, he graduated from University of California, Davis, as a Master of Enology, before helping to set up the wine course at Riverina College. Croser first used the Petaluma label (the name of a small Californian town) for the wines he made at Riverina in the mid-1970s. The winery came about when Croser was a consultant to the Evans Wine Company, which had just purchased vineyards in Clare and Coonawarra. Croser selected Piccadilly in the Adelaide Hills for the winery he designed and the first commercial Petaluma wine was made in 1979.

Today the winery is surrounded by 60 hectares (148 acres) of vines. Croser has a magical touch with white wines and is becoming the sole producer of classic sparkling wine in Australia, but every style of wine can be recommended. Coonawarra is a stylish Cabernet-Merlot blend of varying proportions, but consistent quality. The Chardonnay is always rich and buttery with a smoky-oak complexity and plenty of acidity. But if Petaluma should be singled out for one variety, then it is Riesling. The dry Rhine Riesling is racy and delicate when young, yet gains a honeyed-petrol richness after time in bottle. Depending on the vintage, the Botrytis Riesling can be almost Californian in style, with succulent fruit-pie-juice flavours, or complex and raisiny-rich like a *Trockenbeerenauslese*.

Coonawarra

Chardonnay

Botrytis Riesling

RENMANO WINES

Chairman's Selection Merlot

Chairman's Selection Chardonnay

Part of the Berri Estates operation since 1982, the Renmano wines have retained their high quality. However, they are sold at relatively inexpensive prices, making them extraordinary value, particularly those under the Chairman's Selection label. The Merlot is a soft and juicy wine with a touch of smoky complexity. The Chairman's Selection Chardonnay is a rich and ripe wine with bags of tangy fruit and a touch of smoky-toasty oak.

ROUGE HOMME WINES

Coonawarra Cabernet Sauvignon

Although part of the large Lindeman's combine since 1965, the integrity of these wines has been maintained. The label might look a bit old-fashioned and garish, but behind it lies one of Coonawarra's finest wines. They are all recommended, but the intense, cedary-*cassis* Coonawarra Cabernet Sauvignon is in a class of its own.

ST HALLETT

Old Block Shiraz

This property was purchased and planted in 1912 by Karl Richard Lindner, the Australian-born son of a German immigrant family, and a winery was built six years later. Still owned and run by the Lindner family, whose Old Block is considered to be one of the Barossa Valley's finest Shiraz wines. It is deeply coloured and has a sweet, soft bouquet, a concentrated fruit flavour and a cedary complexity.

SALTRAM WINE ESTATES

Pinnacle Selection Cabernet Malbec

Pinnacle Selection Coonawarra Auslese Rhine Riesling

This winery, founded in 1859 by William Salter of England, was bought by the giant Canadian-based Seagram Group in 1979. With less than 30 hectares (74 acres) of vineyard, most of the half-million cases produced here each year are from purchased grapes. The Pinnacle Selection label is used for top-of-the-range wines. The Cabernet Malbec used to be sourced from Saltram's own vineyard at Angaton, but no longer states Barossa on the label, so can be blended. It has kept, however, its rich, lingering flavour and still has its classy, toasty-oak finesse. The Coonawarra Auslese Rhine Riesling has a fabulously rich, honeyed-petrol Riesling character.

SEAVIEW WINERY

Méthode Champenoise Brut

Established as Hope Farm in 1850 by Englishman George Pitches Manning, the estate became Seaview when it was purchased in 1970 by Allied Vintners and has belonged to the Penfolds Group since 1985. Some of the *méthode champenoise cuvées* can have a fine biscuity autolytic character, but, as with all Australian sparkling wines, there is a tendency to use wines that are simply too rich.

SEPPELT

Barooga, Padthaway, Barossa Valley Chardonnay

Salinger Champagne Brut

Premier Vineyard Chardonnay-Sauvignon Blanc

With some 2,000 hectares (4,942 acres) of vineyards and an annual production of 2.5 million cases, this old established winery, which has roots stretching back to 1851, is one of the key companies in the Australian wine industry today. Despite its huge production and bewildering range of labels, Seppelt manages to produce more than their fair share of medal-winning wines. The Gold Label Chardonnay is a rich, but elegant wine, with a fresh, tropical fruit flavour and fine acidity. Seppelt makes typically good examples of Australian sparkling wines, with the Champagne-method Salinger its very best. Seppelt's Premier Vineyard Chardonnay-Sauvignon Blanc is an excellent food wine, combining the richness of Chardonnay with the grassiness of Sauvignon Blanc and giving it a gentle oaky uplift.

STANLEY LEASINGHAM

Winemakers Selection Fumé Blanc

Winemakers Selection Bin 56 Cabernet Malbec

S. SMITH & SONS

This firm dates back to 1849 and today owns 565 hectares (1,396 acres) of vineyard. There is a vast range of styles and qualities under four label categories. Yalumba is for non-estate wines, but includes some premium products. Wines from the family's own vineyards are sold under the Hill-Smith Estate label. Pewsey Vale and Heggies labels are for wines grown in these high-altitude, cool-climate vineyards. The Hill-Smith Chardonnay is a commercial blend of fruit and oak. The Heggies Cabernet is a rich, cedary-minty-berry-flavoured blend of both Cabernets plus a dash of Merlot. The Heggies Rhine Riesling has a lime-blossom and tropical fruit aroma, fine varietal fruit and a crisp finish. Pewsey Vale Rhine Riesling is an even more intense wine.

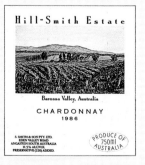

Hill-Smith Estate Chardonnay

Heggies Vineyard Cabernets

Pewsey Vale Rhine Riesling

Stanley Leasingham CONTD

The Leasingham range was created by Tim Knappstein when the Stanley Wine Company was under his family's ownership. Since the firm was bought by Hardy's in 1987, some of its vineyard has been sold off. Most Stanley wines are given the Leasingham name, but the best wines are sold under the Winemaker's Selection label. The Fumé Blanc is light and fresh, with the creamy-oak influence not overplayed. The Bin 56 Cabernet Malbec has a slightly herbaceous, freshly crushed *cassis* character and a certain cedary-oak complexity.

TOLLANA WINES

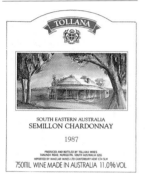

South Eastern Australia
Semillon Chardonnay

This old-established winery once produced entirely estate-bottled wines, but now blends with wines from other sources. The quality remains good, however, as shown by this peachy-tasting Semillon Chardonnay.

TOLLEY'S PEDARE

Late Harvest
Muscat à Petits Grains

Selected Harvest Cabernet Sauvignon

Established in 1893, this privately owned estate has a substantial 180 hectares (445 acres) of vineyard in production. The style is an elegant one, and this comes through in the exquisite richness and perfumed intensity of the Late Harvest Muscat à Petit Grains. The Selected Harvest Cabernet Sauvignon has a fat, ripe bouquet and soft, velvety fruit.

WIRRA WIRRA VINEYARDS

Church Block Cabernet-Shiraz-Merlot

Wirra Wirra was established in 1893 by Robert Wigley, whose wines were greatly appreciated in London at the turn of the century. Wigley died in 1924 and his family sold off most of the vineyards, leaving the rest to fall into disuse. Greg and Roger Trott purchased the property in 1969 and began to ressurrect it. The vibrant, complex Cabernet-Shiraz-Merlot is a superb example of the high standard set by these hand-crafted wines.

WYNNS

Coonawarra Estate
Cabernet Sauvignon

Coonawarra Estate Chardonnay

Established by David Wynn in the early 1950s, but now part of the giant Penfolds Group, Wynns still has one of the best international reputations of any Australian winery. Its legendary Cabernet Sauvignon has adopted a lighter, more herbaceous style since the early 1970s, yet remains one of the finest reds made in Australia, although the deeper, richer John Riddoch Cabernet Sauvignon is finer. Another top wine is Wynns' lovely lemony Chardonnay with its splendid spicy, buttered-toast oak complexity.

WOODSTOCK

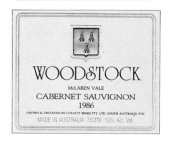

McLaren Vale Cabernet Sauvignon

McLaren Vale Chardonnay

This small vineyard was named after the town in Oxfordshire, England by Arthur Townsend, who settled in McClaren Vale in 1859. Yet the Woodstock winery was not created until 1974, when it was founded by Doug Collett. The Cabernet Sauvignon is rich and oaky; the Chardonnay buttery and toasty, but it is the luscious, honeyed Noble Dessert Wine (sold originally as Botrytis Sweet White Wine) that is this winery's greatest wine.

YALUMBA

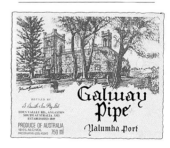

Galway Pipe Yalumba Port

This estate is now owned by S. Smith & Sons. The original vineyard was founded in 1849 by Samuel Smith, who named it Yalumba, which is Aboriginal for "all the land around". The Galway Pipe Yalumba Port is a fine, rich example of this style of Australian fortified wine.

WESTERN AUSTRALIA

THE REMARKABLE IMPACT made in recent years by wines from Margaret River might suggest that Western Australia is a newly developed viticultural area. In fact the first settlers in Western Australia preceeded their counterparts in South Australia and Victoria by five years, when they established the new colony in the 1820s. However, until the late 1960s the state possessed only one principal wine-growing area, which was in Swan Valley on the eastern outskirts of Perth: the location for the successful and well-established wineries of Houghton Wines and Sandalford. Western Australia experienced a viticultural boom with the opening up of the cooler growing areas at Margaret River and further south in Frankland River and Mount Barker, when a rush of small wineries came into being.

Margaret River

The Margaret River region is centred around the town of Margaret River, 320 kilometres (200 miles) south of Perth, on a peninsular promontory. Its vineyards are clustered along the seaward edge. The climate is temperate with a high rainfall, the heat of the long, dry summers being moderated by the sea breezes. Attention is entirely concentrated on classic varieties and an exciting range of wines is produced which includes Cabernet Sauvignon, Chardonnay, Sémillon, Sauvignon Blanc, Rhine Riesling, Shiraz, Pinot Noir and Zinfandel.

Frankland River and Mount Barker

The Frankland River and Mount Barker areas lie south-east of Margaret River, some 300 kilometres (185 miles) from Perth. They are close to the southern seaboard and are the coolest of Western Australia's growing areas. Vines were first planted on Mount Barker experimentally in 1965 under the supervision of the State Department of Agriculture. When the scheme succeeded, other growers moved into the region, establishing numerous small vineyards, often quite remote from each other. The best results have been achieved so far with light, elegant Rhine Rieslings and full-bodied Cabernet Sauvignons. Plantings also include Chardonnay, Pinot Noir and Malbec, and the region is expected to make an increasingly important contribution to Australia's quality wine production.

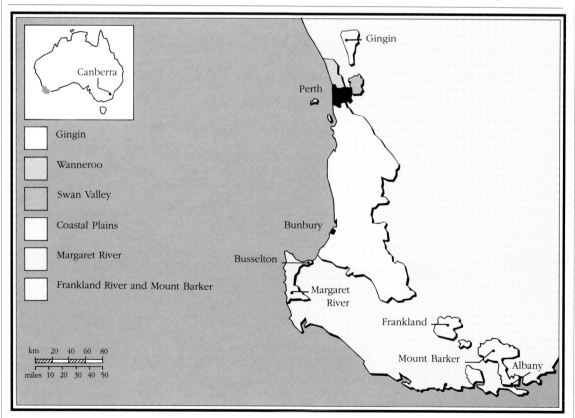

Australia's south-western tip The vineyards in the Margaret River region are planted entirely with classic grapes. South of Margaret River are the districts of Frankland River and Mount Barker; these three areas have now taken over from Swan Valley as the most important quality wine-producing areas of Western Australia.

ALKOOMI

Frankland Cabernet Sauvignon

Limited Release Frankland Malbec

Sheep farmers Mervyn and Judy Lange turned their hand to wine-making and their fresh, fruity, rich-flavoured wines are an excellent indication of the potential of the up-and-coming Frankland area. The Cabernet Sauvignon is a big wine with lots of rich, cedary-minty fruit and fine, spicy-oak underlay. The Limited Release Malbec is another full-bodied wine. It has an opaque colour, dense, gamey fruit and rich, spicy-tobacco complexity.

CAPE CLAIRAULT

Margaret River Semillon Sauvignon Blanc

Margaret River Sauvignon Blanc

Ian and Ani Lewis established this estate in 1976. Ex-geologist Ian Lewis chose the site for the potential in its slopes and soil. The Semillon Sauvignon Blanc has a delicious, exotic fruit flavour, with just the right touch of ripe, creamy oak. The Sauvignon Blanc hits between the eyes with its brash, upfront, elderflower style.

CAPEL VALE

Shiraz

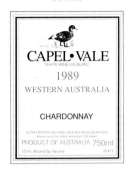

Chardonnay

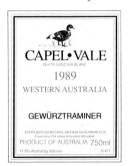

Gewürztraminer

CAPE MENTELLE

This top-performing estate was established in 1970 by David Hohnen, one of Australia's most talented, yet charmingly modest, winemakers. His Zinfandel can be admired by the most chauvinist of European palates, even those who claim not to like the grape. It has nothing to do with Californian renditions of Zinfandel and everything to do with classic winemaking technique. Hohnen has been meticulously working away at his Shiraz, shaving off the porty-weight that can typify so many Australian versions of this grape. The wine has extraordinary elegance and an increasing complexity. The top Cape Mentelle wines are, however, Hohnen's Cabernet Sauvignons, which alone could make Western Australia famous. They are typified by their complex herbaceous-*cassis* and sweet mulberry flavour, beautifully integrated oak and soft, chalky tannins.

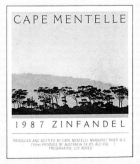

Zinfandel

Shiraz

Cabernet Sauvignon

This rapidly up-and-coming winery is another example of how blissful ignorance of viticulture and oenology can lead to great success when starting up your own winery. Dr Peter Pratten, a Bunbury radiologist, had no experience whatsoever when he began making wine on the banks of the Capel River, but his delicious wines are some of Western Australia's finest. The Shiraz can be variable, but when successful is vibrant and fruity, with lots of sweet-ripe, stone-fruit and berry flavours. However, it is Capel Vale's white wines that are its true forté. The Chardonnay is a tangy, exotic wine, with plenty of ripe pineapple and peach fruit. Even the Gewürztraminer can excel, its aromatic and delicately spicy character being of a far more classic, much less exotic nature than most New World versions of this grape.

CHATEAU XANADU

Margaret River Chardonnay

Margaret River Semillon

Modern-day winemaking in the Margaret River area was established by Dr Tom Cullity in 1967. Since then, a veritable surgery of medical men have followed in his footsteps. No more so than at Chateau Xanadu, which was founded in 1977 by two doctors, John and Eithne Shirden. Their typically tight, but buttery-rich, pineapple-and-peach-flavoured Chardonnay is Chateau Xanadu's top wine, but their intense-flavoured Semillon runs a close second, with its firm, purposeful, bone-dry finish.

CULLENS

Margaret River Cabernet Sauvignon Merlot

Margaret River Chardonnay

Di and Kevin Cullen established this well-known vineyard in 1971. Kevin, another doctor, tends to take the back seat, with Di and Vanya, her Roseworthy-trained daughter, constituting a formidable winemaking team. The range of wines is large and the quality good, sometimes exceptional. The Margaret River Cabernet Sauvignon Merlot is rich and classy, with fabulous herbaceous-chocolatey-capsicum fruit and an amazingly Bordeaux-like style. The Sauvignon Blanc has rich gooseberry fruit; the Margaret River Chardonnay has a vivacity of fruit and a soft, seductive, creamy-toasty, oaky complexity.

EVANS & TATE

Swan Valley Margaret River Gnangara Shiraz

Margaret River Cabernet Sauvignon

Founded in 1972 by John Evans and John Tate, this winery is now solely owned and run by John and Toni Tate. They are in the process of producing an increasing selection of stunning wines that expertly combine richness with finesse. The Gnangara Shiraz is a gloriously rich wine with savoury-smoky fruit that sometimes needs 10 or more years to peak. The Margaret River Cabernet Sauvignon is a much softer, silkier wine, with an elegant, spicy-herbaceous finesse.

JANE BROOK ESTATE WINES

Cabernet Sauvignon

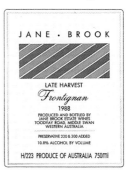

Late Harvest Frontignan

David and Beverley Atkinson named their estate after the brook which runs through their Swan Valley property. The Cabernet Sauvignon is a brilliant, cedary-*cassis* wine with fruit that is almost sweet with ripeness. The Chardonnay is tight and toasty, the Sauvignon Blanc is fresh and grassy and the Late Harvest Frontignan is a succulently soft and aromatic wine with rich peachy-grapey fruit.

HOUGHTON WINES

In 1824 King William IV granted over 3,000 hectares (7,413 acres) of the Swan Valley to Henry Bland, who sold it to a trio of British officers stationed in India. Colonel Houghton, the senior officer, never saw the property, but named it after himself. Now owned by Hardy's, the best-seller is White Burgundy, sold as Houghton's Supreme on some export markets. It remains a remarkable ambassador for Western Australia. Softer now, with Chardonnay-like peachy fruit, it is still made from Chenin Blanc and Muscadelle. The Cabernet Sauvignon is grossly underrated, remaining ripe and fresh for more than 10 years in bottle. The Moondah Brook Estate Cabernet Sauvignon is fuller, spicier and more serious. The Moondah Brook Estate Verdelho is a rich, tropical-fruit-flavoured wine that is delightful when young, assuming a honeyed character after a few years.

White Burgundy

Moondah Brook Cabernet Sauvignon

Moondah Brook Estate Verdelho

LEEUWIN ESTATE

Margaret River Chardonnay

Margaret River Cabernet Sauvignon

This high-tech winery, established with advice from Robert Mondavi, produces a Chardonnay with creamy bouquet, expansive flavour and stunning acidity. It also makes one of the finest Cabernet Sauvignons in Australia. Deep, dark and opaque, it has a complex, herbaceous bouquet and rich, chocolatey fruit, with a firm chalky-tannin structure.

DOMAINE MOSS WOOD

Margaret River Pinot Noir

Margaret River Semillon

The second wine estate to be established in the Margaret River region, this 10-hectare (25-acre) vineyard at Willyabrup was first planted in 1969 by Dr Bill Pannel. Virtually every wine to come out of this winery has been of exceptional quality. The classy Pinot Noir has a soft, sensuous, strawberry fruit and pure, elegant, varietal style. It is one of the finest Pinot Noirs produced anywhere in the New World. The Semillon is a full-blown wine with rich, smoky fruit and a spicy-buttery oak uplift that improves well in bottle.

PEEL ESTATE WINES

Sauvignon Blanc

Cabernet Sauvignon

Located on its own at Baldivis in the all-encompassing Coastal Plains region, this 12-hectare (30-acre) vineyard was planted by William Nairn in 1974 and produced its first wine in 1980. This Sauvignon Blanc is deliciously dry, with fresh, herbaceous fruit and a crisp, elegant finish. The Cabernet Sauvignon has lots of ripe *cassis* fruit, spicy-cedary oak and a firm tannic backbone.

PIERRO

Chardonnay

This small vineyard at Willyabrup was established in 1980 by Dr Michael Peterkin, a partner in the same medical practice as Dr Kevin Cullen, whose eldest daughter he married. The Cabernet Sauvignon has a fine, elegant, cedary-herbaceous style; the Pinot Noir has a bouquet like that of a strawberry jam pot and the Riesling Spatlese is exotic and tangy. But the Chardonnay has wonderfully fresh and vibrant fruit with a creamy-spicy oak uplift.

PLANTAGENET

Mount Barker Chardonnay

Mount Barker Cabernet Sauvignon

Mount Barker Rhine Riesling

This was one of the first winemaking enterprises in the Mount Barker district. Now it covers almost 30 hectares (74 acres) and is renowned for the quality of its cool-climate wines. The Chardonnay is a tightly packed wine that has excellent natural acidity and improves in the bottle. The ripe and spicy Cabernet Sauvignon is

another wine that ages well, but the Rhine Riesling is best drunk young because, although it develops a classic petrol-Riesling bouquet in the bottle, it loses fruit in the process.

REDGATE WINES

Margaret River Reserve Cabernet

Margaret River Oak Matured Sauvignon Blanc

This vineyard on the Boodjidup Road in Margaret River was first planted in 1977 by Bill Ullinger. He now has some 16 hectares (40 acres) under vine. The soil situation at Redgate is a very complex one. The Reserve Cabernet demonstrates the potential longevity of his Cabernet Sauvignon, which is often underrated in the normal release form because of its relatively light and elegant style, but it can develop a fine spicy-minty-cedary intensity. The Oak Matured Sauvignon Blanc is not overwhelmed by the wood, but has rather fresh, striking and crisp herbaceous fruit.

SANDALFORD

Caversham Estate Matilde Cabernet Rosé

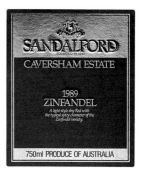

Caversham Estate Zinfandel

Planted by John Septimus Roe in 1840, this is the oldest vineyard in Western Australia. It was wholly owned and run by the family until 1969, when David Roe, the founder's great-grandson and Sandalford's winemaker, died. A public company was formed, and this is now controlled by the Inchcape Group, although the Roe family have a minority holding. The Maltide Cabernet Rosé is a delightfully dry, fresh and unpretentious wine. The Zinfandel is a soft, supple, easy-drinking wine with light, peppery-raspberry fruit.

VASSE FELIX

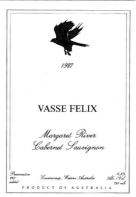

Margaret River Cabernet Sauvignon

This winery was established in 1967 by Dr Tom Cullity, a Perth heart specialist. He was helped from the outset by Englishman David Gregg, who emigrated to Western Australia in 1969 to take a position within the dairy trade, but soon found himself making wine. Cullity sold out to Gregg in 1984, but when Gregg realized he had insufficient funds to operate the estate he sold Vasse Felix to Robert Holmes a'Court in a deal that enabled David and Anne Gregg to continue running the estate. They have not looked back since, and neither have the wines. The Cabernet Sauvignon is the most famous wine here, a big, *cassis*-rich wine with a fine minty-herbaceous complexity.

~ NEW ~
ZEALAND

THE WINE INDUSTRY IN New Zealand is almost entirely the product of the twentieth century. Most of the more important wineries, with the exception of such as Babich, Corbans, Delegat's, Nobilo's and Te Mata, did not come into being until the late 1960s, 1970s and 1980s. One of the largest and best known, Montana, with an output of some 1.5 million cases from 950 hectares (2,347 acres), did not set up in business until 1964. Many producers are boutique wineries with 100 hectares (247 acres) or less - often much less.

The major wine-growing areas started historically in the North Island around the principal centre of population, Auckland. Auckland still accounts for 802 hectares (1,980 acres), including the well-known Huapai Valley. Two-thirds of the grapes for the country's wines are grown on the east coast of the North Island at Gisborne and Poverty Bay (predominantly for whites) and in the Hawkes Bay area (for both reds and whites). New plantings have been made - initially by Montana - at the north end of the South Island, at Nelson and significantly in Marlborough, and now further south in the Canterbury area around Christchurch. The results, from Sauvignon Blanc and Chardonnay, challenge the finest white wines anywhere else in the world. The South Island is also beginning to produce some fine Pinot Noir.

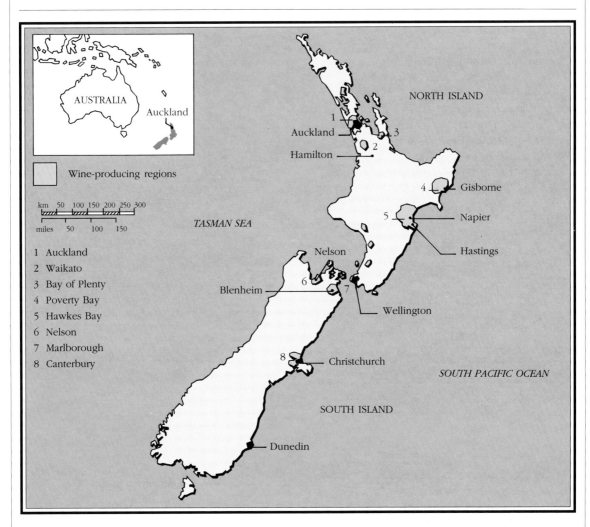

1 Auckland
2 Waikato
3 Bay of Plenty
4 Poverty Bay
5 Hawkes Bay
6 Nelson
7 Marlborough
8 Canterbury

Climatic conditions *Both islands offer a wide variety of generally cool climates influenced by the ocean.*

High humidity from the heavy rainfall, as well as cyclonic damage, can afflict the North Island causing

grape rot. Marlborough, on the South Island, is generally cooler with plenty of sunshine and a lighter rainfall.

There is a basic climatic similarity between New Zealand and Germany - identified by no less an authority than Dr Helmut Becker, the distinguished German viticulturalist. The cool-climate regions of the North and South Islands straddle the 40th parallel South like a peg on a line. Despite this, the Rhine Riesling does not acquire the great prominence in New Zealand that it does in Australia. The predominant grape is still the Müller-Thurgau, on which the modern New Zealand wine industry was built, but in quality terms for world markets it is outclassed by a range of classic grape varieties. These include Chardonnay and Sauvignon Blanc among the whites, and Cabernet Sauvignon and Pinot Noir among the reds. Other whites grown in any quantity are Palomino, Chenin Blanc, Chasselas, Gewürztraminer, Muscat and Sylvaner. Reds - which also include Merlot, Pinotage and Gamay - account for less than 20 per cent of the country's total output. Today, 95 per cent of vines planted are *vitis vinifera*, and the remaining 5 per cent are hybrids.

Changes in demand

The New Zealand wine industry increased its output of better quality wines in 1986, when the Government encouraged the uprooting of many vineyards planted with lesser varities, like Müller-Thurgau. This immediately reduced the overall vineyard area by a quarter and, unfortunately for the domestic market, was followed by a low-yielding harvest in 1987. It accompanied, however, a reduction in consumer demand at home and a swing away from the bulk supplies of cask wines based on Müller-Thurgau towards better quality varietal wines. At the same time, an escalating demand developed for quality wines in overseas markets, especially in the UK and Australia. New plantings of classic varieties were undertaken and by 1989 were beginning to show results. The 1989 grape harvest showed an overall increase in quantity, producing a total of some 45 million litres (5 million cases), with the significant increases in total yields coming from those varieties principally exported. The yield from Chardonnay was up by a massive 64 per cent, with similarly large increases in Sauvignon Blanc and Pinot Noir. The output of Gewürztraminer doubled, and there was a sizeable increase in the quantity of Merlot which is now playing a more significant role as a blending partner with Cabernet Sauvignon.

Whites of international standing

The international reputation of New Zealand's white wines was initially established on the outstanding quality of its Sauvignon Blanc with its rich, fresh, fruity and complex varietal character. Now Chardonnay is coming to the fore as a formidable competitor. The Western Australian winemakers at Cape Mentelle recognized the suitability of the benign but cool climate at Marlborough on the South Island. They stunned the world with their trail-blazing Cloudy Bay Sauvignon Blanc and have shown the superb quality that can be achieved with Cloudy Bay Chardonnay. Their achievement is currently being emulated by other top producers, including Corbans (who now own Cooks) and Montana which, despite their size - they account for 85 per cent of New Zealand wines - still make exemplary wines. New Zealand wineries use winemaking methods adopted elsewhere in the New World, combining new technology with oak-ageing where appropriate.

New wine styles

Recently some notable late-harvest Rhine Rieslings and Gewürztraminers have emerged with perhaps more potential to challenge those of Germany and Alsace than examples from other New World countries. Among the reds, Cabernet Sauvignon has already had some successes, and great promise is now being shown by the Cabernet/Merlot blends which offer an attractive alternative to the straight Cabernet varietal. The suitability of the climate in the South Island for planting Pinot Noir should produce good results in the future and also encourage the current attempts to create top-class New Zealand Champagne-method sparkling wines from a classic Chardonnay and Pinot Noir blend.

NEW ZEALAND VINTAGES

YEAR	CHARACTER
1989	Fine, plentiful vintage in all areas
1988	Smaller harvest, with whites generally of good quality, and some fine reds
1987	Cyclonic damage on east coast of North Island with mixed results and low yields. Good wines from the South Island
1986	High-quality wines from small harvest
1985	A good year, producing wines for the medium term
1984	Low-yielding harvest with white wines performing better than reds
1983	High-yielding, very ripe harvest, well balanced wines
1982	Rain caused problems at harvest time and quality very variable
1981	Generally an excellent vintage, but lower than average yield

BABICH WINES

Gisborne Semillon/Chardonnay

Hawke's Bay Cabernet Sauvignon

Joseph Babich planted his first vineyard at Kaikino, near Cape Reinga, in 1916, moving to Henderson three years later. It is now run by his two sons, Peter and Joe Junior. Best known for its white wines, such as the ripe and juicy Henderson Valley Chardonnay and the superb, smoky, creamy-rich Gisborne Semillon/Chardonnay, Babich has made increasingly excellent Hawke's Bay Cabernet Sauvignon since the 1985 vintage.

BROOKFIELDS VINEYARDS

Sauvignon Blanc

Hawke's Bay Cabernet Merlot

Since this one-time "Sherry" winery was purchased from founder Richard Ellis in 1977, the emphasis has successfully switched to unfortified wines. The Sauvignon Blanc is a fresh, floral wine with a grassy-peardroppy flavour and understated creamy-oak. The Gewürztraminer is soft, ripe and gentle, with a muted, cool-fermented aromatic fragrance. The best wine here is the Cabernet Merlot, which can be big, rich and oaky with smoky-toffee complexity in years like 1986 or ripe, seductive and luxuriant in a year like 1987.

CELLIER LE BRUN

Daniel Le Brun Brut

Daniel Le Brun Blanc de Blancs Brut

In 1980, Frenchman Daniel Le Brun purchased this property just outside Renwick in Marlborough. Planting his vineyard with traditional Champagne varieties - his family still makes Champagne near Epernay - he set about making a sparkling New Zealand wine according to the methods that had been tried and tested by twelve generations of Le Bruns. The result was one of the first New World bubblies to have a true and full autolytic character. The wines caused a sensation in New Zealand, but they lacked finesse and the greatly admired Blanc de Blancs was simply too hefty to have any class. Since then, he has steadily adapted his methods, both in the vineyard and the cellar, to suit growing conditions completely different from Epernay. He is now well on course to establishing Daniel Le Brun *Méthode Champenoise* as one of the New World "*grands crus*" of the 1990s.

CLOUDY BAY

Owned by Western Australia's Cape Mentelle, this winery developed an immediate cult-following for its Sauvignon Blanc, from the launch of its first vintage in 1985. It had 100 per cent distinctive, piercing varietal character. This style was successfully replicated in 1987, but New Zealand is a cool-climate viticultural area and subject to variations in vintage, thus the 1986 and 1988 were much more subdued in style. On an even higher quality level is Cloudy Bay's Chardonnay. This wine was launched with the rich, pineappley 1986 vintage and followed up with the more serious 1987, which quickly showed-off a little barrel-fermented, smoky-oak complexity. The latest, and perhaps greatest, addition to the Cloudy Bay stable is its Cabernet Merlot, a deep-coloured wine with classic spicy-*cassis* Cabernet character fattened out with ripe, juicy Merlot fruit.

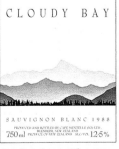

Sauvignon Blanc

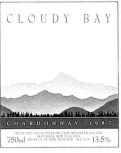

Chardonnay

Cabernet Merlot

COLLARD BROTHERS

Rothesay Vineyard Sauvignon Blanc

Rothesay Vineyard Chardonnay

This firm was founded by English horticulturist J. W. Collard in 1910 and is still in family ownership, under brothers Bruce and Geoffrey Collard. Wines labelled Rothesay Vineyard are amongst the best and come from Collard's own vineyard in the Waikoukou Valley. The Sauvignon Blanc has a typically fresh and exciting gooseberry flavour that begs to be drunk as young as possible. The Rothesay Vineyard Chardonnay is the softest and most subtle of Collard's three different Chardonnays, yet has the most lingering flavour.

COOKS

Hawkes Bay Chenin Blanc

Winemakers Reserve Hawkes Bay Chardonnay

The full name is Cooks McWilliams Ltd, Cooks having taken over its competitor McWilliams in 1984. Then in 1987 Corbans purchased Cooks McWilliams. As Cooks have one of the most prominent ranges of New Zealand wine on the international market, Corbans have sensibly maintained its individual identity. They are well known for inexpensive yet consistently well-made wines, such as the fruity Chenin Blanc, which is made in a fresh, easy-drinking style. Cooks Chardonnay is fine by any standards; its Winemakers Reserve is a gem.

COOPERS CREEK VINEYARD

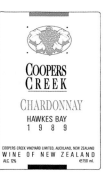

Hawkes Bay Chardonnay

Gisborne Gewurztraminer

This 4-hectare (10-acre) vineyard at Huapai was established in 1981 by a partnership led by Californian winemaker Randy Weaver, whose superb, hand-crafted wines made an immediate impact on the Auckland restaurant trade. Weaver departed in 1988, leaving the majority shareholding in the hands of Andrew Hendry, who has maintained the high quality of these wines. Chardonnay has always been the top Coopers Creek wine. It is dominated by creamy-smoky new oak in its youth and remains dramatically young and vital while other excellent Chardonnays are dropping like flies. The Gewurztraminer is classier than most New World renditions of this grape and has crisper varietal definition.

CORBANS ESTATE

Private Bin Fumé Blanc

Private Bin Gewürztraminer

Marlborough Chardonnay

Forty years before Gaston Hochar established one of the seven wonders of the modern wine world, Château Musar, another Lebanese by the name of Assid Abraham Corban set sail for New Zealand. At the time, Assid could not have contemplated that wine might be his destiny, for he was merely a humble stonemason. But, after 10 years and as many jobs, Assid realized he would not carve out a living for himself plying his old trade, so in 1902 he purchased some land in the Henderson area, planted a vineyard and made wine. Corban was a natural, his business flourished and soon became one of the largest wineries in New Zealand, acquiring Cooks and McWilliams in the process. Corbans Private Bin Fumé Blanc is a gooseberry flavoured wine that develops a rich, tomato taste in bottle. The piercing varietal aroma and flavour consistently found in Corbans Gewürztraminer Private Bin makes it one of the most successful versions of this hard-to-capture variety in the New World. Corbans Premium Class Marlborough Chardonnay has a broad, soft, buttery richness.

Delegat's Wine Estate

Hawkes Bay Sauvignon Blanc

Gisborne Chardonnay

Established in 1947 by Nickola Delegat, this winery had a somewhat low profile until a young Australian winemaker by the name of John Hancock was hired in 1979. The quality and reputation soared, but it was at the time of New Zealand's crazy discount battle, so prices plummeted and Delegat's nearly went under. Wine-merchant Neil Wilson came to the rescue, but the Delegat family retained a significant share and are very much in day-to-day control today. Although Hancock left to run his own venture, Morton Estate, he has been replaced by the very talented Brent Marris. These wines are brilliant across the board, whether the Hawkes Bay Sauvignon Blanc, which is made in the distinctive, piercing, Cloudy Bay style or the Proprietor's Reserve Gisborne Chardonnay, which is attractively rich in its youth, but has the extract and acidity to greatly improve in the bottle.

De Redcliffe Estates

Hawkes Bay Rhine Riesling

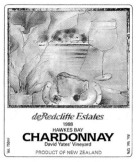

*Hawkes Bay Chardonnay
David Yates' Vineyard*

This attractive riverside vineyard was first planted in 1976 by Chris Canning, whose apprenticeship abroad lasted 20 years and included France and Tuscany. The lively Hawkes Bay Rhine Riesling has its admirers, but, in recent years, it has been de Redcliffe's Hawkes Bay Chardonnay that has attracted most attention, with its elegant buttered-apple flavour, fine fruit acidity and subtle, smoky-oak complexity.

Esk Valley

Hawkes Bay Sauvignon Blanc

*Hawkes Bay
Cabernet Sauvignon/Merlot*

Originally founded as Glenvale Vineyards in 1933, this estate built its reputation on fortified wines but changed emphasis to table wines in the 1970s. Its success attracted the eye of George Fistonich, the owner of Villa Maria and Vidal, and he bought the property in 1987. The Sauvignon Blanc has ripe, soft, tropical fruit flavours, with a certain grassy edge. The Cabernet Sauvignon/Merlot is a smooth wine with stylish fruit and fine cedary-vanilla oak underlay.

Goldwater Estate

*Waiheke Island
Sauvignon Blanc Fumé*

*Waiheke Island Cabernet,
Merlot, Franc*

Founded in 1978 by Kim and Jeanette Goldwater, this tiny island vineyard has a privileged micro-climate. The Sauvignon Blanc Fumé is made in a soft, refined style, with a very delicate varietal flavour that is gently underpinned with oak. The Cabernet, Merlot, Franc is a classy, soft, stylish wine that has evolved from the Goldwater's earlier pure Cabernet Sauvignon wines, which were very good, but lacked the balance of this very fine wine.

Hunter's Wines

Marlborough Chardonnay

Marlborough Sauvignon Blanc

After learning the ropes from wine-maker Almuth Lorenz, Irish-born Ernie Hunter was successfully chiselling out a name for this small Marlborough vineyard when he was killed in a car-crash. His viticulturist wife Jane Hunter was determined to see Ernie's dreams come true, and with the help of John Belsham, her extremely talented winemaker, she has succeeded. The most outstanding wine ever produced here was the extraordinary Botrytis Chardonnay. Its elegant peaches and cream fruit, superb acidity and rich, botrytis complexity defy any expert to identify the variety. The standard dry Hunter's Chardonnay is a very attractive wine, with delicious, delicately ripe fruit with creamy-smoky vanilla oak influence. The Sauvignon Blanc is made in the classic rasping style with a fine, mineral aftertaste.

KUMEU RIVER WINES

Chardonnay

Merlot Cabernet

After passing his oenology course at Roseworthy in Australia with honours, young Michael Brajkovich spent his study tour in California, Italy and France. It is these skills that show through in his winemaking at Kumeu River. Widely regarded as the most talented winemaker, his broad knowledge of wine was acknowledged in 1989 when he became the first (and so far, only) New Zealander to become a Master of Wine. The entire range can be confidently recommended, but the two wines here are stunning yardstick examples of the Kumeu River style. The Chardonnay is ripe and vibrant, with creamy-exotic fruit. The Merlot Cabernet is a stylish wine of great finesse that reflects Brajkovich's time with Moueix of Château Pétrus.

LINCOLN VINEYARDS

Hawkes Bay Chenin Blanc

Brighams Creek Vineyard Sauvignon Blanc

This family-owned 30-hectare (74-acre) vineyard was founded in 1937 by Peter Fredatovich, whose grandsons Peter and John are now in charge. Apart from Lincoln's widely appreciated Old Tawny Port-style wine, it is the white table wines that are best known. The Hawkes Bay Chenin Blanc is a soft, fruity wine; the Brighams Creek Vineyard Sauvignon Blanc has depth of varietal flavour.

MARTINBOROUGH VINEYARD

Chardonnay

Pinot Noir

Just across the water from Marlborough, on the southern tip of North Island, this winery has been so active in opening up viticulture at Wairarapa that it is now more commonly referred to as the Martinborough area. The Chardonnay has a firm, citrussy fruit with a restrained spicy-oak uplift. The Pinot Noir is a delightful, soft and delicately fruity wine, with good spicy-strawberry-cherry varietal character.

MATAWHERO WINES

Gewürztraminer

Cabernet Sauvignon Merlot

Denis Irwin produced his first vintage in a converted chicken shed in 1976 and was winning gold medals within a couple of years. Matawhero is primarily known for its German-influenced white wines, such as this Gewürztraminer, a grapey, aromatic wine with an attractive residual sweetness that lengthens the spicy aftertaste. The Cabernet Sauvignon Merlot is lighter than average for a Gisborne red and this belies its considerable depth of fruit.

MATUA VALLEY WINES

Judd Estate Chardonnay

Matua Valley Wines CONTD

*Cabernet Sauvignon
Dartmoor-Smith Estate*

Founded in 1974, this high-tech winery produces wines that are a joy to drink. The Judd Estate Chardonnay from Gisborne has lovely acidity, tight, lime fruit and a hint of toasty oak. Matua Valley was the first winery to produce a Cabernet Sauvignon with true *cassis* intensity in New Zealand with its stunning 1985 vintage and the Dartmoor-Smith Estate Cabernet Sauvignon is a step up.

MONTANA WINES

Marlborough Sauvignon Blanc

*Marlborough Sauvignon Blanc/
Chenin Blanc*

This range was often the only alternative to Cooks on export markets in the early-1980s. With almost 1,000 hectares (2,470 acres) and two huge, high-tech wineries, this is New Zealand's largest wine company. Among the reds, the Marlborough Cabernet Sauvignon/ Pinotage is an intense and herbaceous wine of some class. Montana's recent venture with Deutz & Geldermann, the *Grande Marque* Champagne house, has every chance of producing one of the finest *méthode champenoise* in the New World. The Marlborough Sauvignon Blanc is very rasping and can be extremely rich. In a more elegant vein, however, is the ripe and flowery Marlborough Sauvignon Blanc/Chenin Blanc, which has very good acidity.

MORTON ESTATE

Fumé Blanc

Hawkes Bay Chardonnay

Founded in 1982 by former Woolworth's trainee, ex-car salesman and kiwi-fruit trader Morton Brown, this winery has been firmly established as one of the great *"grands crus"* of the New World by former Delegat's winemaker John Hancock. From this vineyard, which now exceeds 40 hectares (100 acres), Hancock produces some of New Zealand's finest wines, specializing in barrel-fermented whites of great quality and complexity, such as this Fumé Blanc. The Hawkes Bay Chardonnay Winemakers Selection is a living lesson in how to squeeze so much flavour into a wine and still have elegance and finesse.

NGATARAWA

This small vineyard is planted on the vast and expansive 2,400-hectare (5,930-acre) Washpool estate, which is a sheep station presently under the ownership of the Glazebrook family. Founded in 1981, Ngatarawa (simply ignore the "g" when pronouncing the name of the vineyard) is a venture managed jointly between the Glazebrooks and the Corbans. Ngatarawa is run by Alwyn Corban, who is a quiet and intelligent man and one of New Zealand's talented young winemakers. His Hawkes Bay Alwyn Chardonnay is a deliciously rich wine with a sweet-creamy oak complexity that develops relatively quickly on the palate, but that requires a good four or five years of ageing to fulful completely this promise on the bouquet. The Hawkes Bay Riesling Botrytised Selection is an extremely elegant wine with concentrated, spicy-peachy fruit and excellent acidity. Without doubt, however, the greatest wines from this vineyard are a fine Cabernet Sauvignon by the name of Stables Red and an even finer Hawkes Bay Glazebrook Cabernet Merlot.

*Hawkes Bay
Alwyn Chardonnay*

*Hawkes Bay Riesling
Botrytised Selection*

*Hawkes Bay Glazebrook
Cabernet Merlot*

Nobilo Vintners

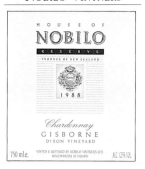

Dixon Vineyard
Gisborne Chardonnay

Hawkes Bay Sauvignon Blanc

This 145-hectare (358-acre) vineyard was first planted in 1943 by Dalmation immigrant Nickola Nobilo. Very much a family-run affair today, most Nobilo wines are rich and characterful, but can lapse into a heavy-handed style. This may be due to an over-zealous search for quality, but a good Nobilo is a great Nobilo, and the Dixon Vineyard Gisborne Chardonnay is a very good Nobilo wine, with its concentrated, satisfying Chardonnay flavour and excellent acidity. Nobilo is particularly successful with Sauvignon Blanc. The Hawkes Bay is a beautiful wine with fine, gentle, mellow pineapple flavour, while the Marlborough is a leaner, more rasping wine, with ultra-fresh, lychee and gooseberry fruit.

Penfolds

Fumé Blanc Ne Plus Ultra

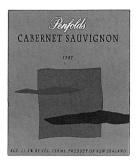

Cabernet Sauvignon

Founded by the Abel family, this winery was taken over by the Australian Penfolds operation and is now a subsidiary of Montana. There are no vineyards, but the firm has contracts with growers owning about 1,000 hectares (2,470 acres). The Fumé Blanc Ne Plus Ultra is a soft, gooseberry flavoured wine that was aged in Nevers oak and is best drunk young. The Cabernet Sauvignon has fine, ripe fruit with an attractive herbaceous-*cassis* character.

St. Helena

Canterbury Pinot Noir

Canterbury Pinot Blanc

This 24-hectare (60-acre) estate was established in 1978 by potato farmers Norman and Robin Mundy. Under the auspices of Danny Schuster, their first winemaker, St. Helena produced its first wines in 1981 and established a reputation as New Zealand's leading Pinot Noir exponent, making a wine that combines varietal purity with satisfying fruit - still a rare combination in this pioneering Pinot country. When Schuster moved on, he was replaced by former Penfolds man Mark Rattray,

who, in effect, has done for St. Helena Pinot Blanc what Schuster did for Pinot Noir. Matured in oak, it is a good substitute for Chardonnay, and its lighter balance makes it considerably more flexible with food.

Selak Estate

Sauvignon Blanc

Marino Selak Founders Selection Cabernet Sauvignon

Founded in 1934 by Dalmatian Marino Selak, this winery is now run by his nephew Mate Selak and his two sons. The Selaks moved from the winery at Te Atatu to their present premises in 1969. The Sauvignon Blanc has a fruity aroma and a rich and lengthy flavour. The Marino Selak Founders Selection Cabernet Sauvignon is a well-coloured wine with a promising, *cassis* flavour and some cedary-herbaceous complexity.

Stoneleigh Vineyard

Marlborough Chardonnay

Marlborough Rhine Riesling

Stoneleigh CONTD

This is the premium range from Corbans. These wines of finesse, rather than size, are amongst the best currently produced in New Zealand. The Sauvignon Blanc is fresh, fragrant and grassy. The Chardonnay is ripe, with excellent acidity, and its creamy-vanilla new oak influence develops into fine, creamy-spicy oak complexity after a year or two in bottle. The Rhine Riesling is a fine, dry wine with attractive orange-blossom aromas.

STONYRIDGE

Larose Waikeke Island Cabernet

This small winery on Waiheke Island was established by Stephen and Jane White in 1982. The Larose Cabernet is a Bordeaux-style blend of Cabernet Sauvignon and Merlot, topped up with a little Cabernet Franc and Malbec. The aroma is sweet and elegant, reminiscent more of mulberries than blackcurrant, although the fruit on the palate is rich in *cassis*, with a classic cedary complexity. In Bordeaux tradition, they make a second label wine named Airfield after the neighbouring airstrip.

TE MATA ESTATE

Coleraine Cabernet/Merlot

Hawke's Bay Elston Chardonnay

Established in 1896, Te Mata Estate is the oldest winery in New Zealand. It was purchased by John Buck, a former member of the British wine trade, and his wife Wendy, in 1978. Despite a very low-key marketing approach, the intrinsic quality and exceptional character of these wines is hard to ignore. The Coleraine Cabernet/Merlot is a great wine by any yardstick. Deep in colour and packed with spicy-cedary *cassis* fruit, it has astonishing finesse for its weight. It has considerable longevity and achieves great complexity. The Elston Chardonnay is a big, firm wine, rich in buttery-toasty fruit, with lots of smoky-toasty complexity.

VIDAL

Private Bin Hawkes Bay Cabernet Sauvignon Merlot

Reserve Chardonnay

This winery was established by Spanish immigrant Anthony Vidal in 1905, but was sold to George Fistonich of Villa Maria in 1976. It consistently produces some of the most exciting wines in the Hawkes Bay area, including the fine, aromatic Cabernet Sauvignon Merlot, which has silky-fragrant fruit, yet develops well in the bottle. The Reserve Chardonnay does not claim the Hawkes Bay appellation, but it is a superb wine with huge extract and great acidity, which offers great ageing potential.

VILLA MARIA ESTATE

Under George Fistonich, this has become the largest privately-owned winery in the country. With the talented winemaker Kym Milne, it is now one of the best. Modern techniques enhance fruit and freshness and where oak is used, the touch is light and the balance perfect. The Private Bin Sauvignon Blanc is a very ripe wine, cut by a certain herbaceous edge. The Reserve Chardonnay is a full-bodied wine with sweet, buttery fruit, a touch of barrel-fermented smokiness and a big toasty finish. The Reserve Cabernet Sauvignon is a rich wine with intense cedary-*cassis* fruit and the classic tannin structure to enable it to develop well in bottle.

Private Bin Sauvignon Blanc Gisborne Region

Reserve Chardonnay Barrique Fermented Chardonnay

Reserve Cabernet Sauvignon Humatao Region

GLOSSARY OF TECHNICAL AND TASTING TERMS

Unless in common usage worldwide, foreign terms are listed in the introductions to individual countries.

Acid/acidity   Primarily *tartaric*, *malic* and lactic acids; a certain amount is necessary for *balance* and potential to age.

Aftertaste   Also called finish or length; taste that remains after the wine has been swallowed. Long aftertaste usually implies a fine wine.

Aggressive   High in *acid* or *tannin* or both. Usually applied to young, immature wines. May refer to an excess of a component like *oak*.

Alcohol   In wines primarily ethanol (ethyl alcohol). Unless *fortified*, most wines contain between 9 and 14 per cent by volume.

Appellation   The legally defined origin of a wine.

Aroma   The primary, fruit smell associated with young wine; sometimes used synonymously with *bouquet*.

Austere   Strong character; rather dry, but acceptable in young wine. In older wines, it implies a lack of fruit.

Autolysis   Breakdown of *yeast* cells; imparts specific flavours to wines bottled *sur lie* and sparkling wines.

Balance   Relationship between all elements in wine - primarily sugar, *acid*, alcohol and *tannin*, but also fruit and flavour components.

Barrel-fermented   A wine fermented in wooden, often oak, barrels.

Big   Large-framed or large-boned wine; such wines are often high in *alcohol*, *extract*, and deeply fruity.

Blind tasting   A tasting where the name of the wine is not known.

Blowzy   Attractive, but rather loose-knit wine, lacking *finesse* and *elegance*.

Body   The sense of weight and fullness of a wine in the mouth; wines that are full-bodied are ripe and rich in *extract*, alcohol and glycerine.

Botrytis cinerea   Fungus that causes rot to black and sometimes white grapes. In the right conditions it becomes *noble rot* and is responsible for some of the world's finest dessert wines.

Bottle age   Time spent in bottle. "Good bottle age" implies that the wine has had sufficient time to mature in the bottle.

Bouquet   Sometimes used synonymously with *aroma*; denotes the smells a wine obtains from the way it has been matured.

Butt   A term used mainly for Sherry casks.

Buttery   The smell and taste that is usually associated with oak-aged Chardonnay.

Cap   When fermenting crushed black grapes, the cap of skins floats to the top; various methods are used to submerge it to extract colour, *tannins* and flavours.

Cassis (Fr.)   Blackcurrant; often discernable on the the bouquet of young Cabernet Sauvignon, especially from Bordeaux.

Cedarwood   A characteristic of the bouquet often associated with Cabernet Sauvignon-based wines in Bordeaux, particularly from St Julien and Pauillac.

Cépage (Fr.)   Grape variety.

Chaptalization   The addition of sugar to the fermenting *must* to increase the final *alcohol* content. Legal in parts of Europe.

Chewy   A high-*extract* wine with dense, viscous *body* and high glycerine content.

Classification   Hierarchy of wine-producing estates.

Clean   Well-made wine lacking non-wine flavours - a complimentary statement.

Complexity   Wines with subtle flavours and aromas; a sign of high quality.

Cool-fermentation   *Fermentation* at a low temperature (usually below 18°C/64°F); mainly for white and rosé wines.

Coulure   The failure of vine flowers to set into grapes. Reduces the quantity but may improve the final quality of the harvest.

Crisp   A fresh, firm wine with positive *acidity*; an attractive quality in white wines.

Deep/depth   Associated with both aroma and taste; refers to the *complexity* of the wine and suggests many layers of flavour.

Delicate   Light and subtle; usually a complimentary term, especially in white wine.

Disgorgement   Removal of sediment after second *fermentation* of Champagne or Champagne-method sparkling wines.

Elegant/elegance   Of high quality, with finesse and usually good length.

Extract   Substances in wine, apart from *alcohol*, sugar and *acidity*, that give *body* and flavour.

Exuberant   Full of life; fruity and vigorous.

Fat   A big, soft wine, often high in glycerine; from a ripe vintage or warm climate. Wines lacking fat may be mean and *hollow*; wines with too much fat become flabby.

Fermentation   The conversion of sugar to *alcohol* through enzymatic action of *yeast*.

Finesse   High quality and breed.

Fining   Clarification of *must*, or more often wine, before bottling. A fining material is added that attracts impurities, enabling them to be removed more easily.

Finish   The final impression of the wine before swallowing.

Firm   Usually asssociated with unresolved *tannin* discernible at the end of the palate. Relates mainly to young wines.

First pressing   The first pressing of white grapes gives the cleanest, freshest juice.

Fleshy   Plenty of *body*, *alchohol* and *extract*, which conceal the *acid* and *tannin* structure in young wines.

Flinty   Gun-flint aroma that is discernible in certain white wines, particularly in some young Sauvignon Blancs and Chardonnays.

Flor   A film of *yeasts* that forms on the surface of certain wines in barrel or vat and gives them their characteristic flavour; notable in Fino Sherries.

Floral   Pleasant aromatic quality; usually associated with Riesling and Muscat wines.

Fortified   Wines that have had their *alcohol* levels increased by adding grape spirit before, during or after *fermentation*.

Forward   Young, undeveloped wines that are nevertheless attractive and easy to drink.

Fresh   Young wine showing no off-flavours; often high in *acidity*; also describes old wines that remain lively and youthful.

Fully fermented   A wine with virtually no residual sugar remaining after *fermentation*.

Generous   Full of flavour and character.

Graft   *Vitis vinifera* vines are grafted to American root stocks to protect against attacks from *phylloxera*.

Grams per litre   Measurement used for all components in wine - particularly useful for the amount of sugar remaining in wine.

Green   Wines from under-ripe grapes, which are high in malic acid. Can describe older wines not yet ready for drinking.

Hard   Young wines in which the *tannins* and *acidity* are pronounced.

Hectolitres per hectare Measurement of yield of wine in hectolitres (1 hectolitre = 100 litres) per hectare (2.47 acres) of vines.

Herbaceous(ness) Usually refers to the aroma that may be reminiscent of certain herbs, such as thyme, rosemary, basil etc.

Hollow Lacking depth and concentration, especially of fruit in the middle palate.

Hybrid A vine that is a cross between *vitis vinifera* and an American vine species. Seldom for high-quality wines.

Jammy Usually associated with very ripe fruit picked in hot conditions. Can be a complimentary term, but often suggests a lack of definition and class in the wine.

Lees Sediment of dead *yeast* cells at the bottom of a cask/vat after *fermentation*.

Lively/liveliness A fresh, young wine with good *acidity* balance. May refer to an older wine that is still fresh.

Long/length High-quality wine in which the flavours remain in the mouth for a considerable time after swallowing.

Luscious A soft, sweet, fruity, ripe wine that is well-*balanced* and not cloying.

Maceration The period when *must*/wine is in contact with the grape skins. Increasingly used pre-fermentation for whites to extract extra flavour. For reds a necessary process during and after *fermentation* to extract colour, *tannins* and flavours.

Malic acid One of wine's natural acids. If not converted to lactic acid (see *malolactic*) may be tasted as an appley *acidity*.

Malolactic Malolactic fermentation may take place during or after *fermentation*. Bacteria convert *malic acid* to the weaker, softer-tasting lactic acid. Most reds undergo this *fermentation*. In whites it may be prevented to retain extra *acid* intensity.

Meaty A *rich, chewy, ripe* wine, usually quite heavy and full of *extract*.

Méthode Champenoise (Fr.) Method of making sparkling wines using a second fermentation in bottle, as in Champagne. May not be used on the label after 1994.

Micro-climate The combination of position (altitude, proximity of water etc.), soil and climatic conditions that affects a particular vineyard site.

Mousse The sparkle in Champagne and sparkling wines.

Mouth-filling A *big, rich,* concentrated wine that literally seems to fill or coat the inside of the mouth. Full of flavour.

Must Grape juice before or during *fermentation*.

Must weight Amount of natural grape sugar in the *must*.

Noble rot A fungus (see *Botrytis cinerea*) that attacks certain white grape varieties in warm and humid conditions when the grape is ripe; it concentrates sugar, acids and flavours in the grape.

Oak/oaky The flavour and aroma dervied from the use of new oak barrels in the maturation of the wine. Usually a positive characteristic, but over-oaking can result in harshness and lack of fruit in the wine.

Oechsle Scale of measurement used (particularly in Germany) to determine the amount of sugar (and thus potential *alcohol*) in grapes or grape *must*.

Oenology Science of wine.

Overblown/overripe An undesirable characteristic where the grapes lack *acidty* and wines become imbalanced, with heavy dried-fruit flavours.

Peak A wine at its peak will not develop further and should be drunk immediately.

Peppery Black pepper aroma; often in young red wines, particularly Rhônes.

Petrol/petrolly A positive character on the *bouquet* of certain Rhine Riesling wines after some development in bottle.

Phylloxera Louse that attacks *vitis vinifera* vines and caused devastation in the late nineteenth and early twentieth century. Can be prevented by grafting *vinifera* vines on to American root stocks.

Press wine Wine pressed from mass of grape skins after red-wine *fermentation*. Deep-coloured and *tannic*, part may be used in a blend with the free-run wine.

Racking Transferring wine from one vessel to another, leaving sediment behind and aerating the wine.

Racy A wine of distinction and breeding. High quality; fine and *fresh*.

Rancio The distinctive flavour of wine that has been in barrels which are exposed to the air and sun.

Residual sugar Amount of sugar remaining after *fermentation* is completed and the wine is made.

Rich High in *extract,* flavour and fruit; for white wines, implies sweetness.

Ripe A wine made from grapes gathered at the optimum level of maturity; a wine that has just reached its maturity point.

Robust Rich, full and strong in alchohol.

Sappy A touch of *greenness* associated with the grape stems, which may have been used in the pressing and fermentation of the grapes. A quality that should tone down, but can be a fault.

Second label/wine Another wine from a property that produces one main wine (particularly Bordeaux); it may be from younger vines or lesser blends and may mature more quickly than the main wine.

Sharp An over-acid wine, often bitter and angular and made from unripe grapes.

Smoky An aroma associated with certain wines, usually derived from oak barrels.

Smooth A soft, silky wine with no rough characteristics.

Soft Describes mature red wines in which the *tannins* and *acidity* have mellowed. Can imply lack of grip in a young wine.

Spicy Aromas associated with various spices like pepper and cinnamon. May be derived from the wood or the grape variety.

Sturdy Wine of good size and quality, needing time to develop.

Subtle A delicate or refined quality that is not immediately apparent.

Supple A soft, velvety wine that is very pleasant to drink.

Table grape Grapes used for eating, not making wine.

Table wine May be a legal definition implying a non-quality wine of no specific origin; alternatively it is a wine that has not been *fortified* with spirit.

Tannic/tannin Derived from grape skins, pips and stalks, and also from oak casks. A *tannic* taste may be astringent when a red wine is young, but it helps the wine to age and softens it as it does so.

Tartaric acid The principal acid in wine.

Tartrates Tasteless crystals formed in wine from *tartaric acid*. They may be precipitated in low temperatures and appear in the wine or on the cork as clear, white crystals.

Terroir (Fr.) The complete growing environment of a vineyard.

Thin Unbalanced wine lacking fruit and *body*, usually made from under-ripe grapes.

Tight Undeveloped, but usually promising fine future development.

Toasty An aroma from the charring of oak barrels in which the wines are aged. Also found in certain Champagnes or sparkling wines through yeast *autolysis*.

Tobacco An attractive aroma found in certain red wines, particularly red Graves in Bordeaux.

Vanilla The flavour and aroma imparted to the wine by the vanillin in oak barrels during maturation.

Varietal A particular grape variety.

Vegetal An undesirable characteristic, usually associated with wines made from under-ripe grapes, which give the wine an unpleasant vegetable smell and flavour.

Véraison (Fr.) The ripening period of the grape on the vine, from when it starts to change colour and ripen, until it is ready for harvest.

Viniculture The technique of growing grapes and making wines.

Vinification Process of winemaking.

Viticulture Methods of vine-growing.

Vitis vinifera The species of vine (often known as European) that includes all classic wine grape varieties.

Yeast Microscopic organisms responsible for *fermentation*.

INDEX

C

ACKNOWLEDGMENTS

Dorling Kindersley would like to thank all the producers featured in this book for providing labels; all the many UK wine importers who obtained labels or bottles; all the London-based government trade offices for each wine-producing country for help with contacts and telephone numbers - special thanks to Nicola Speakman at Wines from Spain and Kate Ponté at the Wine Institute of California; Bureau Interprofessionel des Vins de Bourgogne; Oregon Wine Advisory Board; Washington State Wine Institute; Robert Geddes, David Gummer and Elizabeth Lucas for wine expertise; Sarah Matthews for assistance obtaining labels from Burgundy; Elizabeth Bertocco for assistance obtaining labels from Italy.

We are grateful for permission to reproduce wood engravings by David Gentleman (pages 60, 79, 84, 134, 162, 170, 193, 204, 211, 216, 240, 261, 270) from the 1961 wine list of Harveys of Bristol; and illustrations (pages 1 and 2) from the Christian Brothers Collection at The Wine Museum of San Francisco.

Dorling Kindersley would like to thank the following people for their help in producing this book:
Stephen Oliver for photography; Janos Marffy for maps; Siân Protheroe and Brian Rust for design help; Stephanie Jackson and Mark Ronan for editorial help; Diana LeCore for the index. Special thanks also to Jill Norman and Debbie Rhodes.